Studien aus dem Max-Planck-Institut
für Sozialrecht und Sozialpolitik

Volume 83

Ulrich Becker | Irene Domenici [Eds.]

Life in Dignity

A Comparison of National Approaches to Minimum Income Protection

Nomos

Open Access funding provided by Max Planck Society.

Die Deutsche Nationalbibliothek verzeichnet diese Publikation in der Deutschen Nationalbibliografie; detaillierte bibliografische Daten sind im Internet über http://dnb.d-nb.de abrufbar.

1. Auflage 2025

Publiziert von
Nomos Verlagsgesellschaft mbH & Co. KG
Waldseestraße 3–5 | 76530 Baden-Baden
www.nomos.de

Gesamtherstellung:
Nomos Verlagsgesellschaft mbH & Co. KG
Waldseestraße 3–5 | 76530 Baden-Baden

ISBN (Print): 978-3-7560-3633-2
ISBN (ePDF): 978-3-7489-6398-1

DOI: https://doi.org/10.5771/9783748963981

Onlineversion
Nomos eLibrary

Preface

The present study begins with a seemingly trivial yet fundamental question in view of social reality: Do states guarantee minimum subsistence to individuals under their jurisdiction? Despite the abundance of legal and socio-political promises, combatting poverty remains an unachieved goal to this day. Addressing this question touches on the core responsibilities of the welfare state and reveals the underlying normative conceptions about the relationship between the political community and individuals in need. We explore this question by analysing social benefits designed to ensure a minimum income, which form part of the social protection architecture of many countries. These benefits have grown in importance in the face of the transformations and crises over the past two decades, from the lasting impact of the financial crisis to the pandemic, the rise of non-standard forms of employment, and the current challenges posed by inflation and rising energy and living costs.

The idea for this collective project, bringing together experts from different countries across the globe, took shape building on these reflections. It began with a workshop held in Munich in November 2022 and evolved into a fruitful dialogue. Most of the chapters reflect the legal and policy landscape as of late 2024. The scientific exchange has been very stimulating, and our first heartfelt thanks go to all the contributors. We are deeply grateful for their enthusiastic commitment to this ambitious endeavour and for the smooth collaboration.

The publication of this book would not have been possible without the support and dedication of other colleagues. We are grateful to Monika Queisser and Herwig Immervoll from the OECD for their thoughtful feedback. Our sincere thanks also go to Christina McAllister and Niki Rodousakis for proofreading, and to Matthias Elbert, Jil Sophie Maier, and Oumar Diallo for their assistance with the editing process. We also thank Nomos Verlag for their professional support throughout the publication process.

Munich, June 2025
Ulrich Becker, Irene Domenici

Table of Contents

Part IV: Asian Perspective

Part V: Conclusions

Part I:
Introduction

Life in Dignity Through Minimum Income Protection: Introduction

Ulrich Becker

I. Starting Point: A Thorny Question

1. States have the obligation to protect all persons residing within their territory. This obligation certainly holds true for protection against physical harm. But what about protection in a socio-economic sense, specifically the guarantee of a minimum level of subsistence?

On the one hand, there are compelling arguments supporting the notion that the State has a normative obligation to ensure the socio-economic conditions necessary for a life in dignity. The evolution of the welfare state and the creation of legal instruments to protect social rights reflect this normative imperative. On the other hand, poverty alleviation remains an unfulfilled goal. From the perspective of those fortunate enough to be born and living in a country with comprehensive social security systems where those in poverty receive benefits and support for societal participation, this goal may seem nearly achieved. However, even in countries with well-established social security systems, the extent of minimum social protection remains a subject of ongoing societal and political debate. The situation is markedly different in countries where social protection schemes are rudimentary or partly absent. The notion of the State's obligation to provide an effective safety net may either be under discussion in these countries, lack acceptance, or may be facing other barriers that prevent the realisation of such a safety net.

This situation is not an exception. At the global level, the United Nations (UN) has made strides to end extreme poverty, initially through the *Millennium* and now the *Sustainable Development Goals* (SDGs). However, after decades of poverty decline, the 2020 pandemic marked a turning point to the worse.[1] In the European Union (EU), the 2008 financial crisis revealed that not all Member States had a universal social safety net in the form of an effective social assistance system in place.[2] Although this is changing, one fifth of the Union's population continues to be at risk of poverty or social exclusion.[3]

2. This raises a simple and fundamental question: How do states guarantee a minimum income? In particular, what benefit schemes are in place to achieve this goal? To this end, we must take stock of the institutions that provide financial support to individuals unable to independently cover their basic living costs. Such support has traditionally been delivered through social assistance schemes, often described as the final 'safety net'. However, this safety net may also be provided through other types of social benefits beyond assistance in the technical sense. We take this into account by using the term "minimum income protection". The focus is on financial support to cover basic living costs, while intentionally leaving open the question of how such financial means are delivered (see II.4.).

The question we are interested in is how states legally define a collective responsibility to support individuals in need. A general obligation to provide minimum income protection needs to be implemented. One of the most important steps in this process is the establishment of subjective legal rights. This means translating the State's abstract obligation into concrete and binding legal conditions and instruments. It comprises two

1 See: United Nations, 'Goal 1: End poverty in all its forms everywhere' (2025) < https://www.un.org/sustainabledevelopment/poverty/> accessed 9.6.2025.

2 See U. Becker, 'Conclusions from a Comparative Perspective', in: U. Becker and A. Poulou (ed.), *European Welfare State Constitutions after the Financial Crisis* (Oxford University Press 2020), pp. 338, 341, 354.

3 See: Eurostat, 'Living conditions in Europe - poverty and social exclusion' (April 2025) < https://ec.europa.eu/eurostat/statistics-explained/index.php?title=Living_conditions_in_Europe_-_poverty_and_social_exclusion#Source_data_for_tables_and_graphs> accessed 9.6.2025. See for the technical pros and cons of EU-SILC data H. M. Adzakpa, *Realising the Human Right to a Social Minimum? A Comparative Socio-Legal Study of EU Member States* (Nomos 2024), pp. 116 ff.

elements: first, specifying entitlement in terms of types and amounts; and second, establishing the administrative structures necessary to deliver these subjective rights. At the same time, the administrative concretisation and operationalisation of the State's constitutional obligation sheds light on the conceptualisation of welfare. Provisions on social benefits, how they are calculated and adjusted, reflect the State's normative understanding of how responsibilities are shared between a political community and its individuals. They reflect fundamental notions about the fair and just organisation of a political community, particularly with regard to the legitimacy of public interventions. Such provisions must be checked against and interpreted in line with constitutional obligations and human rights standards. Nevertheless, they possess their own normative meaning and impact, and provide insights into what can be described as the legal practice of social solidarity.

3. Comparison as a method offers a suitable approach to describing and analysing the legal framework surrounding the State's obligation to guarantee a minimum level of subsistence. It must be based on legal facts, such as current laws and regulations, as well as their functions and practical operation. In this context, the collection of legal materials can be guided by the shared social policy goal of ensuring a minimum income, as previously mentioned.

This "function" can be achieved through various types of social protection and benefit schemes. In most countries, these systems have evolved over time in response to specific historical events rather than as the outcome of a comprehensive social policy strategy or a masterplan of the welfare state. This is why minimum income protection is often delivered through a variety of benefits drawn from different schemes, requiring an analysis of their interactions. Secondly, to understand how responsibilities are shared between the political community and the individual, it is necessary to consider not only the definition of minimum income and how it is calculated, but also how it is maintained over time through regular adjustments. Equally important are the conditions attached to these benefits. These conditions reflect societal views on what constitutes basic needs. At the same time, they provide insights into the obligations expected of those applying for benefits. This concerns, in particular, activation measures, which have become widespread since the end of the last century.

Before outlining our research approach and the structure of this book (see Section III), we first contextualise our research questions against their legal and socio-political backgrounds by providing an overview of the historical development, normative foundations and institutional frameworks of minimum income protection (see Section II.).

II. Background: Developments, Standards and Institutions

The assumption of the State's obligation to guarantee a minimum level of subsistence rests on factual and normative developments: the origins of State responsibility to address poverty trace back centuries and are now widely recognised as part of a catalogue of human rights. However, these developments have not changed the need to implement, and potentially enhance, social policy measures: preventing poverty and ensuring participation in society continue to represent the most urgent and relevant goals.

1. From Charity and the Legal Order to Subjective Rights and Activation Measures

A widely recognised starting point for comprehensive State action in this regard is the English Poor Law. The 1601 Act for Relief of the Poor introduced the role of "overseers of the poor" in each parish. They were tasked with putting "to work all such persons married or unmarried, having no means to maintain them" and raise funds "by taxation [...] in such competent sum and sums of money as they think fit" a "convenient stock of [...] necessary ware and stuff to set the poor on work, and also competent sums of money, for, and towards the necessary relief of the lame, impotent, old, blind, and such other among them being poor, and not able to work, and also for the putting out of such children to be apprentices".[4] The Poor Law marked a turning point: with the emergence of states as political communities, charity gradually lost its predominance as a means of providing support to the poor. Another milestone in later developments at the end of the Enlightenment was the Prussian *Allgemeines Landrecht* of 1794, which established the State's obligation to provide food and sustenance to those citizens who were unable to support themselves.[5] However, the

4 The Statutes Project, '1601: 43 Elizabeth 1 c.2: Act for the relief of the poor' (2025) < https://statutes.org.uk/site/the-statutes/seventeenth-century/1601-43-elizabeth-c-2-act-for-the-relief-of-the-poor/> accessed 9.6.2025.

5 Teil II, Titel 19, § 1: "Dem Staate kommt es zu, für die Ernährung und Verpflegung derjenigen Bürger zu sorgen, die sich ihren Unterhalt nicht selbst verschaffen, und

development of a legal foundation did not imply recognition of a subjective right. Poverty was rather regarded as a disruption to the legal order, and the poor had to be protected from the "danger of perishing".[6] This was particularly evident at the onset of industrialisation, as illustrated by the English Poor Law Amendment Act of 1834, which established workhouses and a more centralised administration.[7] The new law was a reaction to the debate on how to fight poverty.[8] This question continued to be discussed, as it had by no means been resolved with the establishment of the State's responsibility to provide support for the poor. As captured by *Hegel*: "The important question, how poverty is to be done away with, is one which has disturbed and agitated society, especially in modern times."[9]

The most significant steps towards the introduction of subjective rights to social assistance followed in the years after the Second World War. At the international level, the Declaration of Philadelphia of 1944 played a particularly important role. It became part of the International Labour Organization's (ILO) Constitution and laid the foundation for a rights-based approach to social protection, grounded in the belief "that lasting peace

denselben auch von andern Privatpersonen, welche nach besonderen Gesetzen dazu verpflichtet sind, nicht erhalten können", available at: < https://digital.staatsbibliothek-berlin.de/werkansicht?PPN=PPN725960604&PHYSID=PHYS_0484&view=overview-toc&DMDID=DMDLOG_0001> accessed 9.6.2025.

6 N. Senior, 'Poor Law Commissioners' Report of 1834, part II, section 1, para 3' (2025) < http://econlib.org/library/YPDBooks/Reports/rptPLC11.html> accessed 9.6.2025.

7 By introducing "The Poor Law Commissioners for England and Wales", Amendment Act 1834 available at: <https://www.workhouses.org.uk/poorlaws/1834act.shtml> accessed 9.6.2025.

8 See N. Senior (n 6), part II, section 1, para. 5: "But in no part of Europe except England has it been thought fit that the provision, whether compulsory or voluntary, should be applied to more than the relief of indigence, the state of a person unable to labour, or unable to obtain, in return for his labour, the means of subsistence. It has never been deemed expedient that the provision should extend to the relief of poverty; that is, the state of one, who, in order to obtain a mere subsistence, is forced to have recourse to labour."

9 "Die wichtige Frage, wie der Armut abzuhelfen sei, ist eine vorzüglich die modernen Gesellschaften bewegende und quälende", G. W. F. Hegel, *Grundlinien der Philosophie des Rechts oder Naturrecht und Staatswissenschaft im Grundrisse* (1821), §§ 244, 149, Zusatz (citation from suhrkamp taschenbuch wissenschaft 1976). Translation taken from *Hegel's Philosophy of Right*, translated by S. W. Dyde (George Bell and Sons 1896), available at: <https://archive.org/details/cihm_50473/page/n7/mode/2up?ref=ol&view=theater > accessed 9.6.2025.

can be established only if it is based on social justice".[10] This development was also reflected at the national level. In 1954, the German Federal Administrative Court issued a decision on social assistance, declaring that the era of former Prussian law, where support for the poor was granted solely in pursuit of public interest and recipients were treated as mere objects of administrative action,[11] had come to an end. If a law required an administrative body to provide a given benefit, then those persons who fulfilled the legal conditions also had a right to that benefit.[12] Persons in need of support had to no longer beg for help but were now entitled to access support.[13]

This does not mean that the right to social assistance had to be free of obligations. By the end of the last century, activation had gained in importance. Originally rooted in labour market policy, it was incorporated into minimum income protection schemes.[14] At its core, activation requires recipients of social assistance to take up employment or, if necessary, undertake measures to improve their employability. On the one hand, this development could be perceived as an excess of neoliberalism, as a risk for solidarity and for the above-mentioned principle of social justice.[15] On the other, neoliberal policies follow different pathways. Even if they have a market-oriented focus, their actual outcome with regard to inequalities depends to a considerable degree on the design of the social protection

---

10 < http://www.ilo.org/wcmsp5/groups/public/---asia/---ro-bangkok/---ilo-islamabad/documents/policy/wcms_142941.pdf > accessed 9.6.2025.

11 Or as an object of moral improvement, see for social welfare in cities in the 1920ies W. Rudloff, 'The Welfare State and Poverty in the Weimar Republic', in: L. Raphael (ed.), *Poverty and Welfare in Modern German History* (Berghahn 2017), pp. 105, 144 ff.

12 Judgement of 24 June 1954, V C 78.54, BVerwGE 1, 159.

13 See also K.-J. Bieback, Die Entwicklung der „social assistance" in Deutschland, Frankreich und im Vereinigten Königreich – von den „armen Armen" zu den „berechtigten Armen"; in: U. Becker (ed.), *Rechtsdogmatik und Rechtsvergleich im Sozialrecht I* (Nomos 2010), pp. 217 ff.

14 See also A. Eleveld, T. Kampen and J. Arts (eds.), *Welfare to Work in Contemporary European Welfare States. Legal Sociological and Philosophical Perspectives on Justice and Domination* (Bristol University Press 2020); for arguments against conditionality A. Moreira, *The Activation Dilemma. Reconciling the fairness and effectiveness of minimum income schemes in Europe* (Cambridge University Press 2008).

15 See A. Supiot, *The Spirit of Philadelphia – Social Justice vs. the Total Market* (Verso 2012).

system.[16] Activation is intended to incentivise labour market participation;[17] with it, the State assumes additional responsibility, even if it pursues a public interest goal through increased labour market participation. It is no coincidence that the EU supports activation policies.[18] The broader process of European integration is often viewed critically from a social policy perspective. Yet, it is important to note that it does not necessarily undermine social policy as such but rather helps push it in a specific direction to reconcile economic objectives with social policies.[19]

Activation should not, of course, lead to a regression from the establishment of subjective rights.[20] It might also be used to promote a more comprehensive approach, for example by incentivising continued education. In this vein, a specific scheme in Denmark provides minimum income protection for individuals under the age of 30 without education.[21] Before we return our attention to social policy, we will first briefly discuss the human rights foundations for guaranteeing a minimum income.

2. Human Rights

a) International Level

As already mentioned, the monitoring of the State's obligations began to be placed in the hands of the people themselves[22] after the Second World

---

16 See M. Fourcade-Gourinchas and S. L. Babb, 'The Rebirth of the Liberal Creed: Paths to Neoliberalism in Four Countries' American Journal of Sociology 198 (2002), pp. 533 ff.

17 See W. Eichhorst, O. Kaufmann and R. Konle-Seidl (eds.), *Bringing the Jobless into Work? Experiences with Activation Schemes in Europe and the US* (Springer 2008).

18 See Principle 14, Sent. 2 of the European Pillar of Social Rights: "For those who can work, minimum income benefits should be combined with incentives to (re)integrate into the labour market."

19 See U. Becker, 'Sozialstaatlichkeit in der Europäischen Union', in: A. Hatje (ed.), *Verfassungszustand und Verfassungsentwicklung in der Europäischen Union*, EuR Beih. 2 (2015), pp. 19, 31 ff.

20 For a critical assessment, see P. Larkin, 'The New Puritanism: The Resurgence of Contractarian Citizenship in Common Law Welfare States' Journal of Law and Society 41 (2014), pp. 227 ff.

21 Educational assistance, whereas the general scheme for assistance is also applicable for individuals under 30 with education, see J. Kvist, *ESPN Thematic Report: Access to social protection for young people*, (European Commission 2021), pp. 16 ff.

22 See H. Lauterpacht, *An International Bill of the Rights of Man* (Columbia University Press 1945).

War. One cornerstone of this development was the Universal Declaration of Human Rights (UDHR) of 1948.[23] Art. 22 links minimum income to social security, explicitly affirming the entitlement "to realization, through national effort and international co-operation and in accordance with the organization and resources of each State, of the economic, social and cultural rights indispensable for his dignity and the free development of his personality." The International Covenant on Economic, Social and Cultural Rights (ICESCR) of 1966[24] stipulates that states "recognize the right of everyone to an adequate standard of living for himself and his family, including adequate food, clothing and housing, and to the continuous improvement of living conditions" (Art. 11(1), Sent. 1). A separate provision on the right to social security (Art. 19) should, according to the Committee on ESCR, also be interpreted as requiring the State to provide social assistance.[25] This blurs the boundaries between different types of social benefit systems, making the rights under Articles 11 and 19 difficult to distinguish.[26] However, it can be explained by a certain State practice (see also below, Section 4) and the need to organise social security effectively.

These general human rights provisions are supplemented by other agreements.[27] They cover specific groups of individuals, and occasionally make

23 Of 10 December 1948, GA res. 217 A (III), available at: < https://www.un.org/en/about-us/universal-declaration-of-human-rights> accessed 9.6.2025.

24 Art. 11(1) ICSCR: "The States Parties to the present Covenant recognize the right of everyone to an adequate standard of living for himself and his family, including adequate food, clothing and housing, and to the continuous improvement of living conditions. The States Parties will take appropriate steps to ensure the realization of this right, recognizing to this effect the essential importance of international cooperation based on free consent". Treaty text available at: < https://www.ohchr.org/en/instruments-mechanisms/instruments/international-covenant-economic-social-and-cultural-rights> accessed 9.6.2025.

25 General Comment No. 19 of the Committee on ESCR to Art. 19 ICESCR, para. 50: 'States parties will need to establish non-contributory schemes or other social assistance measures to provide support to those individuals and groups who are unable to make sufficient contributions for their own protection', available at: < https://digitallibrary.un.org/record/618890?v=pdf> accessed 9.6.2025.

26 Although Art. 11 covers a broad range of aspects, it is often restricted to (the expressly mentioned) food and water, on the one hand, and clothing and housing, on the other, see B. Saul, D. Kinley and J. Mowbray, *The International Covenant on Economic, Social and Cultural Rights* (Oxford University Press 2014), pp. 861 ff.

27 Overview of international standards on the pages of the special rapporteur on extreme poverty and human rights, available at: < https://www.ohchr.org/en/special-procedures/sr-poverty/international-standards> accessed 9.6.2025.

use of similar terms such as "adequate standard of living"[28] or include a non-discrimination principle.[29] They also comprise regional instruments such as the Additional Protocol to the American Convention on Human Rights in the Area of Economic, Social and Cultural Rights[30] or the European Social Charter (ESC) of 1961 with its revision of 1996 (RESC)[31].[32] The latter contains an obligation of the parties, "with a view to ensuring the effective exercise of the right to social and medical assistance", to "ensure that any person who is without adequate resources and who is unable to secure such resources either by his own efforts or from other sources, in particular by benefits under a social security scheme, be granted adequate assistance, and, in case of sickness, the care necessitated by his condition" (Art. 13(1) ESC and RESC).

All of these provisions share the limitation that they neither define the minimum level of subsistence or an adequate standard of living,[33] nor do they establish specific subjective rights.[34] The monitoring bodies, i.e. those

---

28 Art. 28 on adequate living and social protection of the UN Convention on the Rights of Persons with Disabilities, < https://www.ohchr.org/en/instruments-mechanisms/instruments/convention-rights-persons-disabilities> accessed 9.6.2025.

29 Art. 23 on public relief of the Convention relating to the Status of Refugees, < https://www.ohchr.org/en/instruments-mechanisms/instruments/convention-relating-status-refugees> accessed 9.6.2025.

30 Available at: < https://www.oas.org/juridico/english/treaties/a-52.html> accessed 9.6.2025.

31 ETS No. 35 and No. 163. The RESC and the Additional Protocol to the ESC Providing for a System of Collective Complaints, ETS No. 158, have not yet been ratified by all EU Member States (see: < https://www.coe.int/en/web/european-social-charter> accessed 9.6.2025).

32 In the African Charter on Human and Peoples' Rights (available at: < https://au.int/en/treaties/african-charter-human-and-peoples-rights> accessed 9.6.2025), there is no specific right to social assistance, but a right to the best attainable state of health (Art. 16) as well as a "right to existence" (Art. 20(1), Sent. 1) and an obligation to "assist the family" (Art. 18(2), the latter without any direct link to positive rights.

33 See C. O'Cinneide, 'Giving Legal Substance to the Social Minimum', in: T. Kotkas, I. Leijten and F. Pennings (eds.), *Specifying and Securing a Social Minimum in the Battle Against Poverty* (Bloomsbury Publishing 2019), pp. 183 ff.; J. Gilman, 'The rights to social security and social assistance in the European Social Charter: Towards a positive content ... but what sort of content?' EJSS 26 (2024), pp. 411 ff.; see for the progressive realisation clause (with far-reaching conclusions) O. De Schutter, 'Public Budget Analysis for the Realization of Economic, Social and Cultural Rights', in: K. Young (ed.), *The Future of Economic and Social Rights* (Cambridge University Press 2019) pp. 527 ff.

34 At least as far as concrete benefits are concerned; see for other individual legal positions (with regard to Art. 9 ICECSR) M. Kradolfer, 'Verpflichtungsgrad sozialer

bodies mandated in the treaties to report on the progress of the realisation of human rights,[35] may contribute to defining the substance of the respective rights and obligations.[36] However, their implementation cannot depend on the legal enforcement by the persons concerned.[37] Even when international courts intervene[38] or when social rights are strengthened through their combination with other rights, such as under the European Convention on Human Rights (ECHR),[39] or when they are part of a legal order that supersedes national laws, e.g. the EU Charter of Fundamental Rights (EU CFR),[40] the situation remains largely unchanged. While international

---

Menschenrechte' Archiv des Völkerrechts 50 (2012), pp. 255 ff.; for the necessity of qualitative standards G. Vonk, *Welfare state dystopia as a challenge for the right to social security*, (Maastricht University 2024), < https://doi.org/10.26481/spe.20240925gv > accessed 9.6.2025.

35 See for the work of those bodies contributions in U. Becker, B. v. Maydell and A. Nußberger (eds.), *Die Implementierung internationaler Sozialstandards* (Nomos 2006); R. Brillat, 'The Supervisory Machinery of the European Social Charter: Recent Developments and their Impact', in: G. de Burca, B. de Witte and L. Ogertschnig (eds.), *Social Rights in Europe* (Oxford University Press 2005), pp. 31 ff.

36 See for a detailed analysis H. M. Adzakpa (n 3), pp. 182 ff. and 217 ff.; also A. Eleveld and G. Katrougalos, 'The right to social security and social assistance in the 'case law' and conclusions of the Social Rights Committtee', in: F. Pennings and G. Vonk (eds.), *Research Handbook on European Social Security Law* (2nd ed. Edward Elgar Publishing 2023), pp. 64 ff.

37 But see also with regard to "structural shortcomings" G. Vonk and M. Olivier, 'The fundamental right to social assistance: A global, regional (Europe and Africa) and a national perspective (Germany, The Netherlands and South Africa)' EJSS 21 (2019), pp. 219 ff.

38 See contributions in C. Binder, A. Hofbauer, et al. (eds.), *Social Rights in the Case Law of Regional Human Rights Monitoring Institutions: The European Court of Human Rights, the Inter-American Court of Human Rights, the African Commission of Human and Peoples' Rights* (Neuer Wissenschaftlicher Verlag 2016).

39 Convention for the Protection of Human Rights and Fundamental Freedoms, ETS No. 5 of 1950 < https://www.coe.int/en/web/conventions/full-list?module=treaty-detail&treatynum=005> accessed 9.6.2025. For the interaction with the ESC, see I. E. Koch, 'Economic, Social and Cultural Rights as Components in Civil and Political Rights: A Hermeneutic Perspective' The International Journal of Human Rights 10 (2006), pp. 405 ff.; U. Becker, 'European Human Rights Protection: Towards a Multi-Level and Interdependent System based on Cooperation', in: F. Pennings and G. Vonk (eds.), *Research Handbook on European Social Security Law* (2nd ed. Edward Elgar Publishing 2023), pp. 85, 88 ff. See for the concept of human dignity used by the European Court of Human Rights V. Fikfak, L. Izvorova, 'Language and Persuasion: Human Dignity at the European Court of Human Rights' Human Rights Law Review 22 (2022) 3, pp. 1 ff.

40 First solemnly proclaimed on 7 December 2000, OJ C 364/1.

law can have binding effects in individual cases, it cannot guarantee an effective right to a minimum income. There is a lack of competence at the international level due to the existing structures of democratic legitimacy, which also applies within the EU. The EU CFR addresses, inter alia, social assistance (Article 34(3)),[41] but does not contain enforceable social rights for EU citizens, given its scope of application[42] and the distinction between 'rights' and 'principles'.[43]

Ultimately, the implementation of the obligation to guarantee a minimum income under international law rests largely on national processes through which international human rights standards are integrated into domestic legal systems, whether through political decisions and legislative acts or through court decisions that interpret national provisions in light of these standards.

b) National Level

Social rights can also derive their legal foundation from national constitutions. The national level is where their story began. The first constitutional foundations were laid in the early 20th century in the Constitutions of Mexico (1917), the Russian Soviet Federated Republic (1918) and Germany (1919). Today, many constitutions around the world enshrine social rights,[44] often introduced after revolutions, as witnessed in countries such as India, Spain, Portugal or South Africa.

To better understand these rights, it does not suffice to focus solely on the wording of the relevant provisions. The right to a minimum level of

---

41 'In order to combat social exclusion and poverty, the Union recognises and respects the right to social and housing assistance so as to ensure a decent existence for all those who lack sufficient resources, in accordance with the rules laid down by Union law and national laws and practices.'.

42 Art. 51, para. 1, Sent. 1 CFR; see ECJ of 6 March 2014, Case C-206/13 *Cruciano Siragusa v Regione Sicilia* [2014] ECLI:EU:C:2014:126, paras. 24 and 25.

43 Art. 51, para 1. Sent. 2, Art. 52, paras. 2 and 5 CFR.

44 See C. Jung, R. Hirschl and E. Rosevear, 'Economic and Social Rights in National Constitutions' AJCL 62 (2014), pp. 1043 ff.; E. Rosevear, R. Hirschl and C. Jung, 'Justiciable and Aspirational Economic and Social Rights in National Constitutions', in: K. Young (ed.), *The Future of Economic and Social Rights* (Cambridge University Press 2019), pp. 37 ff.; J. King, 'Social rights in comparative constitutional theory', in: G. Jacobsohn and M. Schor (eds.), *Comparative Constitutional Theory* (Edward Elgar Publishing 2018), pp. 144 ff.

subsistence can even be derived from a provision that does not explicitly contain a social right. It is the courts that are driving such developments.[45] A prominent example is a 2010 decision of the German Federal Constitutional Court, which derived a "fundamental right to the guarantee of a subsistence minimum" from the right to human dignity (Art. 1(1) of the Basic Law) in conjunction with the social state principle (Art. 20(1) of the Basic Law).[46]

This example will not be examined in greater detail here. This book does not aim to explore the role of constitutional social rights from a doctrinal point of view, nor to argue whether the right to dignity should entail a positive dimension.[47] Our focus instead lies in assessing whether, and to what extent, such rights influence the creation and implementation of minimum income protection. Before turning our attention to the national level, however, we must first review efforts to establish a political—or from another perspective, a *soft law*—framework for minimum income protection at the international level.

---

45 See A. Mameli, 'Judicial review, social antagonism and the use of litigation as a tool for combating poverty', in: L. Williams, A. Kjønstad and P. Robson (eds.), Law and Poverty: The Legal System and Poverty Reduction (Zed Books 2003), pp. 139 ff.; J. King, *Judging Social Rights* (Cambridge University Press 2012).

46 Judgement of 9 February 2010, 1 BvL 1/09, available at: < https://www.bundesverfassungsgericht.de/SharedDocs/Entscheidungen/EN/2010/02/ls20100209_1bvl000109en.html> accessed 9.6.2025. See for the importance of this judgment also C. O'Cinneide, 'The Present Limits and Future Potentials of European Social Constitutionalism', in: K. Young (ed.), *The Future of Economic and Social Rights* (Cambridge University Press 2019), pp. 324, 349.

47 See R. Alexy, *Theorie der Grundrechte* (Suhrkamp 1986), pp. 395 ff.; R. Alexy, 'Social Constitutional Rights and Proportionality', in: M. Langford, K. Young (ed.), The Oxford Handbook of Economic and Social Rights, online ed. (18 Aug. 2022) < https://doi.org/10.1093/oxfordhb/9780197550021.013.27 > accessed 11 June 2025; C. Fabre, *Social Rights Under the Constitution: Government and the Decent Life* (Oxford University Press 2010). See also S. Huster, 'The Universality of Human Dignity and the Relativity of Social Rights', in: D. Grimm, A. Kemmerer and C. Möllers (eds.), *Human Dignity in Context. Explorations of a Contested Concept* (Nomos 2018), pp. 415 ff.; and in a comparative perspective S. Civitarese Matteucci and G. Repetto, 'The expressive function of human dignity: A pragmatic approach to social rights claims' EJSS 23 (2021), pp. 120 ff. On the situation in Britain, see C. Gearty, 'Socio-Economic Rights, Basic Needs, and Human Development: A Perspective from Law's Front Line', in: C. McCrudden (ed.), *Understanding Human Dignity* (Oxford University Press 2013), pp. 1565 ff. Without focus on positive rights or state obligations for minimum income protection, see P. Becchi, K. Mathis (eds.), *Handbook of Human Dignity in Europe* (Springer 2019).

3. Recommendations

Due to the open wording of human rights provisions, the distribution of competences, and the inherently complex nature of poverty prevention as a socio-political task, binding legal obligations may be supplemented and specified by recommendations. These recommendations can influence social policy at the national level.[48] Since their potential impact will be dealt with in the following chapters, a more detailed analysis is not necessary here.

At the global level, the ILO has introduced the concept of "social protection floors" in response to the recognition that ILO Convention 102,[49] referred to as the "Magna Carta of social security", is no longer sufficient to address future challenges, as it excludes emerging social risks and does not take evolving developments such as activation policies and privatisation into account.[50] Although the ILO continues to use the term "social security", it now recommends Member States to establish and maintain social protection floors that include "basic income security" for children, working-age persons who are unable to earn sufficient incomes, and older persons.[51] According the recommendation, "basic income security should allow life in dignity".[52]

48 On the postulation that 'soft law' plays a considerable and at least supplementary role for implementation, see A. Supiot, 'The Position of Social Security in the System of International Labor Standards', Comparative Labour Law and Policy Journal 27 (2006), pp. 113, 116 ff.

49 Of 1952, available at: < https://normlex.ilo.org/dyn/nrmlx_en/f?p=NORMLEXPUB:12100:0::NO::P12100_ILO_CODE:C102> accessed 9.6.2025.

50 See U. Becker, F. Pennings and T. Dijkhoff (eds.), *International Standard-Setting and Innovations in Social Security* (Wolters Kluwer 2013).

51 Paras. 4 and 5 of Social Protection Floors Recommendation No. 202 of 2012, available at: < https://normlex.ilo.org/dyn/nrmlx_en/f?p=NORMLEXPUB:12100:0::NO:12100:P12100_INSTRUMENT_ID:3065524:NO> accessed 9.6.2025. See for the approach and case studies T. Dijkhoff and L. G. Mpedi (eds.), *Recommendation on Social Protection Floors: Basic Principles for Innovative Solutions* (Wolters Kluwer 2018).

52 Para. 8(b), Sent. 1 of Rec. 202 of 2012 (fn. 51), with the following addition (Sent. 2): "Nationally defined minimum levels of income may correspond to the monetary value of a set of necessary goods and services, national poverty lines, income thresholds for social assistance or other comparable thresholds established by national law or practice, and may take into account regional differences."

The EU has developed various instruments to influence national social policies,[53] including the Open Method of Coordination and the European Semester.[54] The latter has served as a platform for Member State-specific recommendations aimed at enhancing budgetary discipline. In some cases, it has also been used as a platform for recommendations on improvements in social assistance schemes.[55] To provide a broader foundation for EU social policy, EU institutions proclaimed the European Pillar of Social Rights (EPSR) in 2017.[56] According to the European Commission, the EPSR is intended to deliver "new and more effective rights for citizens", although its content is described as comprising "key principles".[57] This "Pillar" is not cast in stone but is a legally non-binding social policy programme.[58] Nevertheless, it formulates shared expectations for robust social protection through a comprehensive catalogue of principles, partly building on previous measures and partly introducing new objectives. One such new objective is Principle 14, Sent. 1: "Everyone lacking sufficient resources has the right to adequate minimum income benefits ensuring a life in dignity at all stages of life, and effective access to enabling goods and services."

The concept of "minimum income" was chosen over the traditional term "social assistance" to take account of future developments.[59] Even without advocating for a universal basic income or citizens' income, such flexibility

53 For a detailed analysis, see A. Aranguiz, *Combating Poverty and Social Exclusion in European Union Law* (Routledge 2022).

54 On the development, see U. Becker (n 19), pp. 27 ff. See also S. Smismans, 'How to Be Fundamental with Soft Procedures? The Open Method of Coordination and Fundamental Social Rights', in: G. de Burca, B. de Witte and L. Ogertschnig (eds.), *Social Rights in Europe* (Oxford University Press 2005), pp. 217 ff. For a European and comparative social policy perspective M. Jessoula and I. Madama (eds.), *Fighting Poverty and Social Exclusion in the EU, A Chance in Europe 2020* (Routledge 2020).

55 See Communication from the Commission, Country Report Bulgaria, 2017 European Semester, SWD(2017) 68 final/2.

56 See for the booklet: < https://commission.europa.eu/document/download/e03c60e7-4139-430b-9216-3340f7c73c20_en?filename=social-summit-european-pillar-social-rights-booklet_en.pdf> accessed 9.6.2025.

57 European Commission 'The European Pillar of Social Rights in 20 Principles' (24 October 2023) < https://employment-social-affairs.ec.europa.eu/european-pillar-social-rights-20-principles_en > accessed 9.6.2025.

58 For a detailed analysis of its contents, character and legal as well as political functions, see U. Becker, 'Die Europäische Säule sozialer Rechte' ZÖR 73 (2018), pp. 525, 528 ff.; see also F. Hendrickx, 'The European Social Pillar: A first evaluation' European Labour Law Journal 9 (2018), pp. 3 ff.

59 Commission Staff Working Document, Accompanying Communication on Establishing a European Pillar of Social Rights, SWD (2017) 201 final, p. 56.

is appropriate. Different social security systems exist in Member States, which guarantee both conditional and unconditional minimum social protection (see II.4.). Securing "life in dignity" as the underlying goal of social protection aligns with the EU CFR (see II.2.), which recognises "human dignity" as a constitutional starting point (Art. 1) and describes the aim of assistance benefits as ensuring "a decent existence" (Art. 34(3)).

As a step towards realising the EPSR,[60] the Council adopted a Recommendation "on adequate minimum income ensuring active inclusion" in early 2023.[61] It recommends Member States to "provide and, where necessary, strengthen robust social safety nets that guarantee life in dignity at all stages of life, by combining adequate income support – through minimum income benefits and other accompanying monetary benefits – and in-kind benefits, and giving effective access to enabling and essential services" and to "set the level of minimum income through a transparent and robust methodology defined in accordance with national law and by involving relevant stakeholders" (paras. 3 and 4). The overall goal, according to the Recommendation is to combat "poverty and social exclusion" (para. 1).

The underlying concept of poverty is not based on a universal absolute minimum income as used by the UN to define "extreme poverty" in the context of the SDGs (see above, I.1.),[62] but follows a relative threshold. This is generally a suitable approach, as both the physical and socio-cultural costs of the minimum level of subsistence vary from country to country. However, it is debatable[63] whether a cross-country standardised "poverty

---

60 See also S. Akarçeşme, A. Aranguiz, et al., 'Reaching the European 2030 Poverty Target: The Imperative to Balance the EU Social Agenda' EJSS 26 (2024), pp. 347 ff.

61 2023/C 41/01 of 30 January 2023, OJ C 41, p. 1, replacing Council Recommendation 92/441/EEC of 24 June 1992 on common criteria concerning sufficient resources and social assistance in social protection systems (OJ L 245, 26.8.1992, p. 46). See on the Recommendation of 1992 P. Guibentif and D. Bouget, *Minimum Income Policies in the European Union* (Uniao des Mutualidades Portuguesas 1997), pp. 83 ff. The EU lacks the competence to adopt the initially planned directive, see U. Becker (n 58), pp. 525, 535; but see also A. Van Lancker, A. Aranguiz and H. Verschueren, *Expert Study on a Binding EU Framework on Adequate National Minimum Income Schemes* (EAPN Study 2020).

62 Defined (at present) as "surviving on less than $ 2.15 per person per day at 2017 purchasing power parity", see < https://www.un.org/sustainabledevelopment/poverty/> accessed 9.6.2025.

63 On questions about the definition of poverty, see S. Marchal and I. Marx, *Zero Poverty Society: Ensuring a Decent Income for All* (Oxford University Press 2024), pp. 1 ff. and 181 ff.; E. Eichenhofer, 'Poverty Measurement and Poverty Alleviation between Norm-Setting and Empirical Inquiries', in: T. Kotkas, I. Leijten and F.

threshold" can accurately reflect the societal and economic realities of deprivation. Eurostat applies such a threshold to calculate the "at-risk-of poverty rate", setting it "at 60 % of the national median equivalised disposable income after social transfers".[64] This threshold does not define poverty. As an indicator, it has been refined by the "at risk of poverty or social exclusion" (AROPE), which includes "persons who are either at risk of poverty, or severely materially and socially deprived or living in a household with a very low work intensity".[65] In this context, the "severe material and social deprivation rate" (SMSD) is an EU-SILC indicator "showing an enforced lack of necessary and desirable items to lead an adequate life, distinguishing between individuals who cannot afford a certain good, service or social activities".[66]

These indicators contribute to a multifaceted concept of poverty, serving as a suitable tool for identifying situations in which social policy measures are necessary. However, they are likely less useful when legislators must determine the calculation of specific social protection benefits.[67]

Pennings (eds.), *Specifying and Securing a Social Minimum in the Battle Against Poverty* (Bloomsbury Publishing 2019), pp. 111 ff.; I. Becker, 'Armut und Reichtum im Teilhabediskurs – die Frage nach den Grenzen', Sozialer Fortschritt 73 (2024), pp. 843 ff. See for the use of reference budgets C. Deeming, *Minimum Income Standards and Reference Budgets: International and Comparative Policy Perspectives* (Policy Press 2021). For poverty as discrimination, S. Jørgensen, 'Social assistance and the end of poverty' EJSS 26 (2024), pp. 27 ff.

64 See Eurostat, 'Glossary: At-risk-of-poverty rate' < https://ec.europa.eu/eurostat/statistics-explained/index.php?title=Glossary:At-risk-of-poverty_rate > accessed 6.9.2025.

65 Serving as the "main indicator to monitor the EU 2030 target on poverty and social exclusion", see Eurostat, 'Glossary: At risk of poverty or social exclusion (AROPE)' < https://ec.europa.eu/eurostat/statistics-explained/index.php?title=Glossary:At_risk_of_poverty_or_social_exclusion_(AROPE)> accessed 6.9.2025.

66 Defined as the "proportion of the population experiencing an enforced lack of at least 7 out of 13 deprivation items (6 related to the individual and 7 related to the household)", see Eurostat, 'Glossary: Severe material and social deprivation rate (SMSD)' < https://ec.europa.eu/eurostat/statistics-explained/index.php?title=Glossary:Severe_material_and_social_deprivation_rate_(SMSD)> accessed 9.6.2025.

67 Which is a step that involves political decisions on the "appropriateness" of benefits; see A. Briggs, 'The Welfare State in Historical Perspective' European Journal of Sociology 2 (1961), pp. 221 ff.; and those decisions raise the question of democratic legitimisation; see also rather generally F. I. Michelman, 'Social Minimums and Democracy', in: M. Langford and K. Young (eds.), *The Oxford Handbook of Economic and Social Rights* (Oxford University Press 2022).

4. Institutions

Most welfare states have a variety of social protection schemes. Social protection is used here as a broad term, encompassing all types of social benefits and various forms of governmental interventions. From a comparative perspective, certain fundamental characteristics of these schemes have developed over time, shaped by their intended functions and the need for effective administrative institutions to manage the distribution of social benefits. This has led to a typology of social protection schemes, even though their actual architecture and the combination of schemes vary significantly across countries. Social protection schemes can be grouped by their specific functions: (1) social insurance provides protection against social risks; (2) social support delivers benefits in situations of (positive) social need, such as education for children; (3) social assistance addresses (negative) social needs resulting from poverty; (4) social compensation covers damages in cases of shared societal responsibility. In a narrower sense, the term social security refers mainly to social insurance and certain support benefits, namely family allowances. As a rule, social insurance is funded by contributions, while other types of schemes are usually financed from the general State budget, i.e. taxes. Yet, there are some exceptions to this, as many social insurance schemes are subsidised by the State, as is the essential infrastructure they rely on, such as hospitals and care homes.

Social assistance systems lie at the heart of minimum income protection,[68] and are therefore central to the following chapters. These systems are typically universal in terms of personal coverage and are usually means-tested, meaning that eligibility for social assistance benefits depends on a person's financial need.

However, it should be noted that systems designed for a specific primary function can also serve a secondary social policy function.[69] In some coun-

---

68 From a social policy perspective, see M. Natili, 'Worlds of last-resort safety nets? A proposed typology of minimum income schemes in Europe' Journal of International and Comparative Social Policy 36 (2020), pp. 57 ff.; A. Noel, 'The Politics of Minimum Income Protection in OECD Countries' Journal of Social Policy 48 (2019), pp. 227 ff.; F. Neumann, *Soziale Mindestsicherung in Europa: Leistungsprofile im Vergleich* (LIT 2016).

69 And that the question how social security benefits relate to social assistance benefits always has been one of concern, see for the early post-WWII development in the UK, R. M. Titmuss, 'The Welfare State: Images and Realities' The Social Service Review 37 (1963) 1, pp. 8 ff.

tries, for instance, certain old-age pension systems effectively operate as family benefits. More relevant to our context is the fact that, in many countries, old-age pension systems are designed not only to maintain a certain standard of living for pensioners but also to ensure a minimum income.[70] The above-mentioned State subsidies may facilitate this dual purpose. In a sense, social insurance can, to some extent, be universalised. Within health insurance systems, governments can guarantee access to healthcare by covering the contributions of those who cannot afford them. Family and housing benefits primarily support families and help secure adequate housing, but they may also contribute to ensuring specific elements of a minimum income. This functional overlap often results in intersecting social benefits. As a result, coordination between different schemes can become problematic, especially since these schemes may apply to different population groups and operate under varying conditions. Such complexity makes implementation, and sometimes even the identification of a specific social policy objective, difficult.

What we do not expect to find are systems providing a Universal Basic Income (UBI). Although the terminology and specific design of such transfer systems may vary, the underlying idea of detaching social protection from economic activity is not new. It flares up periodically,[71] particularly in the current context of ecological transformation and the digitalisation of labour.[72] Without discussing their respective advantages and disadvantages

---

70 See U. Becker, 'Leistungen für langjährige Rentenversicherte in Südeuropa – Eine rechtsvergleichende Analyse' ZIAS 26 (2012)1, pp. 1, 13 ff.; S. Devetzi (ed.), *Minimum Income in Old Age. A Legal Comparison of Selected European Countries* (Sakkoulas Publications 2023); S. Devetzi and F. Pennings, 'Minimum income schemes for the elderly: A comparative analysis of benefit conditions that may affect their right to live in dignity' EJSS 27 (2025), pp. 3 ff.

71 See P. van Parijs and Y. Vanderborght, Basic Income: A Radical Proposal for a Free Society and a Sane Economy (Harvard University Press 2017); G. Allègre and P. van Parijs (eds.), *Pour ou contre le revenu universel?* (puf 2018); P. Alston, 'Universal Basic Income as a Social Rights–Based Antidote to Growing Economic Insecurity', in: K. Young (ed.), The Future of Economic and Social Rights, (Cambridge University Press 2019), pp. 377 ff.; M. Torry, *Basic Income: A History* (Edward Elgar Publishing 2021); M. Torry, *Unconditional, Towards Unconditionality in Social Policy* (Edward Elgar Publishing 2024); for other publications from the same author see: < https://torry.org.uk/basic-income> accessed 9.6.2025.

72 In the context of the platform industry, see U. Becker and O. Chesalina, 'Social Protection of Platform Workers in a Comparative and European Perspective', in: ibid. (eds.), *Social Law 4.0: Update* (Nomos 2025), pp. 117, 131 ff.; see for an "emergency

here, UBI initiatives have remained limited to small-scale experiments.[73] To date, UBI remains more a concept than a reality, and there are strong reasons to assume that it will not replace traditional social benefit systems in the foreseeable future.

III. Substance and Outline

1. Aims and Definitions

a) Research Questions

The aim of this book is to analyse the obligations of the State to protect individuals residing within its territory by guaranteeing a minimum level of subsistence, both in terms of its normative foundations and its practical implementation from a legal perspective.[74]

The underlying questions are:

- What social benefit systems exist with the aim of guaranteeing a minimum income?
- How is minimum subsistence defined, and to what extent does it include participatory elements?
- What is the legal background—relevant constitutional provisions, as well as global and regional international law—with regard to guaranteeing a minimum income?
- To what extent do normative guidelines (human rights and policy recommendations) influence the respective national legislation?
- Is the provision of benefits based on enforceable subjective rights?
- To what extent are courts involved?

---

income" contributions in: J. De Wispelaere and T. Henderson (eds.), 'Themed double issue: Emergency basic income: Distraction or opportunity?' ISSR 77 (2024), pp. 3 ff.

73 For experiments, see J. Chrisp and J. De Wispelaere, 'Parading Utopia on the road to nowhere? An introduction to the special issue on the policy impact of the European basic income experiments' EJSS 24 (2022), pp. 167 ff. See for calculations in the US-American context M. P. Fleischer and D. Hemel, 'The Architecture of a Basic Income' The University of Chicago Law Review 97 (2020), pp. 625 ff.

74 See for a social policy perspective G. Standing (ed.), *Minimum Income Schemes in Europe* (International Labour Organization 2003); T. Bahle, V. Hubl and M. Pfeifer, *The Last Safety Net, A Handbook of Minimum Income Protection in Europe* (Policy Press 2011).

- What are the access conditions for receiving minimum income protection benefits?

Implementation is considered only in terms of how different social benefit systems interact, as this interaction can create difficulties (see II.4.), yet understanding it is essential to grasp the national social protection architecture as a whole. This concept of implementation does not extend to practical issues such as take-up rates, redistributive effects,[75] administrative efficiency of social benefits[76] or the practical effects of activation policies. Instead, it focuses on the legal conditions that shape the scope of application and, as a result, determine where overlaps or gaps exist between social benefit systems.

b) Limitations

To focus on the issues outlined above, various aspects of minimum protection have been excluded from the scope of research. This is not to suggest that these aspects are not important. On the contrary, they would require a separate analysis.

This applies primarily to benefits in kind. While they are mentioned in the following chapters, they are not described or analysed in depth. They are, of course, of major significance to the practical implementation of minimum income support. However, including them in our study would necessitate a detailed examination of a set of legal relationships between administrative bodies and benefit providers, between benefit providers and recipients, as well as of the interactions between these relationships.[77] Such an analysis lies outside the scope of this study.

---

75 See OECD, 'Income support, redistribution and work incentives' < https://www.oecd.org/en/topics/income-support-redistribution-and-work-incentives.html> accessed 9.6.2025.

76 See OECD estimates for 14 OECD countries, 'How reliable are social safety nets in situations of acute economic need?' < https://www.oecd.org/en/publications/how-reliable-are-social-safety-nets-in-situations-of-acute-economic-need_568bb35b-en.html> accessed 9.6.2025. With a view to crisis resilience, Federal Ministry of Labour and Social Affairs, *Minimum income support systems as elements of crisis resilience in Europe, Final Report* (January 2023), pp. 23 ff.

77 For the legal construction with a view to care, see U. Becker, 'Long-Term Care in Europe: An Introduction', in: U. Becker and H.-J. Reinhard (eds.), *Long-Term Care in Europe: A Juridical Approach* (Springer 2018), pp. 1, 11 ff.

The second limitation concerns the personal scope of provisions, namely special provisions for certain population groups. As mentioned above (see II.3.), poverty reduction policy has also developed a focus on barriers to social participation. To overcome such barriers, targeted social policy measures for especially vulnerable groups are needed.[78] Such measures, in particular special benefits for persons with disabilities, are not the primary focus here, as our aim is to identify general principles for supporting individuals in need. Nevertheless, such provisions are mentioned in some chapters, depending on their relevance for the national social protection framework.

A third limitation also relates to the personal scope of application of the relevant provisions, but not in relation to personal physical or mental conditions, but to nationality. We only touch briefly on the question whether, and if so, under what conditions, foreign nationals are entitled to a right to a minimum income. This question would warrant a separate, detailed analysis, as it raises fundamental questions about inclusion and exclusion within society,[79] as well as the personal and territorial responsibility of a political community[80]. It also involves considerations of solidarity,[81] human rights, and the principle of non-discrimination. These issues have become particularly relevant and widely discussed within the context of the EU due to the free movement of persons, and are important for community building as well as for the Union's political role. Initially, the CJEU emphasised the relevance of primary law and the principle of non-discrimination,[82] but later shifted its focus to secondary law and the need to prevent social assistance-driven migration between Member States.[83] More recently, the

78 See L. Ratti (ed.), *In-Work Poverty in Europe: Vulnerable and Under-Represented Persons in a Comparative Perspective* (Wolters Kluwer 2022).

79 See H. F. Zacher, 'Die Bundesrepublik Deutschland als Sozialstaat: Eine Geschichte des sozialen Einschlusses im Zeichen von Nationalisierung und Internationalisierung' ZIAS 16 (2002)3, pp. 193 ff.

80 See U. Becker, 'The Challenge of Migration to the Welfare State', in: E. Benvenisti and G. Nolte (eds.), The Welfare State, Globalization, and International Law (Springer 2003), pp. 1 ff.

81 See with a view to European integration, A. Sangiovanni, 'Solidarity in the European Union' Oxford Journal of Legal Studies 33 (2013), pp. 213 ff.

82 For a summary, see U. Becker, 'Freizügigkeit in der EU – auf dem Weg vom Begleitrecht zur Bürgerfreiheit' EuR (1999), pp. 522 ff.

83 ECJ of 11 November 2014, Case C-333/13 – *Dano*; of 15 September 2015, Case C-67/14 – *Alimanovic*; of 25 February 2016, Case C-299/14 – *García-Nieto*; see U. Becker, 'Migration und soziale Rechte' ZESAR (2017)3, pp. 101 ff.

Court rightly stressed, by referring to the EU CFR, that all individuals residing in a Member State's territory are entitled to fundamental rights, including the right to human dignity, and that these rights must not be violated by denying social benefits.[84]

2. Selection of Countries

The selection of countries included in this book did not follow the well-known categories of welfare[85] and welfare state models[86] which are still frequently used, including in the context of minimum income protection.[87] Instead, the selection was made based on the specific characteristics of minimum income protection and its legal and social policy background. This approach resulted in a selection of countries that covers different geographical regions and diverging conceptions of the welfare state.

In a sense, *Germany* served as a starting point, not least because the question raised at the outset (see I.) is particularly relevant there, given that the right to a minimum standard of living is guaranteed under German constitutional law, albeit not explicitly in the country's Constitution itself, but through case law (see II.2.b)). The *United Kingdom* is included in the study because its social assistance and social support systems underwent a major reform, with different schemes unified under the "Universal Credit".[88] The three Southern European states—*Italy*, *Spain* and *Greece*—are included for a similar reason: major reforms were introduced to establish

84 ECJ of 15 July 2021, Case C-709/20 – *CG*; see H. Verschueren, 'The right to social assistance for economically inactive migrating Union citizens: The Court disregards the principle of proportionality and lets the Charter appease the consequences' Maastricht Journal of European and Comparative Law 29 (2022), pp. 483 ff.; F. Wollenschläger, 'An EU Fundamental Right to Social Assistance in the Host Member State? The CJEU's Ambivalent Approach to the Free Movement of Economically Inactive Union Citizens Post Dano' European Journal of Migration and Law 24 (2022), pp. 151 ff.

85 G. Esping-Andersen, *The Three Worlds of Welfare Capitalism* (Princeton University Press 1990).

86 See W. A. Arts and J. Gelissen, 'Models of the Welfare State', in: F. G. Castles, S. Leibfried, et al. (eds.), *The Oxford Handbook of the Welfare State* (Oxford University Press 2010), pp. 569 ff.

87 Although taking benefit-specific models into account, see Federal Ministry of Labour and Social Affairs (n 76).

88 See P. Larkin, 'Universal Credit, 'Positive Citizenship', and the Working Poor: Squaring the Eternal Circle?' The Modern Law Review 81 (2018), pp. 114 ff.

(stronger) universal social assistance benefits, although Italy has recently taken a step backwards.

To gain a more comprehensive picture of Europe's minimum income protection, we included countries from different regions and of varying sizes. These are *Bulgaria, France, Ireland, Norway, Poland* and *Slovenia,* listed in alphabetical order.

Last but not least, as this book aims to deepen the understanding of the normative and state-philosophical foundations of minimum income protection, we sought to broaden the horizon by including case studies from other regions of the world. In this context, it was important to select countries that already have comprehensive social benefit systems in place. We therefore included *Brazil, Chile* and *Mexico* for Latin America, as well as *Japan* and the *Republic of Korea* for Asia.

3. Structure of the Chapters

Every chapter begins with a brief introduction highlighting the relevance of the research questions, along with an overview of political debates, the historical and socio-economic contexts and legal developments in the country.

The second section provides an overview of the landscape of social protection and its normative background. This includes substantial aspects such as the importance of global and regional human rights, policy recommendations and national constitutions, as well as institutional components, for example subjective rights and access to courts. The overview of minimum protection schemes focuses on their structures, their role in guaranteeing a minimum income, and on their interactions with other social benefit schemes.

The subsequent analytical section of each chapter highlights cross-cutting issues as well as national peculiarities including specific features of minimum income protection and protection of specific groups of persons. Through this approach, the individual chapters aim to provide detailed information that lays the groundwork for a comparative analysis of different legal systems. At the same time, the chapters are designed to present a picture of minimum income protection that can stand and be read independently, showcasing the distinctive features of each country.

The book's final chapter presents our conclusions from a comparative perspective.

Part II:
European Perspective

On the Search for Dignity Amidst Restrictiveness: Minimum Social Income in Bulgaria

Teodora Petrova and Yaroslava Guenova

I. Introduction

Bulgaria has long been plagued by considerable poverty levels especially when compared to the rest of the EU Member States. Analyses often focus on the statistics of the low benefit amounts and thereby say little to nothing about the legal questions and the institutional structure behind the minimum income systems in the country. So far, the question on how minimum income is defined in legal terms in Bulgaria has been largely omitted. In addition, no sufficient attention has been paid to the constitutional influence on minimum income benefits and whether there are related subjective rights following from the Constitution in the respective social law and policy discussions.

Still, the relevance of such questions is considerable given that 22.1% of the population in the country fall below the at-risk-of-poverty threshold.[1] The alarming poverty rates have been accompanied by polarised political discussions during the years. Some have openly argued against expanding the restrictive character of the social assistance system. Given the dire socio-economic situation in the country, the state should not motivate the receiving of social assistance and enable it to become a "professional occupation".[2] In contrast, the European Commission has criticised the low minimum income benefits that were based on executive decision instead of utilising objective calculation criteria.[3] Against this criticism, the reform of the minimum income schemes has been included as one of the points in Bulgaria's Recovery and Resilience Plan following the COVID-19 pandemic.[4]

Accordingly,[5] the social assistance legislation has recently been reformed to reflect the national at-risk-of-poverty threshold as a more objective quality of life indicator.[6] The recent reform thus makes an effort to modernise minimum income mechanisms in the country. National social assistance legislation had long been characterised by considerable fragmentation that also used to mix the functions of minimum income provision and social services, which include tax-funded social integration services. From a his-

1 National Statistical Institute, 'Poverty and Social Inclusion Indicators in 2021' (2021) <https://nsi.bg/sites/default/files/files/pressreleases/SILC2021_en_6IY8TD4.pdf> accessed 12.11.2024.

2 National Assembly of the Republic of Bulgaria, 'Transcript of Parliamentary Plenary Session No. 60, 20/01/2010' (2010) <https://parliament.bg/bg/plenaryst/ns/7/ID/659> accessed 12.11.2024.

3 European Commission, 'Country Report Bulgaria 2017' (28 February 2017) <https://commission.europa.eu/system/files/2017-03/2017-european-semester-country-report-bulgaria-en_3.pdf > accessed 12.11.2024.

4 European Commission, 'Bulgaria's Recovery and Resilience Plan' (2022) <https://commission.europa.eu/business-economy-euro/economic-recovery/recovery-and-resilience-facility/country-pages/bulgarias-recovery-and-resilience-plan_en> accessed 12.11.2024.

5 National Assembly of the Republic of Bulgaria, 'Transcript of Parliamentary Plenary Session No. 48, 17/11/2022' (2021) <https://parliament.bg/bg/plenaryst/ns/55/ID/10709> accessed 12.11.2024.

6 The at-risk-of-poverty rate is the share of people with an equivalised disposable income (after social transfers) below the at-risk-of-poverty threshold, which is set at 60% of the national median equivalised disposable income after social transfers. In Bulgaria, the amount is set by a decree of the Council of Ministers on the proposal of the Minister of Labour and Social Policy. Pursuant to Decree No. 286 of 21/09/2022, the poverty line in the country in 2023 equalled BGN 504.

torical point of view, various forms of care and assistance for the sick and infirm in Bulgaria have always been inherent in charity, which has led to the existing of this unified legislative approach. The functional differentiation between these two systems was finally recognised by the legislature[7] and normativised by way of setting the social services apart in a separate legislative and institutional framework in 2019.[8]

The current chapter evaluates how adequate the existing schemes are for the purpose of securing (subsistence) incomes and whether this could contribute to securing a "life in dignity" in Bulgaria. To answer this question, this chapter reveals the levels and extent of interaction of the different tax-financed as well as contribution-based social protection schemes of relevance to minimum income. Bulgaria has various mechanisms in place to provide a minimum income or supplement citizens' incomes that are grounded in varying functionalities. The mechanisms have different coverages and contribute to varying degrees to the idea of guaranteeing a minimum income and social inclusion. The legal basis, the administrative organisation and the qualifying conditions related to these social schemes also vary. The chapter provides an analysis of the interplay between all of these different systems that could contribute to a minimum income, thereby demonstrating the limited extent of their interaction.

On the one side, social assistance benefits, minimum statutory pensions and social non-contributory pensions all aim at providing some minimum income level. On the other side, child and family allowances can also serve to provide minimum income levels or supplement income through targeting childcare expenses; however, as opposed to social assistance, the above allowances do not have poverty alleviation as their main goal. Disability allowances can likewise supplement one's income but also do not officially function as minimum income provision. There are further auxiliary mechanisms such as specific tax reliefs, assumption of health insurance contributions on behalf of certain risk groups, as well as additional healthcare mechanisms that could contribute to improved basic living necessities of the materially disadvantaged.

7 National Assembly of the Republic of Bulgaria, 'Motives in Draft of the Law on Social Services, No. 802-01-57' (2018) <https://parliament.bg/bg/bills/ID/156809> accessed 12.11.2024.

8 Law on the Social Services, SG 24/22.03.2019 (with later amendments).

II. Overview

1. Normative Background

States must generally comply with constitutional provisions when organising social protection in the event of a constitutional requirement to provide social protection rights.[9] Of course, the mere constitutional proclamation of certain rights does not clarify what the actual impact of these rights on the legal implementation will be. The impact of social rights depends on the constitutional traditions[10] and institutional structures[11] that encompass them. Apart from constitutional rights, in the case of Bulgaria, the examination of social rights with influence on the minimum income also requires the inclusion of social rights stemming from international law instruments that have been ratified according to Article 5(4) of the Constitution and have thus become part of national law.

a) Constitutional Law

Concerning relevant constitutional provisions, Art. 51 para. 1 of the Constitution provides that citizens have the right to social security and social assistance. Additional constitutional content relevant to the branches of social protection identified above include provisions regarding the family and children. In this respect, Article 47 deals with the general protection of children and mothers. This issue also appears in the Constitution as a state objective in Article 14, which declares that mothers, children and the family are under the protection of the state and society. Article 47 para. 1 postulates that the upbringing of children to the age of majority is the right and duty of parents and is supported by the state. Article 47 para. 2 then reiterates, but also reinforces, the state's purpose in Article 14 of providing "special protection" to mothers. This includes the guarantee of prenatal and postnatal leave, the provision of free obstetric care, adjusted working conditions, and other social assistance.

9 U. Becker, 'Security from a Legal Perspective' Rivista del Diritto della Sicurezza Sociale (2015)3, pp. 515, 517.

10 C. Bruzelius, 'How EU Juridification Shapes Constitutional Social Rights' Journal of Common Market Studies 58 (2020)6, pp. 1488, 1492.

11 U. Becker, 'Introduction', in: U. Becker and A. Poulou (eds.), *European Welfare State Constitutions after the Financial Crisis* (Oxford University Press 2020), pp. 5 ff.

So far, there has not been abundant constitutional case law concerning minimum income benefits. The Constitutional Court has not had the opportunity to rule on issues specifically concerning the conformity of the social assistance legislation with the constitutional right of social assistance. Cases brought before the Court have primarily addressed social security or medical insurance. However, throughout its case law in the field of social rights, the Bulgarian Constitutional Court has provided various insights that affect minimum income mechanisms. Like the right to social security, the right to social assistance embodies an objective obligation to adopt a system that is capable of implementing this right in case of need.[12] This objective state requirement is a prerequisite for the subjective realisation of the right to social security.[13] The bearer of the subjective right to social assistance is the person who has fallen into material hardship. This remains to be the case irrespective of the reason that has led to the difficult material situation.[14]

The Constitutional Court has openly stated that constitutional social rights are "difficult to enforce".[15] Namely, their realisation depends on the current economic conditions of the state and cannot always provide immediate entitlements for the individual subject. However, in different case law, the Court has made clear that social rights are still full-fledged rights and cannot be reduced to mere policy development objectives.[16] Hence, the complexity of implementing these rights does not absolve the state of its obligation to ensure their fulfilment through concrete measures. The realisation of these rights is subject to a wide margin of appreciation on the part of the legislature. The latter possesses the ability to assess the necessary needs of the social protection system on the basis of available resources in order to design the most corresponding implementation.

The conditions determining the need for social assistance are not specified in the constitutional text. Similarly, the Constitution does not define

12 V. Mrachkov, 'The Right to Social Assistance – A Fundamental Citizens' Right/ Правото На Социално Подпомагане – Фундаментално Право На Гражданите', in: N. Gevrenova (ed.), *Actual Problems of the Labour and Social Insurance Law. Social Assistance: Problems and Perspectives, Vol. X/Актуални проблеми на трудовото и осигурителното право. Социално подпомагане: проблеми и перспективи, Том X* (University of St. Clement Ohrdski 2018), p. 58.

13 Constitutional Decision No. 12/1997 on Case 6/1997.

14 Constitutional Decision No. 2/2006 on Case 9/2005.

15 Constitutional Decision No. 2/2007 on Case 12/2006, para. III.

16 Constitutional Decision No. 13/2003 on Case 11/2003.

the range of persons in need, nor the type, amount or methods of assistance. Due to the diversity of life conditions and situations and the dynamics of the economic possibilities of citizens and society, such regulation is only possible through laws and regulations of a lower rank.[17] The legislature is free, after assessing the necessities of those in need and the capacities of society, to modify these regulations, including by repealing existing legal texts, within the general objective of creating a social state. Such reforms, however, are subject to the condition that they abide by constitutional principles, such as proportionality, and do not encroach upon already acquired subjective positions.[18] Constitutional social rights therefore entail obligations for the legislature, primarily in relation to the requirement to establish institutional frameworks for the realisation of social rights in ways that are constitutionally acceptable.[19] In sum, while the Constitution acknowledges the legislature's margin of discretion in regulating social protection systems, social rights act as a fundamental constraint.

As regards, in particular, minimum income maternity and child benefits, the constitutional case law has been quite limited. The Court has made it clear that in the event that a woman does not qualify for the maternity rights provided by the public social insurance system, the state is obliged to provide social assistance. Moreover, for (expecting) mothers in material need, the family-relevant constitutional rights and state goals result in the obligation of the state to secure auxiliary mechanisms. Namely, additional medical support systems need to realise the subjective right to free pre-obstetric care derived from Article 47, para. 2, of the Constitution.[20]

In addition, the constitutional case law reveals that the principle of the social state[21] also bears relevance for social policy on minimum income.

---

17 Ibid.

18 Constitutional Decision No. 12/1997 on Case 6/1997.

19 Constitutional Decision No. 5/2000 on Case 4/2000; Constitutional Decision No. 10/2012 on Case 15/2011; Constitutional Decision No. 9/2020 on Case 3/2020.

20 Constitutional Decision No. 2/2006 on Case 9/2005, para. 14.

21 Y. Stoilov, *The Principles of Law, Theory and Application/Правните принципи – теория и приложение* (Sibi 2017), pp. 76-77: The author explains that there was a severe debate in the National Assembly during the preparation works for the new democratic Bulgarian Constitution about the phrase "social state". Some of the "fathers" of the Constitution wanted Bulgaria to be proclaimed as "social state" in a special constitutional article. But others insisted that the Bulgarian state should not be named "social state" at all. As a compromise the "social state" is mentioned only in the Preamble. The author says that "the social state" is not a principle of Bulgarian law but remains only a guideline for social politics. Cf. however, V. Mrachkov, *Social*

The social state is enshrined in paragraph 5 of the Preamble to the Constitution, which proclaims the establishment of a "democratic, just and social state". Being part only of the Preamble, the social state has long been considered by the legal scholarship as lacking the same normativity as, for instance, the provisions on fundamental human rights.[22] However, the social state is a binding programmatic principle. According to constitutional case law, the social state occupies a leading place in policy in terms of matters relating to the material condition and standard of living, as well as to the conditions of work and life, and to the satisfaction of the basic living needs.[23]

In addition to providing safety nets related to biological survival, the social state must also be concerned with "the satisfaction of [the individual's] spiritual needs".[24] The Court further points out that the creation of a social state is not a one-off act, nor is it a campaigning task.[25] Rather, the constitutional text proclaims the social state as a permanent goal of social policy that goes hand in hand with the other two values mentioned in the Preamble, namely human dignity and democracy. An important element of the social state is that it requires special care provision for vulnerable groups. These include citizens who, for reasons beyond their control, such as relating to health, age and family, are disadvantaged in relation to other citizens in society. Such people in society include children, the elderly, the mentally and physically impaired and those in material need.

b) International Law

As mentioned above, international law instruments can become part of the national legal framework on the basis of Article 5, para. 4 of the Constitution. The norms enshrined in such instruments take precedence over contradicting norms of the ordinary law. The Constitutional Court has indicated that the Bulgarian legal framework has "openness" towards

---

Security Law/Осигурително право (Sibi 2010) pp. 47-49: this author, specialised in labour law and social security law, maintains that the "social state" is the main leading idea for the orientation of the politics of the state.

22 E. Tanchev and M. Belov, *Comparative Constitutional Law/Сравнително конституционно право* (Sibi 2009) p. 289.

23 Constitutional Decision No. 8/2012 on Case 16/2011.

24 Ibid., para. V.

25 Ibid., para. V.

international law provisions due to different constitutional provisions.[26] Moreover, international law provisions for whose implementation no specific mechanisms are required can generally be applied directly and thus courts can rely on such international law instruments when faced with contradicting administrative or judicial practice.[27]

When it comes to social law, international law instruments tend to be unable to substantiate subjective rights due to their predominantly open character. Nevertheless, there were instances when international law instruments were able to also yield subjective positions that needed to be reflected in the national legislation.[28] Namely, the Constitutional Court established that norms enshrined in ILO conventions on insurance periods for invalidity insurance were in conflict with the more restrictive national law.[29] The conclusion resulted in the obligation of the legislature to address the discrepancy in line with the margins of the conventions.

While, in relation to minimum income, international law instruments predominantly serve as programmes for legislative action, this does not diminish their overall influence on social protection. On the contrary, the international law instruments have taken independent significance and have served as benchmarking tools in the development of certain minimum income and support and social inclusion benefits.[30] A finding of the European Committee of Social Rights of a violation of the right to social assistance in the ESCR[31] led to the abolition in the national law of the time restrictions for the granting of minimum income benefits for people of working age.[32] International law norms stemming from the ICESCR

---

26 Constitutional Decision No. 3/2004 on Case 3/2004.

27 Z. Stalev, 'The Constituton and the International Human Rights and Freedoms Treaties/Конституцията и международните съглашения за човешки права и свободи' Juridical World/Юридически свят (1999)1, pp. 13, 14.

28 For an in-depth examination of the influence of international law on the social rights framework in Bulgaria, see T. Petrova, *Social Protection in Bulgaria: Functional Systematization and Influence of Constitutional, International, and European Union Law* (Nomos 2024), pp. 165 ff.

29 Constitutional Decision No. 5/2000 on Case 4/2000.

30 T. Petrova, *Social Protection in Bulgaria: Functional Systematization and Influence of Constitutional, International, and European Union Law* (Nomos 2024), pp. 165 ff.

31 'Decision of the Merits, European Roma Rights Centre v. Bulgaria, Complaint No. 48/2008' (2009) para. 46.

32 This reform was also accompanied by a plethora of political considerations. For more on this reform and the international law influences, see T. Petrova, *Social Protection in Bulgaria: Functional Systematization and Influence of Constitutional, International, and European Union Law* (Nomos 2024), pp. 174 ff.

were instrumental when it came to defining some key minimum income concepts in the respective legislation such as the "basic needs of life".[33] Similarly, the UN CRPD contributed to the modernising of the national legislation in different ways, including by motivating the introduction of more comprehensive and individualised support measures.[34] Although neither the Constitution nor the international agreements incorporated into Bulgarian law explicitly recognise the right to a minimum social income or the obligation to establish it as a safeguard against poverty, the social rights enshrined in the Constitution provide a foundation for the development of legislation aimed at ensuring a decent standard of living for those in need.

2. Social Benefits

In Bulgaria, different mechanisms can have a direct bearing on the provision of a minimum income for citizens. The mechanisms stem from different social protection branches that bear different functionalities. The following overview begins by looking into the main tax-financed social assistance, support and social inclusion benefits that have a common administrative setup. Social assistance ultimately addresses the classical risk of poverty. Simultaneously, support and social inclusion benefits, like family benefits and disability allowances, aim at supporting certain groups as an expression of certain public policy goals and/or aim at greater social integration of particular groups. Next, the social security mechanisms providing minimum income are examined. Finally, the overview looks into the auxiliary tax and healthcare mechanisms of relevance to the securing of basic living needs.

a) Social Assistance, Support and Social Inclusion Benefits

Social policy in the fields of social assistance, support and social inclusion is determined at the highest level by the Council of Ministers, which sets the overarching goals and guidelines. The Minister of Labour and Social Policy is responsible for further developing, coordinating and implementing measures within this framework. The Agency for Social Assistance (ASA) is an executive agency of the Minister of Labour and Social Policy

33 Ibid., pp. 173 ff.
34 Ibid., pp. 177 ff.

and implements state policy on social assistance. ASA has the status of a legal entity and is headed by an Executive Director. Pursuant to Article 19(4) of the Law on Administration, the Executive Director has the status of an executive authority but is subordinate to the relevant line minister. The financing of social assistance is carried out with funds from the state budget.

Structurally, the ASA has a central administration based in the capital Sofia. There, as part of the specialised administrative units, the General Directorate of Social Assistance is located. Its territorial subdivisions are the regional directorates for social assistance in the cities which are the centres of the 28 administrative districts of Bulgaria, and a further 147 directorates for social assistance – one for each of several neighbouring municipalities. Overall, the system of Social Assistance Directorates (SAD) of ASA is charged with numerous and diverse social functions, some of which are related to social services, the rights of persons with disabilities, child protection, the implementation of employment programmes, and others.

The provision of social assistance and support and social inclusion benefits is one of the main tasks of the SAD territorial units. They carry out the overall activity of granting, paying, refusing and terminating all types of social assistance referred to in Article 12, para. 1 of the Social Assistance Act (SAA),[35] as well as family allowances for children under the Family Allowances for Children Act (FACA).[36] For this purpose, the SADs are also tasked with identifying persons and families in need of social assistance, managing the application documents and carrying out on-the-spot checks, as well as examining documentation and collecting information on social assistance provision.

The SADs also manage the lump-sum and monthly family allowances for children. These tax-financed payments represent financial expressions of the demographic policy and are intended to stimulate birth rates and to support the responsible fulfilment of parental care and education obligations. Most of them are granted irrespective of family income and only two of the benefits regulated by the FACA aim at guaranteeing a minimum income, namely the lump sum pregnancy allowance (Article 2, para. 2, item 1) and the monthly allowance for raising a child up to one year of

---

35 Social Assistance Act/Закон за социалното подпомагане, SG/ДВ 56/19.05.1998.

36 Family Allowances for Children Act/Закон за семейните помощи за деца, SG/ДВ 32/29.03.2002.

age (Article 2, para. 3, item 1). These are means-tested and are designed as a benefit substitute for those who do not qualify for the pregnancy and childbirth allowance provided by the social security system (Articles 48a-50 of the Social Insurance Code (SIC))[37]. The SADs also administer a means-tested monthly childcare allowance that is paid until the completion of secondary education.

Furthermore, the ASA through its local SADs is charged with some key functions in relation to the tax-financed integration support for persons with disabilities. According to the Disabled Persons Act (DPA),[38] the SADs have specialised departments which prepare individual comprehensive social assessments of the respective persons with disabilities. The SADs issue a conclusion on the supportive measures needed in the specific case based on the data collected on the functional difficulties of the person with a disability and their impact on the way of life and living conditions. The measures are varied and may include various social services, personal assistance and other actions, which are regulated in separate laws.

b) The Social Security System

The social insurance system also includes mechanisms to guarantee a certain minimum income that is often, but not always, subjected to the presence of a sufficient contribution record. In terms of the system's institutional organisation, the National Social Security Institute (NSSI) is the main public insurance institution in Bulgaria. The NSII "manages the public social security" (Art. 33, para. 1 of the SIC), most notably by administering mandatory insurance and benefit payment for the risks of general sickness and maternity, unemployment, occupational accidents and diseases, disability, old age, and death. The collective decision-making body of the NSSI, the Supervisory Board, is staffed on a tripartite basis with an equal number of representatives of the executive and of the representative trade union and employers' organisations. The NSSI manages the pay-as-you-go social security funds that are mainly collected from insurance contributions and flow into separate funds according to the type of insured risks.

In the social security system, the provision of minimum income is carried out through numerous mechanisms targeting various social situations

37 Social Insurance Code/Кодекс за социално осигуряване, SG/ДВ 110/17.12.1999.
38 Disabled Persons Act/Закон за хората с увреждания, SG/ДВ 105/18.12.2018.

and groups. While normally the amount of social security transfers varies for each beneficiary depending on their contributions, a minimum income function can be provided through different guaranteed minimum amounts for some short or long-term payments, such as the guaranteed minimum amounts of unemployment benefits, disability benefits and pensions due to general sickness or occupational disease/accident. The provision of a minimum income in old age is guaranteed by various measures and schemes. Persons entitled to public pensions under the statutory scheme are guaranteed benefits of at least the statutory minimum pension level. The minimum amount of the retirement pension as of the beginning of 2023 was BGN 467,[39] which is itself below the official at-risk-of-poverty threshold of BGN 504.[40] After 1 July 2024, the situation looked a little better – with the minimum amount of this type of pensions being BGN 580.57 and the at-risk-of-poverty threshold being BGN 526. Still, for some other types of pensions, like the widow's and orphan's pensions, the minimum is calculated as 75% of the minimum for the old age pension, i.e. in 2024 this amounts to BGN 435.42.

The system also foresees tax-financed minimum income mechanisms for people who lack a sufficient insurance record, such as non-contributory pensions. Destitute elderly persons who are at least 70 years of age and are not entitled to any other type of pension can qualify for the social old age pension, as provided by Article 89a of the SIC. The eligibility conditions are based on some of the factors used to assess eligibility for social assistance benefits. In particular, the beneficiaries' income or their family's annual income must be equal or less than the amount of the monthly income that is the social assistance base line for the preceding 12 months (Art. 89a, para. 1 of the SIC). The assessment of income for the social old age pension does not include social assistance benefits granted so that it could enable the transition from social assistance to the entitlement to the non-contributory pension. The flat-rate amount is determined by a decision of the Council of Ministers and equals BGN 276.64 in 2023, and BGN 307.07 from 1 July 2024.[41] As of 31/12/2022, a total of 5050 persons have been receiving this

39 Art. 10, item 1, Law on the Budget for the Public Social Insurance for 2022/Закон за бюджета на държавното обществено осигуряване за 2022, SG/ДВ.

40 See below, Section III.1.b).

41 Resolution No. 94 of 27 June 2023 on Determining a New Amount of the Social Old Age Pension/Постановление № 94 от 27 юни 2023 г. за определяне на нов размер на социалната пенсия за старост, SG/ДВ 56/30.6.2023, in force from 01/07/2023.

type of pension, of whom 1034 were granted this payment in 2022. This has cost the non-contributory pension fund of the NSSI an amount of BGN 13,030,593.[42]

There are two further pensions belonging to the group of non-contributory pensions regulated in the Code of Social Security which also serve to guarantee a minimum income in some exceptional situations. These include the personal pensions under Article 92 of the SIC for mothers with many children and for long-term carers of a disabled family member in need of assistance. These pensions are subjected to the same income criteria as the social old age pension. Apart from the means-testing aspect, a common requirement for both pensions is that the beneficiary must not be entitled to any other pension (Art. 89a of the SIC). Qualifying conditions also include minimum age requirements that, similarly to the social old age pension, are heightened in comparison to the statutory contributory pensions. Accordingly, in 2023, the minimum age for personal pensions was 67 for both sexes. The flat-rate amount of the benefit equals 90% of the amount of the social old age pension. The pensions are granted by decision of the Council of Ministers and the number of pension recipients on 31/12/2022 was 1241.[43]

The social disability pension (Article 90a of the SIC) represents a further pension granted on condition that no other pension is received. The social disability pension is not means-tested and covers persons above the age of 16 with permanent and a high percentage work incapacity. The benefit may be cumulated with income from other sources, including wages, if the person can use his/her residual working capacity. Accordingly, this type of pension does not always have the role of a minimum income mechanism. In the period 2000-2012, the social disability pension, reduced by half, was granted even to persons with disabilities who received a further type of pension. This decision was governed by the logic that the 50% of the determined social disability pension were added to the basic type of pension to compensate for the increased costs resulting from the presence of a permanent disability. Hence, the incomplete payment of the social disability pension de facto acted as a social integration supplement for pensioners with disabilities. This practice was permanently abolished in 2019, when the

---

42 National Social Security Institute, 'Statistical Bulletin – Pensions/Статистически бюлетин –Пенсии' (2023), p. 18 <https://www.nssi.bg/wp-content/uploads/STATB4 2022.pdf> accessed 12.11.2024.

43 Ibid.

same function was taken over by the monthly disability allowance provided under the DPA. However, the statutory social security system continues to provide for a supplement designed to offset a necessary assistance expense arising from a pensioner's disability. This is the supplement under Article 103 of the SIC for persons with disabilities to a degree of over 90% who are in permanent need of care.

In terms of interplay of the different schemes, the relationship between the social and personal pensions and the social and family allowances for children granted by the SAD is established in such a way that the situation of social and/or family assistance does not, in principle, exclude the possibility of granting or necessarily leading to the loss of the corresponding pension. The means-testing for the granting of the pensions does not take into account granted social assistance payments as well as most of the social inclusion benefits for persons with disabilities and the family benefits for children.[44] The only exception to this rule is the family monthly allowance for raising a child up to one year, which is included in the means-testing.

c) Complementary Mechanisms – Healthcare and Tax Systems

Different healthcare and tax mechanisms contribute to the goal of securing minimum income. In Bulgaria, health insurance is organised in a separate insurance system. It is administered by the National Health Insurance Fund (NHIF) on the basis of the Health Insurance Act (HIA),[45] the annual NHIF Budget Act and framework agreements between the NHIF and the professional organisations of doctors and dentists. The system is pay-as-you-go-financed with health insurance contributions forming 8% based on income.

Access to health care and medicines provided under the public health insurance may be considered in some hypotheses as an additional mechanism to guarantee basic living standards although in terms of functionality their primary goal is to contribute to public healthcare. The state budget

44 Pursuant to Art. 8 (1) of the Pensions and Contribution Record Ordinance, the annual income of a family member for the purposes of applying the income threshold for entitlement to the social old age pensions and to personal pensions does not include the care assistance supplement, social assistance benefits, nor the one-off family allowances, nor the monthly allowances for raising a child up to the completion of secondary education and for raising a child with a disability under the SAA, nor the financial allowances provided under the DPA.

45 Health Insurance Act/Закон за здравното осигуряване, SG/ДВ 70/19.06.1998.

covers health contributions for citizens who are eligible for monthly social assistance benefits and targeted heating allowances under the SAA if they are not insured on other grounds (Article 40, para. 3, item 5 of the HIA). The same applies to persons who are beneficiaries of social or integrated health and social services for residential care and social services for shelter financed by the state budget. All beneficiaries of the public pension system, but regardless of the type and amount of the pension, are also health-insured at the expense of the state budget (Article 40, para. 1, item 4 of the HIA). This also applies to children up to the age of 18 and full-time students up to the age of 26 (Art. 40, para. 3, items 1-3 of the HIA). Pursuant to Art. 37, para. 4 of the HIA, children and persons receiving social assistance benefits are also exempted from paying fees for doctor's visits and hospital treatment.

In addition to health insurance, the healthcare system provides tax-financed services. In terms of their functionality, these services are part of the healthcare obligations of the state and are not a minimum income mechanism, but could also contribute to the basic living standards of those in material need. Some of these benefits are provided in case of interrupted health insurance status and can thus contribute to preserving the basic living standards. Such services include medical care related to pregnancy and childbirth, intensive care, psychiatric treatment, and communicable venereal and skin diseases (Art. 82, para. 1 of the Health Act[46]). These services are instead covered by the public health insurance should the person have regular health insurance rights. Other benefits are provided regardless of whether the health insurance rights are interrupted. These benefits include emergency medical care, organ, skin and cell transplants, assisted reproduction, compulsory vaccinations and others.

Apart from the healthcare system, the tax regulation also contributes to guaranteeing a minimum income for citizens through tax exemption measures. Namely, the benefits obtained from the public social security, including all of the public pension benefits, are exempted from taxation. In addition, the social assistance benefits, the family and child benefits, and the disability allowance are also exempted from income taxation.

---

46 Health Act/Закон за здравето, SG/ДВ 70/10.08.2004.

III. Analysis

1. Minimum Income for Single Individuals with Working Capacity

The following section focuses on the general minimum income options available to working-age adults with the capacity to work who are not disabled and live alone (without children, a spouse, or other household members). Such individuals in material need can either rely on social assistance benefits or unemployment benefits from the social security system. However, to obtain the right to unemployment benefits, the requirement is that they have previously lost their job and have reached a sufficient contributory period with the unemployment fund of the NSSI. The basic relationship between social insurance and social assistance is one of mutual exclusion and this is evidenced in the very limited possibilities for interaction between the systems providing social income for people of active working age. People registered as unemployed who have lost their jobs receive unemployment benefits from the NSSI if they meet the requirement of at least 12 months of unemployment insurance contributions in the previous 18 months. The time limit for receiving this benefit varies between 4 and 12 months depending on the length of insurance. The minimum monthly amount in 2023 was BGN 400 and the maximum was BGN 1880; in 2024, the minimum has stayed the same but the maximum has been increased to BGN 2357.08. While receiving unemployment insurance benefits, the unemployed person has resources exceeding the differentiated social assistance income. Only in extremely severe social hypotheses, in which the minimum unemployment benefit is the only own source of support for an entire household including two or more other members without any income, will the right to a monthly social assistance also arise; this will supplement the difference between the social insurance benefit of BGN 400 and the total sum of the differentiated minimum income for the cohabitants of BGN 157.80 (in 2024) multiplied by the number of the family members. Hence, social assistance for unemployed persons, especially those living alone, is regulated as an exclusive and last-resort safety net to guarantee a minimum income; this monetary assistance is generally not activated in the presence of unemployment insurance benefits.

a) Beneficiaries

Article 2(1) of the SAA establishes an obligation for Bulgarian citizens to take care of their living needs. The same applies to foreigners with a long-term or permanent residence permit in Bulgaria, asylum-seekers, refugees or beneficiaries of humanitarian protection, and persons with temporary protection. Whenever persons with a work capacity, between the age of 16 and the general retirement age, are unable to provide for themselves and their families, social assistance is the only potential source of social income for them. The main prerequisite is that they are at some point unable, for reasons beyond their control, to meet their own basic living needs through income from work or property, and that, in general, all possibilities of self-support have been exhausted.

b) Means Test

Social assistance is subject to tight qualifying conditions. Apart from stringent means-testing, the conditions include the requirement that one should have exhausted the extensive maintenance possibilities according to Article 140 of the Family Code[47] prior to turning to social assistance. In addition, the law contains further requirements such as rules regarding the size of the occupied dwelling by the applicant and the amount of savings. Social assistance is conditional, in principle, on the person's inability to meet the basic needs of life, either through work or income from property, but also through maintenance by a spouse or relatives obliged under Article 140 of the Family Code. Pensioners often have immovable property and also a close family circle from which they can, in theory, claim maintenance. According to Article 142(1) of the Family Code, the amount of maintenance shall be determined according to the needs of the person entitled to maintenance and the means of the person who owes it. If it is not provided voluntarily, maintenance orders must be sought in court. According to Article 11(2) of the Regulation for the Implementation of the SAA, persons whose relatives are legally obliged to financially support them are not entitled to monthly social benefits at all.

47 Family Code/Семеен Кодекс, SG/ДВ, 47/23.06.2009: "Article 140. (1) The person entitled to maintenance may seek it in the following sequence: 1. children and spouse; 2. parents; 3. former spouse; 4. grandchildren and great-grandchildren; 5. siblings; 6. grandparents and ancestors more times removed".

In terms of means-testing, people used to be able to qualify for social assistance benefits if their income was lower than the legally defined levels. For a long time, the definition of the levels was based on the so-called normatively defined "guaranteed minimum income". The monthly amount of the guaranteed minimum income was determined by the Council of Ministers. This legislative solution was criticised for its lack of reliance on objective indicators based on the costs of living in the country.[48] The definition of the minimum income threshold has thus been recently reformed with the new changes in the law having come into force as of 01/06/2023.[49] The reform foresees that instead of relying on the guaranteed minimum income as a base value, minimum income levels will now be determined in relation to a social assistance base line. The social assistance base line equals 30% of the at-risk-of-poverty threshold[50] established by the government for the given year. For 2023, for instance, the at risk-of-poverty threshold was established at BGN 504 resulting in BGN 151.20 for 2023 as a social assistance base line. This is double the amount of the guaranteed minimum income of BGN 75,[51] which was used as a reference base for social assistance for several years despite increasing living costs.

The threshold amount of the social assistance base line is then discerned in differentiated thresholds to detect a greater need for support based on the individuals' health conditions and family situation. The means test for assessing entitlement to monthly social assistance is to find evidence that the income of the person or of the cohabitants for the previous month is lower than the differentiated income defined in the Regulation for the Implementation of the SAA, or the sum of the differentiated incomes. For a person living alone, the differentiated income is 165% of the social

48 For instance, see European Commission, 'Country Report Bulgaria 2017' (28 February 2017) <https://commission.europa.eu/system/files/2017-03/2017-european-semester-country-report-bulgaria-en_3.pdf > accessed 12.11.024.

49 Law Amending and Supplementing the SAA/Закон за изменение и допълнение на ЗСП, SG/ДВ 102/23.12.2022.

50 The at-risk-of-poverty rate is the share of people with an equivalised disposable income (after social transfers) below the at-risk-of-poverty threshold, which is set at 60% of the national median equivalised disposable income after social transfers. In Bulgaria, the amount is set by a decree of the Council of Ministers on the proposal of the Minister of Labour and Social Policy. Pursuant to Decree No. 286 of 21/09/2022, the poverty line in the country in 2023 equalled BGN 504.

51 Ordinance of the Council of Ministers/Постановление на Министерски съвет №305/19.12.2017, SG/ДВ 102/22.12.2017.

assistance base line. For each cohabitant, the differentiated income would be 100% of the social assistance base line.

c) Benefits

The Social Assistance Act defines the term "basic necessities of life" as "sufficient food, clothing and housing, according to the socio-economic development of the country" (§1, item 1, supplementary provisions, SAA). The provision of these basic necessities is carried through via means-tested monthly, targeted and one-off benefits. The main type of benefit is the monthly cash benefit under Article 9 of the Regulation for the Implementation of the SAA.[52] The beneficiary will receive the benefit in an amount that covers the difference between his/her own income and the differentiated income thresholds. The individual's own income received in the previous month is subtracted from the differentiated income.[53] The resulting difference shall be supplemented by a monthly social allowance in that amount.

The same Regulation provides for the monthly targeted allowance for renting a municipal dwelling under Article 14 that also addresses the function of securing basic living needs. The targeted heating allowance for individuals and families during the heating season can also be included in the present analysis as it is based on the concept of securing 'basic income for heating', thus representing a specific type of minimum income for the energy poor.[54]

Those eligible for monthly social assistance benefits and targeted heating allowances are covered by health insurance at the expense of the state budget. They are also exempted from paying patient fees for doctor's visits and hospital stays. In this way, the health insurance system, in turn, contributes to guaranteeing the material prerequisites for a decent life, but above all, in this way, the state's obligation to guarantee citizens the right to health is fulfilled.

---

52 Regulation for the Implementation of the SAA /Правилник за прилагане на Закона за социално подпомагане, SG/ДВ 133/11.11.1998.

53 Art. 9, para. 1, Regulation for the Implementation of the SAA, SG/ДВ 133/11.11.1998.

54 Provided for under Ordinance No. 07-5/16.05.2008 (Наредба № РД 07-5/16.05.2008 г.).

d) Conditionalities

Potential social assistance beneficiaries who have working capacity and are of working age need to comply with some further conditionalities. Such persons need to be registered as unemployed with the State Employment Office. Registration as unemployed must have been made and maintained for at least 3 months before applying for monthly social assistance. The beneficiaries obtain the right to apply for social assistance 3 months after registration if they have not found work, nor refused a proposal for work or educational training made by the Employment Office. An exception is made for students in a field of study for which attendance is required. While unemployed, adults are obliged to perform 40 hours of work per month within the frame of skills training state programmes or work for the municipality, as well as to participate in literacy and/or educational training, during which time they do not perform the above work. In the event of refusal to perform community service, the monthly allowance shall be suspended for a period of two months from the 1st of the month in which the refusal is made. In the event of a repeated refusal within the previous 3 years, the monthly benefit shall be suspended for 6 months.

Unemployed persons receiving monthly social assistance are also obliged to participate in employment programmes approved by the Minister of Labour and Social Policy. These programmes are implemented jointly by municipal administrations, state, municipal and private enterprises and other legal entities, labour offices and SAD territorial units. Refusal to participate in employment programmes is sanctioned by deprivation of monthly benefits for a period of 6 months, unless the reason is a care commitment for a sick or needy family member in need of permanent care assistance. Termination of registration with the Employment Office due to failure to fulfil in good faith the obligations under the individual action plan drawn up for the person by the Office intermediary leads to the impossibility of re-registration in the following 3 months. This entails the loss of entitlement to monthly social assistance for that person and requires a specific reassessment of the continuation of assistance for the other assisted persons living with him/her.

e) Evaluation

As the illustration of benefits has revealed, the social assistance system in itself offers very limited subsistence amounts and is subject to tight conditionality. While the 2023 legislative changes raised the income threshold for monthly social assistance and eased the requirements for community service, these benefits are still limited to only the most destitute individuals – those with incomes in the lowest 30% below the poverty line. This means that social assistance reaches only a small fraction of those living in poverty, covering less than half of those in need. As a result, the assistance provided does not meet even the most basic subsistence needs, leaving many beneficiaries trapped in extreme poverty.

It is questionable to what extent it is at all possible for a single person, living alone, to physically survive on an income, for example, equal to 165% of the social assistance base, i.e. BGN 249 in 2023, raised to BGN 260.37 in 2024. The question has a categorically negative answer if the cost of food has to be added to the cost of rent and household bills.

The chapter has revealed that entitlement to social assistance is subjected to sanctions in the form of deprivation of monthly social benefits in the absence of registration as unemployed or upon refusal to participate in labour activation programmes. Apart from the sanctions, the recent changes in the social assistance legislation introduced a monetary incentive for the reintegration of beneficiaries into the labour market.[55] According to Article 11a of the Regulation for the Implementation of the SAA, any assisted unemployed person who starts work under an employment relationship is entitled, in the following 3 months of the calendar year, to continue to receive social assistance in an amount equal to the last social assistance received before starting work. This is a real support for social inclusion and encourages, albeit with a modest amount, the exit from a situation of marginalisation.

The analysis reveals that for people with working capacity the subsistence on monthly social benefits, although a subjective right, is not considered a normal situation but rather an emergency and temporary situation in the legislative framework. The considerably low levels of support clearly serve to incentivise beneficiaries to leave the social assistance system as quickly as possible and to support themselves by returning to the labour

55 Law Amending and Supplementing the SAA/Закон за изменение и допълнение на ЗСП, SG/ДВ 102/23.12.2022.

market or by finding other legitimate sources of income. The SAA sets as its objectives the satisfaction of the basic necessities of life and the support of social inclusion of persons in difficult situations. However, the social income provided through the monthly social assistance benefits still does not fully fulfil the function of guaranteeing sufficient purchasing power for food, clothing and housing, in line with the socio-economic development of the country, and does not effectively promote real social inclusion of the beneficiaries.

In 2022, only 19,620 individuals and families benefited from the main type of material support – the monthly cash social assistance.[56] The low number of beneficiaries could be examined against the background of the tight qualifying conditions and the low level of the guaranteed minimum income value. A study of 2021 established that only 4.6% of those with incomes under the at-risk-of-poverty threshold are recipients of social assistance benefits.[57] After the reform of the definition of the minimum income thresholds, the government foresees that this change will allow for a threefold increase in beneficiaries of social assistance[58] as it will result in higher income thresholds used in the means-testing. And data have already confirmed these expectations.[59]

56 Social Assistance Agency, 'Report on the Activities of the Social Assistance Agency for 2022/ Отчет за дейността на Агенцията за социално подпомагане за 2022г.' (14 March 2023), p. 7 <https://asp.government.bg/uploaded/files/7129-YearlyASP-podpisan.pdf> accessed 12.11.2024.

57 Institute for Market Economy, 'Opinion on the Council of Ministers' Draft Amending and Supplementing the Regulation for the Implementation of the SAA/ Относно проект на Постановление на Министерския съвет за изменение и допълнение на Правилника за прилагане на Закона за социалното подпомагане' (21 July 2021), p. 2 <https://ime.bg/var/images/IME_GMI_july2021.pdf> accessed 12/11/2024.

58 Ministry of Labour and Social Policy, 'Partial Pre-Impact Assessment/Частична предварителна оценка на въздействието' (2023) p. 4 <https://www.strategy.bg/PublicConsultations/View.aspx?lang=bg-BG&Id=7515> accessed 12.11.2024.

59 The government expects that in 2025 the total number of people and families receiving social aids will be near 58,000. That is 5% more than stated in the data for 2024, see Ministry of Labour and Social Policy, 'Новата линия на бедност ще увеличи с 21% финансовата подкрепа за 700 000 хора с увреждания' (2024) <https://mlsp.government.bg/eng/novata-liniya-na-bednost-shche-uvelichi-s-21-finansovata-podkrepa-za-700-000-khora-s-uvrezhdaniya> accessed 12.11.2024.

2. Children and Families

a) Social Income Related to Maternity

Pregnant women with Bulgarian citizenship during the last 45 days of pregnancy are, if they are not entitled to maternity allowance from the social security system and have a taxable income per family member for the previous year lower than the threshold provided for in the State Budget Act (BGN 610 in 2023, BGN 810 in 2024) entitled to a lump sum allowance in the amount specified in the same Act (BGN 150 in 2023, BGN 255 in 2024). Moreover, as only income from work and property is taken into account, the receipt of this assistance cannot be prevented by the fact that the woman and her family may have been beneficiaries of income from social protection sources in the previous 12 months. Under the same conditions, a monthly allowance in the amount of BGN 200 in 2023 (unchanged in 2024) is granted until the child reaches the age of one if the non-working mother takes care of the child, resides in Bulgaria for at least 183 days of the year and takes the child for compulsory immunisations and paediatric examinations.

The transition from social assistance in the preceding 12 months to family benefits from the end of pregnancy until the child reaches the age of one is statutorily intended to be seamless. In addition to cash, these benefits may also be granted in the form of goods and/or services that the child needs, at the discretion of a social worker. This is always done in the case of minor mothers, as well as in the case of neglect of child care duties and abuse of the cash assistance. Both benefits are a social substitute for maternity insurance payments under the social security system. They are arranged so that they can be received not only by unemployed women from materially deprived families, but also by women with a slightly higher household standard of living, including those insured under the social security system, but without sufficient insurance periods to receive the maternity benefit.

This type of family support is a separate and independent form of guaranteed social income for mothers. The grounds for its payment are strictly specific – maternity as a vulnerable period of life during which there is a functional incapacity for work due to advanced pregnancy and subsequent care of a baby for up to 12 months. However, its monetary amount makes it only a partial maternity support, in contrast to the maternity benefit under the social security system, which consists of 90% of the woman's average income assessed over the previous 24 months. Hence, the monthly allowance for childcare for up to 12 months is not a sufficient source of support for the life of the woman and her child if they cannot rely on other taxable income and/or financial support from the father.

The benefits granted under the FACA – compared to maternity insurance benefits provided by the social security system – offer lower amounts and cannot fulfil the purpose of a social income for a decent life if the woman and her child rely solely on them. Separately, the system of general social assistance cannot be added onto family assistance so as to lead to an increase in the social income of mother and baby. There is no statutory prohibition on the simultaneous receipt of monthly social assistance under the SAA and the family allowances received by the mother for pregnancy and child-rearing for up to one year. In practice, however, such a combination is only possible in situations of drastic material deprivation.[60] The reason is that all the benefits under the FACA, further sources such as child support awarded to children, and possibly the pensions of other family members, are taken into account in the social assistance means-testing. Regardless of the fact that the aggregated amount of such sources could be lower than the at-risk-of-poverty threshold, the sum usually exceeds the even lower income and property limit set to access social assistance. Nevertheless, even in the specific situation of poor single mothers, if the combination of family benefits with monthly social assistance becomes possible, the interplay of the systems does not guarantee a sufficient social income and does not constitute effective material prevention against the risk of baby abandonment.

b) Monthly Childcare Allowance

A monthly childcare allowance is granted until the completion of secondary education. The allowance represents a benefit essentially linked to the social risk of 'responsibility for bringing up children' within the meaning of Article 40 of the ILO Convention No. 102 (Minimum Standards), 1952. In

60 For example, in 2023 a single mother with one child under 12 months of age and a total income of only BGN 250 from family benefits was entitled to receive social assistance up to the amount of BGN 332.64 – the sum of the differentiated income for social assistance of her and the baby, but only in the case that the child does not have an income of its own from an award of maintenance from the other parent.

reality, entitlement to the allowance can start at the same time as the mother's receipt of the monthly childcare allowance until the age of one, because the maximum income threshold for both types of benefits coincides.[61] The amount of this type of monthly childcare allowance is set in the annual budget law and, because of its additional birth incentive function, also depends on the number of children in the family (BGN 50 for one child, BGN 110 for two, BGN 165 for three, BGN 175 for four, increasing by BGN 20 for each additional child). Benefit entitlement is also conditional on the fulfilment of conditions related to the responsible upbringing and education of the child.

The one-off and monthly child allowances received by the family, including the monthly allowance for raising a child until the completion of secondary education, are considered as income which is taken into account in the means-testing for assessing entitlement to the various social assistance benefits (§1, item 9, letter "m" and item 10, letter "c" of the Regulation on Implementing the SAA).[62] This is an important correlation between family and social assistance, demonstrating the limited interaction between the two systems. Separately, families with children and children with disabilities are also encouraged financially through tax reliefs (Art. 22 "c" and Art. 22 "d" of the Personal Income Tax Act (PITA))[63]. The amount of the refunded tax relief is not enforceable by creditors of the parents (Art. 22 "c", para. 10, PITA). This confirms the refund's purpose as a specific type of child-rearing aid. These tax reliefs do not serve to guarantee a minimum income, because cash sums are returned only to families with taxable income.

61 The full amount of the monthly allowance for raising a child until the completion of secondary education is granted if the family income is up to BGN 510. And if the income is between BGN 510.01 and BGN 610, the amount of the allowance is reduced by 20%. In 2024, these income thresholds have been increased to BGN 710, and for the reduced allowance to between BGN 701.01 and BGN 810. The amount of the allowances has not been increased this year.

62 Exceptions are the one-time universal birth allowance and the one-time universal allowance for a child starting the first year of school education.

63 Personal Income Tax Act/Закон за данъците върху доходите на физическите лица, SG/ДВ 95/24.11.2006.

c) Social Assistance for Families with Children

Social assistance is intended for families with children following the same general idea as assistance provided for other materially disadvantaged groups and single individuals with working capacity. Monthly social benefits are not designed to provide beneficiaries with an income sufficient for the family to have a decent standard of living, but rather function as a minimal financial emergency support for a difficult life situation. In addition to families with children, beneficiaries of monthly social benefits may be Bulgarian citizens and equivalent groups of foreigners cohabiting with others and registered at the same home address, whether or not they have a family relationship.

The differentiated incomes for the means test are different for families than for single individuals. The differentiated income for access to monthly social assistance for pregnant women (starting from 45 days before the estimated due date) and for a parent raising a child up to the age of 3 is 120% of the social assistance base line. Thus, in 2023 such income had to be below the amount of BGN 181.44, and in 2024 it was set at BGN 189.36. For each child in the family, the upper income threshold is equal to the social assistance base line, i.e. BGN 151.20 for each child, plus an allowance supplementing the difference between the threshold and the income is granted. For a single parent raising a child or children up to the age of 18, and if the children are in education, the monthly support can be received up to the age of secondary education but not exceeding the age of 20. The maximum income threshold for the benefit is 120% of the social assistance base line.

In the case of a hypothetical two-parent family with children over 3 years of age, the upper income threshold for receiving social assistance is set for each member at 100% of the social assistance base line, which is BGN 157.80 per person in 2024. Under the thresholds thus established, in practice, families with one or two parents are mainly entitled to monthly social assistance if they are unemployed and if all family members have no income, including from other social security or social sources (i.e. pensions, financial support for disability, scholarships, alimony), with the exception of monthly childcare allowances until the completion of secondary education. While families with minor children receive these monthly childcare allowances, they are not intended to serve as sufficient financial support for raising children in poor families. In fact, the primary purpose of these allowances is to promote childbirth, rather than to ensure the financial stability of poor families. The amount provided – BGN 50 for one child, and up to BGN 175 for four children – remains very low, and is far from sufficient to help families escape poverty.

Assisted parents, if able to work, must actively seek to regain the ability to support themselves. Evidence of this is the requirement for all parents of children over 3 years of age to register with the Employment Office, to participate in employment and skills training programmes and to undertake 40 hours of community service per month. In cases where an unemployed family member – a parent or child older than 16 years with completed compulsory education – has not registered or refuses to register with the Employment Office Directorate, this not only leads to the termination of the assistance; it also means that the monthly assistance for the remaining family members is granted only after an assessment of the objective situation carried out by a committee of two social workers, with the social report describing in detail the reasons for the refusal to seek work.

A special condition for the granting of social assistance to families with children is the requirement of regular attendance at a compulsory pre-school and school establishment, if the child's health permits. Absences from school classes and complete dropout from school lead to a drastic reduction in the monthly social assistance granted to the family – by as much as 70% and 80% respectively. The assistance is reduced by 50% if a child aged 16 to 18 does not continue his/her education but also does not look for a job. When determining the amount of the targeted heating allowance for families under the current regulations, the differentiated income for children also varies much depending on additional factors such as whether they are in education, whether they have a permanent disability to a degree of 50% or more, whether they are orphans, whether they are being raised by their parents or are in foster care.

As a general conclusion, two features stand out in terms of the social assistance of families with children of school age, namely the low benefit amounts combined with the clearly defined function of encouraging parents not to abdicate their two most important responsibilities: the responsibility for securing the material maintenance, and the education of their children. However, so far, this has not yielded undeniable practical results as to whether this approach effectively incentivises responsible parental behaviour.

3. Life in Dignity and the Elderly

Loss of working capacity due to old age exposes the elderly to a serious risk of poverty. The measure of the social system designed to counteract this is public pension provision. According to figures presented by the Minister of Labour and Social Policy during a parliamentary scrutiny in October 2022, the total number of pensioners in Bulgaria was 2,303,988. Of these, 306,460 were below the 2022 at-risk-of-poverty threshold.[64] The receipt of statutory old age pension does not provide a full guarantee that an elderly person will have sufficient resources to lead a dignified and independent life. This is particularly true for those who live alone in a household. The minimum amount of this type of pension was BGN 523.04 per month in 2023 and has been BGN 580.57 per month from 1 July 2024.[65] The minimum amounts of the other contributory pensions (i.e. for disability due to general sickness or occupational disease/accident)[66] are equal to or slightly higher than the minimum statutory old age pension. Given that the at-risk-of-poverty threshold in 2023 was BGN 504, and BGN 526 in 2024, virtually all persons with minimum amounts of contributory pensions receive a benefit that is only slightly over the at-risk-of-poverty threshold. These persons can still be considered as poor if they do not also receive income from other sources or do not live in a common household with a person with a higher income. Simultaneously, elderly persons with minimum pensions cannot, in practice, supplement their income with monthly social assistance due to the low means-testing thresholds for social assistance.

The receipt of any non-contributory pension is considered as income for the purpose of calculating the income threshold for social assistance and family benefits (§1, item 9, letter "c" and §1, item 2 of the supplementary provisions of the SAA). Therefore, despite the new way of determining the social assistance basis and the new percentage of the differentiated income for social assistance, the calculations show that a single pensioner with a

---

64 T. Petkova, 'More than 300,000 pensioners are below the poverty line/Под линията на бедност са над 300 000 пенсионери' (18 November 2022) <https://nova.bg/news/view/2022/11/18/390820/лазаров-под-линията-на-бедност-са-над-300-000-пенсионери/> accessed 12.11.2024.

65 The pensions are annually indexed according to the rule laid down in Article 100 of the SIC.

66 It should be borne in mind that these disability pensions are granted on the basis of disability, irrespective of age, and are therefore often cumulated with earnings from employment if the pensioner has not reached the general retirement age and has retained partial capacity to work.

social old age pension will not qualify for social assistance. Specifically, the social old age pension in 2023 was BGN 276.64, compared to the social assistance base of BGN 151.20 used to determine eligibility for social assistance. In 2024, the amounts have slightly increased to BGN 307.07 for the pension and to BGN 157.80 for the social assistance base, but this still does not affect the outcome. In essence, the current amount of the social old age pension exceeds the differentiated minimum income for social assistance, excluding pensioners from qualifying for additional support. This situation also applies to personal pensions, even though their amounts are lower than the social old age pension.

The issue lies in the fact that, while these pensioners may not qualify for social assistance, their income remains far below the at-risk-of-poverty threshold, which is set at BGN 526. Living solely on a social old age pension of BGN 307.07 leaves individuals well below the poverty line, making them economically vulnerable. However, the social assistance system is designed to support only those in extreme poverty within the broader category of poor individuals, meaning that pensioners living just above the differentiated minimum income threshold are left without additional financial aid despite their precarious financial situation.

Of all the social assistance benefits, only the targeted heating allowance is specifically designed to be used by pensioners with low pensions. To this end, when determining eligibility for targeted heating allowances, the amount of the pension is first reduced by multiplying it by a factor of 1.384.[67] After this reduction, it is assessed whether the pensioner's average monthly income for the preceding 6 months before the month in which the application is submitted is less than or equal to the differentiated heating allowance. However, in order to be eligible for heating assistance, pensioners must also meet the negative preconditions for social assistance already outlined in the social benefits section. Such aspects additionally limit the coverage of social assistance for the elderly.

Most elderly people, in addition to their natural incapacity for work due to old age, have health problems leading to permanent disability. The increased costs associated with disability are also an identified impoverishment risk among persons in the older age group, who are most often also

67 For each new heating season, by order of the Minister of Labour and Social Policy, the coefficient is updated on a chain basis with a percentage equal to or greater than the percentage determined under the rule of Art. 100, para. 1 of the SIC for pension indexation.

pensioners. The examined above allowances for persons with disabilities regulated by the Disabled Persons Act can be received with pensions and thus supplement the income. The previous part revealed that these benefits are calculated as percentages of the at-risk-of-poverty threshold. The legislature recognises that disability has the most severe material impact on the income of pensioners with low pensions who cannot lead independent lives but need constant help from others. Therefore, recipients of the minimum pensions and of the non-contributory pensions can benefit from the disability allowances.

Indirect sources of social income also represent an important tool for guaranteeing material opportunities for a decent life for the elderly. This includes covering the cost of rent if the person is over 70 years of age, lives in council housing, and their income for the previous month does not exceed the at-risk-of-poverty threshold for that year. It should be noted, however, that a very large percentage of older people in Bulgaria live in their own homes. In 2022, a total of 45 persons received rent assistance for council housing, and the data does not specify how many of them were older than 70 years of age.[68] With regard to cost savings, the state supports all pensioners, not just the poorest, by exempting pensions from income tax and health contributions. Pensioners also pay lower patient fees for visits to the doctor and for stays in hospital.[69]

All in all, with regard to the elderly, guaranteeing a social income for a dignified life is a task that is intended to be carried out primarily through the pension insurance within the framework of the statutory old age pension scheme. However, the minimum pension amounts provided for by the social security system are still too close to the statutory and statistical poverty lines. The low amounts of the benefits are further exacerbated by the impossibility for the provision of additional support by the social assistance system. The social protection system allows for the transition of elderly social assistance beneficiaries to non-contributory old age pensions, with the latter providing a greater level of protection than social assistance. In terms of possibilities for combining benefits, the only supplementary payments to the already low pension income are those that cushion the

---

68 Social Assistance Agency, 'Report on the Activities of the Social Assistance Agency for 2022/ Отчет за дейността на Агенцията за социално подпомагане за 2022г.' (14 March 2023), p. 10 <https://asp.government.bg/uploaded/files/7129-YearlyASP-podpisan.pdf> accessed 12.11.2024.

69 Art. 37, para. 2, HIA.

impact of certain specific and significant costs, such as heating benefits and some disability allowances.

4. Financial Support for Persons with Disabilities

Financial support measures for persons with disabilities are designed to compensate for the costs associated with overcoming the difficulties caused by the type and degree of disability and are therefore mainly not means-tested. The amounts are calculated on the basis of the at-risk-of-poverty threshold. These measures include, in the first place, monthly financial support under Article 70 of the DPA, which is tailored to the degree of disability and to the question whether the person is a pension recipient, as well as to the concrete type of pension entitlement and to the question whether the beneficiary is in need of long-term care. The monthly financial support is the highest for elderly people who are in need of personal assistance and are simultaneously entitled to a non-contributory disability pension or survivor's pension due to the lower amounts of these non-contributory pensions. The monthly benefits are further supplemented by targeted benefits under Article 72 of the DPA for the purchase of a private motor vehicle, for the age-appropriate adaptation of housing, for spa treatment and/or rehabilitation services, and for the rent of municipal housing. Only the first two targeted benefits are linked to a family's income threshold. Financial support is exempt from taxes and fees.

The specific purpose of financial support for persons with disabilities has been taken into account in determining its correlation with social assistance. As it is intended to compensate for specific costs related to disability, the benefits are not regarded as income in the means-testing for entitlement to monthly social assistance (§1, item 10, sub-item 'n' of the SAA). The same applies when applying the income threshold for access to certain types of non-contributory pensions.

IV. Concluding Remarks

All in all, Bulgarian social protection contains different mechanisms that can contribute to the basic needs of life. Nevertheless, the mechanisms bearing the functionality of minimum income provision are very limited in their ability to interact with each other. Moreover, the means-testing and the highly restrictive eligibility criteria hinder the social protection mechanisms from contributing to a higher income for recipients of non-contributory pensions or family and child benefits. In addition, the chapter revealed that the minimum unemployment benefits as well as the different minimum contributory pensions are mainly set below the at-risk-of-poverty threshold but are higher than the social assistance threshold. This legislative approach locks the beneficiaries' income under the poverty line while simultaneously banning them from supplementing their income through social assistance measures. Despite the low amounts, however, social assistance provision has finally been reformed so as to include a more transparent and objective indicator in terms of means-testing and the amounts of the benefits. Reliance on the at-risk-of-poverty threshold, albeit in a limited capacity of only 30% of the threshold, will arguably lead to more beneficiaries, certain accounting of the increasing costs of living, and higher benefits.

The constitutional right to social assistance does not result in immediate subjective positions, and the case law of the Constitutional Court has clearly demonstrated the legislature's freedom in designing the provision of minimum income. Instead, the social right to a life in dignity serves as an incentive to establish an institutional structure that expresses certain subjective public law positions. Still, the stringent conditions, minimum interaction between the different schemes, and the insufficient minimum income amounts could hardly be considered an expression of the Constitutional Court's deliberations on the social state. The latter needs to not only secure one's biological survival, but should also strive to enable fulfilment of a person's spiritual needs. As the constitutional jurisprudence has argued, the pursuing of this social policy goal represents a constitutional aim that is inherently connected with the values of human dignity and democracy.

The Quest for a Decent Minimum Income in France

Linxin He

I. Introduction: Poverty in France

"I am not, gentlemen, one of those who believes that suffering can be eliminated from this world; suffering is a divine law; but I am one of those who believes and affirms that misery can be eliminated (...). These are not only wrongs against man, they are crimes against God".[1] With these words, Victor Hugo addressed the National Assembly on 9 July 1849 in support of Armand de Melun's proposal to establish a committee to "prepare laws relating to providence and public assistance". His declaration strongly echoed a commitment to defending human dignity in the face of poverty. The concept of a minimum income has long been a recurring utopian vision, resurfacing throughout history in various forms. First introduced in Thomas More's *Utopia* in the 16th century and picked up by Thomas Paine in the 18th century, the concept has had many variants in France since the 19th century: the Saint-Simonians[2], for example linked the concept of minimum income to employment, while others, such as André Gorz[3], viewed it as a means to eliminate alienation. This chapter revisits France's social assistance laws to fight poverty, with a particular focus on how human dignity is embedded in the overall framework of these laws. While poverty remains a pressing social and economic issue, contemporary approaches increasingly emphasise the need for a more refined understanding of human dignity and its protection in the face of destitution.

1. Developments in the Fight Against Poverty in France

The fight against poverty in France has a long history, and shares common characteristics with its European neighbours. During the Middle Ages[4], poverty relief was largely managed by the Catholic Church in the name of charity. Over time, this responsibility was gradually passed on to secular authorities: efforts to alleviate poverty were first provided through local social services with the establishment of the *Grand Bureau des Pauvres* in Paris in 1545, and later through increased royal interventions, driven by concerns

1 V. Hugo, *Actes et paroles, I: Avant l'exil* (Albin Michel 1937) p. 162.

2 P.-Y. Verkindt, 'Le revenu universel, une question de et pour la Philosophie sociale' Revue de droit sanitaire et social (2020), p. 229.

3 P. Martin, 'Le revenu universel à nouveau : de quoi parle-t-on?' Droit social (2020), p. 770.

4 E. Alfandari and F. Tourette, *Action et aide sociales* (5th ed. Dalloz 2011), p. 5.

over public health and the threat of social unrest.[5] A range of measures was introduced, including the establishment of general hospitals in 1662 to house the poor. Poverty was perceived as an unfortunate condition, but one that was self-inflicted, with the State assuming no obligation for the poor beyond preventing them from becoming a public nuisance. Instead of acknowledging an intrinsic human dignity of the poor, society viewed their dignity as being exclusively derived from divine revelation.[6]

The French Revolution marked a decisive break with the *Ancien Régime*. Influenced by the Philosophers, poverty was no longer perceived as the individual's own fault, but as "a state contrary to that of opulence; one lacks the comforts of life; one is not in control of one's own life" and "it is not a vice in itself".[7] Montesquieu asserted that "some alms offered [...] in the streets do not fulfil the obligations of the State, which owes all citizens an assured subsistence, food, suitable clothing and a way of life that is not harmful to health".[8] Hence, if the poor (or at least some of them) had not fallen into destitution through any fault of their own, then it was the State's duty to provide support and lift them out of poverty. It is therefore not surprising that the revolutionaries initially prioritised assistance for children and disabled persons living in poverty, whose hardship could not be attributed to their own actions. The Constitution of 3 September 1791 therefore declared that "a general establishment for public relief shall be created and organised to raise foundlings, relieve the infirm poor and furnish work for the able-bodied poor who have been unable to procure it for themselves".[9] Article 21 of the Declaration of the Rights of Man and of the Citizen of the Constitution of 24 June 1793 was even more symbolic, proclaiming that "Public relief is a sacred debt. Society owes sustenance to unfortunate citizens, either procuring work for them, or in providing the means of existence for those who are unable to work".[10] Two key obser-

5 D. Roman, *Le droit public face à la pauvreté* (LGDJ 2002), p. 31.

6 J.-B. Bossuet, *De l'éminente dignité des pauvres* (presented by A. Supiot, Mille et une nuits, 2015).

7 D. Diderot and J. Le Rond de l'Alembert, *Encyclopédie vol. II* (1752, text available at < http://enccre.academie-sciences.fr/encyclopedie/article/v2-1093-1/?query=pauvret%C3%A9 > accessed 25.11.2024), p. 213.

8 Quoted by C. Larrère, 'Montesquieu and the poor' Cahiers d'économie Politique 59 (2010), p. 24 (author's translation).

9 Constitution de 1971, text available at < https://www.conseil-constitutionnel.fr/les-constitutions-dans-l-histoire/constitution-de-1791 > accessed 25.11.2024.

10 Constitution du 24 juin 1793, text available at < https://www.conseil-constitutionnel.fr/les-constitutions-dans-l-histoire/constitution-du-24-juin-1793> accessed 25.11.2024.

vations can be made about the Declaration: first, the notion of society's responsibility towards the poor, as established by virtue of the Social Pact, was expanded to cover "every unfortunate citizen"; second, assistance was provided through two means, namely job opportunities for able-bodied persons and sufficient means of subsistence for those unable to work. These principles were also reflected in the work of the Beggars' Committee established by the Constituent Assembly in 1790. The committee proposed several reforms to the welfare system, placing emphasis on the principle of compulsory work for the able-bodied poor: "Every human being has the right to demand from society: *Give me sustenance*, just as society has the right to reply: *Give me your labour*."[11]

With its emphasis on work, social assistance measures in France remained focused on specific categories of marginalised groups, such as children, the elderly, disabled persons, etc.[12] Able-bodied adults were largely left in a legislative void, apart from unemployment assistance introduced by the Law of 22 April 1905.[13] Specific forms of assistance were introduced throughout the 20th century, including personalised housing assistance in 1977 and the expansion of family allowances in 1978. However, the end of the "Thirty Glorious Years" and the emergence of structural unemployment exacerbated poverty in France. According to Julien Damon, "poverty has not exploded in recent decades but has undergone a fivefold transformation: it increasingly affects younger people and women, has become more urbanised and concentrated, is marked by greater dependence on social benefits, and is more prevalent among the workforce. At the same time, a series of initiatives has been introduced: *Revenu minimum d'insertion* (minimum inclusion income) (1988), *Samu sociaux* to assist the homeless (1993), *Loi d'orientation pour la lutte contre les exclusions* (anti-exclusion law) (1998), *Couverture maladie universelle* (universal health care) (1999), *Plan de cohésion sociale* (social cohesion programme) (2004), and *Droit au logement opposable* (right to housing) (2007). The most recent initiative to fight poverty, *Revenu de solidarité active (RSA)* (active solidarity income), was introduced in 2008. The introduction and implementation of the RSA,

11 S. Paugam, 'La société française et ses pauvres' Presses universitaires de France (2002) p. 85.

12 Cf. Decree of 8 July 1793 on the organisation of assistance to be granted annually to children, the elderly and the needy.

13 M. Borgetto and R. Lafore, *Droit de l'aide et de l'action sociales* (11th ed. LGDJ 2021), p. 530.

which established a measurable target for reducing poverty, marked a turning point in France".[14] More recently, the debate over a universal income project (the *Revenue universel d'activité*) gained momentum during and after the 2017 presidential election. While the proposal did not materialise, it heightened the government's awareness of the need to guarantee a decent standard of living for all, placing the issue of living in dignity at the centre of public discourse.

2. Understanding Poverty in France

Understanding poverty is intrinsically linked to understanding the concept of living in dignity. As highlighted in the Introduction of the current volume, measuring poverty is a prerequisite for formulating policies that effectively address poverty. France has taken measures to incorporate poverty reduction targets into law. According to Article L115-4-1 of the *Code de l'action sociale et des familles* (CASF), "the Government defines, for each five-year period (...) quantifiable poverty reduction targets, measured in line with conditions determined by decree by the *Conseil d'Etat*". Article R115-5 CASF outlines several indicators, including monetary poverty, difficult living conditions, poverty among children, young people and the elderly, in-work poverty, barriers to access to housing and healthcare, etc. Poverty has traditionally been assessed using quantitative indicators, but a new participatory approach is gradually emerging.

a) Quantified Assessment of Poverty Using Indicators

France applies a relative threshold to measure poverty (in contrast to approaches using the absolute threshold). The French National Institute for Statistics and Economic Studies (INSEE) used the 50 per cent threshold for many years, but aligned this threshold with Eurostat's at the end of the 2000s.[15] Other institutions, such as the *Observatoire des inégalités*, continue to apply the 50 per cent threshold—including the Organisation for Economic Co-operation and Development (OECD)—on the grounds that the 60 per cent threshold groups together populations that are too heterogeneous.

14 J. Damon, *Éliminer la pauvreté* (Presses Universitaires de France 2010), p. 16.
15 A. Lambert, 'Quelle mesure officielle pour la pauvreté?' Regards croisés sur l'économie (2008), p. 30.

This divergence underscores the subjective nature of defining the relative poverty line. Rather than directly measuring need, the relative threshold is more indicative of economic inequalities within society.

Whether absolute or relative, monetary indicators are often criticised for failing to capture the more complex realities of people's living conditions: the quality of public services, the gap between the living standards of the poor and the general population, etc. Alternative methods have been proposed to address these shortcomings, such as measuring the intensity of poverty and poverty in terms of living conditions. According to INSEE, the intensity of poverty gauges how far the standard of living of poor populations is from the poverty line. Similar to Eurostat, INSEE measures this indicator as the relative gap between the median standard of living of the poor and the poverty threshold.

b) Participatory Evaluation: The Multiple Dimensions of Poverty

More recently, a new "systemic" approach has emerged to replace purely material indicators of poverty. In a 2019 *ATD Quart Monde* report in France, produced in collaboration with international partners, the authors identified eight dimensions of poverty: material deprivation and denial of rights; fear and suffering; deterioration of physical and mental health; social abuse; institutional abuse; isolation; constraints of time and space; and acquired skills that are not recognised.[16]

The research team consisted of four individuals with personal experience of poverty, four professionals working in associations or for individual and collective support structures, and four experts engaged in the field of poverty research.[17] This cross-fertilisation of perspectives helps avoid a one-sided approach, ensuring that poverty is defined in a more balanced way.

16 A. Bendjaballah, C. Consolini-Thiébaud, et al., *Comprendre les dimensions de la pauvreté en croisant les savoirs: "Tout est lié, rien n'est figé"* (ATD Fourth World 2019).

17 Ibid, p. 7.

3. The State of Poverty in France

According to INSEE estimates, 9.2 million people in France live below the poverty line, which is defined as 60 per cent of the median standard of living (around EUR 1,102 per month).[18] The poverty rate in the country is 14.6 per cent, which is lower than the EU average of around 17 per cent. France fares better than its neighbours Germany (14.8 per cent poverty rate), Belgium (14.8 per cent), Italy (20.1 per cent) and Spain (20.7 per cent). The poverty rate has remained relatively stable since the financial crisis of 2008.[19] The only significant rise in poverty was observed in 2018 (up by 0.8 per cent) due to the reduction in the housing benefit.

When reviewing other monetary indicators, we find that the intensity of poverty also remained stable between 2014 and 2019: the median standard of living for those below the poverty line lies at around 80 per cent of the poverty threshold.[20] However, the rate of poverty in living conditions rose slightly by 0.4 per cent in 2019, reaching 12.3 per cent, just below the EU average, trailing behind Germany, Belgium and Italy. The COVID-19 pandemic has made it more difficult to measure poverty, but INSEE expects the poverty rate to have remained stable in 2020 and 2021 as well.[21]

As regards budgetary expenditure in the fight against poverty, benefits amounted to EUR 34.7 billion in 2021, or 4.1 per cent of total social benefits. This amount increased again in 2021 (+6.7 per cent following a rise of +13.2 per cent in 2020 due to the exceptional assistance provided during the health crisis). This increase is due to anti-inflation measures introduced by the government, such as the inflation allowance, which consists of ex-

18 Institut national de la statistique et des études économiques, 'France, portrait social Édition 2021: pauvreté monetaire', < https://www.insee.fr/fr/statistiques/5431755?sommaire=5435421#consulter > accessed 25.11.2024.

19 However, according to a recent INSEE study of July 2025 (<https://www.insee.fr/fr/statistiques/8600989#titre-bloc-13> accessed 14.7.2025), the poverty rate in France rose sharply to 15.4% in 2023, reaching its highest level since the beginning of the measurements in 1996.

20 Institut national de la statistique et des études économiques, 'Intensité de la pauvreté, Données annuelles de 1996 à 2022, < https://www.insee.fr/fr/statistiques/3564980#tableau-figure1> accessed 25.11.2024.

21 Institut national de la statistique et des études économiques, 'En 2020, une mesure de la pauvreté compliquée par la crise sanitaire' < https://www.insee.fr/fr/statistiques/6542073> accessed 25.11.2024.

ceptional, individual payments of EUR 100 for recipients with a monthly income of less than EUR 2,000 net.[22]

II. Overview

1. Normative Background

a) International Commitments

At the international level, France is bound by the International Covenant on Economic, Social and Cultural Rights, which under Article 9 guarantees the right to social security, and Convention 102 of the International Labour Organisation on Social Security of 1952, which provides for non-contributory benefits for the elderly (Article 26) and their surviving spouses (Article 60). France has ratified the revised European Social Charter. Its Article 13 states that "With a view to ensuring the effective exercise of the right to social and medical assistance, the Parties undertake: 1. to ensure that any person who is without adequate resources and who is unable to secure such resources either by his own efforts or from other sources, in particular by benefits under a social security scheme, be granted adequate assistance, and, in case of sickness, the care necessitated by his condition." Article 34 of the EU Charter of Fundamental Rights provides for a right to social and housing assistance. However, these international commitments have a limited effect in France (usually non-discrimination). Next, we turn to French domestic law.

b) Constitutional Standards

aa) Constitutional Social Rights

The French Constitution of 4 October 1958, which remains in force today, in its preamble explicitly refers to both the Declaration of the Rights of Man and of the Citizen of 26 August 1789 and to the preamble of the Constitution of 1946. From this reference, the Constitutional Court deduces the

22 DREES, *Social protection in France and Europe in 2021* (DREES 2022) p. 101.

constitutional value of these two declarations of rights within French law.[23] While the Declaration of 1789 enshrines civil and political rights only, the Declaration of Rights contained in the preamble to the 1946 Constitution has a strong social dimension. In the context of social welfare, paragraphs 10 and 11 of the Preamble of the Constitution are particularly noteworthy.

Paragraph 10 states that "the nation shall ensure to the individual and to the family the conditions necessary for their development". While the wording suggests equal concern for both individuals and families, its interpretation has largely centred on the constitutional protection of the family. The Constitutional Council exercises minimal control over this paragraph, leaving the legislator significant discretion. For example, it has ruled that the introduction of a means test for the payment of family allowances does not violate paragraph 10.[24] The decision to impose such a test lies entirely at the discretion of the legislator and does not affect the allowances' conformity with constitutional requirements. The legislator has broad discretion in social policy.[25] This also applies to paragraph 11.

Paragraph 11 further states that the nation "guarantees everyone, in particular children, mothers and elderly workers, protection of health, material security, rest and leisure. Every human being who, by reason of his age, physical or mental condition or economic situation, is unable to work, has the right to obtain from the community an adequate means of subsistence". The reference to adequate means of subsistence may imply the need for a minimum income. Yet before drawing such a conclusion, it should be noted that the paragraph is a condensed provision that encompasses several rights related to social protection. The Constitutional Council applies it to justify the need for various social security schemes. For example, as regards old-age pensions, the Council examines whether a given legislative measure undermines the system's fundamental principle or structure. If it does not, the measure will usually be accepted.[26] The Council has frequently reiterated that there is considerable room for manoeuvre in the implementation of these principles, stating for example that it "does not have a general power of assessment and decision of the same nature as that

23 Constitutional Council, 16 July 1971, No. 71-44 DC.

24 Constitutional Council, 18 December 1997, No. 97-393 DC.

25 O. Dutheillet de Lamothe, 'Les normes constitutionnelles en matière sociale' Les Nouveaux Cahiers du Conseil constitutionnel 29 (2010), p. 193.

26 Constitutional Council, 20 March 1997, No. 97-388 DC, § 4.

of Parliament".[27] In other words, this does not establish a direct protection of subjective rights. In the fight against poverty, the Constitutional Council often combines paragraphs 10 and 11. When assessing an extension of the minimum income (RSA) for certain population groups under the age of 25, the Council declared that "the constitutional requirements resulting from the aforementioned provisions imply the implementation of a policy of national solidarity in favour of disadvantaged persons; that the legislator retains discretion to determine the concrete arrangements it deems appropriate to meet this requirement; that, in particular, the legislature retains full discretion within the scope of Article 34 of the Constitution to amend or repeal previous enactments and replace them with new provisions where appropriate; that it retains discretion to adopt new procedures aimed at achieving or reconciling constitutional objectives, assessing their appropriateness as necessary, and which may entail amending or deleting provisions deemed excessive or unnecessary; that, however, the exercise of this power may not undermine the constitutional requirements of legal guarantees".[28] This statement by the Council affirms that paragraphs 10 and 11 do not confer direct subjective rights to individuals, but establish "constitutional requirements", the implementation of which lies at the discretion of the legislature. It therefore does not come as a surprise that the Council has never scrutinised the interpretation of "adequate means of subsistence" referred to in paragraph 11. In short, the Council's current case law provides little guidance in determining the appropriate level of social assistance to effectively fight poverty and exclusion.

bb) Constitutional Protection of Dignity

Can the notion of "adequate means of existence" be constructed through the protection of dignity? This approach does not seem any more straightforward. In fact, the protection of human dignity in French constitutional law in itself raises several questions.

Despite the many declarations of human rights that have been issued throughout France's constitutional history, no constitutional provision explicitly enshrines the protection of human dignity. The draft constitution of 19 April 1946 provides some insights. Article 22 of this draft stipulated

27 Constitutional Council, 16 May 2012, No. 2012-249 QPC.

28 Constitutional Council, 29 December 2009, No. 2009-599 DC.

that "every human being within society is entitled to rights that guarantee the integrity and dignity of his person, his full physical, intellectual and moral development. The law organises the exercise of these rights". In the economic and social sphere, Article 27 of the same draft stated that "the duration and conditions of work must not be prejudicial to the health, dignity or family life of the worker". Similarly, Article 28 of the draft asserted that "men and women have the right to just remuneration commensurate with the quality and quantity of their work, and in any event to the resources necessary for them and their families to live in dignity". The strongest recognition of the protection of a dignified life is found in Article 38 of the draft: "No one shall be placed in a position of economic, social or political inferiority that is contrary to his or her dignity and exploitative of others by reason of gender, age, colour, nationality, religion, opinions, ethnic or other origins".

This draft Constitution was unfortunately rejected, and the social rights that were outlined in the Constitution's preamble adopted that same year ultimately remained principles with little binding force. In positive law, the only explicit mention of the term "dignity" is made in Article 6 of the Declaration of the Rights of Man and of the Citizen of 1789, which states that "All citizens, being equal in its eyes, shall be equally eligible to all 'dignities', public positions and employments, according to their ability, and without other distinction than that of their virtues and talents". "Dignities" in this context refers to "membership of a civil or military order", which is relatively far removed from the dignity of the individual.

Nevertheless, the absence of explicit references to human dignity in the French Constitution as found in European and other international legal instruments has not prevented the Constitutional Council from recognising the protection of human dignity as a principle of constitutional value. However, such recognition is confined to the biomedical field, more specifically, the field of medically assisted procreation. In its "Bioethics" decision of 27 July 1994, the Constitutional Council[29] derived the constitutional principle of safeguarding human dignity against all forms of enslavement and degradation from the first sentence of the preamble to the 1946 Constitution, which reads as follows: "In the wake of the victory won by the free peoples over the regimes that attempted to enslave and degrade the human person, the French people once again proclaim that every human being, without

29 Constitutional Council, 27 July 1994, No. 94-343/344 DC.

distinction of race, religion or belief, possesses inalienable and sacred rights". This reading is quite surprising[30], given the proposal of the "Vedel Committee", which had been tasked with refining the French Constitution, and in 1993, proposed the protection of human dignity to be more explicitly represented in the Constitution. As Paul Cassia notes, this recognition implies that human dignity does not hold a foundational or central role in French law, as is the case in other legal systems such as Germany's.[31] While the principle of human dignity can be derived from the preamble to the 1946 Constitution, which incorporates a strong social dimension, it is framed more as a defensive principle that may not be undermined by the legislature. In other words, in positive law, this principle is rarely invoked in the context of social rights. At best, it surfaces in decisions concerning conditions of detention, where the requirement for dignified conditions reflects that for decent housing.[32] According to the Constitutional Council, inmates should have the possibility to request the administrative judge to reverse any undignified conditions of detention. Yet the comparison ends there – although the Constitutional Council recognises access to decent housing as "an objective of constitutional principles" in decisions on the right to decent housing, this objective is far from representing a constitutional right for individuals. The Council again leaves legislators considerable room for manoeuvre.[33]

c) Legislative Standards

Social assistance primarily falls within the competence of the French legislator. While Article 34 of the French Constitution grants the legislature authority over "the fundamental principles of social security", both constitutional and administrative judges have interpreted "social security" as referred to in this article to encompass non-contributory benefits as well.[34] Consequently, the executive's role is limited to the practical implementation of the principles established by the legislator.

30 P. Cassia, *Dignité(s)* (Dalloz 2016), p. 76.
31 Ibid, p. 79.
32 Constitutional Council, 2 October 2020, No. 2020-858/859 QPC.
33 Constitutional Council, 19 January 1995, No. 94-359 DC.
34 M. Borgetto and R. Lafore (n 13), p. 83.

Despite this division of powers, social welfare law has grown increasingly complex over time, involving multiple levels of government and intersecting with different branches of law (education, health, labour, social security, etc.). In response, the legislature has made several attempts to simplify existing laws, for example by overhauling the former Family and Social Welfare Code of 1905. The new *Code de l'action sociale et des familles* (CASF) was introduced by Ordinance No. 2000-1249 of 21 December 2000. Several new laws were introduced prior to the publication of the CASF, such as the Law of 30 June 1975 on guidance for persons with disabilities and on social and medico-social institutions; the Law of 1 December 1988 on the minimum integration income; the Law of 24 January 1997 on specific dependency benefits; the Law of 29 July 1998 on the fight against exclusion, and the Law of 27 July 1999 on universal health coverage.[35] The CASF incorporates laws on families, the elderly, disabled persons, healthcare and social inclusion. It opens with a book on fundamental principles.

Fundamental principles in relation to poverty are outlined in Article L115-1. Accordingly, "The fight against poverty and exclusion is a national imperative based on respect for the equal dignity of all human beings and a priority for all of the nation's public policies. It aims to guarantee effective access for all to fundamental rights in the areas of employment, housing, health protection, justice, education, training and culture, and family and child protection. (...)". The foundation of this article lies in "the equal dignity of all human beings", which might suggest a link with the constitutional principle of safeguarding human dignity. However, we must be very cautious about the normative value of this statement. Notably, the fight against poverty is framed as "a national objective" rather than an enforceable right of individuals. Initially, this article was preceded by a provision closely aligned with paragraph 11 of the preamble of the 1946 Constitution. Some authors claim that the deletion of this former provision represents a shift "from an approach in terms of 'rights to assistance' to one that places greater emphasis on an obligation to integrate based on a duty on the part of the community to contribute".[36]

Somewhat surprisingly, Article L115-3 of the Code places particular emphasis on housing conditions and the basic needs associated with it. The ar-

35 G. Dubreuil, "Le Code de l'action sociale et des familles" Revue de droit sanitaire et social (2001), p. 794.

36 M. Borgetto and R. Lafore, *Code de l'action sociale et des familles annoté et commenté* (18th ed. Dalloz 2022), p. 40.

ticle states that "any person or family experiencing difficulties, particularly in terms of assets, resources or living conditions, has the right to assistance from the community in obtaining access to water, energy, a telephone landline and internet connection (...)". Access to the internet was added by Law 2016-1321 of 7 October 2016 for a Digital Republic. The article also provides for other measures to ensure the continued provision of fundamental services, even in the event of non-payment by the tenant. While it does not explicitly mention the principle of human dignity, this article implicitly recognises that certain services are indispensable to contemporary life.

By establishing these principles, the new Social Action and Family Code offers a framework through which the principle of human dignity can be more effectively integrated into efforts to fight poverty and exclusion. However, for this principle to have a genuine impact, it must be accompanied by practical measures.

2. Social Benefits

As already mentioned (I.1), social assistance benefits in France were initially designed for specific population groups (persons with disabilities, the elderly, unemployed persons, etc.), before being extended to anyone in need with the introduction of the *Revenu Minimum d'Insertion* (RMI) in 1988. This trajectory reveals how complex France's system of minimum social benefits is. The 2016 Sirugue report, "*Repenser les minima sociaux. Vers une couverture socle commune*" (Rethinking minimum social benefits. Towards a common basic coverage), identified ten such benefits,[37] including assistance for specific needs such as housing. Since the introduction of the allowance for asylum seekers (ADA) in summer 2015, the French government has explored ways to simplify the system by creating a single basic benefit. This not only led to the aforementioned Sirugue report,[38] but also to intense debates during the 2017 presidential elections on universal

37 The Revenu de solidarité active (RSA), the Allocation de solidarité pour les personnes âgées (ASPA), the Allocation adultes handicapés (AAH), the Allocation supplémentaire d'invalidité (ASI), the Allocation de solidarité spécifique (ASS), the Allocation veuvage (AV), the Revenu de solidarité outre-mer (RSO), the Prime transitoire de solidarité (PTS), the Allocation temporaire d'attente (ATA) and the Allocation pour demandeur d'asile (ADA).

38 C. Sirugue, C. Cadoret and S. Grobon, *Repenser les minimaux sociaux. Vers une couverture socle commune* (Report to the Prime Minister 2016).

income.[39] While the idea of universal income was ultimately dismissed, the newly elected President Emmanuel Macron pledged in 2017 to introduce a universal activity income, aimed at refining and strengthening the active solidarity income initiative.[40]

The *Revenu de solidarité active* (RSA), which is the most comprehensive benefit designed to ensure minimum income protection, is explored in detail in this chapter. Targeted benefits intended for specific population groups are analysed as well.

a) General Benefit: The Active Solidarity Income (RSA)

The 2008 RSA replaced the *Revenu minimum d'insertion* (RMI) introduced in 1988. As its name suggests, the RMI was designed to supplement financial assistance with an integration component to encourage people to return to work as a path out of poverty. This marked the first step towards activating social assistance policies. However, the integration objective ultimately fell short.[41] Moreover, the system became increasingly complex over time, with a rising number of eligible beneficiaries not claiming benefits. A comprehensive reform of the scheme was therefore necessary, resulting in the establishment of the RSA through the Law of 1 December 2008. The RSA does not call the underlying idea behind the RMI into question, but refines, simplifies and harmonises it.

The RSA serves three primary objectives: i) providing a guaranteed minimum income to ensure a decent standard of living without a time limitation; ii) to incentivising recipients to return to work; and iii) facilitating social support for the return to work. As stated in Article L115-2 of the CASF: "The social and professional integration of individuals facing difficulties contributes to achieving the national imperative of fighting poverty and exclusion. The active solidarity income (...) supplements income from work or provides support to households whose members only earn a minimal income from work and from the rights they have acquired through work, or who are unemployed. It guarantees a minimum income for all, regardless of their capacity for work. RSA recipients are entitled to social

39 M. Borgetto and R. Lafore (n 13), p. 592.

40 J. Damon, 'Le projet de RUA, c'est le projet de RSA' Revue de droit sanitaire et social (2020), p. 238.

41 M. Lelièvre and E. Nauze-Fichet (ed.), *RMI, l'état des lieux (1988-2008)* (La Découverte 2008).

and professional support designed to facilitate their long-term integration into employment". The function of incentivising people to return to work has been absorbed by the activity allowance introduced by the Act of 17 August 2015. However, the general structure has remained unchanged since 2008.

aa) Entitlement to the RSA

To qualify for the RSA, applicants must meet three conditions: i) continuous residency in France; ii) at least 25 years old (with some exceptions), and iii) earning an income that is below the threshold set by decree. According to Article L262-2 of the CASF, "any person residing in France on a continuous and effective basis, whose household income falls below a specified amount, is entitled to the active solidarity income under the conditions defined in this chapter".

Continuous and effective residence means living and conducting business in France. The judge assesses this requirement based on a "bundle of evidence" method. If the recipient resides outside of France for a period exceeding three months, the RSA may be reduced to reflect only the full calendar months spent in France.[42] This requirement does not a priori imply French nationality. Article L262-4 2° specifies an alternative condition: applicants must either "be French nationals or have held a residence permit for at least five years authorising them to work". Exceptions apply to refugees, beneficiaries of subsidiary protection, stateless persons, foreigners with a residence permit or a residence permit granted under an international treaty or agreement that confers equivalent rights, and individuals eligible for the increased RSA. These provisions were challenged before the Constitutional Council. According to the applicant, the requirement for foreign applicants to have held a residence permit for at least five years authorising them to work was contrary to both the principle of equality and paragraph 11 of the preamble to the 1946 Constitution. In its ruling, the Council reiterated the legislature's broad discretion in determining appropriate policy measures. According to the Council, "the legislature could reasonably consider continuous residence in the national territory as one of the key requirements for professional integration; by restricting

42 CE, 30 April 2014, No. 357900.

RSA eligibility to foreign nationals who have held a residence permit for at least five years authorising them to work, the legislature has introduced a difference in treatment between French and foreign nationals, on the one hand, and between foreign nationals, on the other, depending on whether or not they have continuously resided in France. This distinction is directly related to the purpose of the law; it establishes a criterion that is not manifestly inappropriate with reference to the intended objective".[43] Hence, the Constitutional Council upheld the law.

Secondly, the beneficiary must be over 25 or must be the guardian of one or more children which have been born or are expected (Art. L262-4, 1°, CASF). The underlying notion is that young people under 25 should first rely on family support before applying for the RSA. In other words, this is one of the manifestations of the RSA's subsidiary nature. One important exception to this condition is the increased accessibility of the RSA for working young people. A new scheme was introduced following issuance of the Law of 1 December 2008. A "pilot support fund for young people" aged 16 to 25 was established. Subsequently, the 2010 Finance Act expanded RSA eligibility to working young people under the age of 25, provided they were integrated into the labour force (Art. L262-7-1, CASF). That is, young people aged 18 to 25 must have worked full time for at least two years within the three years preceding the date of RSA application. Periods of work, regardless of professional activity, are taken into account, with the exception of civic or voluntary activities. As previously mentioned, the RSA's expansion to include young people under the age of 25 was prompted by the Constitutional Council's ruling on the constitutional requirement to implement a national solidarity policy in favour of disadvantaged persons, affirming that the legislature had discretion to determine the appropriate means for achieving this objective. The extension meets this objective and was therefore deemed to comply with the Constitution.[44] However, pupils, students and trainees remain excluded from the RSA (Art. L262-4, 3°, CASF).

Finally, the most decisive condition concerns the applicant's financial resources. First and foremost, it is essential to emphasise that the RSA is subsidiary in nature. According to Article L262-10 of the CASF, "entitlement to the *revenu de solidarité active* is subject to the household asserting its rights to statutory, regulatory and conventional social benefits, with the

43 Constitutional Council, 17 June 2011, No. 2011-137 QPC.
44 Constitutional Council, 29 December 2009, No. 2009-599 DC.

exception of monthly allowances [for home help]". To determine whether the applicant's own resources exceed the RSA threshold, Article R262-6 of the CASF outlines a wide range of sources of income to be considered: "the resources taken into consideration to determine the amount of the *revenu de solidarité active* include (...) all types of resources, regardless of their nature, of all individuals living in the household, and in particular benefits in kind as well as income from movable and immovable property and capital". More specifically, these resources are categorised as follows:

- Income that is considered in full: this includes professional income (Art. R262-12, CASF; i.e. any income earned from paid employment or self-employment; income from participation in vocational training courses; legal or contractual assistance for employees in short-time work; compensation for statutory maternity, paternity or adoption leave; basic or supplementary social security daily allowances). Family allowances also fall under this category.
- Income that is fully excluded: Article R. 262-13 of the CASF outlines the resources that are excluded from the calculation to determine the applicant's total resources. These include certain social benefits, such as the birth or adoption grant, childcare allowance for young children, back-to-school allowance, health insurance benefits in kind, etc.
- Income that is partially excluded: some benefits are only partially included in the calculation of the applicant's resources. This primarily concerns resources linked to housing. For example, housing benefits in kind are included at a rate of 12 per cent of the flat-rate amount applicable to a single-person household; 16 per cent for a two-person household; and 16.5 per cent for households consisting of three or more people (Art. R262-9, CASF). More interestingly, if the applicant receives personalised housing assistance (social assistance for housing), the amount of RSA will be reduced by a flat rate under the same conditions as the housing benefits in kind (Art. R262-10, CASF). In other words, the personalised housing assistance (APL) can be combined with the RSA, provided that the automatic reduction in the amount of RSA is taken into account.
- Income that is excluded for a limited period: to encourage recipients to return to work, professional income earned during the first three months after rejoining the labour force is generally excluded.

bb) Amount of RSA

The maximum RSA amount is determined annually by government decree. The actual payment is calculated as the difference between the household's total resources and the flat-rate amount. This amount varies based on household composition: it increases by 50 per cent for a two-person household and by 30 per cent for each additional dependant in the household (child or other dependant). However, if the household includes more than two dependent children or persons under the age of 25, the RSA increases by 40 per cent from the 3rd dependant onwards (Art. R262-1, CASF).

From 1 April 2023, the RSA guarantees a monthly income of EUR 607.75 for a single person, EUR 911.63 for a two-person household (a couple or claimant with one child or dependant), EUR 1,093.96 for a three-person household, and EUR 1,276.29 for a couple with two children or dependants. The amount is increased by EUR 243.10 for each additional dependant.[45]

As previously mentioned, the RSA serves two purposes: i) fighting poverty among the working class, and ii) incentivising unemployed persons to return to work. However, the notion of ensuring a dignified existence is not a central element in the fundamental design of the RSA. Its amount is determined in relation to the minimum wage: the RSA must remain low enough to incentivise recipients to return to work, but high enough to prevent them from falling too far below the minimum wage level, which serves as a benchmark for the country's poverty line. By way of comparison, the monthly minimum wage in France on 1 May 2023 was EUR 1,747.20 gross, or EUR 1,383.08 net for a 35-hour work week. We will later analyse whether the RSA amount is sufficient to guarantee a dignified life.

cc) The Activity Allowance

The activity allowance was established by the Law of 17 August 2015, in response to the initial RSA's failure to include an "activity" component. The activity bonus was therefore merged with the "*Prime pour l'emploi*" and replaced the previous "*RSA-activité*". This new single scheme aims to incentivise RSA recipients to enter and remain in employment rather than stay unemployed and consequently trapped in poverty. To achieve its

45 Decrees of 4 May 2023 increasing the flat-rate amount of the revenu de solidarité active, No. 2023-340 and No. 2023-341.

objective, the RSA introduced a relatively complex calculation based on the household's total resources, broadened the scope of beneficiaries, and introduced new bonuses for those who remain in employment.

According to Article L842-3 of the Social Security Code (CSS), "the activity allowance is calculated as the difference between: 1) a flat-rate amount, which varies depending on household composition and number of dependent children, increased by [62 per cent] of the household members' professional income, and which may be subject to one or more bonuses; 2) the household's total resources, which may not be lower than the flat-rate amount referred to in 1". Total household resources are calculated under conditions similar to those applicable for the RSA (Art. R844-5, CSS). As the household's professional income rises, the amount of benefit initially rises before gradually decreasing, with the final phase-out at approximately 1.4 times the monthly minimum wage for a single person.

The monthly flat-rate amount, which is adjusted annually, was set on 1 April 2023 at EUR 595.60 per month for a single-person household, and EUR 892.88 for a two-person household. This amount is increased depending on number of dependants. Additionally, a bonus is granted to each employed household member, which increases with the household's professional income above a certain threshold, i.e. EUR 679.68 in 2023 (Art. D843-2, CSS). The maximum bonus amount is EUR 173.22.

Similar to the RSA, the activity allowance is available to anyone residing in France on a continuous and effective basis, and who earns income from a professional activity (Art. L842-1, CSS). However, unlike the RSA, the minimum age requirement is not 25, but 18 (Art. L842-2, CSS).

dd) The Rights and Obligations of RSA Recipients

Whether through integration under the RMI or activity under the RSA, access to a guaranteed minimum income has always been contingent on the beneficiary's willingness to reintegrate into the labour market. Such reintegration is achieved by means of a contract that defines both the beneficiary's rights to social and professional support (Art. L262-27, CASF) and their obligation to actively look for a job.

According to Article L262-28 of the CASF, "recipients of the *revenu de solidarité active* (RSA) are required, when unemployed or earning income from a professional activity below a threshold set by decree, to seek employment, take the necessary measures to establish their own business or to enhance their social or professional integration". To this end, the legislator requires the president of the departmental council to refer the RSA beneficiary to either the *Pôle emploi* or to other organisations that assist in the provision of access to employment. If such referral to employment is not feasible, other social integration measures will be considered (Art. L262-29, CASF). As some authors have noted, "wherever possible, RSA beneficiaries should be guided towards mainstream structures".[46]

Consequently, RSA beneficiaries who are referred to the *Pôle emploi* (today "*France Travail*", the institution responsible for unemployment services) must adhere to the provisions of the unemployment insurance scheme by drawing up a personalised employment access project (PPAE). This project, introduced by Law No. 2008-758 of 1 August 2008 on the rights and duties of jobseekers, is well-defined: drawn up jointly between the jobseeker and the *Pôle emploi* advisor (Art. R5411-14 of the Labour Code), the PPAE must specify the nature and characteristics of the desired jobs, the preferred geographical area, the expected salary level, and the personalised support measures provided by *Pôle emploi* (Art. L. 5411-6-1, Labour Code). The PPAE is used to determine what qualifies as a "reasonable job offer". This project may be adjusted over time, depending on the jobseeker's circumstances.

If the RSA beneficiary is referred to a public employment service organisation other than *Pôle emploi*, a contract must be concluded with the *Conseil Départemental*, represented by its president, within one month of the RSA beneficiary's referral, which "sets out their mutual commitment in terms of professional integration" (Art. L262-35, CASF). Beneficiaries referred for social integration must also conclude an integration contract (Art. L262-36, CASF). The balance between "guaranteed resources and integration obligations" reaches its peak at this stage.

Following this logic, any beneficiary who does not respect this commitment (for example by rejecting a reasonable job offer) will face sanctions. Article L262-37 of the CASF stipulates that in the event of the beneficiary's failure to draw up a PPAE or a contract within the period set by law and to comply with the agreed commitments, he or she is removed from the list of jobseekers (after rejecting two reasonable job offers). If a beneficiary refuses to submit to monitoring, the President of the Conseil Départemental may

46 M. Borgetto and R. Lafore (n 13), p. 614.

suspend payment of the RSA in full or in part, which is not merely a theoretical threat.

b) Benefits Linked to Specific Circumstances

The Sirugue report found that in 2014, the social benefits schemes with the highest number of recipients following the RSA (1.8 million) were the Disabled Adults Allowance (AAH) (1 million), the Solidarity Allowance for the Elderly (ASPA) (0.55 million) and the Special Solidarity Allowance (ASS) (0.47 million). Next, we will briefly examine these benefits, as well as the Allowance for Asylum Seekers (ATA), to provide an interesting perspective of a dignified standard of living.

aa) Disabled Adults Allowance (AAH)

The Disabled Adults Allowance (AAH), codified in the Social Security Code, is paid by the Family Allowance Funds (or the Agricultural Social Mutual Benefit Fund) (Art. L821-1, CSS). It is a subsidiary form of social assistance. To qualify for this benefit, recipients must be at least 20 years old[47] and have a degree of disability and incapacity for work of at least 50 per cent, representing a "substantial and lasting restriction to access to employment", or of at least 80 per cent in other cases. The degree of disability and incapacity for work is assessed by the *Commission des droits et de l'autonomie des personnes handicapées* (Commission for the Rights and Independence of Disabled People) on the basis of the *guide-barème* for assessing disabilities and incapacities for work of disabled persons set out in Appendix 2-4 of the CASF (Art. D821-1, CSS). Residency in France is also a requirement, with the previous condition of French nationality having been deemed contrary to the European Convention on Human Rights.[48]

The AAH is only paid if the recipient's own resources do not exceed a threshold set by decree. In 2023, this threshold was EUR 11,656.44 for a sin-

47 Disabled persons under the age of 20 are usually entitled to the Education Allowance for Disabled Children (Art. L541-1, CSS). Under certain circumstances (e.g. if the person is no longer dependent on his or her parents), the age of entitlement to the AAH may be reduced to 16.

48 ECHR, 30 September 2003, *Koua Poirrez v France*, No. 40892/98.

gle-person household, and EUR 21,098.16 for a couple. These amounts are increased by EUR 5,828.22 for each dependent child. Income deductions often apply when a household's total resources are taken into account.[49] For many years, a disabled person's resources were assessed together with their spouse's if the disabled person was part of a couple. Since 1 October 2023, only the disabled person's personal resources are considered in the calculation.[50] The former calculation based on "conjugalisation" was abolished to address the decline in purchasing power and demands for individualised payment of the AAH.

If all the eligibility criteria are met, the organisation responsible for paying the AAH (often, the family allowance offices) is informed of the Commission for the Rights and Independence of Disabled People's decision to provide the AAH for a period of between one and ten years, depending on the beneficiary's degree of disability. The AAH recipient is entitled to a monthly allowance equal to one-twelfth of the difference between the amount of the applicable threshold and his or her total annual resources (Art. D821-2, CSS). The maximum monthly AAH amount has been set at EUR 971.37 since 1 April 2023. While additional supplements and higher rates can be provided under certain circumstances, these will not be discussed here.

It is well-known that people with disabilities face challenges in accessing certain social services, such as healthcare. Such barriers may be financial, logistical (e.g. mobility difficulties), or structural (e.g. accessing medical facilities) in nature. The AAH helps mitigate these challenges to some extent. A beneficiary can receive both the RSA and the AAH if he or she meets the eligibility criteria. However, while receiving the AAH, the beneficiary will not be entitled to the full RSA amount, which is reduced by the AAH amount received.

49 Following an exemption period of six months, professional income is subject to a deduction equal to: a) 80 per cent for the portion of income that, on a monthly average, is less than 30 per cent of the monthly minimum wage calculated based on 151.67 hours at rate in effect on the last day of the reference period; b) 40 per cent for the portion of income that, on a monthly average, exceeds 30 per cent of the monthly minimum wage calculated based on 151.67 hours at the rate in effect on the last day of the reference period (D821-9, CSS).

50 Decree No. 2022-1694 of 28 December 2022 on the deconjugalisation of the disabled adults allowance.

bb) Solidarity Allowance for the Elderly (ASPA)

The Solidarity Allowance for the Elderly (ASPA) traces its origins to the Law of 14 March 1941, which established a minimum old-age pension to provide a minimum income for elderly people with a low income. Over time, however, the system became increasingly complex, consisting of both a basic and a supplementary allowance. The Ordinance of 24 June 2004 merged these allowances to create the ASPA (Art. L815-1, CSS).

To qualify for this allowance, applicants must be 65 or older or must have reached retirement age if they are unable to work. They must also have regularly and effectively resided in France, and their income may not exceed a given threshold. When assessing the applicant's total resources, "all disability and old-age benefits, professional and other income, including income from movable and immovable property and assets donated by the applicant in the ten years preceding the application" (Art. R815-22, CSS) are considered. Certain exclusions (such as the applicant's premises, namely his or her principal residence) are specified in the same article. In 2023, the threshold was set at EUR 961.08 for a single-person household and EUR 1,492.08 for a couple. The actual ASPA amount is therefore equal to the difference between household income and the applicable threshold.

The ASPA can be combined with the RSA which will be subject to a reduction.

cc) Specific Solidarity Allowance (ASS)

The Specific Solidarity Allowance (ASS) is a form of social assistance provided to unemployed persons who have exhausted their entitlement to unemployment insurance (Art. L5423-1, Code du travail). Recipients of unemployment insurance benefits aged 50 or older may opt to receive ASS (Art. L5423-2, Code du travail). However, this is relatively uncommon, as the ASS is generally less advantageous than the standard unemployment insurance benefit, the *allocation d'aide au retour à l'emploi.*

Three conditions must be met to qualify for the ASS (Art. R5423-1, Code du travail):

- First, the applicant must provide proof of at least five years of paid employment within the ten years preceding the end of the employment contract that gave rise to the entitlement to unemployment insurance benefits (for individuals who interrupted their (paid) employment to

care for a child, this period is reduced by one year for each dependent child, up to a maximum of three years);
- Secondly, they must demonstrate that they are actively looking for work;
- Finally, as with other social assistance benefits, the applicant's income may not exceed a certain threshold. This limit was set at EUR 1271.90 for a single-person household in 2023 and at EUR 1998.79 for a couple. In addition, the income of the applicant's spouse, civil union partner or cohabiting partner is taken into account (C. trav., Art. R5423-2, Code du travail).

If all these conditions are met, the individual can request *Pôle emploi* to pay him or her the ASS, which amounted to EUR 18.17 euros per day in 2023. If the applicant's total resources—including the ASS—exceed the established threshold, the ASS will be reduced accordingly. Once awarded, the ASS is provided for a renewable six-month period, with no restriction on the number of renewals, provided the eligibility criteria continue to be met.

As with other benefits, the ASS can be combined with the RSA which will be reduced accordingly.

dd) Asylum Seeker's Allowance (ADA)

The asylum seeker's allowance (ADA) was established by the Law of 29 July 2015, based on the "insertion allowance" (Art. D533-1, *Code de l'entrée et du séjour des étrangers et du droit d'asile*). To qualify for the ADA, applicants must possess an asylum application certificate. The asylum seeker must be at least 18 years old. Unaccompanied minors are placed under the care of child welfare services. The applicant's monthly income must be lower than the amount of the RSA. The resources taken into consideration to determine eligibility include the applicant's and, where applicable, his or her spouse's, civil union or cohabitating partner's.

When these conditions are met, the allowance is paid by the French Office for Immigration and Integration (OFII). The amount is a fixed daily rate that varies depending on household size, ranging from EUR 6.80 per day for a single-person household to EUR 37.40 for a family of ten. An additional housing allowance may be added to this daily rate, if the asylum seeker has not been provided accommodation, despite requesting it. Initially set at EUR 4.20 per day, this additional amount has been the subject of two rulings by the *Conseil d'État*, which twice ruled against the administrative determination on the grounds that the amount was insufficient. We will review these decisions in the following section. The ADA cannot be combined with the RSA.

III. Analysis

1. Different Levels of Benefit

Depending on the respective benefit, the maximum monthly amount of benefits for a single-person household in 2023 varied from around EUR 204 per month (ADA for a 30-day period) to EUR 971.37 (AAH). The amount of ASS was set at EUR 545.10 per month (for a 30-day month), the RSA at EUR 607.75 per month, and the ASPA at EUR 961.08 per month. While the amounts of the AAH and ASPA are similar to that of the minimum monthly wage, other benefits fall below this threshold.

The different benefits are calculated using distinct means-testing methods: the RSA considers all of the applicant's sources of income, including all family allowances, while the ADA generally excludes family allowances from the calculation of the applicant's total resources (Art. D553-4, *Code de l'entrée et du séjour des étrangers et du droit d'asile*). The AAH only considers professional income after applying an allowance, while the calculation of the ASPA also includes donations of movable and immovable property made by the applicant within the ten years prior to the application.

The applicant's family situation also influences the benefit amount. The RSA, ASS and ASPA include the spouse or partner's income in the calculation; the amount of the RSA and ASPA increases in proportion to household size. The AAH has been "deconjugalised" (it is now only based on the disabled individual's income to enhance his or her autonomy), though the income threshold is still influenced by the recipient's family situation. For the calculation of the ADA, the partner's resources are also considered, but an increase in household size only leads to a minimal increase in social assistance.

Beyond this complexity, which makes it difficult for recipients to navigate the benefits system, the justification for the difference in treatment is questionable. The Sirugue report of 2016 already highlighted that RSA and ASS recipients are significantly further from the poverty line than AAH or ASPA recipients.[51] A 2021 study by the *Conseil d'Etat* also noted that "the overall

51 C. Sirugue, C. Cadoret, S. Grobon (n 38), pp. 36-37.

observation is that the rules are illegible and extremely complex to follow, despite the fact that the benefits in question are primarily aimed at our fellow citizens who are often the least equipped to navigate them (...). It is therefore necessary (...) to introduce major simplifications".[52]

Finally, it should be noted that the rules governing benefit increases were also unclear for a long time. Some benefits were subject to exceptional increases, for example the AAH and the ASPA in 2008 (an increase of 25 per cent). This inconsistency in how benefits were adjusted to new economic conditions was addressed by the 2016 Social Security Financing Act, which standardised the frequency and method of revaluation. Since then, the benefit amounts have been adjusted annually by the government on 1 April, based on inflation. However, it should also be noted that the revaluation does not apply to ADA, which remains at its initial level.

2. Identifying Needs: The Adequacy of Social Assistance in Question

a) Factual Finding of Inadequacy

Does social assistance provide a path out of poverty? We can answer this question by first reviewing the various monetary definitions discussed earlier (see I, 2). According to a recent report by the *Cour des Comptes*, nearly 65 per cent of RSA recipients remain below the poverty line. This figure has remained relatively stable since 2010. It seems that, regardless of household composition, the total income from social and family assistance (i.e. the RSA and family benefits) has never enabled recipients to rise above 86 per cent of the poverty threshold (*seuil de pauvreté*).[53] When looking at the indicator 'poverty in living conditions', the situation remains largely unchanged: over half of recipients are still considered poor.[54] ASPA and AAH recipients are in a slightly better situation due to the benefits' higher amounts. However, poor living conditions still affect around 50 per cent of recipients of each of these benefits, according to a 2020 report.[55]

In other words, while social assistance helps mitigate the effects of poverty, it does not lift people out of their state of need. One of the questions

52 Conseil d'Etat, *Les conditions de ressources dans les politiques sociales: plus de simplicité, plus de cohérence* (2021), p. 8.

53 Cour des Comptes, *Le revenu de solidarité active* (2022), pp. 77-78.

54 Ibid, p. 81.

55 DREES, *Minima sociaux et prestations sociales* (DREES 2020), p. 98.

put forward to the government is whether the amount of benefits should be reviewed, particularly in the light of the requirement to uphold human dignity.

b) Return of the Absolute Concept of Poverty: The Reference Budget

At present, ensuring a decent income is not directly addressed in legislation. Benefit amounts are determined based on historical contexts and specific, temporary circumstances. For example, the initial amount of the minimum integration income (RMI) when it was introduced in 1988 was simply the result of an election promise. An official at the time recalled that "we were bound by candidate François Mitterrand's 'Letter to the French'. He had set the amount at 2,000 francs for a single person. This reference was not justified by an analysis of the desired corelation between the RMI and the minimum wage or the RMI and the poverty line".[56]

Such an approach is no longer adequate today. An alternative, known as "reference budgeting", has recently emerged. Inspired by British experiences, this reference budget is based on an innovative method that focuses on goods and services (an absolute approach aimed at identifying the criteria for a dignified life) and the involvement of those directly affected, as already seen in the definition of poverty's different dimensions. In the version developed by the *Conseil national des politiques de lutte contre la pauvreté et l'exclusion*, the reference budget is defined as covering "the essential needs to meet the necessities of daily life (food, housing, healthcare, etc.) and to fully participate in social life".[57] The determination of the reference budget also includes applicants' geographical and family circumstances. When determining essential goods and services, the discussions with participating French residents do not focus on essential goods and services' monetary value, which is determined by experts. This final determination is furthermore based on in-depth exchanges and negotiations with the residents. The budget prioritises needs such as housing, equipment (e.g. internet connection), transportation, participation in social life, childcare,

56 B. Fragonard, 'Trente ans après : retour sur les arbitrages initiaux du RMI et leur évolution' Revue de droit sanitaire et social (2020), p. 213.

57 M. Lelièvre, *Les budgets de référence en milieu rural, en ville moyenne et en métropole du grand Paris* (Conseil national des politiques de lutte contre la pauvreté et l'exclusion 2022), p. 78.

etc. For example, the lowest reference budget for Paris is EUR 1,691, rising to EUR 4,459 for a couple with two children.[58]

This outcome stands in strong contrast to the current level of benefits. Advocates of the reference budget propose a twofold objective: "in the short term, to raise the level of minimum social benefits and in the medium term, to develop employment dynamics that offer better protection against job insecurity and very short-term employment".[59] Interestingly, they also challenge the social perceptions of what constitutes essential needs. For example, in the context of environmental challenges, should "organic" products be considered a fundamental component of a decent diet? While there is no immediate answer, such questions deserve to be clearly articulated and openly debated within society.

c) The Judge's Marginal Control over the Amounts Set

In the light of ongoing developments, what role should judges play? Currently, French judges rarely intervene in this debate. As already mentioned, the Constitutional Council grants the legislature significant discretion.[60] This flexibility is so extensive that as long as a solidarity benefit is not abolished, any modifications, regardless of their nature, are generally upheld by the Constitutional Court.

Nevertheless, the *Conseil d'Etat* has exercised a certain degree of control over the executive's determination of the additional ADA amount. This additional amount is granted when the French Office for Immigration and Integration is unable to provide accommodation to applicants. Initially, the government set the additional amount at EUR 4.20 per day in a Decree of 21 October 2015. In an effort to annul this decree, several associations advocating for the protection of asylum seekers invoked Article 17 of EU Directive 2013/33, which mandates the guarantee of adequate material reception conditions.[61] The *Conseil d'Etat* upheld the complaint, ruling that

---

58 Ibid, p. 137.

59 J. Vignon and M. Lelièvre, 'Les budgets de référence, ou la pauvreté vécue comme un manque' Revue de droit sanitaire et social (2020), pp. 269, 282.

60 See above, sec. II.1.b).

61 Article 17 of Directive 2013/33 specifically states that "Member States shall ensure that applicants have access to material reception conditions when they submit their application for international protection (...) and that measures relating to material reception conditions provide applicants with an adequate standard of living which

"the additional amount of EUR 4.20 provided for by the contested decree is clearly insufficient to enable an asylum seeker to obtain accommodation on the private rental market".[62] In response, the regulatory authority raised the additional daily amount to EUR 5.20 in a new decree dated 29 March 2017. However, on the same grounds, the Council annulled this decree as well at the request of several associations.[63] Finally, the government adopted a new decree on 31 May 2018, setting the additional daily amount at EUR 7.80. Not surprisingly, the decree was again contested in court. This time, however, the *Conseil d'Etat* upheld the amount, deeming it not manifestly insufficient.[64] Such a conclusion may leave observers sceptical. On the one hand, the three rulings of the *Conseil d'Etat* were based on the EU Reception Directive rather than on a domestic principle of human dignity. On the other hand, such control is exercised in a minimalist manner, which does not effectively address the inadequacy of protection. With domestic remedies now having been exhausted, one might expect change to come at the European level. In 2020, France was already condemned by the European Court of Human Rights under Article 3 of the Convention (which prohibits inhumane and degrading treatment) for leaving asylum seekers "for months on end, living in the street, without resources, without access to sanitary facilities, without any means of meeting their basic needs, and in constant fear of being attacked and robbed".[65]

3. Activation: Difficult to Achieve

The RSA (and its predecessor, the RMI) and the ASS prioritise integration and activation. Interestingly, recipients of the AAH also benefit from a six-month exemption of their professional income upon resuming work. In what follows, we use the RSA as an example to assess the various activation measures that have been implemented.

guarantees their subsistence and protects their physical and mental health" and that "where Member States grant material reception conditions in the form of financial allowances or vouchers, the amount thereof shall be fixed in accordance with the level or levels established in the Member State concerned, either by law or in practice, to ensure an adequate standard of living for its nationals".

62 CE, 23 December 2016, No. 394819.

63 CE, 17 January 2018, No. 410280.

64 CE, 11 December 2019, No. 422857.

65 European Court of Human Rights, 2 July 2020, N. H. et al. vs. France, n° 28820/13.

a) Limited Impact

The RSA activation mechanism consists of two components: a traditional one, which makes eligibility to the RSA conditional on actively seeking employment; and a second, more incentive-based component, which takes the form of the activity allowance.

The traditional component, often referred to as "conditionality", takes the form of a contract. This "contractualisation" refers to the process of drafting a contract that "binds the recipient to the managing body (...), outlining all relevant information about the benefit, the recipient's rights and duties and the commitments they must fulfil".[66] Initially, the RMI provided for an "integration contract". Despite its name, the benefit's contractual nature was very ambiguous. Today, RSA recipients' rights and duties are outlined in either a personalised employment access project or a reciprocal commitment contract. Despite the legal framework providing for a sophisticated support system, these contracts—particularly commitment contracts—are often treated as a formality in practice.[67] Moreover, the *Cour des Comptes* highlights that no figures are available to assess the application of sanctions, which demonstrates the lack of monitoring. The impact of activation measures on recipients therefore remains fairly limited.

The introduction of the activity allowance in 2015 was a direct response to the failure of the *RSA-activité* of 2008. According to a national report on the evaluation of the RSA published in 2011, 68 per cent of eligible individuals did not claim the *RSA-activité*.[68] Although the structure of the new scheme has been simplified, its calculation remains no less complicated,[69] and though it seems to be more favourably perceived by recipients,[70] access to employment remains just as challenging as before. According to the *Cour des Comptes*, "when they return to work, 68 per cent of non-RSA recipients find lasting employment (i.e. lasting more than six months), compared to only 56 per cent of RSA recipients".[71] People experience a high degree

66 C. Willmann, 'Minima sociaux/RUA à l'épreuve de la contractualisation' Droit social (2020), p. 796.

67 Cour des Comptes, *Le revenu de solidarité active* (2022), pp. 23, 127.

68 Comité national d'évaluation du RSA, *Rapport national d'évaluation du RSA - Rapport final* (2011), p. 52.

69 C. Magord, 'Le revenu universel : une réponse aux freins à l'accès au(x) droit(s) et au non-recours?' Droit social (2020), p. 781.

70 DREES, CNAF, *Rapport d'évaluation de la prime d'activité* (2017), p. 15.

71 Cour des Comptes, *Le revenu de solidarité active* (2022), p. 21.

of instability when exiting the RSA, with two-thirds of former recipients fluctuating between employment and unemployment at least twice within five years. Moreover, 41 per cent of former recipients eventually return to the RSA.[72]

It therefore seems that a system based exclusively on sanctions and financial incentives is insufficient to address the challenge of reintegration into the labour market. As some authors have noted, this approach is based on several questionable assumptions: an economic calculation of the benefits of employment, a robust employment policy, and a simplistic conception of the labour market.[73] However, the government seems to overlook the fact that the activation policies' effectiveness depends more on social than on economic factors, such as vocational training or social integration. The most recent reform proposal aims to step up sanctions against RSA recipients.

b) A New Reform is Underway

The French government's objective to achieve full employment requires a more effective strategy for "remobilising" economically inactive persons. A report published in April 2023 criticises the fact that "only 40 per cent of RSA recipients are registered with *Pôle emploi* and many young unemployed persons, who are neither in education nor in training, are not identified by the public employment service".[74] Like the *Cour des comptes*, this report criticises the fact that RSA sanctions are largely ineffective.

Subsequently, a bill entitled "For Full Employment" was tabled in the Senate on 7 June 2023.[75] The Law on Full Employment was approved in December 2023,[76] to be implemented between 2024 and 2027. After an initial trial period, the new mechanism will be applied across France. Several measures stand out: Article 1 calls on all unemployed persons to be registered with the *France-Travail*, which will replace the *Pôle emploi*. Registration as a jobseeker with the relevant authorities will become automatic

72 Ibid.
73 M. Borgetto and R. Lafore (n 13), p. 618.
74 Thibaut Guilluy, *France Travail* (Report for the Ministry of Labour 2023), p. 52.
75 < https://travail-emploi.gouv.fr/objectif-plein-emploi-presentation-du-projet-de-loi> accessed 25.11.2024.
76 Law No. 2023-1196 of 18 December 2023.

upon applying for the RSA (Art. 3). Article 2 introduces a commitment contract, increasing recipients' obligations. It establishes the obligation to work at least 15 hours per week. [77] If the applicant refuses to conclude a commitment contract or fails to meet certain obligations defined in the contract, Article 3 introduces a measure of temporary suspension of benefits to enforce a more graduated system of sanctions. The duration and scope of suspension shall be set by assessing the beneficiary's circumstances, household size and nature and frequency of violations.[78]

The bill clearly aims to generalise the status of jobseekers to the detriment of a more socially inclusive approach to individuals who find themselves in a difficult situation. The question of minimum income dominates the economic discourse, which should first and foremost guarantee decent living conditions.

4. Non-Economic Conditions

Apart from the conditions linked to specific groups of people (permanent disability rate for the AAH, and the old-age requirement for the ASPA), two non-economic criteria warrant a closer look: the age criterion and the residence criterion.

The RSA sets the minimum age of eligibility at 25, with some exceptions outlined in law. This condition was already adopted for the RMI, and the justification is twofold[79]: on the one hand, young adults between the ages of 18 and 25 are still supported by the family solidarity benefit as stipulated in the Civil Code (for example, the obligation of parental maintenance as set out in Article 371-2 of the Civil Code); on the other hand, the circumstances of young adults are very heterogeneous, calling for a period of stabilisation. These reasons remain valid in the eyes of the legislature, which has not proposed any change to the age requirement in the reform

77 Art. 2: Le contrat d'engagement définit "Un plan d'action, précisant les objectifs d'insertion sociale et professionnelle et, en fonction de la situation du demandeur d'emploi, le niveau d'intensité de l'accompagnement requis auquel correspond une durée hebdomadaire d'activité du demandeur d'emploi d'au moins quinze heures. Il comporte notamment des actions de formation, d'accompagnement et d'appui."

78 Art. 3: "III.-La durée des décisions de suspension et de suppression et le montant concerné sont fixés en prenant en compte la situation du bénéficiaire, notamment la composition de son foyer, et en fonction de la nature et de la fréquence des manquements constatés."

79 R. Lafore, 'Les jeunes majeurs et le "revenu garanti": pas si simple!' Revue de droit sanitaire et social (2020), p. 245.

proposed in June 2023. In fact, this is more of a political than a legal issue. RSA eligibility from the age of 18 would reduce the share of family solidarity, elevating the role of social assistance beyond simply a form of subsidiary support. On the other hand, failure to recognise this requirement is an obstacle to the individualisation of young adults. The benefit is therefore still designed in relation to the family.

The residence criterion is required across all social assistance schemes examined. The importance of this criterion has grown over time. Residence was not initially a condition for entitlement to the predecessor of the ASPA, but this changed in 2004. The increasing importance of this criterion can be understood in relation to the scope of the solidarity community concerning minimum social benefits: they are designed for the national community, which includes all those who regularly and effectively reside on the country's territory. However, French law does not currently provide for a universal income that is applicable for all residents of France. Minimum social benefits remain a conditional form of assistance.

IV. Conclusions

France is often perceived as having a generous social protection system that addresses the different needs of vulnerable populations. This chapter demonstrates that while France does indeed offer a large range of social benefits, they are relatively heterogeneous. This heterogeneity can largely be attributed to the independent evolution of benefits and the lack of a unified legal approach that prioritises human dignity in the formulation of benefits. Despite some emerging practices within civil society (such as the reference budget), neither the legislator nor the judiciary have sought to determine or assess the appropriate benefit amount on the basis of a legal understanding of dignity. The issue has been left to political considerations, which continue to be shaped by an economic discourse centred on full employment. While stable employment is undoubtedly one of the most effective paths out of poverty, focussing exclusively on this option may be detrimental to particularly vulnerable individuals.

The current system's complexity gives rise to inconsistencies and even inequalities (for example the widely disparate effects of different benefits on poverty reduction), calling for a greater coherence of the social protection system.[80] The scenarios presented here are still largely anchored in a bureaucratic (simplification) or an economic (full employment) perspective. Greater attention to dignified living conditions for all is therefore essential.

80 M. Badel, 'Demain, un revenu universel d'activité?' Droit social (2020), p. 791.

Minimum Income Protection in Germany: The Relevance of Fundamental Social Rights in Times of Crisis

Ute Kötter

I. Introduction

German social minimum protection has roots in church and communal charity dating back to the Middle Ages,[1] even though modern systems of social assistance only emerged at the turn of the 18th to the 19th century.[2] Welfare laws for the poor required local authorities to care for "their" poor, thereby establishing poverty relief as a State responsibility. While today's social minimum protection schemes still reflect their roots in Poor Law,[3] they have been considerably influenced by more recent developments.[4] The Federal Social Assistance Act (*Bundessozialhilfegesetz* – BSHG) of 1961 laid the foundation of the current system of subsistence benefits. Based on a new understanding of citizens' legal status under the new Constitution[5], the Basic Law of the Federal Republic of Germany (*Grundgesetz* – GG),[6] this Act established, for the first time, a statutory legal entitlement to social assistance benefits. A means-tested cash benefit for all (*Hilfe zum Lebensunterhalt* – livelihood assistance) was introduced in addition to social and medical services to address specific needs (e.g. in case of illness, old age, disability, in need of care) that cannot be met through personal resources (*Hilfen in besonderen Lebenslagen* – assistance in special life situations). Other features of the social welfare scheme such as tax-based funding, administration by local authorities, and guiding principles including the coverage of individual needs, the principle of human dignity or of

1 For an overview, see M. Stolleis, *Geschichte des Sozialrechts in Deutschland, Ein Grundriss* (UTB 2003), pp. 13–35.

2 The regulation of the General Land Law for the Prussian States (ALR, II, 19, Section 6) is generally regarded as the first law that regarded poor relief as a state task. See Stolleis (n 1), pp. 23 f. Cf. also the Ordinance on Poor Relief of 17 November 1816, Kgl. Baierisches Reg. Bl. 1816, 780, Art. 1, 7 quoted from Stolleis (n 1), p. 24, which transferred the duty to care for the poor to the municipalities.

3 See also C. Sachße and F. Tennstedt (eds.), *Bettler, Gauner und Proleten, Armut und Armenfürsorge in der deutschen Geschichte. Ein Bild-Lesebuch* (Rowohlt Taschenbuch 1983).

4 On the historical development of German legislation on minimum income, especially after 2010, see H. Spindler, 'Dispute over the statutory right to a minimum subsistence in Germany' Labour and Social Security Journal 10 (2019), pp. 10–15 < https://www.pwe.com.pl/pobierz.php?id=2087915698&mode=artykul> accessed 22.3.2025.

5 Cf. BVerwGE 1, 159, paras. 28–30. Critical of the reception of the judgment, K. Hauer, *Die „Fürsorge-Entscheidung" des Bundesverwaltungsgerichts (BVerwGE 1, 159) aus rechtshistorischer Sicht* (Nomos 2020).

6 *Grundgesetz* (Basic Law) as promulgated on 23 May 1949 (Federal Law Gazette 1949, p. 1).

subsidiarity are still evident in recent social minimum income protection schemes. One main difference between the Federal Social Assistance Act scheme and recent social minimum income protections schemes lies in its universal coverage approach. *Anyone* who meets the conditions stipulated by law is entitled to social assistance benefits. The universal coverage of the BSHG was abandoned for the first time in 1993, when— - *inter alia* in response to a sharp increase in the number of refugees from the war in former Yugoslavia[7]—asylum seekers and persons without residence status were excluded from the personal scope of its application. Since then, minimum income protection for asylum seekers and tolerated persons has been provided under the 1993 Asylum Seekers' Benefit Act (*Asylbewerberleistungsgesetz*) at a significantly lower level than that offered under the social assistance scheme. With the enactment of the Act on Means-Tested Basic Income Support in Old Age and in the Event of Reduced Earning Capacity (*Gesetz über eine bedarfsorientierte Grundsicherung im Alter und bei Erwerbsminderung*),[8] which was introduced as a supplement to the pension reforms around the turn of the millennium, another benefit system was separated from the BSHG as of 1 January 2003. Aimed at addressing 'concealed poverty in old age',[9] the law did not provide for recourse for dependants required to pay maintenance for persons in need of assistance, if the dependants' annual income was less than EUR 100,000.

In 2004, the so-called Hartz IV reform[10] replaced the general social welfare scheme under the Federal Social Assistance Act with two categorical schemes of basic income support. It also reintegrated the previously mentioned Basic Income Support in Old Age and in Case of Reduced Earning Capacity. Implemented through the Fourth Law on Modern Services in the Labour Market, the reform was part of a comprehensive package of

7 See W. Bosswick, 'Kriegsflüchtlinge aus dem ehemaligen Jugoslawien nach Zielland' (2022) < https://www.efms.uni-bamberg.de/ds27_2_d.htm> accessed 22.3.2025. Cf. V. Gerloff, *Das Asylbewerberleistungsgesetz für die Soziale Arbeit* (Nomos 2023), p. 12, n 1: Increase in asylum applications in Germany from 193,063 in 1990 to 438,191 in 1992.

8 Act as promulgated on 26 June 2001 (Federal Law Gazette I 2001, pp. 1310, 1335).

9 The term refers to the non-take up of minimum income benefits by the elderly to avoid financial consequences for their children who have maintenance obligations.

10 For an overview, see I. Dingeldey, 'Hartz IV in Context: The German Way to Employability' (18 March 2005) < https://www.realinstitutoelcano.org/en/analyses/hartz-iv-in-context-the-german-way-to-employability/> accessed 22.3.2025.

labour market reforms introduced at the beginning of the 21st century.[11] It fundamentally restructured the traditional system of social assistance with the aim of addressing growing and persistent mass unemployment.[12] The personal scope of application of the two schemes was delimited with the help of the criterion of employability: while the new Book II of the Social Code (SGB II: *Grundsicherung für Arbeitsuchende* – Basic Income Support for Jobseekers)[13] provided benefits for jobseekers capable of working and their partners and children, the target group for social assistance benefits under Book XII of the Social Code (SGB XII: *Sozialhilfe* – Social Assistance)[14] were individuals with no capacity for work, persons of pensionable age and all those in need of assistance whose level of subsistence could not otherwise be secured.

The reform was rooted in a workfare approach[15] that placed strong pressure on employable recipients of basic income support benefits to accept job offers or participate in labour market integration measures, with non-compliance penalised by reductions in basic income support benefits of up to 100 per cent. The reform also reduced the duration of unemployment benefits, abolished unemployment assistance and transferred its recipients to the new basic income support scheme for those with capacity for work under SGB II (*Arbeitslosengeld II*). Insured persons, including long-term insured, were relegated to the subsistence-level support of social assistance once their unemployment benefits expired.

---

11 For a summary of the four Laws on Modern Labour Market Services, see Landeszentrale für politische Bildung, 'Die Hartz-Gesetze. Wie die Gesetze entstanden sind und was sie umfasst haben' (February 2021) < https://www.lpb-bw.de/hartz-gesetze#c65719> accessed 22.3.2025.

12 The unemployment rate in 2005 was 13 per cent for the reunified Federal Republic of Germany, 20.6 per cent in the new Federal States, 11 per cent in the old Federal States, see Statista, 'Arbeitslosenquote der Bundesrepublik Deutschland in den Jahren 1955 bis 2024' (2025) < https://de.statista.com/statistik/daten/studie/1127090/umfrage/arbeitslosenquote-der-bundesrepublik-deutschland> accessed 23.3.2025.

13 For a brief overview, see Federal Ministry of Labour and Social Affairs, 'Citizen's Benefit: Assistance and Needs' (24 April 2024) < https://www.bmas.de/EN/Labour/Basic-income-support-for-jobseekers/basic-income-support-for-jobseekers-art.html> accessed 23.3.2025.

14 For a brief overview, see Federal Ministry of Labour and Social Affairs, 'What is Social Assistance?' (21 February 2023) < https://www.bmas.de/EN/Social-Affairs/Social-assistance/social-assistance-art.html> accessed 23.3.2025.

15 W. Voges, H. Jacobs and H. Trickey, 'Uneven Development – Local Authorities and Workfare in Germany', in: I. Lodemel and H. Trickey (eds.), *An Offer You Cannot Refuse – Workfare in International Perspective* (Bristol University Press 2001), pp. 71–104.

This made the Hartz IV reform one of the most controversial social law reforms in Germany since World War II. The controversy was even brought before the Federal Constitutional Court, with far-reaching implications for social assistance law, prompting multiple revisions in line with the requirements of the Federal Constitutional Court's case law.

Nearly 20 years later, in 2023, several restrictive regulations of the Hartz IV legislation were reversed: under the new name "SGB II – Basic Income Support for Jobseekers, Citizen's Benefit" (*Bürgergeldgesetz*[16]), the regulation on the priority of employment over education, vocational training and professional development was withdraw, the thresholds for income and asset allowances were raised and the six-month limit on the reimbursement of inadequate accommodation costs was extended to one and a half years.

According to the Federal Statistical Office, around 7.3 million of Germany's 84.669.000 inhabitants were receiving basic income support at the end of 2023, which includes 5.5 million recipients of basic income support for jobseekers under SGB II; 1.2 million recipients of basic income support in old age and for those with a reduced capacity for work under SGB XII, and 523,000 recipients of basic benefits under the Asylum Seekers Benefits Act (*AsylbLG*).[17] The rise in the basic income support rate (proportion of benefit recipients in the total population) from 8.0 per cent at the end of 2021 to 8.6 per cent by the end of 2023 is primarily attributed to the influx of refugees from Ukraine who are entitled to subsidiary protection under EU law. Since 1 June 2022, refugees from Ukraine have been entitled to benefits under SGB II or SGB XII. The at-risk-of-poverty rate (proportion of people with less than 60 per cent of the population's median personal net equivalent income) deviates from this by definition: 14.4 per cent of the population were at risk of poverty in 2023,[18] while the share of those at

16 *Zwölftes Gesetz zur Änderung des Zweiten Buches Sozialgesetzbuch und anderer Gesetze – Einführung eines Bürgergeldes (Bürgergeld-Gesetz)* as promulgated on 16 December 2022 (Federal Law Gazette I 2022, p. 2328).

17 The numbers have risen by 22 per cent compared to the previous year (= 88,000, of which 40,000 are from Ukraine): Statistisches Bundesamt, Asylbewerberleistungen (2025) < https://www.destatis.de/DE/Themen/Gesellschaft-Umwelt/Soziales/Asylbewerberleistungen/_inhalt.html> accessed 22.3.2025. For more detailed figures, see Statistisches Bundesamt, 'Zahl der Empfängerinnen und Empfänger sozialer Mindestsicherungsleistungen 2023 um 1,6 % gestiegen' (2025) < https://www.destatis.de/DE/Themen/Gesellschaft-Umwelt/Soziales/Mindestsicherung/aktuell-mindestsicherung.html> accessed 23.3.2025.

18 Statistisches Bundesamt, 'Armutsgefährdungsquote (monetäre Armut) nach Geschlecht und Alter' (2025) < https://www.destatis.de/DE/Themen/Gesellschaf

risk of poverty and social exclusion in the total population (AROPE) stood at 21.3 per cent.[19] Public expenditure on the Citizen's Benefit amounted to around EUR 42,59 billion in 2023.[20]

II. Overview

1. Normative Framework

a) International Law

Although Germany has ratified the International Covenant on Economic, Social and Cultural Rights[21] and the European Social Charter[22]—both of which enshrine traditional social rights such as the right to social security (Art. 9 ICESR, Art. 12 ESC), the right to an adequate standard of living (Art. 9 ICESR)[23] or the right to social assistance (Art. 13 ESC)—their impact[24] on the development of Germany's national social assistance law has remained limited so far.[25]

---

t-Umwelt/Einkommen-Konsum-Lebensbedingungen/Lebensbedingungen-Armutsgefaehrdung/Tabellen/armutsgef-quote-nach-sozialleistung-mz-silc.html> accessed 23.3.2025.

19 Statistisches Bundesamt, 'Gefährdung durch Armut oder soziale Ausgrenzung: AROPE-Indikator nach Geschlecht und Alter' (2025) < https://www.destatis.de/DE/Themen/Gesellschaft-Umwelt/Einkommen-Konsum-Lebensbedingungen/Lebensbedingungen-Armutsgefaehrdung/Tabellen/eurostat-armut-sozialeausgrenzung-mz-silc.html> accessed 23.3.2025.

20 Response of the Federal Government to a minor interpellation by MPs and the AfD parliamentary group dated 4 July 2024, BT-Drs. 20/12225.

21 Federal Law Gazette II 1976, p. 428.

22 Federal Law Gazette II 1964, p. 1261. Germany also ratified the RESC in 2021. It came into force on 1 May 2021.

23 On the content and interpretation, see G. Vonk and M. Olivier, 'The fundamental right of social assistance: A global, a regional (Europe and Africa) and a national perspective (Germany, the Netherlands and South Africa)' European Journal of Social Security 21 (2019)3, pp. 219–240.

24 On the significance of international legal acts for the development of minimum social benefits, see ibid, pp. 223 ff., who particularly highlights the Gaygusuz Judgment of the European Court of Human Rights of 16 September 1996 Gaygusuz v Austria Application No. 19371/90.

25 On the right to strike (Art. 6 AESC) and on fair pay (Art. 4 ESC), see H. Brecht-Heitzmann and M. Sadat Khonsari, 'Beachtung der Europäischen Sozialcharta durch Deutschland' ZESAR 11 (2017), pp. 463–468.

b) European Union Law

Despite Member States' exclusive responsibility for social security legislation, they are required, according to established case law of the European Court of Justice (ECJ), to comply with the principles of EU law when designing their social security systems.[26] This has had a major impact on German social assistance law. Between 2013 and 2019, the ECJ was repeatedly called upon to assess the compatibility of Germany's exclusion of foreign nationals from minimum income benefits under SGB II (Section 7, para. 1, sentence 2 SGB II) with EU law. In a partial departure from its previous, more integration-friendly case law,[27] the ECJ upheld the exclusion of economically inactive foreign nationals (i.e. Union citizens and their family members) from basic income support for jobseekers under SGB II.[28] According to the ECJ's case law, EU citizens are only entitled to equal treatment with the host Member State's nationals if their residence complies with the requirements of the Freedom of Movement Directive (2004/38/EC). Exclusions based on the absence of a substantive right to freedom of movement in accordance with Directive 2004/38/EC are therefore consistent with European law.[29] As already mentioned, the ECJ has upheld the exclusion of foreign nationals (i.e. Union citizens and their family members) from benefits during their first three months of residence in Germany as being in line with European law.[30] However, in its most recent decision[31] on

26 ECJ 28 April 1998 – C 120/96 (Kohll); EuGH 28.4.1998 – C 120/95 (Dekker).

27 ECJ 12 May 1998 – C-85/96 (Sala); ECJ 7.9.2004 – C-45/02 (Trojani); ECJ 20.9.2001 – C-184/99 (Grzelczyk); ECJ 23.3.2004 – C-138/02 (Collins).

28 ECJ 11 November 2014 – C-333/13 (Dano) para. 69; ECJ 15 September 2015 – C-67/14 (Alimanovic), paras. 49–51; on the discussion, see U. Kötter, 'EU-Sozialbürgerschaft oder Menschenrecht auf Gewährleistung eines menschenwürdigen Existenzminimums? – Zur aktuellen Diskussion um das Recht von Unionsbürgerinnen auf soziale Grundsicherung in Deutschland', in: W. Sartorius and H. Weth (eds.), *Rechtsstaat, Markt und Menschenwürde – Herausforderung Armut und Migration* (Lambertus 2016), pp. 43–71.

29 ECJ 11 November 2014 – C-333/13 (Dano) para. 69; ECJ 15 September 2015 – C-67/14 (Alimanovic), paras. 49–51.

30 ECJ 25 February 2016 C-299/14 (Garcia-Nieto).

31 ECJ 6 October 2020 – C 181/19 (J.D. v Jobcenter Krefeld); for a discussion, see S. Devetzi and C. Janda, 'Das Gesetz zur Regelung von Ansprüchen ausländischer Personen in der Grundsicherung für Arbeitssuchende und in der Sozialhilfe' ZESAR 5/6 (2017), pp. 197 ff. and U. Berlit, 'Die Regelung von Ansprüchen ausländischer Personen in der Grundsicherung für Arbeitsuchende und in der Sozialhilfe' NDV 2 (2017), p. 68.

such exclusions under SGB II, the ECJ found that the exclusion from benefits of persons whose right of residence derives from the right of residence of a child under Art. 10 Regulation 492/2011, and for whom they have care responsibilities, is contrary to European law. The Court based its decision on the objective of Regulation No. 492/2011 to integrate migrant workers and their families into the host country's society as effectively as possible. The ECJ's judgments on the exclusion of foreign nationals from SGB II has had an impact on German case law and legislation, extending well beyond the direct affirmation of Germany's legal framework. The Federal Social Court (*Bundessozialgericht*, BSG) initially made social assistance benefits accessible for foreign nationals who fall under the exclusion criteria and are excluded from entitlement to basic security benefits in accordance with Section 7, para. 1, sentence 2 SGB II, by interpreting Section 23 SGB XII as being in conformity with the Constitution.[32] However, this access was blocked by the legislator with the extension of exclusions to SGB XII and the introduction of entitlement to transitional benefits (for 1 month within 2 years) and to loans for travel expenses.[33]

c) Constitutional Law

aa) The Welfare State Principle

In contrast to the Weimar Constitution,[34] the Basic Law of 1949, the Constitution of the Federal Republic of Germany, does not contain a detailed catalogue of fundamental social rights, but only roughly outlines the framework of the German welfare state through the welfare state principle enshrined in Art. 20.1.1 and Art. 28.1.1 of the Basic Law. Like the other foundational principles of the Basic Law, the welfare state principle binds the State directly as the "benchmark for all State action"[35]. Nevertheless,

32 BSG (German Federal Social Court), Judgment of 3 December 2015, B 4 AS 44/15 R.

33 *Gesetz zur Regelung von Ansprüchen ausländischer Personen in der Grundsicherung für Arbeitsuchende (SGB II) und in der Sozialhilfe (SGB XII)* as promulgated on 22 December 2016 (Federal Law Gazette I 2016, p. 3155).

34 Art. 155 Weimar Constitution as promulgated on 11 August 1919 (Reich Law Gazette 1919, p. 1383).

35 H. Zacher, *Sozialpolitik und Verfassung im ersten Jahrzehnt der Bundesrepublik Deutschland* (De Gruyter 1980), pp. 676 ff., 706 ff.

its content is characterised by a high degree of vagueness.[36] In its case law, the Federal Constitutional Court has emphasised the State's obligation to establish a "just social order" and to support persons in need (*Fürsorge für Hilfebedürftige*).[37] Their concretisation lies primarily within the remit of the democratically elected legislator. [38] The welfare state principle thus supplements the constitutional guarantees of individual freedom by addressing the applicable prerequisites and conditions, the organisation of which remains the responsibility of the legislator.

bb) A Fundamental Right to a Guaranteed Subsistence Minimum

Fundamental social rights[39] have traditionally been rejected as non-justiciable in view of their uncertain legal consequences and fiscal risks.[40] According to prevailing opinion, claims to enforceable rights can neither be exclusively derived from the welfare state principle[41] nor from the principle of human dignity pursuant to Article 1.1 of the Basic Law.[42] Initially, the Federal Constitutional Court also interpreted these principles as imposing an obligation on the legislator to create the foundations for a life in dignity, requiring the legislator to exclude income up to the amount of the

36 H. Zacher, 'Das soziale Staatsziel', J. Isensee and P. Kirchhof (eds.), *Handbuch des Staatsrechts der Bundesrepublik Deutschland* (C. F. Müller 1987), pp. 1045 ff., paras. 61 ff.

37 BVerfGE 22, 180 (1st Guiding Principle of the Judgment of the Federal Constitutional Court); 43, 13 (19).

38 H. Zacher (n 36), pp. 1045 ff., para. 440. For the current understanding of the design mandate derived from the social state principle, see J. Heesen, 'Menschenwürde und Existenzminimum', in: U. Berlit, W. Conradis and A. Pattar (eds.) *Handbuch des Existenzsicherungsrechts* (3rd ed. Nomos 2019), paras. 32 ff.

39 For an overview, see Wissenschaftlicher Dienst des Bundestags, 'Soziale Grundrechte – Eine Ausarbeitung' (2007) < https://www.bundestag.de/resource/blob/419210/91fa0b6b3f13da93d5f798346438ab02/wd-3-050-07-pdf-data.pdf> accessed 22.3.2025.

40 J. Isensee, 'Grundrechtsvoraussetzungen', in: J. Isensee and P. Kirchhof (eds.), *Handbuch des Staatsrechts der Bundesrepublik Deutschland* (C. F. Müller 1987), para. 174; on the current discussion, see I. Winkler, 'Interpreting the Right to a Dignified Minimum Existence: A New era in German Socio-Economic Rights Jurisprudence?' Human Rights Law Review 13 (2013)2, pp. 388–401, 394, with further references.

41 Except in cases of evident and arbitrary disregard of the objectives and mandates of the welfare state, see H.-J. Papier, 'Der Einfluss des Verfassungsrechts auf das Sozialrecht', in: B. von Maydell and F. Ruland (eds.), *Sozialrechtshandbuch* (2nd ed. Nomos 2003).

42 BVerfG Decision of 19 December 1951 – 1 BvR 220/51 para. 104.

minimum level of subsistence from taxation.[43] This interpretation changed fundamentally with the landmark ruling[44] of the Federal Constitutional Court of 9 February 2010.[45]. The so-called Hartz IV ruling led to a reorientation of constitutional case law towards fundamental social rights. In this judgment, the Federal Constitutional Court for the first time explicitly recognised a fundamental right to a minimum level of subsistence that ensures human dignity (*Grundrecht auf Gewährleistung eines menschenwürdigen Existenzminimums*). This represents a remarkable constitutional shift,[46] given that the framers of the Constitution had deliberately refrained from including fundamental social rights in the Basic Law and had only granted the legislature a social mandate based on the principle of the social state.[47] Since this ruling, the Federal Constitutional Court has repeatedly intervened to correct legislation governing basic income support for job-seekers.

The fundamental right to the guarantee of a minimum level of subsistence is derived from the principle of human dignity in Article 1.1 of the Basic Law, in conjunction with the principle of the welfare state in Article 20.1 of the Basic Law: "The fundamental right to the guarantee of a minimum level of subsistence that is in line with human dignity (....) ensures that every person in need of assistance receives the material means that are indispensable for his or her physical existence and for minimum participation in social, cultural and political life."[48] The Court emphasised

43 BVerfG Judgment of 19 May 1990, 1 BvL 20/84.

44 The judgment resonated not only in Germany, but also internationally: G. Vonk and M. Olivier (n 23), p. 219; see ESCR, 'Hartz IV GFCC, Judgment of the First Senate of 09 February 2010 – 1 BvL 1/09, 1 BvL 2/09, 1 BvL 4/09' (26 March 2020) < https://www.escr-net.org/caselaw/2020/hartz-iv-gfcc-judgment-first-senate-09-february-2010-1-bvl-109-1-bvl-309-1-bvl-409> accessed 22.3.2025.

45 BVerfG 1 BvL 1/09, 'Judgment of 9 February 2010 (Hartz VI)' (9 February 2010) < www.bverfg.de/entscheidungen/ls20100209_1bvl000109en.html> accessed 22.3.2025.

46 For more details, see U. Kötter, 'Die Rechtsprechung des Bundesverfassungsgerichts der Bundesrepublik Deutschland zum Grundrecht auf Gewährleistung eines menschenwürdigen Existenzminimums: erste Konturen eines sozialen Grundrechts', in: A. Hekimler (ed.), *Festschrift für Otto Kaufmann. Armağanı* (Legal Yayincilik 2021), pp. 751–774.

47 W. Abendroth, 'Zum Begriff des demokratischen und sozialen Rechtsstaates im Grundgesetz der Bundesrepublik Deutschland', in: A. Hermann (ed.), *Aus Geschichte und Politik. Festschrift zum 70. Geburtstag von Ludwig Bergsträsser* (Droste 1954), pp. 279–300.

48 BVerfG Judgment of 9 February 2010 1 BvL 1/09, 1st Guiding Principle of the Judgment of the Federal Constitutional Court.

that "[i]n addition to the right under Article 1.1 GG to respect the dignity of every individual, which has absolute effect"[49], the fundamental right to the guarantee of a minimum level of subsistence, in conjunction with Article 20.1 GG, holds autonomous significance as a right of entitlement. This right is not subject to the legislature's discretion and must be honoured.[50] The right to a minimum level of subsistence includes both physical necessities which, according to the Federal Constitutional Court, include food, clothing, personal and health care, housing, heating, household electricity and household goods,[51] as well as participation in social, political and cultural life and the maintenance of social contacts.

With its 2010 judgment, the Federal Constitutional Court established the fundamental right to the guarantee of a minimum level of subsistence that is in line with human dignity as a justiciable constitutional entitlement for all inhabitants of the Federal Republic of Germany.[52] However, determining and adjusting the level of the "socio-cultural subsistence minimum" (*sozio-kulturelles Existenzminimum*) remains the responsibility of the legislature, "which must align the benefits to be provided with the respective stage of societal development and the prevailing conditions of life".[53] In this respect, the Court exercises limited judicial review, intervening only when the level of benefits is evidently inadequate.[54] At the same time, it outlines detailed guidelines for the procedure to determine the level of benefits: "In order to ascertain the extent of the claim, the legislature must realistically and comprehensively assess all expenditures necessary for subsistence, using a

49 Ibid., 2nd Guiding Principle of the Judgment of the Federal Constitutional Court.

50 Ibid, para. 133

51 BVerfG Judgment of 9 February 2010 – 1 BvL 1/09 para. 135; BVerfG Order of 23 July 2014 – 1 BvL 10/12 para. 90. Cf. J. Heesen (n 38), para. 11.

52 In its judgment of 18 June 2012 (1 BvL 10/10) concerning the level of benefits for asylum seekers, the Court clarified that the fundamental right to the guarantee of a subsistence minimum that safeguards human dignity is not only a citizen's right but a human right that applies to both German and foreign residents alike. Differentiations in the level of benefits are therefore only permissible if the needs of the comparison groups differ. The fundamental right may not be relativised by migration policy considerations. In contrast to the Hartz IV decision, however, the Court found in this case that the benefits, which had not been adjusted to the evolving living conditions in Germany and the inflation rate for nearly 20 years, were manifestly inadequate.

53 BVerfG Judgment of 9 February 2010 1 BvL 1/09, 2nd Guiding Principle of the Judgment of the Federal Constitutional Court.

54 I. Winkler (n 40), p. 398.

transparent and appropriate procedure based on reliable data and plausible methods of calculation."[55]

Accordingly, the Federal Constitutional Court found the provisions regulating the amount of 'Hartz IV' benefits for children to be unconstitutional[56] and instructed the legislature to reassess and set basic income support in a way that complies with the constitutional requirements. Notably, the Court conducted a detailed review of the rules and criteria applicable for defining the "social minimum" and placed particular emphasis on the legislator's procedural obligations.[57]

cc) Self-Responsibility as a Limit to the Fundamental Right

The 2010 judgment was followed by a series of further appeals to the Federal Constitutional Court challenging other provisions of the Hartz IV reform, providing the Court opportunities to consolidate and further develop its case law.

In its 2019 "sanctions" judement,[58] the Federal Constitutional Court dealt with the constitutionality of reducing the level of benefits in the event of a breach of obligations to "cooperate".[59] Reinforcing the principle of subsidiarity through self-help obligations subject to sanctions does not in itself violate the Constitution, provided the person in need of assistance can overcome this need through their own efforts.[60] Reductions in benefits must, however, be reviewed in light of the fundamental right to a guaranteed minimum level of subsistence. Since the benefits intended to ensure such a minimum level that is in line with human dignity are, by definition, already limited to the bare minimum, any reduction exceeding 30 per cent of the standard benefit is not permissible. The judgment recalibrates the relationship between rights and duties in the context of receiving the

---

55 BVerfG Judgment of 9 February 2010 1 BvL 1/09, 3rd Guiding Principle of the Judgment of the Federal Constitutional Court.

56 BVerfG Judgment of 9 February 2010 BvL 1/09, paras. 190–198.

57 See III.1.a.

58 BVerfG Judgment of 5 November 2019, 1 BvL 7/16, 'Judgment of 5 November 2019' (5 November 2019) < https://www.bundesverfassungsgericht.de/SharedDocs/Entscheidungen/EN/2019/11/ls20191105_1bvl000716en.html> accessed 22.3.2025.

59 For a detailed description and assessment, see S. Rixen, 'Abschied vom Sozialstaat der Sanktionen? Das Urteil des BVerfG v. 5.11.2019 zu den Sanktionen im SGB II („Hartz IV")' Die Sozialgerichtsbarkeit (2020)1, pp. 1–7.

60 BVerfG Judgment of 5 November 2019, 1 BvL 7/16, paras. 123 ff.

Citizen's Benefit by limiting the extent to which this can be reduced in case the obligation to cooperate is violated, but at the same time emphasises the fundamental duty of beneficiaries to help themselves. The fundamental right to a decent minimum level of subsistence does not entitle the recipient to an unconditional basic income.

In its decision of 23 September 2024 on the amount of educational assistance provided to individuals during a course of study,[61] the Federal Constitutional Court reaffirmed its established case law on the limitation of the fundamental right to a minimum level of subsistence that is in line with human dignity through the principle of self-help: 'Entitlement to benefits that ensure subsistence under Article 1.1 of the Basic Law in conjunction with the principle of the social state (Article 20.1 of the Basic Law) guarantees a dignified existence for those who are unable to do so on their own and is limited to the means absolutely necessary to achieve this. This entitlement does not exist if this need can be remedied or avoided, for example, by taking up gainful employment that would secure the individual's livelihood, even if the exercise of certain fundamental freedoms, such as the right to pursue a university degree under Article 12.1.1 of the Basic Law, is no longer possible as a result.'

2. Social Benefits

a) A Structured System of Livelihood Benefits

Germany's social security system has evolved over time into a highly structured framework. Its legal foundation is set out in the 13 Books[62] of the German Social Code and other federal laws listed in Section 68 SGB I. Social assistance (*soziale Hilfe*) benefits under SGB II and SGB XII are subordinate to social insurance (*Sozialversicherung*) benefits, social compensa-

61 BVerfG Order of 23 September 2024, 1 BvL 9/21, 1st Guiding Principle of the Order of the Federal Constitutional Court.

62 Recently, social compensation law was codified in Book 14 of the German Social Code. The 13th book is not yet occupied.

tion (*soziale Entschädigung*)[63] and social support (*soziale Förderung*),[64] and are mutually exclusive.

As regards social assistance schemes, SGB II—which applies to around 2/3 of recipients of minimum income benefits—serves as a reference system. However, it is important to bear in mind that the regulatory systems of the SBG II and of Book XII on social assistance (SGB XII) have diverged considerably since the Hartz IV reform.[65] The most important subsistence benefit under SGB II is the Citizen's Benefit (*Bürgergeld*). The Citizen's Benefit is provided to individuals who have capacity for work, as well as to those who are unable to work and live with beneficiaries who are able to work but are not entitled to benefits in accordance with SGB XII.[66]

aa) The Principle of Subsidiarity (Section 2 SGB II, Section 2 SGB XII)

The principle of subsidiarity (*Nachranggrundsatz*) requires those entitled to benefits to first exhaust all possibilities for ending or reducing their need for assistance and to cover their living costs using their own resources and means before claiming benefits intended to secure their livelihood.[67] This principle also directs those affected to utilise assistance from third parties, in particular from persons liable for maintenance, but also from providers of other social benefits.[68] In relation to other social benefits, social assistance benefits therefore have a 'catch-all' function in terms of addressing unmet needs that are not covered by other social benefit schemes. To meet current needs in a timely manner (so-called principle of needs coverage, *Bedarfsdeckungsgrundsatz*), subsistence benefits must also be provided as advance payments (Sections 42 f. SGB I, Section 91 SGB XII), especially

63 On functional overlaps between compensation law and social welfare law, see U. Becker, *Soziales Entschädigungsrecht* (Nomos 2018), p. 5.

64 H. Zacher, 'Grundtypen des Sozialrechts', in: W. Fürst, R. Herzog and D. Umbach (eds.), *Festschrift für Wolfgang Zeidler* (De Gruyter 1987), p. 571, 583 ff.

65 See U. Klerks and W. Conradis, 'Die problematischen Unterschiede der Regelungen nach dem SGB II und SGB XII' info also (2024)3 and 4, pp. 99–106 (part 1) and pp. 147–155 (part 2).

66 See II.c) aa).

67 However, some benefits under SGB XII are not subordinate: this applies to assistance for overcoming specific social difficulties (e.g. counselling and support for homeless persons, persons released from prison or social participation) and to benefits for persons with disabilities under SGB IX. See J. Siefert, 'Sozialhilferecht', in: F. Ruland, U. Becker and P. Axer (eds.), *Sozialrechtshandbuch (SRH)* (7th ed. Nomos 2022).

68 Section 2 SGB II, Section 2 SGB XII.

in cases where institutional responsibility has not yet been determined (Sections 37 f., SGB XII). The right to reimbursement under Sections 102 to 114 SGB X requires the competent institutions to subsequently reimburse the costs incurred.

Entitlement to benefits to cover basic needs is also influenced by regulations governing preferential means, e.g. family law provisions on the amount of child maintenance,[69] but also labour law provisions, such as statutory or collectively agreed provisions on the amount of income from dependent employment (e.g. statutory minimum wages)[70], as well as remuneration provisions for freelance or commercial services.[71]

bb) Interplay with Social Security Benefits

Social insurance laws do not currently contain regulations guaranteeing a minimum level of protection.

Until 2004, unemployment assistance (Sections 190 – 197 SGB III, former version) was provided as a follow-up benefit under the unemployment insurance scheme after the fixed-term[72] unemployment benefit had expired in accordance with the unemployment insurance scheme under SGB III. This benefit was open-ended for those insured under the unemployment insurance scheme, calculated based on their previously earned income and was means-tested only in relation to their own and their spouse's income and assets. The Hartz IV reform reduced both the amount and

69 See the Düsseldorf Table: OLG Düsseldorf, 'Düsseldorfer Tabelle' (1 January 2024) < https://www.olg-duesseldorf.nrw.de/infos/Duesseldorfer_Tabelle/Tabelle-2024/2023_12_11_Duesseldorfer_Tabelle_-2024.pdf> accessed 22.3.2025.

70 *Gesetz zur Regelung eines allgemeinen Mindestlohns* as promulgated on 11 August 2014 (Federal Law Gazette I 2014, p. 1348). In 2024, the statutory minimum wage was EUR 12.41, in 2025 EUR 12.82 per hour. For a 40-hour week it is about EUR 2220 gross per month, see < https://www.dgb.de/service/ratgeber/mindestlohn/> accessed 14.07.2025.

71 For an overview, see S. Heitzer and A. Kaufhold, 'Managervergütung, Mindestlohn, Mietpreisbremse, Vergütungsregelungen als Steuerungsinstrumente in einer sozialen Marktwirtschaft' Der Staat 60 (2021)3, pp. 353–386.

72 The period of entitlement is staggered depending on the beneficiary's previous insurance period and age (Section 147 SGB III). From 1 February 2005, the maximum period of entitlement for older employees was reduced from 36 to 18 months and then increased again to 24 months in 2008, see Institut für Arbeitsmarkt- und Berufsforschung, 'Aktueller Bericht 2016' (March 2016) < https://doku.iab.de/aktuell/2016/aktueller_bericht_1603.pdf> accessed 22.3.2025.

duration of unemployment benefits and abolished unemployment assistance. In its place, a means-tested and comprehensively needs-assessed basic income support for jobseekers (*Grundsicherung für Arbeitsuchende*) was introduced.[73] Once entitlement to unemployment benefits ends, even those who were previously employed in positions subject to social security contributions for many years must accept any form of gainful employment without job or income protection or to rely on transfers of income at the subsistence level and be subject to extensive[74] liquidation of their own or their partner's assets. The associated risk of occupational and social marginalisation are a central point of criticism of the Hartz IV reform.[75]

Even the basic pension supplement in the statutory pension insurance scheme introduced in 2021 does not guarantee a minimum level of security equivalent to the statutory level of minimum subsistence in accordance with SGB II and SGB XII. The basic pension supplement is provided after at least 33 years of contributions or other qualifying periods (child-rearing, caregiving or periods of receipt of social benefits due to illness or rehabilitation) as an increase in the statutory pension calculated according to general rules (Section 76g SGB VI). It is calculated individually and currently amounts to an average of EUR 86 per month for 1.1 million beneficiaries.[76]

Income-replacing social insurance benefits may therefore fall below the minimum level of subsistence due to the insurance principle, e.g. in cases of low incomes earned prior to the onset of risk or short insurance periods, as well as the absence of minimum security provisions. Inadequate social

---

73 Around 10 per cent of the 2 million former recipients of unemployment benefit lost entitlement to state support as a result. See K. Bruckmeier and D. Schnitzlein, 'Was wurde aus den Arbeitslosenhilfeempfängern? Eine empirische Analyse des Übergangs und Verbleibs von Arbeitslosenhilfeempfängern nach der Hartz-IV-Reform' IAB Discussion Paper (2007)24 < http://doku.iab.de/discussionpapers/2007/dp2407.pdf> accessed 22.3.2025.

74 According to the version under Section 12 SGB II at the time, the asset limit was EUR 200 per year of life, with a minimum of EUR 4,100 and a maximum of EUR 13,000, and an additional EUR 200 per year of life for old-age provision after the age of 60. In addition, company pensions, the Riester pension or other statutory pension subsidies as well as owner-occupied residential property are included in the so-called protected assets.

75 See C. Butterwegge, *Hartz IV und die Folgen: Auf dem Weg in eine andere Republik?* (3rd ed. Beltz 2018).

76 Deutsche Rentenversicherung, 'Der Grundrentenzuschlag' (2025) < https://www.deutsche-rentenversicherung.de/DRV/DE/Rente/Grundrente/grundrente.html> accessed 22.3.2025.

insurance benefits must then be supplemented with minimum income benefits.

Since the Hartz IV reform, recipients of subsistence benefits under SGB II are mandatorily insured under the statutory health insurance scheme, which ensures comprehensive coverage in the event of illness (Section 5, para. 1, No. 2a SGB V).[77] Partners and children who are not otherwise insured are covered free of charge through the family insurance of the Citizen's Benefit recipient (Section 10 SGB V). If the recipient of subsistence benefits, e.g. a formerly self-employed person, already has health and long-term care insurance, subsidies may be provided towards the recipient's contributions to statutory or private health and long-term care insurance (Section 26 SGB II). In accordance with SGB XII, there is no compulsory insurance for recipients of minimum income support and/or of care assistance. However, under Section 264 SGB V, they are entitled to statutory health insurance benefits equivalent to those of insured persons, with the costs covered by the social welfare authorities (*Sozialhilfeträgern*).[78]

The regulations on compulsory insurance in long-term care insurance correspond to those of statutory health insurance (Section 20 para. 1 No. 2 a SGB XI). If the limited long-term care insurance benefits, along with the individual's own income and assets and support from those legally obligated to provide maintenance, are insufficient to cover the costs of long-term care, these may be supplemented by long-term care assistance benefits under SGB XII (Sections 61 ff. SGB XII).

cc) Interplay with Social Support (*soziale Förderung*)

The aim of social support benefits is to promote equal opportunities and to reduce disparities in wealth and social disadvantages. These include, in

---

77 Contributions to statutory health insurance are covered by the federal government in accordance with Section 251, para. 4, sentence 1 SGB V.

78 In SGB II, these are the Federal Employment Agency together with the municipal institutions (the district-free cities and districts, Section 6 (1) SGB II), and in SGB XII, the local and supra-local institutions (Section 3 SGB XII). The local institutions are generally the district-free cities and the districts, while the supra-local organisations differ in the various federal states. However, the federal states may deviate from this and they also determine the local institutions. Cf. on this, for example, Art. 80 ff. AGSG of the State of Bavaria.

particular, educational support[79], family support benefits, but also child and youth welfare benefits in accordance with SGB VIII[80] and benefits for persons with disabilities under SGB IX.[81] Since social support benefits effectively contribute to securing beneficiaries' minimum level of subsistence, their distinction from social assistance benefits is controversial.[82] However, social support benefits serve different functions, such as enhancing the social position of individuals, families and groups when there is a fundamentally desired and recognised situation of special need,[83] which may even contribute to the common good.[84] Moreover, the cash benefits associated with social support do not guarantee a minimum level of subsistence in accordance with SGB II and SGB XII. Social support and social assistance benefits are therefore generally mutually exclusive.

This applies in particular to educational support benefits under the *BAföG*, which are intended to secure students' livelihood when their own income and the maintenance provided by parents or spouses who are legally obligated to support them is insufficient. Although these benefits are not intended to ensure subsistence, recipients of *BAföG* benefits are, in principle,[85] excluded from the scope of minimum income support under SGB II (Section 7, paras. 5 und 6 SGB II).[86]

79 The vocational training allowance according to Sections 56 ff. SGB III, as well as the benefits of the *Bundesausbildungsförderungsgesetz (BAföG).*

80 See Art. 1 *Gesetz zur Neuordnung des Kinder- und Jugendhilferechts (Kinder- und Jugendhilfegesetz – KJHG)* as promulgated on 26 June 1990 (Federal Law Gazette I 1990, p. 1163).

81 See F. Welti, 'Recht der Rehabilitation und Teilhabe' in F. Ruland, U. Becker and P. Axer (eds.), *Sozialrechtshandbuch (SRH)* (7th ed. Nomos 2022), paras. 22–23.

82 E. Eichenhofer, 'Kapitel 3: Vorrangige Sozialleistungszweige', in: U. Berlit, W. Conradis and A.K. Pattar (eds.), *Existenzsicherungsrecht* (4th ed. Nomos 2025) p. 47, paras. 12-13. Eichenhofer therefore speaks of special branches of livelihood security, a categorisation that is not followed here, as support benefits have a different function than livelihood-securing benefits, even if they have a livelihood-securing effect.

83 H. Zacher (n 64), p. 588.

84 U. Becker, 'Das Sozialrecht: Systematisierung, Verortung und Institutionalisierung' in: F. Ruland, U. Becker and P. Axer (eds.), *Sozialrechtshandbuch (SRH)* (7th ed. Nomos 2022), p. 53, paras. 21–22.

85 Exceptions apply, for example, for additional needs not covered by *BAföG*, e.g. in the case of pregnancy and single parenthood and in cases of hardship (Section 27 SGB II).

86 On the constitutionality of the exclusion, see III.3.c) below.

Recipients of subsistence benefits under SGB II and SGB XII are generally excluded from benefits under the *Wohngeldgesetz*[87] (Section 7, para. 1, Nos. 1, 5 und 6 WoGG). The housing benefit is provided to low-income, single-person or family households to ensure access to adequate and family-friendly housing. Given that this need is already covered by benefits provided for the actual costs of accommodation, an adequate amount of which must be covered (Section 22 SGB II, Section 35 SGB XII), recipients of minimum income support under SGB II and SGB XII are not entitled to additional benefits under the *Wohngeldgesetz*. An exception applies to the so-called child housing benefit, which can be granted upon request for children living in the household of a Citizen's Benefit beneficiary, if the child's subsistence level is covered using his or her own resources (i.e. the child's own income or the child supplement, if applicable) and the housing benefit (Section 12a SGB II).[88]

The most complex intersection arises between means-tested social assistance benefits and the wide range of family benefits[89] at both the federal and state level.[90] These include child allowance (*Kindergeld*), which is provided as a tax refund to persons who earn a domestic income[91] and as a social benefit to other parents,[92] and a parental benefit (*Elterngeld*) for periods of reduced employment due to child-rearing responsibilities,[93] and advance maintenance payments for children (*Unterhaltsvorschuss*) who do not receive maintenance payments from a liable parent.[94] Cash family

87 *Wohngeldgesetz* as promulgated on 24 September 2008 (Federal Law Gazette I 2008, p. 1856).

88 See Bundesagentur für Arbeit, 'Zweites Sozialgesetzbuch – SGB II, Fachliche Weisungen: § 12a SGB II, Vorrangige Leistungen' (1 January 2023), pp. 10 ff. < https://www.arbeitsagentur.de/datei/dok_ba029240.pdf> accessed 22.3.2025.

89 For an overview, see the documentation of the Conference of the German Social Law Association (Deutscher Sozialrechtsverband) on the topic 'Familienleistungen im Bermudadreieck zwischen Verwaltungs-, Steuer- und Sozialrecht' Sozialrecht Aktuell (2023) Sonderheft 1, pp. 125 ff.

90 See, for instance, the Bavarian State Education Allowance of 9 July 2007, GVBl., p. 442.

91 Section 3 (6) EstG (*Einkommenssteuergesetz*) as promulgated on 8 October 2009 (Federal Law Gazette I 2009, pp. 3366, 3862).

92 *Bundeskindergeldgesetz* as promulgated on 28 January 2009 (Federal Law Gazette I 2009, pp. 142, 3177).

93 *Bundeselterngeld- und Elternzeitgesetz* (BEEG) as promulgated on 27 January 2015 (Federal Law Gazette I 2015, p. 33).

94 *Unterhaltsvorschussgesetz* as promulgated on 17 July 2007 (Federal Law Gazette I 2007, p. 1446).

benefits are considered income under SGB II and SGB XII and are deducted in full (e.g. child allowance or advance maintenance payments), or in part (e.g. parental allowance, Section 10 BEEG) from basic security benefits. The amount of child benefits under SGB II has been controversial since the Hartz IV reform. The legislator introduced additional benefits for education in the amount of EUR 100 for school supplies in 2008[95]—likely in anticipation of the Federal Constitutional Court's decision on the constitutionality of standard benefits for children under SGB II[96]—and expanded these in 2013 to include participation benefits.[97] Benefits for education and participation in accordance with Section 28 SGB II are intended to guarantee equal access to education (only for pupils) and participation for (all) children of households that receive the Citizen's Benefit. Educational benefits cover the costs of school trips, class trips, school transport, learning support (tutoring), even if there is no risk of the pupil having to repeat the year, lump sums for daily school supplies (2025: EUR 130 in the first semester, EUR 65 in the second semester), and costs for communal school lunch. For participation in social and cultural life, minors are eligible for a lump sum of EUR 15 per month upon proof of actual expenses for sports, games, cultural and social activities, arts, creative and cultural education activities, as well as for leisure activities (Section 28, para. 7 SGB II). Since benefits for education and participation have a very low take-up rate[98] due to the bureaucratic hurdles involved in applying for them and the conditions of benefit provision (Section 29 SGB XII), in particular the need to prove the need for assistance to service providers (e.g. tutoring institutions) or third parties (e.g. teachers), they have been repeatedly criticised.[99]

95 Art. 3 *Familienleistungsgesetz* as promulgated on 22 December 2008 (Federal Law Gazette I 2008, p. 2955).
96 For the judgment of the Federal Constitutional Court, see III.3.b) below.
97 Art. 1 *Gesetz zur Änderung des Zweiten Buches Sozialgesetzbuch und anderer Gesetze* as promulgated on 7 May 2013 (Federal Law Gazette I 2013, p. 1167).
98 Deutscher Paritätischer Wohlfahrtsverband, 'Empirische Befunde zum Bildungs- und Teilhabepaket – Teilhabequoten im Fokus' (2020) < https://www.der-paritaetische.de/fileadmin/user_upload/Publikationen/doc/expertise-BuT-2020_web.pdf> accessed 22.3.2025.
99 Answer from the Federal Government, 'Inanspruchnahme der Leistungen im Bildungs- und Teilhabepaket – BT-Drs. 19/31398' (6 July 2021) < https://dserver.bundestag.de/btd/19/313/1931398.pdf> accessed 22.3.2025.

As part of the Hartz IV reform, the so-called child supplement (*Kinderzuschlag)* (Sections 6a, 6b BKGG)[100] was incorporated into Child Benefit Law for parents who are able to cover their own minimum level of subsistence but not that of their children. The child supplement (*Kinderzuschlag*), together with the child allowance and housing benefit, was intended to ensure the minimum level of subsistence for children and thus prevent the need for basic benefits under SGB II.[101] However, the complex access and calculation rules have resulted in high rates of non-take-up.[102]

With the introduction of the Basic Child Benefit (*Kindergrundsicherung*)[103] during the 20th legislative period, the legislator aimed to address the persistently high poverty and marginalisation risk rate of 24 per cent among children under 18,[104] and to increase opportunities for participation of children at risk of poverty.[105] In addition to the Guaranteed Child Benefit (EUR 253) provided for all children, and which replaced the child allowance (*Kindergeld*), the reform[106] envisaged a supplementary child allowance (EUR 153) for all children, which would be graduated in

---

100 *Bundeskindergeldgesetz* as promulgated on 28 January 2009 (Federal Law Gazette I 2009, p. 142), last amended by Article 10 of the *Bürgergeldgesetz* of 16 December 2022 (Federal Law Gazette I 2022, p. 2328).

101 On the child supplement, see W. Conradis, 'Kinder und Jugendliche', in: U. Berlit, W. Conradis and A. Pattar (eds.) *Handbuch des Existenzsicherungsrechts* (4th ed. Nomos 2025), paras. 50 ff.

102 Answer from the Federal Government, Inanspruchnahme des Kinderzuschlags – BT-Drs. 20/5673 (15 February 2023) < https://dserver.bundestag.de/btd/20/056/2005673.pdf> accessed 22.3.2025.

103 For different models of basic child protection, see A. Lenze, 'Kindergrundsicherung – Hintergrund, Kontext, Herausforderungen' Sozialrecht aktuell (2023) Sonderheft 1, pp. 164–170. For the legal arguments in detail, see ibid, pp. 125–178.

104 Statistisches Bundesamt, 'Jedes siebte Kind in Deutschland armutsgefährdet'(1 July 2024) < https://www.destatis.de/DE/Presse/Pressemitteilungen/2024/07/PD24_N033_63.html> accessed 22.3.2025, highlighting the "persistently high poverty and social exclusion risk rate of 24% among those under 18".

105 BMFSFJ, 'Die Kindergrundsicherung – eine Leistung für alle Kinder' <https://www.bmfsfj.de/bmfsfj/service/publikationen/die-neue-kindergrundsicherung-231364 > accessed 30.4.2025.

106 Draft bill of the Federal Government of 6 November 2023, see BT-Drs. 20/9092 < https://dserver.bundestag.de/btd/20/090/2009092.pdf> accessed 22.3.2025. For criticism of the existing system of transfer payments for children, see A. Lenze, 'Die Ermittlung der Bedarfe von Kindern – Probleme, Herausforderungen, Vorschläge: Rechtsgutachten' (May 2019) < https://noa.gwlb.de/receive/noa_mods_00000385> accessed 22.3.2025.

accordance with the parents' and children's income and their age. These would not count towards the minimum level of subsistence. The supplementary child allowance was intended to replace the child supplement, standard benefits and part of the education and participation benefits for children under SGB II and SGB XII. An online tool was supposed to simplify the application for benefits procedure for families. The reform ultimately failed due to political differences within the governing coalition, primarily due to financial sustainability concerns related to the Basic Child Benefit, but also due to the fact that the reform did not make a sufficient contribution to simplifying the application procedure for family benefits.[107] One positive side effect of the discussion surrounding the Basic Child Benefit was the increase in the number of recipients of supplementary child allowance (from 764,900 in January 2023 to 1,045,172 in March 2024), which was likely driven by the heightened media coverage.[108]

b) Requirements for the Citizen's Benefit According to SGB II

aa) Eligibility

Beneficiaries who have capacity for work must be at least 15 years old but may not have reached retirement age, they must have a need for assistance, and their habitual residence must be located in Germany (Section 19, para. 1, sentence 1 SGB II in connection with Section 7, para. 1, sentence 1, nos. 1–4 SGB II). Individuals who are not prevented by illness or disability from working for three hours a day in the foreseeable future under the standard working conditions of the general labour market are considered to have capacity for work (Section 8, para. 1 SGB II). The final decision in the event of disputed capacity for work is made by the Employment Agency after obtaining an expert opinion from the respective pension insurance provider, which is binding for all social benefit providers potentially liable for providing benefits in the event of incapacity for work. In the case of foreign

107 For a critical review, see also I. Vorholz, 'Wege aus dem bürokratischen Irrgarten der Kindergrundsicherung' Sozialer Fortschritt (2024)4, pp. 331–340.

108 For the figures, see Bundesagentur für Arbeit, 'Kindergeld und Kinderzuschlag – Jahreszahlen 2023' (2023) table 1.4, p. 16 < https://statistik.arbeitsagentur.de/Statistikdaten/Detail/202312/famka/famka-jz/famka-jz-d-0-202312-pdf.pdf?__blob=publicationFile&v=2> accessed 22.3.2025.

nationals[109]—apart from EU citizens entitled to the freedom of movement right and their relatives—an employment permit is also required (Section 8, para. 2 SGB II). Habitual residence is established when the person's centre of life is in Germany (Section 30, para. 3, s. 2 SGB I). A place of residence is not required in this regard. This means that homeless people are also entitled to social assistance benefits if they have a postal address, e.g. at a facility for homeless people[110] and are therefore not excluded from receiving benefits under SGB II due to lack of reachability (Section 7b SGB II).

Beneficiaries who are unable to work receive the Citizen's Benefit if they are in need of assistance, live in a community of need with an individual who has capacity for work, and are not entitled to benefits to ensure their livelihood due to old age or reduced earning capacity in accordance with SGB XII (Section 19, para. 1, s. 2 SGB II). According to Section 7, para. 3 SGB II, a community of need includes partners and/or children of those entitled to benefits who have capacity for work. The partners can be married (including different-sex and same-sex couples), in a registered partnership (only for same-sex couples) or in an informal marriage-like or civil partnership-like relationship. Children are considered part of the community of need if they live with an individual who is entitled to benefits and who has capacity for work, if they are the child of an employable beneficiary or of that person's partner, live in the same household, are unmarried and have not yet reached the age of 25. Being a member of a community in need not only determines entitlement to benefits, but also the benefit amount based on classification in a specific standard needs level, on the one hand, and the distribution of income and assets among the community of need members, on the other.

---

109 The proportion of foreigners (individuals without German citizenship, all age groups) among basic income support recipients was around 47 per cent in August 2024. See Bundesagentur für Arbeit, Statistik, Strukturmerkmale von Bedarfsgemeinschaften und Personen, Tabelle 4, < https://statistik.arbeitsagentur.de/SiteGlobals/Forms/Suche/Einzelheftsuche_Formular.html?nn=15024&r_f=ur_Deutschland&topic_f=zeitreihekreise-zr-gruarb > accessed 21.12.2024.

110 Beneficiaries' accessibility to the job centre in accordance with Section 7b SGB II is not a prerequisite for entitlement to benefits, but a reason for exclusion from entitlement to benefits. Accessibility presupposes that those entitled to benefits are in the immediate vicinity of the responsible job centre and are able to receive and respond to its notifications and requests on every working day.

bb) Need for Assistance as a Reflection of the Principle of Subsidiarity

The subsidiarity principle is applied on a case-by-case basis by means of an individual assessment of the need for assistance. A person is considered in need of assistance if they are unable (or only partially able) to cover their living expenses using their own income and assets or through third-party benefits (e.g. maintenance payments or overriding social benefits), as stipulated in Section 9, para. 1 SGB II.

In case of a community of need, the partner's income and assets are also included in the assessment; in the case of children under the age of 25, the parents' income and assets are also considered (Section 9, para. 2, s. 2 SGB II). The concept of the community of need also extends to the income and assets of individuals who are not liable for maintenance under civil law (unmarried partners or partners living in a civil partnership who are not the parent of the child). After a cohabitation period of no more than one year[111] in the community of need (Section 7, para. 3a, No. 1 SGB II), the income and assets of the partner (who is not the parent of the child) are also included in the calculation of the child's entitlement to benefits. Consequently, children will no longer be entitled to the Citizen's Benefit in the full amount, despite the absence of maintenance obligations of their parent's partner.

In principle, all cash income is considered income, subject to certain deductions (Section 11, para. 1, s. 1 SGB II). These include taxes and mandatory social security contributions, as well as other contributions to compulsory (e.g. motor vehicle liability insurance) or voluntary insurances (e.g. liability insurance, household contents insurance), contributions to private state-subsidised pension schemes and maintenance payments for children who do not live in the same household, and expenses incurred to generate income (e.g. for further vocational training, trade union dues) (see Section 11b SGB II). An additional allowance for gainfully employed persons is intended to incentivise individuals to take up work. It amounts to 20 per cent for incomes between EUR100 and EUR 520, 30 per cent between EUR 520 and EUR 1,000 and 10 per cent for incomes between EUR 1,000 and EUR 1, 200 (or EUR 1,400 for parents of minors). The most recent adjustment to the sliding scale in the income range between EUR 520 and EUR 1,000 as part of the Citizen's Benefit reform aims to

111 The regulation is a legal presumption that can be rebutted by the beneficiaries.

encourage individuals to increase their working hours beyond the threshold for social security contributions (EUR 520 – so-called mini-jobs). Certain types of income are excluded from the assessment (Sections 11a SGB II, Section 1 *Bürgergeld-Verordnung*[112]): these, inter alia, are any benefits in kind (e.g. food banks, clothing banks), monetary donations from voluntary welfare associations (to a limited extent), but also compensation pensions, expense allowances for volunteer work subsidised under tax law and, in the case of students who have not yet reached the age of 25, income from holiday jobs.

According to established case law,[113] the distinction between assets and income follows the inflow principle. All disposable assets available at the beginning of the period of need (the month in which benefits are received) represent the beneficiary's assets. All inflows during the period of need are treated as income. The assets are assessed at their market value (Section 12, para. 5, s. 1 SGB II). However, certain 'protected' assets are excluded, for example, adequate household goods, a reasonable motor vehicle,[114] specific forms of old-age provision, and an owner-occupied home of up to 140 m^2, or an owner-occupied flat of up to 130 m^2 if it is being used by up to four persons (Section 12, para. 1 s. 2 SGB II).[115]

As a result of the experiences with "new" beneficiaries during the coronavirus pandemic,[116] a waiting period of one year from the beginning of the month in which benefits are first received (Section 12, para. 3, s. 1 SGB II) was introduced in 2023. During this waiting period, only substantial assets, namely if these exceed EUR 40,000 for the beneficiary and EUR 15,000 for each additional member of the community in need, are included (Section 12, para. 3, s. 2, para. 4 SGB II). After the waiting period ends, a lower asset allowance of EUR 15,000 per community of need member applies, although

112 *Verordnung zur Berechnung von Einkommen sowie zur Nichtberücksichtigung von Einkommen und Vermögen beim Bürgergeld* as promulgated on 17 December 2007 (Federal Law Gazette I 2007, p. 2942).

113 BSG Judgment of 10 August 2016 – B 14 AS 51/15 R.

114 According to the Federal Employment Agency's administrative regulations, a car is considered reasonable if the sales proceeds after deduction of liabilities would not exceed EUR 15,000, see Bundesagentur für Arbeit, 'Zweites Sozialgesetzbuch – SGB II: § 12 SGB II, Berücksichtigung von Vermögen' (30 April 2025), para. 12.13 < https://www.arbeitsagentur.de/datei/dok_ba015849.pdf > accessed 30.4.2025.

115 In case of more members, the relevant living space is increased by 20 m^2 for each individual.

116 See III.2.b) below.

unused exemptions can be transferred within that community (Section 12, pars. 2 SGB II).

Ultimately, a need for assistance only exists if beneficiaries are unable to secure support from third parties. They must first exhaust preferential social benefits made available by other welfare providers.[117] The obligation to seek recourse from third parties also means that claims for benefits must be made against persons with maintenance obligations or other debtors (e.g. in case of unpaid wages).

c) Scope and Amount of Benefits to Secure Subsistence

In addition to benefits for securing livelihoods (the Citizen's Benefit for those who have capacity for work and for those who are unable to work, benefits for education and participation in social and cultural life), benefits for integration in training and employment[118] and counselling [119] are also provided under SGB II (Section 1, para. 3 SGB II).

The Citizen's Benefit includes standard needs, costs for accommodation and heating and additional needs (Section 19, para. 1, s. 3 SGB II). Moreover, one-off benefits, loans (Section 24 SGB II) or subsidies may also be granted in special cases (e.g. subsidies for health and long-term care insurance for privately insured persons, Section 26 SGB II).

aa) The Standard Needs

Standard needs include, in particular, food, clothing, personal hygiene, household goods, household energy, excluding costs associated with heating and hot water, as well as personal everyday needs, which include an acceptable degree of participation in social and cultural life (Section 20, para. 1, s. 1 SGB II). The standard needs amount is paid as a monthly lump sum, which depends on the beneficiary's categorisation into one of six standard needs levels (Section 20, paras. 2 – 4, Section 23, No. 1 SGB XII).

117 This applies, in particular, to the obligation to apply for a pension, although this has been restricted by the Citizens' Benefits Act to applications for a pension without deductions until 2026 (Section 12a, sentence. 1 no. 1 and sentence. 2 SGB II).

118 See III.1.b) below.

119 See III.1.c) below.

The standard needs levels depend on marital status (single, single parent or with a partner) and age.

The amount of standard needs according to the six standard needs levels in 2025 are:

Standard Needs Levels		Amount
Level1	Single individuals, single parents, persons with a minor partner	EUR 563
Level 2	Partner in a community of need	EUR 506
Level 3	Other employable beneficiaries in a community of need aged 18 and older (SGB II), adults in institutions (SGB XII)	EUR 451
Level 4	Teenagers from 14 – 17 years	EUR 471
Level 5	Children from 6 – 13 years	EUR 390
Level 6	Children up to 5 years	EUR 357

The standard needs amount for each standard needs level is determined using the so-called statistics model using data from the Income and Expenditure Sample (*Einkommens- und Verbrauchstichprobe - EVS*), conducted every five years by the Federal Statistical Office and the statistical offices of the federal states (Section 20, para. 1a SGB II in conjunction with Section 28 SGB XII).[120]

bb) Additional Needs and Alternative Provision of Benefits

Additional needs in accordance with Section 21 SGB II are intended to cover increased needs arising from special life situations (e.g. pregnancy, single parenthood) or special needs (e.g. for schoolbooks or additional costs for dietary needs due to illness). After the 12th week of pregnancy, for example, women are entitled to an additional 17 per cent of their standard needs. Single parents receive an additional 36 per cent of their standard needs if they live with one child under the age of 6 or with two or three children under the age of 16. In all other cases, the benefit amounts to an additional 12 per cent per child, up to a maximum of 60 per cent of standard needs.

Needs not covered by the standard needs benefit, such as initial equipment for pregnancy and birth, or initial equipment for housing, or needs

120 See III.1.a) below.

ranging from repairs to therapeutic devices and equipment, are provided as one-off special benefits (Section 24 SGB II). On the basis of Section 24 SGB XII, in individual cases where an unavoidable need ordinarily covered by the standard need cannot be met (e.g. replacement of a defective washing machine), the necessary amount can be provided as an interest-free loan, which must be repaid by the beneficiary in the following months.

cc) Needs for Accommodation and Heating

The nationwide determination of standard needs is intended to ensure uniform living conditions across Germany, but this objective might fall short, especially in large cities and metropolitan areas with high housing costs. The requirements for accommodation and heating are therefore excluded from the standardised benefit rates. They are covered in addition to the standard needs benefit in their actual amount, provided this amount is considered appropriate (Section 22 SGB II).

The appropriateness[121] of accommodation and heating costs is determined by the responsible local authorities (Section 6, para. 1, No. 2 SGB II) through administrative regulations or in bylaws (Section 22a-c SGB II). According to the Federal Social Court's case law, the determination of an abstract adequacy limit must be based on a "coherent concept"[122] that reflects the actual conditions of the relevant local[123] housing market (e.g. by referring to a rent index). The concept must justify the standard of living to which beneficiaries are entitled by using accommodation that meets simple basic needs as a benchmark in terms of facilities, location and building

121 The absence of a clear legal definition for this undefined legal term and its interpretation by case law and administrative practice raises normative and methodological concerns. See U. Berlit, 'Annäherungen an die Angemessenheit der Unterkunftskosten – das Unterkunftskostengutachten des IWU v. Januar 2017' info also (2017)4, pp. 147 ff. and S. Knickrehm, 'Das schlüssige Konzept im Wandel von Rechtsprechung und Politik' Die Sozialgerichtsbarkeit (2017)5, p. 241, 247 ff.

122 Established case law since BSG Judgment of 7 November 2006 – B 7b AS 18/06 R; cf. U. Berlit, 'Unterkunft und Heizung', in: U. Berlit, W. Conradis and A. Pattar (eds.) *Handbuch des Existenzsicherungsrechts* (3rd ed. Nomos 2019), paras. 58 ff.

123 H. Thomé publishes coherent concepts of various municipal providers on his website, see H. Thomé, 'Bundesweite Mietobergrenzen und KdU Richtlinien' (2025) < https://harald-thome.de/informationen/bundesweite-dienstanweisungen-kdu.html> accessed 22.3.2025.

materials. It must be based on a segment of the housing market that ensures that all beneficiaries have access to housing that meets this standard.[124]

The maximum appropriate gross rent (excluding utilities) is calculated by multiplying the appropriate rent per square metre determined according to the amount of appropriate square metres for a certain number of household members. As long as the rent for a flat remains below the applicable limit for the respective number of household members, it is considered to be appropriate, regardless of any individual factors.[125] In the City of Munich[126] (which has a significantly higher rent level compared to the rest of Germany), the rent appropriateness limits have been set as follows since January 2024:

Persons	Flat size up to m^2	'Rent caps' from 1 January 2024 in euro
1	50	890
2	65	1092
3	75	1286
4	90	1569
5	105	1939
6	120	2188

The statutory minimum level of subsistence under SGB II is partially individualised through reference not only to the regional, but also to the individual[127] housing situation.

124 However, neither SGB II nor SGB XII include an entitlement to the provision of housing as a benefit in kind.

125 For the so-called product theory of the Federal Social Court, see BSG Judgment of 2 July 2009, B 14 AS 36/08 R, para. 14.

126 LH München, 'Kosten der Unterkunft (SGB II)' (8 August 2024) < https://stadt.muenchen.de/dam/jcr:ec15cb97-5642-4f31-90e2-d97c186fbb95/Kosten_der_Unterkunft_SGB_II.pdf> accessed 22.3.2025.

127 A rent that deviates from the abstract appropriateness limit may be individually appropriate, e.g. due to the special needs of those affected (e.g. care by or from relatives who live close by, integration of families with underage children into the social environment). See LH München (n 126), p. 13.

d) Exclusions from Benefits

Despite meeting all eligibility requirements for the Citizen's Benefit, individuals who have capacity for work or who are unable to work, and members of certain groups are excluded from the scope of benefits.

First, certain groups of foreign nationals are excluded from eligibility to benefits according to Section 7, para.1, sentence 2 SGB II. This clause applies, in particular, to foreign nationals who are not workers or self-employed persons and to whom the right of freedom of movement under EU law does not apply for the first three months of their residence in Germany; to foreign nationals who have no right of residence in Germany; to foreign nationals whose right of residence arises solely based on their status as jobseekers; to foreign nationals who have a right of residence derived from their child's right of residence and which is enrolled in a school in Germany; as well as to the family members of the aforementioned groups of individuals.

The exclusion of certain foreign nationals has been the subject of considerable controversy in case law and legal doctrine.[128] While the ECJ confirmed that most of these exclusions from benefits under Section 7, para. 1, s. 2 SGB II were consistent with EU law,[129] the Federal Constitutional Court has not yet issued a ruling on the constitutionality of the exclusionary provisions.[130] Foreign nationals who are excluded from entitlement to the Citizen's Benefit are only entitled to transitional benefits (for one month within a two-year period) and to loans for travel expenses.[131]

Moreover, under Section 7, paras. 4–6 SGB II, individuals who receive an old-age pension or similar benefits; are residents in an inpatient facility (e.g. in a nursing home, addiction treatment centre) and cannot pursue gainful employment in the general labour market for at least 15 hours a week, as well as prisoners and students at state and state-recognised universities and trainees are excluded as well. The livelihoods of these

128 See E. Eichenhofer, 'Kapitel 2: Völker- und europarechtliche Vorgaben an die Existenzsicherung in Deutschland mit weiteren Nachweisen', in: U. Berlit, W. Conradis and A. Pattar (eds.) *Handbuch des Existenzsicherungsrechts* (4th ed. Nomos 2019) and H. Thomé (n 123).

129 See above II.1.b).

130 Cf. on the inadmissibility of the referral, BVerfG, Decision of 4 December 2019, 1 BvL 4/16.

131 *Gesetz zur Regelung von Ansprüchen ausländischer Personen in der Grundsicherung für Arbeitsuchende (SGB II) und in der Sozialhilfe* (SGB XII) of 22 December 2016 (Federal Law Gazette, p. 2016, 3155).

groups are typically ensured through other means, e.g. through a pension, social welfare benefits in accordance with SGB XII (in case of institutional care in a nursing home), benefits in kind for prisoners or corresponding regulations for trainees in vocational training.

Finally, the main issue of contention is the legislative decision to exclude students from entitlement to the Citizen's Benefit, although exceptions are made for individuals not covered by BAföG, such as additional needs in the event of pregnancy or single parenthood or transitional support in emergency situations at the end of their studies (Section 27 SGB II).[132] Students are not entitled to benefits that guarantee their subsistence, as their need for assistance could potentially end or be avoided by taking up gainful employment.[133]

III. Analysis

Social assistance law consistently faces the challenge of striking a fair balance between social solidarity and individual responsibility. The key instruments for achieving this are the determination of benefit amounts and defining beneficiaries' obligation to cooperate, as well as the consequences of non-compliance.

1. Determination of a Minimum Level of Subsistence

a) Procedure to Determine Standard Needs

With the Standard Needs Determination Act (*Regelbedarfsermittlungsgesetz*) of 24 March 2011,[134] a statistical procedure was introduced to determine standard benefits. A distinction is made between so-called levels of standard needs (*Regelbedarfsstufen*), which depend on family status (single, single parent or living with a partner or spouse) and age. The amount of the standard needs for each of the six individual levels is determined by applying the so-called statistical model based on the income and consumption sample (*Einkommens- und Verbrauchsstichprobe*, EVS), which is

132 BVerfG, Order of 23 September 2024, 1 BvL 9/21.

133 1st Guiding Principle of the decision of the Federal Constitutional Court of 23 September 2024. See below for details.

134 Federal Law Gazette I 2011, p. 453.

carried out every five years by the Federal Statistical Office of Germany. The EVS is a voluntary survey of around 80,000[135] private households that collects data on their financial and real estate assets, their living conditions and their ownership of selected consumer goods. It is conducted as a quota sample to ensure representation of various population groups. Among others, participating households maintain a diary for three months to record the type and amount of their income and expenditures. The data collected and extrapolated to the general population serve as the basis for the special evaluations conducted by the Federal Ministry of Labour and Social Affairs to determine the standard needs levels. Only the expenditure of low-income households is considered in the special evaluations. For single-person households, the expenditure of the lowest 15 per cent of households, stratified by income, is considered, and in the case of family households, the expenditures of the lowest 20 per cent are used.

To avoid circular reasoning, households that only receive subsistence benefits under SGB II, SGB XII or *AsylbLG* are excluded from the assessment. The sum of the average expenditure values in various categories, such as food, drinks, tobacco products or clothing and shoes, determines the standard needs of a single-person or family household. The results of the special evaluation are then defined as the standard needs in the Standard Needs Determination Act (*Regelbedarfsermittlungsgesetz*).[136] The special evaluation does not consider all consumption expenditures of the surveyed households, but only the so-called standard needs-relevant expenditures (Section 28, para. 4 SGB XII). Expenditures on items such as gambling, domestic help or all-inclusive holidays, for example, are excluded from the assessment. These exclusions, as well as the procedure and results of the statistical model, have long been subject to criticism for both methodological [137] and socio-political reasons. [138] However, the Federal Constitutional

135 This figure is provided by the Federal Statistical Office for the 2023 EVS. Around 55,000 households participated in the most recent EVS in 2018.

136 *Regelbedarfsermittlungsgesetz* as promulgated 9 December 2020 (Federal Law Gazette I 2020, p. 2855), which was amended by Art. 12 sec. 13 of the Act of 16 December 2022 (Federal Law Gazette I 2022, p. 2328).

137 This is partly because it does not take the compensation of higher expenditure in one area by lower expenditure in another area into account. See I. Becker, 'Existenzsicherung und Armutsforschung', in: U. Berlit, W. Conradis and A. Pattar (eds.) *Handbuch des Existenzsicherungsrechts* (4th ed. Nomos 2025), paras. 11 ff.

138 The Paritätische Wohlfahrtsverband regularly calculates significantly higher standard needs in its reports: EUR 813 for a single-person household in 2024 instead of EUR 563 (Der Paritätische/Paritätische Forschungsstelle: 'Regelbedarfe

Court has upheld the empirical-normative approach for determining the socio-cultural minimum level of subsistence with the help of the EVS's assessment as well as the exclusion of individual consumption goods, to be constitutionally valid.[139] The legislator's responsibility is to guarantee a dignified subsistence level. The legislator must therefore record the needs that are necessary to cover the socio-cultural minimum level of subsistence in a timely and realistic manner and justify these in a sustainable manner. However, there is room for manoeuvre both in the methodology used and in assessing actual living circumstances and necessary needs, and the legislator is not required "to make an optimal determination of the minimum level of subsistence by including all conceivable factors".[140] Consequently, the subsequent exclusion of individual items from the statistical calculation of the minimum level of subsistence by the Standard Needs Determination Act is also deemed constitutional, insofar as the standard needs are calculated in such a way that ensures the minimum level of subsistence is met, whether through internal equalisation of shortfalls, by saving or by additional benefit entitlements.[141]

b) Indexation

Between the periodic EVS reassessments, the standard needs are adjusted annually based on the development of wages and salaries (30 per cent) and prices (70 per cent) using a mixed index and a two-stage procedure. First, the national average rate of change is calculated for both the prices of goods and services relevant to the standard needs and the net wages and salaries per employee during the period from 1 July of the previous

2024, Fortschreibung der paritätischen Regelbedarfsforderung' (December 2023) < https://www.der-paritaetische.de/fileadmin/user_upload/Publikationen/doc/expertise_regelsatzberechnung-2023.pdf> accessed 22.3.2025.

139 See BVerfG, Decision of 23 July 2014 (1 BvL 10/12, 1 BvL 12/12 BvR 1691/13), paras. 76 ff.

140 BVerfG of 23 July 2014 1 BvL 10/12, 1 BvL 12/12, 1 BvR 1691/13.

141 Ibid, 2nd guiding Principle.

year to 30 June of the year before last[142] and published in a regulation.[143] The 2023 Citizen's Benefit Act introduced a second stage for calculating the rate of change. This allows for a more up-to-date adjustment of standard benefits by comparing the development of wages and prices during the three-month period from 1 April to 30 June of the previous year with the same period of the year before last, in line with the Federal Constitutional Court's demand for a regular and timely adjustment of standard needs.[144] This is intended to more accurately capture current developments such as the recent sharp price increases as a result of the COVID-19 pandemic and the war in Ukraine.

2. Between Poverty Reduction and Labour Market Integration

a) Activation

As a result of the Hartz IV reform, the function of social assistance underwent a shift. While the fight against poverty and providing social support remain the primary focus of SGB XII, under SGB II, the fight against poverty was reduced to the function of providing basic income (*Grundsicherung*),[145] together with integration into the labour market (under the political motto 'support and demand') as the central function of the system. By adopting the workfare approach, which "require(s) people to work in return for social assistance benefits", [146] the relationship between the rights and duties in social assistance was recalibrated and the welfare

142 For a critical review of the determination and the updating procedure, see I. Becker, 'Regelbedarfe im Konzept des neuen Bürgergelds – das Fortschreibungsverfahren' (4 November 2022) < https://netzwerk-sozialrecht.net/regelbedarfe-im-konzept-des-buergergelds-das-neue-fortschreibungsverfahren/> accessed 22.3.2025, with further references to the discussion.

143 Most recently, Federal Law Gazette, 'Regelbedarfsfortschreibungsverordnung' (2024) < https://www.recht.bund.de/bgbl/1/2023/287/VO> accessed 22.3.2025.

144 BVerfG, Decision of 2 September 2010 – 1 BvL 1/09, paras. 204, 209.

145 The term itself indicates a departure from the "aid" (Hilfe) concept of social assistance. In the original version of Section 1 SGB II, the reference to the fulfilment of a dignified minimum level of subsistence that was added later was missing.

146 On the definition, see I. Lodemel and H. Trickey (eds.), *An Offer You Cannot Refuse – Workfare in International Perspective* (Bristol University Press 2001), p. 6.

conditionality[147] in the Law on Basic Income Support for Jobseekers was significantly tightened.

The Hartz IV reform prioritised the labour market integration of employable beneficiaries as a means of ensuring their livelihood.[148] In addition to prioritising employment placement over potential integration benefits (Section 3, para. 1 SGB II), this shift was primarily reflected in the expansion of beneficiaries' obligations to cooperate and the tightening of sanctions for breaches of duty.[149]

At the centre of the special obligation to cooperate under Section 31 SGB II is the duty to take up and continue reasonable work, training or work opportunities.[150] In addition, beneficiaries are subject to reporting obligations, such as complying with summonses from the job centre, e.g. to verify eligibility for benefits or to attend a medical or psychological assessment. This obligation to cooperate must be formalised in an integration agreement between the job centre and the beneficiary, which may be replaced by an administrative act if the individual refuses to participate. The threshold of reasonableness in the basic income support for jobseekers has been lowered considerably compared to that in unemployment insurance (Section 140 SGB III): beneficiaries are generally expected to accept any type of work, regardless of their qualifications or previous occu-

147 B. Watts and S. Fitzpatrick, *Welfare Conditionality* (Routledge 2018); N. Harris, 'Unfavourable Conditions: Highlighting Welfare Conditionality' Journal of Social Security Law 25(2018) 3.

148 Draft bill of the parliamentary groups SPD and Bündnis 90/Die Grünen, BT-Drs. 15/1516, p. 44 < https://dserver.bundestag.de/btd/15/015/1501516.pdf> accessed 22.3.2025.

149 For a comprehensive description of the Hartz IV reform, see U. Becker, '"Hartz IV" und was sich dahinter verbirgt – Ziele, Inhalt und Bewertung des SGB II', in: T. Tomandl and W. Schrammel, *Sicherung von Grundbedürfnissen* (Wilhelm Braumüller Universitätsverlag 2007), pp. 23–61.

150 Work opportunities also include those with additional expenses ("1-euro jobs"), which are controversial not only from a workfare perspective, but also because of their displacement effects on the regular labour market. See H. Spindler, 'Fordern und Fördern – zur Eingliederung arbeitsuchender Arbeitsloser in den Arbeitsmarkt', in ArchSozArb (2008), pp. 70–80; G. Stahlmann, 'Die Zusätzlichkeit bei Arbeitsgelegenheiten ohne Arbeitsvertrag nach § 16 Par. 3 SGB II' ZFSH/SGB (2008), pp. 337–346 (part 1) and pp. 403–424 (part 2); W. Spelbrink, 'Gelingt durch die neuen Instrumente die Integration von Langzeitarbeitslosen in den Arbeitsmarkt?' Die Sozialgerichtbarkeit (2008)8, pp. 445–45.

pation, [151] the distance between their place of residence and the place of employment or less favourable working conditions (even if the pay is below the collectively agreed or local wage). Until the introduction of the statutory minimum wage ten years after Hartz IV,[152] individuals were expected to accept reductions in income up to the limit of an exploitative wage.[153]

While the obligation to cooperate already existed in principle under the Federal Social Assistance Act (BSHG), unlike workfare schemes in other countries, social assistance benefits in Germany were not directly tied to community work[154] (with the exception of some pilot schemes).[155] Compared to the BSHG, however, the relationship between the rights and obligations has assumed a new quality through the new focus on the priority of labour market integration in SGB II, which is now primarily oriented towards the beneficiary's employability.[156]

Despite fierce political resistance from unemployment initiatives[157] and social welfare associations[158], a high rate of successful legal challenges against job centre decisions[159], and multiple minor legislative amend-

151 J. Greiser, 'Zumutbare Arbeit i.S.d. § 140 SGB III und des § 10 SGB II. Gibt es noch einen Berufsschutz im SGB III und SGB II?' Vierteljahreschrift für Sozial- und Arbeitsrecht (2021)1, pp. 1–21.

152 Gesetz zur Einführung eines allgemeinen Mindestlohns as promulgated on 11 August 2014, Federal Law Gazette I 2014, p. 1348.

153 H. Spindler, 'Grenzen der Zumutbarkeit für Sozialhilfebedürftige bei Niedriglöhnen und Lohnwucher' info also (2003)2, < https://tacheles-sozialhilfe.de/aktuelles/archiv/grenzen-der-zumutbarkeit-von-arbeit-fuer-sozialhilfeberechtigte-bei-niedrigloehnen-und-lohnwucher.html > accessed 22.3.2025.

154 H. Spindler, 'Arbeiten für die Grundsicherung, Für die Gewährung des Existenzminimums wird zunehmend eine Gegenleistung verlangt' Soziale Sicherheit (2008)11, p. 366.

155 C. Heinz, C. Hense, et al, 'Modellversuch Bürgerarbeit. Zwischen Workfare und Sozialem Arbeitsmarkt' IAB Forschungsbericht (2007)14 < https://doku.iab.de/forschungsbericht/2007/fb1407.pdf> accessed 22.3.2025.

156 U. Becker (n 149), p. 26.

157 See unemployment and social assistance association, Tacheles e.V. (2025) < www.tacheles-sozialhilfe.de> accessed 22.3.2025.

158 In particular, the Paritätische Wohlfahrtsverband, 'Schwerpunkt: Armut und Grundsicherung' (2025) < https://www.der-paritaetische.de/themen/sozial-und-europapolitik/armut-und-grundsicherung/> accessed 22.3.2025.

159 Legal Tribune Online, 'Leichte Entspannung bei Hartz IV-Verfahren. Justizbelastung am Sozialgericht Berlin' (18 April 2018) < https://www.lto.de/recht/justiz/j/sg-berlin-hartziv-verfahren-belastung-pilotprojekt-elektronischer-rechtsverkehr> accessed 22.3.2025. Approximately 35 per cent of complaints against SGB II notices are successful (Haufe, Jobcenter: 'Rückgang bei Klagen und leichter Anstieg der Widersprüche' (11 January 2024) < https://www.haufe.de/sozialwesen/sgb-rec

ments,[160] the legislator significantly weakened the workfare components of the Hartz IV reform only as late as 2023. The introduction of the Citizens' Income Act was the legislature's response to the high and stagnating number of long-term unemployed,[161] which drew attention to the failure of integration measures to meet their objective and to the neglect of the major differences in the standards of living of the beneficiaries.[162]

Recipients of the minimum income benefit include full-time or part-time workers whose income is insufficient to cover their own and their families' subsistence (so-called "top-up workers"), part-time parents, single parents and caregivers who, due to their family obligations and often limited access to other care options, are restricted in their ability to participate more fully in working life. This group also includes employees across all qualification levels who are 'laid off' during times of economic and other crises, as well as young people facing difficulties transitioning from school to work or addicts and those with mental illnesses who, despite having capacity for work within the meaning of the SGB II, are unable to meet the heightened demands of the modern labour market.[163] Their inclusion in the labour market requires a broad range of measures for (re)integrating them into the labour market, from job application training, literacy and language acqui-

---

ht-kommunal/jobcenter-widerspruech-und-klagen_238_534016.html> accessed 22.3.2025.

160 For a chronological overview of the amending laws, see < https://www.buzer.de/gesetz/2602/l.htm> and for a chronology of significant changes to the basic income support for jobseekers < https://www.portal-sozialpolitik.de/index.php?page=Grundsicherung-fuer-Arbeitsuchende> both accessed 22.3.2025.

161 Statista, 'Anzahl der Langzeitarbeitslosen im Zeitraum von 2010 bis 2024' (2025) < https://de.statista.com/statistik/daten/studie/666199/umfrage/anzahl-der-langzeitarbeitslosen-in-deutschland/> accessed 22.3.2025. The long-term unemployed are defined as individuals who have been out of work (working less than 15 hours a week) for over a year. They make up around 50 per cent of the 1.7 million unemployed people receiving the Citizen's Benefit. See B. Fitzenberger, 'Warum die aktuelle Bürgergelddebatte nicht die richtigen Schwerpunkte setzt' (11 March 2024), p. 3 < https://www.iab-forum.de/warum-die-aktuelle-buergergelddebatte-nicht-die-richtigen-schwerpunkte-setzt/ > accessed 22.3.2025. According to a well-founded estimate, between January 2005 and December 2014, around 1 million people were continuously dependent on basic security benefits. H. Seibert, A. Wurdack, et al., 'Typische Verlaufsmuster beim Grundsicherungsbezug: für einige Dauerzustand, für andere nur eine Episode' IAB-Kurzbericht (2017)4.

162 See the draft bill of the Federal Government, 10 October 2022, BT-Drs. 20/3873, p. 1.

163 Paritätischer Wohlfahrtsverband (ed.), *Wer die Armen sind* (Der Paritätische Gesamtverband 2018) < https://www.der-paritaetische.de/fileadmin/user_upload/Schwerpunkte/Armutsbericht/doc/2018_armutsbericht.pdf> accessed 22.3.2025.

sition, vocational training and long-term pedagogically-supported interventions aimed at overcoming difficult life circumstances. This also includes job placement and follow-up support. SGB II provides for a variety of integration services to facilitate this process, although their implementation is largely at the job centre's discretion. The obligation to participate in integration measures was to be specified in an integration agreement, which could be formalised in an administrative act in case of the beneficiary's refusal to participate. The integration agreement was replaced by the non-legally-binding 'cooperation plan' introduced by the Citizen's Benefit Act. After the *Sofort-Angebot* (immediate offer) under Section 15a SGB II was abolished in 2018,[164] the Citizen's Benefit Act enhanced the opportunities of sustainable labour market integration, above all, by abolishing the priority of job placement over the completion of educational qualifications and participation in integration and language courses, but also by (re-)introducing holistic support through individual coaching (Section 16k SGB II).

b) Sanctions

Since the obligation to cooperate under SGB II constitutes—from a legal standpoint—a duty to cooperate that is not reciprocally linked (i.e. not in synallagma) to the entitlement to basic income support, fulfilling this obligation is not a prerequisite for receiving basic income benefits. However, non-compliance with the obligation to cooperate may result in a reduction of benefits, in which case the legal subsistence level is not met, even over extended periods. This applies in particular when benefit reductions coincide with claims for reimbursement of overpaid benefits (Section 42 SGB II in connection with Section 50 SGB X), claims for repayment of a loan granted by the job centre (Section 42a SGB II) or claims for compensation, e.g. due to anti-social behaviour prior to receiving benefits[165] or due to periods of ineligibility for unemployment insurance (Section 31, para. 2, No. 3 SGB II). Pursuant to the original version of Sections 31 et seq. SGB II,

164 Art. 1 of the 9th *Gesetz zur Änderung des Sozialgesetzbuchs* as promulgated on 26 July 2016 (Federal Law Gazette I 2016, p. 1824, 2718) < https://www.bgbl.de/xaver/bgbl/start.xav#__bgbl__%2F%2F*%5B%40attr_id%3D%27bgbl116s1824.pdf%27%5D__1742664246074> accessed 22.3.2025.

165 Section 43 No. 2 in conjunction with Section 34 SGB II. Such claims were discussed but rejected by case law in the case of a lorry driver's drunk driving incident outside working hours, leading to unemployment, as well as payments made by a later recipient of the Citizen's Benefit to a romance scammer. See U. Klerks, 'Ausgewählte

reductions in the standard benefit ranging from 30 per cent to 100 per cent were possible in the event of breaches of the obligation to help oneself, e.g. by refusing an offered job, training position or integration measure. As a consequence, violations of the obligation to cooperate could result in extended periods during which recipients were denied a minimum level of subsistence adequate to uphold human dignity.

The situation changed following the Federal Constitutional Court's 2019 "sanctions" ruling,[166] in which the Court affirmed that benefit cuts must comply with the fundamental right to a guaranteed minimum level of subsistence. In response, the legislature initially issued a one-year moratorium on sanctions for breaches of the duty under SGB II, which came into force in July 2022.[167] Subsequently, the Citizen's Benefit Act of 2023 amended Section 31a SGB II Sanctions to meet constitutional requirements. The Act limited the sanctions, which were renamed into 'reduction in benefits' to a maximum of 30 per cent in the event of a breach of the obligation to cooperate. However, on 28 March 2024,[168] this regulation was corrected again by the new provision reducing the benefits to zero (Section 31a, para. 7 SGB II) for so-called 'total objectors' who deliberately refuse to accept an actual and direct offer of employment.

3. Lessons from the Coronavirus Crisis

The legislator has also incorporated lessons learned from the coronavirus crisis into the Citizen's Benefit reform. Due to the pandemic-related restrictions, many self-employed persons and small business owners, as well as employees in marginal employment in sectors heavily impacted by the lockdowns (such as gastronomy and culture), lost their livelihoods and had to apply for basic income support, as they lacked overriding claims to unemployment or short-time working benefits. The number of communities

---

Fragen zum Ersatzanspruch wegen sozialwidrigen Verhaltens gem. § 34 SGB II' info also (2021), pp. 3–8 and 56–60.

166 See Sec. II.1.c).cc).

167 *Elftes Gesetz zur Änderung des Zweiten Buches Sozialgesetzbuch* (11. SGB II-*Änderungsgesetz*, so-called "Sanktionsmoratorium") as promulgated on 19 June 2022 (Federal Law Gazette I 2022, p. 921) < https://www.bgbl.de/xaver/bgbl/start.xav#__bgbl__%2F%2F*%5B%40attr_id%3D%27bgbl122s0921.pdf%27%5D__1742664432219> accessed 22.3.2025.

168 Art. 5 *Zweites Haushaltsfinanzierungsgesetz* 2024 as promulgated on 27 March 2024 (Federal Law Gazette I 2024, No. 107).

in need (single or multiple-person households) increased by around 1.2 million.[169] The legislator facilitated access to basic income support and social assistance for this new category of individuals in need by means of a waiting period of one year within which inadequate accommodation costs could be covered and non-substantial assets are excluded from assessment,[170] as stipulated in the first social protection package.[171]

As part of the measures introduced in response to the pandemic and in anticipation of the introduction of a basic child benefit, an immediate supplement of EUR 20 for children in receipt of the minimum income benefit was also introduced to improve children's chances of participating in society, in education, and in training and labour market integration.[172] This measure was intended to serve as a temporary bridge until the introduction of the basic child benefit. After the failure of the child benefit reform in the last legislative period the benefit was increased by EUR 5 on 1 January 2025.[173]

The adoption of revised waiting periods for assessing the adequacy of coverage of accommodation costs and the increase in exemption of assets in the Citizen's Benefit Act allowed for cushioning the loss of financial stability for a limited period while receiving the Citizen's Benefit and thus made basic income support accessible to jobseekers belonging to socio-politically vulnerable groups in case of future crises as well. Due to the different political majorities in the Bundestag and Bundesrat, however, longer waiting periods and the introduction of a one-year waiting period without the risk of sanctions could not be implemented.

---

169 BT-Drs. 19/1807, p. 5.

170 Section 67 (1) in conjunction with 2–5 SGB II as amended by the Act of 27 March 2020.

171 Art. 1-5 *Gesetz für den erleichterten Zugang zu sozialer Sicherung und zum Einsatz und zur Absicherung sozialer Dienstleister aufgrund des Coronavirus SARS-CoV-2* as promulgated on 27 March 2020 (Federal Law Gazette I 2020, p. 575).

172 *Gesetz zur Regelung eines Sofortzuschlages und einer Einmalzahlung in den sozialen Mindestsicherungssystemen sowie zur Änderung des Finanzausgleichsgesetzes und weiterer Gesetze* as promulgated on 23 May 2022 (Federal Law Gazette I 2022, p. 760).

173 Art. 5 *Steuerfortentwicklungsgesetz* as promulgated on 30 December 2024 (Federal Law Gazette I 2024, No. 449).

IV. Conclusions

Since the Hartz IV reform entered into force, its provisions have been controversial. The political dispute is fuelled by the inherent contradiction between the two functions of basic income support for jobseekers, namely guaranteeing a minimum level of subsistence and promoting labour market integration, driven by divergent political goals, concepts of poverty and views of society. The Federal Constitutional Court has not resolved the fundamental functional conflict within the basic income support system through its rulings. However, it has affirmed the right to social assistance as an individual fundamental right and has delineated its boundaries based on the Basic Law's fundamental value judgments. At the same time, the constitutional framework provides the legislature with room to adapt basic income support measures to different economic and social requirements in times of crisis.

The relationship between the legislation and the Federal Constitutional Court in the design of social assistance is therefore not so much an endless constitutional tale of woe[174] but rather an example of successful 'social self-regulation'.[175] The constitutional requirement that legal measures aimed at regulating the behaviour of benefit recipients be grounded in empirical evidence of their effectiveness[176] can foster a more objective political discourse on the balance between rights and obligations in the context of means-tested benefits, one that also considers the complex and diverse life situations of individuals experiencing poverty in Germany.

174 Rixen (n 59), p. 1.

175 I. Ebsen, *Das Bundesverfassungsgericht als Element gesellschaftlicher Selbstregulierung. Eine pluralistische Theorie der Verfassungsgerichtsbarkeit im demokratischen Verfassungsstaat* (Duncker & Humblot 1985).

176 Implemented in Section 55 SGB II.

Guaranteed Minimum Income in Greece: The Transition from Fragmented Measures to Comprehensive Constitutional and Legislative Protection

Anastasia Poulou

I. Introduction

In 2022, 26.3 per cent of the Greek population was at risk of poverty or lacked access to essential goods and services.[1] This figure indicates that a life in dignity—defined as a life where individuals have adequate financial and material resources considered indispensable for maintaining health, well-being and active participation in economic and social life—may not necessarily be guaranteed for a significant share of the population. Even though poverty is not a new phenomenon in Greece, social protection measures to fight it have historically not been prioritised by the Greek State. As has been the case in other social security systems in Southern European countries, Greece's welfare state has long been centred around safeguarding its residents against old-age risks, as reflected in the disproportionately high pension expenditure compared to other forms of social spending. In this

1 See Hellenic Statistical Authority, 'Risk of poverty 2022 Survey on Income and Living Conditions (Income reference period: 2021)' (8 May 2023) < https://www.statistics.gr> last accessed on 12.02.2024.

vein, the fight against poverty and social exclusion was largely overlooked for many years and any related social assistance measures were fragmented and underdeveloped.

The landscape of Greek social protection has only recently undergone a transformation, which was largely driven by external pressure during the euro crisis,[2] prompting social policy reforms as part of broader financial recovery measures. Initially introduced as a pilot scheme in 2014, Greece adopted a nationwide guaranteed minimum income scheme in 2017. This non-contributory, means-tested safety net serves as a last resort for persons without sufficient resources.[3] The scheme is designed to support individuals and families facing extreme poverty, providing beneficiaries with income support combined with social reintegration measures.

Against this background, this chapter explores the constitutional and legislative protection of a life in dignity in Greece. First, we present the constitutional framework of social protection in Greece, tracing its gradual development from providing indirect protection to formal constitutionalisation of the guaranteed minimum income benefit. Second, we analyse the legal framework of social protection, which encompasses both social services and the transition from fragmented social assistance to a universal minimum income scheme. Third, we review the recently introduced Greek guaranteed minimum income scheme, focusing on its coverage, eligibility criteria and adequacy of support provided.

II. Overview

1. The Constitutional Law Background: From Indirect Protection to the Constitutionalisation of the Guaranteed Minimum Income

a) Human Dignity

In Greek law, the notion of a life in dignity or a decent standard of living is primarily protected by Article 2, para. 1 of the Greek Constitution, which enshrines the principle of human dignity. It reads: “Respect for and protec-

2 See further U. Becker and A. Poulou (eds.), *European Welfare State Constitutions after the Financial Crisis* (OUP 2020).

3 See also Art. 2 of Council Recommendation of 30 January 2023 on adequate minimum income ensuring active inclusion (2023/C 41/01).

tion of human dignity is the primary obligation of the State". The position of this constitutional provision within the Greek Constitution is indicative of its normative significance: human dignity is not safeguarded in the second part of the Constitution, which addresses individual and social rights, but is included in the first part, which contains "basic provisions" and defines the constitutional framework, thus giving human dignity an anthropocentric character. Consequently, human dignity is not a merely a declaratory principle in Greek constitutional law, but a fundamental principle of law that requires all state institutions to respect and protect the intrinsic value of the human person.[4] This provision establishes human dignity as the ultimate criterion for the legitimacy of the actions of state institutions, ensuring that no rule of law can be interpreted or applied contrary to the principle of respect for and protection of human dignity. All fundamental rights and principles, such as democracy, equality, the rule of law and the welfare state, aim to protect human dignity, given that the value of the human being takes precedence over all other legal principles. Article 2, para. 1 of the Greek Constitution requires respect for human beings to prevail in the exercise of any authority.[5]

At the same time, human dignity has evolved into a subjective right, empowering individuals to limit state interventions or to demand positive measures for its protection. A basic defining element of human dignity is personal self-determination, that is, the freedom to choose one's own path and status in life. Since self-determination depends on the existence of robust socio-political institutions and conducive practices, Article 2, para. 1 of the Greek Constitution establishes the obligation of the State to guarantee a minimum subsistence level for every individual. This means that the State is expected to create the socioeconomic, political, cultural and environmental conditions and circumstances under which employment relationships are established and income is earned, with the aim of ensuring that the basic needs of both individuals and society as a whole are met. These conditions include ensuring human well-being in all stages of life, supported through the social security system, healthcare, infrastructure development and environmental protection.

---

4 See Areios Pagos judgment 40/1998, 17 December 1998.

5 For a detailed analysis of Article 2 of the Greek Constitution, see T. Ziamou, 'Article 2', in: F. Spyropoulos, X. Contiades et al. (eds.), *Commentary on the Greek Constitution* (Sakkoulas 2017), p. 20 (in Greek).

The principle of human dignity has served as a benchmark in many cases before the Greek courts. First, it served as a benchmark for the Greek Council of State when reviewing the constitutionality of wage and pension cuts during the debt crisis. Reductions in wages and pensions were reviewed in the light of Article 2, para. 1 of the Greek Constitution to determine conformity with the subsistence necessary for a decent standard of living. More specifically, the Council of State ruled that the claim alleging infringement of Article 2 of the Constitution, which protects human dignity, as a result of the reductions in wages and pension benefits introduced by Law 3845/2010, must be rejected as unfounded, as this constitutional provision does not guarantee the right to a specific level of wage or pension, except where such a reduction represents a risk to a decent standard of living.[6] The Court found that the applicants had failed to substantiate that the respective reductions placed them at such a risk.[7] Moreover, in a subsequent decision on the introduction of a new salary scale for public servants by Law 4024/2011, the Council of State reviewed a claim that this pay scale —in combination with the wage cuts introduced by the aforementioned Law 3833/2010—would result in reductions exceeding half of the applicants' total remuneration. The applicants argued that these measures jeopardised their and their families' ability to maintain a dignified standard of living in violation of Article 2, para. 1 of the Constitution. The Court dismissed the claim, ruling that in the context of the budgetary crisis, the contested intervention could not be considered a burden that compromised the applicants' ability to live in dignity, since, first, the application of the new salary scale did not entail a reduction in the basic salary of civil servants in relation to the previously applicable system and, second, the greater percentage reduction in the applicants' salary compared to that of other civil servants was attributable to the fact that they had received particularly high special allowances.[8] Nevertheless, the Council of State clarified that this assumption in no way precludes a different conclusion in the event of future salary reductions that might lead to a further deterioration in civil servants' standard of living.[9] Furthermore, Article 2, para. 1 of the Constitution has been invoked as a legal foundation for the protection of a decent standard of living in cases of tax exemptions. The Council of State has ruled

6 Symboulio tis Epikrateias, judgment 668/2012, 20 February 2012, para. 35.
7 Ibid.
8 Symboulio tis Epikrateias, judgment 3177/2014, 26 September 2014, para. 8.
9 Ibid.

that Article 2, para. 1 establishes a fundamental obligation of the State to safeguard a decent standard of living, which may not be compromised by the imposition of taxes and other financial burdens; these must be levied in line with each taxpayer's taxpaying capacity. More specifically, the Court maintained that an individual's taxpaying capacity refers to his/her ability to pay taxes without compromising the minimum threshold for a dignified standard of living, established in Article 2, para. 1 of the Constitution, and is determined on the basis of objective criteria, such as income or property, and subjective criteria, including the individual's personal, family and social situation, as well as the taxpayer's health and age. Consequently, the amount of income required to cover the taxpayer's and his/her family's needs for a decent standard of living, in accordance with the above criteria, should remain tax-exempt.[10]

b) Social Rights

Beyond the protection of human dignity, the Greek Constitution embraces a human-centred and socially-oriented conception of law and the State. Without calling into question the market economy, it incorporates a series of general provisions and specific social rights that define the foundations of the Greek welfare state. More precisely, the 2001 amendment of the Constitution of 1975 introduced the principle of the welfare state in Article 25.[11] The principle of the welfare state, to be guaranteed and promoted by the State, complements the social rights outlined in the Constitution, providing a constitutional foundation for social rights that are not explicitly enshrined therein. In this vein, the principle of the welfare state could serve as a foundation for the right to a guaranteed minimum income.[12] Furthermore, the Greek Constitution includes an extensive catalogue of social rights. Article 22, para. 5 of the Constitution enshrines the right to social securi-

10 Symboulio tis Epikrateias, judgment 1087/2017, 10 April 2017.

11 Article 25 of the Greek Constitution reads as follows: "1. The rights of a person as an individual and as a member of society and the principle of the rule of law of the welfare state are guaranteed by the State. All state institutions shall be required to ensure their unconstrained and effective exercise. (...)".

12 C. Anthopoulos, 'Aspects of constitutional democracy. In the example of Article 25 para. 1 of the Constitution', in: D. Tsatsos, E. Venizelos and X. Contiades (eds.), *The New Constitution* (Ant. Sakkoulas 2001), p. 159 (in Greek).

ty,[13] establishing a constitutional mandate and an institutional guarantee, ensuring that social security is organised according to specific principles of organisation, operation, administration and financing. The legislator has the obligation to uphold its core principles and substance. More precisely, social security in Greece is founded on six fundamental principles: i) universality, ii) compulsory participation, iii) compulsory insurance, iv) reciprocity, v) protection of insurance capital, and vi) solidarity.[14] The interaction of these principles and their coherent expression in the social security system's institutional design implies a framework that is immune to regulatory interventions by the legislator. Second, Article 21, para. 3 of the Constitution establishes the State's obligation to take measures to protect public health, recognising healthcare as a social right that encompasses citizens' physical and mental well-being, and includes both prevention and treatment.[15] As a universal right, access to healthcare guarantees a minimum level of state intervention to protect health.[16] The maintenance of an organised public system that provides healthcare services and supervises private healthcare providers reflects the State's constitutional commitment to safeguard public health.

Moreover, the right to social protection derives from a number of constitutional provisions, namely Article 21, paras. 1, 2, 4 and 6 of the Constitution, which establish the State's obligation to provide "special care" and to adopt "special measures" for several vulnerable social groups, are to be read jointly. More precisely, Article 21, para. 1, subpara. a of the Constitution recognises the family as the foundation for the preservation and advancement of the nation, placing it, along with marriage, maternity and childhood, under the protection of the State.[17] Furthermore, Article

---

13 Article 22, para. 5 of the Greek Constitution reads as follows: "5. The State shall provide for the social security of workers as prescribed by law."

14 See A. Stergiou, 'Article 22 para 5', in: S. Vlachopoulos, X. Contiades and G. Tasopoulos (eds.), *Commentary on the Greek constitution*, < https://www.syntagmawatch.gr> accessed 12.2.2024 (in Greek).

15 Article 21, para. 3 of the Greek Constitution reads as follows: "3. The State shall provide for the health of its citizens and shall take special measures for the protection of youth, old age, disability and for the care of the most deprived."

16 For a detailed analysis of the right to healthcare in the Greek Constitution, see P. Pararrigopoulou, 'Article 21', in: F. Spyropoulos, X. Contiades, C. Anthopoulos et al. (eds.), *Commentary on the Greek Constitution* (Sakkoulas 2017), p. 536 (in Greek).

17 Article 21, para. 1, subpara. a of the Greek Constitution reads as follows: "1. The family, as the foundation of the preservation and promotion of the nation, as well as marriage, maternity and childhood are under the protection of the State. (...)".

21, para. 2 of the Constitution reserves special treatment for large families, persons with disabilities, individuals with physical or mental impairments, the elderly, as well as widows and orphans of those who have died in war.[18] Although these social groups are included in Article 21, para. 2 of the Constitution without further distinction, Decision 1095/2001 of the Greek Council of State holds that the reference to large families in this constitutional provision should be considered separately from the other vulnerable social groups. While the special care assistance provided by the State to the other vulnerable social groups is undoubtedly welfare-based—implying that means-testing may be considered legitimate, if not mandatory—the constitutional right of large families to special care assistance primarily aims to address the country's demographic challenges. It is therefore considered unconstitutional to limit or downgrade the scope of special care assistance for large families on the basis of income criteria, unless there are compelling reasons to do so.[19]

For a detailed analysis of the protection of family in the Greek Constitution, see A. Kotzampasi, 'Article 21', in: F. Spyropoulos, X. Contiades, C. Anthopoulos et al. (eds.), *Commentary on the Greek Constitution* (Sakkoulas 2017), p. 527 (in Greek).

18 Article 21, para. 2 of the Greek Constitution reads as follows: "2. Large families, war and peacetime disabled persons, war victims, widows and orphans of those who have fallen in war, and those suffering from incurable physical or mental illness are entitled to special care from the State." For a detailed analysis of Article 21, para. 2 of the Greek Constitution, see P. Pararrigopoulou, 'Article 21', in: F. Spyropoulos, X. Contiades, C. Anthopoulos et al. (eds.), *Commentary on the Greek Constitution* (Sakkoulas 2017), p. 536 (in Greek).

19 Based on this interpretative approach, Article 39, paras. 1-3 of Law 2459/1997, which introduced income criteria for granting benefits to large families, was deemed unconstitutional by the Greek Council of State in its Decision 1095/2001. Consequently, the joint ministerial decision implementing this legislative provision was annulled. The decision was criticised by Greek academia, which argued, first, that if childcare benefits are intended as a tool of demographic policy, their effectiveness for wealthy families is questionable, given their relatively low level. Second, concerns were raised about whether the court had the legitimacy to rule on the necessity of imposing income criteria for such benefits or whether the balance between the social protection of large families and demographic policy should have been left to the legislator's discretion. In a similar vein, the Greek Council of State in its Decision 1175/2008 held that imposing income criteria for the granting of lifelong pensions to mothers of large families is contrary to Article 21, para. 2 of the Constitution. The significance of this case law lies primarily in its affirmation of the normative content of a right to social welfare, which had previously been considered to be of a "weak", merely programmatic nature, to draw important conclusions for legislative policies in a critical area of social protection.

Article 21, para. 4 of the Constitution guarantees the right to housing.[20] The State has the obligation to provide housing assistance to citizens, not necessarily as an *in rem* entitlement, but as a form of support, including free or subsidised housing or financial aid for the purchase, rental or renovation of accommodation for those in need.[21] Finally, Article 21, para. 6 of the Constitution enshrines the right of persons with disabilities to measures that safeguard their autonomy and facilitate their professional integration and participation in the country's social, economic and political life.[22] Hence, special constitutional treatment is reserved for persons with disabilities, recognising their personal freedom and dignity, while ensuring they receive individualized and adequate assistance from the State. One important consequence of such preferential constitutional protection for this social group is consistent recognition in case law that specific policy measures, such as tax privileges, the granting of licenses or exemptions from the principle of meritocracy in public sector recruitment, are legitimate means that serve the public interest by safeguarding the protection of persons with disabilities in society.[23]

The abovementioned constitutional provisions (Article 21, paras. 1, 2, 4, and 6 of the Constitution) establish the framework for the social protection of specific groups with distinct social characteristics, providing guidance to the legislature, public administration and the judiciary in shaping and evaluating the constitutionality of all related measures. Given that these provisions address specific social groups as right holders, the question arises whether the Constitution only guarantees fragmentary protection for these specific social groups or whether a more general right to social protection can be inferred. The abovementioned constitutional provisions could, in fact, be read as a list of narrowly defined individual rights, granted exclusively to the specified social groups and tied to specific forms of protection, without establishing the obligation to provide protective measures

20 Article 21, para. 4 of the Greek Constitution reads as follows: "4. The acquisition of housing by those who lack it or are inadequately housed shall be the subject of special care by the State."

21 For a detailed analysis of the right to housing in the Greek Constitution see P. Pararrigopoulou (n 18).

22 Article 21, para. 6 of the Greek Constitution reads as follows: "Persons with disabilities have the right to enjoy measures that ensure their autonomy, professional integration and participation in the social, economic and political life of the country."

23 See Council of State 1635/2012, 3729/2011.

to other population groups as well.[24] However, a systematic interpretation of the key provisions of Article 21, paras. 1, 2, 3, 4 and 6 of the Constitution, in conjunction with the principles of human dignity, the right to personal identity and, in particular, the rule of law, leads to the conclusion that constitutional protection is *not* limited to specific, narrowly defined social groups. On the contrary, Article 21 of the Constitution enshrines a general right to social protection, which is articulated through specific forms of protection granted to the social groups explicitly mentioned in the Constitution. At the same time, however, Article 21 guarantees the right of every individual to sufficient resources to meet their basic needs.[25] In this context, the explicit reference in Article 21, para. 3, inter alia, to the most deprived social groups is of particular significance, as it provides a constitutional foundation for guaranteeing a minimum standard of living for all.[26]

c) Minimum Income Protection in the 2019 Constitutional Revision

While it can be argued that the guaranteed minimum income already had a sufficient constitutional foundation in Greece, the constitutional revision of 2019 representes an important cornerstone of the right to a dignified life. This revision introduced a new constitutional provision (Article 21, para. 1, subpara. b), which stipulates that "The State ensures that all citizens enjoy decent living conditions through a minimum guaranteed income system, as provided by law". Although all political parties agreed on the necessity of this provision, disagreements arose regarding its systematic positioning within the Constitution. The governing leftist party at the time, "Syriza", advocated for incorporating the new right in Article 21, para. 1, which, as mentioned above, traditionally focused on the protection of family, marriage, motherhood and childhood, to emphasise the welfare-oriented nature of the right to a decent standard of living. In contrast, the conservative party " New Democracy" suggested incorporating the new right in Article 25 of the Greek Constitution, which enshrines the principle of the welfare state, first, to highlight that it was not intended as a subjective right

24 I. Glykofrydis, 'Social rights in the Greek Constitutions' EDKA (1979), p. 1, 4 (in Greek).

25 K. Kremalis, *The right of a person to social protection* (Ant. Sakkoulas 1991), p. 155 (in Greek); P. Pararrigopoulou (n 18), p. 540; X. Contiades, *Courses on social administration and social security law* (Papazisis Publications 2023), p. 202 (in Greek).

26 X. Contiades (n 25), p. 204.

and second, to place more emphasis on private income as the primary means of ensuring a decent standard of living rather than focusing on social protection. Other political parties voiced concerns that this provision might lead the State to replace universal social services, such as free education or access to healthcare, with cash benefits for the poor. Ultimately, these disagreements were resolved by including an explicit reference to the State's obligation to guarantee a decent standard of living for all citizens through a guaranteed minimum income scheme in Article 21, para. 1, subpara. b of the Constitution.

The constitutional guarantee of social protection primarily imposes an obligation on the legislator, who, while enjoying broad discretion in implementing this right, must adopt an individualised approach to addressing social needs. Moreover, the gradual legislative development of specific institutions and structures in the field of social protection establishes an institutional guarantee. Within this scope, it would not be constitutionally acceptable to significantly reduce public welfare services, diminish the State's regulatory, coordinating and monitoring role in the field of social welfare, prohibit or impose unjustified restrictions on private or voluntary sector entities providing welfare services.[27] Likewise, abolishing the guaranteed minimum income scheme or imposing excessive limitations on its amount and tightening eligibility criteria would be inconsistent with the Constitution, even though the latter does not stipulate a specific level of guaranteed minimum income. Furthermore, the constitutional protection of the right to social welfare justifies certain restrictions on other constitutional rights, such as the freedom of enterprise and the principle of equality, allowing for the adoption of positive measures in favour of protected social groups.

2. Social Benefits

The Greek welfare state uses two main mechanisms to address social risks. The first mechanism is social security, predominantly funded through contributions,[28] with a focus on mitigating the risks associated with old

27 Ibid.

28 For an overview of the Greek social security system, see M. Bakavou, 'Salus Rei Publicae Suprema Lex Esto? Welfare State Reforms Before the Greek Courts', in: U. Becker and A. Poulou (eds.), *European Welfare State Constitutions after the Financial Crisis* (OUP 2020), p. 151.

age. Just like social security systems in Southern European countries more generally, the Greek welfare state prioritises protection against old-age risks, as evidenced in the disproportionately higher levels of pension expenditure compared to other forms of social spending. This focus on the pension problem has come at the expense of the fight against poverty and social exclusion. However, in the context of declining full-time employment and the increasing prevalence of flexible forms of work, including a growing share of teleworking, social security remains necessary but insufficient to guarantee a decent income for all.

Against this background, despite the fact that the Greek welfare state is fragmented and underdeveloped, its second mechanism for addressing social risks is the establishment of a network of social support benefits that is based on a category-based approach, aimed at covering all possible risks through composite, specialised or personalised benefits. Additionally, guaranteed minimum income schemes have been established, which are based on income criteria, i.e. benefits are allocated on the basis of a means test, with the aim of preventing extreme poverty and ensuring that no one is deprived of life's basic necessities. Within the broader framework of social protection, the provision of social support services has historically been sidelined compared to the provision of income support.[29] In particular, the transfer of responsibility for the care of the elderly and for persons with disabilities from the respective families and the private sector to specialised social services has not been sufficiently achieved.

As regards social welfare benefits, a range of distinct income schemes that provide supplementary cash benefits to specific groups have been introduced. These schemes were initially established in a fragmented and uncoordinated manner, each with its own eligibility criteria, benefit calculation methods and adjustment mechanisms. This lack of uniformity reproduces income inequalities between different beneficiary groups. An important step towards ensuring equal and effective access to welfare-based income support to all was the establishment of the Organisation for Welfare Benefits and Social Solidarity (OPEKA) in 2018.[30] OPEKA's objective is the provision of welfare benefits, allowances, financial assistance and social services to financially support beneficiaries and promote social integration. The governing body of OPEKA consists of the Board of Directors and its

29 X. Contiades (n 25), p. 81.

30 OPEKA is the universal successor of the welfare responsibilities of the former OGA and the Agricultural Estias Account (Law 4520/2018).

Governor, while its structure also includes a Central Office and Regional Directorate services. It is primarily funded through the state budget and supplemented by revenues from its assets and reserves.

The category-based minimum income schemes primarily target unprotected children, uninsured women during maternity, large families, uninsured elderly persons, people with disabilities and the homeless. Cash benefits are the main form of support within all category-based minimum income schemes. The category-based structure of welfare cash benefits has one major disadvantage, however: it excludes certain population groups and economically vulnerable individuals from access to such schemes. Although several complex social security benefits were introduced alongside welfare cash benefits, such as pension thresholds, the Social Solidarity Benefit for Pensioners, basic pensions for former members of the Agricultural Insurance Organisation, family allowances, additional disability insurance benefits and special benefits for persons outside the labour market, these measures did not sufficiently compensate for the absence of a general guaranteed minimum income scheme. This gap was ultimately addressed with the late introduction of a universal guaranteed minimum income scheme, which has since become Greece's main instrument of social protection.

The universal guaranteed minimum income scheme, which is also provided by OPEKA, does not replace category-based minimum income schemes. In fact, receipt of other social benefits does not necessarily preclude eligibility from the guaranteed minimum income scheme. On the contrary, certain allowances, such as non-contributory disability benefits, education, vocational training and job-search allowances for unemployed persons, emergency financial assistance for natural disaster victims and support for labour market integration of homeless persons and domestic violence victims, are excluded from the calculation of household income, as defined in the income criteria for eligibility to the universal minimum income scheme.[31] Old-age pensions, disability pensions, unemployment benefits, family allowances and other social security benefits are included in the calculation of a household's income,[32] which means that if a household's total income falls below the income threshold set by law, its members—even if they receive other social benefits—are additionally eligible for universal minimum income protection. Category-based minimum income

31 See in detail below under III.3.

32 Ibid.

schemes thus coexist with the recently introduced universal minimum income scheme in the Greek social welfare system.

III. Analysis

1. Introduction of the Guaranteed Minimum Income

Greece has only recently introduced a nationwide guaranteed minimum income scheme. The introduction of minimum income protection was one of the conditions Greece had to meet to receive financial assistance during the euro crisis. This requirement was first outlined in the second Memorandum of Understanding (MoU) adopted by Greece. A pilot guaranteed minimum income scheme was introduced by Law 4093/2012 in January 2014 and was piloted in 13 regions of the country with different socio-economic characteristics, and defined in a ministerial decision.[33] It targeted individuals and families living in extreme poverty, providing not only income support but also social reintegration measures to beneficiaries. The total expenditure for the pilot scheme did not exceed EUR 20 million and was ultimately implemented for six months.

The pilot guaranteed minimum income scheme provided three forms of support for beneficiaries: a) income support, b) improved and guaranteed access to social services, and c) provision of goods and labour-market integration or reintegration measures. The maximum monthly income support was EUR 200 per adult and EUR 50 per minor, with the first dependent minor in a single-parent family counted as an adult. Hence, the annual guaranteed minimum income for a single adult was EUR 2,400, EUR 5,400 for a couple or for one adult and one dependent minor. The amount of financial support was determined in accordance with common practices among EU member states. The maximum financial support (EUR 200 for a single adult) corresponded to approximately 24 per cent of the median equivalised income and 40 per cent of the net minimum wage (EUR 489).

Under the framework of the 3rd MoU signed by Greece, the government was required to implement the guaranteed minimum income scheme nationwide. Article 235 of Law 4389/2016 renamed the Guaranteed Minimum Income into the Social Solidarity Income. Until 31 December 2016, the

33 KYA 39892/ΓΔ1.2 B΄ 30182014.

scheme was limited to only 30 regions across the country, and as of 01 January 2017, it was expanded to all of the country's municipalities.[34]

Finally, following this introductory phase, the legal framework for minimum income in Greece was further strengthened. Specifically, Article 29 of Law 4659/2020 amended Article 235 of Law 4389/2016, renaming the Social Solidarity Income back to Guaranteed Minimum Income, which remains the official term in the Greek legal order today. Ministerial Decision Δ13/οικ./33475/1935/15.06.2018 outlined the details of the scheme, was amended by three subsequent decisions,[35] and was ultimately revised by Ministerial Decision Δ13/οικ. 53923/23.07.2021 (Β΄ 3359). Thus, the Greek Guaranteed Minimum Income scheme is currently regulated in Article 29 of Law 4659/2020 in conjunction with Ministerial Decision Δ13/οικ. 53923/23.07.2021 (Β΄ 3359).

2. Coverage and Eligibility Criteria

Under Greek law, beneficiaries of the guaranteed minimum income are classified into three categories. The first category includes single-person households, defined as any adult who lives alone, excluding adults up to 25 years old who are enrolled in a university, school, vocational or training institution in Greece or abroad. The second category comprises multi-person households, which include all persons residing in the same accommodation, including a) guests or a host family, provided that this hosting arrangement was declared in the most recent (cleared) tax declaration[36], and b) adults up to 25 years old who are enrolled in university, school or a vocational or training institution, regardless of their place of residence. Moreover, Greek law also recognises single-parent families as potential beneficiaries within this category. For the purpose of the guaranteed minimum income scheme, a single-parent family is strictly defined as a single parent (unmarried, widowed or divorced[37]), who has sole or exclusive custody of

34 Article 22 of Law 4445/2016.

35 Δ13/οικ./54653/2701/18.10.2018 (Β΄ 4837 2018), Δ13/οικ.25150/557/03.06.2019 (Β΄ 2194 2019) and Δ13/οικ. 16250/321/24.04.2020 (Β΄ 1655 2020).

36 "Guests" are persons residing in the household, who are not classified as dependants for tax purposes. For instance, an adult (over the age of 25), a non-disabled child, who still resides in the parental home is no longer a dependant and is classified as a "guest".

37 Or due to the detention of the other parent in a penitentiary facility.

one or more minors.[38] The third category comprises homeless persons who either live on the street or in an unsuitable accommodation, provided they are registered with the municipal social services or community centres, or who stay in hostels, transitional shelters or facilities for women who are victims of violence. Homelessness cannot be solely determined by means of a tax declaration.[39] In September 2021, 3.5 per cent of all beneficiary units were classified as homeless.[40] On the other hand, certain categories of individuals are excluded from the scheme and are not considered members of the household. These include: a) individuals residing or being cared for in a residential care or assisted living facility, b) individuals staying in a psychosocial rehabilitation facility or beneficiaries of the Protected Apartments programme established under Article 9 of Law 2716/1999, c) individuals living in monasteries, d) persons incarcerated in penitentiary institutions, and e) individuals residing abroad.[41]

The Greek guaranteed minimum income scheme is designed to support households, a concept that encompasses one or more members of a nuclear or extended family, who reside in the same accommodation, regardless of their legal relationship. Thus, it is irrelevant whether the family has been established through marriage or a civil partnership between same-sex or opposite-sex couples. The provisions indirectly include informal cohabitation under the category of 'hosted individuals'. Against this background, the Greek guaranteed minimum income scheme embraces a modern concept of family, which covers different household types and sizes. However, by defining the household as the primary beneficiary of the guaranteed minimum income, Greek law necessarily focuses on the economic needs of families rather than individuals, assessing poverty at the family level.

Every household that is legally and permanently established in Greece is eligible to apply for the minimum income scheme.[42] This means that access to guaranteed minimum income is not determined by nationality (citizenship), but by the criterion of permanent residence. Greek legislation does not require a specific previous period of residence to be eligible for the guaranteed minimum income, as is the case for other non-contributory

---

38 Article 2, para. 2 of Ministerial Decision Δ13/οικ. 53923/23.07.2021.

39 Article 2, para. 1 of Ministerial Decision Δ13/οικ. 53923/23.07.2021.

40 See Joint Report prepared by the Social Protection Committee (SPC) and the European Commission (DG EMPL), *The 2022 Minimum Income Report Country Profiles Volume II*, p. 34.

41 Article 2, para. 6 of Ministerial Decision Δ13/οικ. 53923/23.07.2021.

42 Article 3, para. 3 of Ministerial Decision Δ13/οικ. 53923/23.07.2021.

benefits (such as birth allowance or housing benefit). In addition to the permanent residence requirement, applicants' tax residence must be in Greece, because they must possess a tax registration number and file an annual income tax return.[43] This highlights the strong link between tax law and social protection. The application for minimum income must be submitted by the person responsible for filing the household's annual income tax return, their spouse or their cohabiting partner. If all adult household members filed separate tax returns, the application for guaranteed minimum income must be submitted collectively.[44] Applications can be made in person at a municipal or community centre, or online. Homeless persons, households hosting guests, single-parent families, and those with unprotected children[45] can only apply in person.[46]

3. Income and Property Criteria

The guaranteed minimum income is regulated by the welfare principle of subsidiarity, i.e. it is granted only after all other available protection mechanisms have been exhausted. In particular, eligibility presupposes a lack of sufficient income from work, non-receipt of other social security benefits, depletion of personal savings and assets, and inability to obtain family assistance. As previously mentioned, poverty is assessed at the family level, with family income and family assets taken into account to determine eligibility. To ensure effective targeting of the guaranteed minimum income scheme, means-testing is used as a tool to set a threshold for the applicant's maximum total income (e.g. from work or existing benefits) and certain assets (e.g. property). Against this background, a household must cumu-

---

43 Article 6, para. 1 and Article 9, para. 1 of Ministerial Decision Δ13/οικ. 53923/23.07.2021.

44 Article 6, para. 1 of Ministerial Decision Δ13/οικ. 53923/23.07.2021.

45 Unprotected children are minors within a household, who are orphans or whose parental care cannot be provided by either parent due to illness, disability, incarceration or military service. In such cases, custody must been legally assigned to a member of the household by court decision. For example, a grandmother who has been granted custody of her grandchildren would declare them as unprotected children.

46 Article 6, para. 1 of Ministerial Decision Δ13/οικ. 53923/23.07.2021.

latively meet specific income and property criteria to be eligible for the guaranteed minimum income.[47]

First, as regards the income criterion, the declared household income for the six months preceding the application may not exceed six times a legally prescribed amount, which varies depending on household type. The threshold for the maximum total income of each household type in the six months preceding the application is presented in the following table:

Single-person household	EUR 1,200
Household consisting of two adult members or a single-parent family with one minor member	EUR 1,800
Household consisting of two adults and one minor member or a single-parent family with two minor members	EUR 2,100
Household consisting of three adult members or two adult and two minor members or a single-parent family with three minor members	EUR 2,400
Household consisting of three adults and one minor member or two adults and three minors or a single-parent family with four minor members	EUR 2,700
Household consisting of four adult members or two adult and four minor members or a single-parent family with five minor members	EUR 3,000

In this context, 'declared income' refers to total income from all sources of both domestic and foreign origin, before taxes, but after the deduction of social security contributions received by all members of the beneficiary unit in the six months preceding the submission date of the application for inclusion in the guaranteed minimum income scheme.[48] The declared income includes all allowances and benefits, as well as exempt income or income taxed under special provisions.[49] This means that old-age pensions and disability pensions, unemployment benefits, family allowances and other social security benefits are included in the household's declared income for determining eligibility to the guaranteed minimum income. Nevertheless, foster care allowances, non-contributory disability allowances granted by the State, education, vocational training and job-search allowances provided to unemployed persons, emergency financial assistance for natural disaster victims and for homeless persons participating in a labour market integration programme and victims of domestic violence, as

47 The inclusion of family assistance is reflected as an increase in the income and asset thresholds. The financial control is mainly carried out through electronic cross-checks with a GIS database.

48 Article 2, para. 8 of Ministerial Decision Δ13/οικ. 53923/23.07.2021.

49 Ibid.

well as the total income for two reference periods are excluded from the calculation of declared income.[50]

It is important to note the Greek Ombudsman's statement that the exclusion of disability allowances from the calculation of declared income, while disability pensions are included, results in unequal treatment of individuals who find themselves in similar situations, especially in the light of Article 28 of the Convention on the Rights of Persons with Disabilities (CRPD),[51] which recognizes the right of persons with disabilities to an adequate standard of living without discrimination on the basis of disability.[52]

Moreover, the calculation of declared income excludes 20 per cent of the applicant's net earnings from salaries, community service programmes or any other work-related programme.[53] This provision ensures that an individual who earns minimum wage or a low salary does not automatically disqualify from eligibility to the guaranteed minimum income. The scheme covers not only unemployed persons but also serves as a supplement for those who earn insufficient income from low-paid work, extending its reach to the so-called working poor. Additionally, the possibility to simultaneously earn minimum wage or a low salary helps prevent the minimum income scheme from becoming a disincentive to work.

Second, as regards the property criterion, household assets are assessed on the basis of the applicant's tax return for the previous year. The total taxable value of the household's assets may not exceed EUR 90,000 for a single-person household, increased by EUR 15,000 for each additional household member, and up to a maximum ceiling of EUR 150,000.[54] Moreover, the imputed annual taxable income related to passenger cars owned by the household members may not exceed EUR 6,000.[55] At the same time, their total capital income from bank deposits in Greece or abroad may not exceed the thresholds outlined in the following table:[56]

50 Ibid.
51 The CRPD was transposed into the Greek legal order by Law 4074/2012.
52 Report of the Greek Ombudsman on the application of the CRPD, 2019, p. 30.
53 Article 2, para. 9 of Ministerial Decision Δ13/οικ. 53923/23.07.2021.
54 Article 3, para. 2a of Ministerial Decision Δ13/οικ. 53923/23.07.2021.
55 Article 3, para. 2b of Ministerial Decision Δ13/οικ. 53923/23.07.2021.
56 Article 3, para. 2c of Ministerial Decision Δ13/οικ. 53923/23.07.2021.

Single-person household	EUR 4,800
Household consisting of two adults or a single-parent household with one minor member	EUR 7,200
Household consisting of two adults and one minor member or a single-parent household with two minor members	EUR 8,400
Household consisting of three adults or two adults and two minors or a single-parent household with three minor members	EUR 9,600
Household consisting of three adults and one minor member or two adults and three minor members or a single-parent household with four minor members	EUR 10,800
Household consisting of four adults or two adults and four minor members or a single-parent household with five minor members	EUR 12,000
Household consisting of four adults and one minor member or two adults and five minor members or a single-parent household with six minor members	EUR 13,200
Household consisting of five adults or two adults and six minors or a single-parent household with seven minor members	EUR 14,400

Furthermore, households in which any member according to the most recent (cleared) income tax return falls under the following categories do not qualify for the guaranteed minimum income, namely individuals who: a) are subject to the provisions of the luxury tax, b) report expenses for yacht crews, c) report expenses for tuition fees for private schools, d) report expenses for domestic helpers, chauffeurs, tutors and other staff.[57]

4. Benefit Amount

The amount of guaranteed minimum income is, in principle, determined by the household's size and composition. The benefit amount lacks a clear legislative justification and seems to reflect fiscal constraints rather than a calculation based on poverty thresholds or actual living costs. Under the scheme, each household, depending on the number and age of its members, receives: a) EUR 200 per month for a single-person household, b) EUR 100 per month for each additional adult household member, and c) EUR 50 per month for each minor household member.[58] In single-parent households, as defined above, the oldest minor member is considered an adult in the calculation of the guaranteed minimum amount.[59] This ensures that single-parent families are not placed in a worse position than a cou-

57 Article 3, para. 2 of Ministerial Decision Δ13/οικ. 53923/23.07.2021.
58 Article 2, para. 7 of Ministerial Decision Δ13/οικ. 53923/23.07.2021.
59 Ibid.

ple without children. Similarly, in a household with unprotected children, each unprotected child is considered an adult for the calculation of the guaranteed minimum amount.[60] Regardless of household composition, a ceiling of EUR 900 per month is set as the maximum benefit amount. If the beneficiaries have another source of (low) income, they are not eligible to the full amount of guaranteed minimum income. More precisely, the amount of guaranteed minimum income they are eligible to is calculated as the difference between six times the full guaranteed minimum income and the household's declared income over the previous six months, calculated for the purpose of inclusion in the scheme, divided by six.[61]

If the total monthly benefit is equal to or exceeds EUR 100, 50 per cent of the amount must be exclusively spent using the beneficiary's prepaid bank card, which can be used without restriction for purchases (including online transactions) or payments.[62] As a result, at least half of the benefit amount is exclusively intended for the purchase of consumer goods and may not be saved. The remaining 50 per cent can be withdrawn in cash from a credit institution's bank branches (where the beneficiary has an account) and/or by debit card from automatic teller machines (ATMs). Beneficiaries of the scheme are not charged issuance or transaction fees for using these cards, except for cash withdrawals from ATMs of banks other than their own.

While means-testing is conducted at the household level, it often overlooks the financial situation of individuals within the household, potential disparities in family income distribution and the desire for personal autonomy. This disproportionately affects women who are more likely to have a lower income, earn lower pay and carry greater caregiving responsibilities. Without necessarily altering the means-testing approach and increasing the overall household benefit amount, solutions should be explored to ensure that individual household members receive a fair share of the income support. Such measures could promote gender equality, enhance economic independence and improve income security for women, young adults and persons with disabilities.

The guaranteed minimum income benefit is provided for a period of six months.[63] This short duration allows the administration to conduct regular assessments of beneficiaries' eligibility, particularly with regard to any

60 Ibid.
61 Article 2, para. 10 of Ministerial Decision Δ13/οικ. 53923/23.07.2021.
62 Article 8, para. 4 of Ministerial Decision Δ13/οικ. 53923/23.07.2021.
63 Article 2, para. 11 of Ministerial Decision Δ13/οικ. 53923/23.07.2021.

changes in their income. After this six-month period, beneficiaries must reapply, which initiates a reassessment of their eligibility. To ensure that its intended purpose is met, the minimum income benefit is protected from all debt obligations. It is tax-free, exempt from any deductions, confiscations or set-offs against debts owed to the State or credit institutions, excluded from income limits and the calculation for determining eligibility to other social or welfare benefits.[64]

5. Package of Benefits (Composite Benefit)

The modern understanding of poverty has evolved beyond the mere lack of income and has transformed into a multifaceted condition of social exclusion. While absolute poverty can be equated with lack of income, relative poverty (social exclusion) is understood as a broader lack of economic and non-economic goods (cultural goods, education, new technologies). Adopting this latter concept of poverty, the Greek guaranteed minimum income scheme was not conceived solely as a financial support mechanism. It is embedded in a more comprehensive policy against social exclusion, combining financial assistance with social care and healthcare services, as well as measures to promote employment.[65]

More specifically, the Greek minimum guaranteed income scheme comprises three pillars. The first pillar provides financial income support, as described above. The second pillar ensures access to complementary social benefits and services, depending on the beneficiaries' needs. More precisely, individuals eligible for the minimum income scheme have access to a) free medical care for the uninsured,[66] b) social care and support structures and services, c) programmes and social initiatives for poverty reduction, d)

64 Article 15 of Ministerial Decision Δ13/οικ. 53923/23.07.2021.

65 Linking the guaranteed minimum income with complementary social services, benefits and goods begins with the local authorities informing beneficiaries. During the application process and submission of supporting documents, municipal or community centre officials inform applicants about the availability of additional social services, benefits and goods, provided they meet the legal requirements. .

66 In Greece, Law 4368/16 grants uninsured and vulnerable social groups the right to free access to public healthcare services, including inpatient/medical care (Article 33). This provision unified all groups previously excluded from the health protection system (unemployed, insured persons with fund debts, migrants, vulnerable citizens). Access to care is not contingent on income or asset thresholds, except for economically weak persons who are exempt from contributing to the cost of medication.

measures implemented under the Operational Programme of the European Aid Fund for the Most Deprived, e) social tariffs for electricity providers, f) social tariffs for water providers, and g) social tariffs for municipalities and municipal enterprises.[67] The scheme's third pillar includes measures targeting household members, if they are able to work, promoting their integration or reintegration into the labour market, which may include, inter alia: a) support with obtaining a proposed job, b) participation in community service programmes, c) participation in vocational training programmes, d) participation in programmes to gain work experience, and e) integration or return to the education system and second-chance schools.[68]

6. A Benefit with Obligations

As part of the third pillar described above, beneficiaries of the minimum income scheme are required to return to the labour market. This provision aligns with the prevailing understanding in contemporary social policy that any individual who receives social assistance must contribute to society in return (workfare). Given that the combination of passive income policies with labour market integration measures is considered best practice, the right to receive minimum income is conditional on participation in active labour market measures designed to prevent beneficiaries from playing a passive role only, which may give rise to long-term dependency.

The legal framework regulating the Greek minimum income scheme specifies which beneficiaries are subject to the work obligation. Two categories of beneficiaries of guaranteed minimum income are considered incapacitated for work by the respective legal framework: a) persons with disabilities who have been certified as being unable to work by the Disability Certification Committee, and b) full-time students, apprentices in vocational schools or those practicing in a vocational training programme without an employment relationship.[69] All other beneficiaries who do not fall into the above categories and who are aged between eighteen (18) and sixty-five (65) are considered capable of working.[70]

67 Article, 1 para. 2 of Ministerial Decision Δ13/οικ. 53923/23.07.2021.
68 Article, 1 para. 3 of Ministerial Decision Δ13/οικ. 53923/23.07.2021.
69 Article 2, para. 12 of Ministerial Decision Δ13/οικ. 53923/23.07.2021.
70 Article 2, para. 13 of Ministerial Decision Δ13/οικ. 53923/23.07.2021.

Beneficiaries deemed able to work, as described above, are required—in line with the applicable regulatory framework—to register with the Greek Labour Employment Office by the end of the month following approval of their application for minimum income support and renew their unemployment status.[71] Moreover, they are required to attend meetings with employment counsellors of the Greek Labour Employment Office, who provide personalised support services. More importantly, they must accept suitable employment opportunities proposed by the Greek Labour Employment Office or participate in any employment promotion activities such as vocational training, counselling and entrepreneurship initiatives.[72] Lastly, should the beneficiaries of guaranteed minimum income be employed, they may not voluntarily and unjustifiably quit their jobs.[73]

In view of the above, pressing questions arise regarding the nature of jobs that can be proposed as a condition for continuing to receive the benefit. Specifically, it remains unclear whether such work must be exclusively paid employment or whether other forms of work such as community service outside the formal labour market are included, as well as whether the scope of such work must be full time or part time, and whether a low-paid job is also included. Here we argue that "suitable work", which the recipient of the minimum income has to accept, may not only fall within the broader professional sector, but must meet additional objective criteria, such as reasonable proximity between the workplace and the beneficiary's place of residence, fair remuneration and balanced working hours. More generally, suitable work is considered decent work, ensuring that the risk of occupational downgrading is, in principle, removed.

Furthermore, given the strong link between poverty and education, beneficiaries of the minimum income scheme, who are adults up to 45 years old and have not completed compulsory education, are required, upon notification, to either sit for exams to obtain a primary school graduation certificate or to enrol in second-chance schools or evening secondary schools.[74] Beneficiaries must also ensure that any minor household members attend compulsory education.[75] More precisely, if the household includes minor members who meet the conditions for attending compulsory

---

71 Article 9, para. 3 of Ministerial Decision Δ13/οικ. 53923/23.07.2021.

72 Ibid.

73 Article 9, para. 3 of Ministerial Decision Δ13/οικ. 53923/23.07.2021.

74 Article 9, para. 6 of Ministerial Decision Δ13/οικ. 53923/23.07.2021.

75 Article 9, para. 7 of Ministerial Decision Δ13/οικ. 53923/23.07.2021.

education, the minimum income will only be granted on the condition that these minors are enrolled in and actively attend school, and only if the minor member is not required to repeat the same grade due to a high number of absences.[76] Given the potentially problematic nature of the provision's rigid wording, it is envisaged that exceptions will be introduced, particularly if the pupil's absences are due to health-related reasons. If a pupil fails to meet the obligation of adequate school attendance due to unjustified absences, the household may resubmit an application for the minimum income scheme six months later, provided the pupil is enrolled in the new school year.[77] It is noteworthy that while the legislator establishes this obligation, the coverage of education expenses are not accounted for in the calculation of the guaranteed minimum income.

Furthermore, all members of the beneficiary household are required to file an annual income tax return and to consent to a social survey, including home visits by municipal or Community Centre officials for on-site verification of the household's composition and living conditions.[78] Lastly, beneficiaries must comply with notices concerning personalised support services, such as psychosocial counselling or vocational guidance by qualified professionals.[79]

If a beneficiary of the minimum income scheme fails to meet the obligations described above, his/her entitlement to the minimum income benefit is revoked.[80] In this case, the household may resubmit an application one month following the month in which the relevant obligations are met. Similarly, receipt of the minimum income is automatically suspended if electronic cross-checks reveal discrepancies.

IV. Concluding Remarks

As a latecomer among European countries, Greece's guaranteed minimum income scheme has been in operation for only a few years. Given that shortly after its introduction, a new constitutional provision was adopted, stipulating protection by the State of citizens' right to a decent standard

76 Article 235, para. 8 of Law 4389/2016 and Article 4, para. 1 of Ministerial Decision Δ13/οικ. 53923/23.07.2021.
77 Article 4, para.2 of Ministerial Decision Δ13/οικ. 53923/23.07.2021.
78 Article 9, para. 1 and 2 of Ministerial Decision Δ13/οικ. 53923/23.07.2021.
79 Article 9, para. 5 of Ministerial Decision Δ13/οικ. 53923/23.07.2021.
80 Article 11, para. 2 of Ministerial Decision Δ13/οικ. 53923/23.07.2021.

of living through a guaranteed minimum income scheme, the legislative framework of Greece's guaranteed minimum income scheme benefits from special constitutional protection. Any future reform of the existing scheme must therefore be examined in the light of this constitutional norm. Its abolishment could only be considered if an equivalent mechanism were introduced in its place.

From its operation, the greatest challenge facing the guaranteed minimum income scheme has been the adequacy of benefits provided. The thresholds for means-testing are very rigid, and exclude an important segment of the population, which struggles to meet their basic needs. At the same time, with the rising cost of living, the sufficiency of the benefit amount in ensuring a dignified standard of living for recipients is questionable. Overall, the newly introduced guaranteed minimum income scheme marks a transformative step for Greece's previously fragmented and underdeveloped social protection system, but still calls for further upgrading to meet the needs of contemporary standards of decent living.

Life with Dignity: Minimum Income Support in Ireland

Elaine Dewhurst

I. Introduction

There is no doubt that the protection of minimum income in Ireland is a social priority. The at-risk-of-poverty rate in Ireland is currently 13.1%, which indicates that a significant percentage of the population has nominal equivalised disposable incomes which are under the at-risk-of-poverty threshold (defined as "*60% of the median nominal equivalised disposable income*")[1]. Those most at risk are those who are unemployed (35.2%), those who cannot work due to health-related problems (35.2%), those who are over the age of 65 years (19%), and those who live alone (age 65+ 33.6%, under 65 years 32%). 17.7% of people experience enforced deprivation in Ireland, which is defined by reference to eleven types of deprivation[2] and

1 Central Statistics Office, 'Survey on Income and Living Conditions 2022' < https://www.cso.ie/en/releasesandpublications/ep/p-silc/surveyonincomeandlivingconditionssilc2022/poverty/> accessed 05.12.2024.

2 These include being: unable to afford to replace any worn out furniture, unable to have family or friends for a drink or a meal once a month, unable to afford a morning, afternoon or evening out in the last fortnight, unable to afford new (not second-hand)

5.3% of people are living in consistent poverty.[3] This measure is correlated to employment status with the rate being highest amongst those who are unemployed and those who cannot work due to ill-health.[4] Therefore, the need for a minimum income protection is real but as this chapter reveals is not constitutionally protected and while legislation exists, is not indexed or benchmarked and is subject to both economic and non-economic conditions which can impact on its effectiveness.

This chapter provides an overview of the legal (both constitutional and legislative) protections of minimum income in Ireland, followed by a more detailed excursus into the existing protections and their subtleties. The chapter analyses four specific aspects of minimum income protections, namely the benefit and its adaptation, the economic and non-economic conditions attached to such protection and the importance of activation in the development of social protection mechanisms. The main purpose of social protection in Ireland today (for those of working age) is to mitigate against social risks i.e. to replace income temporarily lost due to periods of unemployment, injury, disability, sickness or maternity.[5] Additionally, minimum income in old age is secured through either contributory or assistance-based schemes.

---

clothes, having been without heating at some stage in the past year, unable to keep the home adequately warm, unable to afford to buy presents for family or friends in the past year, unable to afford a roast joint (or equivalent) once a week, unable to afford two pairs of strong shoes, unable to afford a warm waterproof coat, unable to afford a meal with meat, chicken, fish (or vegetarian equivalent) every second day. Central Statistics Office, 'Survey on Income and Living Conditions: Enforced Deprivation 2022' (23 November 2022) < https://www.cso.ie/en/releasesandpublications/ep/p-silced/surveyonincomeandlivingconditionssilcenforceddeprivation2022/deprivationitems/> accessed 21.11.2024.

3 Defined as being at risk of poverty and experiencing enforced deprivation. See Central Statistics Office, 'Survey on Income and Living Conditions 2022' < https://www.cso.ie/en/releasesandpublications/ep/p-silc/surveyonincomeandlivingconditionssilc2022/poverty/> accessed 05.12.2024.

4 Central Statistics Office, 'Survey on Income and Living Conditions 2022' < https://www.cso.ie/en/releasesandpublications/ep/p-silc/surveyonincomeandlivingconditionssilc2022/poverty/> accessed 05.12.2024.

5 Commission on Taxation and Welfare Secretariat, 'Introduction to the Irish Social Protection System' (18 June 2021), p. 6.

II. Overview

1. Normative Background

a) Historical Context

Social protection in Ireland has suffered in some ways from its rather non-traditional start. Grappling with the management, establishment, and development of national priorities in the aftermath of independence from the United Kingdom, the official provision of social protection was deferred, and existing systems remained in place to serve the needs of the newly independent population. This meant that colonial legacies, such as the British Poor Laws, provided the new Irish citizens with modest rates of social protection with low contributions. This was supplemented by support from the Catholic Church in maintaining certain social services. It was not until 1947 that the Department of Social Welfare was finally established and the beginnings of the modern social protection principles we see today were expounded.

The implications of this turbulent beginning are that the Irish social protection system has been impacted by many conflicting influences in its development: a Catholic focus on charity and voluntarism, an Anglo-Saxon liberal focus on market privilege and individual responsibility and, upon joining the EU in 1972, the EU ideals of income replacement, social insurance and comprehensive public services. The effect of this confluence of, often contradictory, ideologies has been that the system of social protection in Ireland has developed in a rather piecemeal way, developing hybrid forms of protection which reflect differing rationales and ideologies.[6]

b) Constitutional Law and Constitutional Case Law

Constitutional protections in Ireland do not expressly address issues of minimum income support.[7] This is not unusual as many constitutional documents shy away from such specificities. The Irish Constitution is no different and there are no express rights to social protection arising from it.

---

6 M. Cousins and G. Whyte, *Social Protection Law in Ireland* (3rd ed. Kluwer Law International 2021).

7 Ibid., para. 31.

Impliedly, it is possible to ground such a claim on other constitutional articles. The basis for these arguments could arise from Article 40.3 (the right to dignity), Article 41.2.1 (a gender specific provision protecting the role of mothers in the home) and, potentially, Article 43 (the right to property). All these constitutional provisions could provide a basis for a potential constitutional right to minimum income. However, there are significant obstacles to such claims.

Firstly, while Article 40.3 provides that the State guarantees "*in its laws to respect, and, as far as practicable to defend and vindicate the personal rights of the citizen*", which has been held to include a right to dignity[8], such a right is mired in functionality. This means that the right to dignity has only ever been interpreted as a right to be treated with dignity[9] which would be an uneasy foundation for a right to be provided with minimum income. Additionally, even if it could be invoked, this right is not absolute and is subject to justification on a number of grounds including the common good, protection of public order and morality, the protection of the rights and freedoms of others and the best interests of children or vulnerable persons.[10] Where issues involving legislative budgetary considerations have arisen in the past, the judiciary have traditionally shied away from interfering in these decisions given that the legislature is often in a better position to assess what might be in the common good. In fact, the enforcement of socio-economic rights has been stymied by such rationales. For example, in the case of *O' Reilly v Limerick Corporation*[11], it was held that socio-economic claims should be "*advanced in Leinster House rather than in the Four Courts*", a nod to the fact that this is in effect a legislative rather than a judicial matter. Therefore, it is arguable that Article 40.3 and a right to dignity would not be an obvious ground for a claim for minimum income in Ireland.

Secondly, there is a potential claim arising from Article 41.2.2 (recently the subject of an unsuccessful constitutional referendum) which provides that the "*State shall, therefore, endeavour to ensure that mothers shall not be obliged by economic necessity to engage in labour to the neglect of their*

8 E. Dewhurst, 'Human Dignity in Ireland', in: P. Becchi and K. Mathis (eds.), *Handbook of Human Dignity in Europe* (Springer 2019), pp. 431-451.

9 High Court, *MX v Health Service Executive* [2012] IEHC 491; *PP v Health Service Executive* [2014] Unreported High Court No. 10792P.

10 E. Dewhurst (n 8), pp. 443-445.

11 High Court, *O' Reilly v Limerick Corporation* [1989] ILRM 181.

duties in the home". This could arguably be a basis of social protection and minimum income claim as it imposes a positive (albeit gender specific) duty on the state to ensure that women have sufficient economic support to engage in labour within the home[12], a potential foundation of a right to social protection. However, the prevailing academic opinion is that such a right is a "*protective guarantee*"[13] only and unlikely to impose "*financial obligations on the State to support mothers in the home given that tax and social welfare impact on public expenditure*" [14]. This certainly chimes with the approach of the courts with respect to socio-economic rights already discussed previously.

There is an argument that the right to social protection could be regarded as a property right under Article 43. Cousins[15] notes that while this has not been expressly litigated, there is an argument that if an applicant meets all the eligibility criteria for a social protection payment and is not excluded by any relevant exceptions, then a property right may arise in Irish constitutional law. He bases this assertion on the implication in the Supreme Court decision in *Re Article 26 and the Health Amendment (No 2) Bill 2004*[16] which implied that such a right might be a chose in action which may be actionable as an infringement on the right to property. Whether this could be translated into a right to minimum income though is doubtful. The Supreme Court in *PC v Minister for Social Protection*[17] held that a statutory welfare payment was not a property right as the entitlement could be varied by the legislature. The discretionary and means-tested nature of minimum income requirements may mean that the legislature could argue that the right to a specific quantity of payment is not protected by the property rights in the Constitution being a matter exclusively within the preserve of the legislature. [18]

At a legislative level, the Social Welfare (Consolidation) Act 2005 to the present day, provides for the legislative right to social protection. Addition-

12 Irish Human Rights and Equality Commission, 'Policy Statement on Article 41.2 of the Constitution of Ireland' (2018), p. 9.

13 The Convention on the Constitution, 'Second Report of the Convention on the Constitution' (2013), pp. 12-13.

14 Ibid., pp. 12-13.

15 M. Cousins and G. Whyte (n 6), para. 33.

16 Supreme Court, Re Article 26 and the Health Amendment (No 2) Bill 2004 [2005] IESC 7.

17 Supreme Court, *PC v Minister for Social protection* [2018] IESC 57.

18 M. Cousins and G. Whyte (n 6), para. 33.

ally, this legislation is supplemented by Ministerial Regulations which detail the payments to be provided and the specifics of the payments, including definitions and transitional provisions. The Department of Social Protection also issues guidelines on certain aspects relating to the provision and application of social protection.[19] The legislation is guided constitutionally by Article 45 of the Constitution entitled the Directive Principles of Social Policy. Article 45 is non-justiciable but provides that the "*State shall strive to promote the welfare of the whole people by securing and protecting as effectively as it may a social order in which justice and charity shall inform all the institutions of the national life*" and "*pledges itself to safeguard with especial care the economic interests of the weaker sections of the community, and, where necessary, to contribute to the support of the infirm, the widow, the orphan, and the aged*". In case of *TD v Minister for Education*[20] it was stated that these principles are an "*ingenious method of ensuring that social justice should be achieved while excluding the judiciary from any role in the attainment of that objective*". Therefore, while not justiciable, they should act as a guide to the legislature on their decision-making in these areas.

c) International Law and International Case Law

As a dualist state, Ireland incorporated the European Convention on Human Rights into Irish domestic law in 2003.[21] The ECHR is not a "shadow Constitution"[22] but rather the Act provides that courts must attempt to interpret domestic law in line with the ECHR in as far as is possible.[23] However, this only applies to statutory law. The only potential argument which could arise in the Irish context would be in relation to Article 1, Protocol 1. According to the interpretation of this provision by the European Court of Human Rights, Member States have the freedom to decide whether to provide a particular social protection scheme and, more importantly, to set the type and amount of benefits which can be afforded under any particu-

19 Ibid., para 33.
20 Supreme Court, *TD. v Minister for Education* [2001] IESC 101.
21 European Convention on Human Rights Act 2003.
22 Department of Justice, Equality and Law Reform 2003 introducing the European Convention on Human Rights Act, see < https://emn.ie/legislation/european-convention-on-human-rights-act-2003> accessed 05/12/2024.
23 European Convention on Human Rights Act 2003, Section 2.

lar scheme.[24] Therefore, there is no minimum level which is imposed by membership of the Council of Europe which could be enforced judicially in Ireland.

d) Discretion in Minimum Income Protection

An analysis of the constitutional, legislative and international protections of minimum incomes in Ireland reveals two important points. Firstly, it would require some very creative judicial interpretation to provide a justiciable right to minimum income. Secondly, even where such protections might exist these are tempered by a judicial reluctance to interfere with the democratic legislative process. This in turn impacts on the manner in which social protection in Ireland is determined whether by the legislature or by those who administer social protection. The lack of constitutional and legislative protection coupled with judicial reluctance to interfere with legislative decision-making essentially means that there is a lot of discretion left to both the legislature (which is subject to political machinations) and the administrators of the systems (mainly Deciding Officers within the Department of Social Protection). Such discretion and subjectivity permeate the system and leads to inconsistency, and with that potential inequality. The protections which do exist are essentially too weak to mitigate against these inadequacies.

2. Social Benefits

a) Overall Structure of the System

The system of social protection Ireland, including the right to minimum income, has developed over time into a tripartite model based on three distinct systems: universal benefits, contribution-based and social assistance, with an overarching right to Supplementary Welfare Allowance which is means-tested right to social protection where income (from whatever source) falls below a certain minimum level. Essentially this payment is available where there is no or other income available (subject to the means

24 European Court of Human Rights, *Sukhanov and Ilchenko v. Ukraine* (2014) Applications Nos. 68385/10 and 71378/10, para. 36; *Fedulov v. Russia* (2019) Application No. 53068/08, para. 66.

test). Where recipients have an income which is below that of Supplementary Welfare Allowance, they will be given an amount which allows them to be brought to the level of such allowance. Supplementary Welfare Allowance is only available for as long as no other social protection payments are available. Once an applicant becomes entitled to another payment, Supplementary Welfare Allowance is then withdrawn. To a certain respect then, Supplementary Welfare Allowance is only meant as a temporary, stop-gap measure to ensure that each person has a minimum income essentially equivalent to the rate of this allowance. The rate is set each year in the national budget, is not indexed or benchmarked but is a matter of political discretion. Table 1 illustrates how the existing systems in Ireland currently interact.

Social insurance or contribution-based benefits are based on two inter-related principles: contribution and solidarity. The central idea is that individuals contribute during their lifetime when they are economically active which entitles them to benefits in the event of inactivity or retirement. The solidarity principle recognises that there is a "*long-standing social contract between employers, employees, the self-employed and the State. Social insurance contributions are collected over time from income and then redistributed to provide income support for contributors who, at a given point, are facing one of a set of contingencies covered under social insurance (e.g. unemployment, illness, caring responsibilities or reaching pension age)*"[25]. Social assistance payments, on the other hand, are based on ensuring a minimum floor of protection for those who do not satisfy the conditions for a contributory payment. The aim of these provisions is to cover gaps in the social protection system.[26] Finally, universal payments are provided to all persons regardless of contribution or means. They are based on meeting certain criteria but once these are met the payments are made universally. Supplementary welfare allowance is essentially a base minimum income payment which is payable either to those who have no income, or as a top-up to those whose family income falls below the rate of this minimum payment to bring it in line with this basic minimum.

25 Commission on Taxation and Welfare Secretariat, 'Irish Social Protection System' (n 5), p. 7.

26 Ibid., p. 8.

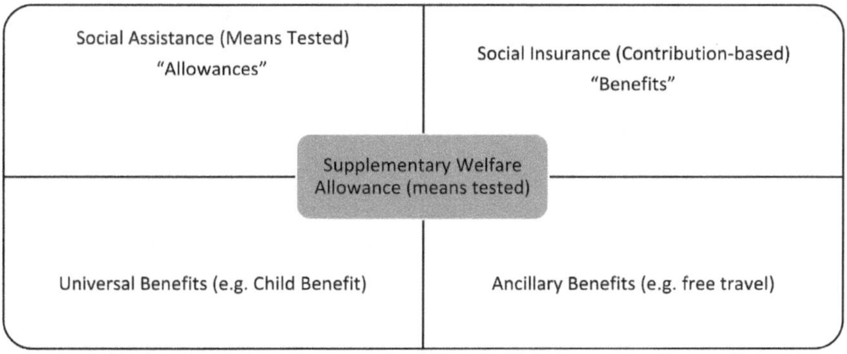

Overall, these benefits, allowances and universal payments are categorical (dependent on individual life circumstances), are flat rate in nature and are provided as low-level cash transfers with additional top-ups. They are also supported by ancillary services, many of which are underdeveloped in many respects. Education is generally free, but some schools do request voluntary contributions from parents/guardians in respect of their children to cover certain school costs or to provide additional services. Healthcare is a hybrid system with 47% of the population relying on private health insurance[27] while the rest are entitled to either free GP or hospital care or both (this is generally means-tested except for those over 70 or under 18 years). Childcare is a persistent issue because of a '*lack of affordable, accessible and available childcare provision*'[28]. The National Childcare Scheme has alleviated this to some extent, but it still remains a barrier for many working parents, particularly women. There is an increasing reliance also on Housing Assistance Payment, Rental Accommodation Scheme and Rent Supplement due to the lack of affordable housing in Ireland.

Table 2 outlines the different payments available in Ireland and whether they are insurance-based, universal or assistance-based.

27 Statista, 'Share of population with private health insurance coverage in Ireland from 2012 to 2023' (26 April 2024) < https://www.statista.com/statistics/1399880/private-health-insured-share-in-ireland/#:~:text=In%202021%2C%2047%20percent%20of,Ireland%20from%202002%20to%202021> accessed 21.11.2024.

28 National Economic and Social Council, 'The Future of the Irish Social Welfare System: Participation and Protection' (November 2020), p. 24.

Universal	**Contribution-Based**	**Assistance-Based**
Child Benefit	State Pension (Contributory)	Disability Allowance
	Widow's, Widower's and Surviving Civil Partner's Contributory Pension	Job Seeker's Allowance
	Invalidity Pension	State Pension (Non-Contributory)
	Illness Benefit	Carer's Allowance
	Job Seeker's Benefit	One-Parent Family Payment
	Maternity Benefit	Family Income Supplement/Working Family Payment
		Housing Assistance Payment / Rent Supplement
		Supplementary Welfare Allowance) (temporary until a claim for another social protection payment is confirmed – it can be combined with other allowances but only as a far as it does not exceed the rate of Supplementary Welfare Allowance)
		School supports
		Fuel Allowance

b) Old-Age Protection

With respect to older persons over the retirement age in Ireland (currently 66 years), the State Pension (Non-Contributory) is available. This is a means-tested social assistance payment financed from general taxation. The means test includes an assessment of both cash income and capital (excluding the personal home). If a person is entitled to a State Pension (Contributory), funded from their national insurance contributions over many years, they cannot also claim a State Pension (Non-Contributory). However, some individuals with limited contributions may decide to forfeit their State Pension (Contributory) in favour of the non-contributory payment where it is more financially lucrative to do so. In addition, to the State Pension (Non-Contributory) or a low-rate State Pension (Contributory) certain social protection payments are also available which are generally means-tested. This so-called Basic Income Support in Old Age includes payments such as Rent Supplement, Living Alone Increase, Household Benefits Package, Free Travel Pass, Fuel Allowance, Island Increase and Centenarian's Payment.

c) Protection for Job Seekers

Individuals who are unemployed and seeking work can apply for the contribution-based job seeker's benefit or for the assistance-based job seeker's allowance, which is means-tested. The job seeker's benefit is paid for 6 or 9 months, depending on the previous contribution period. If a recipient is entitled to contributory benefit, they will be able to apply for the allowance once their payment period has ended. Moreover, some individuals who are only entitled to a reduced rate of job seeker's benefit[29] may decide to apply for job seeker's allowance right away.

d) Uptake

The general uptake of all social protection payments is significant. The Irish State spent €24.6 billion in 2022 on social protection payments, over half of which (€12.8 billion) was spent on social assistance payments. Pensions were naturally the highest proportion of this expenditure (38.2%), with working age supports (15.3%), illness, disability and caring payments (21.6%), universal child benefit payments (11.6%) and supplementary welfare payments (4.5%) accounting for the majority of the rest of the expenditure.[30] Almost 65% of the population were beneficiaries of the social protection system in 2022.[31] When examining how this transfers to households, it is estimated by the Central Statistics Office that 14.8% of gross income per household per week arises from social transfers.[32]

III. Analysis

The technical administration of the social protection system in Ireland is complex but is based on a rationale of providing minimum floors of

---

29 Recipients with less than 300 euros weekly earnings see table 4.

30 Department of Social Protection, 'Statistical Information on Social Welfare Services 2022' (2022), p. 11 < https://www.gov.ie/pdf/?file=https://assets.gov.ie/262944/3bdd325b-db94-4daf-90c3-b6c00682a7d9.pdf#page=null> accessed 21.11.2024.

31 Ibid., p. 24.

32 Central Statistics Office, 'Survey on Income and Living Conditions 2022. Household Income' (22 February 2022) < https://www.cso.ie/en/releasesandpublications/ep/p-silc/surveyonincomeandlivingconditionssilc2022/householdincome/> accessed 21.11.2024.

protection. As such, means-testing is commonplace (outside of the insurance-based system) and non-economic conditions are also attached to many payments. Activation is a common goal of work-related payments, but this has not yet filtered into other social protection payments. There is no indexation or benchmarking of social protection payments, and this has had the effect of reducing the effectiveness of these payments in meeting their basic functions as a minimum floor of protection, especially during a cost-of-living crisis. This section reviews the benefits and adaptation of social protection payments, the economic and non-economic conditions attached to such payments and an assessment of functionality.

1. Benefits and Adaptation

The rationales for social protection in Ireland are twofold: (a) providing a minimum floor of protection for those who may need support due to a certain life situation (such as disability or unemployment) via social assistance which is generally means-tested and (b) providing solidarity for those who have contributed to social protection systems at economically active points in their lives via contribution-based social benefits. There is also the universal child benefit which is related to individual circumstances.

The main *social assistance payments* and their personal weekly rates (excluding top-ups) are:

Table 3

Allowances (non-insurance-based)	**Personal rate per week**
Disability Allowance	€232 per week
Job Seeker's Allowance	€232 (over the age of 25) €141.70 (18-25 years)
State Pension (Non-Contributory)	€266 (66-80 years) €276 (80+ years)
Carer's Allowance	€248 (under 66 years caring for 1 person) €372 (under 66 years caring for 2 or more persons) €286 (over 66 years caring for 1 person) €429 (over 66 caring for 2 or more persons)
One-Parent Family Payment	€232

Allowances (non-insurance-based)	**Personal rate per week**
Working Family Payment	This payment provides 60% of the difference between the working family payment income limit for your family size and your assessable income.
Rent Supplement	Amount paid is based on ensuring that income, after paying rent, does not fall below a minimum level.
Supplementary Welfare Allowance	€230 individuals above 18 and living independently €141.70 (18-24 and not living independently) Top-ups are available for qualified adults (at a rate of €154), children under 12 (€46) and those over 12 (€54).
School supports	Rates and supports available depend on each situation
Fuel Allowance	€33 for 28 weeks per year

The main *contribution-based payments* and the weekly personal rates (excluding top-ups) are:

Table 4

Contribution-based benefits	**Personal rate per week**
State Pension (Contributory)	Maximum is €277.30 per week
Widow's, Widower's and Surviving Civil Partner's Contributory Pension	Maximum is €277.30 per week over 66 / €237.66 per week under 66 years
Invalidity Pension	€237.50
Illness Benefit	Depends on weekly earnings but those earning maximum €300 or more will receive €232
Job Seeker's Benefit	Depends on weekly earnings but those earning €300 or more will receive €232
Maternity Benefit	€274

Universal payments include:

Table 5

Child Benefit	Monthly rate: 1 child: €140 2 children: €280 3 children: €420 4 children: €560 5 children: €700 6 children: €840 7 children: €980 8 children: €1,120

Despite much debate around indexation in Ireland, there is currently no formal system of indexation or benchmarking for the determination of social protection payments. These are determined instead annually as part of the budgetary process. In 2001 the Social Welfare Benchmarking and Indexation Working Group (SWBIG)[33] was established and agreed that social protection rates should be benchmarked, particularly that they should be index-linked to Gross Average Industrial Earnings (GAIE) despite the limitations of this approach. The National Anti-Poverty Strategy in 2002 set key targets, namely 30% of GAIE. In Budget 2007 this benchmark was finally reached although not formally applied. The Government made a commitment in the National Action Plan for Social Inclusion to "maintain relative value of the lowest social welfare rate at least at €185.80 in 2007 terms, over the course of this Plan (2007-2016), subject to available resources"[34].

Since then, increments have been made on social protection payments annually based on political discretion but no formal attention to benchmarking has been paid. In the most recent Budget 2025, for example, the Government announced the largest social welfare package in the history of the State but this was based purely on where they perceived need to be i.e. assisting households through a mix of cost of living payments, targeted supports and across the board increases to weekly payments. This has the effect of limiting long-term planning and can be particularly precarious for those facing retirement.

33 Economic and Social Research Group, 'Final Report of the Social Welfare Benchmarking and Indexation Group' (September 2001).

34 Office for Social Inclusion, 'National Action Plan for Social Inclusion 2007-2016' (February 2007), p. 14.

2. Economic Conditionality: Situation of Need (The Means Test)

Whereas contribution-based benefits are paid on the basis of the number of contributions accrued in active employment, social assistance payments are based on the individual circumstances of the applicant, often achieved by way of a means test. This fits well with the rationale for such payments which is based on need to ensure that individuals do not fall below a certain minimum income threshold. The rate of social assistance is determined on a sliding scale dependent on need. There are two main assessments which take place in determining means in individual cases: household income and capital. In general, this is the same for all social assistance payments with some minor variations discussed in the table below.

Household income is assessed through an examination of all sources of income available to the applicant, including all cash income expected, in the coming year. Cash income includes income from employment or self-employment, including farm income, income from a social protection pension from another country and maintenance payments. Income from other social assistance or benefits payments are not taken into account. The test is based on individual circumstances but also takes account of household structures.[35] This means that any income arising from partners, spouses, civil partners or cohabitants are taken into account for the purposes of the means test. It has been pointed out that the corollary of this is that "*the presence of a spouse or partner, and any children, is a factor in determining the final payment rate through the payment of extra amounts for adult and child dependants*"[36].

Capital is also assessed as part of the means test.[37] The rationale for this is that there is an "expectation that people with reasonable amounts of capital and property are in a position to use that capital, or to realise its value, to support themselves without having to rely solely on a means-tested welfare payment".[38] The capital assessment includes the value of savings, investments, shares and any property, excluding the main residence. A formular has been developed to assess the value of capital for social welfare payments. The first €20,000 is not assessed. After this the next €10,000

35 Commission on Taxation and Welfare Secretariat, 'Irish Social Protection System' (n 5), p. 9.
36 Ibid., p. 9.
37 Although not for all social assistance payments, see Table 6 below.
38 Commission on Taxation and Welfare Secretariat, 'Irish Social Protection System' (n 5), p. 9.

is assessed at a rate of €1 per €1,000, followed by the next €10,000 being assessed at a rate of €2 per €1,000. Any balance beyond this is assessed at €4 per €1,000. There is a slightly different calculation for those on Disability and/or Carer's Allowance where the first €50,000 is excluded from the means test and for Supplementary Welfare Allowance where the first €5,000 is not taken into account.

This table indicates which payments are subject to a means test, whether household income is assessed and whether and to what extent capital is assessed.

Table 6

Means-Tested	**Household Income Assessment**	**Capital Assessment**
Disability Allowance	Yes	Yes, except for the first €50,000
Job Seeker's Allowance	Yes	Yes, standard formula applies
State Pension (Non-Contributory)	Yes	Yes, standard formula applies
Carer's Allowance	Yes	Yes, except for the first €50,000
One-Parent Family Payment	No, single-person assessment	Yes, standard formula applies
Working Family Payment	Yes	No
Rent Supplement	Yes	Yes, standard formula applies
Supplementary Welfare Allowance	Yes	Yes, except first €5,000
School supports	Yes	Yes, standard formula applies
Fuel Allowance	Yes, assessable income limit applied (this means income must be less than the State Pension (Contributory) plus €200)	No

However, some income and assets are protected from being assessed as part of the means test. These are commonly referred to as "disregards". For most payments, the standard formula is that the principal residence of the applicant is not assessed as part of a means test unless the applicant receives an income from it. If an applicant rents a room, any rental income over

€14,000 per years is assessable. Other payments have different disregards. For example, rental income under €14,000 is generally disregarded unless you are renting to an employee or immediate family member. Additionally, for those receiving non-contributory pensions, any income from rent is disregarded.

3. Non-Economic Conditionality: Age and Habitual Residence

While most conditions for accessing social protection payments are economically focussed (insurance contributions, activation, means test), there are other non-economic conditions which often determine access to a payment. The two most common in the Irish context are age and residence.

Age is clearly a condition for accessing pension-related payments but it can also be applicable to other payments such as job seeker's allowance. Age may, for example, reduce or increase payments depending on the particular payment in question, which is common in respect of work-related payments. Additionally, the general application of minimum ages of eligibility for certain selected payments is widespread. For child benefit there is no minimum age of eligibility but this is to be expected considering its universal application. However, other payments are restricted to those over 16 (disability allowance) or 18 (all working age payments) or pension age (state pension). Other schemes have even higher minimum ages attached such as 66 in the context of the free travel scheme, 70 for household benefits packages and 80 for pension increases.

The habitual residence condition is another common condition attached to many social protection payments, including those that are universal in nature.[39] While there is no official legal definition in Irish law, it is commonly agreed that in practice such a condition means that the applicant has a proven link with Ireland. This implies that the applicant must have been in Ireland for some time and there is also an intention to remain. The applicant must prove their own entitlement to the social welfare payment so the onus is on the applicant to prove all of these conditions. Ryan and Power discovered that interactions with applicants are very limited and decisions

39 Section 246, Social Welfare Consolidation Action 2005 (as amended). However, Deciding Officers and Designated Persons must also have regard to S.I. No. 548/2015 – European Communities (Free Movement of Persons) Regulations 2015.

are often made "based purely on the documents submitted by applicants"[40]. The law is clear that if you have no legal right to reside in Ireland, then habitual residence cannot be established.[41] Once residence is established, five conditions must be met to determine whether an applicant is habitually resident: (a) length and continuity of residence, (b) length and purpose of any absence from Ireland, (c) nature and pattern of employment, (d) main centre of interest, and (e) future intentions to live in Ireland as it appears from the evidence.[42] These criteria are checked by a statutorily appointed Deciding Officer based in the Department of Social Protection who have full discretion in their determination. An appeal is available in all social protection matters to the Social Welfare Appeals Office. This office operates independently of the Department of Social Protection. A further appeal is also available to the High Court on a point of law or by way of judicial review. Harmon and Garrett have identified that the administrative discretion is subjective and open to "inconsistent interpretation"[43] leading inevitably to unfair results in some cases.

A recent case from 2020[44] illustrates the very strict application of this principle by Social Welfare Appeals Officers in Ireland. The applicant was a single mother of two children who had arrived in Ireland in 2013, seven years earlier. She had claimed asylum and was granted refugee status in 2019. She had resided in Ireland for the duration of this application. She applied for a One Parent Family payment to support childcare costs so that she could pursue an educational course. Her initial application was refused on the grounds that she had not satisfied the habitual residence condition due to the fact that her presence in the State was not in accordance with

40 M. Ryan and M. Power, 'Understanding how decision makers practice discretion in the context of Habitual Residence Condition in the Republic of Ireland' Irish Journal of Sociology 28 (2020)2, pp. 143, 144.

41 Section 15, Social Welfare and Pensions (No. 2) Act 2009 amending section 246 of the Social Welfare Consolidation Act 2005 by inserting section 246(5).

42 Social Welfare and Pensions Act 2007, Section 30. See also Community Law and Mediation, 'Thematic Note G0116: Right to Reside and Habitual Residence Condition' (2020) < https://communitylawandmediation.ie/casebase/thematic-note-g0116-right-to-reside-and-habitual-residence-condition/> accessed 21.11.2024.

43 A. Harmon and P. Garrett, "It's like Weber's "iron cage"': Irish social workers' experience of the Habitual Residence Condition' Critical and Radical Social Work 3 (2015)1, pp. 35, 37.

44 Community Law and Mediation, 'Social Welfare Appeal G0128: One Parent Family Payment/Habitual Residence Condition' (2020) < https://communitylawandmediation.ie/casebase/social-welfare-appeal-g0128-one-parent-family-payment-habitual-residence-condition/> accessed 21.11.2024.

her permission-to-remain which had been subject to the condition that she would make every effort to gain employment and not become a burden on the State. As she was not in employment at the time of the application, the Appeals Officer took the view that she had failed to satisfy the habitual residence condition. The applicant appealed to the Chief Appeals Officer on the grounds that the decision was erroneous by reason of some mistake in fact. During this time the applicant had become employed as a cleaner. As a result of this, the Chief Appeals Officer overturned the decision following a review of all the facts. The decision illustrates the fact that habitual residence decisions can turn not only on permanence and intention but also on the basis of following the conditions of their residence in the State.

4. Activation

For the most part, activation policies (a focus on active assistance to return to the labour market rather than merely income support) are targeted at those receiving unemployment allowances or benefits of some kind with the aim of encouraging people to return to the labour market. Social protection in Ireland aims to encourage activation in three main ways. The first is through facilitation of people to join the labour market. The second is to assist unemployed people to find work. The third is to incentivise progression from part-time to full-time work.[45] These policies apply regardless of whether the applicant is in receipt of social insurance payments or assistance payments.

There is activation conditionality to the receipt of job seeker's allowance and job seeker's benefit (contributory payment). For those who apply for such payments, they must be able to demonstrate that they are "*capable of work and be available for and genuinely seeking work*". This is a mandatory condition which will otherwise reduce the rate of payment. This has been interpreted as meaning that an applicant must be willing to accept any reasonable offer of employment (based on their skills, qualifications and experience), willing to accept any reasonable offer of training, re-training, work experience or education to improve their prospects of finding employment, and be able to show that they have taken reasonable steps to ensure they have the best prospects of getting employment. The core

45 Commission on Taxation and Welfare Secretariat, 'Activation and the Public Employment Service' (19 November 2021), p. 3.

activation work is carried out by the Department of Social Protection and the Irish Public Employment Service (Intreo). Therefore, the process of activation is essentially two-way: the jobseeker must "*maintain contact with the labour market and take up opportunities available to them*" and the public employment service must provide "*income support, job search assistance and an evidence-based set of interventions that improve*" job-seeking prospects.[46] The sanction for non-compliance is a reduction in the rate of payment.

While currently activation measures are reserved mainly for those in receipt of job seeker's payments, there has been some discussion of extending this to other cohorts namely, adult dependents of people in receipt of job seeker's payments and recipients of other income support payments.[47] Modified activation measures have recently been extended to lone parents in receipt of income support. This was achieved by reducing the child qualifying age criteria for the One Parent Family Payment from 18 years to 7 years. Once their child reaches the age of 7, they no longer qualify for this payment but can avail of Jobseeker's Transitional Payment, which involves a labour activation component (they must be capable of work but does not require them to work given their caring responsibilities).[48] One Parent Family Payment recipients are subject to a maximum weekly earnings limit but there is no such limit for Jobseeker's Transitional Payment. This means that there is capacity to increase their hours worked and income. The Institute for Labor Economics has concluded that these reforms have led to an increased in working hours for lone parents[49] which has in turn led to an increase in household income of between 8-12%. Overall, these lone parents saw an increase of between 20-29% in earnings from employment and a 10-13% reduction in poverty.[50] Extending activation to other cohorts is more challenging given the multiple inequalities they face. Indeed, ques-

46 Ibid., p. 12.

47 Ibid., p. 12.

48 P. Redmond, S. McGuinness and C. Keane, 'The Impact of One Parent Family Payment Reforms on the Labour Market Outcomes of Lone Parents', in:IZA Institute for Labor Economics, *Discussion Paper Series* (April 2020), p. 1 < https://docs.iza.org/dp13109.pdf > accessed 21.11.2024.

49 An increase of between 2-5 hours per week. See P. Redmond, S. McGuinness and C. Keane (n 48), p. 1.

50 P. Redmond, S. McGuinness and C. Keane (n 48), p. 1.

tions such as whether this is desirable or what economically valuable work is, need to be answered first.[51]

IV. Concluding Remarks

The fundamental rationale underpinning social protection in Ireland is to provide a minimum floor of protection. In 2021, the Commission on Taxation and Welfare developed a briefing paper on social protection which included an impact assessment of the social protection system.[52] Using a variety of measures they assessed a number of working age payments against the 'at-risk-of-poverty' rate which measures the impact of social transfers in reducing poverty. This stands currently at 13% in Ireland but if all social transfers and pension income was excluded it would be in excess of 40%. This indicates that social transfers play a significant role in reducing poverty. However, Ireland is facing a number of crises which threaten the effectiveness of the system. Crises exist with housing, the cost-of-living and high inflation and these generate "a risk of increasing poverty and inequality,[53] with structurally vulnerable groups known to experience inflation at a higher rate than the official measure"[54].[55] The Irish Human Rights and Equality Commission recently called for indexation of welfare payments which has the potential to "uphold living standards for the most structurally vulnerable members of society, offsetting the effect of

51 Commission on Taxation and Welfare Secretariat, 'Public Employment Service' (n 45), p. 14.

52 Ibid., p. 19.

53 Parliamentary Budget Office, 'Inflation Issues for Ireland 2022' (2022), p. 2.

54 These groups included lower-income households, households that rent their home from a local authority, households renting privately, one-parent households, households where the dwelling is owned outright, and rural households. See Central Statistics Office, 'Estimated Inflation by Household Characteristics' (September 2022).

55 Irish Human Rights and Equality Commission, 'Policy Statement on the Index Linking of Welfare Payments (Welfare Indexation)' (03 February 2023), p. 4 < https://www.ihrec.ie/documents/policy-statement-on-the-index-linking-of-welfare-payments-welfare-indexation/> accessed 26.11.2024.

cost of living increases[56]".[57] This call has been supported by the Oireachtas Committee on Budgetary Oversight[58] and would contribute significantly to social inclusion.[59]

Despite the lack of indexation, Ireland follows other continental countries in providing contribution-based and assistance payments. It also attaches economic (means test) and non-economic (habitual residence and age) conditionality to its protection system. Activation in Ireland is primarily focused on job seeking but considerations are being given to extending these policies outside the unemployment realm. In the spirit of social inclusion and understanding intersectional inequalities, movements to extend activation are being led by more theoretical discussions on what the purpose of the social protection system is and what the State conceives to be economically valuable. These moves are to be commended as they fit strongly with the ethos of the Preamble to the Irish Constitution which calls for the promotion of the common good, so that "the dignity and freedom of the individual may be assured".[60]

---

56 Quoting Social Justice Ireland, 'Social Welfare Rates Budget 2022: The case for benchmarking and indexation' (September 2021), p. 5; See also T. Callan, C. Keane and M. Regan, 'Assessing the distributional impact of budgetary policy: The role of benchmarks and indexation' Budget Perspectives No. 2020/2, the Economic and Social Research Council (2019), p. 3 where it states that "[i]f benefit payment rates do not keep pace with price inflation, welfare recipients experience losses of real income.".

57 Irish Human Rights and Equality Commission, 'Policy Statement on the Index Linking of Welfare Payments' (n 55), p. 5.

58 The Committee recommended that indexation would provide greater certainty and planning for fixed and low-income households. Committee on Budgetary Oversight, 'Work Programme November 2021-October 2022' (2021), p. 6.

59 Government of Ireland, 'Roadmap for Social Inclusion 2020-2025: Ambition, Goals, Commitments' (2020), p. 15.

60 Constitution of Ireland, Preamble.

In Search of a Guaranteed Minimum Income: Continuity and Discontinuity in Ensuring Dignified Subsistence Benefits in Italy

Eva Maria Hohnerlein[*]

* I am particularly grateful to *S. Borelli, P. Bozzao, I. Domenici* and *M. d'Onghia* for their invaluable help in providing research material.

I. Introduction

Italy has a long tradition of neglecting poverty as a central concern of social policy. Responsibility for the poor and destitute was left to charities, if not to family and relatives.[1] Public efforts to provide dignified means of subsistence remained fragmented and inefficient. Under the Constitution of 1948, the State continued to deny responsibility for citizens lacking sufficient financial resources. In practice, social protection largely relied on contributory social security schemes for regular workers, offering only minimal protection to those outside or at the margins of the labour market. The general lack of national minimum income protection (further exacerbated by the notorious weakness of social services at the local level) has been attributed to the ambivalence of the Constitution of 1948 with regard to the protection of social rights, and in particular by its strong emphasis on the protection of workers. While the Constitution enshrined a wide range of social and economic rights, the provision of social assistance and minimum income protection was limited to specific groups deemed "deserving" of State support, namely the elderly and those with reduced capacity for work.

In 2017, after several unsuccessful attempts[2] and proposals to reform social assistance[3], Italy introduced an ambitious measure known as "Inclusion Income" (*Reddito di Inclusione, REI*)[4], aimed at progressively establishing a universal minimum income following an initial phase of limited coverage. Despite plans to gradually increase benefit amounts, it remained quite

1 An early exception was The *Bourbon Hospice for the Poor* (*Albergo Reale dei Poveri*), also known as *il Reclusorio*. The facility, established in 1751, functioned as a self-sufficient community where the poor and sick could reside, learn trades and engage in work.

2 None of the proposals were successful, partly due to the fragmentation of the public social assistance system, and partly because of a widespread public attitude that attributed poverty to individual failings rather than structural factors.

3 Several Poverty Commissions (1984-2012) produced recommendations on poverty, yet no tangible policy reforms ensued. In the same vein, a comprehensive reform proposal for the Italian welfare state, including the introduction of a "*Reddito Minimo Vitale*" for the most impoverished, put forward by the Commission for the Analysis of the Macroeconomic Compatibility of Social Expenditure in 1997, remained largely confined to paper. For an overview of previous reform attempts, cf. A. Brandolini, 'Il dibattito sulla povertà in Italia, tra statistica e politica', in: L. Chies, M.D. Ferrara, E. Podrecca (ed.), *Le dimensioni della povertà. Aspetti economici e giuridici* (Torino 2021), pp. 47-49; C. Saraceno, D. Benassi and E. Morlicchio, *Poverty in Italy: Features and Drivers in a European Perspective* (Policy Press 2020), pp. 43 ff.

4 Legislative Decree No. 147 of 15 September 2017, implementing enabling Act (*legge delega*) No. 33/2017.

modest, with the financial resources allocated to this scheme remaining under 0.15 per cent of the country's gross domestic product (GDP). It was only with the introduction of the "Citizenship Income" (*Reddito di Cittadinanza, RdC*) in April 2019 that public funding on a scale comparable to those in other European countries were allocated, ranging from 0.3 per cent to 0.4 per cent of GDP.

However, only few social benefits in Italy have sparked as much controversy as the Citizenship Income. Its design raised several concerns, particularly the restrictive residence requirements.[5] Moreover, its implementation was considered ineffective, while the job search requirement was deemed too lenient. Ambivalent public attitudes favoured a narrative that the new scheme encouraged idleness and fraudulent behaviour. Although the 2022 Budget Law had already introduced tighter conditionality features of the instrument,[6] the Meloni government, which took office in October 2022, abolished the *RdC* altogether. As of 2024, it has been replaced by the far more limited Inclusion Allowance (*Assegno di Inclusione, ADI*).[7]

Survey data on living conditions and household income confirm that poverty remains a structural phenomenon in Italy. In 2023, 22.8 per cent of the population (around 13.4 million people) were at risk of poverty or social exclusion (according to the composite indicator Europe 2030).[8] This marks a slight improvement from 2022 (24.4 per cent), primarily driven by a reduction in the population at risk of poverty[9] (which stood at 18.9 per cent in the previous year), combined with a marginal increase in severe material and social deprivation,[10] which rose to 4.7 per cent (approximately 2.8 million individuals) compared to 4.5 per cent in 2022. Southern Italy and the islands continue to exhibit the highest rates of poverty and social

5 They were declared contrary to European law because of indirect discrimination of non-EU citizens, cf. ECJ Judgment of 29 July 2024, C-112/22, C-223/22.

6 Law No. 197/2022 (Budget Law for 2022).

7 The abolition of the *RdC* was announced by the Budget Law for 2023 and implemented by Decree Law (DL) No. 48 of 4 May 2023, converted by Law No. 85 of 3 July 2023, with amendments.

8 Combining the three indicators for relative income poverty, severe material and social deprivation, and very low work intensity.

9 The share of persons with a disposable income below the risk-of-poverty threshold, set at 60 per cent of the national median equivalised disposable income (after social transfers).

10 Presenting at least seven signs of deprivation out of the 13 indicators identified by the new Europe 2030 indicator.

exclusion (39 per cent).[11] While the overall risk of poverty and social exclusion declined across most household types, it increased in particular among large households with five or more members. Vulnerability remains high among those who primarily rely on income from pensions and/or social benefits (31.6 per cent) and among individuals in households with at least one foreign national (40.1 per cent).[12]

The Italian Institute for Statistics (ISTAT) measures relative and absolute poverty incidence in a different way, based on household expenditure for a reference basket of goods and services.[13] In 2023, the incidence of relative household poverty remained stable at 10.6 per cent compared to 2022, with over 2.8 million households living below the poverty threshold. However, the incidence of individual relative poverty rose slightly to 14.5 per cent (up from 14.0 per cent in 2022), affecting nearly 8.5 million individuals.[14] Absolute poverty, based on consumption needs, affected just over 2.2 million households in 2023 (8.4 per cent of total resident households, up from 7.7 per cent in 2021). Nearly 5.7 million individuals were living in absolute poverty (9.7 per cent of the population, up from 9.1 per cent in 2021). The absolute poverty rate was particularly high among households with at least one foreigner (30.4 per cent compared to 6.3 per cent for households composed of Italian nationals only), families with three or more children (21.6 per cent), young people under 18 (13.8 per cent, or 1.29 million individuals in this age group), and families living in rented housing[15] (21.6 per cent compared to 4.7 per cent among homeowners).[16] The surge in extreme poverty among households

11 Cf. ISTAT, Living Conditions and Household Income, year 2023. Statistiche report, 7 May 2024.

12 ISTAT, ibid., p. 3.

13 The relative poverty threshold for a two-member household is determined as the average expenditure per person. For absolute poverty thresholds, ISTAT has developed a sophisticated set of indicators, where the thresholds vary according to household size, its composition in terms of age, geographical area and the size of the municipality of residence, ISTAT, Le statistiche dell'Istat sulla povertà in Italia, Anno 2023. Statistiche report, 17 October 2024, p. 10 f; A. Cutillo, M. Raitano, I. Siciliani, 'Income-Based and Consumption-Based Measurement of Absolute Poverty: Insights from Italy' Social Indicators Research161 (2022), pp. 689–710. https://doi.org/10.1007/s11205-020-02386-9.

14 In 2023, the relative household poverty threshold defined by ISTAT was EUR 1,211 for a two-person household, EUR 1,610 for a three-person household, and up to a maximum of EUR 2,906 for a seven-person household. Cf. ISTAT (n 13), p. 7.

15 In Italy, 18.1 per cent of households are rented homes, while 72.8 per cent are homeowners; the remainder reside under usufruct or free use arrangements.

16 For details on absolute poverty rates, cf. ISTAT (n 13).

whose reference person is an employee is particularly alarming: the incidence reached 9.1 per cent in 2023 (up from 7.7 per cent in 2021), despite the increase in employment recorded in 2023.[17]

II. Overview

1. Normative Background

a) Constitutional Law Framework

The Italian Constitution does not explicitly establish a duty for the State to guarantee minimum income protection for citizens and residents. It highlights fundamental principles, declaring that the "Republic is founded on labour" (Art. 1), that the State is responsible for removing any economic and social obstacles which, by limiting the freedom and equality of citizens, prevent the full development of the natural person (Art. 3, para. 2), and that the State must uphold the right of all citizens to work, promoting the necessary services to ensure this right is effectively realised (Art. 4). "Human dignity" is closely linked to the principle of equality as "equal social dignity" (Art. 3, para. 1), and to the right of workers to remuneration which is to ensure them and their families "a free and dignified existence" (Art. 36, para. 1). This reflects a strongly labour-centred (*ergo-centric*) imprint of the Constitution and a constitutional promise to effectively implement the right to work for all.

Art. 38 (paras. 1 and 2) of the Constitution recognises the rights to social assistance and social security. Its interpretation is contested among legal scholars, particularly whether a claim to general minimum income protection as *ius existentiae* derives from the provision's para. 1 or para. 2.

Pursuant to Art. 38, para. 1, "Every citizen unable to work and lacking the necessary means of subsistence shall have the right to maintenance and social support."[18] This wording seems to limit the right to public income

17 Cf. Caritas Italiana, 'La povertà in Italia, Report statistico nazionale 2024' (2024) < https://archivio.caritas.it/materiali/Rapporti_poverta/report_statistico_2024.pdf > accessed 22.1.2025, p. 34, where it is also noted that nearly half of all families living in absolute poverty (47 per cent) do not face a "lack of work" issue, as the head of the household is reported to be employed.

18 Ogni cittadino inabile al lavoro e sprovvisto dei mezzi necessari per vivere ha diritto al mantenimento e all'assistenza sociale.

support to individuals who, on the one hand, do not possess the necessary means of subsistence and are incapacitated for work, on the other, either due to old age or a physical disability. The constitutional text does not recognise a general social right to income support based exclusively on lack of sufficient means of subsistence. The Constitution primarily fights poverty through work. Art. 38, para. 2 states that "workers shall have the right to envisaged and assured adequate means for their subsistence needs in the event of an accident, illness, disability, old age and involuntary unemployment", establishing the constitutional foundation for a higher level of protection for workers, guaranteed primarily—albeit not exclusively—through the social insurance system. The principle of adequacy of benefits is the only explicit requirement imposed on the legislator, with the clear objective of addressing inappropriate benefit levels of post-war social insurance schemes. Still, the criteria for determining adequacy remain unclear. The interpretation of what constitutes adequate means depends on various factors, including availability of public resources. In any case, ensuring an adequate level of support over time requires a mechanism to index benefit amounts, thereby preventing a significant decline in purchasing power.[19]

The majority of legal scholars support the compatibility of national minimum income benefits with the Constitution, albeit based on different arguments. Some advocate for an interpretation of Art. 38, para. 1 that goes beyond its literal wording.[20] A broader interpretation would allow for the inclusion of individuals who have capacity for work but are unable to sustain themselves because they cannot find work.[21]

As regards the constitutional foundations of a social right to minimum income, some scholars argue that the state has a duty to lift citizens excluded from the labour market out of a condition of "indigence" by guaranteeing access to adequate means of subsistence and drawing on a broader

19 Cf. Corte Cost., sent. No. 497/1988 (declaring the lack of an adjustment regulation for unemployment benefits unconstitutional).

20 In favour of a literal approach, cf. E. Ales, G. Canavesi, D. Casale et al., *Diritto della Sicurezza Sociale* (Giappichelli EDU 2021), pp. 14 ff.; M. Ferraresi, 'L'Assegno di inclusione tra vincoli costituzionali ed europei in tema di reddito minimo garantito' LavoroDirittiEuropa (2024) 1, pp. 6 ff.

21 C. Tripodina, 'Reddito di cittadinanza come "risarcimento per mancato procurato lavoro". Il dovere della Repubblica di garantire il diritto al lavoro o assicurare altrimenti il diritto all'esistenza' costituzionalismo.it, (2015)1, pp. 20 ff.; C. Tripodina, *Il diritto a un'esistenza libera e dignitosa* (Giappichelli 2013); M. Vincieri, 'Verso la tutela della povertà: l'ipotesi del reddito di inclusione' Lav.dir. (2017), p. 302.

understanding of social security as stipulated in Art. 38, para. 2.[22] This argument is reinforced by several fundamental constitutional principles, particularly by the principle of general solidarity (Art. 2), which underpins the right to a free life in dignity.[23] Some scholars justify the need to introduce minimum income provisions by re-interpreting the Constitution in light of European Union law.[24] The debate continues about whether the Italian Constitution mandates or merely legitimizes a minimum income scheme, i.e. whether such a scheme is constitutionally an obligation of the legislature or in fact optional.

The Constitutional Court's case law falls short of establishing a social right to an adequate minimum income for citizens living in poverty. The concept of human dignity as a constitutional principle has been acknowledged—albeit to a limited extent—in relation to the right to housing, which is considered an integral component in ensuring the minimum conditions necessary for a life in dignity.[25]

As regards the content of the right to social assistance, the Constitutional Court stated in 1986 that this right "guarantees citizens the existential minimum or subsistence level necessary to meet the basic needs of daily life —that is, to cover essential dietary needs—as the irreducible core of guar-

---

22 E.G. M. Persiani, *Diritto della previdenza sociale* (CEDAM 2009), pp. 14 ff.; M. Cinelli, *Diritto della previdenza sociale* (Giappichelli 2022), p. 4; P. Bozzao, 'Reddito base e cittadinanza attiva nei nuovi scenari del welfare' Riv.giur.lav (2014)2, p. 333; F. Ravelli, *Il reddito mínimo* (Giappichelli 2018), p. 83.

23 On the fundamental principles of dignity, equality and solidarity (Art. 2, 3 and 4, combined with Art. 38 of the Constitution) requiring the State to create conditions guaranteeing *ius existentiae* (understood as the right to a free life in dignity), cf. F. Ravelli (n 22), pp. 90 ff.; P. Bozzao, 'Quale e quanto intervento pubblico nel contrasto alla povertà? Rileggendo Claudio Franchini' RDSS (2022), pp. 127 ff., 138; P. Bozzao, 'Reddito di cittadinanza e laboriosità' Giornale di diritto del lavoro e di relazioni industriali 165 (2020)1, pp. 1 ff.; S. Caffio, *Povertà, reddito e occupazione* (ADAPT Labour Studies 2023), pp. 9 f.

24 G. Bronzini, 'Il reddito minimo garantito e la riforma degli ammortizzatori sociali' WP C.S.D.L.E. "Massimo d'Antona".IT 270 (2015).

25 Corte Cost. No. 217/1988 (concerning access to social housing) stated that "creating the minimum conditions of a welfare state, helping to guarantee a fundamental social right such as the right to housing for as many citizens as possible, helping to ensure that every person's life reflects the universal image of human dignity every day and in every respect, are tasks that the State cannot evade under any circumstances". See C. Domenicali, 'Quale garanzia per il diritto all'abitazione? Il caso dell'edilizia popolare', in: A. Morrone, *Il diritto costituzionale nella giurisprudenza* (9th ed. Wolters Kluwer 2022), p. 209.

antees due to those who are fully incapacitated for work".[26] The national legislator has a similar responsibility of ensuring access to benefits deemed indispensable for alleviating situations of *extreme* need, in particular in relation to food. The State also has the duty to define both the qualitative and quantitative components of such benefits to uphold the irreducible core of this fundamental social right.[27] In practice, however, decisions that recognize a constitutional right to minimum income protection have been limited in scope: Constitutional Court rulings have either defined the content of this right in terms of mere subsistence levels, addressed very specific situations, including cases of severe disability,[28] or specific State responsibilities, including custodial sentences with domestic detention.[29]

Both constitutional guarantees—the right to social security and the right to social assistance—are linked to the State's obligation to maintain budgetary equilibrium (Art. 81) and the principle of sound administration (Art. 97). These provisions could potentially weaken the enforceability of social rights due to budgetary constraints.[30] Only under exceptional circumstances can the right to income support from the State take precedence over budgetary constraints.[31]

---

26 Corte Cost. No. 31/1986 (on minimum pension guarantees). In its early decision, the Court held that the term "adequate means of subsistence" should not be limited to basic subsistence or social assistance levels, but must also ensure the fulfillment of needs related to workers' standard of living, in addition to dietary needs.

27 Corte Cost. No. 10/2010 on the Social Card, ex Art. 81 (29 ff.) of d.l. n. 112/2008, based on the fundamental principles of Art. 2 and 3, para. 2; Art. 38 and Art. 117, para. 2 (m) Constitution. Cf. F. Pizzolato, 'La "social card" all'esame della Corte costituzionale' Riv.dir.sic.soc. (2010), pp. 349 ff.

28 Corte Cost. No. 152/2020 addressed the adequacy of benefits provided to individuals with disabilities aged 18 to 59, who are fully incapacitated for work, affirming their right to minimum subsistence.

29 Corte Cost. No. 137/2021. The Court found a provision unconstitutional that revokes social assistance benefits as an ancillary penalty of individuals convicted of crimes, who are serving alternative measures to prison detention. The Court held that such revocation, based on the legislator's notion of "unworthiness", undermines the constitutional foundations of the right to social assistance. It emphasised that withdrawing essential benefits could jeopardise the convicted person's ability to live in dignity, thereby violating his or her right to "minimum vitale".

30 Art. 81 Cost., as amended in 2012, establishes the duty to maintain financial equilibrium, forming the constitutional basis for the financing of the social security system. For the Constitutional Court's position on the relationship between Art. 81 Cost. and the social security system, cf. Judgments No. 12/2018 and No. 20/2018; No. 88/2014.

31 C. Cost. No. 152/2020. Even in the case of benefits based on social insurance schemes, constitutional case law has emphasised that the definition of "adequate" benefits is

Guaranteeing the right to a minimum income is further complicated by the division of competences between the State and the Regions (and the Autonomous Provinces), a division that was reinforced by the 2001 constitutional reform. Accordingly, the State retains exclusive competence over social security, while healthcare falls under the shared competence between the State and the Regions. Social assistance and social services are the exclusive responsibility of the Regions, except in cases where such services are defined as "essential levels of benefits" (*livelli essenziali di prestazioni, LEPs*). The State is responsible for ensuring their uniform provision across the national territory and for financing them through national public resources.[32] Since no general, comprehensive definition of these essential standards had been adopted until the end of 2021,[33] highly diverse social assistance schemes (including minimum income benefits) developed not only at local and regional levels, but at state level as well.[34]

b) International Law Standards

Although Italian constitutional law does not provide a strong foundation for holding the State responsible for guaranteeing adequate minimum income benefits, this obligation could instead derive from international and European human rights instruments, particularly the European Social Charter (ESC) and the EU Charter of Fundamental Rights.

---

left to the discretion of the legislator. A rare exception was the historic ruling of the Constitutional Court No. 497/1988, which found unemployment insurance benefits inadequate due to the absence of an indexation mechanism. For an overview of Constitutional Court Judgments regarding the interaction between Art. 81 Cost. and the social security system, see M. Faioli, 'Beyond the Formal Principle of Intergenerational Sustainability in the Italian Social Security System', in: E. Kasagi (ed.), *Solidarity Across Generations* (Springer 2020), pp. 59 ff.

32 The Constitutional Court clarified that the LEPS indicate the constitutionally required threshold of expenditure necessary to provide social benefits of a fundamental nature, as well as the non-reducible core of minimum guarantees to ensure the effectiveness of these rights (Judgment No. 220/2021).

33 For social assistance, Article 1, para. 159 of Law No. 234/2021 (Budget Law for 2022) defines the Essential Levels of Social Benefits (*LEPS*) as "the interventions, services, activities and integrated benefits that the Republic ensures and which have universal character throughout the national territory, with the aim of guaranteeing quality of life, equal opportunities, non-discrimination, and the prevention, elimination or reduction of conditions of disadvantage and vulnerability".

34 See below, sect. II.2.

Italy has ratified the European Social Charter of 1961, its additional protocols as well as the revised Charter of 1996, and is one of 16 European states that has ratified the 1995 Protocol on Collective Complaints. Italy is also among the few states that has accepted all provisions of Part II of the ESC, with the exception of one.[35] The European Committee of Social Rights has repeatedly stated that Italy fails to comply with the Charter provisions on the protection of the right to social security (in particular, Art. 12, para. 4), the right to social assistance (Art. 13, para. 1), the right of the elderly to social protection (Art. 23), and the right to protection against poverty and social exclusion (Art. 30). The level of social assistance was found to be insufficient, with gaps in coverage for persons in need (Art. 13, para. 1), i.e. the level of contributory and non-contributory old-age pensions was deemed inadequate to guarantee a dignified existence for elderly persons (Art. 23 RESC).[36] The social rights enshrined in the European Social Charter can serve as an intermediary parameter for judges when assessing the constitutionality of laws pursuant to Art. 117, para. 1 of the Italian Constitution. Although the Constitutional Court of Italy has acknowledged this possibility, it has rejected the obligation of national judges to follow the interpretations of Charter provisions issued by the European Committee on Social Rights, with some rare exceptions that are not applicable to minimum benefits.[37]

c) Evolution of the Legislative Framework

While social protection under the post-war Constitution was predominantly based on contributory social security schemes for regular workers, the level of social protection remained inadequate for those who were not—or only marginally—participating in the labour market.

The shift in minimum income protection started in the 1990s during a period of prolonged economic recession, with the first experimental minimum income scheme, the *Reddito Minimo di Inserimento* (*RMI*) of 1998,

35 The only provision that has been rejected is Art. 25, which protects workers' rights in terms of their claims in the event of insolvency of their employer.

36 For details, see G. Palmisano, *L'Europa dei diritti sociali. Significato, valore e prospettive della Carta sociale europea* (Il Mulino 2022), pp. 275, 280-283.

37 The exception only applies to decisions of the ECSR in collective complaint procedures involving Art. 24 of the ESC (protection against dismissal).

initially implemented in 39 municipalities and later extended to a total of 306 municipalities (1999–2007).[38] Although the Framework Law on Social Services (No. 328/2000)[39] provided for the extension of the *RMI* to the entire national territory, the project was discontinued in 2002. In 2008, a national anti-poverty instrument known as the "Social Card" (*Carta Acquisti*) was introduced. Based on extended legislative powers, several regions launched their own social assistance programmes, especially following the international financial crisis in 2008. Regional minimum income schemes adopted various names and displayed significant heterogeneity in terms of benefit amounts, eligibility criteria, obligations of the beneficiaries and duration of benefits.[40]

With the economic crisis persisting beyond 2010, a new era of social policy reform began: unemployment protection was gradually expanded, and a limited minimum income scheme called "Support for Active Inclusion" (*Sostegno per l'inclusione attiva, SIA*) was proposed in 2013 to address extreme poverty. The establishment of the National Fund against Poverty by the Budget Law for 2016 and the introduction of a new scheme known as "Inclusion Income" (*Reddito di inclusione, REI*)[41] in 2017 marked a turning point, although REI was never fully implemented. In April 2019, the REI scheme was replaced by the new "Citizenship Income" (*RdC*), which extended coverage and provided higher benefit amounts, with the allocation of public resources for *RdC* being three times higher than under the *REI* scheme.

During the COVID-19 pandemic (2020–2022), Italy adopted a series of temporary ad hoc measures, including special flat-rate allowances to

38 In the absence of a national minimum income scheme, several municipalities introduced minimum income benefits, e.g. Turin in 1978, Ancona in 1982, Bari in 1983, Milan in 1989, cf. C. Saraceno, D. Benassi, E. Morlicchio (n 3), p. 123.

39 Law No. 328/2000 introduced an "integrated system of social interventions and services", which included social services and financial benefits aimed at eliminating and overcoming situations of indigence and hardship, as defined in Art. 128 of D.lgs. No. 112/1998.

40 For example, *Reddito di Solidarietà* in Emilia Romagna; *Reddito di Dignità* in Apulia; *Reddito di Inclusione Sociale* in Sardinia; *Reddito Minimo di Cittadinanza* in Molise; *Reddito di Garanzia*, later absorbed into the *Assegno Unico Provinciale* of the Autonomous Province of Trento. For details of these schemes and other complementary regional measures, cf. M. Matarese, 'Le misure regionali di reddito mínimo', in: M. Ferraresi, *Reddito di inclusione e reddito di cittadinanza. Il contrasto alla povertà tra diritto e política* (Giappichelli 2018), pp. 51, 62 ff., F. Ravelli, *Il Reddito Minimo. Tra universalismo e selettività delle tutele*, (Giappichelli 2018), pp. 150 ff.

41 Legislative Decree No. 147 of 15 September 2017, implementing enabling Act (*legge delega*) No. 33/2017.

ensure a minimum income for several professional groups, as well as a novel "Emergency Income" (*Reddito di emergenza*)[42] for low-income households without access to *RdC* benefits or other forms of minimum income support. None of these emergency measures were transformed into a permanent component of minimum income protection.

Despite some efforts to improve minimum income protection for households unable to support themselves in the period 2018–2023, Italy experienced a significant setback in minimum income protection in 2023. The newly elected government discontinued the Citizenship Income and introduced the Inclusion Allowance (*Assegno di inclusione, ADI*) as a new minimum income benefit starting in 2024, accompanied by a new Training and Work Benefit (*SFL*) in September 2023.[43] Estimated annual costs for both cash benefits range between EUR 6.8 billion and EUR 6.6 billion, significantly lower than the nearly EUR 9 billion that were allocated to the *RdC* scheme.[44] This major policy shift has led to a resumption of regional minimum income programmes.[45] The abolition of the Citizenship Income has again left Italy without a universal minimum income scheme. The recent reform introduced another categorical protection scheme for selected households in addition to the already existing ones, but has reduced the target group of beneficiaries, and now excludes a significant number of former beneficiaries from minimum income protection.[46] New eligibility criteria for the *ADI* scheme are expected to decrease average benefit amounts by 11 per cent (around

42 Cf. DL 34/2020, converted by Law No. 77/2020; extended by DL 137/2020, 149/2020, 154/2020 and 157/20, converted by Law No. 176/2020; in 2021 by DL 41/2021; DL 73/2021. The monthly amount varied between EUR 400 and maximum EUR 804.

43 The new "Support for Training and Work" (*Supporto per la formazione ed il lavoro, SFL*) scheme does not constitute a minimum income benefit: it is an instrument to promote the integration of individuals, who are deemed to have capacity for work, into the labour market. For details, see below sec.. II.2.a) aa) (for ADI) and 2.b) cc) (for SFL).

44 EUR 5.8 billion annually for ADI and EUR 1.3 for SFL compared to EUR 8.8 billion annually for the RdC (only cash benefits), see G. Bovini, E. Dicarlo, A. Tomasi, 'La revisione delle misure di contrasto alla povertà in Italia', in: Banca d'Italia (ed.), *Questioni di Economia e Finanza* (Occasional Papers) No. 820/2023, p. 6; Senato della Repubblica, XIX legislatura, Servizio del Bilancio, Nota di lettura No. 53, «A.S. 685: "Conversione in legge del decreto-legge 4 maggio 2023, n. 48, recante misure urgenti per l'inclusione sociale e l'accesso al mondo del lavoro"», May 2023, pp. 5, 25, 38, 41.

45 For example, the Region of Apulia relaunched the "*Reddito di Dignità*" scheme of 2016; Sardinia accelerated the implementation of its "*Reddito di Inclusione Sociale*"; Campania and Sicily have envisaged similar proposals.

46 G. Bronzini, 'La controriforma dell'assegno di inclusione: dalla protezione di diritto al welfare caritatevole' RGL, Giurisprudenza online, Newsletter 1 (2024).

EUR 12,300 annually), with reductions of up to EUR 4,000 per year for households in the poorest decile.[47] The recent shift towards stricter workfare conditions, combined with more rigid eligibility criteria for who is considered 'deserving' of support as well as an increased emphasis on reliance on family, intentionally excludes individuals in need who are deemed capable of supporting themselves through labour market participation, thereby withdrawing adequate State protection from them.

2. Social Benefits

a) Main Minimum Income Benefits

aa) Inclusion Allowance

Inclusion allowance[48] is defined as a "national measure to fight poverty, 'fragility' and social exclusion of weak groups through social inclusion, training, employment and active labour policies".[49] The scheme is limited

47 G. Bovini, E. Dicarlo, A. Tomasi (n 44).

48 The benefit scheme is regulated in Art. 1 - 11 of the "Labour Decree", DL No. 48/2023, of 5 May 2023 (*Misure urgenti per l'inclusione sociale e l'accesso al mondo del lavoro*), converted into Law No. 85 of 3 July 2023, with amendments; for implementation details, see Decree of the Ministry of Labour and Social Policies, D.M. No. 154 of 13 December 2023 ("Assegno di inclusione"), INPS, Circular No. 105 of 16 December 2023, and Decree of the Ministry of Labour and Social Policies, D.M. No. 160 of 29 December 2023. For initial commentaries, cf. M. Ferraresi, 'L'Assegno di inclusione tra vincoli costituzionali ed europei in tema di reddito minimo garantito' LavoroDirittiEuropa (2024) 1; F. De Michiel, 'Le misure di contrasto alla povertà nel c.d. decreto lavoro (commento agli artt. 1-13, d.l. 4 maggio 2023, n. 48, conv. con modif. dalla l. 3 luglio 2023, n. 85' LavoroDirittiEuropa (2024) 1; S. Caffio (n 23), pp. 192 ff.; G. Bronzini (n 46); M. Ricci, 'Dal reddito di cittadinanza all'assegno di inclusione tra poche luci e molte ombre' ArgDirLav (2023) 6, pp. 1105 ff.; H. Caroli Casavola, 'Il congedo del reddito di cittadinanza e il passaggio al Welfare condizionale' Giornale Dir. Amm. (2023)5, pp. 603 ff.; M. M. Cellini, 'Assegno di inclusione e isee' Il Lavoro nella Giurisprudenza (2023) 10, pp. 877 ff.; A. Di Filippo, 'Assegno di inclusione, la nuova frontiera per il contrasto alla povertà e alla esclusione sociale' Aziendítalia (2023) 10, pp. 1205 ff.; E. Dagnino, C. Garofalo, G. Picco et al. (eds.) *Commentario al d.l. 4 maggio 2023 n. 48 c.d. "decreto lavoro", convertito con modificazioni in l. 3 luglio 2023, n. 85* (Adapt Labour Studies 2023); P. Tridico, 'La riforma del Reddito di cittadinanza e del Decreto dignità. Criticità e conseguenze' LavoroDirittiEuropa (2023) 3.

49 "Misura nazionale di contrasto alla povertà, alla fragilità e all'esclusione sociale delle fasce deboli attraverso percorsi di inserimento sociale, nonché di formazione, di

to households with certain "fragile members": at least one household member must either be under the age of 18; over the age of 60; have a disability; or "in serious bio-psycho-social distress" (*in grave disagio bio-psico-sociale*) and enrolled in a care and assistance programme duly certified by the public administration.[50]

To qualify for the inclusion allowance, applicants must meet specific criteria. Italian citizenship is one such requirement; EU citizens must hold either the right of residence or be permanent residents, while third-country nationals must possess a long-term EU residence permit[51] or international protection status.[52] The applicant must have resided in Italy for at least five years[53], with the last two years being continuous. A new requirement for households with children under the age of 18 is that the children must be attending school regularly.[54]

Furthermore, entitlement to the inclusion allowance is conditional upon the applicant's honesty and integrity: access is denied to those who are

---

lavoro e di politica attiva del lavoro", Art. 1, para. 1 DL 48/2023. The term "*fasce deboli*" refers to persons who need or 'deserve' special protection and support.

50 The new category of beneficiaries was introduced by the conversion Law No. 85/2023, explicitly including victims of gender-based violence. The eligibility criteria are defined in Art. 3, para. 5 of the Decree of the Ministry of Labour and Social Policies No. 154 of 13 December 2024. These include individuals in the care of mental health facilities; those under the charge of disability or addiction facilities; individuals receiving assistance as victims of gender-based violence or human trafficking; persons under the supervision of the Offices for External Penal Execution, including those admitted to alternative measures to detention, or former prisoners released within the past year who remain under the care of the State; individuals identified as particularly vulnerable and placed in reception facilities or emergency housing programmes; homeless persons under the charge of support services; young adults between the ages of 18 and 21, who live outside their family home based on a provision from the judicial authorities placing them in residential communities or alternative foster care, and who are under the supervision of social or healthcare services.

51 The Constitutional Court confirmed the constitutional legitimacy of this requirement, cf. sent. No. 19/2022, with a critical note by F. De Michiel, 'Il reddito di cittadinanza alla prova della Corte costituzionale: una sentenza previdibile in tema di accesso al beneficio da parte degli stranieri extra-UE' Dir. Rel. Ind. 32 (2022) 3, pp. 856 ff.

52 Political asylum or subsidiary protection pursuant to Legislative Decree No. 251 of 19 November 2007.

53 The residency requirement for the abolished citizenship income was ten years. ADI beneficiaries lose entitlement after two continuous months of absence from Italian territory, or after a total of four months of absence over an 18-month period.

54 Art. 2, para. 3-*bis* DL 48/2023.

subject to certain measures under criminal law, including preventive measures.[55] Households with a member who is subject to activation obligations and who has been unemployed for 12 months following voluntary resignation, are also excluded from access to the benefit.[56] This exclusion is not limited to the individual who resigned, but to his or her entire household.

The economic requirements for benefit eligibility are based on a combination of several criteria: the applicant's household must possess a valid ISEE (Equivalent Economic Situation Indicator)[57] value that does not exceed EUR 9,360; the household's annual income must be below EUR 6,000, multiplied by the corresponding parameter of the ADI equivalence scale.[58] This threshold increases to EUR 7,560 per year, if the household consists exclusively of persons aged 67 or older, or of persons of this age group and other family members all with a severe disability or who are not self-sufficient. The annual family income threshold is in that case increased by EUR 2,000 for each additional household member, up to a maximum of EUR 10,000 for the entire household, with an additional increment for each minor beyond the second child.[59] The same thresholds apply to movable assets.[60] In addition, the total value of real estate assets may not exceed EUR 30,000. No member of the household may be the owner or have full availability of certain high-value movable goods.[61]

---

55 This preclusion exists regardless of the severity of the criminal offence committed.

56 Art. 2, para. 3 DL 48/2023. Exceptions are possible, e.g. in case of resignation with just cause.

57 ISEE (*Indicatore della situazione economica equivalente*) is a tool used to assess household income and assets for eligibility to social subsidies and support for different household sizes, regulated in DPCM No. 159/2013. The general ISEE value is based on the household's total income, plus 20 per cent of all movable and immovable assets, divided by the applicable parameter of the scale of equivalence.

58 A benefit-specific equivalence scale is applied to determine both the household income threshold for accessing the ADI benefit and the benefit amount, as defined in Art. 2, para. 4 of DL 48/2023. The coefficients used are less generous than those applied in the calculation of the ISEE. See below, sec. III.2.b).

59 Further increases apply to each minor beyond the second one, and for each household member with a disability.

60 Additional increases to the upper capital threshold are provided for household members with a disability, with further increases for members with a severe disability or requiring long-term care.

61 Motor vehicles with an engine capacity exceeding 1600 cc. or with a displacement over 250 cc., if registered for the first time within the 36 months preceding the application; no household member may possess such a vehicle or have full availability of yachts and pleasure boats, or aircraft of any kind.

The standard monthly allowance is set at maximum EUR 500 for a single-person household (or EUR 630, if the person is at least 67 or severely disabled).[62] The second component consists of a monthly supplement for rental costs, amounting to a maximum of EUR 280 (and up to EUR 150 for households composed exclusively of elderly and/or severely disabled persons).[63] The benefit amount is calculated by multiplying the "standard" amount by a scale of equivalence with specific coefficients that reflect the household's composition and account for various forms of "fragility" or disability among the household members.[64]

In general, household members aged 18–59 years are only included in the scale of equivalence if they qualify as either caregivers, as persons with a disability or suffer from a severe distress as defined by law. The duration of the allowance is limited to 18 months, with the possibility of renewal for an additional 12 months following a one-month break.[65] The benefit can only be used to purchase food, pharmaceutical and para-pharmaceutical products from (physical) retail channels within Italy, and to pay rent and utility bills. Monthly cash withdrawals are restricted to EUR 100 per adult.

The allowance can be combined with unemployment insurance benefits and various social assistance benefits that are not counted as income. It is, moreover, fully compatible with the universal child benefit (*assegno unico universale*).[66]

Conditionality measures aimed at encouraging recipients to enter the labour market have been tightened, primarily through a sanctions regime. Eligibility for the benefit now depends on participation in an activation project designed to promote social and labour market inclusion.[67] The

62 Art. 3, para. 1 DL 48/2023. The maximum annual subsistence benefit is EUR 6,000 (or EUR 7,560) to be multiplied by the scale of equivalence. The minimum annual amount is EUR 480 (EUR 40 per month).

63 Art. 3, para. 1 DL 48/2023, the annual amounts of the supplement for rental costs are maximum EUR 3,360 or EUR 1,800. The scale of equivalence is not applied to this supplement.

64 Subject to an upper limit.

65 There is no limitation to the number of renewals, but the benefit is always suspended for one month after a 12-month period has ended.

66 For the interaction rules, cf. Art. 2, para. 2, litt. b) n. 2; and para. 7 of DL 48/2023; Art. 2, para. 7, litt. a of DL 48/2023.

67 Exemptions from the activation requirement apply to employed persons, people attending a regular course of studies, household members aged 60 or older, those with a reduced capacity for work of more than 45 per cent (Law No. 68/1999), individuals with an oncological disease, those with care duties (for children under

central instrument is the "Personalized Social and Professional Inclusion" initiative, coordinated by local social services. Beneficiaries are required to register on the multifunctional digital platform (Information System for Social and Labour Inclusion, SIISL),[68] and sign two agreements, namely the Digital Activation Agreement[69] and the "Personalised Service Agreement".[70]

Beneficiaries aged 18 to 59 who are subject to activation measures may be required to participate in public utility projects (PUC)[71], which are organised by local authorities and third sector entities. Those between the ages of 18 and 29 who have not completed mandatory schooling are required to enrol in adult education programmes.[72] Strict conditionalities apply to the job offers beneficiaries must accept (Art. 9 DL 48/2023).[73] Non-compliance with any of the activation obligations will result in forfeiture of the benefit in full, while non-compliance with cooperation duties leads to temporary

the age of three, or for at least three children, or for a severely disabled or not self-sufficient family member), and individuals participating in special programmes to escape gender-based violence.

68 Established at the Ministry of Labour and Social Policies and implemented by INPS, Art. 5 DL 48/2023. The Information System aims to facilitate beneficiaries' engagement in independent job searches and skills enhancement, and serves as a tool for analysis, monitoring, evaluation and control of the Inclusion Allowance.

69 The agreement authorises the transmission of data to the public employment services (*Centri per l'impiego*) and to other bodies involved in activities to promote labour market integration, Art. 4 DL 48/2023.

70 *Patto di attivazione digitale* (PAD), Art. 4 DL 48/2023. Benefit entitlement starts in the month following the signing of the Digital Activation Agreement.

71 Art. 6, para. 5-*bis* of DL 48/2023; Ministerial Decree No. 156 of 15 December 2023. Such projects can be carried out in the cultural, social and environmental spheres, the organisation of training activities or the maintenance and restoration of common areas. Participation in such projects may not entail any kind of subordinate, para-subordinate or self-employed activity.

72 Art. 3, para. 11 DL 48/2023 and Art. 1, para. 316 Law No. 197/2022 (Budget Law for 2023).

73 Including open-ended employment relationships anywhere within the national territory (except for parents of children under the age of 14); full-time or part-time employment relationships equal to at least 60 per cent full-time working hours; remuneration may not be lower than the minimum wages established by the collective agreements referred to in Legislative Decree No. 81 of 15 June 2015; fixed-term employment contracts, including temporary agency work, if the workplace is located within 80 km of the individual's residence (or can be reached in no more than 120 minutes by public transport).

suspension[74] of benefit payments. The sanctions regime also includes imprisonment to prevent fraudulent behaviour.[75]

bb) Minimum Income Benefits for the Elderly

Italy guarantees a set of minimum income benefits through separate schemes that target different categories of senior citizens. Coverage and entitlement criteria primarily depend on the individual's former employment history.

A supplement to contributory pensions which fell below the minimum pension level was introduced in 1952 (*pensione integrata al minimo*).[76] The benefit aimed at reducing poverty among former workers (largely women) with discontinuous and often irregular work histories. The 1995 pension reform abolished this minimum pension supplement for new entrants to the labour market as of January 1996. Pensioners who entered employment before 1996 (and are subject to the pre-reform pension calculation rules) remain entitled to the guaranteed (contributory) minimum pensions. This supplement is subject to a dual means test, which comprises an assessment of both the individual's and the couple's income if married.[77] Beneficiaries are guaranteed an amount of maximum EUR 615 per month, paid in 13 instalments in 2024.[78] The income thresholds for eligibility to the benefit are set at twice the minimum pension for pensioners who live in a sin-

74 For example, violation of a child's compulsory school attendance.

75 For example, in case of false declarations with the intent to obtain the cash benefit; or omission of required information. Prison sentences are two to six years in the former, one to three years in the latter case. Detention of more than a year results in forfeiture of the benefit.

76 Law No. 218/1952; Law No. 638/1983. In 1981, the amount of the minimum pension level was set at 30 per cent of the average *de facto* contractual minimum wage for industrial workers, Art. 22 Law No. 119/1981.

77 Beneficiaries with a personal annual income of less than or equal to EUR 7,782, and if married, with a marital income of less than or equal to EUR 23,246 received the maximum amount in 2024. If these thresholds are exceeded, pensioners received a progressively decreasing benefit. Entitlement to the benefit is lost if personal income lies above EUR 15,563 or marital income above EUR 31,128 annually in 2024. Higher income limits apply if pension payments started in or before 1994.

78 INPS, Circular Letter No. 1 of 2 January 2024. The Budget Law for 2023 allowed for an additional re-adjustment amounting to up to EUR 16, added to the benefit amount resulting from ordinary re-adjustment (EUR 599).

gle-person household, and four times the minimum pension amount for married pensioners.[79]

The 1995 pension reform replaced the traditional supplement to low contributions-based pensions by two distinct forms of benefits: on the one hand, partial compensation is provided through special pension increases for pensioners with a lengthy insurance period (so-called 14th instalment), which is subject to a personal means test.[80] On the other hand, the 1995 reform also introduced a non-contributory social allowance for senior citizens with little or no income. In 2024, eligibility for this old-age social allowance (*assegno sociale*)[81] required the beneficiary to be at least 67 years old (subject to adjustments for changes in life expectancy) and guarantees a minimum income of EUR 534 per month, paid in 13 instalments (EUR 6,947.33 annually) for elderly persons without sufficient means.[82] In addition to either Italian or EU citizenship, eligibility for this benefit requires legal residence in Italy of at least 10 years.[83] Third-country nationals must possess a long-term residence permit.[84] The old-age social allowance is subject to a stringent dual means test,[85] which not only considers the applicant's pension income but also most other sources of income, including income exempt from IRPEF income tax and maintenance payments. The

79 Art. 6 Law No. 638/1983; Art. 4 Legislative Decree No. 503/1992; Art. 2, para. 14 Law 335/1995.

80 "*Quattordicesima*" introduced by Art. 5, paras. 1-4 DL 81/2007, converted by Law No. 127 of 3 August 2007. After coverage extension by Law No. 232/2016 (Budget Law for 2017), the benefit is paid to pensioners aged 64 and older, amounts are differentiated depending on the beneficiary's income bracket, i.e. up to 1.5 times or up to 2 times the minimum contributory pension. Benefits vary according to the duration of the insurance period and personal income thresholds; in 2022, the average benefit amounted to EUR 484 annually.

81 Art. 3, paras. 6 and 7, of Pension Reform Law No. 335/1995; Art. 38, para. 1 of Law No. 448/2001.

82 If the benefit recipient is admitted to an institution and the costs are covered by the State or public bodies, the benefit is reduced. If the costs are borne entirely by the State, the reduction is 50 per cent.

83 The extensive residence clause has applied since 2009, pursuant to Art. 20, para. 10 of Law No. 133/2008.

84 The legitimacy of the requirement for possession of a long-term residence permit was confirmed in Constitutional Court ruling No. 50/2019. By the Decision of 30 April 2024, the Constitutional Court submitted to the EU Court of Justice the question of compatibility with EU law of the rule that prevents holders of a single work permit from applying for the old-age social allowance.

85 The personal annual income threshold for the full benefit in 2024 was EUR 7,115.29 for single-person households, rising to EUR 14,897.22 for married couples.

benefit cannot be denied on the grounds that the applicant's hardship is self-inflicted or the result of a voluntary lifestyle choice.[86] Both the benefit amount and income thresholds for eligibility to the minimum contributory pension and to the old-age social allowance are adjusted annually to reflect changes in the cost of living. No limit to the duration of the benefits applies, but payment of the social allowance is suspended if the recipient resides outside Italy for more than 29 consecutive days, and entitlement is permanently revoked if the recipient's stay abroad exceeds one year.

In addition to the minimum contributory pension and the old-age social allowance, age-related benefit increases (*maggiorazione sociale*) may be provided, subject to strict means-testing criteria.[87] The traditional increments are fixed flat-rate amounts and depend on a dual means test, with the income thresholds adjusted annually for inflation. Starting at age 70, all recipients of a contributory pension or of the old-age social allowance can apply for the so-called "increment to the million", which is also subject to a dual means test in the case of applicants who are married.[88] The respective amounts are determined by law, and vary depending on type of benefit subject to the increment. The provisions guarantee a minimum income that is based on the level of the INPS minimum pension, which is increased by a fixed amount set in 2008. Both the components defining the guaranteed minimum income and the corresponding income thresholds are adjusted to changes in the cost of living.[89] Under certain conditions, the age requirement of 70 years for recipients of a contributory pension may be reduced by up to 5 years.[90] Additionally, pensioners receiving a

86 Cass.civ. Sez. lavoro, sent. No. 7235/2023; Cass. No. 23305/2022; Cass. No. 24954/2021.

87 "*Maggiorazione sociale*", e.g. Art. 1 of Law No. 544/1988, modified by Art. 69, para. 3 of Law No. 388/2000; Art. 38 of Law No. 448/2001, modified by Art. 5, para. 5 of Law No. 127/2007. Coverage is excluded for self-employed workers who are exclusively insured under the special scheme for atypical workers (*gestione separata*) created by the 1995 pension reform. The benefit increases (paid in 13 instalments) amount to EUR 25.83 per month as of the age of 60, and to EUR 82.64 per month as of the age of 65.

88 The increase was introduced as "*incremento al milione*", Art. 38 of Law No. 448/2001, to guarantee a minimum pension of 1 million lire at that time.

89 For recipients of a contributory INPS old-age pension, the monthly increment is not adjusted for inflation, but remains fixed at EUR 136.44, which is reduced to EUR 124 for INPS pensioners entitled to the so-called 14th pension instalment. Recipients of the old-age allowance are granted an increment that guarantees a minimum income level of up to EUR 735 in 2024.

90 Reductions of 1 year for every 5 years of insurance contributions.

contributory pension equal to or below the minimum pension amount may be eligible, under income tax law, to a small increase to the 13th monthly instalment, provided they are unable to claim tax deductions due to their low pension.[91]

cc) Minimum Income Benefits for Persons with Disabilities

Special minimum income schemes are available for individuals with a severely reduced capacity for work (of 74-99 per cent) or a full incapacity for work (100 per cent) and who are not or only insufficiently covered by the statutory pension insurance system.[92] Entitlement to this benefit is conditional on Italian citizenship and residence in Italy, while foreign nationals must possess a residence permit for work or a residence permit for at least one year.[93] The general (non-contributory) minimum income benefit for "disabled civilians" (*invalidi civili*) aged 18 to 67 years amounted to maximum EUR 333.33 per month in 2024 (13 instalments). It is only subject to the personal means test.[94] The benefit and income threshold are adjusted annually in line with inflation. Upon reaching the age of 67, the benefit is automatically converted into the old-age social allowance for senior citizens (*assegno sociale*). This conversion does not affect the applicable income threshold, provided the status of invalidity was officially recognised before the beneficiary reached statutory retirement age.

91 The benefit was introduced by Art. 70, para 7 of Law No. 388/2000. The total annual amount (EUR 155 in 2023) is subject to a dual means test (1.5 times the contributory minimum pension for a pensioner living in a single-member household; three times the minimum pension, if the pensioner is married). The 'no tax' amount for pensioners has been set at EUR 8,500 annually since 2022.

92 Law No. 118/1971 (*Nuove norme in favore dei mutilati ed invalidi civili*). For details see M. Persiani and M. d'Onghia, *Fondamenti di diritto della previdenza sociale* (3rd ed. Giappichelli 2019), pp. 342 ff. Distinct minimum income schemes continue to exist for the blind. Special benefits to cope with impairments or the loss of self-sufficiency fall outside the scope of this chapter.

93 According to the Constitutional Court's case law, benefit schemes for persons with disabilities do not have to be in possession of a qualified long-term residence permit: Corte Cost. No. 11/2009; No. 40/2013 (*pensione di inabilità*); No. 187/2010 (*assegno mensile).*

94 The income threshold is EUR 5,725 per year in case of partial invalidity, which is a criterion for eligibility to the allowance called *assegno mensile*, and EUR 19,461 in case of full incapacity for work, which is required for eligibility to the *pensione di inabilità*.

Since 2002, recipients of the pension for disabled civilians aged 60 and older have been entitled to the special "increment to the million", initially established for individuals aged 70 and above.[95] In 2020, the Constitutional Court[96] ruled that this increment must extend to all disabled civilians aged 18-59 years who are fully incapacitated for work.[97] Hence, civilian invalids and beneficiaries of the contributory invalidity pension who meet the necessary requirements are now entitled to an increased minimum income of up to EUR 735 per month in 2024 (with 13 instalments).

dd) Ordinary "Social Card"

In 2008, the legislator introduced the first electronic "Social Card" (*carta acquisti ordinaria*) as a tool for the most impoverished to meet their most basic needs, such as food, energy and healthcare.[98] The benefit, amounting to EUR 80 every two months requires inscription in the municipal register (*anagrafe municipale*); non-EU citizens must possess a long-term EU residence permit.[99] Eligibility is limited to households with children under the age of three and to senior citizens aged 65 or older, and is subject to strict economic criteria linked to assets,[100] income and the ISEE. While the ISEE threshold and income limits are adjusted annually for inflation,[101] the bene-

95 Unlike the "basic" benefit, the increase is subject to both personal and couple-based income thresholds. The annual couple-based income threshold for eligibility to an increase of EUR 402 is set at EUR 16,503 (2024).

96 Corte Cost., sent. No. 152/2020. This case was one of the rare instances in which the Court corrected the legislator by extending the personal scope of minimum social protection.

97 Art. 15 of DL 104/2020. The increase also applies to contributory invalidity pensions under Law No. 222/1984.

98 Art. 81, paras. 29-32 of DL 112/2008, converted into Law No. 133/2008 (with amendments). For the dispute on legislative competences, see Corte Cost., sent. No. 10/2010.

99 Initially, coverage was limited to Italian citizens only. Law No. 147 of 27 December 2013 extended the personal scope to EU citizens and third-country nationals in possession of a long-term residence permit.

100 Beneficiaries may be owners of only one residence and only one motor vehicle; account holder (individually or together with their spouse) of only one electricity and gas utility bill, and have less than EUR 15,000 in savings.

101 The 2024 ISEE threshold and the annual personal income threshold was EUR 8,053 for senior citizens aged 65-69 (increased to EUR 10,737 for those aged 70 and above).

fit amount remains fixed. The Card can be used in affiliated commercial establishments to purchase food, pharmaceutical and para-pharmaceutical products, and to pay utility (electricity and gas) bills.[102]

b) Additional Benefits

aa) Universal Child Benefit

In 2022, Italy introduced a new family allowance for dependent children, designed to significantly expand both child benefits and coverage.[103] The new single and universal child benefit applies to all dependent minor children (starting from the seventh month of pregnancy) until they reach adulthood. Under specific conditions, coverage is extended up to the child's 21st birthday.[104] Only parents with Italian or EU citizenship who have resided in Italy for at least two years are eligible for this benefit.[105] In addition to the residence requirement, third-country nationals must possess an open-ended permanent residence permit or have an employment contract of at least six months.

The amount of benefit depends on the household's financial situation, as assessed through the ISEE indicator, as well as on the number and age of dependent and/or disabled children. For families with an ISEE below EUR 15,000, the maximum monthly amount in 2022 was EUR 175 per child (reduced to 85 EUR for adult children under the age of 21).[106] For higher ISEE levels, the benefit amount gradually decreases, reaching a minimum of 50 EUR per child for households with an ISEE level of EUR 40,000 or more. Flat-rate supplements are provided for each dependent child beyond

102 Social Card holders are entitled to reimbursement for milk and nappy expenses, Law No. 9/2009.

103 See Legislative Decree No. 230 of 29 December 2021, implementing enabling Act (*legge delega*) No. 46/2021.

104 The age-related extension also applies to children registered as unemployed at a job centre who are actively searching for a job; or if they are volunteering for the social services (*servizio civile universale*).

105 On 25 July 2024, the EU Commission decided to refer Italy to the Court of Justice of the European Union for the restrictions on access to the child allowance benefit for foreign workers.

106 Art. 4 Legislative Decree No. 230/2021 and subsequent modifications. Due to adjustments to inflation, the 2024 amounts correspond to a maximum of EUR 199 for one child under the age of 18, and EUR 97 for each dependent child aged 18-20.

the second child[107] and in case of early motherhood. The Budget Law for 2023[108] introduced additional increases for children during their first year of life, and for children aged 1-3 years that are raised in large families with three or more dependent children. Additional supplements are provided to large households with four or more children and for families in which both parents are employed.[109]

Both the monthly benefit amounts and the ISEE thresholds are adjusted annually in line with changes in the cost of living.[110]

bb) Support for Housing Costs and Essential Services

According to Art. 47, para. 2 of the Constitution, the Republic is entrusted with the task of "promoting access to housing", including through social support measures. In practice, national social legislation has paid little, if any, attention to such support. Home ownership is traditionally widespread, and measures to facilitate access to home ownership for particular categories of individuals or families with a low income have typically been funded through annual budget laws. On the other hand, "social housing" has steadily declined over time, with social rented housing only accounting for around 5.5 per cent and private rented housing for 16.3 per cent of the national housing stock (2015).[111]

National social legislation does not provide any direct housing benefits to support rental costs for low-income tenants, with the exception of a flat-rate rent subsidy included in the ADI benefit, which has been in effect since January 2024.[112] State legislation only offers indirect support for tenants by

107 Art. 4, paras. 3 and 7 of Legislative Decree No. 230/2021.

108 Budget Law for 2023, Law No. 197/2022.

109 Art. 4, paras. 8 and 10 Legislative Decree No. 230/2021. Special supplements are provided for children with disabilities.

110 Art. 4, para. 11 Legislative Decree No. 230/2021. The initial annual threshold of EUR 15,000 for the maximum amounts was raised to EUR 17,090 as of 2024.

111 Housing Europe, *The State of Housing in the EU 2015*, (2015), p. 62. On the different meanings of "social housing" in Italy and its evolution, see N. Caruso, *Policies and Practices in Italian Welfare Housing* (Springer 2017), pp. 23 ff., 40 ff.

112 Regions, autonomous provinces or municipalities can provide direct subsidies to support vulnerable groups at the local level. For example, as of November 2023, the Autonomous Province of Bolzano provides a standard monthly allowance of up to EUR 195 to help cover rent and incidental expenses. Beneficiaries of the minimum pension who are aged 65 or older and live in a single-member household, are

way of a contribution aimed at reducing rent for low-income households.[113] Funding depends on the financial resources allocated through the annual state budget laws.[114]

Special bonuses were introduced in 2008 to ensure access to essential public services for low-income households, including the electricity and gas bonuses (initially only available for households with an ISEE below EUR 7,500).[115] In 2015, a similar measure was introduced to guarantee access to water,[116] exempting low-income households (with an ISEE below EUR 8,265 EUR or EUR 20,000 for families with at least four dependent children) from payments for the "minimum amount of water deemed vital for the satisfaction of essential needs". Another social bonus to reduce the waste tax for low-income households was introduced by the 2020 Budget Law. Since 2018, a reduced fee for telephone and internet access has been available for low-income households. Public transport fare reductions are available in some regions on the basis of varying eligibility conditions.[117] The ISEE threshold for energy bonuses was raised to EUR 15,000 in 2023, while the personal scope of application was reduced in 2024.

cc) Income Support for Training and Employment

The income support for training and employment (*supporto per la formazione e il lavoro, SFL*) is a targeted measure that was introduced on 1 September 2023 to promote the employment of persons at risk of social and labour market exclusion. The benefit is granted to those enrolled in

entitled to an increased allowance (up to EUR 240), provided their pension income does not exceed EUR 10,000 and they do not possess any other significant assets beyond their home, cf. Art. 20 of Presidential Decree of the Provincial Government No. 30 of 11 August 2000, as amended.

113 Art. 11 of Law No. 431/1998, as amended. The measure cannot be accessed directly but is granted according to a distinct municipal ranking list, with priority given to tenants whose overall annual income does not exceed twice the minimum pension of INPS, and for whom rent is at least 14 per cent of their income. The municipality is also responsible for determining the access criteria and amount.

114 The budget laws may also provide relief through special tax deductions (e.g. Budget Law for 2024).

115 Interministerial Decree of 28 December 2007 (Bonus electricity); Art. 3 of Law No. 2/2009 (Bonus gas).

116 Law No. 221/2015.

117 For an overview, see M. Raitano, M. Natali et al., *Access to essential services for low-income people. Italy* (European Commission 2020).

training programmes, vocational and reskilling courses, career guidance programmes, job placement services, and other active labour market policies.[118] It targets individuals aged 18 to 59 who are deemed to have "capacity for work" ("*occupabile*") but do not qualify for the ADI benefit. The residence and economic eligibility criteria are the same as for the ADI benefit, particularly the requirement for a low ISEE below EUR 6,000 (adjusted in line with the scale of equivalence). Applicants must follow the same activation procedures as those required for the ADI benefit, including participation in work activation initiatives.

The modest monthly flat-rate amount of EUR 350 is only provided during periods of participation in a training programme and is limited to maximum 12 monthly payments, i.e. it is not renewable.[119] Unlike the ADI benefit scheme, the SFL does not include any housing-related support.

dd) Ad-hoc Measures in Crisis Situations

During periods of increased economic pressure, the Italian State continues to rely on ad-hoc interventions to support families or individuals facing financial hardship.

Under the Budget Law for 2023[120], the government introduced a new solidarity card (*carta solidale "Dedicata a Te"*) for the purchase of basic necessities, as a special one-off benefit to help households cope with the rising cost of living. The benefit, amounting to EUR 460 in 2023 and raised to EUR 500 in 2024, is paid by INPS to households consisting of at least three members with an ISEE below EUR 15,000. The benefit is intended to cover food, fuel and public transport costs. Households already receiving another

---

118 Art. 12 DL 48/2023. For details, see F. Nardelli, 'Il supporto per la formazione e il lavoro. Prime riflessioni sullo strumento introdotto dal c.d. decreto lavoro' Il lavoro nella Giurisprudenza (2023)10, pp. 884 ff.; L. De Menech, M. Ruggiero 'Il supporto per la formazione e l'occupazione: un faro per l'inclusione e lo sviluppo professionale in Italia e in Europa' LavoroDirittiEuropa (2024) 1.

119 From 2025, the SFL scheme was slightly improved, with Law No. 207/2024 (Budget Law for 2025) introducing higher income limits, raising the benefit amount up to EUR 500 and extending the maximum duration by an additional 12 months.

120 Art. 1, para. 450, of Law No. 197 of 29 December 2022 (Budget Law for 2023), as amended by Art. 2, para. 1 (a) and (b) of Decree-Law No. 131, converted, with amendments, by Law No. 169 of 27 November 2023; Art. 1, paras. 2, 3, 4 and 5 of Law No. 213 of 30 December 2023; Interministerial Decree of 4 June 2024; INPS, Message No. 2575/2024.

form of income support are excluded from eligibility. The Budget Law for 2023 also introduced a new experimental measure called "food income" (*reddito alimentare*) aimed at assisting people living in poverty through the distribution of food items and to fight food waste.[121] Eligibility for this programme is limited to households with an ISEE below EUR 15,000.

c) Interaction of Different Benefits

The interaction between traditional and newly introduced minimum income schemes depends on the specific rules governing each scheme. Whether benefits can be combined often hinges on income thresholds and on which types of benefits are included or excluded from the income test defined by each scheme.

In general, the compatibility rules for traditional welfare pensions such as those for senior citizens and for disabled civilians are quite restrictive. Cumulation with other benefits is often not possible, with the exception of family allowances and specific disability-related supplementary benefits or provisions that are not subject to any means testing. However, entitlement to a minimum pension or to a social allowance for elderly or for civilian invalids frequently opens access to additional bonus payments and other benefits (for instance, a bonus for electricity costs and other essential services, a bonus for medical expenses, discounts for public transport, etc). The complexity increases further when considering the combinations between national minimum income measures and financial assistance provided at the local or regional level.

The interaction between minimum income schemes and other welfare benefits becomes even more complex when eligibility depends not only on means testing, but also on meeting the ISEE threshold. This is the case with the ADI scheme which regulates the compatibility of the minimum income benefit with other social benefits and services (Art. 2, para. 7 DL 48/2023), including the new single child benefit (*assegno unico e universale*)[122], other

121 Budget Law for 2023, Art. 1, para. 434 f.; Ministerial Decree (D.M.) No. 78, 26 May 2023.

122 Legislative Decree No. 230/2021. For the total amount when both benefits are combined, cf. G. Bertoluzza, 'Contrasto alla povertà: il ruolo delle Caritas nel contesto delle politiche pubbliche in mutamento', in: Caritas Italiana (ed.), *Tutto da perdere. Rapporto su povertà ed esclusione sociale in Italia* (Palumbi 2023), p. 187.

national or regional anti-poverty measures,[123] benefits for involuntary unemployment,[124] benefits granted in the form of service vouchers in lieu of social services, or cash benefits for conditions related to disability. Social benefits provided in addition to the ADI benefit may entail subsequent eligibility restrictions, given that such benefits are considered an additional income in the subsequent ISEE declaration, if ISEE regulations do not stipulate an exemption. This problem could also arise with respect to the new child allowance.

III. Analysis

1. Defining the Standard for a Dignified Life

Social legislation on minimum income benefits rarely refers explicitly to the guarantee of a life in dignity. This legislative reluctance is evident, for instance, in the minimum income guaranteed by the contributory minimum pension for former workers which should correspond to the constitutional parameter of "adequacy to the needs of life", yet the precise content of this principle remains subject to debate, given the legislator's broad discretion to define the minimum level of protection.[125] The minimum wage cannot serve as a benchmark, as Italy has still not introduced a statutory minimum wage, even though the *Corte di Cassazione* set the "constitutional" minimum wage at EUR 650 per month for full-time employment in 2023.[126] This amount falls short of guaranteeing freedom from want, and certainly

123 For example, the ordinary Social Card or the Dignity Income (*Reddito di Dignità*) introduced by Regional Law (Apulia) No. 3 of 14 March 2016, revised in 2019 to extend coverage.

124 In particular, the benefits paid under the New Social Insurance for Employment (NASPI), DIS-COLL (unemployment benefit for workers in a coordinated collaboration relationship) and other income support measures are compatible with the ADI. However, the ADI benefit is not compatible with short-time work benefits, the maternity or paternity benefit, or sick leave benefit.

125 P. Bozzao, 'Sistema pensionistico', in: *Digesto delle Discipline Privatistiche. Sezione Commerciale*, Aggiornamento IX (UTET 2022), pp. 369-395, 378 ff.

126 Cass. civ., Sez. lav., 2/10/2023, n. 27711; Cass. civ., Sez. lav., 2/10/2023, n. 27713; Cass. civ., Sez. lav., 2/10/2023, n. 27769; Cass. civ., Sez. lav., 10/10/2023, n. 28320; Cass. civ., Sez. lav., 10/10/2023, n. 28321; Cass. civ., Sez. lav., 10/10/2023, n. 28323 affirming the possibility that wages dictated by collective agreements can be disapplied by the judge and replaced with more appropriate amounts.

does not meet the standard of a free life in dignity as enshrined in Art. 36 of the Italian Constitution.[127]

The 2013 bill on the "Institution of the Citizenship Income" envisioned "a system aimed at reducing social exclusion and enhancing each individual's opportunity for development within modern society", guaranteeing "a minimum subsistence level" while also "incentivising personal and social growth". These objectives should be pursued "with respect for the dignity of the individual".[128] However, the concept of an adequate minimum level of subsistence to promote the "personal and social growth of the individual" has not been incorporated into the legislative objectives of the 2024 allowance scheme. This is evident in the technical parameters defining the amount and duration of the benefit, as well as in the restrictive access criteria, resulting from the definition of dependent family members and the excessive emphasis on family responsibility. The principles underlying the rules on "suitable work" and activation are closely linked to the workfare approach, in which dignity is assumed to be based on and derived from work. This is perceived as the key criterion for 'deserving' public support.

A key parameter for determining whether and to what extent Italian minimum protection schemes can guarantee a decent standard of living is the definition of absolute poverty thresholds developed by ISTAT for statistical purposes.[129] The ISTAT thresholds serve as an important reference point in Italian social policy debates. The absolute poverty thresholds vary depending on household size[130], age composition, geographical area and the size of the municipality of residence. The indicator is derived from a fixed basket of goods and services considered essential for a household to achieve a minimally acceptable and decent standard of living. These basic

127 M. Tufo, 'I working poor in Italia' RDSS (2020), pp. 185-214.

128 Cf. d.d.l. n. 1148/2013 per l'Istituzione del reddito di cittadinanza nonché delega al Governo per l'introduzione del salario mínimo orario" del *Movimento 5 Stelle*, cited by M. Altamiri, 'Tra assistenza e solidarietà: la liberazione dal bisogno nel recente dibattito político parlamentare', in: M. Ferraresi (ed.), *Reddito di inclusione e reddito di cittadinanza. Il contrasto allá povertà tra diritto e politica* (Giappichelli 2018), pp. 114, 116.

129 On the methodological approach to determine absolute poverty, see ISTAT, *Le statistiche dell'Istat sulla povertà in Italia, Anno 2023. Statistiche report* (2024), pp. 10 f; A. Cutillo, M. Raitano, I. Siciliani, 'Income-Based and Consumption-Based Measurement of Absolute Poverty: Insights from Italy' Social Indicators Research 161 (2022), pp. 689–710.

130 Calculated using the Carbonaro scale of equivalence (ranging from 0.6 for a single-person household to 2.4 for 7 and more household members), cf. ISTAT (n 129), p. 9.

needs include adequate food, access to housing that fits the size and needs of the household, equipped with heating, basic services, durable goods and household accessories, as well as the minimum necessities in terms of clothing, communication, information technology, mobility, education and healthcare.

This approach results in a wide range of absolute poverty thresholds: for a single adult aged between 30 to 59 years, it can range from EUR 718 (if residing in a small village in Apulia) to EUR 1,217 (if residing in a metropolitan municipality in Lombardy).[131] A second challenge in assessing whether an adequate minimum income is guaranteed lies in the complexity of the various cash and/or in-kind benefits provided at national, regional or local levels.[132]

2. Level of Benefits and Access to the ADI Scheme

a) Standard Benefit Level Compared to Absolute Poverty Thresholds

The ADI scheme implemented in 2024 maintained the same standard benefit amount for a single-person household (EUR 500 EUR or EUR 630 for those aged 67 or above) as was the case under the RdC scheme from 2019 to 2023. When combined with the rental subsidy of EUR 280 (EUR 150 for beneficiaries aged 67 and above), the maximum monthly amount of EUR 780 recalls the guaranteed minimum income benefit initially proposed by the *Movimento 5 Stelle* in 2013. This early proposal was based on the concept of a "median income" as a benchmark for determining the benefit amount, aiming to guarantee "an income in accordance with household size and the official EU monetary poverty indicator of 6/10 of the median equivalised household income". In 2013, when the bill was proposed, the median income in Italy was calculated by ISTAT to be approximately EUR 15,000, making the 60 per cent threshold equivalent to

131 According to ISTAT estimations, based on 2022 data from the Household Consumption Expenditure Survey, cf. ISTAT (n 129), p. 11.

132 On the fragmented and intermittent minimum income schemes at various levels, see C. Saraceno, D. Benassi, E. Morlicchio (n 3), pp. 123 ff. Provision is not always guaranteed as a legal entitlement, but may depend on the availability of public funds, or granted for a limited period, as in the case of the "Liberty Income" (*Reddito di Libertà*) of EUR 400 per month, paid to victims of gender-based violence for up to 12 months, cf. DL 34/2020 and DPCM of 17.12.22020, now converted into a structural benefit by the Budget Law for 2024.

EUR 750 per month.[133] Thus, a benefit level similar to the relative poverty benchmark proposed in 2013 was reintroduced a decade later under the ADI minimum income scheme to fight poverty. However, when measured against the absolute poverty thresholds calculated by ISTAT for 2022,[134] the standard basic amount of EUR 500 or EUR 630 per month (provided in 2024) falls short of ensuring a life in dignity, especially in light of the persistent rise in the cost of living.[135] Even when the rental subsidy is added, an adequate benefit level relative to the absolute poverty threshold is not guaranteed due to the absence of a realistic assessment of actual housing costs. This flat-rate increase does not take household size into account, nor does it provide support for homeowners' mortgage costs. This approach raises serious concerns about the legislator's commitment to guaranteeing an adequate minimum income that supports a life in dignity.

There is no publicly available information explaining the rationale behind the chosen benefit levels or their calculations. It is assumed that the calculations were primarily determined by the need to distribute a predetermined amount of tax revenue across a selected group of potential beneficiaries. In other words, the legislator's approach was driven by a logic of balancing the potential number of recipients with budgetary considerations, prioritizing the reduction of public spending in light of Italy's substantial public debt.[136] With the introduction of the ADI minimum income scheme, the government opted for a significant reduction in public expenditure compared to the previous RdC scheme. Further evidence of the normative aim to reduce State spending can be found in the technical provisions on the calculation and duration of benefits.

133 M. Altamiri (n 128), p. 116. Other parliamentary initiatives proposed lower minimum income levels, e.g. a monthly amount of EUR 600 as in DDL No. 1683/2013 or 500 EUR in DDL No. 1919/2015 ("Disposizioni per l'introduzione di una misura universale di contrasto alla povertà denominata reddito minimo". When the *Movimento 5 Stelle* joined the coalition government in 2018, the same amount of minimum income as proposed in 2013 (EUR 780) was used for the Citizenship Income adopted in 2019.

134 More recent absolute poverty thresholds for 2024 (updated for inflation rates) have not yet been published.

135 The annual inflation rate was 8.74 per cent in 2022, 5.9 per cent in 2023, cf. Eurostat data.

136 In 2023, Italy's public debt reached 134 per cent of the country's GDP. According to Eurostat, Italy had the highest government deficit of all EU Member States recorded in 2024.

b) Limitations to Benefits due to Calculation and Duration Rules

The ADI benefit is not an individual but a family entitlement, determined by household size. A new mechanism referred to as the scale of equivalence is used to calculate both the benefit amount and the income threshold based on six coefficients.

However, these coefficients are at the discretion of the legislator and do not accurately reflect the actual cost or burden of additional household members, like a genuine scale of equivalence would, such as the one used in the ISEE.[137] Unlike the ISEE, which applies an open-ended equivalence scale, the ADI coefficient is capped at 2.2, irrespective of family size (2.3 if a household member has a disability or lacks self-sufficiency).[138] This upper limit restricts the scheme's ability to meet a larger family's essential needs. As such, the instrument cannot be considered a genuine scale of equivalence but rather a simplified scale intended to reflect varying forms of fragility. The ADI equivalence scale excludes able-bodied individuals aged between 18 and 59, who are not caregivers as defined by the scheme[139], apart from the first household member. While this option appears to align with the legislator's decision to allocate the benefit to households with members of particular fragility, the scale of equivalence does not reflect the actual composition of the family unit, underscoring the legislator's refusal to provide adequate means of subsistence. Moreover, the ADI scale of equivalence paradoxically reduces the weighting of minors in a regressive manner,[140] with a negative impact on large families. Based on these

137 The ISEE scale of equivalence applies the following parameters: 1 for a single-person household, 1.57 for 2 household members, 2.04 for 3 household members, 2.46 for 4 household members, 2.85 for five household members, and an additional 0.35 for any subsequent household members. These parameters are increased for larger households (0.2 for families with 3 children, 0.35 for those with 4 children, 0.5 for households with 5 children; 0.2 for families with children under the age of 18, and which may reach 0.3 under specific conditions. See F. Pesaresi (ed.), *Il nuovo ISEE e i servizi sociali* (Maggioli 2015), p. 44 f.

138 The coefficient cap is slightly higher than under the Citizenship Income scheme.

139 Qualifying caregivers are allocated a coefficient of 0.4, persons with a serious distress a coefficient of 0.3.

140 0.15 for the first and second child under 18, further reduced to 0.10 for any subsequent child, while dependent children aged 18-21 years are excluded. By way of comparison, the modified OECD equivalence scale assigns a coefficient of 1 to the first household member, 0.5 for any additional member aged 14 or older, and 0.3 for each child under the age of 14.

findings, it can be concluded that the calculation mechanism falls short of covering the true costs of each additional household member, and is fraught with numerous paradoxes and inequities.[141] Due to contradictory interactions between exclusions and coefficients, the new parameters defining which household members 'count' and to what extent, ultimately undermine the provision of adequate minimum income protection for many disadvantaged households.[142]

The provisions governing the duration of ADI benefits also undermine adequate minimum income protection. Benefits are granted for an initial 18-month period, but before they can be renewed for an additional 12 months—and provided the eligibility criteria continue to be met, a one-month suspension period applies, regardless of whether hardship continues to persist. This rule is especially challenging for pensioners and diverges from the generally unlimited duration of minimum income benefits typically available to the elderly or individuals with a disability who are fully incapacitated for work. The suspension of payments reveals that the State does not ensure continuous minimum income protection throughout the entire period of economic hardship.

c) Relevant Family Units and Economic Requirements

The primary reason for exclusion from benefit eligibility under the ADI scheme lies in its new classification criteria, which effectively exclude all households that are not classified as "fragile". According to some estimates,

141 For instance, a coefficient of 1.7 for a couple with two children, if one of them is under the age of 3, and the other is under the age of 18, will amount to a minimum monthly income of up to EUR 850. If both children are between 3 and 18, the coefficient drops to 1.3, and the monthly income will be EUR 650. If the couple has three children under the age of 18, the coefficient is increased to 1.8, amounting to a monthly income of EUR 900. For a couple with one child over the age of 3 and one adult child, the coefficient reduces to 1.15, and the monthly income is EUR 575.

142 Under the ADI benefit regime, adult family members who are neither severely disabled, over the age of 60, nor have care responsibilities for a child under the age of 3 are fully excluded from the coefficients used to calculate whether the household's disposable income falls below (and if, to what extent) the threshold for benefit eligibility. On the impact of these rules, see C. Saraceno, 'Così il nuovo reddito ha punito i più fragili' La Stampa (6 February 2024).

this change in criteria affects over 1/3 of former RdC recipients.[143] The ADI benefit scheme not only requires a condition of personal "fragility" to be met, but ties eligibility to the benefit to the presence of "fragile" members in the household.[144] The criteria "fragility" echoes earlier welfare schemes related to specific indicators such as age, disability, or the presence of children under the age of three. The ADI scheme introduces additional eligibility criteria based on the presence of household members classified as belonging to the group of severely, non-economically disadvantaged persons. This category was added to mitigate the impact of the new selection criteria that would have significantly reduced the protection of those with a reduced capacity for work.

In addition, a set of other economic and non-economic eligibility criteria may result in the exclusion of both impoverished family units and individuals from adequate minimum income protection. As regards means testing, the income thresholds applicable to households are very low at EUR 6,000 per year (500 EUR per month), with a higher income threshold only applicable if all household members are at least 67 years old (statutory retirement age in 2024). Notably, the income threshold is not higher if the household resides in rented accommodation (notwithstanding entitlement to a rental supplement in case all relevant conditions are met). This exclusion is problematic, as it risks excluding a large number of households in genuine need of support.[145] Asset testing is also more stringent than under the RdC benefit scheme, with a new cap on the home's value, which is now set at EUR 150,000, as well as an extension of the scope of durable goods[146] that are excluded from the calculation for eligibility for the ADI benefit.

Another factor limiting access to minimum income protection lies in the definition of the relevant family unit, particularly in the case of unmarried and childless single adults who do not live with their parents. If such individuals have no income of their own, they are considered financially dependent on their parents and thus as part of their parents' household

143 A. Sartori, 'Misure di inclusione sociale e lavorativa dopo il reddito di cittadinanza. Back to the future or to the past?' RDSS (2023), p. 741, 751.

144 The Parliamentary Budget Office estimated that these new eligibility criteria would deprive 42 per cent of all families benefitting from the RdC from access to the ADI benefit.

145 Law No. 207/2024 (Budget Law for 2025) introduced higher income limits (including for rental/ housing) which reduced economic access restrictions to the scheme from 2025.

146 Such as recently acquired vehicles above a certain engine capacity.

for the purposes of calculating the ISEE and all other economic eligibility requirements, i.e. even if they have been living in their own household for many years.[147] As a result, the applications of such individuals for the ADI benefit often fail the statutory means test, especially if the applicant's parents receive a pension and are homeowners.

Another factor that has the potential of restricting access to benefits (or reducing their amount) is the narrow definition of individuals who face a "serious disadvantage". While households with such a member are, in principle, eligible for the ADI benefit, access may still be denied due to the additional condition that the individual facing serious disadvantage must be part of a specific social programme. This ties eligibility not to the condition of need itself, but to the availability or the local administration's discretion to establish and provide the required programmes.[148] This condition, set out in the Ministry's guidelines, withdraws protection from households in need if the relevant programme ends or is discontinued due to lack of funding. The narrowly defined term 'caregiver', which is restricted to adults who are caring for a child under the age of three or who have parental responsibilities for at least three children under the age of 18 or for disabled family members or other family members in need of care, may also lead to reductions in the benefit amount: even if caregiving responsibilities continue once the child has reached the age of three, the legally defined eligibility criteria are no longer being met and the individual with the parental responsibilities is therefore no longer considered a 'caregiver' in the household composition.

---

147 Under these circumstances, the relevant household is defined in accordance with Art. 3, para. 5 of DPCM No. 159/2013, a provision adopted in 2013 to prevent individuals from claiming exemptions from university fees, even if they were in fact being supported by their parents, or to avoid paying municipal real estate tax (*Imposta comunale sugli immobili, ICI*) on a second home. This rule was not applied under the RdC regime, in an effort to promote the autonomy of young people and adults more generally. However, under the ADI scheme, adults of advanced age who are not legally entitled to parental maintenance are classified as "dependent members" of the parental household.

148 G. Bronzini (n 46).

d) Restrictions Related to Sanctions and the Use of Benefits

A lack of protection may also result from the harsh sanction regime governing the ADI scheme, which provides for a suspension or cancellation of ADI benefits. If even just one household member fails to comply with the activation obligations, the entire household forfeits eligibility to the ADI benefit, highlighting the household's collective responsibility for the action of all its members.[149] In this case, a new application can only be submitted six months after the date of revocation.[150] This sanction applies when a household member fails to attend appointments with the social services without a justified reason. Even in the absence of a summons, beneficiaries are required to report to social services within the legally established timeframe. Failure to do so results in a suspension of the benefit, which may, however, be reinstated retroactively. While the temporary suspension of benefits is less severe than a cancelation of access to adequate means of subsistence, it nevertheless reflects the same principle of holding the entire household collectively accountable for the actions of all its individual members.

Compared to recipients of unemployment benefits, ADI beneficiaries are subject to stricter work conditionality, particularly in terms of the definition of "suitable" job offers for those who have capacity for work (Art. 9). They must accept any job offer that provides 1) an employment contract of indefinite duration anywhere within the national territory, without restrictions on distance; 2) a full-time or part-time contract amounting to at least 60 per cent of regular working hours; 3) an employment contract with a remuneration that is not below the minimum levels established by a collective agreement; 4) a fixed-term employment contract (including those offered through a temporary work agency), if the workplace is located within 80 km of the beneficiary's residence or is reachable within 120 minutes by public transport. The first (unjustified) refusal of such a job offer results in the loss of the ADI benefit. This strict conditionality is only attenuated for households with children under the age of 14. In this case, the obligation to accept low-paid jobs anywhere in the country is limited to positions located within 80 km of the place of residence or reachable withing 120 minutes by

149 Art. 8, para. 6 DL 48/2023; Decree of the Ministry of Labour, No. 156 of 15/12/2023. Cf. S. Caffio (n 23), p. 232.

150 Art. 8, para. 9 of DL 48/2023.

public transport. Even this reduced condition may conflict with caregiving duties.

The new rules exacerbate the workfare logic not only by increasing mobility demands and extending the maximum commuting time to 120 minutes (up from 100 minutes under the previous rules), but more significantly by failing to define quality criteria, such as the minimum duration of fixed-term employment contracts and the lack of any proportionality between the ADI benefit and the minimum salary offered. Moreover, the beneficiary's "educational and training experiences and previous professional competences" are likely to be sidelined, as they are inevitably subordinated to "the job offers, training courses, projects of public utility, internships and other activation measures available."[151]

Ultimately, the reform's conditionality requirements fail to take the long-lasting dysfunctions and structural limitations of the employment service system into account. As employment services fall under regional jurisdiction, territorial disparities in terms of efficiency and outcomes continue to persist. The preferred instrument for promoting employment at the national level has been State-funded relief in the level of social insurance contributions by employers instead of providing training and reskilling or upskilling measures This "institutional" shortfall is most pronounced in regions with high unemployment rates and limited labour demand, namely in regions where support for an adequate minimum income and social inclusion is most urgently needed.

In addition to sanctions for non-compliance with activation requirements,[152] the ADI scheme imposes the (unusual) requirement that beneficiaries must not have been convicted of any criminal offence, including fraudulent declarations or failure to provide required information. Moreover, beneficiaries who have been sentenced to a prison term of at least one year are barred from access to ADI benefits for ten years.[153] This rule reflects the normative assumption that such individuals are in a self-inflicted situation, which seems to justify the State's refusal to assume responsibility for providing minimum income protection, leaving former prisoners

---

151 For a critical analysis of conditionality provisions, see F. De Michiel, 'Le misure di contrasto alla povertà nel c.d. decreto lavoro' LavoroDirittiEuropa (2024) 1; G. Bronzini (n 46).

152 Art. 8, para. 9 of DL 48/2023: if benefits are withdrawn due to less serious offences, the recipient is not allowed to submit a new application before six months have elapsed.

153 Art. 8, para. 3 of DL 48/2023.

dependent on charity or family support.[154] This denial of State support constitutes a secondary sanction beyond the criminal sentence itself, and is rooted in the notion of "undeservingness", which stands at odds with the principle of human dignity.

The human dignity of minimum income benefit recipients is not only undermined by inadequate benefit amounts, but also by the modalities linked to the payment of benefits, particularly through public control mechanisms that limit personal autonomy in spending decisions. The ADI scheme prohibits recipients from making online purchases or to purchase goods outside Italy, a restriction that also applies to the ordinary Social Card scheme. Such restrictions are at odds with the principle of financial autonomy as an element of dignity.

The reform signals a re-interpretation of social citizenship grounded in mutual obligations, marked by a strong punitive logic and a tendency to shift responsibility for income security back to family solidarity.[155] The emphasis lies primarily on the objective of preventing opportunistic or fraudulent behaviour and avoiding so-called 'poverty traps'. However, the risks that arise from shortcomings in employment services, public activation measures,[156] or the lack of decent working conditions are being shifted onto economically disadvantaged individuals and their families. Several patterns of family responsibility are emerging: on the one hand, normative assumptions are holding families accountable for the actions of each household

---

154 A final conviction of the beneficiary for a non-culpable offence carrying a prison sentence of at least one year, as well as the imposition of a preventive measure by judicial authorities, leads to the automatic and immediate forfeiture of the benefit. The beneficiary is also required to repay any unduly received benefit amounts. The automatic forfeiture applies irrespective of the nature of the offence committed. The ADI benefit is suspended in case of violation of family support obligations (Art. 570 of the Criminal Code) and in case of violation of compliance with a minor's compulsory school attendance until regular school attendance resumes. On the political abuse of criminal law and exemplary, disproportionate penalties (already stipulated in the RdC regime), cf. G. Picco, 'L'apparato sanzionatorio nel "Decreto Lavoro"' Il lavoro nella Giurisprudenza (2023)8-9, pp. 792 ff.

155 This rationale was already incorporated in the RdC scheme. See the analysis of M. D'Onghia, 'Il Reddito di Cittadinanza un anno dopo' Labor. Il lavoro nel diritto (2020)1, pp. 27, 42 ff.

156 On critical elements of Italian employment services, cf. P. Bozzao, 'Politiche attive per l'occupazione e Centri per l'impiego', in: P. Curzio (ed.) *Diritto del lavoro contemporaneo. Questioni e tendenze* (Cacucci 2019), p. 171; P. Bozzao, 'Il reddito di cittadinanza. Un primo bilancio a tre anni dal suo avvio', in: CNEL (ed.), *XXIV Rapporto mercato del lavoro e contrattazione collettiva* (2022), pp. 243, 251 f.

member and for reconciling activation requirements with caregiving duties for children over the age of three. On the other hand, the system reflects normative assumptions associated with traditional family structures, only recognising caregivers as relevant household members if they are providing care for a child under the age of three, for at least three children, or for other family members classified as 'fragile', reflecting traditional family structures as a substitute for comprehensive public support.

3. Minimum Income Levels Guaranteed by "Traditional Schemes"

In comparison to the ADI benefit, traditional minimum income schemes introduced in the previous century offered a more adequate level of protection, particularly for beneficiaries aged 70 and older. The combination of the 'increment to the million' and the traditional contributory and non-contributory minimum pensions provide up to EUR 735 per month (2024), which with 13 monthly payments brings income levels close to the absolute poverty threshold. However, younger beneficiaries of contributory pensions and even more so beneficiaries of non-contributory old-age pensions, may not receive an adequate amount of benefits that would allow for a life in dignity across all regions of the country. In metropolitan areas, in particular, the guaranteed minimum amount may remain below the absolute poverty threshold, even when accounting for the 13th monthly instalment and the modest "*maggiorazione sociale*" supplement.

The special minimum income scheme targeting disabled civilians without any capacity for work traditionally provided only modest support to cover their basic needs. This form of support increased substantially when social legislation extended eligibility for the "increment to the million", initially reserved for beneficiaries of an old-age pension aged 70 and older, to recipients of the civil invalidity pension aged 60 and above in 2002, and subsequently to those aged 18 and older in 2020. In contrast, the minimum income benefit for impoverished, disabled individuals with a partial, albeit significantly reduced, capacity for work remains very modest and must be deemed inadequate to ensure a life in dignity.

The economic eligibility criteria for accessing various minimum income schemes reveal substantial disparities arising from fragmented social legislation and different approaches to means testing. While some schemes only apply income tests with varying thresholds, they do not consider movable or immovable assets and do not require an ISEE declaration: not surprisingly, the most generous access rules apply to the guaranteed minimum income scheme for contributory old-age pensioners, as well as to recipients of a minimum pensions for invalids and who are fully incapacitated for work.

Stricter means-testing rules apply to the non-contributory minimum pension (*assegno sociale*). However, movable or immovable assets are excluded from the means test. The use of comparatively more lenient means tests — often limited to individual or partner-related income, and in some cases to personal income only, without considering any potential assets — reflects a traditional notion of presumed 'deservingness', associated with stronger State responsibility.

Finally, the benefit levels provided by the "Social Card" introduced in 2008, along with the corresponding economic eligibility requirements, are insufficient to guarantee a life in dignity. The scheme is designed to only cover the most basic needs such as food, energy and healthcare. In addition to meeting the ISEE threshold, beneficiaries must also fulfil additional means-testing criteria such as limits to household income and financial assets, albeit excluding durable goods as in case of the ADI scheme.

4. Indexation Rules

An adequate minimum income can only be sustained over time if indexation rules ensure protection against inflation. Mechanisms that preserve the purchasing power of benefits are a fundamental component of adequate subsistence support, but not all minimum income schemes provide such safeguards.

Only the "traditional" minimum income schemes for old age or for reduced capacity for work provide automatic annual adjustments to benefit levels (and income thresholds). These adjustments are based on changes in the Consumer Price Index as calculated by ISTAT for the preceding calendar year. This mechanism is also applied to statutory pensions and the universal child benefit. In periods of high inflation, the legislator supplements regular adjustments with special ad-hoc corrections or deviations from the regular schedule.[157] Increases in old-age pensions and those receiving an invalidity pension for full incapacity for work serve as an additional

157 For example, the Budget Law for 2023 introduced a "*bonus perequativo*" of 2.7 per cent on the minimum pension. In 2024, the application of this bonus increased the guaranteed contributory minimum pension of EUR 599 by EUR 16 to a total of EUR 615 (with 13 payments).

mechanism for raising minimum income levels and ensuring a decent standard of living.

Conversely, the new ADI and the ordinary Social Card schemes do not include a mechanism for regular benefit adjustment, resulting in an erosion of their original value over time. The income threshold of the ADI scheme is not indexed to inflation either, resulting in a reduction of the number of potential beneficiaries. Individuals may be excluded from the benefit scheme despite the fact that their subsistence needs are not met. This risk is not present in the Social Card scheme, as its income threshold is subject to annual adjustment. The absence of regular adjustment mechanisms only confirms the ambiguity surrounding minimum income protection and the reluctance to recognize it as a responsibility of the State. Additional protection through ad-hoc interventions is often left to the discretion of the legislator, e.g. through one-off bonus payments for specific needs (e.g. energy costs). In this respect, access to adequate minimum income is not guaranteed as a structural element within the legal framework, but depends on the government's discretion to allocate public resources through annual budget laws.

5. Residence-Related Conditions

Non-economic eligibility criteria are frequently used as a selection mechanism to control public expenditure by limiting access to a last-resort safety net at the expense of economically disadvantaged individuals and households. One salient feature of Italy's minimum income schemes is the restricted access for foreign nationals. This exclusionary approach has also been taken by the ADI minimum income scheme under DL 48/2023, and excludes many immigrant families from minimum income protection, despite the reduction in the duration of residence requirement.

Many minimum income schemes require beneficiaries to be in possession of a long-term residence permit and extended residency conditions as proof of rootedness in Italy, but they also effectively limit access as an indirect exclusion mechanism.

Traditional minimum income guarantees in contributory schemes and minimum income protection for disabled civilians without work capacity do not require prolonged legal residence as an eligibility criterion. However, since 2009, the non-contributory social allowance for the elderly has included a residence requirement of ten years (with at least the last two years being continuous). While the Constitutional Court has declared several regional welfare provisions with similar residence requirements as unconstitutional, it upheld the ten-year residence requirement for access to the *assegno sociale*.[158] It found that social allowance represents "support from the community in which (the beneficiaries) have worked (...), and also reflects a solidaristic recognition of their dutiful contribution to the material or spiritual progress of society". The Court's argument is based on a logic of corrispectivity, which is typically not applied to welfare benefits for individuals who lack the means of subsistence. The Italian government has reduced the residence requirement for the ADI scheme to five years, aligning it more closely with the minimum residency period required to obtain a long-term (permanent) residence permit under EU law. Despite this relaxation, many migrant families (in particular third-country nationals) remain excluded from access to minimum income protection.

A notable problem is the requirement to possess a qualified long-term residence permit as a condition for access to minimum income benefits. This requirement applies to the old-age social allowance, the ordinary Social Card and the ADI scheme. In contrast, beneficiaries of the welfare pension for disabled civilians without work capacity (and other welfare benefits for disabled persons) are exempt from this stricter requirement; they only need to have been in possession of a residence permit for at least one year.[159]

The requirement to have been in possession of a qualified residence permit to be eligible for non-invalidity-based guaranteed minimum income benefits is a contentious issue. While the Constitutional Court upheld the constitutionality of this requirement in relation to the RdC benefit,[160] it also reprimanded the legislature to fulfil its duty "of implementing the constitutional principles set out in Articles 2, 3 and 38(1) to guarantee the

158 Corte Cost., sent. No. 50/2019 found that the restrictive residence clause was in conformity with Art. 3 of the Constitution. In April 2023, the Court of Cassation again questioned the constitutional legitimacy of the residence requirement citing a violation of EU law, supported by recent case law of the European Court of Justice (C-350/2020 of 2/09/2021).

159 Corte Cost., sent. No. 22/2015, and INPS, Message No. 6456 of 20 October 2015. See also INPS Message No. 1268 of 3 April 2023, specifying that the accrual of the 10-year residency requirement is interrupted in the event of the individual's absence from Italian territory for a period equal to or exceeding six consecutive months or for a total of ten months within a five-year period. Exceptions to this interruption apply for serious and proven reasons.

160 Corte Cost., sent. No. 19/2022.

right of every individual to a life in dignity and a minimum level of subsistence". However, the ADI scheme has replicated the same residence permit requirement. This raises questions about conformity with EU law, though a judgment in a preliminary ruling by the European Court of Justice on this matter is still pending.[161]

IV. Concluding Remarks

With the adoption of DL 48/2023, Italy's minimum income policy has suffered a serious setback. The reform divides potential beneficiaries of minimum income support into two groups: i) those eligible for the ADI benefit, and ii) those who can only access the new "Support for Training and Work" benefit, which does not qualify as a minimum income benefit. This distinction, based on an actual or presumed capacity for work, places many households and individuals at risk of losing their right to a life in dignity. The new eligibility criteria for access to the minimum income benefit are linked to specific "fragilities" within the family unit. The ADI scheme not only establishes yet another categorical benefit that is associated with a specific classification, it also signals a shift away from State responsibility towards increased reliance on the family.

The analysis of the protective functions of "traditional" and newly introduced categorical schemes reveals significant differences in the State's guarantee of an adequate minimum income for a life in dignity. Notable disparities exist in the guaranteed benefit amounts for different population groups, the criteria used to determine their resource insufficiency, the duration of benefits, and the mechanisms for benefit re-adjustment.

Traditional minimum income schemes for the elderly and the disabled civilians provide benefit levels that, in some cases, ensure a decent standard of living. The degree of adequacy varies depending on factors such as age-related increases in protection, the provision of 13 (or even 14) monthly instalments per year, automatic benefit adjustments, and more generous income thresholds. Means testing excludes assets but is limited to personal and/or couple-based income thresholds. Constitutional Court case law has contributed to enhancing the level of protection, particularly for disabled civilians who are fully incapacitated for work. Other groups of disabled civilians (e.g. those with only a partially reduced capacity for work) do not

161 European Commission, Infringement Case No. INFR (2022) 4113.

enjoy the same level of minimum income protection, despite the legislator's special attention to the need of disability-related protection in DL 48/2023.

As regards traditional minimum income schemes for the elderly and disabled persons, two problems are cause for concern regarding their ability to ensure a decent standard of living for the target population in the future. The first problem concerns the adequacy of guaranteed minimum contributory pensions, when the transitional phasing-out period of the INPS minimum pension scheme ends. Without any changes, future old-age pensioners with a small pension will need to rely on the social allowance for the elderly, which imposes extended residence requirements, or on the ADI benefit scheme, which has less strict residence conditions but applies more stringent economic criteria and provides lower benefit amounts. This situation falls short of the constitutional commitment to enhanced worker protection under Art. 38, para. 2 of the Constitution. The second problem relates to the extensive residence requirements imposed by the social allowance for the elderly.[162]

The ADI scheme has a drastically limited scope of application, targeting only households that consist of members of a specific age, with specific health or social conditions. Compared to the previous minimum income scheme, its standards of protection have been reduced, resulting in substantial income losses for those in the lowest income decile. Moreover, the exclusion of family members deemed capable of participating in the labour market (or in public utility activities) from minimum income protection risks undermining the right to a decent standard of living for many individuals with a very low or no income.

From a broader perspective, the shift towards a contractual interpretation of the right to minimum income is particularly striking. This approach prioritises strict conditionality and punitive measures, framing support as contingent on a *quid pro quo* logic, whereby individuals facing economic hardship must meet specific obligations to access the resources they need for subsistence. The enhanced workfare approach echoes the rationale of 18th-century poor laws, and draws a line of continuity in the historical tendency to view an individual's condition of poverty with suspicion, to punish deviant attitudes, and exclude "outsiders". As in the past, the poor are held personally accountable for their condition, while the structural causes of poverty continue to be disregarded. Activation is treated as a form of total mobilisation of individuals, creating strong social unease and

162 See above (n 83).

further deepening marginalisation. Substantial cuts in public spending on minimum income protection call into question the State's responsibility to guarantee a life in dignity, not only for a narrowly defined group of "deserving poor", but for all individuals in need.

Constitutional Change and Minimum Social Protection in Norway

Anika Seemann and Henriette Sinding Aasen

I. Introduction

Norway has one of the most developed welfare states in the world, belonging to the Social Democratic 'Nordic' welfare state family typically associated with universalism, financing through taxation, high levels of redistribution and generous welfare support. The universal and generous provisions of the Norwegian welfare state typically ensure more than a mere minimum of social protection. At the same time, the Norwegian welfare state is built on an assumption of active labour market participation, bringing all those who *can* contribute into a collective of taxpayers subject to high levels of taxation.

The Norwegian welfare state's overall generosity makes the question of how the 'minimum' for a 'life in dignity' is defined a fascinating one. Focusing on minimum social protection in Norway can provide important insights into the normative foundations of the Norwegian welfare state, and cast light on how questions of poverty, inclusion and minimum protection are negotiated in wealthy societies. Despite regulations to combat social inequality, poverty is not uncommon in Norway. According to the Norwegian Statistical Bureau, 10,9 per cent of the population are at risk of poverty, with a disposable income of less than sixty per cent of the national median.[1] The Committee on Economic, Social and Cultural Rights has expressed concern about the 'continued increase in the incidence of poverty, particularly among children, as a result of the increase in income inequality'.[2] Lack of adequate housing and homelessness among vulnerable groups are also highlighted.[3] English-language analyses of the Norwegian welfare state have typically focussed on the overall system of welfare schemes and their comparative generosity. The question of how the Norwegian welfare state defines the *minimum* which an individual should have access to, by contrast, has so far not been explored in much detail.

This chapter aims to provide an understanding of the idea of 'minimum social protection' in the Norwegian welfare state, focusing in particular on the relationship between the country's Constitution (*Grunnloven*) and ordinary social law. Originally, Norway's Constitution – adopted in 1814 and the second-oldest existing constitution in the world – had enshrined only some core liberties and political rights. While select human rights were added to the Constitution throughout the 20th century, it continued to lack the type of full human rights catalogue typically included in 20th century European constitutions, in particular those of the post-1945 era. This changed in 2014, when, on the occasion of its 200th anniversary, the Constitution's human rights catalogue was expanded and, among the addition of other rights, for the first time came to include a number of social rights. Most significantly in the context of this chapter, a provision was added that includes the right to a minimum level of subsistence (§ 110).[4] This provision will form a central focus of this chapter, analysing the arguments for including it in the Constitution, and asking what role this provision plays in practice.

In addition, the chapter discusses how social assistance is regulated at the ordinary social law level. A particular focus will be on how the concept of minimum social protection is understood and determined in the legal bases for social assistance, and what types of benefits and benefit levels the individual schemes provide in practice. Furthermore, the analysis extends

1 A. Hattrem, Statistisk Sentralbyrå, 'Hvor mange er fattige i Norge' (15 April 2024), <https://www.ssb.no/inntekt-og-forbruk/inntekt-og-formue/artikler/hvor-mange-er-fattige-i-norge> accessed 30.8.2024.
2 Concluding observations on the sixth periodic report of Norway (2020) (E/C.12/NOR/CO/6), para. 32.
3 Ibid. para. 34.
4 § 110 Grunnloven.

to how the social assistance schemes interact with the social insurance schemes of the Norwegian National Insurance System (*Folketrygden*). The chapter in particular highlights the differences in how social assistance and the regular social insurance schemes are regulated and how benefit levels are determined. Whereas social insurance schemes follow a set calculation based on the figure "G" (determined once yearly by the Government), there is some more flexibility in setting benefit levels for social assistance in that municipalities have discretion in determining the precise amount an individual receives. This can be problematic from the perspective of legal certainty and equality. However, as this contribution shows, the municipalities receive very detailed guidelines from the Ministry of Labour and Social Affairs, which in turns limit strong variations in the exercise of discretion.

In the conclusion, the chapter offers some reflections on the future relationship between the constitutional guarantee for minimum social protection and the practical application of social law.

II. Overview – The Norwegian Constitution and the Social Benefit System

1. Normative Background

a) Historical Development – The 1814 Constitution and the Norwegian Welfare State

The adoption of the 1814 Norwegian Constitution long precedes the establishment of the country's modern welfare state.[5] When the Constitution was promulgated in Eidsvoll, just outside Kristiania (now Oslo) on 17 May 1814, this occurred in a context in which social questions had yet to become a political priority. Norway's Constitution played a central role in the formation of its nationhood and ambitions for independence from both Denmark and Sweden. For this reason, the Constitution was centred around the institutions of the state, Norwegian sovereignty and the traditional freedom rights of the nineteenth century. This is reflected in the structure of the Constitution, in which the first chapters concerned the form of state and the division of powers between the different organs of the state. As was the case with most Constitutions adopted in the nineteenth century, human

5 For an English-language introduction to Norwegian constitutional law, see: M. Langford and B. K. Berge, '*Norway's Constitution in a Comparative Perspective*' Oslo Law Review 6 (2019) 3, pp. 198-228.

rights – or 'citizen rights' (*borgerrettigheter*), as they were called in the Constitution – were placed further towards the end of the document, and they tended to focus on liberal freedoms. In the case of the 1814 Norwegian Constitution, the rights catalogue was found in Chapter E, running from § 96 to § 105, although this chapter also contained a number of unrelated provisions. These paragraphs were left virtually untouched until the 2014 anniversary.

The Norwegian welfare state developed without the Constitution having any direct influence. The poor relief system was retained for the remainder of the nineteenth century. In 1845, Norway adopted the first national poor relief act.[6] This was followed by further poor laws in 1863 and 1900. Around the turn of the century, Norway also adopted its first more encompassing social protection systems, including a set of work accidents schemes (1908, 1911 and 1915), health insurance (1909) and unemployment insurance (1906).[7] Throughout the twentieth century, Norway developed an expansive welfare state of the classical 'Nordic' type – with large welfare bureaucracies, generous benefit levels, access based on residency and employment/work, and a high degree of taxation and redistribution. While its social policy measures had initially, at least to some extent, been influenced by the insurance schemes found in continental Europe, following the Second World War they became more universalist and taxation became the main financing mechanism. Most significantly, the Scandinavian schemes were never limited to industrial workers, but almost from the outset included farmers as well.[8] During this time of expansion, no relevant provisions in the Constitution were invoked in advocating for an expansion of the welfare state. Nevertheless, one can argue that there was a more indirect influence of the Constitution in that the principles of equality and human

6 A.L. Seip, *Sosialhjelpstaten blir til – norsk sosialpolitikk 1740-1920* (Oslo 1984), pp. 52-64.

7 Ibid., pp. 87-106. Note that the elements of redistribution and universalism were important early on in Norwegian social policy discourses, which is why the schemes were renamed 'trygd' ('protection') rather than continuing with the term 'insurance', which had been used initially: A. Hatland, *De sosiale rettighetenes frammarsj gjennom 200 år*, p. 96.

8 S. Kuhnle and N. Kildal, 'Velferdsstatens idégrunnlag i perspektiv', in: A. Hatland, S. Kuhnle, T.I. Romøren (eds.), *Den norske velferdssstaten* (Oslo 2011), pp. 15-39, 17.

dignity enshrined in the Constitution led to a form of thinking that furthered the advancement of social policy.[9]

With the adoption of the Social Insurance Act (*Folketrygdloven*) in 1966, the various social security schemes with individual entitlements in place at the time were integrated into one act of law.[10] A little later, the expansion of the welfare state was further bolstered by the discovery of oil off the Norwegian West coast. Over the following decades, the formerly agrarian country would become one of the wealthiest states per capita in the world. The oil reserves could cushion any fluctuations in welfare expenditure. Throughout this period, the Constitution again did not play a decisive role in shaping the development of the welfare state. A new labour-market related provision was added to the Constitution in 1954 (the obligation of the State to create the conditions for every capable individual to provide for themselves through labour, § 110, in part a response to the high unemployment rates of the interwar period), but that remained one of the few obligations on the state to be added to the Constitution until later in the twentieth century. The Constitution was, of course, of central symbolic value in the country. It was also always more than a political document of symbolic significance. The Norwegian Supreme Court has the right and duty to review the constitutionality of legislation and other measures, a power which was long recognised in the customary law of the country and also referenced in a series of laws.[11] Since 2015, the right and obligation of courts to perform constitutional review has been laid down in § 89 of the Constitution. Over the decades, the courts have interpreted the provisions of the constitution further, giving them new contours and adapting them to societal changes. However, the Supreme Court overall uses this power restrictively, not taking on a role in shaping laws and policies that for example the German Federal Constitutional Court does. Given the comparative absence of social rights and other rights directly related to the welfare state,

9 H. S. Aasen, 'Fra rettsstat til velferdsstat: Grunnloven og den moderne samfunnskontrakten', in: H. S. Aasen and N. Kildal (eds.), *Grunnloven og velferdsstaten* (2014), pp. 183-197, 187-188. Note that while the term "human dignity" was not directly included in the Constitution, it was generally agreed to have underlain the Constitution, at least for those parts of the population covered by its human rights catalogue.

10 Lov 17. juni 1966 nr. 12 om folketrygd; Ø. Bjørnson and I. E. Haavet, *Langsomt ble landet et velferdssamfunn – Trygdens historie 1894 – 1994* (Oslo 1994), p. 291; NOU 1990:20 Forenklet folketrygdlov, Chapter 0.1.6.

11 Rt. 1976 s. 1; it was first referred to in the so-called Plenumsloven of 1926, E. Sandmo, *Siste Ord – Høgsterett i norsk historie 1814-1965, Bind II, 1905-1965* (Oslo 2006), p 52.

there was less of a role to play for the Constitution in this domain than in other areas, such as criminal law.

Towards the end of the twentieth century, political figures began to call for reforms of the Constitution, which they argued was beginning to seem out of step with the social and political realities that defined contemporary Norwegian society. It was not surprising that, given its age and the specific context in which it was adopted, it did not fully reflect developments in modern society. In comparison to other countries' more modern constitutions, especially those adopted in the wake of the Second World War and decolonialisation, the Norwegian Constitution began to seem dated. For this reason, politicians made repeated calls to change the Constitution. Over the years, there was a "steady stream" of reform proposals for the constitution to better reflect the post-war values of the Norwegian state.[12] Some rights indeed were added, such as the right to freedom of religion on the 150th anniversary of the Constitution in 1964, and a right protecting the cultural rights of the Sami in 1988.[13] At the same time, it was not considered highly problematic from a *legal* perspective that the Constitution did not encompass many of the rights and principles upon which Norwegian society functioned. Norway was already a signatory to a long list of international conventions, including the UN Human Rights treaties and the European Convention on Human Rights, and recognised as legally binding in § 110c of the Constitution (§ 92 after the 2014 reform). The European convention and the two UN conventions on economic, social and cultural rights, and civil and political rights, were incorporated into the domestic legal order by the Human Rights Act[14] in 1999. The convention on the rights of the child, and the convention on the elimination of all forms of discrimination against women, were later included in the Human Rights Act. This Act granted the selected conventions precedence over domestic law in case of a conflict between international law and domestic regulations.

To sum up, the relationship between the Norwegian Constitution and the development of its welfare state was not one in which constitutional

12 Stortinget, Dokument 16 (2011-2012), Rapport fra Menneskerettighetsutvalget om menneskerettigheter i Grunnloven (19 December 2011), p. 49. See also: T. Opsahl, 'Trenger Norge en ny grunnlov?', in: T. Opsahl, *Statsrett og menneskerett* (Oslo 1995), p. 607, referenced in: O. Mestad, *Grunnlovshistoria – eit oversyn*, p. 51, fn 81.

13 On the history of the Constitution in the second half of the twentieth century, see: O. Mestad, *Grunnlovshistoria – eit oversyn*, p. 48.

14 Act May 21, 1999, No. 30 (Lov om styrking av menneskerettighetenes stilling i norsk rett).

provisions or the constitutional doctrine developed by the Supreme Court drove the development. Nevertheless, one may argue that the 1814 Constitution was central in generating the conditions in which a modern welfare state could emerge: a society based on principles of democratic participation, equality and human dignity.

b) The 2014 Constitutional Reform and the (Constitutional) Right to Minimum Protection

In 2014, new provisions were introduced into the Norwegian constitution that specifically concern the right to a minimum subsistence: a new provision in § 110 and the new § 104. The introduction of the right to minimum subsistence was part of an overall amendment of the Constitution upon its 200th anniversary in 2014 with a more updated human rights catalogue (an expansion of "Chapter E"), which includes the minimum social subsistence guarantee enshrined in § 110 and a particular provision on children in § 104. This followed years of parliamentary deliberations. The anniversary had long been seen as a fitting moment to give human rights a more central place in the Constitution, and to bring it more into alignment with the human rights obligations Norway already had under international law. Following a comprehensive deliberation process by the so-called Human Rights Committee (*Menneskerettighetsutvalget*), appointed by the Norwegian Parliament (*Storting*) on 18 June 2009, a report was published in 2011 recommending the adoption of a new human rights catalogue.[15] However, each of the new rights was introduced only after careful consideration by the Committee and Parliament. The question of why certain rights were chosen and others were not can provide key insights into the meaning of the articles chosen for the national self-image and identity of Norway today, including the values and principles underpinning its welfare regulations.

The Human Rights Committee had been appointed with the mandate of exploring if and how the fundamental rights protection in the Norwegian Constitution should be expanded.[16] It consisted of a number of senior politicians and legal experts, including academics. In its report, the Committee found that in terms of human rights the 1814 Constitution had only been

15 Stortinget, Dokument 16 (n 12).
16 Ibid., p. 17.

updated "to a modest degree" since its adoption.[17] In addition, it found that the language used was frequently outdated and difficult to understand for many individuals.[18] Those who read the Constitution, the Committee argued, could therefore receive a "skewed and incomplete picture of the values on which Norwegian society is founded".[19] The overall state of human rights in the Constitution was one of 'fragmentation', which the Committee feared could lead to legal uncertainty. The Committee argued that it would be preferable for the Constitution to better reflect Norway's commitments under international law. In addition, the Committee stressed that it was important that Norwegian courts would be able to solve legal disputes within its domestic legal order to prevent an overburdening of international bodies in resolving conflicts.[20] While the international provisions were already incorporated into national law,[21] a direct inclusion of human rights into the Constitution would provide a higher degree of legal certainty and visibility of Norway's human rights commitments.

The relationship between international law and the domestic legal (constitutional) order was a central concern in the Committee's report. As a signatory to, among others, the UN Declaration of Human Rights in 1948, and having ratified the later UN human rights conventions, as well as the European Convention on Human Rights, Norway was already party to a long list of human rights treaties. In particular, the Committee asked what rights needed to be expressly included in the Constitution, and which ones could remain unmentioned, but which would still be binding through the general incorporation mechanisms. It ruled out a complete incorporation of *all* human rights that Norway was bound by under international law. The considerations concerning the relationship between international law and the Constitution that explain the central role of international human rights treaties in the Committee's deliberation process on what rights to include in the Constitution. In addition, the Committee looked at the human rights protection in a series of national constitutions. Regarding the question of which rights should be expressly included, the Committee emphasised that any new constitutional rights should reflect

17 Ibid., p. 13.
18 Ibid.
19 Ibid.
20 Ibid.
21 Lov 21. Mai 1999 nr. 30 om styrking av menneskerettighetenes stilling i norsk rett (menneskerettsloven).

> *Norwegian tradition and Norwegian values, both with a view to making visible the values on which Norwegian society is founded and with a view to ensuring that the Constitution is better suited to meeting Norway's future challenges.*[22]

In arguing for which rights should be included, the Committee therefore placed particular emphasis on the fact that the new provisions should reflect the "core values that are fundamental in Norwegian society".[23] While it did not see the reform as introducing any material changes to the existing law, it did see a potential long-term effect beyond the symbolic: Most centrally, it argued that those rights that were to be included in the Constitution would provide an additional safeguard against short-term political fluctuations, as the threshold for changing the Constitution is significantly higher than for ordinary legislation.[24] Overall, the Committee considered its mandate to be that of identifying the most central human rights to which Norway had subscribed, which would then be included in the Constitution. Its deliberation process was therefore about identifying the most central human rights principles, while it was of the view that more detailed provisions could remain at the international level. At the same time, the Committee stressed that the provisions should not be too detailed and thereby unduly bind future generations.[25]

In relation to social rights, there was some disagreement within the Committee. A minority member representing a more conservative political line argued that including too many paragraphs that were programmatic in nature, "programmatic statements that most people consider to be unrealistic dreams without legal consequences", could lead to a weakening of those provisions that contained 'hard' rights.[26] Such declaratory provisions, he argued, were found in particular with regard to social rights, and they should therefore be treated with caution and not be included in the Constitution's human rights catalogue. For this reason, the minority member voted against the inclusion of any social rights into the Constitution.[27] However, the Committee's majority advocated the inclusion of a set of

22 Stortinget, Dokument 16 (n 12), p. 14. Unless specified otherwise, all translations from Norwegian into English are made by the authors.
23 Ibid., p. 48.
24 Ibid.
25 Ibid., p. 62.
26 See: '11.4.2, Særmerknad fra Carl I. Hagen', Stortinget, Dokument 16 (n 12), pp. 62-63.
27 Stortinget, Dokument 16 (n 12), p. 63.

social rights, including the right to education and cultural rights. With regard to minimum protection specifically, a majority within the Human Rights Committee proposed the inclusion of the following social rights in the Constitution (emphasis added by the authors):[28]

> § 104 The Right of Children[29]
> *Children have the right to respect for their human dignity. They have the right to be heard in questions that concern them, and due weight shall be attached to their views in accordance with their age and development.*
> *For actions and decisions that affect children, the best interests of the child shall be a fundamental consideration.*
> *Children have the right to protection of their personal integrity.* The authorities of the state shall create conditions that facilitate the child's development, including ensuring that the child is provided with the necessary economic, social and health security, preferably within their own family.
> *§ 110*[30]
> *The authorities of the state shall create conditions under which every person capable of work is able to earn a living through their work or enterprise.* Those who cannot themselves provide for their own subsistence have the right to support from the state.
> *Specific provisions concerning the right of employees to co-determination at their work place shall be laid down by law.*
> *§ 111*[31]
> *It is incumbent on the state authorities to respect and ensure the right to a satisfactory standard of living. Likewise, it is incumbent on the state authorities to promote the health of the population and ensure the right to necessary health care.*

Regarding the general provisions – those covering the entire population and not children specifically – we see an interplay between § 110 and § 111, in that the provisions together were meant to cover minimum social protection. The Committee's majority saw the rights in § 110 and § 111 as

28 In addition, the Committee proposed a series of rights that also fall into the category of 'social, economic and cultural rights', such as the cultural rights of the Sami and the right to a healthy environment.
29 This paragraph was entirely new in 2014.
30 The second sentence in this paragraph was new in 2014.
31 None of the proposed provisions in § 111 were included in the Constitution.

an integrated whole, derived from the same normative basis (see below), and in concert ensuring social protection, a satisfactory standard of living and of health (*sosial trygghet, tilfredsstillende levestandard og helse*). These rights are covered by the International Covenant on Economic, Social and Cultural Rights (ICESCR), which is incorporated into Norwegian law and given priority in case of conflict.[32] For children, § 104 adds an additional safeguard concerning minimum social protection, drawing on the UN convention on the rights of the child. This convention is also incorporated into Norwegian law with priority.

And yet, in the end, the Parliament opted not to include § 111 and therefore voted for a more minimal scope of social rights in the Constitution than the Committee had suggested. In particular, the conservative parties blocked the inclusion of § 111 in Parliament. This was based on an argument that this could risk too high a financial burden on the state by the open wording of § 111. It is, however, likely that the rejection of § 111 was also due to a general resistance towards including social rights in the Constitution,[33] despite the Human Rights Committee's explanation that § 111 should be interpreted restrictively: The proposed § 111 was, in accordance with the ICESCR, directed towards the State institutions, requiring them to recognize the right of everyone to the protected goods and to put in place a sufficient infrastructure to this end. Paragraph 111 was formulated in a similar way, not intended as an *individual* right. The Committee had also argued that the term "satisfactory" should be defined objectively and that it only covered a *minimum*, not a "good" living standard. However, in the end, only the right to a minimum subsistence was included in § 110.

c) Interpreting the New Constitutional Provisions

The Norwegian Parliament approved the changes to the Constitution on 13 May 2014, four days ahead of the Constitution's 200th anniversary.[34] As we have seen, § 111 was ultimately abandoned. A new provision in § 110 on the other hand was included, but here, too, different parties advocated for different versions. Ultimately, Parliament adopted the provision as proposed by the Human Rights Committee following its reasoning. For this reason,

32 Paragraph 3 cf. paragraph 2 No. 2 of the Human Rights Act 21 May 1999 No. 30.

33 For an example of a more hesitant reasoning by a Committee member from the political right see: Stortinget, Dokument 16 (n 12), p. 63.

34 Kunngjøring av Stortingets vedtak 13. mai 2014 om endringer i Grunnloven.

the report of the Human Rights Committee can serve as an interpretative tool for understanding how the provision was intended. The right to minimum social protection is now laid down in the second sentence of the first section of § 110 of Norway's Constitution.

To understand the right to minimum social protection, and the Norwegian welfare contract more generally, however, section one of § 110 has to be read in its entirety:

> *The authorities of the state shall create conditions under which every person capable of work is able to earn a living through their work or enterprise. Those who cannot themselves provide for their own subsistence have the right to support from the state.*

The overall idea enshrined in the first section of § 110 is that work or enterprise is to be the primary source of income for all adults until retirement. The right to support from the state is only to be invoked by those who *cannot* provide for themselves,[35] and the State has adopted strict activation measures to encourage and direct people into work (the Norwegian 'work line'[36]). In its deliberations, the Human Rights Committee stressed that the primary way of securing income should be through work. In Norway, as in the other Scandinavian countries, this extends to men and women.[37] In terms of the minimum social protection guarantee in the second sentence, the wording of the provision ensures subsistence for those who "cannot" provide for themselves, meaning a lack of will to do so would not suffice. This implies that conditions set in social law[38] do not provide an obstacle to meeting the standards of the constitutional provision as long as the core of the right is safeguarded.[39]

In its report, the Human Rights Committee had also proposed an alternative formulation of § 110, although it stated that it was in favour of the version that was ultimately adopted.[40] In the second alternative, it had pro-

---

35 Stortinget, Dokument 16 (n 12), p. 239.

36 H. S. Aasen, '§ 110', in: O. Mestad and D. Michalsen (eds.), *Grunnloven, Historisk kommentarutgave 1814-2020* (Oslo 2021), p. 1236.

37 Ibid., p. 1236.

38 The Social Service Act 18 December 2009 No. 131 paragraphs 20 and 20a give the authorities power to reduce or take away social benefits if the benefit recipient does not fulfil certain obligations, such as taking on "suitable work" or other work promoting activities.

39 H.S. Aasen, '§ 110' (n 36), p. 1236.

40 Stortinget, Dokument 16 (n 12), p. 240.

posed to insert the words: "anyone who, due to illness, age, unemployment, childbirth or similar circumstances, is unable to provide for their own subsistence." The Human Rights Committee had argued that this added a risk to the provision that it may not capture all social risks. Parliament concurred and opted for the neutral version that did not state any concrete social risks, thereby also providing a certain degree of political flexibility in terms of how such a need is defined. This wording also means that the provision is intended to reflect only an abstract minimum rather than to safeguard the currently existing social protection schemes. A further alternative was proposed but also abandoned again during the legislative process. It would have included the following wording: "every person has a duty to endeavour to provide for their own subsistence".[41] The only party supporting it was the Labour Party. Although the proposal was abandoned without a debate, this was presumably because it may have placed an undue pressure on individuals who may have a wish to opt for a more traditional family model such as a single breadwinner model.[42]

In terms of eligibility for the minimum social protection guarantee, the wording of § 110 ("Den", which means any person) indicates that basic social protection should not be limited to individuals who are insured in the obligatory Norwegian Social Insurance system (*Folketrygden*).[43] However, illegally residing adult immigrants are not legally entitled to primary healthcare and regular social assistance. They have, however, a right to emergency healthcare as well as care in connection with pregnancy and birth and infection prevention.[44] Illegally residing children are entitled to the full range of healthcare services, except the right to be registered with a permanent doctor. Illegally residing immigrants do not have a right to work, and they only have a right to necessary social services for a limited period until he/she in practice could have left the country.[45] Asylum seekers are (as long as their asylum application has not been rejected) entitled to almost the same benefits as Norwegians regarding healthcare and social assistance.

41 Stortinget, Innstilling til Sortinget fra kontroll- og konstitusjonskomiteen 187 S (2013-2014), forslag 6.

42 H.S. Aasen, '§ 110' (n 36), p. 1234.

43 H.S. Aasen, 'Grunnloven og de sosiale rettighetene', in: H.S. Aasen and N. Kildal (n. 9), p. 155; H.S. Aasen, '§ 110' (n 36), p. 1235.

44 Regulation 16 December 2011 No. 1255 to the Patient and User's Rights Act 2 July 1999 No. 63.

45 Regulation 16 December no. 1251 to the Social Service Act.

In terms of what it is that individuals can request, the constitutional provision is neutral. The means through which the minimum subsistence levels can be provided are left open – meaning that they could be provided through cash payments or benefits in kind.[46] Because it is a subsidiary provision (the primary responsibility of the individual is to provide for themselves, as laid down in the first part of § 110, only if they are unable to do so do the rights on minimum subsistence become relevant), the Human Rights Committee felt able to formulate the provision as an individual right.[47] Due to its nature as an individual right, it is in principle possible for individuals to bring their cases to court for constitutional review. The minimum level enshrined in § 110 of the Constitution generally falls far below the current social protection levels in place in the Norwegian welfare state, which means that it was unlikely at the time the provision was introduced that it would be tested much in court. However, groups who are legally or practically excluded from health and social protection, or live on the margins of the welfare state, are in principle given a possibility to use the legal system to secure his or her right to basic social support.

The Human Rights Committee considered the normative bases of the social rights it proposed (both § 110 and § 111),[48] including the provision concerning minimum social protection, and stated that

> *In order for individuals to live a life in dignity and at the same time utilise the freedom that all human beings are born with, it is essential that the most elementary and basic human needs are covered.*[49]

It is thus human dignity and freedom that form the basis of this set of rights. In terms of what this means in practice, the Committee lists "food, water, clothes, housing and healthcare".[50] This suggests that its idea of minimum social provision was centred on the basics, rather than guaranteeing a more encompassing type of access to social life and culture. The Committee stressed the importance of these basics being available in particular to children, as well as to anyone who for reasons of sickness, unemployment, old age "or similar" cannot provide for themselves. While political partici-

46 Stortinget, Dokument 16 (n 12), p. 240.

47 Ibid., pp. 239-240; H.S. Aasen, 'Grunnloven og de sosiale rettighetene' (n 43), p. 155.

48 While the Committee had proposed two provisions (§§ 110 and 111), which taken together were meant to reflect these normative bases, these reflections still give us some important insights into the normative foundations for § 110.

49 Stortinget, Dokument 16 (n 12), p. 238.

50 Ibid., p. 238.

pation and social inclusion are not listed as part of this basic right, access to "food, water, clothes, housing and healthcare" are intended to ensure that the individual *can* participate in a democratic society and exercise their right to education.[51] The Committee concluded that: "If democracy is to be safeguarded and developed, and if individual human dignity is to be protected in our society, people's basic needs must be met."[52] The social rights in question were therefore intended to safeguard both the individual's dignity as well as to ensure the stability of the country's democracy. In this reading, therefore, the provision intends to secure more than the bare minimum for survival.

Generally, the Committee deemed its proposed rights to be overarching and argued that individual rights would have to continue to be regulated in the social security laws.[53] The Parliamentary committee agreed, stating that

> *The idea is that the Constitution should express the fundamental principles, while details in ordinary legislation must be continuously adapted to different circumstances, such as socio-economic conditions, technological development, changes in living patterns, changes in moral perceptions and, not least, changes as a result of changing political majorities.*[54]

While the Committee did not intend for the inclusion of social rights to bring about a material change in the individual social protection schemes or the status quo of protection levels, it still argued that they would have a legal effect in that courts could now assess whether the constitutional provisions were satisfied, and develop a new benchmark, against which any future changes in the ordinary legislation would have to be measured.[55] It is these considerations that need to be borne in mind when assessing the relationship between the Constitution after the 2014 changes and the regular social security and social assistance legislation.

In addition to the ordinary right to a minimum subsistence level enshrined in § 110, the Constitution also contains § 104, which covers, among other rights, a right to minimum subsistence for children. The provision includes the following passages that are relevant for the purposes of this chapter:

---

51 Ibid.
52 Ibid., p. 239.
53 Ibid.
54 Stortinget, Innstilling 187 S (n 41), p. 3.
55 Stortinget, Dokument 16 (n 12), p. 239.

> *The authorities of the state shall create conditions that facilitate the child's development, including ensuring that the child is provided with the necessary economic, social and health security, preferably within their own family.*

One reason why an additional provision on children was added to the Constitution was that Norway had always been one of the leading countries in safeguarding the rights of children. The Human Rights Committee therefore argued that a separate provision in the Constitution would reflect this historical legacy and the values upon which Norwegian society is founded today.[56] Additional reasons included the potential of such a provision to increase protection levels for children. The above provision concerning the child's development (the first half of the sentence) needs to be understood as a programmatic declaration and not as a subjective right.[57] The second half of the sentence, which includes the word "ensuring" ("sikre") meanwhile, is generally thought to be enforceable in court.[58]

In constitutional law terms, the new provisions in §§ 110 and 104 have not been in place for a long time. For this reason, it is not possible to assess in any meaningful way the impact these provisions have had. Nevertheless, a few first reflections can be offered on the relationship between the new constitutional provisions and the existing schemes for minimum social protection:

A survey of High Court and Supreme Court decisions reveals that since the introduction of § 110, the provision has been invoked by the claimants in only about a dozen cases. However, in no case did this lead to a change in outcome. In fact, the courts did not engage with the provision in any detail. Instead, the courts tend to resolve via Social Insurance Act or mention Constitution only briefly.[59] Paragraph 104 has been one of the new constitutional provisions most frequently cited in court. Nevertheless, this has so far not involved the right of children to minimum subsistence.[60] While this may seem disappointing from a human rights perspective at first glance, it is, in fact, in line with the way the provision was intended. The minimum subsistence guarantees in § 104 and § 110 were not intended as a remedy to any acute problems and was not seen as bringing about

56 T. Haugli, '§ 104', in: O. Mestad and D. Michalsen (n 36), pp. 1167-1177, 1172.
57 Ibid.
58 Ibid.
59 These claims are based on a search of relevant case law in Lovdata.no.
60 Ibid., p. 1177.

changes to the functioning of the welfare state. Rather, as we have seen, they were designed to bring the Constitution up to speed with the present-day functioning of the welfare state, so that the Constitution better reflects the current values of the Norwegian state. In addition, it was intended to add a constitutional safeguard for the future, in case of a change in politics and a serious deterioration of the current standards of minimum protection to be found in the welfare system.

In assessing the relationship between the Norwegian constitution and the right to minimum subsistence, one will therefore need to distinguish between the short and long-term effects of the 2014 amendments. While there has been no direct constitutional influence on the emergence of the schemes, § 110 certainly reflects a particular normative idea of the welfare state and has made it more difficult for future legislators to deviate from it. In addition, the deliberation process ahead of the constitutional reform of 2014 has also allowed for an open reflection on the normative bases of the Norwegian welfare state. And finally, at least in principle, it has given those who might need it the most, individuals suffering hardship and who may in some way fall between the cracks of the Norwegian welfare state, a tool to seek redress in court.[61]

2. Social Benefits – Legal Foundations, Benefit Calculation and Benefit Schemes

The main acts of the Norwegian welfare state regulating the minimum levels of protection are, first and foremost the Social Insurance Act (*Folketrygdloven*),[62] the Act on Social Services (*Lov om sosiale tjenester*),[63] the Patient and User's Rights Act regulating access to health and care services (*Lov om pasient- og brukerrettigheter*) and the Child Benefit Act (*Barnetrygdloven*).[64]An understanding of these key legal texts is essential to understanding how the overall legal framework for minimum social protection works.

Folketrygdloven is Norway's central piece of legislation in the area of social protection. It is the legal foundation of the Norwegian welfare state,

61 In many cases, however, this access to justice will in practice be hampered by high legal costs and the general challenges faced by individuals with low resource levels.

62 Lov 28. februar 1997 nr. 19 om folketrygd (folketrygdloven).

63 Lov 18. desember 2009 nr. 131 om sosiale tjenester i arbeids- og velferdsforvaltningen (sosialtjenesteloven).

64 Lov 8. mars 2002 nr. 4 om barnetrygd (barnetrygdloven).

regulating all social insurance schemes. The Act accordingly regulates, among others, the schemes for unemployment benefits, sickness benefits, disability benefits, parental benefits and the public old-age pension scheme. All individuals ordinarily resident in Norway are members of the Social Insurance System, the *Folketrygden.* In addition, a small group of individuals based overseas are also members, such as individuals in the diplomatic service. *Folketrygdloven* is complemented by the Act on Social Services (*Lov om sosiale tjenester*), which in particular regulates social assistance and social services. Finally, the Child Benefit Act (*Barnetrygdloven*) regulates child benefits, and therefore has an important role in regulating the income of families.

The calculation of benefits within the general social security system (*Folketrygden*) is centred on a key figure, the so-called Basic Amount (*Grunnbeløpet*, abbreviated to "G"), which has been in existence since the introduction of the Social Insurance Act in 1967.[65] Norwegian social legislation contains fixed references to G, which is adjusted by way of government guidelines on an annual basis to match income growth. The Social Insurance Act states that it has to be adapted according to expected income growth, and to be adjusted for any discrepancies between previously expected income growth and actual income growth in the preceding two years.[66] For 2024, G amounted to 124,028 NOK (approx. 10.567 €). Within the Social Insurance Act, it is therefore easy to see the relationship between benefit levels and calculation bases in the various insurance schemes. Parental benefits, for example, cover an individual's previous salary, up to 6G annually. Sickness and disability benefits are paid at the level of 66 % of previous salary up to 6G annually, whereas pension rights are accrued for income of up to 7,1G annually. For social assistance, meanwhile, the level of benefits is ultimately discretionary on the part of the municipalities and not regulated with reference to G.[67] The social assistance benefits are therefore not universal across the country, and they are also less predictable compared to the social security benefits provided by *Folketrygden.* This also means that social assistance does not necessarily rise in line with other

65 For the yearly figures of the Base Amount since 1967, see: NAV, "Grunnbeløpet i folketrygden": <https://www.nav.no/grunnbelopet#> accessed 30.8.2024.

66 § 1-4 folketrygdloven.

67 According to the Act on social assistance § 3, the municipality is responsible for the provision of services, including economic assistance. The state is, however, responsible for providing guidelines etc., cf § 8.

benefit levels in times of increasing prices and costs, implying a significant risk that recipients of social assistance fall even further behind.

Social assistance is subsidiary to the schemes of the *Folketrygden*. A number of schemes will typically be applicable before an individual falls back on social assistance. The most important schemes shall be outlined here briefly to give the reader an understanding of when the eligibility period for social assistance begins in cases of a) sickness, injury and disability, and b) unemployment:

a) Sickness, Injury and Disability

In cases in which an individual is unable to work due to sickness, injury or disability, there are a number of schemes in place within the framework of the Social Insurance Act (*Folketrygdloven*). The work assessment allowance (*arbeidsavklaringspenger*) is paid during an active treatment for sickness or other event that has resulted in a reduced ability to work (by at least 50 %).[68] The aim must be that the individual returns to employment. The benefit is usually paid for a maximum of three years.[69] The benefit amounts to a minimum of 2G. Sickness benefits (*sykepenger*) are paid when an individual is unable to work due to sickness or injury. The benefit can be paid for up to 248 days in any three-year period. The daily benefit level of sickness benefits amounts to 1/260 of the 'sickness benefit basis' (*sykepenge-grunnlag)*, which is the previous salary up to an amount of 6G.[70] If the ability to work has been permanently reduced by at least 50 %, a disability benefit may be paid (*uføretrygd*), after a thorough and often lengthy process of assessing if, how and to what degree the impairment impacts on the person's ability to work. The benefit is calculated on the basis of the three best income years of the previous five years, up to 6G.[71] The minimum payment is 2,28G. There is no upper limit for how long it can be received, and the benefit can therefore be paid up to retirement age.

All of these schemes recognise the obligation of the welfare state to secure the individual in the case that they are unable to work due to any of the listed social risks. They do, however, go beyond the protection levels envisaged in § 110 of the Constitution in that the economic protection of persons

68 § 11-5 folketrygdloven.
69 § 11-12 folketrygdloven.
70 § 8-10 folketrygdloven.
71 § 12-11 folketrygdloven.

with long- and full-time employment and high salaries provide more than a minimum level of subsistence as protected by the constitutional provision. For other persons, only when an individual reaches the end of their eligibility period, or before disability pension is granted, would social assistance step in and provide a minimum income (see below). In addition, there are several benefit schemes in place to cover the specific cost of additional expenditure in relation to long-term illness and special care needs, including the Basic Benefit (*grunnstønad*) and Assistance Allowance (*hjelpestønad*), as well as Higher Rate Assistance Allowance (*forhøyet hjelpestønad*). These ensure that individuals with special needs can sustain a decent standard of living despite the added expenditure their condition entails. Despite these regulations, many persons with disabilities, injuries and illness experience severe economic and administrative challenges trying to handle not only their own condition but also the communication and struggle with the welfare system, which has a strict control function as well as the service function.

b) Long-Term Unemployment and Low Income

With regard to the risk of long-term unemployment without any exacerbating factors such as sickness or disability, but rather owing to market demands, the unemployment insurance scheme applies. The Norwegian unemployment insurance system differs from that of Sweden and Denmark (the so-called "Ghent model") in that it is not optional. Instead, individuals who are a member of the Social Insurance System (*Folketrygden*) are automatically insured. When an individual meets the qualifying thresholds, a daily rate of 2,4 per mill of the 'unemployment benefit basis' (*dagpengegrunnlaget*) is paid out.[72] The base salary is calculated on the basis of the individual's salary in the preceding 12 months, up to a salary of 6G.[73] Unemployment benefits can be paid out for a maximum period of 104 weeks.[74] After that, social assistance from the municipality takes over as the social protection alternative, if other alternatives in the Social Security Act are not available.

72 § 4-11 folketrygdloven.
73 § 4-11 folketrygdloven.
74 § 4-15 folketrygdloven.

III. Analysis

As regards minimum income, the most important schemes in Norway are social assistance, specific child benefits and the minimum pension (*minste-pensjon*) within the pension system of the *Folketrygden.*

1. Social Assistance

Social assistance is regulated in the Act on Social Services (*Lov om sosiale tjenester*). The purpose of the law is:

> *[...] to improve the living conditions of disadvantaged people, contribute to social and economic security, including giving individuals the opportunity to live and reside independently, and promote transition to work, social inclusion and active participation in society.*[75]

The quote reflects the Norwegian – and Nordic – 'work line', but also ideas of human dignity through the emphasis on living conditions and independence. The Act "*is intended to contribute to greater equality of human worth and social status, and to prevent social problems*".[76] This wording precedes the provision introduced in § 110 of the Constitution in 2014. However, we see here the same type of aims that the Human Rights Committee had also considered to be the normative bases for minimum protection. In this way, § 110 is in harmony with the pre-existing laws and their purposes of promoting equality and stabilising democratic society. We also see an additional reference to these considerations in § 12 of the Act, which concerns the general responsibilities of municipalities: "*The municipality shall seek to facilitate the development and strengthening of social community and solidarity in the neighbourhood*".[77]

Section 18 of the Social Services Act regulates who has the right to minimum subsistence: "*Those unable to support themselves by working or exercising financial rights are entitled to financial support.*" The means test is strict, and includes the following assets: "*bank deposits, wealth and investment income, outstanding funds, realisable assets, rental income, inheritance,*

75 § 1 sosialtjenesteloven.
76 § 1 sosialtjenesteloven.
77 § 12 sosialtjenesteloven.

gifts and gains, compensation, legacies and similar".[78] However, a certain degree of discretion can be exercised, and whether all of these assets need to be monetised to become eligible also depends on how long or short the estimated period of dependence on social assistance will be.[79] In other words, if the situation suggests that an individual will only be dependent on support for a short period of time, it would be unreasonable to expect all existing assets to be sold. In addition, people will not be required to move if their home is seen as necessary to accommodate the family in a reasonable manner and is not too expensive to keep. An individual also cannot be expected to take out a loan to cover their life expenses in lieu of social assistance.[80] In relation to households, those living in house shares are to be considered singles, while married couples' assets are usually considered together (exceptions apply in cases of actual separation or domestic violence).[81]

The level to be paid is discretionary. The municipalities receive annual guidelines issued by the state, but caseworkers ultimately set the amount, taking into account the specific circumstances of the individual concerned, including family responsibilities. The exercise of discretion by case workers is not without challenges and problems from an equality perspective and as regards predictability of outcome. Research has shown that a wide range of factors may determine caseworkers' discretion and decision-making.[82] This carries the risk of biased or inconsistent decision outcomes.

At the same time, the ministerial regulations for social assistance are detailed, and give suggested rates to be paid. This indicates that the application of the social assistance regulation can be expected to show a certain level of consistency across the country and from case to case. For 2024, the monthly rate to be paid to singles under the state guidelines was 7,850 NOK (approx. 657 €), and 13,100 NOK (approx. 1,096 €) for couples.[83] For indi-

78 Rundskriv til Lov om sosiale tjenester i NAV (R35-00), NAV – Arbeids- og velferdsetaten, 22 June 2012, 4.18.2.19.

79 Ibid.

80 Ibid.

81 Ibid., 4.18.2.4, 4.18.2.5.

82 On this topic in the specific context of social assistance in Norway, see for example: A. Bjelland, *Skjønn og økonomisk sosialhjelp i NAV – En kvalitativ studie om betydningen av skjønnsvurderinger i saksbehandling av søknader om økonomisk sosialhjelp* (Master's Dissertation, University of Agder, 2021).

83 Regjeringen, Rundskriv A-3/2023 Statlege rettleiande retningslinjer for økonomisk stønad for 2024. Note that the Norwegian Krone is very weak at the time of writing, which means that the figures may seem surprisingly low when converted into €.

viduals living in shared housing, the rate is 6,600 NOK (approx. 552 €).[84] These figures do not include housing costs (see below), as the costs for housing varies so much that they need to be assessed on an individual basis. Since 2006, the figures recommended by the state have been adapted yearly in accordance with expected changes in consumer prices. As of 2023, 54,779 individuals had social assistance as a main income source (out of a population of 5,550,200), meaning 0.99 per cent of the population.[85] In total, 152,645 individuals received social assistance as *a* form of income source (2.75 per cent of the population). The average monthly social assistance rate amounted to 12,078 NOK (approx. 1,010 €).[86]

The law is unclear on what specifically is meant by "subsistence". However, this has since been defined by the interpretative guidelines issued by the authorities. The ministerial regulations for social assistance, issued annually by the Ministry of Labour and Social Inclusion, provide a good sense of what the minimum comprises:

> *expenses for very basic needs, such as food, clothing, communication, household items and hygiene and more, and also [...] other aspects of daily life, such as leisure and social needs.*[87]

This means that even in what is traditionally the least generous of schemes in a welfare state, the 'last safety net' of social assistance, several dimensions of human life are factored into determining benefit levels. Beyond the most basic needs for survival such as food and clothing, there is a participative dimension through the focus on communication. In addition, with daily life, leisure and social needs being considered, we see a further emphasis on participation and cultural and social wellbeing. This corresponds to the normative foundations that the Human Rights Committee had identified, and the role of minimum social protection in also ensuring the stability and development of democracy. We can therefore see that the Norwegian idea of 'minimum protection' contains an element of participation, placing the individual within their social environment. Thus, the concept of minimum

84 Regjeringen, Rundskriv A-3/2023 (n 83). On the situation when there are children in the household, see below, pp. 19-20.

85 Statistisk sentralbyrå, "Økonomisk sosialhjelp": <https://www.ssb.no/sosiale-forhold-og-kriminalitet/trygd-og-stonad/statistikk/okonomisk-sosialhjelp> accessed 10.9.2024.

86 Ibid.

87 Regjeringen, Rundskriv A-3/2023 (n 83).

subsistence is based on an idea of human dignity that goes beyond mere physical survival.

This is also emphasised in the interpretative guidelines issued by the Norwegian Welfare Authority (NAV) for the Social Services Act:

> *The purpose of the Act forms the basis for the lower limit for an acceptable benefit level. The benefit must be at a level that helps to realise the objectives of the Act for the individual. The term "subsistence" therefore involves more than covering basic needs such as food and shelter. Coverage of expenses should make it possible to maintain a standard of living at a reasonable and sober level, adapted to general welfare developments and the local community of which the service recipient is a part. The concept of subsistence is therefore a dynamic concept.*[88]

The guidelines highlight the variability of what this means:

What constitutes a reasonable subsistence level will vary depending on personal circumstances, such as family situation, household size, place of residence, living situation, age and health. [...]

> *The considerations that form the basis for the assessment of what constitutes justifiable subsistence for the individual must be justified on a concrete and individual basis. If this is not done, or if the assessment is not within the purpose and framework of the law, the result may be that the requirement of justifiability is not met.*[89]

The significant space for discretion implies less predictability compared to fixed schemes but also allows for individual concern and assessment of situation. The guidelines also take into account that expenses may vary according to health status, age and individual life situation. This is to be factored in in the case worker's exercise of discretion:

> *The calculation of financial support must take into account expenses that are common for people of a similar age and life situation. If the service recipient is young and in the early stages of adulthood, their needs will be different from those of recipients who are well into adulthood. For young adults, it will be common to acquire household goods and other assets as finances allow, and this can be taken into account in the benefit calculation for service recipients in this age group. For older service recipients with*

88 Regjeringen, Rundskriv NAV (R35-00) (n 78), 4.18.1.1.

89 Ibid.

no possibility of a future increase in income, it would be reasonable to take into account that the financial situation is permanent and that the standard of living for the age group is higher than for young adults.[90]

The guidelines state that, typically, the subsistence needs include food and drink, clothes and shoes, household and hygiene products, media and communication, leisure activities, transportation and housing and electricity. The guidelines stress that clothing allowances need to match the needs for clothing in different seasons and should also factor in clothes for special occasions such as Christmas and birthdays. With regard to food, special allowances can be made for special dietary requirements.

In return for social assistance, the municipality is entitled to demand that individuals perform some form of work in their municipality.[91] For individuals under the age of 30, the municipality *has to* demand work in return for social assistance.[92] In this way, the Norwegian 'work line' is central even in relation to the most basic form of subsistence. The political intent behind this is that in particular younger individuals should be strongly discouraged from staying away from the labour market for too long, which could endanger their employability on a long-term basis. For those who do not comply with activation obligations, sanctions can be issued.[93] It should also be mentioned that, while § 110 includes all those on Norwegian territory, the social assistance granted under the Act on Social Services is only available to individuals *legally* resident in Norway. Special regulations apply to those groups who fall outside of this category, such as immigrants without legal residence or who lack valid documentation of their membership in the European transborder health schemes.[94] As is the case in *Folketrygden*, this highlights the strong distinction the Norwegian welfare state makes between 'insiders' and 'outsiders'.

In sum, therefore, we observe that the Norwegian social assistance system is rather flexible. Not only is social assistance paid out in a discretionary manner, the guidelines issued by the welfare authorities also stress the wide range of different factors that must be taken into account when exercising discretion in each case. This flexibility is not always unproblematic, as the wide scope for discretion by municipality case workers can make

90 Ibid., 4.18.2.8.
91 § 20 sosialtjenesteloven.
92 § 20a sosialtjenesteloven.
93 §§ 20, 20a sosialtjenesteloven.
94 See above in section II.1.c).

social assistance recipients dependent on good-will and they become more vulnerable to power abuse compared to citizens with a regular income.[95] Still, the detailed guidelines also limit variations in decision-making, ensuring that the same factors are taken into account across the country and from case to case.

2. Childhood and Parenthood

As we have seen, a special provision on the rights of children was added as part of the 2014 Constitutional reform (§ 104). This was meant to reflect, not least, that the rights of children have a central position in Norwegian society. Several schemes are in place in the Norwegian social law system that have the purpose of ensuring that children's minimum subsistence needs are met. This includes the regular child benefit (*barnetrygd*) and extended child benefit (*udvidet barnetrygd*) for single parents. Eligibility for these benefits is not dependent on a means test, however, and in most cases, the benefit will contribute to more than a mere minimum subsistence level.

Social assistance, however, is a means-tested benefit (see above on the general system), which factors in children in the household. For children between 0 and 5 years of age, the state guidelines for social assistance recommend in 2024 a payment of 3,850 NOK (approx. 281 €). This rises to 3,950 NOK (approx. 290 €) for children aged between 6 and 10, and to 5,150 NOK (approx. 381 €) for children aged between 11 and 17.[96] The particular position of children in the family is highlighted in the accompanying documents to the Act on Social Services. The interpretative guidelines of the Welfare Agency (NAV) stress:

> *If the service recipient has children, special consideration must be given to their needs. Children and young people must be ensured a safe upbringing and be able to participate in normal school and leisure activities, regardless of whether their parents are in financial difficulties. This means that expenses for children and young people may be included in the cost of living, even if similar expenses for adults are not.*[97]

95 E. Nilssen and I. Voll, 'Rettslig proseduralisering og 'governmentality' i norsk aktiveringspolitikk [Legal proproceduralization and 'governmentality' in Norwegian activation policy]', Retfærd 153 (2016) 3, pp. 58-71.

96 Regjeringen, Rundskriv A-3/2023 (n 83).

97 Rundskriv NAV (R35-00) (n 78).

The guidelines also state that, in the case of families, children's income in their spare time and holidays is not to be counted in the means-testing or calculation of benefits. The same applies to the child benefit.[98] The law is therefore conscious of not limiting children's opportunities in society and within the labour market, and that their possibilities for participation in society are not limited through their parents' or caregiver's dependence on social assistance. A general risk with both the child benefit and the rates for social assistance paid for families with children in the household, meanwhile, is that it is difficult to ensure that the benefits paid actually reach the children.

Finally, for children who have lost one or both of their parents, a children's pension is paid until they are 20 years of age. According to the Social Insurance Act, the purpose of the child pension is "to secure income for children when one or both parents have died".[99] From 1 January 2024, children who have lost one parent receive an amount equivalent to 1 G per year 124,028 NOK (approx. 10.567 €). Children who have lost both of their parents will receive 2.25 G annually (279,063 NOK, approx. 23,369 €). The children's pension is therefore also directed at securing a minimum subsistence level of children in need.

3. Retirement

The Norwegian pension system ensures a minimum protection level also for individuals in old age. While § 110 is mainly directed at the working age population, and those of retirement age are not expected to work, the Norwegian pension system contains a minimum level of pension benefits (*grunnpensjon*) which ensures that individuals do not risk suffering financial hardship in the way seen in pension systems without a corresponding minimum level. The entitlement to full pay of the minimum protection level (*grunnpensjon*) is secured through being a resident of Norway for 40 years,[100] and can be taken out from age 67. From 1 January 2024, the level has been 223,358 kroner annually (approx. 18,707 €). This figure is also referred to as minimum pension level (*minste pensjonsnivå*). A slightly lower rate applies for individuals living in shared households. Those with shorter periods of residence in Norway receive a sum proportionate to

98 Rundskriv NAV (R35-00) (n 78), 4.18.1.
99 § 18-1 folketrygdloven.
100 § 3-2 folketrygdloven.

their period of residence. They are entitled to an additional benefit to top up the difference. However, unlike for those who meet the residency requirement, the additional benefit is means-tested. Since the pension level of the lowest pension amounts to approx. 18,613 NOK (1,559 €) monthly, it is higher than the minimum level recommended in the guidelines for social assistance (around 657 €). Clearly, the minimum pension level provides more than what is considered the minimum level to live a 'life in dignity' (note, on the other hand, that it needs to cover all expenditure, including for housing). Within the pension system, there is therefore an additional element of recognition of an individual's lifetime contributions to society, and an idea that retirees should receive more than that which is considered the minimum deemed essential to survive.

IV. Conclusion

As this chapter has shown, there is a comprehensive system in place in Norway for guaranteeing minimum social protection for individuals in need. The exact benefit levels are determined on a case-by-case basis. While scenarios in which case workers need to exercise discretion will always lead to some outcomes that are perceived as unduly harsh, the detailed guidelines issued by the Ministry of Labour and Social Affairs and the Norwegian Welfare Agency aim to ensure that individuals in need can live a 'life in dignity'. Since 2014, the right to a minimum subsistence has been enshrined in § 110 of the Norwegian Constitution, highlighting that it is one of the guiding principles of the welfare state. While this did not have a particular impact on the ways in which minimum income schemes work today, the Parliament nevertheless affirmed the centrality of this dimension of the welfare state by adding this provision to its Constitution. Note, however, that more encompassing rights such as the right to health and a decent standard of living were abandoned in the legislative process implying that the social rights in the Constitution do not fully reflect the scope of the Norwegian welfare state today.

By forming a guarantee enshrined in the Constitution, the right to minimum subsistence has become part of the fabric of the Norwegian Constitutional order. Most significantly, § 110 provides a safeguard against an erosion of minimum social protection levels and it has granted individuals a subjective right to have their case tested in court. At the same time, the importance of this should not be overstated. Through a wide range of schemes, the Norwegian welfare state today offers significantly higher social protection levels for most individuals than those laid down in the Constitution's § 110. One can hope, therefore, that court cases in which individuals need to invoke § 110 will remain few and far between.

Ensuring a Dignified Life in Polish Law

Agnieszka Górnicz-Mulcahy, Monika Lewandowicz-Machnikowska and Ariel Przybyłowicz

I. Introduction

Social protection in Poland is pursued through an extensive and diversified system of social benefits. The system is quite developed and provides various forms of benefits, which include a basic role of social insurance, supplemented by assistance of a monetary and non-monetary nature. In particular, the 2004 reform of social assistance generally improved the support for people in need by simplifying the previous system of means-tested benefits and reducing the margins of discretion in the benefits amount.[1]

Despite the existence of numerous instruments of social protection, the number of people living in poverty in Poland is still consistent. Based on Eurostat data, EAPN concluded that extreme poverty was still at 4.7% in 2022.[2] Data show that poverty has recently increased in particular for elderly persons (an increase from 3.8 to 3.9 per cent) and children (an increase from 5.3 to 5.7 per cent).[3] This persistent poverty highlights ongoing challenges to the effectiveness of current social protection measures. Current discussions focus on the adequacy of existing thresholds and benefits. There is a growing debate on whether the current income thresholds adequately reflect the cost of living and protect individuals from poverty, emphasizing the need for more frequent adjustments to these thresholds.

Against this framework, the purpose of this study is to present the Polish solutions aimed at providing means of subsistence or support to ensure better living conditions for groups in need, and to assess whether the benefits provided for in various benefit systems allow us to conclude that the Polish legislator actually ensures a life in dignity.

The study will be divided into two main parts. In the first part, we will present the constitutional conditions, as the superior source of Polish social law is the Constitution of the Republic of Poland of 1997. This basic legal act contains a number of provisions that, on the one hand, constitute the basis for the activity of the legislator in the area of social law and, on the other hand, also define its obligations as regards the creation of specific solutions.

We will also present an outline of the Polish social law system, i.e. we will point to the existing benefit systems, the main assumptions of these systems and their mutual relations. In this section, we consider it necessary to cite the legal regulations on the minimum wage, the aim of which is to ensure that every person in gainful employment receives a wage that guarantees a life in dignity.

---

1 I. Wóycicka, 'Poland: Minimum Income Schemes. A Study of National Policies' (2009), pp. 3-4 < https://ec.europa.eu/social/BlobServlet?docId=9038&langId=en > accessed 14.11.2024.

2 EAPN, 'Poverty Watch 2023. Monitoring of Poverty and Anti-Poverty Policy in Poland 2022-2023' (17 October 2023) <https://www.eapn.eu/wp-content/uploads/2023/10/eapn-EAPN-PL-English-version-2023-PW-5823.pdf> accessed 14.11.2024.

3 Ibid.

In the second part of the study, we will analyse and discuss some important detailed solutions. We will focus on those insurance and assistance benefits which we find the most important for the purpose of the study. We have chosen them on the basis of the function they perform in the system of social law – they are benefits that provide a livelihood for people who, for various reasons (age, illness, family or life situation), cannot independently provide for themselves the means to ensure a certain minimum of life, or whose aim is to ensure a slightly higher standard of living than merely that of biological survival. These benefits therefore either replace the income that the person concerned does not earn on his or her own for various reasons, or supplement the income earned on his or her own when it is too low to ensure the necessary minimum and a dignified life. Benefit receipt is, in some cases, subject to specific income criteria, while in other cases it is granted regardless of such criteria, but the purpose and legal structure of these benefits make it possible to classify them as benefits ensuring a dignified life.

II. Overview

1. Normative Background

a) Dignity and Social Justice in the Constitution

Article 2 of the Constitution[4] states that the Republic of Poland is a democratic state governed by the rule of law, implementing the principles of social justice. The concept of social justice involves, among other things, ensuring social security and securing basic conditions of existence for those who, for reasons beyond their control, remain unemployed. The principle of social justice is normatively and axiologically linked to the principle of human dignity that is formulated explicitly in Article 30 of the Constitution. Both principles are invoked in the jurisprudence of the Constitutional Court, in order to specify the scope of the legislator's freedom in defining

4 Constitution of the Republic of Poland of 2 April 1997 <https://isap.sejm.gov.pl/isap.nsf/download.xsp/WDU19970780483/U/D19970483Lj.pdf> accessed 14.11.2024.

social rights, such as the right to social security referred to in Article 67 of the Constitution.[5]

Pursuant to Article 30 of the Constitution, inherent and inalienable human dignity is the source of human and civil liberties and rights. It is inviolable, and its respect and protection are the duties of public authorities. This is considered a fundamental principle of the political system; it links the fundamental human and civil rights and freedoms to dignity, and is normative in nature, which means that it constitutes an independent benchmark for constitutional control.[6] One of the aspects of the obligation to respect dignity is to provide the material conditions for a humane existence.[7] According to the Constitutional Court, an obligation to respect and protect human dignity has been imposed on public authorities. A prerequisite for the respect for human dignity that is understood in this way is, among other things, the existence of a certain material minimum that ensures the individual's ability to function independently in society, as well as the creation of opportunities for each person to fully develop their personality in the surrounding cultural and civilisational environment.[8] These general constitutional norms are therefore important for the specific solutions adopted by the legislator within the framework of social law.

As elucidated in the next paragraphs, the provisions of the Constitution of the Republic of Poland not only make the principle of human dignity a fundamental principle of the political system, but by regulating a number of social rights therein also serve as an expression of the so-called "socialisation of human dignity". This means that human dignity cannot be fully guaranteed without establishing appropriate instruments of social protection. In turn, the constitutional norms oblige the legislator to create appropriate specific solutions and benefit systems that will guarantee an adequate level of social security and thus also life in dignity. Of particular importance here is the constitutional entrenchment of the issue of minimum wages and social security in the event of old age or incapacity, which

---

5 See Judgment of the Constitutional Tribunal of 6 October 2015, Case SK 19/14, OTK-A 2015/9/141.

6 L. Bosek, 'Zasady ogólne', in: M. Safjan and L. Bosek (eds.), *Konstytucja RP, Tom I Komentarz. Art. 1-86* (C.H. Beck 2016), pp. 735 ff.

7 L. Garlicki, 'Komentarz do art. 30', in: L. Garlicki and M. Zubik (eds.), *Konstytucja Rzeczypospolitej Polskiej. Komentarz. Tom II* (Wydawnictwo Sejmowe 2016), note 29.

8 See Judgment of the Constitutional Court of 4 April 2001, K 11/00, OTK 2001/3/54 <https://ipo.trybunal.gov.pl/ipo/Sprawa?sprawa=3483&dokument=184> accessed 14.11.2024.

compels the legislator to adopt specific solutions and at the same time provides the population with a legal basis for a constitutional assessment of these solutions by the Constitutional Court. They provide a model of constitutional control.

b) Constitutional Foundations of Social Security

Detailed regulations on social rights aimed at ensuring economic security and a life in dignity for individuals are included in the Constitution of the Republic of Poland in the chapter on economic, social and cultural freedoms and rights. The following provisions of the Constitution should be noted here: Article 65(4), which deals with the establishment of a minimum wage, provisions guaranteeing the right to social security (Article 67), the right of persons with disabilities to special protection through state assistance in securing their existence (Art. 69), the right of a family in a difficult material and social situation to special assistance from public authorities (Article 72), the right to individual assistance for pupils and students aimed at ensuring equal access to education (Article 74), and the right of a child deprived of parental care to care and assistance from public authorities (Article 72(2)).[9] In addition, we should also mention Article 18, concerning the protection of marriage, family, and motherhood. By establishing certain social rights in the Constitution, the state defines the priorities of its social policy and the scope within which the ordinary legislator is obliged to act when creating legal regulations on social benefits.

aa) Programmatic Nature of Social Rights and Justiciability

As a rule, no claims for specific benefits arise for citizens from constitutional regulations. These provisions most often contain only programmatic norms addressed to the ordinary legislator so that it may achieve the goals set forth in the Constitution. Moreover, most of the provisions on social rights are listed in Article 81 of the Constitution, which stipulates that the rights set forth in the provisions listed therein can be asserted within the limits set by law. Thus, it is only from statutory norms that an entitled person can derive a specific subjective right, in particular to a social benefit.

9 M. Lewandowicz-Machnikowska, *Regulacja prawna socjalnego wsparcia dla osób o niskich dochodach* (Wydawnictwo Uniwersytetu Wrocławskiego 2013), pp. 63 ff.

The references to ordinary laws used in the Constitution are in two forms, and the limits and nature of this reference are not the same in both cases. Firstly, the aforementioned Article 81 of the Constitution explicitly specifies which rights can be asserted within the limits set by the law, and secondly, the contents of some provisions on social rights not mentioned in Article 81 of the Constitution, such as Article 67 on the right to social security, refer explicitly to the law and indicate that the scope and forms of exercising the right mentioned therein are determined by law. This means that the determination of the content of the individual rights included in Article 81 is left to the discretion of the legislator. In the case of the second type of references, on the other hand, the essential elements and limits of the law are shaped directly by the Constitution, and only their concretisation and the manner of implementation are left to the ordinary legislator.[10] However, it should be emphasised that the rights listed in Article 81, such as the right to assistance in securing the existence of persons with disabilities (Article 69), the right to special assistance to families in a difficult material and social situation (Article 71(1)), the right to special assistance to a mother before and after childbirth (Article 71(2)), and the right to security of a citizen's housing needs (Article 75) are constitutional rights, and can therefore be asserted by the entitled party at least to the extent of the minimum of this right, which is determined by its essence.[11]

In this sense, it is important to note that the Constitution guarantees citizens the right to a court procedure, i.e. the right to a fair and public examination of a case without undue delay by a competent, impartial and independent court (Article 45), as well as the right to appeal judgments and decisions issued at first instance (Article 78). Furthermore, anyone whose constitutional freedoms or rights have been violated has the right, on the principles set out in the law, to file a complaint to the Constitutional Court regarding the conformity with the Constitution of a statute or other normative act on the basis of which a court or organ of public administration has made a final decision on his/her freedoms or rights or on his/her obligations specified in the Constitution (Art. 79). Constitutional regulations are of particular importance with regard to the protection of citizens' rights

10 J. Oniszczuk, 'Problemy realizacji wolności i praw socjalnych gwarantowanych w Konstytucji RP', in: L. Wiśniewski (ed.), *Wolności i prawa jednostki oraz ich gwarancje w praktyce* (Wydawnictwo Sejmowe 2006), p. 206.

11 J. Trzciński, 'Komentarz do art. 81 i art. 68 Konstytucji', in: L. Garlicki (ed.), *Konstytucja Rzeczpospolitej Polskiej. Komentarz* (Wydawnictwo Sejmowe 2003).

to social benefits – any decision refusing to grant a benefit may always be challenged and verified through a two-instance procedure.[12]

bb) The Right to Social Security

Article 67 of the Constitution stipulates that a citizen has the right to social security in the event of incapacity to work due to illness or disability and upon reaching retirement age. The scope and forms of social security are determined by law (sec. 1). A citizen who is unemployed not of their own free will and who has no other means of subsistence has the right to social security, the scope and forms of which are set by law (sec. 2).

The Polish legislator has used the explicit phrase "right to social security", to which a citizen is entitled in several life situations specified in Article 67 of the Constitution. This provision does not create any subjective rights of the individual in relation to the state, as it is left to the ordinary legislator to specify the "scope and forms" of social security. The legislator is therefore obliged by means of ordinary laws, using social security techniques of its choice, to establish the benefits that will allow individuals to exercise their right to social security.

The Constitution imposes an obligation on the ordinary legislator to determine the scope and forms of social security. This means that its actions should result in creating a whole system of benefits, of diverse scope, constituting the content of this notion.

This system, as a whole, is intended to enable citizens with no capacity to work due to illness or disability, who have reached retirement age, or who are unemployed not of their own will, and have no other means of subsistence, to fully exercise their right to social security.[13] What transpires from the right to social security is that every citizen should be guaranteed the right to benefits in the event of incapacity to work due to illness, disability, reaching retirement age, being unemployed involuntarily and having no other means of subsistence. It is understood that Article 67 is the

12 Decisions of organs granting benefits from non-insurance systems are always subject to appeal to a higher authority and then to an administrative court (also a two-instance procedure). On the other hand, in the case of decisions of the Social Insurance Institution (ZUS) regarding social insurance benefits, an appeal can be filed to the common court – the social insurance court (also here the proceedings are two-instance).

13 See Judgment of the Constitutional Tribunal of 25 September 2019, SK 31/16, OTK-A 2019/53.

basis for establishing and distinguishing the scope of social security from its minimum, which constitutes the essence of the right to entitlements that go beyond this scope. Thus, the legislator has a certain amount of freedom to shape the entitlements under the right to social security. However, the lower limit of this freedom is the obligation to guarantee the minimum of the right – its essence.

Article 67 is violated when the legislator has not granted the persons indicated therein the benefits that ensure their subsistence at the minimum level of existence. The content of the right to social security under Article 67 is determined on the basis of the content of this provision and sources of international law, which Poland is obliged to respect, e.g., ILO Convention No. 102 on Minimum Standards of Social Security.[14]

One of the basic issues concerning the content of the right to social security in the Constitution is what social risks are covered by this right. Although the provision of Article 67 does not list all traditional social risks, this does not mean that these situations are not covered by the concept of social security or do not require protection by the Polish state. This is because, as a rule, Article 67 was not created to define the concept of social security and should be read together with other provisions of the Constitution concerning social rights and international obligations assumed by Poland.[15] Firstly, as it transpires from the wording of the provision, a citizen has the right to social security in the event of incapacity to work due to illness or disability. The constitutional provision in question deals with the risk of incapacity to work regardless of the legal basis for its provision and the related incapacity to provide for one's livelihood through one's own labour, which can arise from two separate factual situations – illness or disability (also if they are caused by an accident at work or occupational disease[16]). Sickness and disability differ in that sickness is transient and requires the provision of periodic benefits, and disability is rather permanent and requires the provision of long-term benefits. Sickness and disability also involve other social risks which are unrelated to work, and which are

14 K. Ślebzak, 'Komentarz do art. 67', in: M. Safjan and L. Bosek (eds.), *Konstytucja RP, Tom, I Komentarz. Art. 1 – 86* (C.H. Beck 2016), p. 1511.

15 H. Pławucka, 'Prawo do zabezpieczenia społecznego w orzecznictwie Trybunału Konstytucyjnego', in: T. Kuczyński and Z. Kubot (eds.), *Z zagadnień prawa pracy i prawa socjalnego. Księga jubileuszowa Profesora Herberta Szurgacza* (Difin 2011), p. 504; and M. Zieleniecki, 'Prawo do zabezpieczenia społecznego' Gdańskie Studia Prawnicze 13 (2005), pp. 566 ff.

16 K. Ślebzak (n 14), p. 1513.

protected in separate benefit systems. Their foundation is Article 68 (right to health care) and Article 69 (right of persons with disabilities) of the Constitution. The benefits included in the above systems are not related to the loss of means of subsistence, but rather to the need to obtain benefits from the health care system or the need to cover costs incurred as a result of increased expenses.

A separate social risk protected under the right to social security in the Constitution is the risk of incapacity to work after reaching retirement age. The legislator is supposed to provide an adequate benefit to replace income from work to a person who has reached a certain age and has the relevant merit. Exercising the right to social security therefore requires that the conditions for acquiring and exercising the right to an old-age pension be indicated in the law. Article 67 of the Constitution itself does not contain detailed conditions for the acquisition of benefits or the manner of determining their amount. However, the Constitutional Court has repeatedly stressed that the legislator, when implementing the provisions of the Constitution concerning security and related to incapacity to work due to reaching retirement age, should take into account the postulate, arising directly from the principle of social justice, to maintain fair proportions between the size of the pension, which is a 'meritorious' benefit, and the size of this 'merit'. This merit is determined by two elements: the length of the period of professional activity leading to the acquisition of the right to a pension, and the income earned from this activity.[17] Furthermore, no citizen who finds themselves in one of the situations indicated in Article 67 of the Constitution, including incapacity to work after reaching retirement age, may be deprived of a benefit that guarantees them the receipt of at least the social minimum.[18]

Another risk protected under the right to social security is being unemployed not of one's own will and having no other means of subsistence. This, in practice, is combined with the risk of unemployment. The protection, however, is limited to those cases where a person is capable of working and he or she can work, and their unemployed status quo is independent of the will of the unemployed person. Moreover, the person should have no other means of subsistence. As for other social risks, it is assumed that, for

---

17 Judgment of the Constitutional Tribunal of 8 May 2000 SK 22/99 OTK 2000/4/107.

18 See Judgments of the Constitutional Tribunal: 8 May 2000, case file no. SK 22/99, OTK ZU no. 4/2000, item 107; 7 February 2006, case file no. SK 45/04, OTK ZU no. 2/A/2006, item 15; 27 January 2010, case file no. SK 41/07, OTK ZU no. 1/A/2010, item 5.

example, the risk of a family losing its breadwinner has been included in the constitutional right to social security, since it is of a substitutive nature for incapacity benefits due to age or incapacity to work, i.e. for the benefits previously received by a breadwinner who died.

Another important issue is how social security law benefits are related to the minimum subsistence and human dignity. Constitutional protection is given to the value of the benefit at the time of its determination, which means that benefits should provide maintenance at the level of the minimum subsistence. The preservation of the real value of the benefit by means of a valorisation mechanism is also protected, with the legislator having considerable freedom in choosing the relevant valorisation methods.[19]

cc) Special Assistance for Families

Another important provision from which social rights are derived is Article 71 of the Constitution. According to this provision, the state shall take into account the welfare of the family in its social and economic policies. Families in a difficult material and social situation, especially families with many children or single-parent families, are entitled to special assistance from the public authorities. These provisions do not provide grounds for constructing individual claims of the individual against the state. What distinguishes the provisions of Article 71(1), second sentence, is that we are here dealing with a constitutional determination of the scope of benefits for families in difficult situations.[20] This provision specifies that assistance to families in difficult financial and social situations, especially those with many children and single-parent families, is supposed to be of a "special" nature, i.e. should go beyond the usual assistance provided to others.

19 Cf. Judgments of the Constitutional Tribunal on (case file no.): K. 14/92, OTK in 1993, part II, item 35; K. 23/95, OTK in 1995, part II, item 33; K 8/96 OTK ZU No. 4/1996, item 32; K. 4/99, OTK ZU No. 7/1999, item 165.

20 See grounds of Judgment of the Constitutional Tribunal of 13 April 2011, SK 33/09, OTK-A 2011, no. 3, item. 25, pp. 366 ff.

dd) The Minimum Wage

A fundamental means of ensuring a dignified existence is to guarantee working people an adequate wage that enables them and their families to secure their justified needs. The minimum wage provisions, which have their source in the Constitution, are intended to serve this purpose. Article 65(4) of the Constitution of the Republic of Poland stipulates that the minimum amount of remuneration for work or the method of determining this amount shall be set by law. Due to the autonomous nature of constitutional terms, this provision refers to the performance of any gainful work, and therefore not only to work performed based on an employment relationship.[21] The remuneration for work should be a fair remuneration – it should be sufficient to meet the justified basic needs of the individual (the minimum standard of a life in dignity).

c) What Shall Be the Minimum? The Issue of Quality-of-Life Measures and Income Thresholds

Before proceeding to the illustration of benefits, it is necessary to consider what criteria can and should be adopted when evaluating individual solutions, including the number of benefits and income thresholds (in the case of benefits that depend on this criterion, which is especially the case in the group of social assistance and social support benefits). In Poland, there are four poverty thresholds and income benchmarks that can be used to assess social needs and poverty levels. They are set by the Institute of Labour and Social Affairs and are: the social intervention threshold (Próg Interwencji Socjalnej – PIS), family income support (Wsparcie Dochodowe Rodzin – WDR), social minimum (Minimum Socjalne – MS) and subsistence minimum (Minimum Egzystencji – ME). The common feature of these criteria is that they are minimum consumption thresholds determined using the method of basic needs and the corresponding basket of goods and services (also known as the basket method). These four measures serve as important benchmarks for guiding policy decisions and framing discussions on social protection.

---

21 A. Krzywoń, *Konstytucyjna ochrona pracy i prawa pracowniczych* (Wolters Kluwer 2017); A. Sobczyk and K. Kulig, 'Komentarz do art. 65', in: M. Safjan and L. Bosek (eds.), *Konstytucja RP, Tom, I Komentarz. Art. 1-86* (C.H. Beck 2016), p. 1477.

The subsistence minimum (ME), also called the biological minimum, defines the level of satisfaction of consumption needs, below which there is a biological threat to human life and psychophysical development.[22] Satisfying needs at this level and within this material range enables nothing more than survival. This means that this category can be considered the lower limit of the poverty scale. The basket of basic subsistence needs includes only expenses related to food, clothing and footwear, housing costs, children's education costs, hygiene and health care products at a level that allows biological survival. This means that social benefits should always be available to people whose income is below the designated subsistence level.

The type and level of needs met at the level of the social minimum (MS), on the other hand, should ensure such conditions as to enable the reproduction of life forces of a human being, upbringing of children and maintenance of social bonds during work, study and leisure. Therefore, the social minimum (MS) determines a level of expenditure, the achievement of which also enables participation in social life (provides better housing conditions, better food, allows to pay for leisure and recreation).[23] For this reason, the basket of basic needs also includes expenditure on culture, sport and leisure, transport and other areas. The social minimum thus sets the limit of household expenses that measure a decent living standard at the minimum level[24], which in turn allows beneficiaries to maintain ties with society.[25]

When evaluating the adopted detailed solutions of the social law in terms of living a life in dignity, a more adequate criterion would be the social minimum (MS). A life in dignity should be based not only on biological survival, but also on participation in social life, and therefore should also take social inclusion into account. Ensuring income at the level of the

---

22 L. Deniszczuk and B. Sajkiewicz, 'Kategoria minimum egzystencji', in: S. Golinowska (ed.), *Polska bieda II. Kryteria – Ocena – Przeciwdziałanie* (Instytut Pracy i Spraw Socjalnych 1997).

23 B. Szatur-Jaworska, 'Diagnoza, diagnozowanie, badania diagnostyczne w polityce społecznej', in: G. Firlit-Fesnak and J. Męcina (eds.), *Polityka społeczna* (Wydawnictwo Naukowe PWN 2018).

24 P. Kurowski, *Koszyki minimum socjalnego i minimum egzystencji – dotychczasowe podejście* (2002), p. 2 <https://www.ipiss.com.pl/wp-content/uploads/2022/11/rola_funk_min_soc_egz.pdf> accessed 14.11.2024.

25 L. Deniszczuk and B. Sajkiewicz (n 22).

subsistence minimum (ME) does not remove problems that generate social exclusion.[26]

The social intervention threshold (PIS) represents the minimum income level below which a household or individual is considered to require social assistance, while the family income support (WDR) is a benchmark used to define income criteria in family benefits.

Importantly, the subsistence minimum is linked to the category of the social intervention threshold, which typically defines the income criterion in social assistance. Legal mechanisms for increasing these criteria are to ensure that social assistance benefits are available to people in need and that their value does not fall below the subsistence minimum[27] (in practice, PIS are close to ME in a certain period, while WDR thresholds, used to define income criteria in family benefits, are set more or less as an average of ME and MS). However, while the subsistence and social minimum criteria are reviewed on an ongoing basis (annually – ME, and even quarterly – MS), the WDR and PIS are set every three years (as provided for in the Act on Family Benefits and the Act on Social Assistance). At such a value, they are taken into account in order to establish income criteria for social assistance (PIS) and family benefits (WDR) for the next 3 calendar years, which means that the current income criteria in these benefit systems are based on prices and costs from several years ago, which, especially in the light of high inflation, raises doubts as to whether these systems can fulfil their function of protection against poverty. The (too) rare valorisation of PIS, WDR and, as a consequence, income thresholds in social assistance and family benefits is subject to criticism. In the light of rapidly rising prices and wages in Poland (both minimum and average wage), it appears that many people actually living in poverty (or even in extreme poverty – with incomes below the subsistence minimum level) do not have access to benefits that are supposed to protect them from poverty because they are 'too rich' to do so. Among other things, it has been proposed to introduce an annual valorisation of the criteria in question and of the income thresholds for benefits in the Act on Social Assistance.[28] This question is

26 R. Babińska-Górecka, 'Problem wykluczenia społecznego a system świadczeń z pomocy społecznej', in: J. Blicharz and J. Boć (eds.), *Prawna działalność instytucji społeczeństwa obywatelskiego* (Kolonia Limited 2009), p. 520.

27 P. Kurowski, 'Rola progów minimalnej konsumpcji w polityce społecznej w Polsce', Polityka Społeczna 4 (2019), p. 44.

28 K. Nowakowska, 'Pomoc społeczna w Polsce jest pełna absurdów: Skrajnie ubodzy zbyt bogaci na zasiłki i miliony, które nie eliminują biedy' <https://www.gazetaprawn

reasonable when considering that PIS (important for social assistance) in particular tend to be closer to the subsistence minimum (ME) than the social minimum (MS). However, it must be stressed that, in general, the normative anchoring of the ME and MS thresholds, followed by the WDR and the PIS, is assessed positively in science, and the criteria themselves are an important part of the social debate and social dialogue.[29] Another question is whether it is purposeful to complicate the system, and whether it would not be possible to use the ME and MS criteria directly for the purposes of the Social Assistance Act and the Family Benefits Act, since ME and MS are determined by the Institute for Labour and Social Affairs anyway, and much more frequently than PIS and WDR. This would allow for a better shaping of income thresholds and the availability of benefits from these benefit systems.

Below, we present the amounts of the social minimum (MS) and the subsistence minimum (ME) for 2023, in PLN.[30] It is to note that every 'per person' amount has increased compared to the 2022 figures (so year by year) by around PLN 200 (MS) and around PLN 120 (ME). At this time, the income thresholds for social assistance and family benefits were not changed and the values adopted in 2019 were in force, based on WDR and PIS data from previous years. It should be emphasised that the amount of the income criterion entitling to social assistance benefits (PLN 776 for a person running a household alone and PLN 600 per person in a family) are currently lower than the subsistence minimum (!), which raises significant doubts from the point of view of the fulfilment by social assistance of its fundamental role. The same remark applies to family benefits, where the income threshold is PLN 674 per person in a family (or PLN 764 if there is a disabled child in the family) – much below the social minimum and even below the subsistence minimum (ME). The result is that many people whose incomes are below the subsistence minimum thresholds are unable to obtain social assistance benefits and are thus condemned to live in extreme poverty.

a.pl/praca/artykuly/9567365,pomoc-spoleczna-w-polsce-jest-pelna-absurdow-skrajnie-ubodzy-zbyt-bog.html> accessed 14.11.2024.

29 P. Kurowski (n 27), p. 45, p. 47.

30 Own compilation based on data published by Instytut Pracy i Spraw Socjalnych (Institute for Labour and Social Policy) <https://www.ipiss.com.pl/wp-content/uploads/2024/04/MS-srednioroczne-2023-1.pdf> and <https://www.ipiss.com.pl/wp-content/uploads/2024/04/ME-srednioroczne-2023.pdf> both accessed 14.11.2024.

Social minimum (MS) level – 2023							
	Employee households					Pensioner households	
	1-person	2-person	3-person	4-person	5-person	1-per-son	2-person
In total	1717.41	2906.84	4292.76	5586.52	6885.10	1684.33	2849.81
Per per-son in the family	1717.41	1453.42	1430.92	1396.63	1377.02	1684.39	1424.91

Subsistence minimum (ME) level - 2023							
	Employee households					Pensioner households	
	1-person	2-person	3-person	4-person	5-person	1-per-son	2-person
In total	901.04	1547.38	2240.55	3143.69	4044.23	854.08	1453.49
Per per-son in the family	901.04	773.69	814.85	785.92	808.85	854.08	726.74

To enable the reader to relate the above data to the Polish realities, the amounts of remuneration should also be indicated. The average remuneration (net of social security contributions and taxes) was PLN 5540.25 (2022) and PLN 6246.13 (2023) gross and the minimum remuneration was PLN 2209.56 (2022) and PLN 2783.86 (2023) gross (net of social security contributions).[31] This means that a single parent of a child under the age of 18 earning the minimum wage had an income that was well above the subsistence minimum but slightly below the social minimum. This income, however, was supplemented with certain social benefits (e.g. child support benefit in the amount of PLN 800 per month), thanks to which the income of such a household also exceeded the defined social minimum.

2. Social Benefits

To meet its obligations resulting from the Constitution, the Polish legislator has created a social security system which is relatively vast in terms of both the number of potential benefit recipients and the subject of the benefits. The system includes not only cash benefits, but also benefits in the form

31 In 2024, the minimum wage is PLN 3261.53 gross (net of social security contributions and taxes). This significant increase in the minimum wage in previous years was due to high inflation in Poland.

of services, e.g. care services for dependent persons, placement in a social assistance home, and especially health care benefits, in the form of certain activities.

a) Social Insurance

The basis of this system is social insurance, based on contributions, laid out by the Act on the Social Insurance System.[32] The idea behind it is to create a state fund based on a separate part of the national income generated by working people, who contribute to its foundation to varying degrees, which then has consequences in terms of shaping their right to the benefits they may receive.[33] The social insurance system includes old-age pension insurance (old-age pension insurances together with nursing compensatory allowances), disability pension insurances (disability pension and training pension, nursing compensatory allowance, survivor's pension, supplementary allowance for complete orphans), sickness and maternity insurance (sickness benefit, rehabilitation benefit, compensatory allowance, maternity allowance, care allowance) and work accident and occupational diseases insurance (sickness allowance, rehabilitation benefit, compensatory allowance, disability allowance, training allowance, survivor's pension lump-sum compensation), nursing compensatory allowance and supplementary allowance for complete orphans, covering the costs of dental care and vaccination, and supplying them with orthopedic items within the scope set forth by the law. In principle, social insurance is of a comprehensive nature, which means that the legislator's goal was to cover the widest possible group of people who make their living from work and earn income from it, with the exception of a few professions for which separate schemes have been created to cover typical social risks. Social insurance coverage is based on the so-called insurance entitlements that are related to gainful activity, e.g. work performed on the basis of an employment contract or conducting non-agricultural business activity, and entitlements which are not related to gainful activity, but which are important from the point of

32 Act of 13 October 1998 on the social insurance system, Journal of Laws of 2022, item 1009, consolidated text.

33 I. Jędrasik-Jankowska, *Pojęcia i konstrukcje prawne ubezpieczenia społecznego* (Wolters Kluwer 2020), p. 52.

view of the state's social policy, e.g. providing personal care for a child or a dependent family member.[34]

Farmers however are covered by a separate social insurance system (which is insurance only by name, because its expenses are, in about 90% of cases, covered from the state budget). Outside the basic social insurance system, there are also selected professional groups, such as judges and prosecutors who receive emolument when retired, as well as soldiers and officers of the uniformed services, e.g. the police, whose social security in the event of a social risk is provided using the pension provision method.[35] The risk of unemployment is also secured through the provision method and, among other things, through the payment of unemployment benefits, as well as some disability-related benefits, i.e. social pension, or benefits for people who are caregivers for family members with disabilities.

b) Social Support

Due to their significant development in the recent period, attention should be paid to benefits referred to as 'social support benefits', the purpose of which is primarily to supplement income and meet socially justified needs. They include nursing allowances, family allowances, benefits from the Maintenance Fund, housing benefits, scholarships for pupils and students.[36] These benefits are also aimed at ensuring an appropriate standard of living and development, e.g. a child support benefit. The legal structure of most of these benefits (i.e. dependence on income criteria) means that they are intended to be available to persons/families in need of such support due to their financial situation. However, the exception is the child support benefit, for which the income criteria have been completely eliminated.

34 G. Uścińska, *Prawo zabezpieczania społecznego* (C.H. Beck 2021), p. 60.
35 K. Ślebzak, in: A. Wypych-Żywicka (ed.), *System prawa ubezpieczeń społecznych. Część ogólna* (Wolters Kluwer 2020), p. 529.
36 M. Lewandowicz-Machnikowska (n 9), p. 33 ff.

c) Social Assistance

People who cannot provide for their livelihoods through their own work and who do not meet the requirements necessary to receive benefits on the account of social insurance and find themselves in a difficult life situation that they are unable to overcome using their own rights, resources and opportunities, may apply for social assistance benefits. Therefore, one can speak of the complementary role of social assistance in the social law system in the sense that it complements the protection provided by other benefit systems.[37] Hence, the two systems work together to provide a comprehensive safety net for individuals in need. Benefits from social assistance and social insurance can generally be cumulated. As a rule, if an individual is receiving social insurance benefits, they can still be eligible for social assistance if their total income from social insurance and other sources is below the threshold required for social assistance.

Some social assistance benefits are obligatory (and claim-based), which means that if the person applying for the benefit meets the conditions on which the right to receive the benefit depends, the authority is obliged to grant it in a strictly defined amount, e.g. permanent allowance. Other benefits, on the other hand, are discretionary and depend on the needs and individual situation of the person applying for assistance, e.g. purpose-specific allowance.

d) Minimum Wage

Although the minimum wage cannot be considered a social benefit per se, in Poland it remains a fundamental tool of ensuring a dignified existence. Minimum wage is currently regulated by the Act of 10 October 2002 on the minimum wage.[38] This law specifies the procedure for determining the annual amount of the minimum wage and the criteria to be considered in determining this amount (which is the rate of price increase (inflation)

---

37 K. Stopka, 'Refleksje nad rolą pomocy społecznej w polskim systemie zabezpieczenia społecznego', in: R. Babińska-Górecka, A. Przybyłowicz, et al. (eds.), *Prawo pracy i prawo socjalne. Teraźniejszość i przyszłość. Księga jubileuszowa dedykowana Profesorowi Herbertowi Szurgaczowi* (E-Wydawnictwo, Prawnicza i Ekonomiczna Biblioteka Cyfrowa, 2021), pp. 351-363.

38 Consolidated text, Journal of Laws 2020, item 2207, as amended.

forecast for the following year and – if the minimum wage is less than half the national average – also by two-thirds of real economic growth).[39] The amount of the minimum wage is negotiated annually by the Social Dialogue Council[40]. Until 2017, the Act only defined the monthly amount of the minimum wage applied only to employees, i.e. those employed under an employment relationship. As a result of an amendment that came into force in 2017, those employed under civil law contracts were subsequently also protected. A minimum hourly rate is set annually for these contracts.

III. Analysis

1. Old-Age, Unemployment and Disability Support

a) The Problem of the So-Called New Old-Age Pensions

Social insurance is the basic pillar of the social system in Poland. Bearing in mind the solutions adopted in social insurance, benefits from this system are not particularly interesting from the point of view of ensuring a minimum decent life. The amount of social insurance benefits is generally determined as a derivative of the income (remuneration) earned during the period of professional activity. This means, in principle, the social insurance system provides benefits at a relatively high level, depending on the amount of a person's earnings. However, it is crucial to draw attention to the growing problem of poor old-age pensioners in Poland, who receive an old-age pension benefit below the so-called "minimum old-age pension" (the amount of the minimum benefit set by law and valorised every year, to ensure a social minimum).

The problem is the result of the 1999 old-age pension scheme reform. At that time, a new old-age pension scheme was introduced in Poland, under which an old-age pension at statutory retirement age is received if only one condition is met – reaching the retirement age of at least 60 for women and 65 for men. The amount of the benefit is strictly dependent on

39 In the event of a forecast inflation rate of more than 5%, two dates are set for the change of the minimum wage and the minimum hourly rate: as of 1 January, and as of 1 July. That was the case in 2023 and 2024.

40 The Social Dialogue Council is the most important institution of national social dialogue in Poland. It constitutes a forum for tripartite dialogue and cooperation between the representatives of employees, the representatives of employers and the representatives of government, functioning at the central level.

the amount of old-age pension contributions paid. Acquiring the right to an old-age pension is not determined by a certain length of qualifying insurance period. The method of determining the amount of the new old-age pension (dividing the amount of accumulated and valorised contributions by the expected life expectancy in months), results in the fact that if a given insured person has ever been subject to old-age pension insurance and has paid at least one contribution, the right to an old-age pension is established. In extreme cases, this old-age pension thus amounts to literally a few PLN. The guarantee of the so-called "minimum old-age pension" (in 2024 it is PLN 1620.65 net) covers only those whose qualifying insurance period is a minimum of 20 years (women) or 25 years (men). Taking into account the subsistence minimum and social minimum criterion indicated above, the minimum pension significantly exceeds the subsistence minimum threshold and is slightly lower than the social minimum for pensioner households.

Unfortunately, currently more than 340,000 people in Poland already receive an old-age pension amounting to less than the minimum old-age pension, and nearly 19,000 people receive a benefit of less than PLN 400.[41] This results in the old-age pension not serving its purpose and not allowing those who receive such low benefits to support themselves. Paying old-age pensions below the minimum subsistence thresholds results in old-age pensioners being forced to rely on social assistance benefits to meet their most basic needs anyway (if they met the income thresholds for social assistance, which is not always the case).

b) Unemployment Benefits

In most cases, losing a job results in losing a livelihood. For this reason, it is important to provide a minimum of assistance to the unemployed while

41 Structure of the amount of benefits paid by Social Insurance Institution after the March 2022 valorisation; Zakład Ubezpieczeń Społecznych, 'Struktura wysokości świadczeń wypłacanych przez ZUS po waloryzacji w marcu 2022 roku' (2022) <https://www.zus.pl/documents/10182/39637/Struktura+wysoko%C5%9Bci+%C5%9Bwiadcze%C5%84+wyp%C5%82acanych+przez+ZUS+po+waloryzacji+w+marcu+2022+r..pdf/75b859ca-4130-0372-9d23-27c1882aced6?t=1653904662501> accessed 14.11.2024.

they are searching for a new job.[42] What works as such assistance is the unemployment benefit, serving as an expression of treating unemployment from a social perspective.[43] In Poland, this benefit is defined as a lump-sum benefit. Its amount does not depend on the amount of previous earnings[44], since it is not a social insurance benefit.

Unemployment benefit is granted to persons within the meaning of the Act of 20 April 2004 on employment promotion and labour market institutions.[45] However, the mere possession of the legal status of an unemployed person is not equivalent to obtaining the right to unemployment benefits. The benefit is only available to unemployed persons who have lost their jobs and, before registering at the labour office, had been performing the type of gainful work specified by the law, for at least 365 days during the 18 months for which "contributions" to the Labour Fund were paid by the employer, and whose earnings were not less than the minimum wage. The amount of the benefit depends on the length of service and the period of its receipt (180 or 360 days), as it is assumed that in the case of long-term unemployment, social assistance benefits are a more appropriate form of assistance. This is because long-term unemployment creates a risk of deprivation, and what comes as a form of mitigating this risk is essentially social assistance (especially periodic allowance).[46]

The relatively low amount of the benefit (compared to the average or even the minimum wage) is supposed to motivate people to effectively look for a new job (the so-called motivational function of the benefit).[47] It should be noted, however, that the amount of the benefit significantly exceeds the subsistence minimum for a one-person household and oscillates around the social minimum thresholds: from 01/06/2024, the basic monthly amount of the unemployment benefit amounts to PLN 1512.42

42 See more in: M. Paluszkiewicz, 'Świadczenia dla bezrobotnych i poszukujących pracy', in: M. Włodarczyk (ed.), *System prawa pracy. Tom VIII. Prawo rynku pracy* (Wolters Kluwer 2018), pp. 1122 ff.

43 K. Jaworska, *Socjalne traktowanie bezrobocia* (Wydawnictwo Uniwersytetu Warmińsko Mazurskiego 2017), p. 10.

44 As a result, the Polish model of securing unemployment can be described as a hybrid one, combining elements of the insurance assistance technique (due to the partly contributory model of financing the benefit) – see more in: K. Jaworska (n 43), pp. 212-213.

45 Consolidated text, Journal of Laws of 2022, item 690, as amended.

46 W. Sanetra, *Zatrudnienie i bezrobocie. Przepisy i komentarz* (Wydawnictwo Prawnicze 1993), p. 86.

47 K. Jaworska (n 43), pp. 183-184.

net for the first three months and PLN 1187.73 for the remaining period.[48] It is also worth pointing out that in the case of unemployment benefits, the legislator has introduced a mechanism of automatic valorisation by the average annual index of prices of total consumer goods and services in the previous year. This allows to make the number of benefits more realistic, and the amounts of benefits after valorisation are announced by the Minister of Labour. Moreover, in the system of support for the unemployed, there is the possibility of drawing a benefit and, in combination, receiving a salary from gainful activity. This only applies to unemployed persons who are entitled to unemployment benefit. These recipients, in the event of taking up employment, may receive a so-called activation allowance of up to half the amount of the unemployment benefit to which they are entitled for half the period for which they would be entitled. This applies in particular to the unemployed who have found a job on their own. This is intended to encourage the self-motivated seeking of employment.

Unemployment benefits are available not only to Polish citizens, but also to foreigners living in the territory of Poland on the basis of legal residence permits indicated in the Act.

c) Social Pension

The purpose of the social pension is to compensate for the incapacity to acquire entitlement to benefits from the social insurance system due to the fact that total incapacity to work arose before entering the labour market. A social pension is granted to any adult who is totally incapable of working (i.e., unable to perform any work) due to impairment of bodily functions, which arose before the age of 18 or 25 (during school or higher education). The law does not provide any income criterion for receiving a social pension, but it is only available to people who cannot earn a living through their own efforts. This benefit is available not only to Polish citizens, but also to foreigners living in the territory of Poland on the basis of legal residence permits indicated in the Act. This benefit is intended to be a source of subsistence for the entitled person and, in a way, takes priority over social assistance benefits; it especially takes precedence over the permanent benefit (the Act on Social Assistance expressly provides that

48 However, depending on the number of years of employment, the benefit for a given unemployed person may be 80%, 100% or 120% of the amounts indicated.

a person entitled to a social pension is not entitled to a permanent benefit even if he or she fulfils the conditions for its granting. However, it is not possible to exclude the receiving of social pension and periodic benefit if the social pensioner meets the conditions, including income criteria, for periodic benefit. This is not possible in the case of single persons, but in the case of multi-person households it is possible).

The social pension amount is equal to the amount of the minimal complete incapacity pension (in 2024, it is PLN 1620.27 net). By linking the amount of the social pension to the amount of the minimum complete incapacity pension, the benefit is subject to annual automatic valorisation. There is also an ongoing discussion (and legislative work) regarding the increase of the social pension to the amount of the minimum wage, which would significantly change the financial situation of recipients of this benefit.

d) Benefits Granted by the President of the Social Insurance Institution in Exceptional Cases

Socially insured persons and their surviving family members who, as a result of special circumstances (e.g. they are a few weeks short of the required contribution periods), do not meet the conditions required to obtain the right to an old-age or disability pension and are unable to take up employment or activities covered by social insurance and do not have the necessary means of subsistence due to their total inability to work or their age may, by way of exception, be granted special benefits by the President of the Social Insurance Institution. Their amount in practice is equal to the amount of the minimum old age pension; they are also valorised annually like all social insurance pensions. These benefits cannot be considered as social insurance benefits, as they are financed from the state budget. Their receipt is not subject to income criteria; however, a condition for their granting is the lack of the necessary means of subsistence, which is examined in the course of the procedure for granting this benefit. These benefits are therefore intended to provide a certain minimum for a decent life for those who cannot provide for themselves.

2. Social Assistance Programmes

a) Permanent, Periodic and Purpose-Specific Allowance

Social assistance is described as a "low-lying social safety net that protects against a hard fall to the bottom if one slips down the rungs of the social ladder and fails to stop at higher levels of protection"[49]. It is intended to support individuals and families in their efforts to meet their essential needs and enable them to live in conditions commensurate with human dignity. From the point of view of the subject matter of this study, it can be said that all social assistance benefits are therefore in the nature of benefits ensuring a life in dignity, but it is not possible to discuss them all: the Act on Social Assistance defines 7 types of cash benefits and a dozen or so types of non-cash benefits which include, among others, provision of shelter, meals, necessary clothing, etc. We have therefore decided to present the basic cash benefits – permanent benefit, periodic benefit and purpose-specific benefits.

Social assistance benefits are available not only to Polish citizens, but also to foreigners living in the territory of Poland based on legal residence permits indicated in the Act.

aa) Permanent Allowance

Permanent allowance is a social assistance benefit aimed at providing income to a single adult or an adult in a family who is unable to provide it through their own efforts. The lack of such an opportunity results from complete incapacity to work or incapacity to work[50] due to reaching retirement age. This means that the permanent allowance is granted to an adult who is unable to provide sufficient means of subsistence (due to age, disability or incapacity to live independently) and whose material situation does not allow for a dignified existence. It is also necessary in cases where a difficult life situation has occurred combined with the incapacity to overcome it independently. This allowance is available to a person who does not meet the conditions for obtaining a social insurance pension or social

49 J.Jończyk, *Prawo zabezpieczenia społecznego* (Zakamycze 2001), p. 390.
50 That is a formal declaration of incapacity for work, which is one of the conditions for receiving a social security pension.

pension and, in this sense, it has a subsidiary role in the social law system, just like most social assistance benefits.

Granting the right to a permanent allowance requires that an income criterion is met. As mentioned above,[51] income thresholds for social assistance are revised every 3 years, taking into account the result of the social intervention threshold (PIS) study carried out by the Institute of Labour and Social Affairs upon indications of the Minister competent for social protection.[52] In 2023 and 2024, the PIS was significantly lower than the subsistence minimum (ME) set by the Institute of Labour and Social Affairs, as a result of which some of the people who live below the subsistence minimum cannot apply even for social assistance benefits. Thus, the existing mechanisms for the valorisation of income criteria (every 3 years) must be considered inadequate as it fails to ensure a dignified life for those in real need. According to the most recent update, for social assistance benefits to be received, a person running a household alone must now show an income lower than PLN 776, with the amount of permanent allowance not lower than PLN 100 nor higher than PLN 1000[53] per month – it should be the difference between 130% of the income threshold amount and the applicant's income. The period for which the permanent allowance is granted is determined by the social assistance institution at its discretion, considering the duration of the circumstances which justify granting the benefit. A permanent benefit can be defined as a benefit that replaces a pension for people who are not entitled to it, or that supports a pensioner if the amount of the pension is so low that the recipient meets the social assistance income criterion.

bb) Periodic Allowance

Periodic allowance is another social assistance benefit that aims to provide means of subsistence. It is granted, in particular, due to long-term illness, disability, unemployment or the possibility of maintaining or acquiring entitlements to benefits from other social security systems. It may be received by a single person or a family whose income does not exceed the statutory income criterion (PLN 776 for a single person, or PLN 600 per person in

51 See Sec. II.1.c).

52 Art. 9 paras. 1 and 2 of the Social Assistance Act.

53 The amounts indicated apply from 2024 – previously, for many years, it was PLN 30 and PLN 719 respectively.

the family) and in the event of the occurrence of one or more difficult life situations justifying the granting of a social assistance benefit. The amount of periodic allowance granted depends on the income of the person or family. The allowance is paid up to the difference between the income criterion established in accordance with the Social Assistance Act and the income which the applicant actually earns. In the case of a person running the household alone, the periodic allowance may not be higher than the amount of the income criterion per person in the family. The period for which a periodic allowance is granted depends on the individual situation of the person or family. In practice, this allowance is most often paid to unemployed persons who are not entitled to unemployment benefits. It can also be received by persons who are able to work (contrary to the permanent allowance, which persons who are able to work are not entitled to). It is also sometimes granted to persons who have no source of income due to protracted proceedings for other benefits (e.g. social security pensions).

cc) The Purpose-Specific Allowance

The purpose-specific allowance[54] may be granted in order to satisfy an essential living need (i.e. a need justified in terms of preservation of life, health, fulfilment of social roles, function of a family member)[55], in particular to cover partial or full costs of food purchases, medicines and treatment, heating, including fuel, clothing, necessary household items, minor repairs and renovations in the flat, as well as funeral costs. In addition, the homeless and other persons who have no income and no possibility of obtaining health care benefits may be granted a purpose-specific allowance to cover part or all of their expenses for health care services. The granting of a purpose-specific allowance depends on the income criterion and the occurrence of a difficult life situation and the incapacity to overcome it independently.[56] The right to the special-purpose allowance is fully based on how the discretion of the administrative social assistance body is constructed.[57]

54 I. Sierpowska, 'Kommentarz do art. 39', in: I. Sierpowska (ed.), *Pomoc społeczna. Komentarz* (Wolters Kluwer 2021).

55 I. Sierpowska, 'Przesłanki nabycia prawa do świadczeń', in: I. Sierpowska (ed.), *Meritum. Pomoc społeczna. Wsparcie socjalne* (Wolters Kluwer 2016), p. 78.

56 Ibid, p. 40.

57 W. Maciejko 'Komentarz do art. 39', in: P. Zaborniak and W. Maciejko (eds.), *Ustawa o pomocy społecznej. Komentarz* (Lexis Nexis 2013).

Discretion is manifested in the possibility of choosing the content of the decision depending on the circumstances of the case, and in particular on the income received by people applying for assistance, the scope and type of their needs, as well as the funds available to the authorities for benefits and the number of people applying for them.[58] The authority decides both on granting the purpose-specific allowance and its form and amount.[59] The legislator has not even specified the amount of this benefit, so that it is left to the granting authority to determine the amount of the purpose-specific allowance.[60] The addressee of the benefit is a single person, a person in a family or a family. If the need is of an individual nature (e.g. purchase of medicines), the benefit will be addressed to a specific person; if the allowance is to meet the needs of an entire family (purchase of firewood), then the addressee of the benefit will be the family.[61] The benefit in question is always granted for a specific purpose, and not to cover the full monthly living costs of the beneficiary. It is therefore of an *ad hoc* nature, aimed at a specific living purpose and is a lump-sum benefit (unlike a permanent or periodic allowance).[62] It is not a source of subsistence, but is used to meet a very specific need, here and now, which for some reason the person is unable to meet on his or her own (e.g. buying winter fuel, food, medicine). It is about meeting the most basic needs of life to enable a person's existence. In this sense it helps provide a life in dignity.

A special-purpose allowance may also be granted in the event of a loss suffered by a person or family as a result of a fortuitous event or as a result of a natural or ecological disaster – even if the income thresholds are exceeded. In this case, the social assistance institution is obliged to assess whether the party actually suffered losses as a result of a fortuitous event, natural or ecological disaster, and assess their scale, which requires the applicant to prove such a loss.[63] Granting special purpose-specific allowance in the amount which does not exceed the income criterion of a single person or a family, respectively, is also possible in particularly justified cases. Assessing whether given circumstances constitute a particularly justified

58 I. Sierpowska (n 54).

59 G. Uścińska, Prawo zabezpieczenia społecznego (C.H. Beck 2021), p. 492.

60 Ibid.

61 I. Sierpowska (n 54).

62 I. Sierpowska, 'Kommentarz do art. 40', in: I. Sierpowska (ed.), *Pomoc społeczna. Komentarz* (Wolters Kluwer 2021).

63 I. Sierpowska, 'Kommentarz do art. 41', in: I. Sierpowska (ed.), *Pomoc społeczna. Komentarz* (Wolters Kluwer 2021).

case is the responsibility of the social assistance institutions and is made within the administrative discretion, considering both the needs reported by the applicant (and other applicants) and the institution's financial capacity.

Due to the way in which the amounts of benefits are determined, there is no mechanism for automatic valorisation. It is therefore always a political decision and does not guarantee an increase in the level of benefits and their adaptation to current socio-economic conditions.

b) Activation Mechanisms

Social assistance benefits are provided on the basis of the subsidiarity principle according to which social assistance is an institution of the state social policy aimed at enabling persons and families to overcome difficult life situations which they are unable to overcome using their own entitlements, resources and possibilities, and persons and families benefiting from social assistance are obliged to co-operate in solving their difficult life situation (Art. 2, para. 1 and Art. 4 of the Social Assistance Act).

In general, therefore, in social assistance, undertaking gainful activity will lead to loss of benefits if the earned income exceeds the income thresholds. The Act does not provide for mechanisms that would encourage gainful activity in the form of continued entitlement to benefit. On the contrary: if there is any change in the personal, income or property situation, which is related to the basis for granting benefits, persons and families benefiting from social assistance benefits are obliged to immediately inform the body that granted the benefit. Bearing in mind the low-income criteria, even low earned income may result in deprivation of the right to social assistance benefits or in inability to obtain them due to exceeding income thresholds. This is downright demotivating and may, in practice, encourage people to work in the black economy.

In social assistance, we have one exception to this rule. This is the periodic benefit collected when a person covered by a social contract takes up employment, as it is continued to be paid regardless of income, up to the date resulting from the decision granting the periodic benefit – but no longer than for a period of two months from the date on which the person was employed.[64] A social contract is a contract concluded by a social assistance body with a person or family in order to strengthen their activity and independence in life, at work or to counteract social exclusion.[65] The conclusion of a social contract is at the discretion of the social assistance body. The social worker dealing with the case of a person claiming social assistance benefits must always individually assess its effectiveness. In particular, it has to be considered whether the person, due to their situation or other circumstances and conditions, will be able to independently and consciously work out the common provisions of the contract with the social worker and implement them. The assumption is that since the content is negotiated and therefore agreed upon with the beneficiary, they should feel more obliged to fulfil the provisions of the social contract, although it is assumed that the contract is not a civil law contract, but rather an administrative contract (which is rarely used in Polish law).

3. Family and Child Support

a) Family Allowance with Supplements

The Act of 28 November 2003 on family benefits[66] mentions a number of benefits aimed at providing financial support to families with lower incomes. Their essence is to meet the basic needs of the family and ensure that its members live at a level that is commensurate with human dignity.[67] These benefits are financed from the state budget. The basic benefit is family allowance. It is available to both Polish citizens and foreigners legally residing in the territory of Poland, and its purpose is to partially cover the expenses of maintaining a child. It is granted to one or both parents or the child's legal guardian.

Family allowance is a benefit granted to low-income families, as its receipt is conditioned by an income criterion[68]: the income per person in

---

64 The possibility of combining earnings with a periodic allowance derives from Art. 38 (para. 4a) of the Social Assistance Act.

65 Art. 108 of the Social Assistance Act.

66 Consolidated text, Journal of Laws of 2022, item 615.

67 A. Kawecka, 'Rozdział 1. Przepisy ogólne', in: K. Małysa-Sulińska (ed.), *Ustawa o świadczeniach rodzinnych. Komentarz* (Wolters Kluwer 2015), p. 21.

68 M. Lewandowicz-Machnikowska, 'Zasiłek rodzinny i dodatki do zasiłku rodzinnego', in: I. Sierpowska (ed.), *Meritum. Pomoc społeczna. Wsparcie socjalne* (Wolters Kluwer 2016), p. 242.

the family cannot exceed certain amounts (in 2023 this was PLN 674, and PLN 764 if a family member is a child with a certain degree of disability; these amounts have not been changed since 2018, as no changes were made to the income threshold amounts or to the benefits themselves during their verification in 2021). As of 2016, exceeding the income threshold does not mean that the benefit cannot be granted, as the "1 PLN for 1 PLN" rule was introduced at that time. According to this rule, in such a situation, the benefit is paid in the amount of the difference between the amount of family benefits (i.e. family allowance and supplements to this allowance) and the amount of income exceeding the income thresholds.[69] The "zloty for zloty" (PLN 1 for PLN 1) mechanism can be regarded as a mechanism encouraging economic activity. In this case, a slight exceeding of income thresholds does not result in deprivation of the right to benefits, but in their proportional reduction (e.g. exceeding the income threshold for family benefit by 50 PLN will not result in deprivation of the benefit, but in its payment to be reduced by 50 PLN). The allowance is paid for each child in the family who has not reached the age of 18. After reaching this age, the allowance is also paid if the child continues to study (for no longer than until the age of 21). The amount of the benefit depends on the age of the child (ranging from PLN 95 to PLN 135).

Family allowance is often supplemented by a number of payments, which include allowances for childbirth (PLN 1,000); for child care during parental leave[70] (PLN 400 per month); for single parenting (PLN 193 per month for each child, but no more than PLN 386 per month); for raising a child in a large family (PLN 95 per month for the third and subsequent children in the family); for education and rehabilitation of a disabled child (PLN 90 or PLN 110 per month, depending on the age of the child).

The law does not provide a mechanism for an automatic valorisation of income thresholds and benefit amounts in the family allowances system. Changes are made by an ordinance of the competent minister and should take place every 3 years, but in practice the amounts are revised less frequently (e.g. when revising the income thresholds and benefit amounts in 2021, they were left unchanged). The lack of valorisation for 6 years with a significant increase in the minimum and average wages in Poland

69 Ibid, p. 243.

70 It is one of the types of leave granted to employees to enable them to provide personal care to a child; it can last up to 36 months (and up to 72 months in the case of care of a disabled child). It is an unpaid leave (no remuneration from the employer is paid and no sickness insurance benefits are granted during this time).

has resulted in a significant decrease in the number of family benefits granted – fewer and fewer families meet the income criteria. Perhaps the government wanted to effectively extinguish the family benefits system due to the introduction of the child support benefit in 2016.

b) Child Support Benefit

The child support benefit is a relatively new benefit, introduced by the Act of 11 February 2016 on state aid in raising children[71], which is part of the system of material aid for families raising children.[72] It was meant to increase fertility rates by reducing the financial burden on the family which results from raising children.[73] This benefit is intended to provide partial coverage of expenses related to satisfying the basic needs and raising children. The primary goal (to increase the fertility rate) has not been achieved, but the benefit has made it possible to reduce the poverty of Polish families and ensure a higher standard of living.[74] Polish citizens and foreigners legally residing in the territory of the Republic of Poland are entitled to this benefit.

The group of eligible persons includes, first of all, the mother or father if the child resides with and is their mother's or father's dependant (but also that of an actual guardian or the legal guardian in certain cases). It is granted until the child reaches the age of 18. As per 2024, each child is entitled to one benefit in the amount of PLN 800 (previously, since 2016, in the amount of PLN 500 per month, hence the colloquial term "500+" for the benefit). The amount is determined by the Act itself. It does not provide

71 Consolidated text, Journal of Laws of 2022, item 1577, as amended.

72 A. Nowicka-Skóra, 'Pojęcie i cel świadczenia wychowawczego', in: I. Sierpowska (ed.), *Meritum. Pomoc społeczna. Wsparcie socjalne* (Wolters Kluwer 2016), p. 408.

73 Parliamentary paper no. 216 – Uzasadnienie projektu ustawy o pomocy państwa w wychowywaniu dzieci z projektami aktów wykonawczych p. 1-6 <https://www.sejm.gov.pl/sejm8.nsf/druk.xsp?nr=216> accessed 14.11.2024.

74 A. Kaczmarek and W. Kudela, *Analiza i skutki ustawy o pomocy państwa w wychowywaniu dzieci, tzw. program "Rodzina 500 plus"*, Przegląd Prawa Publicznego 6 (2018), pp. 8, 21. Although in the cited text, the authors point to an apparent pronatalist effect in 2016 and 2017, this effect was no longer apparent in subsequent years (see the Statistical Information of the Central Statistical Office, Główny Urząd Statystyczny, 'Rocznik Demograficzny 2021', in the section 'Population. State and structure and natural movement in territorial' in 2021 as of 30 June, p. 8 <https://stat.gov.pl/obszary-tematyczne/roczniki-statystyczne/roczniki-statystyczne/rocznik-demograficzny-2021,3,15.html> accessed 14.11.2024.

for an automatic valorisation mechanism, but authorises the Council of Ministers to increase the benefit (to date, the Council of Ministers has not used such authorisation).

Initially, the benefit was unconditionally granted for the second and each subsequent child in the family, and for the first child only if the income threshold criterion per person in the family was met, but in the run-up to the 2019 parliamentary elections, this condition was abolished, and the benefit is now not subject to an income threshold.

The child support benefit is financed from the state budget. It is worth noting that the child support benefit is not included in the income on which the granting of other income-supplementing benefits (such as family benefits or social assistance benefits) depends. It is worth mentioning that there is an ongoing discussion as to whether this benefit should not, however, be made conditional on an income threshold again and whether it should only be granted if at least one parent is working. Such a solution would have an activating character and would motivate beneficiaries to work. In our opinion, however, it is doubtful whether it would be politically feasible to push through such a solution.

c) Maintenance Fund Benefits

Pursuant to the Act of 7 September 2007 on assistance for persons entitled to maintenance, benefits from the maintenance fund are state-funded support for children entitled to child support whose parent is evading the obligation of drawing on this benefit. A person entitled to the maintenance fund benefit is a child who has been awarded child support from a parent, but where its enforcement is ineffective.

The maintenance fund benefit is available to an eligible person until he or she reaches the age of 18, or 25 if he or she is studying at school (including a higher education institution). In special cases, it may be granted indefinitely (if the eligible person has a certificate of significant disability). The benefit depends on the income criterion, which in 2024 is PLN 1209 per person in the family.[75] This amount will be subject to increases every 3 years by the valorisation rate (the first verification took place in 2023, previously the income criterion was PLN 900). The income criterion is

75 Which puts a single parent with one child and earning the minimum wage over the indicated income threshold.

judged to be too low (a single mother with one child, for example, is not entitled to the benefit, even if she only earns the minimum wage).

It is important for eligible persons that the "zloty for zloty" rule applies here as well (it has applied since 2020). Maintenance fund benefits are paid on a monthly basis. They are paid in the amount of child support currently established by the court or as part of a child support settlement, but they amount to no more than PLN 500 per month. Both Polish citizens and foreigners legally residing in Poland are entitled to them.

4. Support Benefit for Persons with Disabilities in Need of Support and Nursing Benefit

If there is a person in the family that is incapable of unaided existence, he or she usually requires constant care and maintenance. This is often provided by family members of the dependent person. To provide care, they often give up gainful work, in return for which they receive certain benefits. In 2024, a major reform of benefits related to the care of dependent persons was passed. Firstly, a cash benefit was introduced, which dependent persons receive directly if they demonstrate a certain level of need for assistance. The purpose of the support benefit is to provide assistance to persons with disabilities who have a need for support in order to partially cover the expenses associated with meeting their special needs in life. The amount of support benefit in 2024 ranges from PLN 712 to PLN 3920 and is related to the amount of social pension. Such a link will result in an automatic annual valorisation of the benefit, as the social pension is subject to annual valorisation.

Secondly, the reform has changed the benefit system for the caregivers. Previously, the nursing benefit was only addressed to carers who gave up paid work to provide care. The recipients were not allowed to perform any gainful work, even if doing so would not interfere with care. This solution has been heavily criticised in the scientific literature, but also by publicists.[76] The benefit could then be considered as an income replacement benefit, as this was a source of livelihood for the caregiver. In this way, the state supported those who, by taking care of persons with disabilities,

76 For more about these provisions, see: A. Przybyłowicz, 'The Legal Position of Persons Dependent on Long-Term-Care in the Republic of Poland', in: U. Becker and H. Reinhard (eds.), *Long-Term Care in Europe. A Juridical Approach* (Springer 2018), pp. 400 f.

assume the obligations actually imposed on the state.[77] Since 2024, the requirement to give up gainful employment has been removed and carers can combine earning and care work. However, the nursing benefit is only available to carers of children under the age of 18 who have a certified, significant degree of disability or a certificate of disability together with the following indications: the need for permanent or long-term care or assistance from another person in connection with significantly limited possibilities of independent existence and the need for permanent participation of the child's guardian in the child's everyday life in the process of treatment, rehabilitation and education. Special benefits for caregivers of older persons, which existed prior to the reform, are no longer available. However, a recipient of support benefit him/herself or his/her family can decide how to spend the support benefit, and it can also be given to the caregivers.

Both nursing benefit for caregivers and especially support benefit for dependent persons should be classified as life-in-dignity benefits, even if obtaining them does not require meeting any income criteria. The caregivers of dependent children often cannot work full-time and the nursing benefit is still an important source of their livelihood, even if they work. The support benefit should secure the required care for dependent persons who need constant support in their daily lives. Professional care services are expensive and even well-off pensioners often cannot afford them. On the other hand, the person in need of support is free to transfer the amount of the benefit to the family members who actually provide care (in Poland, in practice, care is usually provided by family members, and most often by the daughters of dependent persons). The benefits provided are available to both Polish citizens and foreigners living in the territory of Poland based on the legal residence permits indicated in the Act.

IV. Conclusions

The Polish legislator is obliged to create a legal system ensuring a standard of living which reflects respect for human dignity. Such an obligation results from several provisions of constitutional rank, although detailed solutions and methods have been left to the ordinary legislator.

77 B. Chludziński, 'Komentarz do art. 16', in: P. Rączka (ed.), *Świadczenia rodzinne. Komentarz* (Wolters Kluwer 2021).

In our opinion, the Polish legislator generally fulfills these obligations by creating an extensive and diversified system of social benefits, using various methods to secure the existing needs. The basic framework of the system is a social insurance system that is universal in terms of the benefit recipients. It provides benefits in the event of common social risks. These benefits replace income in the event of the occurrence of typical risks (maternity, incapacity to work, reaching retirement age) at a relatively high level, usually depending on the amount of previous earnings. For selected professional groups, separate systems of securing such risks are created, which also provide benefits at a relatively high level. In this context, important reservations are raised regarding the above-mentioned solutions in the old-age pension system, resulting in the acquisition of the right to even symbolic old-age pensions. There is no doubt that they cannot be a sufficient source of income after ceasing gainful activity upon reaching the retirement age (in more and more cases they are even below the subsistence minimum). Such old-age pensioners are forced to use other benefit systems, primarily social assistance, to meet their basic needs.

The Polish legislator also considers the needs of people who are unable to earn money for reasons other than the occurrence of typical social risks covered by the social insurance system. The legislator provides, for example, certain benefits to caregivers of dependent people or to dependent people themselves who have not had the opportunity to enter the labour market, as well as to unemployed people. When taking into account the criteria of the social minimum or the subsistence minimum, the amount of these benefits (social pension, nursing benefit, unemployment benefit) basically allows us to think that in most typical life situations these benefits should ensure life at least at the level of the subsistence minimum (which allows biological surviving), and in most cases at the level of the social minimum. Valorisation mechanisms are provided for most of these types of benefits, which allows them to maintain their actual value. Where this mechanism is automatic, with the conditions of indexation specified, it generally fulfils its role.

In addition to the benefits that are an essential source of livelihood, we cannot forget the benefits of a supportive nature. Their purpose is to equalise opportunities or meet a larger spectrum of needs so that a more decent standard of living is ensured. These include family benefits, benefits from the maintenance fund, the "500+/800+" child benefit, and to some extent social assistance benefits. These benefits mostly depend on meeting income criteria, although there are some exceptions (e.g. concerning child support benefit). As regards these benefits, although certain valorisation mechanisms or verification of income thresholds are provided for, they usually require specific legislative actions (issuing a regulation or amending the Act). Even if certain authorities are obliged to verify the number of benefits or income thresholds during certain periods of time, in practice this is not always the case. This is of significant practical importance, especially in recent years, with the rapidly growing minimum and average remuneration for work and high inflation. In many cases, even receiving the minimum remuneration from work will exclude the possibility of obtaining such benefits due to exceeding the income thresholds (although introducing the "PLN 1 for PLN 1" mechanism in some acts should be considered a positive change).

However, as we indicated above, although such mechanisms are provided for, in practice they do not always fulfil their role. An example is the solutions adopted in social assistance and family benefits. Income thresholds and benefit amounts are not subject to automatic annual valorisation in these benefit systems. The statutory provisions provide for a mechanism of their verification every 3 years, taking into account the value of the social intervention threshold (PIS) and the income support of families (WDR). The increase takes place by means of executive acts – i.e. regulations passed by the relevant minister. With the rapid growth of wages in Poland and high inflation in the years 2022-2024, it turns out that these mechanisms are not sufficient. Income thresholds and benefit rates set on the basis of amounts in force many years earlier are in force. This results in the exclusion, in practice, of the possibility of applying for social assistance benefits (which are aimed at helping those most in need) by people who have incomes even below the current values of the subsistence minimum and thus live below the lower poverty line (i.e. in extreme poverty). Their physical existence is even threatened. The mechanism in use in these systems therefore needs to be rethought and amended so that social assistance in particular can fulfil its function in practice. Social assistance provides benefits aimed at meeting the basic needs, mostly by ensuring benefits that allow people to live at the minimum subsistence level, which allows them to survive biologically, but not necessarily to participate in social life. When these benefits are not available for people who live below the subsistence minimum, social assistance is not fulfilling its primary task. It is worth adding here that the Social Assistance Act actually provides that if, in a particular calendar year, the amount of the income criterion is equal to or lower than the subsistence minimum, the Social Dialogue Council may apply to the Council of Ministers to verify the amounts of the income criteria also before the expiry of the 3-year period of the income thresholds. So far, this solution has not been applied in practice, even in 2023-2024.

Another thing is that, in our view and according to the definition of a social minimum, living a life in dignity is not only about biological survival, but also about participation in social life. This means that people receiving social assistance who are not granted the social minimum often live in poverty and are socially excluded. This comment is particularly important in the context of two years of high inflation (in 2022, the average annual inflation rate was 14.4%), as the social assistance income criteria in force from 2022, based on the social intervention threshold calculated in 2021 based on 2019 prices, now seem inadequate and exclude the possibility of receiving benefits even with a view to persons living in poverty who were previously managing financially.

It should also be added that since 2015, there has been a significant increase in the instrumental treatment of social legislation for election purposes. Depending on the political election cycle, the government makes numerous social transfers, often without objective justification, which only partially achieve social objectives (e.g. the 800+ benefit for each child regardless of family income; the so-called 13th pension for each person entitled to a pension, regardless of the amount of pension). Although the declared goals are poverty reduction, it is obvious that the real goal is to 'buy' electoral votes. An example is the granting of the 500+ benefit for the first child a few months before the 2019 elections, retroactively, and its payment literally a few weeks before the elections with compensation for 3 months. At the same time, there is a lack of reflection on a rational and comprehensive system for supporting Polish families that could encourage people to have children (the issue of the system of family allowances, dependent on income thresholds, which have remained unchanged since 2018, is the best example here).

Minimum Income Protection in Slovenia: A Dignified Life Beyond Social Assistance

Luka Mišič and Grega Strban

I. Introduction*

Measures preventing poverty and social exclusion in Slovenia are exercised within the functionally centralised, tax-funded social assistance scheme. It provides a subsidiary safety net in respect to the functionally decentralised, contribution-funded social insurance scheme and other types of social security benefits, e.g. family benefits. The Slovenian social security system namely consists of three general parts, as is the case in numerous (continental) European countries. The first is the social insurance system, composed of a mandatory health insurance, pension and disability

* This research is part of the research project Linguistic Accessibility of Social Assistance Rights in Slovenia (J5-50169) and the research programme Incorporation of the EU Legal Terminology into the Slovenian Legal System (P5-0217) funded by the Slovenian Research and Innovation Agency.

insurance, unemployment insurance, and parental protection insurance scheme. In 2021, the Long-Term Care Act (ZDOsk)[1] was passed, adding a new, independent social insurance scheme to the system. However, the act's application has been delayed by the newly elected Parliament a year later, with the deferral subject to a legislative referendum.[2] In 2023, an amended Long-Term Care Act (ZDOsk-1)[3] was passed and is now applicable. Next to the Bismarckian social insurance system, a subsidiary social assistance scheme is in place. It represents, as mentioned, a safety net for all persons and families who are facing poverty and social exclusion. Before claiming income support, beneficiaries have to claim, as will be discussed below, every available right from the social insurance scheme, e.g. unemployment benefits, sickness cash benefits, alimony or family benefits, and accept paid work.[4] The social assistance scheme also shares some characteristics with the third system, providing family benefits which are aimed at reducing child-rearing costs, since benefits under both schemes are generally tax-financed and provided on a means-tested basis. With the traditional categories of social insurance, social assistance, and family benefits, the Slovenian social security system is part of a larger social protection system.[5] The system also comprises a number of social advantages and social compensation schemes (partially introduced due to the COVID-19 epidemic[6]) that are commonly means-tested and paid on behalf of the state budget and are thus similar to social assistance.

Even though the fight against poverty and social exclusion is primarily reserved for social assistance benefits, provided both in cash and in kind, only a coordinated assurance of all types of social security benefits can lead

---

1 *Zakon o dolgotrajni oskrbi*, Official Gazette of the RS, No. 196/21.

2 *Zakon o spremembah in dopolnitvah Zakona o dolgotrajni oskrbi* (Act Amending the Long-Term Care Act), EVA 2022-2611-0048. The amendment entered into force on 28 December 2022.

3 *Zakon o dolgotrajni oskrbi*, Official Gazette of the RS, No. 84/23.

4 A. Bubnov Škoberne and G. Strban, *Pravo socialne varnosti* (GV Založba 2010), p. 364. See also Decision of the Constitutional Court of the Republic of Slovenia, No. U-I-110/15 of 1 March 2018.

5 G. Strban, 'Systematisierung des slowenischen Rechts der sozialen Sicherheit im Vergleich zur Systematisierung des deutschen Sozialrechts', Zeitschrift für ausländisches und internationales Arbeits- und Sozialrecht (ZIAS) 4, (2010/2011), p. 353.

6 See G. Strban and L. Mišič, 'Social Protection and the Pandemic in Slovenia: Between Income Protection, Social Policy and Politics', in: U. Becker and A. Seemann (eds.), *Protecting Livelihoods: A Global Comparison of Social Law Responses to the COVID-19 Crisis* (Nomos 2022), pp. 427 ff.

to an adequate level of social protection for all persons, families or groups of the population. Since traditional income replacement benefits, like pensions, sickness cash benefits or unemployment benefits, do not follow only the principle of reciprocity but also the principles of horizontal, vertical and intergenerational solidarity,[7] they may have a strong redistributive effect themselves, just like their income support counterparts. In this sense, they also prevent poverty and social exclusion. In this respect, the challenge of offering means for a dignified life to all members of society seems much broader than the challenge of offering minimum income protection alone.

However, it is the variety of so-called *social transfers* that mostly contribute to the alleviation of poverty and social exclusion in Slovenia. Until austerity measures that limited, reduced or even suspended the provision of several social assistance benefits were introduced around 2012,[8] they played a significant role in lowering the risk of poverty and social exclusion in Slovenia. In 2009, 11.3% of the population lived below the poverty threshold, with the number of poor and socially excluded residents increasing to 12.7% in 2010, 13.5% in 2012 and 14.5% in 2013.[9] In 2009, social assistance benefits still reduced the risk of poverty and social exclusion by 50%, whilst the numbers kept falling from 2011 onwards, when 44% of cases were prevented. In the years following the recession, the material deprivation rate increased as well, most notably in 2008, when it reached an all-time record of 17%, lasting more or less up until 2013, with the then EU-wide average of 19.6%. Despite a number of austerity measures introduced in the field of social assistance at the time, the level of income inequalities remained comparably low during the economic crisis.[10] Interestingly, the number of persons living below the at-risk-of-poverty threshold remained steady after said period, even though Slovenia has been experiencing record high employment rates in the recent years.[11] In 2023, 12.7% of residents were at risk of poverty, similar to the crisis years of 2009 and 2010. Even more residents (13.7%) were at risk of social exclusion, considering not only

---

7 Solidarity between generations is mentioned also by Article 3 Treaty on European Union (TEU), Official Journal of the EU, No. C 326, of 26 October 2012.

8 B. Kresal, K. Kresal Šoltes, G. Strban, *Social Security Law in Slovenia* (Wolters Kluwer 2016), p. 213.

9 See ibid, p. 21.

10 See ibid.

11 See, for example, Republic of Slovenia Statistical Office, 'More Residents Below the At-Risk-of-Poverty Threshold' (10 February 2023) < https://www.stat.si/StatWeb/en/News/Index/10898> accessed 4.07.2024.

the poverty line of EUR 10,832 per year in 2023 but also the level of work productivity. Last year, 264,000 residents lived below the poverty line whilst 62,000 of households faced energy poverty.[12]

Even so, there has been little public discussion on poverty and social exclusion in the recent years. Instead, record high employment rates (3.4% in the first quarter of 2024)[13] and a constant lack of job seekers were being put in the forefront. This changed temporarily during the summer of 2023, when Slovenia experienced the most devastating floods in its recorded history, leading to several legislative measures in the field of emergency social assistance and social compensation schemes.

II. Overview

1. Normative Background

a) Constitutional Provisions

The Slovenian Constitution, as inspired by international social law documents, contains no explicit reference to the right to social assistance. However, according to the Slovenian Constitutional Court, a lack of such reference in Article 50 on the right to social security does not mean that no constitutional protection is afforded. Conversely, following its well-established case law, the Court notes that Slovenia is a social state and that the legislator is thus obliged to offer appropriate assistance to persons in need. It is the aim of Articles 50(1) and 50(2) of the Constitution (general provision on the right to social security, regulation of social insurance schemes) that individuals enjoy economic protection and human dignity.[14] Therefore, the provision of social assistance remains subject to key constitutional safeguards, like the principle of legality, equality of treatment and possibly the protection of legitimate expectations, even if the right itself is not contained within the basic law. Article 34 of the Slovenian Constitution also guarantees the right to personal dignity and safety to everyone.

12 Republic of Slovenia Statistical Office, 'Income, Poverty and Social Exclusion' (2024) < https://www.stat.si/StatWeb/Field/Index/10/39> accessed 4.07.2024.

13 Republic of Slovenia Statistical Office, 'Labour Market' (2024) < https://www.stat.si/StatWeb/Field/Index/3> accessed 4.07.2024.

14 Decision of the Constitutional Court of the Republic of Slovenia, No. U-I-110/15 of 6 May 2021.

The right to personal dignity represents the foundations for one's free personal development and life-plan creation. According to the Slovenian Constitutional Court,[15] it guarantees to the individual the recognition of his or her value as a human being, from which his or her ability of self-determination is derived. The right is also a guarantor of personal rights. According to the Court, even the name of this set of rights itself suggests that they are granted to the person as such. Respect of personal rights also guarantees the protection of all elements of one's personality which are not explicitly protected by other constitutional provisions, like the freedom of conscience, freedom of expression, etc., and which offer to the individual means for their free personal development and a life grounded in autonomous decision-making. Since personal dignity and equal opportunities for all, coupled with the prevention of poverty and social exclusion, represent the core of all social assistance benefits, Article 34 is commonly recognised as one of its constitutional cornerstones,[16] next to the social state principle from Article 2 (Germ.: *Sozialstaatsprinzip*) of the Slovenian Constitution. This basic principle is included in the same article as the rule of law principle, marking Slovenia as a normative social state that provides social protection and personal dignity by means of statutory legislation and within the limits of the law.[17] At the core of the social state principle lies the principle of solidarity that represents no difference between public (social) and private insurance, but also a legal argument that has often been used by the Slovenian Constitutional Court when determining the constitutional meaning of social security rights and obligations. The Court has, for example, referred to the solidarity between persons with higher and persons with lower income in parental care insurance or, for example, decided that the legislator followed the solidarity principle when it determined the lowest and the highest calculation base within the pension and disability insurance scheme.[18] Next to the notion of vertical solidarity, i.e. solidarity of high-earners with low-earners, the Court explicitly referred to the principle of intergenerational solidarity, and, for example, the principles of mutuality

15 Decision of the Constitutional Court of the Republic of Slovenia, No. U-I-226/95 of 8 July 1991.

16 See B. Kresal, K. Kresal Šoltes, G. Strban (n 8), p. 214.

17 See G. Strban, 'Constitutional Protection of the Right to Social Security in Slovenia', in: M. Wujczyk (ed.), *The Right to Social Security in the Constitutions of the World: Broadening the Moral and Legal Space for Social Justice*, ILO Global Study, Volume 1: Europe (International Labour Organization 2016), p. 244.

18 See ibid, pp. 246-247.

and solidarity, unfortunately with no clear boundaries established in this respect.[19]

In social security, the principle of solidarity manifests itself in an interpersonal redistribution of risk-based burdens within the compulsorily insured community, possibly forming a community distinguishable from the society as a whole.[20] According to Pieters, it all boils down to the question of who belongs to the scope of application *ratione personae* in the distributing function of social security.[21] Even so, the Slovenian Constitutional Court argued that social insurance is a type of insurance which is not completely based on the principle of mutuality (as is private insurance) but also on the principle of solidarity,[22] interpreting the latter beyond its sole risk-pooling function. Interestingly, the personal scope of the constitutional right to social security is grammatically restricted to Slovenian citizens. Foreigners, even EU citizens, lawfully residing or even employed in Slovenia are not expressly protected. However, since Article 50 has to be read in line with international and EU law, as well as other constitutional provisions (such as the right to private property, applied for example in the field of pensions),[23] such narrow interpretation of its personal scope may be applied in the field of minimum income protection only.[24] The concept of membership, limiting the personal scope of social solidarity that guarantees the financial stability of national welfare systems,[25] is strongest in the field of social assistance, where access to rights is generally grounded in one's permanent and actual residence in the territory of Slovenia.

19 See ibid, p. 247.

20 U. Becker, 'Solidarity, Financing and Personal Coverage', The Japanese Journal of Social Security Policy 6 (2007)1, p. 1.

21 D. Pieters, *Social Security: An Introduction to the Basic Principles* (Kluwer Law International 2006), p. 21.

22 G. Strban (n 17), p. 247. On the notion of (social) solidarity see also L. Mišič, 'Theories of Political Philosophy as Guiding Principles in Social Security', Studies on Labour Law and Social Policy 25 (2018)3, p. 272 ff.

23 G. Strban, 'Lastninsko varstvo socialnih pravic' Podjetje in delo 41 (2015)6-7, p. 1251.

24 See G. Strban (n 17), p. 248.

25 K. Lenaerts, 'European Union Citizenship, National Welfare Systems and Social Solidarity', Jurisprudence 18 (2011)2, p. 398.

b) The Principle of Need

According to Dean, whenever we take *wants, preferences, desert* or *merit* as the prime organising principles in society, all of the above still amount to different interpretations or approaches to the principle of *need*.[26] On the one hand, a humanistic or humanitarian approach may be followed, on the other hand, it may be the paternalistic approach that prevails.[27] The economistic or market-oriented approach, as suggested by Dean, is concerned not with needs but with economic opportunities and consumer preferences. It expresses need in terms of the opportunities that people have to satisfy their wants and the preferences that they express in the marketplace, prioritising between jobs, homes, leisure pursuits and relationships.[28] From a liberal point of view, which is commonly concerned with persons' active participation in the free market, it is the friction between individuals' liberties and obligations towards the common good or considerations for the other that is triggered by the establishment of solidarity-based social security and (especially) social assistance schemes. The first are primarily shaped by the principle of equivalence whilst the second depend fully on the criterion of need, legitimising the distribution of wealth to the point in which social exclusion and poverty are effectively prevented.[29] Such philosophical underpinnings are important for the discussion since according to the Slovenian Constitutional Court, the legislator is faced with the difficult task of, on the one hand, fairly redistributing public funds according to criterion of personal and family needs and in line with the particular goal of a given benefit (i.e. assistance should be granted to those truly in need, and made available in appropriate from) whilst on the other hand protecting an economically-sound and effective public expenditure.[30] According to the Court, the constitutional right to personal dignity is related to the provision of certain minimum funds for the satisfaction of persons' cultural and other personal needs. A complete absence of such possibilities could be regarded

26 H. Dean, *Understanding Human Need* (The Policy Press and the Social Policy Association 2016) p. 4. On different criteria of just redistribution see also D. Miller, *Principles of Social Justice* (Harvard University Press 2003).

27 H. Dean (n 26), p. 5.

28 Ibid.

29 L. Mišič, 'Theories of Political Philosophy as Guiding Principles in Social Security' Studies on Labour Law and Social Policy 25 (2018)3, p. 281.

30 Decision of the Constitutional Court of the Republic of Slovenia, No. U-I-110/15 of 1 March 2018.

as a violation of the right to human dignity and, in this sense, the right to social security.[31] According to the Slovenian Constitutional Court, the social state principle on the one hand obliges the state to consider the *social interests* of individuals and groups of the population and to pass active measures as to afford everyone a *life in dignity*.[32] On the other hand, the Court also followed a narrow, less idealistic interpretation of the benefit's legislative intent, i.e. the abovementioned coverage of the most immediate basic needs.[33]

Regardless of the two almost contradictory approaches towards the minimum income benefit from 2006 and 2007, the legislator enjoys a broad margin for appreciation (using the language of international human rights law and of the Slovenian Constitutional Court) in the field of social security, especially in the field of social assistance, where it redistributes funds raised from general taxation and not funds raised from earmarked social security contributions that are (re)distributed within the more or less autonomous insurance group. Any constitutional review is thus refrained or limited, following the traditional division between positive and negative rights or human rights of the first and the following generations.[34]

2. Social Benefits

a) Between Social Security and Assistance

Uncodified and regulated by several legislative acts from different fields of social security law, alongside the basic law of the Constitution, the Slovenian social law refers to a 'system' of social security in a single provision. Article 58 of the Labour and Social Courts Act (ZDSS-1)[35] defines a social dispute as a dispute concerning rights, obligations, and benefits of physical, legal, and other persons who can be bearers of rights and obligations within the social security system, and for which the social courts are competent. According to Article 7, their competence extends to the fields of pension and disability, health, long-term care, unemployment, and parental

31 See B. Kresal, K. Kresal Šoltes, G. Strban (n 8), p. 214.
32 Decision of the Constitutional Court of the RS, No. U-I-11/07 of 13 December 2007.
33 See Decision of the Constitutional Court of the RS, No. U-I-116 of 9 February 2006.
34 See L. Mišič and G. Strban, 'ESL in EKČP: bremena človekovih pravic druge generacije in kako jih preseči' Delavci in delodajalci 21 (2021)4, pp. 515 ff.
35 *Zakon o delovnih in socialnih sodiščih*, Official Gazette of the RS, No. 2/04 to 196/21.

insurance, the field of family benefits, and the field of social benefits (Sl.: *socialni prejemek*) which comprise (monetary) social assistance benefits[36] and any other type of benefits that concern the social protection status of the beneficiary and are, as explicitly stipulated by the act, means-tested. On the one hand, procedural social law is referring to an open number of social assistance benefits stemming from material legislation. On the other hand, the inclusion of social assistance benefits within the social security system, as derived from a simultaneous reading of Articles 58 and 7 of the Labour and Social Courts Act, replaces, at least to a certain extent, the absence of the right to social assistance in the Slovenian Constitution.[37]

As mentioned above, the Slovenian Constitution does not explicitly recognise minimum income protection as part of the right to social security. However, the distinction between social security and social assistance is today somewhat fluid since elements of minimum income protection are commonly found in social security (insurance) benefits as well. Furthermore, the statutory right to social assistance is a subjective and enforceable legal right.[38] Even if discretionary decision-making powers of social assistance carriers, following their means-tested nature and a targeted, reactivation-based approach (e.g. granting benefits in kind instead of cash benefits), represent an integral part of social assistance legislation, a person or a family (household) will be entitled to any form of social assistance if the legislative conditions are met and if there exists no proof of misuse. Such powers must be exercised strictly within the margins of the law and cannot lead to plain discretion or arbitrary decision making and unequal treatment.[39] In case of a rejected claim, parties to the social administrative procedure can first complain to the competent ministry, then bring forward an individual social dispute. Judicial protection is afforded by specialised labour and social courts and by the Slovenian Constitutional Court, since the right so social assistance forms part, even if only implicitly, of the constitutional right to social security. Following limited constitutional provisions, social assistance benefits are also dispersed, as mentioned, through various pieces of statutory legislation.

---

36 Social courts are generally not competent in the field of social services and related emerging disputes.

37 *Ustava Republike Slovenije*, Official Gazette of the RS, No. 33/91-I to 92/21.

38 G. Strban (n 17), p. 244.

39 See A. Bubnov Škoberne and G. Strban, *Pravo socialne varnosti* (GV Založba 2010), p. 364.

b) Statutory Legislation on Social Assistance

The Slovenian social assistance scheme comprises both cash benefits as well as benefits in kind (e.g. social services). It represents a complex system of rights aimed at tackling a variety of persons' or families' social challenges, especially poverty and social exclusion. Its complexity is furthered by the fact that the applicable legislation is dispersed through numerous legal acts and is frequently amended.[40]

The Social Assistance Payments Act (ZSVarPre)[41] represents the main source of law for cash benefits in the field of social assistance. It regulates monetary social assistance (Sl.: *denarna socialna pomoč*), extraordinary monetary social assistance (Sl.: *izredna denarna socialna pomoč*), and the social assistance allowance (Sl.: *varstveni dodatek*). It also contains provisions on the assistance and attendance allowance (Sl.: *dodatek za pomoč in postrežbo*), primarily regulated in pension and disability, and now mostly in long-term care insurance legislation. If the person is not entitled to the latter allowance under sectoral legislation, their monetary social assistance may be increased by the amount of such allowance under the ZSVarPre. The main social assistance cash benefit is the monetary social assistance, which is aimed at alleviating the poverty of individuals and their dependent family members.

In 2012, a new type of social assistance was introduced. The legislator removed the state pension (Sl.: *državna pokojnina*) from the pension and disability insurance scheme – since it was provided on a means test basis – and created the so-called social assistance supplement, regulated by a special act.[42] When this happened, most beneficiaries shifted from one system of social security to the other almost automatically. Today, the social assistance supplement is regulated by ZSVarPre.

In 2014, two additional types of extraordinary social assistance were introduced with the aim of covering funeral costs.[43] They were once part of the health insurance legislation. The first benefit covering funeral costs (Sl.: *pogrebnina*) equals two basic amounts of minimum subsistence income (EUR 930.70) and may not surpass actual costs, whilst the second bereave-

40 See B. Kresal, K. Kresal Šoltes, G. Strban (n 8), p. 214.

41 *Zakon o socialnovarstvenih prejemkih*, Official Gazette of the RS, No. 61/10 to 196/21.

42 *Zakon o varstvenem dodatku*, ZVarDod (Minimum Pension Support Act), Official Gazette of the RS, No. 10/08 to 61/10.

43 B. Kresal, K. Kresal Šoltes, G. Strban (n 8), p. 221.

ment benefit or death grant (Sl.: *posmrtnina*) amounted to EUR 465.35 in 2023. Several means-tested benefits that are not included in ZSVarPre, like state scholarships or the right to a child benefit, are in part regulated by the Exercise of Rights from Public Funds Act (ZUPJS)[44].

The aim of ZUPJS is that persons take advantage of a variety of social assistance and associated benefits in a fixed order: child benefit, monetary social assistance, social assistance supplement, state scholarship. If the applicant does not follow the prescribed order, the public officer considers amounts of benefits that were available to the applicant as if they were granted, meaning that they count as personal income, potentially going beyond the threshold for a lower-ranked social assistance benefit or reducing its amount.[45] This adds to the complexity of the regulation whilst further limiting access to at least some social assistance or associated benefits. The Act also gives competence to territorially competent Social Work Centres (SWCs) to decide on several different cash benefits and social subsidies or incentives that do not strictly fall within the realm of social assistance. They are, however, means-tested and paid on behalf of the general state budget. They comprise subsidies for kindergarten care, school meals, partial or full exemption from the payment for a number of social services, like institutional care or co-payment for family assistants.[46] ZUPJS thus established a single-entry point into the world of different types of means-tested benefits, laying down uniform rules concerning the assessment of income, property or number of dependent family members, that accompany ZSVarPre. The legislator also enacted a number of social policies, for example in the field of taxation, employment or housing as to further the socio-economic status of the population whilst at the same time developing different regions in Slovenia.[47] ZUPJS also partially regulates family benefits, more precisely the child benefit or child allowance (Sl.: *otroški dodatek*), and its relationship to other rights like reduced kindergarten fees, or state scholarships. Systematically, all family benefits, aimed at reducing the costs of childrearing to

---

44 Zakon o uveljavljanju pravic iz javnih sredstev, Official Journal of the Republic of Slovenia, No. 62/10, 40/11, 40/12.

45 See ibid.

46 B. Kresal, K. Kresal Šoltes, G. Strban (n 8), p. 223.

47 See A. Bubnov Škoberne and G. Strban, *Pravo socialne varnosti* (GV Založba 2010), p. 377.

prevent poverty and social exclusion, are part of the Parental Protection and Family Benefits Act (ZSDP-1),[48] as discussed in the analysis.

If, on the one hand, ZSVarPre and ZUPJS regulate monetary social assistance and other means-tested cash benefits, a number of social services are, on the other hand, regulated by the Social Assistance Act (ZSV).[49] They also belong to the Slovenian social assistance scheme; however, they are aimed at preventing and eliminating social challenges that are not of a financial nature.[50]

III. Analysis

1. Access to Benefits

The first issue of the Slovenian social assistance scheme relates to its level of complexity. The understanding of rights and obligations as well as being able to effectively claim them is commonly difficult for the average beneficiary,[51] let alone for vulnerable groups of persons. Even if special administrative procedure rules favour claimants as weaker parties,[52] effective access to social rights remains limited. Since 2012, SWCs serve as single-entry points for most means-tested benefits as well as subsidies,[53] whilst public officers have a statutory obligation to check whether beneficiaries are eligible for any other benefit, either in cash or in kind. However, they cannot initiate a social administrative procedure on behalf of the party or, even more so, on behalf of a potential beneficiary who is not (yet) a party.

The application for social assistance or other means-tested benefits is filed by way of a single form, together with the documents proving eligibility.[54] This form should facilitate access to benefits and inform claimants on a variety of rights that are available according to the law. However, the form is complex and requires at least some familiarity with the legal terminology

---

48 *Zakon o starševskem varstvu in družinskih prejemkih*, Official Gazette of the RS, No. 26/14 to 153/22.

49 *Zakon o socialnem varstvu*, Official Gazette of the RS, No. 23/07 to 196/21.

50 B. Kresal, K. Kresal Šoltes, G. Strban (n 8), p. 214.

51 Ibid.

52 G. Strban, 'Country Report on Slovenia', in: U. Becker; D. Pieters et al. (eds.): *Security: A General Principle of Social Security Law in Europe* (Europa Law Publishing 2010), p. 419.

53 B. Kresal, K. Kresal Šoltes, G. Strban (n 8), p. 214.

54 Ibid, p. 223.

and basic notions in the field of social security. It is thus important that ZSV, among others, stipulates the right to first social assistance (Sl.: *prva socialna pomoč*) as a special type of social service that is aimed at recognising persons' needs and offering first advice in the matter. Unlike other social assistance benefits, it may be claimed from any SWC, regardless of their territorial competences that generally go by the claimant's place of permanent residence.

Public officers are thus namely well-informed on the socio-economic landscape in a particular area. Together, 16 SWCs cover the territory of roughly 20,300 square kilometres and roughly 2,000,000 potential beneficiaries. In 2023, for example, around 50,000 persons were entitled to receive monetary social assistance, whilst the benefit, granted to the individual whilst covering the needs of his or her dependent family members as well, comprised around 75,000 beneficiaries.[55] According to the Employment Services of Slovenia, 29,312 or 44.4% of unemployed persons were recipients of monetary social assistance at the end of 2021. In the three largest cities, Ljubljana (300,000 inhabitants), Maribor (100,000 inhabitants) and Celje (40,000 inhabitants), municipal SWCs have been established, whilst the rest cover regions or parts of regions. Some SWCs also partake in special social projects, like the regional SWC Posavje, which is involved with the Roma population.[56] In 2021, 3 SWCs also had in place special programmes for the social inclusion and activation for employment of the Roma.[57] According to Article 49a ZSV, SWCs not only carry out duties of municipal significance but also cooperate with competent NGOs. Nevertheless, they do not hold competence to act *ex officio* on behalf of a potential beneficiary who did not themselves initiate a proceeding. Conversely, SWCs may *ex officio* start proceedings against social assistance recipients if the circumstances regarding their eligibility have changed or if misuse is suspected.[58]

55 See STA, 'Prejemnikov denarne socialne pomoči oktobra skoraj 49.500' (4 February 2023) < https://www.sta.si/3135138/prejemnikov-denarne-socialne-pomoci-oktobra-skoraj-49-500> accessed 11.05.2023.

56 See < https://www.gov.si/zbirke/projekti-in-programi/vecnamenski-romski-centri/ > accessed 25.10.2024.

57 <https://irssv.si/wp-content/uploads/2022/10/Spremljanje_izvajanja_programov_socialnega_varstva_porocilo_o_izvajanju_programov_v_letu_2021.pdf > accessed 17.11.2022.

58 See B. Kresal, K. Kresal Šoltes, G. Strban (n 8), p. 224.

2. Benefits, Amounts and Conditions

a) Monetary Social Assistance

The second issue of the social assistance scheme relates to the amount of provided benefits, especially the amount of monetary social assistance, stipulated by ZSVarPre. Monetary social assistance or minimum income benefit represents the central social assistance (cash) benefit aimed at alleviating poverty not only of the individual, but also of his or her dependent family members. According to Article 2 ZSVarPre, the minimum income, alongside the social assistance supplement, is available to those who cannot make a living due to circumstances beyond their control. According to Article 8 ZSVarPre, the basic amount of minimum subsistence income is set at EUR 392.75 and reflects the at-risk-of-poverty threshold. Monetary social assistance is namely always tailored to persons' financial needs, since it is provided as a difference between personal income of the individual or family and minimum income as set by the line of poverty.[59] It is adjusted according to the Act Regulating Adjustments of Transfers to Individuals and Households in the Republic of Slovenia (ZUTPG).[60] Like a number of other thresholds, the amount is adjusted annually, following the increase in consumer prices from the previous year as determined by the Statistical Office of the Republic of Slovenia. Thus, in 2023, the amount of the benefit was set at EUR 465.34 net for an adult person without any income, whilst being increased according to the number of dependent as well as partially economically active members of the family. In comparison, the legislatively prescribed minimum salary for full working time reached EUR 878.48 net (EUR 1,203.36 gross) in January 2023, following an almost EUR 200 gross increase from 2022.

It is difficult to imagine how this amount can effectively prevent poverty and social exclusion, let alone enable persons to actively participate in public life and lead, if not a fulfilling, at least a decent life. According to Article 4 ZSVarPre, the benefit is aimed at offering to the beneficiary material means that are sufficient to cover their *immediate basic needs* and to make a living. From the reading of Article 4 ZSVarPre, it is clear that the

59 G. Strban, 'Pravni vidiki nove ureditve sistema socialnega varstva' Pravnik, 66 (2011)3-4, p. 171.

60 *Zakon o usklajevanju transferjev posameznikom in gospodinjstvom v Republiki Sloveniji*, Official Gazette of the RS, No. 114/06 to 153/22.

right is not aimed at enabling the individual to lead a free and fulfilling life, according to a rationally selected life-plan. Its aim is to cover one's basic needs only, which may also represent a violation of the social state principle when interpreted in a broader sense, i.e. through the prism of protecting one's personal dignity. From this perspective, need-based redistribution of societal wealth, where one's needs are understood as a bare minimum for survival, can hardly live up to the standard of a dignified life, unless a person's wants, wishes or desires coincide with their basic needs only.[61]

Social assistance, including monetary social assistance, is often not adapted to the local social and economic environment either (prices of, for example, housing, services, public transport), nor to the geographic and demographic characteristics of the beneficiary's place of residence. Different living costs in different cities, municipalities or regions may lead to differences in the impact of a given social assistance benefit. Even more so, especially bigger or richer municipalities commonly introduce special social assistance benefits or[62] subsidies for their (permanent) residents, making one's socio-economic status partly dependent on their place of residence even if key benefits, aimed at tackling poverty and social exclusion, are provided at the level of the unitary state within a functionally (semi-)centralised social assistance scheme.[63]

To prevent the so-called poverty trap and to promote work, economically active persons who work from 60 to 128 hours per month are entitled to a higher benefit of EUR 586.33 net. Persons who work more than 128 hours monthly receive EUR 702.66 net as an important incentive to remain or become economically active, whilst not immediately losing the right to monetary social assistance. Minimum income legislation follows a broad notion of persons' economic activity, recognising not only employment and self-employment, but also voluntary work, work of family assistants or carers and work within rehabilitation programmes, thus also following a broad notion of *merit* or *desert*, accompanying the central distributional

61 See, for example, L. Mišič, 'Theories of Political Philosophy as Guiding Principles in Social Security' Studies on Labour Law and Social Policy 25 (2018)3, p. 284 ff.

62 Article 21 of the Local Self-Government Act, *Zakon o lokalni samoupravi* (ZLS), Official Gazette of the RS, No. 94/07 to 80/20 refers to monetary assistance.

63 On the division of competences in the field of social security in Slovenia see L. Mišič and G. Strban, 'Devolution and Decentralisation in Social Security: The Situation in Slovenia', in: G. J. Vonk and P. Schoukens (eds.), *Devolution and Decentralisation in Social Security: A Comparative European Perspective* (Eleven International Publishing 2019), pp. 165 ff.

criteria of *need.* Whenever possible, social assistance benefits stipulated in ZSVarPre follow the logic of economic reactivation since they are of a purely financial nature. They are paid in limited duration and subject to review before periodical renewal, whilst recipients generally must register with the Employment Services of Slovenia and become or remain active job seekers. This does not apply to some groups of the population, like the elderly and permanently incapacitated male (65 years of age) and female (63 years of age) beneficiaries who may exceptionally receive permanent monetary social assistance. According to Article 28 ZSVarPre, unemployed persons claiming monetary social assistance also must prove that they have become unemployed against their will (e.g. no dismissal agreement with their employer with exceptions,[64] objective reason behind self-employed persons' unemployment) or without their fault (e.g. no culpable reason behind termination of employment contract). They are also not entitled to, may lose, or even have to pay back the obtained benefits if they, for example, refuse suitable employment, do not claim other rights that would positively affect their social and economic situation (e.g. maintenance allowance), lose other means of subsistence or income for reasons that were not beyond their control, or if they become incarcerated. Two types of suitable employment, determined by working time, distance from the person's home, level of education, etc., are found in the Market Regulation Act (ZUTD)[65], which regulates a variety of active employment measures alongside the Slovenian unemployment insurance scheme.

On the one hand, ZSVarPre stipulates the rights and obligations concerning key social assistance benefits, whilst on the other hand ZUPJS sets thresholds and the order of considered income within the means test, also for several other social rights like family benefits, subsidies and incentives (e.g. scholarships) or benefits of a mixed nature (coverage of medical costs). According to Article 17 of the Exercise of Rights from Public Funds Act (ZUPJS),[66] different types of property are considered when granting the right to monetary social assistance and other social assistance rights (real estate, movable assets, stocks, etc.), with some types of property excluded by law, e.g. real estate used as one's dwelling up to a certain amount in value, car or other transport vehicle up to a certain amount in value,

---

64 For example, if the claimant or beneficiary terminates the contract of employment due to family violence, and moves to a different and remote place of residence.

65 *Zakon o urejanju trga dela,* Official Gazette of the RS, No. 80/10 to 109/23.

66 *Zakon o uveljavljanju pravic iz javnih sredstev*, Official Gazette of the RS, No. 62/10 to 54/22.

etc. Differences between municipalities or regions are problematic with respect to housing prices, since homeowners who own and reside in real estate that exceeds EUR 120,000 may become eligible to receive monetary social assistance under special conditions only. Additionally, if a deceased monetary social assistance recipient owned and resided in a house or apartment surpassing the said threshold, his heirs will have to return the entire amount of received income support to inherit the property before the state.

The means test by which the amount of monetary social assistance and several other social assistance benefits is decided considers, as mentioned, the number of family members, with different criteria set for different types of members, e.g. the first adult person, the first adult person who is economically active, first child, etc. It also considers assets, like bank account savings, real estate, valuable movables, business and/or stock ownership, motor vehicles and vessels, etc., with different thresholds or exemptions set for different types of more common assets, like real estate (e.g. house or apartment up to EUR 120,000, as discussed regardless of the average price of real estate in the area, municipality, region, agricultural land, forest) according to value, motor vehicle according to value, bank loans if granted in respect to homeownership, additional pension insurance savings, general savings (up to EUR 2,500 or 3,500, depending on one's family status or age) etc. As discussed, monetary social assistance as well as other social assistance benefits are granted only to persons and families who could not ensure the necessary means of subsistence themselves and due to an objective reason and who have exhausted recourse to all other rights, e.g. social insurance rights or maintenance allowance that could have protected their livelihood. Therefore, all social security and other benefits are generally considered when determining the amount of the claimants' or beneficiaries' personal income. The discretionary decision-making powers of the SWC's follow the basic social assistance principle according to which everyone is primarily personally responsible for themselves and their family members in respect to preventing poverty and social exclusion.[67] However, potential beneficiaries might feel reluctant to claim some types of rights that could secure their livelihood, e.g. maintenance allowances following separation from violent spouses.

67 See B. Kresal, K. Kresal Šoltes, G. Strban (n 8), p. 213.

Since it is a tax-funded benefit and grounded in the redistribution of societal wealth within a one-sided social relationship between the individual and the state, monetary social assistance beneficiaries must hold permanent residence and actually reside in Slovenia for the necessary link between the individual and the tax community to be present. This applies both to Slovene citizens as well as foreigners, whilst special conditions are laid down for persons who were granted international protection.[68] According to Article 7(2) of the Regulation (EU) No. 492/2011 on freedom of movement for workers within the Union,[69] monetary social assistance should also be available, if meeting other conditions provided by law, to foreign workers, since they are entitled to the same social and tax advantages as national workers.

b) Social Assistance Supplement

Unlike monetary social assistance covering immediate needs of the person and family, the Social Assistance Supplement is aimed at covering living costs that have emerged gradually or over longer time periods, like home maintenance costs. It is granted to permanently unemployable persons or persons who lost their working capacity and who are older than 63 (women) or 65 (men) years of age. To obtain the said benefit, a person either must be a monetary social assistance recipient or fulfil the more lenient conditions for the obtainment of the allowance (EUR 684.05 for a single person in 2023). The social assistance supplement is means-tested and tax-funded, with the maximum income ceiling increased by criteria depending on the personal circumstances of the respective recipient.[70] Like in the case of monetary social assistance, the person is entitled to the difference between their personal income and the abovementioned threshold (max. EUR 218.71).[71] Since the benefit depends on the social risks of disability and/or old age, it is theoretically not clear which EU social security coordination rules should apply, i.e. general rules that exclude

68 See, for example, G. Strban and L. Mišič, "Migrants' Access to Social Protection in Slovenia', in: J. M. Lafleur and D. Vintila (eds.), *Migration and Social Protection in Europe and Beyond. Comparing Access to Welfare Entitlements* (Springer 2020), pp. 391 ff.

69 Official Journal of the EU, No. L 141/1 of 27 May 2011.

70 B. Kresal, K. Kresal Šoltes, G. Strban (n 8), p. 222.

71 See Ibid.

social assistance from the material scope of coverage, or rules on special non-contributory cash benefits (SNCBs). According to the latter, *lex loci domicilii* and the non-exportability of benefits rules apply. However, when the social assistance supplement was first transferred from the pension and disability insurance into the social assistance legislation, the Slovenian government also excluded it from Annex X to the Regulation (EC) No. 883/2004,[72] arguing that it has now become a traditional social assistance benefit. Insertion into the Annex is a constitutive element for the SNCBs according to Article 70 Regulation (EC) No. 883/2004.

c) Extraordinary Social Assistance

Unlike the social assistance supplement, which is aimed at covering ordinary but long-term costs, the right to extraordinary social assistance is aimed at covering unforeseen costs. The benefit stipulated in Article 33 ZSVarPre can be granted as a one-off earmarked payment (e.g. roof replacement due to hail damage) or a periodical payment over the duration of 3 or 6 months. The benefit may not exceed the monetary social assistance amount for a single person or family granted monthly, nor may it exceed five times the amount on a yearly basis. Additionally, three minimum amounts may be granted to cover costs incurred as a result of natural accidents or force majeure. From the wording of Article 33(3) ZSVarPre, it is not clear whether the benefit may be granted as a one-off payment in the amount of three monthly or three yearly maximum amounts when such costs are incurred. However, since the yearly amount cannot exceed the amount of five monthly amounts and since very high costs may result from natural disasters or other events, it may be concluded that the maximum amount comprises three yearly amounts and may reach several thousand euros. In 2023, the benefit was limited to EUR 465.34 monthly and EUR 2,326.70 annually for a single, economically inactive person.

72 Regulation (EC) No 883/2004 of the European Parliament and of the Council of 29 April 2004 on the coordination of social security systems, Official Journal of the EU, No. L 166 of 30 April 2004.

d) Social Insurance Benefits

An important characteristic of the Slovenian social security system is also the fact that several measures preventing poverty and social exclusion are found not in social assistance but in social insurance legislation, even after the latter was stripped of most income support benefits. Insurance-based cash benefits for low-income contributors are commonly increased according to the principle of vertical solidarity, i.e. solidarity of high-earners with low-earners, and are paid in higher amounts that they would have been paid if the insurance principle was followed to a greater extent. They are mostly found in the pension and disability insurance legislation. However, some insurance benefits are paid in amounts that may lead to poverty and social exclusion, triggering the subsidiary social assistance safety net.

Article 36 of the Pension and Disability Insurance Act (ZPIZ-2)[73], for example, stipulates that the minimum calculation base must amount to 76.5% of the average monthly gross wage in the previous calendar year. Following the principle of vertical solidarity, the highest calculation base cannot exceed four times the minimum. It also stipulates minimum pension conditions. The benefit cannot be lower than 29.5% of the minimum calculation base. Additionally, beneficiaries meeting general retirement conditions (60 years of age and 40 years of insurance with no purchased period)[74] are entitled to a guaranteed pension of EUR 653.75 (in October 2022), whilst the invalidity pension, obtained under general conditions, cannot be lower than 41% of the minimum calculation base. The said provisions are aimed at preventing poverty and social exclusion. However, the amounts that they guarantee are in some cases too low to effectively prevent the application of subsidiary social assistance provisions. According to the Slovenian Constitutional Court, the elements of mutuality and solidarity are a constitutionally permissible part of the insurance scheme since the Constitution defines the pension insurance as a type of social insurance and explicitly mentions the right to a pension as a social insurance benefit. Despite the proprietary characteristics of the right to an old-age pension, the Constitution however does not safeguard the right in a particular amount. Nevertheless, the lowest pension insurance benefits ought to protect the social minimum which

73 *Zakon o pokojninskem in invalidskem zavarovanju*, Official Gazette of the RS, No. 48/22.

74 The other general condition is 65 years of age and 15 years of insurance. In this case, the calculation percentage is only 29.5% of the calculation base.

cannot be understood as a basic subsistence minimum only as found in social assistance legislation, but as a minimum that provides the recipient with a certain living standard based on their work and the amount of contributions paid during their career.[75] As put forward by the Court in as early as 2003, the legislator, following the broad margin of appreciation in the field of social security and the principle of solidarity, is free to prescribe both the minimum as well as the maximum calculation base, as well as the ratio between them.[76] However, a flat-rate minimum pension for all beneficiaries would go against the constitutional right to social security from which social insurance benefits are derived, first and foremost, as proportional, income-sensitive cash benefits that do not reflect one's needs, but the previous standard of living.

Some benefits aimed at preventing poverty and social exclusion are part of the health insurance legislation, showcasing a broad legislative approach to income support. According to the Healthcare and Health Insurance Act (ZZVZZ),[77] some persons, for example those meeting poverty thresholds set in social assistance legislation, enjoyed full coverage of particular medical care even if they had not concluded supplementary health insurance for once rather extensive co-payments. In 2024, the system of co-payments was abolished.[78] Then, SWCs also granted the right to full payment of medical care on behalf of the general state budget which took on the costs borne either by private insurance groups, offering supplementary health insurance, or by the patients themselves, whenever no such insurance was concluded. The right that depended on one's entitlement to monetary social assistance was granted under the conditions set in ZUPJS. This also stipulates the conditions for the payment of social security contributions in the field of health insurance, since persons who are not economically active nor recipients of income-replacing social security benefits that lead to insurance must enter the insurance scheme by means of individual registration and pay a monthly insurance fee. The health insurance legislation also comprises benefits that are increased in cases of low-income contributors. Sickness

75 Decision of the Constitutional Court of the Republic of Slovenia, No. U-II-1/11 of 10 March 2011.

76 Decision of the Constitutional Court of the Republic of Slovenia, No. U-I-36/00 of 11 December 2003.

77 *Zakon o zdravstvenem varstvu in zdravstvenem zavarovanju*, Official Gazette of the RS, No. 72/06 to 141/22.

78 The system of co-payments, along with supplementary health insurance, was abolished in 2023 with ZZVZZ-T, Official Gazette of the RS, No. 78/23 of 19/7/2023.

cash benefits, for example, cannot be lower than 60% of the minimum wage.

Conversely, some insurance-based cash benefits are provided in amounts so low that they do not necessarily prevent poverty and social exclusion, let alone allow for the proportionate continuation of the beneficiary's lifestyle during times of an occurred contingency. Even if paid from a social insurance scheme, they are provided in amounts that may expose the person and their family members to the risk of poverty and social exclusion. According to Article 62 of the Labour Market Regulation Act (ZUTD),[79] no unemployment insurance benefit may exceed EUR 892.50 gross. First, the cash benefit fully neglects the insurance principle of reciprocity and, even more so, falls below the amount of the minimum salary, which in 2023 reached EUR 1,203.36 gross. Even if unemployment insurance contributions are significantly lower than contributions paid within most other insurance branches, thus making the scheme almost exclusively dependent on the state budget, the reactivating idea behind the provision seems to go up against the liberal-egalitarian ideal of equal opportunities, since the need for sustained labour market participation fully disregards the notion of *desert*. Put differently, a worker or self-employed person who becomes fully unemployed after earning a Slovenian average salary of EUR 2,144.72 gross or EUR 1,399.03 net at the beginning of 2023, receives around EUR 650 net, even if 80% of his or her salary, which is the calculated amount for the first 3 months of entitlement, would entitle the unemployed person to more than EUR 1,000 net. The principle of reciprocity only sets in after three months, when the person is entitled to 60% of his or her salary, which amounts to approximately EUR 800 net and falls below the upper limitation. In this sense, an unemployed person with, for example, a part-time working spouse and two dependent children may claim monetary social assistance straight after losing employment, unless they surpass the property threshold. Conversely, the amount of unemployment benefits cannot be lower than EUR 540,19 gross, which leads to the great paradox of the legislator who, on the one hand, tried to afford minimum insurance-based benefits that were to prevent poverty and social exclusion, and, on the other hand, failed to effectively prevent the provision of social assistance benefits of unemployed persons who may be entitled to the maximum amount of benefits. Additionally, current domestic legislation allows for much higher

79 *Zakon o urejanju trga dela*, Official Gazette of the RS, No. 80/10 to 59/22.

unemployment benefits to be paid to Slovenian-resident frontier workers, setting more than a double maximum threshold (EUR 1,785 gross) for whenever higher-income member states of last employment (commonly Austria, Italy and Germany) reimburse the benefits paid by Slovenia as the competent member state of residence.[80] It comes as no surprise that the competent ministry recently proposed substantial increases to both the minimum and the maximum amount of unemployment benefits. According to the Slovenian Constitutional Court, which also recognised the principle of adjusting the law to changing social relations as a sub-principle to the rule of law principle,[81] social security rights, e.g. insurance-based long-term care benefits paid from the emerging independent branch of insurance, have to provide (proportional) continuity of one's standard of living,[82] whilst social assistance benefits (and social services) should provide the amount of protection needed in order to alleviate poverty and social exclusion and enable the free development of every individual and the society.[83]

e) Family Benefits

As mentioned, measures aimed at preventing poverty and social exclusion are also a key feature of the Slovenian legislation on family benefits. They are generally means-tested, with the amounts dependent on the amount of personal income and number of children (e.g. child benefit), and granted either to parents who are not entitled to income replacement benefits from the parental protection scheme or those who fulfil other special conditions, like raising a large family (e.g. large family supplement), raising a child with disabilities (e.g. special child-care allowance, partial compensation for loss of income), etc.

---

80 See L. Mišič, 'Unemployment Benefits in the EU: Is Slovenia Fighting the Good Fight or Just Trying to Get Away with a Free Lunch?' (7 April 2021) < https://www.europeanlawblog.eu/pub/unemployment-benefits-in-the-eu-is-slovenia-fighting-the-good-fight-or-just-trying-to-get-away-with-a-free-lunch/release/1?readingCollection=37e593b8> accessed 25.10.2024.

81 G. Strban (n 17), p. 244.

82 Decision of the Constitutional Court of the Republic of Slovenia, No. U-II-1/11 of 14 March 2011.

83 See Strban (n 17), p. 244.

ZSDP-1 also provides parents with a one-off flat rate payment in case of every childbirth (EUR 421.97). The benefit could be disputed since it is an earmarked benefit the use of which cannot be controlled effectively, whilst being granted to all parents regardless of their socio-economic situation. From this perspective, an earmarked and means-tested benefit would ensure far better targeting, even if on the account of additional administrative work by the SWCs. Just like social assistance benefits, family benefits were either lowered or not adjusted to the rising costs of living during the economic crisis, with fiscal restrictions relaxed around 2015.[84]

f) Temporary Benefits

Most recent amendments in the field of social assistance, however, mostly came about as emergency measures only. Just like during the 2008 recession and the COVID-19 epidemic,[85] in which new and *sui generis* social rights commonly categorised as a mix of social assistance benefits, social advantages and social compensations were introduced, the legislator once again relied on novel, temporary means-tested benefits to tackle the energy crisis and inflation in 2022 and 2023. The Act Determining Temporary Measures to Remedy the Consequences of Higher Living Costs of the Most Vulnerable Population Groups (ZZUOPD),[86] for example, introduced a special energy allowance for monetary social assistance and social assistance supplement beneficiaries, as well as a special energy allowance for disabled persons, and formed a special regime for the exclusion of this benefit from one's relevant income concerning the means test for other social assistance benefits. According to governmental data, around 13,500 individuals will be eligible to receive the said benefit which can be calculated online.[87] Additionally, the legislator raised all pensions and wages in the public sector by 4.5%, as well as some other elements of one's work remuneration, to remedy the negative effects of long-term inflation. Excessive use of emergency legislation, which has in the recent years also become a norm in the field

84 See B. Kresal, K. Kresal Šoltes, G. Strban (n 8), p. 97.

85 See G. Strban and L. Mišič (n 6), pp. 427 ff.

86 *Zakon o začasnih ukrepih za odpravo posledic draginje za najbolj ranljive skupine prebivalstva*, Official Gazette of the RS, No. 117/22.

87 Republic of Slovenia, 'Ukrepi za omilitev draginje za ranljive skupine in družine' (11 May 2023) < https://www.gov.si/zbirke/projekti-in-programi/ukrepi-za-omilitev-draginje/ukrepi-za-omilitev-draginje-za-ranljive-skupine-in-druzine/> accessed 25.10.2024.

of healthcare, may violate the rule of law principle and its subprinciples, e.g. legal clarity and certainty, the predictability of law, and the systematic nature of the legal order itself.

3. Emerging Challenges

a) Social Services and Long-Term Care

A third issue of the Slovenian social security system that has an important impact in the field of social assistance is the dispersion of long-term care benefits and social services not only throughout different pieces of legislation but also different parts of the social security system, whilst necessarily offering comprehensive coverage. Social as well as long-term care services are important in any debate on poverty and social exclusion since they, whenever provided at the expense of the state or social insurance carriers, increase the disposable income of care recipients, therefore limiting the chances of income support provision. Like other social assistance benefits, need- and income-sensitive social services are afforded on grounds of citizenship and/or permanent residence. They are non-profit and exercised as part of the public social care service network, established and maintained by the state or, in some cases, municipalities. Several social services provided institutionally or at home commonly represent a mix of social inclusion, social care and healthcare measures. In this respect, social services like domestic care,[88] residential or semi-residential care (day care centres) and others, will gain importance soon. In October 2022, the average old-age pension amounted to EUR 777.72, and to EUR 971.09 net for 40 years of insurance, whilst the average invalidity pension amounted to EUR 663.46.[89]

88 Domestic or at-home care comprises assistance with activities of daily living, like personal hygiene, dressing, toileting, household assistance, like cooking or cleaning, and assistance with social interaction. It is one of seven social care services provided by the Social Assistance Act. However, it in itself comprises a variety of sub-services or sub-rights. At the same time, the regulation in the field of *family assistance* might appear similar to the regulation in the field of *personal assistance* even if there exist several paradigmatic differences between the two. The latter is regulated by the Personal Assistance Act, *Zakon o osebni asistenci* (ZOA), Official Gazette of the RS, No. 10/17 to 172/21.

89 Pension and Disability Insurance Institute of Slovenia, 'Mesečni statistični pregled' (2024) < https://www.zpiz.si/cms/content2019/-mesecnistatisticnipregled-koledar-objav> accessed 25.10.2024.

An average pension recipient who is not a homeowner and who cannot rely on their family members as social buffers can barely make ends meet, let alone make out-of-pocket payments for a variety of care services that are also available in the free market. Homes for the elderly, for example, are either public (13,501 places with 59 providers) or private (5,476 places with 43 providers),[90] with different municipalities potentially co-financing such care in different amounts. In 2022, the average daily costs of basic care amounted to EUR 23.06 (EUR 21.20 in public and EUR 25.52 in private homes for the elderly). The costs for the highest category of care amounted to EUR 34.49 daily in public, and to EUR 38.71 daily in private homes for the elderly.[91] Relatively small differences in price between public and private providers (around EUR 60 monthly for basic and EUR 128 monthly for advanced care) can be ascribed to the fact that private providers act as concessionaires within the public network. However, since the average old-age pension amounted to less than EUR 800 net in October 2022, and to less than EUR 1000 net for 40 years of insurance, the average retired person can barely afford institutional care in old-age. After paying for the most basic care according to the average daily costs of public providers, he or she is left with around EUR 80 of disposable income from the average old-age pension, whilst he or she cannot pay for the average daily costs of private providers (around EUR 776 monthly), nor afford advanced care, which may amount to over EUR 1,200 monthly. In comparison, the average invalidity pension amounted, as mentioned, to just over EUR 660 net in October 2022. According to Article 100 ZSV, the right to first social assistance, victim support and institutional care within SWCs, providing special training, are the only social services that are provided free-of-charge. However, some persons, like permanent recipients of monetary social assistance, receive all services free-of-charge, apart from institutional care, where organised care supplements or substitutes one's home and family functions (accommodation, nutrition, healthcare, etc.). Full or partial exemption from payment of social services may be claimed in from SWCs, whilst exemption criteria are stipulated by a governmental decree. In 2011, only 11.9% of the Slovenian population above the age of 65 were receiving long-term care benefits. 5.0% received care institutionally, whilst

90 Skupnost socialnih zavodov Slovenije, Splošno o domovih za starejše (2024) < https://www.ssz-slo.si/splosno-o-domovih-in-posebnih-zavodih/> accessed 25.10.2024.

91 < https://www.ssz-slo.si/splosno-o-domovih-in-posebnih-zavodih/cene-oskrbe-1-3-2022/> accessed 25.10.2024.

6.9% received long-term care benefits within their home environment. 2.1% of beneficiaries received informal, i.e. unprofessional care, covered by cash benefits paid to carers.[92] Long-term care benefits that were received within the home environment, however, mostly consisted of healthcare and had no social dimension.[93] A similar trend was observed in 2019, when around EUR 360 million of long-term care expenses emerged as healthcare costs, whilst only EUR 185 million figured as costs of social services. 23,227 beneficiaries received long-term care services within an institution, whilst 23,395 did at home.[94] On the one hand, long-term dependency should be perceived as an independent contingency and distinguished from sickness, injury, invalidity or old age.[95] On the other hand, it should be accompanied by all types of benefits that allow persons to live a dignified life during all of its stages, irrespective of the challenges they face. The provision cannot be limited to healthcare only. Additionally, at-home assistance is not provided free of charge, with prices varying from municipality to municipality. As mentioned, persons at risk of poverty and social exclusion may apply for full coverage of the right by their municipality, which co-finances (to a proportion of 50% or more) the scheme alongside its users. However, the payment of such costs (average costs for user per hour is EUR 5-6)[96] for those not entitled to the exemption may also trigger the poverty trap, with necessary recourse to monetary social assistance. This also makes the amount and/or type of provided social or other services potentially dependent on the socio-economic situation of the family, since close family members generally possess maintenance obligations under family law.

92 See M. Nagode, E. Zver et al., 'Dolgotrajna oskrba – uporaba mednarodne definicije v Sloveniji', Delovni zvezek UMAR 23 (2014)2, p. 38.

93 See ibid.

94 Republic of Slovenia Statistical Office, 'Long-Term Care Expenditure and the Number of Recipients of this Care Higher than in 2018' (15 December 2021) < https://www.stat.si/StatWeb/news/Index/10027> accessed 25/10/2024.

95 For an in-depth analysis see: G. Strban, 'Legal Aspects of Long-Term Care in Slovenia' in: U. Becker and H.-J. Reinhard (eds.), *Long-Term Care in Europe. A Juridical Approach* (Springer 2018), pp. 440 ff.

96 Republic of Slovenia Government, 'Pomoč na domu' (23 July 2024) < https://www.gov.si/teme/pomoc-na-domu/> accessed 7.07.2024.

b) Housing

One of the reasons for the rather low level of poverty and social exclusion considering severely low amounts of monetary social assistance or guaranteed wage can be ascribed to the high levels of homeownership. Historically, homeownership represented a *de facto* pension pillar of its own and is without a doubt still the most important and most common form of saving or investment or, put in other words, the most common and most important means of private income protection, especially in old age. Currently, 92.1% apartments in Slovenia are owned by natural persons. However, the statistics do not reveal how many natural persons own several apartments, with 36,400 apartments built between 2011 and 2021.[97] Nevertheless, in 2021 real estate prices grew by almost 17%.[98] According to the Deloitte Property Index, buyers in Slovenia have to put aside between 8 and 10 gross annual salaries to purchase a new own apartment, which amounts to between EUR 190,000 and 235,000 and is the overall country average, with real estate prices significantly higher in Ljubljana, the governmentally, economically and culturally centralised capital. By comparison, in Denmark, Portugal, Belgium and Norway, citizens need to put aside between 4 and 6 gross annual salaries only.[99] It is thus becoming increasingly difficult for young persons and families to rent, let alone own decent housing. As stipulated in Article 78 of the Slovenian Constitution, the state shall create opportunities for citizens to obtain proper housing. In this regard, special attention will have to be afforded by the government and legislator to the challenges of decent and affordable housing soon, otherwise housing costs may have a detrimental long-term negative effect on the levels of poverty and social exclusion.

97 Republic of Slovenia Statistical Office, 'Število naseljenih stanovanj se je povečalo' (1 January 2021) < https://www.stat.si/StatWeb/News/Index/10265> accessed 25.10.2024.

98 Republic of Slovenia Statistical Office, 'Dwelling Prices Continue to Rise' (23 June 2022) < https://www.stat.si/StatWeb/News/Index/10232> accessed 25.10.2024.

99 Deloitte, 'Property Index' (2022) < https://www2.deloitte.com/content/dam/Deloitte/de/Documents/real-estate/Property-Index-2022.pdf> accessed 25.10.2024.

IV. Conclusions

Minimum income protection in Slovenia is not limited to the field of social assistance alone. Measures aimed at offering material and other means for a dignified life to all members of the community are found both in poverty-preventing social insurance and poverty-alleviating social assistance legislation, as well as in the field of family benefits. This also applies to the field of taxation (the so-called *hidden welfare state*),[100] which has not been discussed in this contribution. Social assistance benefits are included in ZSvarPre and ZSV, whilst ZUPJS, the act setting income and other criteria concerning social assistance rights, very much broadened the competences of SWCs, which decide on several other means-tested benefits provided on behalf of the state budget. This requires a broad research approach to the topic of minimum income protection, a field in which the legislator enjoys a wide margin of appreciation with respect to the basic constitutional provisions that do not, as mentioned, directly govern the right to social assistance. Several benefits like subsidies or incentives as well as *ad hoc* or emergency measures are also of a mixed legal nature and do not fully fall within the established category of social assistance, where the right to monetary assistance represents the key cash benefit. It is accompanied, as mentioned, several other cash benefits as well as social services which follow different purposes (e.g. basic needs coverage, social activation, social inclusion) and sometimes share an important link with long-term care services. Generally, all benefits stem from the social state principle enshrined in Article 2 of the Slovenian Constitution but are associated with different constitutional rights, like the right to social security (Article 50), the right to healthcare (Article 51), or the right to personal dignity and safety (Article 34), depending on the legal nature of every benefit. Even if protected by the Constitution, some social assistance benefits are in practice, however, not high enough to effectively prevent poverty and social exclusion. Even more so, this applies to some social insurance benefits too, like unemployment benefits or invalidity pensions. The legislator thereby potentially violates the right to personal dignity and safety as well as the right to social security, especially with respect to social insurance benefits.

100 Taken from C. Howard, *The Hidden Welfare State. Tax Expenditures and Social Policy in the United States* (Princeton Studies in American Politics: Historical, International, and Comparative Perspectives 1999).

In the future, a rising demand for long-term care and the lack of affordable housing will add to the challenges in the field of social and economic rights and may have, if not considered by the legislator to safeguard timely and effective access to benefits, a detrimental effect on the socio-economic situation in the country and on its social assistance scheme. Even if granted a broad margin of discretion by the Constitution in the field of social security, the legislator must take the necessary action to adapt the legislation to relevant social change and, in doing so, fulfil its positive obligations towards citizens and other potential beneficiaries.

Minimum Income in a Decentralised State: The Complex Articulation between the Regional and State Level in Spain

Cristina Sánchez-Rodas Navarro and María Dolores Ramírez Bendala

I. Introduction

The need to guarantee a minimum income so that people can live in dignity is not at all a new idea: one of the aims of social security, already described by Beveridge[1], was to provide a guaranteed minimum income to any person, an objective now assumed to be among the socio-political values that permeate both the policies of the European Union[2] and those of the Member States, including Spain. In fact, the attainment of "providing for existence" of citizens while maintaining the capitalist production system will be the most outstanding target that modulates the concept of the social state (which Spain adheres to) that intends to guarantee individuals minimum levels of protection.

As the Council of the European Union recognises, "all Member States have social safety nets in place but the design varies across Member States, reflecting different national traditions and the overall architecture of social protection systems"[3]. Due to the heterogeneity in this field, it should be anticipated that when we refer to minimum income schemes in Spain, we always refer to cash benefits provided by the social security or the social assistance system, not addressing other rights related to people's welfare such as the right to free public health care, free public pre-university education or local services that can provide temporary shelter to vulnerable persons.

Minimum income schemes arrived in Spain three decades ago with Law 26/1990 establishing social security non-contributory disability and retirement pensions, as well as non-contributory family benefits. According to the Preamble to Law 26/1990, its aim was to establish and regulate a non-contributory level of economic benefits of the social security system, as a development of the guiding principle contained in Article 41 of the Constitution, which entrusts the public authorities with the maintenance of a "public social security system for all citizens". The unbreakable link between non-contributory benefits and solidarity was already present in that law, which states that the new benefits are "an expression of the general

1 In the Spanish translation: Lord Beveridge, *Seguro Social y Servicios Afines* (Ministerio de Trabajo y Seguridad Social, 1989), p. 15.

2 "With a view to ensure a life in dignity at all stages of life, this Recommendation aims at combatting poverty and social exclusion and at pursuing high levels of employment by promoting adequate income support, in particular by means of minimum income" says the first recital of the Council Recommendation of 30 January 2023 on adequate minimum income ensuring active inclusion.

3 Recital 20 of the Council Recommendation of 30 January 2023 on adequate minimum income ensuring active inclusion.

solidarity with people with fewer resources". There was no reference to dignity in this law.

Since 1990 to the present day, the list of (social security and social assistance) non-contributory and means-tested benefits has been expanding.

Social security[4] minimum incomes regulated by the state coexist with social assistance minimum incomes regulated by the 17 Autonomous Communities and the two Autonomous Cities (Ceuta and Melilla). This follows from the fact that Spain is a decentralised country and that the Autonomous Communities may assume competences over social assistance. With regard to minimum income schemes, it must be taken into account that all Autonomous Communities and Cities have passed relevant laws in this respect.

Moreover, the Spanish National Strategy to Prevent and Combat Poverty and Social Exclusion 2019-2023, approved in March 2019, announced the introduction, by 2023 at the latest, of a Minimum Vital Income (MVI).[5] However, the economic crisis resulting from the pandemic accelerated its implementation: Royal Decree-Law 20/2020 established the Minimum Vital Income, aimed at preventing the risk of poverty and social exclusion of persons living alone or integrated into a cohabitation unit when they are in a situation of vulnerability due to lack of sufficient economic resources to cover their basic needs. The MVI is a non-contributory means-tested social security benefit, not a basic income guaranteed to all citizens regardless of their economic resources. Since its implementation in 2020, the social security system has spent EUR 10 billion on the payment of MVI benefits[6].

The improvisation in approving the MVI and the lack of a prior reform of the pre-existing non-contributory benefits explains why the regulation was born with many deficiencies and gaps and has been subject to continuous reforms since its approval.[7] Nowadays, the MVI is regulated by Law

---

4 On the definitions of social assistance and social security in Spain see below, sec. II.2.a).

5 Minister of Social Rights and 2030 Agenda, 'National Strategy for Preventing and Fighting Poverty and Social Exclusion 2019-2023' (2019) <https://www.mdsocialesa2030.gob.es/derechos-sociales/inclusion/contenido-actual-web/estrategia_en.pdf> accessed 13.10.2024.

6 La Moncloa, 'La nómina del Ingreso Mínimo Vital llega a 575.000 hogares en marzo, 125.000 prestaciones más que hace un año (3 April 2024) <https://www.lamoncloa.gob.es/serviciosdeprensa/notasprensa/inclusion/Paginas/2024/030424-nomina-ingreso-minimo-vital-marzo.aspx> accessed 03.04.2024.

7 M. García Macías, 'El Ingreso Mínimo Vital y los Vaivenes del legislador' Revista de Estudios Jurídico Laborales y de Seguridad Social 5 (2022), pp. 205 ff.

19/2021 but reforms to the text have continued. There are few benefits that have seen so many changes in such a short period of time. Despite all this, the combined action of different minimum income schemes did not prevent high percentages of poverty in Spain.[8] In 2023, 26.5% of the Spanish population, i.e., around 12.7 million people, lived at risk of poverty and/or social exclusion.[9]

This latest failure cannot be blamed on the coronavirus pandemic, since already in February 2020 – a month before the Spanish government decreed a "state of alarm" (*estado de alarma*) – the European Commission had confirmed that the poverty rate in the country was 4.4 percentage points above the EU average and inequalities in disposable income remained among the highest in the EU.[10] Particularly worrying was the fact that among the Spanish working population the proportion of employed people at risk of poverty was 3.4 percentage points above the EU average. Just as in other EU countries, in Spain the threat of poverty is proportionally linked to the educational level of the head of household and his/her socio-professional status. Nationality is another factor to be taken into account as in cases where the head of household does not have the nationality of an EU Member State the risk of poverty is higher than average.[11]

In Spain, the national debate on minimum income has never been linked to the concept of human dignity. The topics addressed by the doctrine and the courts are basically computable and non-computable incomes, and European coordination under Regulation 1408/71 and 883/2004. Another recurring theme in the national debate is whether minimum incomes may discourage job search or encourage work in the underground economy.

8 Although this is not an exclusively Spanish problem: according to the European Commission, in 2017 around 25% of the population in the European Union were at risk of poverty and social exclusion. In 2021, over 95.4 million people still remained at risk of poverty or social exclusion in the European Union according to recital 11 of the Council Recommendation of 30 January 2023 on adequate minimum income ensuring active inclusion. The Union and the Member States are a long way from achieving the Europe 2020 target, which Spain has also failed to meet.

9 EAPN-ES, 'El Estado de la Pobreza. Seguimiento de los indicadores de la Agenda UE 2030' (June 2024) <https://www.eapn.es/estadodepobreza/ARCHIVO/documentos/Informe_AROPE_2024_completo.pdf> accessed 13.10.2024.

10 Eurostat, 'At Risk of Poverty or Social Exclusion in the EU-27' (2019) <ec.europa.eu/eurostat/cache/infographs/PovertyDay/PovertyDay_2019/index.html> accessed 13.10.2024.

11 C. Sánchez-Rodas Navarro, 'El Ingreso Mínimo Vital a la luz del derecho de la Unión Europea y de los Convenios Internacionales de Seguridad Social vigentes en España' Cuadernos de Derecho Transnacional 1 (2023), p. 631.

II. Overview

1. Normative Background

a) Dignity in the Spanish Constitution

One of the purposes included in the Preamble of the currently valid 1978 Constitution is to promote the well-being of all members of the Spanish Nation.[12] The "welfare of the individuals that compose it" was already mentioned as a goal for the government in Article 13 of the first Spanish Constitution of 1812. But such an ambitious goal did not spawn a minimum income regulation at the time.

With regard to the expression "human dignity", this has only recently appeared in Spanish constitutional texts. Of the seven constitutions that have been promulgated in Spain to date, only the current Constitution of 1978 includes the expression "human dignity" once, when proclaiming in Article 10.1: "The human dignity, the inviolable and inherent rights, the free development of the personality, the respect for the law and for the rights of others are the foundation of political order and social peace"[13].

Dignity is considered by the Spanish Constitutional Court "a fundamental legal value and the germ or core of certain rights that are inherent to it".[14] Although a database search would list more than three hundred rulings of the Spanish Constitutional Court that contain the expression "(human) dignity" in their texts, none are related to minimum income or social security or social assistance. All these judgments are related to a wide range of different issues, for instance privacy and personal freedom, fundamental right to an ordinary judge predetermined by law, permanent reviewable prison, right to freedom of expression, right to equality before the law, among others.

In Judgment 113/1989, the State Attorney – not the Constitutional Court – held that "human dignity must include, as inherent to its meaning, not only certain immaterial rights, but also economic rights which make it possible to ensure a dignified existence. In this sense, these economic rights must be considered within the category of inviolable rights which

12 The official English translation of the Constitution by the Congress of Deputies is available at <https://www.congreso.es/constitucion/ficheros/c78/cons_ingl.pdf > accessed 13.10.2024.

13 In the official English translation, human dignity is the term used.

14 Judgment 53/1985, related to partial decriminalisation of voluntary abortion.

are explicitly mentioned as inherent to human dignity in Article 10.1 of the Constitution". However, the issue under discussion was merely whether or not the rule that social security benefits were unseizable was in conformity with the Constitution.

b) The Constitutional Basis for the Right to Sufficient Benefits in Case of Need

As follows from the above considerations, the obligation to guarantee sufficient resources in case of need is not based on the concept of human dignity but is a consequence of the fact that Spain is constitutionally configured as a social and democratic state (Article 1.1).

From a political point of view, a democratic state will inevitably turn into a social state insofar as it has to attend to and respond to the demands of all sectors of society and not exclusively to those of one part of it.[15] In other words, in a democratic state, the right to vote guaranteed to all citizens makes that they have the capacity to guide, modulate and modify the policies of the leaders who come out of the ballot box and who represent them. And, conversely, in order to attract and keep the electorate's vote the political programmes will pay special attention to social rights. It is no coincidence that the introduction of a non-contributory level of social security was on the Socialist Party's election manifesto in the 1980s, while the introduction of the Minimum Vital Income was the flagship of an extreme left-wing party in the 2019 elections.

The aim of the social state is to "rectify and order directly, within the framework of a democratic system, situations of marked injustice resulting from a competitive society left to the free play of its own forces"[16]. Characteristic of the social state established after the Second World War is the inclusion of social and economic rights in order to provide citizens with areas of welfare and security. One of the basic pillars of the social state proclaimed by Article 1.1 of the Spanish 1978 Constitution is the public social security system. The formal scope of the "social security system" in Spain is not limited to insurance-based social protection, but also encompasses social assistance benefits. According to the Constitutional Court, "the purpose of social security is to reduce, remedy or eliminate situations

15 J.P. Royo, *Curso de Derecho Constitucional* (2nd ed. Marcial Pons 1995), p. 199.

16 S. Martín-Retortillo Baquer, *Derecho Administrativo Económico* (La Ley, 2nd ed. 1977), p. 32.

of need, situations which will undoubtedly have to be determined and assessed in the light of the general context in which they occur, and in connection with economic circumstances, current availabilities and the needs of the various social groups" (Judgment of the Constitutional Court 65/1987). More concretely, Article 41 of the Constitution proclaims that "public authorities shall maintain a public social security system for all citizens which will guarantee adequate social assistance and benefits in situations of hardship, especially in cases of unemployment. Supplementary assistance and benefits shall be optional". According to the Judgment of the Constitutional Court 65/1987, "Article 41 clearly configures social security as state function to meet situations of need that may go beyond the contributory coverage from which the system itself started and that is assigned to the public authorities".

However, Article 41 is not included among the constitutional fundamental rights and public liberties but in Part I, Chapter 3, which is entitled "Principles Governing Economic and Social Policy". This specific location – purposely intended by the drafters of the Spanish Constitution – has a legal consequence, insofar as "recognition, respect and protection of the principles recognised in Chapter 3 shall guide legislation, judicial practice and actions by the public authorities. They may only be invoked before the ordinary courts in accordance with the legal provisions implementing them"[17]. Thus, for the Constitutional Court, Article 41 lacks direct normative efficacy. Indeed, the content of Article 41 "is oriented towards the public authorities as a duty, but without creating individualised subjective rights" (Judgment of the Constitutional Court 68/1982). In other words, Article 41 is not directly applicable and needs to be developed by the legislator, who must enact laws to ensure its compliance.

As noted by the Spanish Constitutional Court, "[i]t is therefore up to the legislator to determine the degree of protection that the different social needs must deserve and to technically articulate the protection systems aimed at covering them" (Judgment of the Constitutional Court 128/2009). Therefore, "the right that citizens may have in the field of social security strictly derived by ordinary legislation and the legislator is free to modulate the protective action of the system in response to economic and social circumstances that are imperative for the very viability and effectiveness of the system" (Judgments of the Constitutional Court 44/2004 and 213/2005).

17 See Article 53.3 of the Spanish Constitution.

We can conclude that there are no direct subjective rights to benefits in situations of hardship other than those that have been expressly regulated by the legislator. However, there are two constitutional limits, that of equality and that of sufficiency.[18] Moreover, the fact that the Constitution specifically dedicates an article to social security has the legal consequence of blocking and limiting changes within the existing social security system.

In particular, Article 41 prohibits the legislator from abolishing the social security system without prior constitutional reform (Judgments of the Constitutional Court 65/1987 and 51/2006). It also implies that the legislator is bound to maintain a social security system respectful to the main principles that arise from Article 41 in the Spanish Constitution: social security, as a public task and a basic pillar of the social state, must be financed by public resources.[19] Therefore, the state is not only obliged to maintain a public social security system but also to finance it. The fact that in Spain social benefits are financed in an important percentile through social contributions[20] does not contravene this obligation, as contributions themselves have a tributary nature.[21]

Moreover, the social security system must be unique and unitary for all citizens and at the same time ensure the equality of all Spaniards in the exercise of their social security rights and duties.[22] This universal personal scope arises from the state's responsibility to maintain a public social security system "for all citizens".[23]

It is the state's responsibility to guarantee adequate social assistance and benefits in situations of hardship through the social security system. The legislator is obliged to regulate social benefits in case of need and not only against specific contingencies. Furthermore, the social benefits guaranteed

18 A. Ojeda Avilés, 'La Garantía de un Régimen Público de Seguridad Social', in: J. Cruz Villalón (ed.), *Las Transformaciones del Derecho del Trabajo en el marco de la Constitución Española* (La Ley 2006), p. 954.

19 M. Alarcón Caracuel, *La Seguridad Social en España* (Aranzadi 2010), p. 66.

20 People prefer to pay social contributions rather than taxes. That is so because they have the feeling that by paying social contributions they are going to be entitled to some kind of benefit in the future. This conclusion, nevertheless, is false because the fact of paying social contributions does not necessarily imply entitlement to social benefits.

21 E. Borrajo Dacruz, *Estudios de Previsión Social* (Aguilar 1962), p. 425.

22 Judgment of the Constitutional Court 124/1989, 7 July 1989.

23 According to the Organic Law on Foreigners, foreigners legally residing in Spain are equal to Spaniards in terms of the contributory and non-contributory levels of social security.

by the state must be adequate, otherwise the constitutional order cannot be achieved.

In sum, there is a constitutional basis for the right to adequate benefits in case of need that is not Article 10.1 of the Constitution (human dignity) but Article 41. In fact, all social security non-contributory benefits, including the Minimum Vital Income[24], have been enacted under Article 41 of the Constitution. And all of them are configured (by the laws that respectively regulate them) as perfect subjective rights.

2. Social Benefits

a) General Structure of the Social Benefits System and Competences

Article 148.1.20 of the 1978 Constitution says that the Autonomous Communities may assume competences over social assistance, while Article 149.1.17 attributes to the state the exclusive competence over the basic legislation and financial system of social security.

When the current 1978 Constitution was enacted, the state social security system established during the Franco era was based on the coverage of contributory risks only.[25] However, the existence since 1974 of a regulation on minimum supplements for beneficiaries of contributory pensions[26] constitutes the express recognition that the mere contributory level of social security can generate pensions that do not cover the basic needs of people who are in a situation of poverty despite having worked and paid contributions.[27] Until 1990, the central social security system was of the Bismarckian type, but with the approval of Law 26/1990 regulating non-contributory pensions, family and disability benefits, it became a mixed system. The

24 Article 2.2 Law 19/2021: "pursuant to Article 41 of the Spanish Constitution, and without prejudice to the aid that may be established by the Autonomous Communities in the exercise of their powers, the Minimum Vital Income forms part of the protective action of the social security system as a non-contributory economic benefit".

25 Judgment of the Constitutional Court 103/1983.

26 Its origin dates back to the Ministerial Order of 26 April 1974. See J. Rivera Sánchez, 'Los Suplementos de las Pensiones Inferiores a la Mínima en el Sistema de la Seguridad Social' Revista Laborum 4 (2015), p. 79.

27 This non-contributory and means-tested supplement is now regulated by the General Social Security system. For the year 2024, the income limits for the recognition of the minimum income supplement are as follows: without a dependent spouse: EUR 8,614 per year; and with a dependent spouse: EUR 10,048 per year. The maximum that can be received as a minimum benefit is EUR 6,402.20 per year.

Socialist Party was in power in Spain at the time. The design of these non-contributory benefits responded to the government's choice of the principle of redistribution, rather than the principle of universalisation.[28] Moreover, a minimum income scheme at the central level was introduced by Royal Decree-Law 20/2020, which incorporated the MVI as a new non-contributory benefit in the social security system.

At the regional level, through their statutes of autonomy, all the Autonomous Communities and the two Autonomous Cities assumed exclusive competences for social assistance outside the state social security system, as well as for social services. Each of them has their own social services laws[29] and there has been no joint plan for the development of them but rather the spontaneous organisation of each one in accordance with the interests and priorities of the autonomous governments. Social services can be benefits in kind or in cash: day care centres for the elderly, day care centres for drug addicts, shelters for transient, homeless or women victims of domestic violence, thermal social vouchers and others. The concept of "entitlement" in social services has a flaw and is not always a perfect subjective right. From 1989 onwards, the Autonomous Communities began to enact a series of programmes to combat socio-labour exclusion and fight poverty. In particular, they regulated social assistance minimum incomes. The models are very different from each other, with substantial variations in their design and especially in their degrees of coverage and level of protection.

In practice, this results in a parallel coexistence between the state public social security system, including the MVI, the social assistance and social services of the Autonomous Communities and those of the two Autonomous Cities.

As a result, the delimitation of competences between the state and the Autonomous Communities in the field of social protection remains formally simple. If the state legislates, the measures fall within the field of social security, if the Autonomous Communities legislate, it is considered to be social assistance. Following this division of competences, the MVI is formally defined as a social security benefit, while the regional minimum incomes are classified as social assistance benefits. However, at least two emblematic

---

28 R. Mota, 'La Política Socialista de Pensiones de Jubilación (1982-1996): entre Gradualismo y Redistribución' Panorama Social 4 (2006), p. 39.

29 EAPN España, 'Análisis de los Servicios Sociales. Las Personas Atendidas y la Perspectiva Autonómica' (2021), p. 11, available at <https://www.eapn.es/publicaciones/487/analisis-de-los-servicios-sociales-las-personas-atendidas-y-la-perspectiva-autonomica > accessed 13.10.2024.

cases show frictions between the Autonomous Communities and the state due to alleged encroachments on the competences of each one regarding non-contributory minimum incomes.

In Judgment 239/2002, the conflict was initiated by the Government of Spain against the Autonomous Community of Andalucía because the latter established the payment of a supplementary economic aid to non-contributory social security old-age and disability pensions in favour of beneficiaries of such pensions who have their habitual residence in Andalucía. The Constitutional Court dismissed the appeal arguing that one feature of the minimum insertion incomes financed by the Autonomous Communities was their compatibility with any other type of income, including pensions, provided that they do not reach the poverty line regulated in each case. Thus, this social assistance minimum income could be received by persons who actually receive non-contributory social security pensions. The Constitutional Court considers "that it is a requirement of the social state that those whose minimum needs are not covered by the non-contributory modality of the social security system should be able to access other benefits or aid of a different nature. This confluence cannot prevent the Autonomous Communities from acting in this common area when they have sufficient competence, especially if it is considered that, in certain economic circumstances, the scope of social security protection could entail limitations in terms of assistance and benefits which, therefore, require complementation with other sources to ensure the principle of sufficiency referred to in Article 41 of the Constitution".[30]

In another case, an Autonomous Community (Cataluña) sued the state before the Constitutional Court when the Minimum Vital Income came into force in 2020 alleging that the state had incorporated into the social security system a social assistance benefit, encroaching on the competences of the Autonomous Communities.

This appeal was dismissed by Judgment 158/2021 because an interpretation of Article 41 of the Constitution permits, together with the "social assistance", provided at the autonomous level, the provision of benefits of a social assistance nature within the realm of the social security system. Through benefits of a non-contributory nature – among which is the MVI

30 Andalucía has continued to pay this supplement which in 2024 amounts to EUR 178.42 to be paid in a single payment. Other Autonomous Communities also pay it, but there is no uniformity in its amount, for example in Galicia it is EUR 218 annually.

– the state fulfils the mandate entrusted to it by Article 41 of guaranteeing sufficient social assistance and benefits in situations of need. In other words, Art. 148 cannot entail an autonomous reservation of all matters of social assistance, since Article 41 allows the state to include an assistance level in the social security system. In short, although Cataluña has statutorily assumed social assistance as its exclusive competence and, in the exercise of its functions, guarantees a minimum income in its territorial scope, this cannot affect the exercise of the competences of the state when these concur with the competences of the Autonomous Community with a view to the same physical space or the same legal object.

b) Social Assistance: Coexistence of Nineteen Social Assistance Minimum Incomes with One State Social Security Minimum Income

aa) Regional Minimum Income Schemes

Nowadays, each Autonomous Community and Autonomous City has its own specific legislation about minimum incomes to combat poverty and exclusion. Between 2022 and 2023, 11 of the 17 Autonomous Communities have introduced changes to their minimum income regulations to adapt them to the MVI and it has been observed that there is a general tendency for regional minimum incomes to be subsidiary to the MVI.[31]

Regional minimum incomes share few common elements: they are non-contributory means-tested social assistance benefits. The calculation of the amount is differential. All of them require that the income of the family unit does not exceed the amount that would correspond to it based on the number of members and characteristics of the family unit.[32]

To live in the territory of the Autonomous Community or Autonomous City that finances the minimum income is a requirement shared by all regional legislations, although they vary as to the time period. Not all legislations require legal residency. No Autonomous Community presupposes

31 Autoridad Independiente de Responsabilidad Fiscal, 'Opinión 2/2023 Ingreso mínimo vital' (June 2023) <https://www.airef.es/wp-content/uploads/2023/06/IMV/230615.-Opinio%CC%81n.-Segunda-Opinio%CC%81n-IMV_AIReF.pdf> accessed 17.04.2024.

32 J. Lázaro, 'Renta Mínima Adecuada. A propósito de la Recomendación 2023/C 41/01, sobre una Renta Mínima que Procure la Inclusión Activa' Temas Laborales 168 (2023), p. 485.

a nationality requirement. Regarding the nationality of the recipients in those Communities that have provided data, 71% of the beneficiaries of minimum income are Spanish, compared to 29% foreign recipients.[33] It is generally not possible to continue receiving the autonomous minimum income when there is a change of residence between Autonomous Communities. Only Asturias, Cataluña, Galicia, Madrid, Murcia and Navarre contemplate the possibility of geographical mobility.[34]

In order to receive regional minimum income, the general rule is that an applicant must be registered as a job seeker. But there are also Autonomous Communities where registration as a job seeker is not mandatory, as in Aragon, Asturias, Extremadura, Madrid and Murcia. With respect to mandatory participation in social and labour insertion programmes this requirement is demanded by most of the Autonomous Communities, although it is not requested in Aragon, Baleares and Navarre.

There is also no uniformity regarding a minimum age requirement for the receipt of a minimum income: it is 26 years in Melilla, 25 years in Andalucía, Canarias and Castilla La Mancha, 23 years in Cataluña and La Rioja, 18 years in Aragon and Asturias, and 16 years in Valencia.[35] Nevertheless, all Autonomous Communities provide for exceptions to access their benefits at lower ages than those established in general.[36] Some Autonomous Communities do not establish an age limit (as Asturias and Cantabria), others do. In the latter case, most of the Autonomous Communities set the limit at 65 years of age (e.g. Aragon and Asturias), although others set it at 64 years of age (e.g. Andalucía and Castilla La Mancha).

With regard to the duration of the benefit receipt, 13 Autonomous Communities have no specific time limit, so the general rule is that the regional minimum income can be collected for as long as the requirements that gave rise to its concession subsist.[37]

The regional schemes have different parameters for calculating the poverty line, to the point that there is not even coincidence between the

33 Ministerio de Derechos Sociales, *Informe Rentas Mínima de Insercion en España* (2022), p. 27.

34 Ibid, p. 13.

35 Exceptional situations are usually foreseen by all Autonomous Communities to allow for access to the benefit at a lower age.

36 P. Burriel Rodríguez-Diosdado, 'El Desencuentro entre las Rentas Mínimas de las Comunidades Autónomas y el Ingreso Mínimo Vital: Decreciente Protección y Regulación Confusa' Revista de Trabajo y Seguridad Social 468 (2022), p. 72.

37 Ministerio de Derechos Sociales, *Informe Rentas Mínima de Insercion en España* (2022), p. 11.

computable or excluded resources, which are different depending on where the applicant resides. To give some examples: as a general rule, the value of the habitual residence does not compute in most of the Autonomous Communities, but it does in Cataluña. Scholarships do not count in most of the Autonomous Communities, but they do in Cataluña and Madrid. Ownership of motor vehicles counts in some Communities (as Cataluña and Galicia) and not in others (as Andalucía and Baleares). Only Aragon applies the same poverty line as the MVI.

With respect to the amount of these regional minimum incomes there is also no coordination: in Andalucía, the amount of the "Renta Mínima de Inserción Social" coincides now with the amount of the non-contributory old-age social security pension paid in 12 payments: EUR 604.21 monthly increased by 30% for each member of the family unit up to a maximum equivalent to 220% of such benefit, i.e., EUR 1,329.26 monthly. In the case of a single-parent or single-parent family units and family units with disabled persons, it is increased by 22%.[38] In Madrid, the minimum income is called "Renta Mínima de Inserción". One person living alone, with no other income, would receive EUR 469.93 per month, two people EUR 587.41, and three people EUR 662.52, up to EUR 965, which is the maximum amount to be received. In Pais Vasco, the minimum income is called "Renta de Garantía de Ingresos" and a recipient living alone would be entitled to EUR 840.29. A cohabitation unit of one adult with a dependent minor would be entitled to EUR 1,148. A couple with one child could receive EUR 1,288 and, if there were two children, EUR 1,456. One adult and four minors receive EUR 1,652.57. It is paid monthly.

As for the reference index used to calculate the regional benefit, some Autonomous Communities use the MVI (e.g. Andalucía); others use the Minimum Interprofessional Wage (e.g. Valencia), others the Public Multiple Effect Income Indicator[39] (e.g. Galicia) and only Cataluña uses an

38 The coexistence of the MVI and the Andalusian minimum income led to the adoption of legal reforms of the latter by Decree-Law 14/2022. Taking the amount of non-contributory social security pensions as a reference was one of the novelties.

39 The "*Indicador Público de Renta de Efectos Múltiples*" is an index used in Spain as a reference for the granting of aid, subsidies or unemployment benefits. It was created in 2004 to replace the Minimum Interprofessional Wage as a reference for these benefits. Monthly amount: EUR 600.

indicator specific to its Autonomous Community: the Sufficiency Income Indicator of Cataluña.[40]

It must be outlined that in all Autonomous Communities and Autonomous Cities, without exception, the percentage of women beneficiaries of the autonomous minimum income is much higher than that of men.[41]

bb) Compatibility between Regional Minimum Incomes and MVI

In 2022, the expenditure on regional minimum incomes was 5% less than the previous year, as practically all Autonomous Communities and Cities have decreased their spending. Of note is the decrease in Aragon, which has disbursed 67.38% less than the previous year, as well as in the Autonomous City of Melilla (-62.26%) and in the Community of Madrid (-56%).[42] This decrease does not mean that the number of people in need has decreased, but rather that the expense has been assumed by the state by paying the MVI.

The compatibility or incompatibility between each of the regional minimum incomes and the MVI depends on what the regional legislation establishes. For example, the MVI and the Andalusian minimum income are incompatible: applicants for the Andalusian minimum income must have a negative decision on their application for the MVI in order to be eligible for the Andalusian benefit.[43] As a result, the number of applications for this regional minimum income has fallen in recent years as has expenditure: 32,712 beneficiaries and a budget of EUR 77,223,918 in 2022 vs. 110,397 beneficiaries and a budget of EUR 107,673,708 in 2020. This incompatibility also exists, for instance, in the Baleares, Galicia, Cataluña and Cantabria. On the other hand, there are Autonomous Communities whose minimum income schemes are compatible with the MVI, but the amount of the

40 Ministerio de Derechos Sociales, *Informe Rentas Mínima de Insercion en España* (2022), p. 10.

41 Exactly 62.5% of women in 2022, see Ministerio de Derechos Sociales, *Informe Rentas Mínima de Insercion en España* (2022), p. 21. In Andalucía, in 2022, 63.71% were women. By age, the largest group is women over 45 years, see Junta de Andalucía, 'Memoria de la Renta Mínima de Inserción Social en Andalucía (RMISA)' (May 2022) <https://www.juntadeandalucia.es/sites/default/files/inline-files/2023/06/Memoria%20RMISA22.pdf> accessed 10.04.2024.

42 Ministerio de Derechos Sociales, *Informe Rentas Mínima de Insercion en España* (2022), p. 21.

43 Decree-Law 3/2017.

MVI counts as income to determine the poverty line to get these regional minimum incomes. This, for example, is the case in Madrid, País Vasco, Navarre, Asturias, Canarias and Valencia.

The advantage of the regional minimum income compared to the MVI is that all beneficiaries are entitled to a minimum amount (which varies greatly from Community to Community), whereas, as will be explained in detail later, in the MVI there is no guaranteed minimum, so the final amount may be very small.

c) State Non-Contributory Minimum Incomes Linked to Typical Social Security Risks and their Relationship to MVI

aa) Old-Age and Disability Pensions

Non-contributory retirement and non-contributory disability pensions were established by Law 26/1990. Both pensions share common elements. They are means-tested and have been listed under Annex X Regulation 883/2004, and must be qualified as special non-contributory cash benefits according to EU law.

To calculate the poverty line, the income and assets of the applicant and the members of his/her cohabitation unit are calculated according to the same criteria.[44] Spanish nationality is not a requirement, but legal residence in Spain is required: 10 years in the case of non-contributory retirement pension and 5 years for a non-contributory disability pension. Persons who do not meet these residency requirements may try to apply for the MVI, since the MVI only requires one year of residence in Spain.

The amount of these non-contributory pensions are determined annually in the General State Budget Act. In 2024, it is EUR 7,250.60 annually in 14 payments. The updated individual amount for each pensioner is established on the basis of the aforementioned amount but depending on the number of beneficiaries living in the same household, their personal income and/or that of their economic unit of cohabitation.[45] Beneficiaries

---

44 See Instituto De Mayores y Servicios Sociales, 'Pensiones no contributivas' (2024) <https://sede.imserso.gob.es/documents/20123/1595507/fpnc_2024.pdf/a614ed0e-7cd9-50e6-d0a3-c78a4bbb7f80> accessed 13.10.2024.

45 The amounts of the resource accumulation limit applicable in 2024 depending on the number of persons in the economic unit can be consulted at: Gobierno de España,

will never receive less than the minimum of 25%[46] of the annual amount. In 2012, a supplement for non-contributory pensioners living in rented accommodation was regulated by Royal Decree 1191/2012.[47] It consists of a one-off payment of EUR 525 per year.

On the other hand, there are also relevant differences between both non-contributory pensions with regard to the age requirement: beneficiaries must be 65 years old for a retirement non-contributory pension while the disability pension requires to be at least 18 years of age and not having reached 65 years of age. When the MVI was introduced, there was an age limit set at 65 years of age, probably because it was expected that at that age the person would be able to collect the non-contributory retirement pension. However, since the requirements for these two non-contributory benefits are different and collecting the MVI did not guarantee that the non-contributory retirement pension could be received, the maximum age requirement was removed for the MVI.

To be eligible for a non-contributory disability pension, the beneficiary must be affected by a disability or chronic illness to a degree of 65% or more.[48] Persons who do not meet this degree of disability have the option of applying for the MVI, since the MVI does not require proof of any degree of disability.

Other differences are that the non-contributory disability pension is compatible with the salary for work up to a limit in 2024 of EUR 14,450.60 per year. If this amount is exceeded, the disability pension will be reduced. Disability pensioners who are affected by a disability or chronic illness to a degree of 75% or more, and who, as a result, require the assistance of another person to carry out the most essential acts of life (such as dressing, moving about, eating and similar) are entitled to a fixed allowance equivalent to 50 percent of the amount of the pension (EUR 258.95 monthly).

Ministerio de Derechos Sociales, Consume y Agenda 2030 (2024) 'Guía resumen de las pensiones no contributivas de la seguridad social. Año 2024' <https://imserso.es/documents/20123/1595507/pncresumen2024.pdf/62e24a0f-cede-5580-326e-2baebbf2ad3c> accessed 08.04.2024.

46 14 instalments of EUR 129.48 each.

47 This is a pension supplement aimed at those persons receiving a non-contributory social security retirement or disability pension who can prove that they do not own their own home and that their habitual residence is a home rented from owners who are not related to them up to the third degree of kinship.

48 The degree of disability or chronic illness shall be determined on the basis of the scale provided for in Royal Decree 1971/1999.

Non-contributory disability pensions and non-contributory retirement pensions are incompatible with each other.

The amount of the pensions and benefits, whether contributory or non-contributory, public or private, are counted as income in order to assess the beneficiary qualifications for the MVI. Therefore, formally, the MVI and non-contributory pensions are not incompatible, but in practice, aggregated income above the poverty line will result in incompatibility. There is no obligation to apply for non-contributory pensions before MVI, nor vice versa.

Here too, it is worth noting that three quarters of non-contributory pension recipients are women.[49]

bb) Family Benefits[50]

A non-contributory benefit is granted for children with a disability of more than a certain degree (33% if under 18 years of age, 65% if over 18 years of age), regardless of the legal nature of the filiation, as well as for minors in permanent foster care or guardianship for the purpose of adoption, who are (financially or in any other way) dependent on the beneficiary and live with him/her. Beneficiaries can be biological or adoptive parents, foster parents and even applicants for adoption in charge of minors.

This benefit is not means-tested. Legal residence in Spanish territory is required for recognition, although no minimum period of residence is required. This benefit has not been listed in Annex X of Regulation 883/2004 and therefore is paid for children and minors residing in countries where EU law applies.

The amount differs according to the age and degree of disability of the dependent child or minor. For the year 2024 the amounts are:

- EUR 1,000 per year (EUR 83.33 monthly) for a dependent child or minor with a degree of disability equal to or greater than 33%;

49 Vicepresidencia Segunda del Gobierno, 'Estadísticas de Prestaciones no contributivas' (2024) <https://www.mites.gob.es/es/estadisticas/prestaciones_ss_otra_proteccion/PNC/welcome.htm> accessed 03.04.2024.

50 Since only a lump sum is granted, the non-contributory allowance for birth or adoption of a child in cases of large families, single parent families and in the case of disabled mothers or fathers will not be analysed here, nor will the economic allowance for multiple births or adoptions.

- EUR 5,647.20 per year (EUR 470.60 monthly) for children over 18 with a degree of disability equal to or greater than 65%;
- EUR 8,469.60 per year (EUR 705.80 monthly) for children over 18 with a degree of disability equal to or greater than 75% and who require the assistance of another person to carry out basic vital acts.

The receipt of this benefit for a dependent disabled child over 18 years of age is incompatible with the child's status as a non-contributory retirement or disability pensioner.

A special maternity allowance, not means-tested and non-contributory, is paid to women who, in the event of childbirth, would meet all the eligibility criteria to receive the contributory maternity benefit except for the minimum contribution period. The amount shall be equal to 100% of the Public Multiple Effects Income Indicator[51] in force (in 2024: EUR 17.93 daily). The duration of the benefit shall be 42 calendar days from the date of birth.

Formally, these two family benefits are not incompatible with MVI, but their amounts are considered in the means-testing for MVI, possibly leading to a sum above the poverty line, which would result in incompatibility.

cc) Unemployment Allowances

For unemployed people who are not entitled to contributory unemployment benefits there is a "second level of protection" consisting of eight different kinds of means-tested unemployment allowances. They share with the non-contributory social security pensions the common purpose of guaranteeing a minimum subsistence income to those who are in real need.[52]

Spanish nationality is only required in the case of Spanish emigrant workers returning to Spain from countries outside the European Econo-

---

51 The "*Indicador Público de Renta de Efectos Múltiples*" is an index used in Spain as a reference for the granting of aid, subsidies or unemployment benefits. It was created in 2004 to replace the Minimum Interprofessional Wage as a reference for these benefits. Monthly amount: EUR 600.

52 S. Barcelón Cobedo, 'Las Prestaciones Autonómicas de Garantía de Ingresos como Cobertura de la Brecha de Protección del Sistema de Seguridad Social en Relación con las Situaciones Reales de Necesidad Económica' Temas Laborales 143 (2018), pp. 13-54.

mic Area. All unemployment allowances are coordinated under Regulation 883/2004.

The amount is fixed: in all cases it is 80% of the Public Multiple Effect Income Indicator[53], i.e., EUR 480 monthly in 2024.

They are means-tested benefits: applicants' incomes on a monthly basis must be less than 75% of the Minimum Interprofessional Wage, excluding the proportional part of two extra payments.[54] Moreover, beneficiaries must be unemployed persons who have been registered as job seekers for a period of one month (waiting period) and who have not refused a suitable job offer and have not refused to take part, except for justified reasons, in promotion, training or vocational retraining activities.

If applicants are of pensionable age it is necessary for them to apply for the pension and not for unemployment allowances.

As a general rule, the benefit is provided for 6 months, extendable for six-month periods, up to 18 months, although there are exemptions. Only the allowance for persons over 52 years of age will be paid until the retirement age is reached.

Theoretically, the MVI is compatible with all unemployment allowances, although not in all cases both can be received simultaneously, nor, even if a person is entitled to receive both, will the same amount be received since the maximum monthly income that can be received for MVI is the difference between the computable income of the applicant and his or her family unit. This income includes the amount of unemployment allowances, so the amount of unemployment allowances is deducted from the total amount that guarantees the MVI. Therefore, whether or not the two minimum incomes (MVI and unemployment allowances) are compatible, in practice depends on the income of the applicant and his or her family unit. In any case, there is no obligation to apply for unemployment benefits before MVI, nor vice versa.

53 The "*Indicador Público de Renta de Efectos Múltiples*" is an index used in Spain as a reference for the granting of aid, subsidies or unemployment benefits. It was created in 2004 to replace the Minimum Interprofessional Wage as a reference for these benefits. Monthly amount: EUR 600.

54 The amount of social assistance benefits granted by the Autonomous Communities will be computed as income.

dd) The Active Insertion Income

It is aimed at the unemployed with special economic needs and difficulty in finding employment. It is a perfect subjective right although is not regulated in the General Social Security Law but in Royal Decree 1369/2006.[55]

The requirement for receiving the Active Insertion Income is to not be entitled to contributory unemployment benefit nor unemployment allowances. Moreover, beneficiaries must be under 65 years of age and have been registered as unemployed at the employment office for 12 months or more.

It is a means-tested benefit: the beneficiaries' incomes must be less than 75% of the Minimum Interprofessional Wage excluding the proportional part of two extra payments.[56] This benefit lasts for a maximum of 11 months and its amount is equal to 80 percent of the public monthly Multiple Effects Income Indicator in force, i.e., EUR 480 monthly in 2024.

The Active Insertion Income is incompatible with the non-contributory retirement and disability pension. However, it is only compatible with the MVI with the same limitations applicable to unemployment allowances. There is no obligation to apply for this benefit before MVI.

ee) Extraordinary Unemployment Allowance

The Social Security Act regulates the Extraordinary Unemployment Allowance for persons who are not entitled to unemployment protection either through the contributory or the assistance level, and also for those who have extinguished the Active Inclusion Income.

Beneficiaries must not have reached the age at which they are entitled to a retirement pension, whether contributory or non-contributory. They must be long-term unemployed workers.[57] It is a means-tested benefit. For 2024, the amount paid is EUR 480 monthly. The allowance is paid for a

55 C. Sánchez-Rodas Navarro, 'La Exportación de la Renta Activa de Inserción ¿Buena práctica legislativa?', in: M. Ramírez Bendala (ed.), *Buenas Prácticas Jurídico-Procesales para Reducir el Gasto Social* (Laborum 2015), pp. 65-93.

56 The amount of social assistance benefits granted by the Autonomous Communities will be computed as income.

57 A long-term unemployed person is a person who has been registered as a job seeker for at least 360 days in the 18 months immediately preceding the date of claiming the benefit.

maximum length of 180 days and cannot be recognised in more than one occasion.

This extraordinary allowance is theoretically compatible with the receipt of the MVI. However, since the calculation of the MVI is differential, this income will reduce the amount of the MVI or may even, when added to other incomes or assets of the applicant, exclude him/her from meeting the economic requirements to apply for the MVI. There is no obligation to apply for it before MVI.

III. Analysis

Since 2020, the social benefits listed above have been coexisting with the Minimum Vital Income, which is the main object of our analysis. According to Article 2.1 Law 19/2021, the Minimum Vital Income is configured as a subjective right, this implies that administrative appeals can be filed in case of denial or rejection of the benefit claim. Further, against the administrative decision, a lawsuit can be filed before the social jurisdiction.

1. Conditions

a) Nationality and Legal Residence Requirements

Spanish nationality is not a requirement to receive the MVI but 82.3% of all recipients are Spanish.[58] MVI is the only non-contributory and means-tested social security benefit that has not been listed under Regulation 883/2004.

MVI beneficiaries[59] must not only legally reside in Spain, but they must also have resided in the country continuously and without interruption for at least one year immediately prior to the date of submission of their application. Requiring a prior period of residence stems from the idea of avoiding "social tourism". The one-year period is not required for two categories of beneficiaries: minors incorporated into the cohabitation unit by

58 Secretaría de Estado de la Seguridad Social y Pensiones, 'El Ministerio de Inclusión publica una nueva estadística del Ingreso Mínimo Vital, que llega a cerca de 1,7 millones de personas en febrero' (29 February 2024) < https://revista.seg-social.es/-/nueva-estad%C3%ADstica-del-ingreso-m%C3%ADnimo-vital-febrero-2024> accessed 13.10.2024.

59 Asylum seekers are excluded from the MVI as well as stateless persons.

birth, adoption, family reunification of sons and daughters, guardianship for the purpose of adoption or permanent foster care; victims of human trafficking and sexual exploitation.

A change of place of residence within the national territory does not affect the collection of MVI. However, it is a cause for the extinction of this right to transfer the residence abroad, even if it is to a state of the European Union.

b) Age

Although the legal age of access to the Spanish labour market is 16, MVI's individual beneficiaries must be, as a general rule, persons of at least 23 years of age. There is no legal explanation as to why the threshold of 23 years of age has been set, since it does not correspond to any legally relevant age. This age limit does not apply in the case of women victims of gender violence, or victims of human trafficking and sexual exploitation.[60] Exceptionally, beneficiaries may also be persons between 18 and 22 years of age who come from residential centres for the protection of minors in the different Autonomous Communities, and who have been under the guardianship of public entities for the protection of minors within the three years prior to reaching the age of majority, or who are absolute orphans, provided that they live alone without being part of a cohabitation unit.

c) Means Test

The MVI is a means-tested benefit. Therefore, benefit holders will have to prove incomes below the poverty line calculated in accordance with the specific and complex rules for calculating incomes and assets[61] contained in Articles 11 and 20 of Law 19/2021. For the computation of income, the

60 Permanent users of a social, health or public health residential service benefit are not entitled to the benefit, except in the case of women victims of gender-based violence or victims of human trafficking and sexual exploitation.

61 Rules for calculating incomes and for calculating assets can be found at this link: Gobierno de España, Ministerio de Inclusión, Seguridad Social y Migraciones, 'Requisitos' (2024) <https://www.seg-social.es/wps/portal/wss/internet/Trabajadores/PrestacionesPensionesTrabajadores/65850d68-8d06-4645-bde7-05374ee42ac7/71a1fba3-daee-4b01-b447-5d6096cb154e/reglasparaelcomputodepatrimonio#Reglasparaelcomputodeingresos> accessed 13.10.2024.

income obtained by the beneficiaries during the fiscal year prior to the application will be taken into account. In case of cohabitation units, the income of all members will be considered. The regional minimum incomes will not be counted as income or revenue. The value of the habitual residence is excluded. Contrary to this, the amounts of pensions and benefits, whether contributory or non-contributory, public or private, will be counted as income.

It is not possible to collect MVI when the applicant is the holder of a net worth valued at an amount equal to or greater than three times the corresponding annual amount of guaranteed income guaranteed by the MVI for an individual beneficiary. In the case of cohabitation units, it will be understood that this requirement is not met if they are holders of a net worth valued at an amount equal to or greater than the amount resulting from applying the scale of increases contained in Annex II Law 19/2021.

Moreover, individual beneficiaries or cohabitation units who own non-corporate assets (without a habitual residence) of a value greater than that established in Annex III Law 19/2021 will be excluded from access to the MVI, regardless of the valuation of the net worth. Also excluded from access to the MVI, regardless of the valuation of net worth, are individual beneficiaries or persons who are part of a cohabitation unit in which any of its members is a legal administrator of a commercial company that has not ceased its activity.

Given the complexity of determining eligibility for MVI, a simulator is available to help potential beneficiaries consider whether or not to apply.[62]

2. Level of Benefits

a) Amount and Child Supplement

The amount of the Minimum Vital Income is the difference between the guaranteed income, fixed by law, and other income that the beneficiaries may have, provided that the resulting amount is equal to or greater than EUR 10 per month (Article 13.1 Law 19/2021). Therefore, the MVI can only be accessed if the beneficiary's income is lower than the guaranteed income, and the amount received will be the amount necessary for the

62 Gobierno de España, Ministerio de Inclusión, Seguridad Social y Migraciones, 'Ingreso Mínimo Vital y Complemento de ayuda a la infancia' (2024) <https://imv.seg-social.es/> accessed 14.04.2024.

beneficiary to reach this economic threshold. In case of cohabitation units, the income of all its members is considered.

In 2024, the guaranteed income in case of one single adult will be 100% of the annual sum of non-contributory social security pensions divided by 12, i.e., EUR 7,250.52 divided into 12 payments (EUR 604.21 monthly). In the case of a cohabitation unit, the above amount is increased by 30% for each additional member, adding EUR 2,175.16 per year (EUR 181.26 per month) to the guaranteed income of the unit.[63] However, as of 5 members, the amount stops increasing, so that the guaranteed income of the cohabitation unit cannot exceed 220% of an individual income. Therefore, for a unit of 5 members or more, the guaranteed income will be EUR 15,951.24 per year (EUR 1,329.27 per month).

The amount thus calculated may be increased by two supplements: in case of a single-parent cohabitation unit[64], 22% of an individual guaranteed income is added to the amount received, i.e., EUR 1,596.11 per year (EUR 132.93 per month). If any member of the unit has a recognised degree of disability equal to or greater than 65%, a supplement of the same amount is added.

Furthermore, a monthly Child Support Supplement will be granted for each minor child member of the cohabitation unit. This supplement had not been foreseen when the MVI was established: it came into force in January 2022 resulting from the fact that the MVI did not adequately protect those who, having family responsibilities, could no longer claim the non-contributory benefit for a non-disabled dependent child or minor.

The government states that this Child Supplement is having a particular impact on reducing child poverty. However, we believe that this is misleading, as practically, what used to be non-contributory family benefits for non-disabled children are now paid under the name of MVI.[65] In fact, Law 26/1990 had introduced non-contributory family benefits for non-disabled dependent children or minors. In 2019, there were a total of 1,223,482

---

63 The specific amounts are available at: Secretaría de Estado de la Seguridad Social y Pensiones, 'Cuantías y otras novedades del IMV en 2024' (4 January 2024) <https://revista.seg-social.es/-/novedades-del-imv-2024> accessed 12.04.2024.

64 In February 2024, there were 98,315 single-parent households.

65 J. Alvarez Cortés and V. Cardeñas Porta, 'Ingreso Mínimo Vital Como Prestación Familiar y La Supresión de las prestaciones familiares por hijos o menores a cargo', in: I. Villar Cañada (ed.), *Renta Mínima y Democrática Sustantiva* (UJA 2001), p. 101: the MVI is essentially a family benefit that aims to provide a level of income that fits many different types of households and is also intended to reduce child poverty.

beneficiaries of these non-contributory social security benefits which guaranteed a benefit of uniform amount throughout the national territory. It was a benefit coordinated by Regulation 883/2004 as a non-contributory social security benefit but not listed in Annex X. Nevertheless, this non-contributory family benefit was not only declared incompatible with the MVI but also destined to become extinct. As of 1 June 2020, the date of entry into force of Royal Decree Law 20/2020, which established the minimum living income, no new applications for the non-contributory family benefit for a child or dependent minor could be submitted. Therefore, former recipients of non-contributory family benefits have now statistically become beneficiaries of the MVI although the number of beneficiaries has decreased as the Child Supplement is not paid for children residing abroad, unlike the previous non-contributory family benefits.

The Child Support Supplement is part of the MVI and recipients are included in the statistics of MVI beneficiaries, although it can also be granted independently to families who, due to their income, are not eligible for the MVI if they meet certain conditions.[66] Statistics show that a total of 964,787 people in Spain received the MVI in February 2024, i.e., 258,619 individually and 706,168 together with the Child Supplement. In addition, there are 705,574 persons who only receive the Child Supplement without MVI.

This supplement is always calculated according to the age of the child at the beginning of the year for which the aid will be granted. In 2024, it is, for children under 3 years of age, EUR 115; for children over 3 years of age and under 6 years of age, EUR 80.50; and for those between 6 and 18 years of age, the aid amounts to EUR 57.50. The Child Supplement is not subject to the pension revaluation rules and its amount in 2024 remains the same

66 Beneficiaries must cumulatively meet the following requirements:1) income below 300% of the thresholds established in the scale of increments for the calculation of the guaranteed income according to the type of cohabitation unit; 2) a net worth of less than 150% of the limits established in the scale of increments for the calculation of the net worth limit applicable according to the type of cohabitation unit; 3) meeting the asset test requirements whose limit for an adult is 6 times the guaranteed income, with a scale of increments equal to that of the income limit according to the type of cohabitation unit. The limits for 2024 can be consulted at: Secretaría de Estado de la Seguridad Social y Pensiones, 'Guía sobre el complemento de Ayuda para la Infancia del Ingreso Mínimo Vita' (07 February 2024) <https://revista.seg-social.es/-/gu%C3%ADa-sobre-el-nuevo-complemento-a-la-infancia-del-imv> accessed 12.04.2024. In any case, the Child Supplement, when paid alone, has higher income and net worth limits than the MVI.

as in 2023; whether it is revalued in the future will depend on budgetary possibilities.

The amount of the beneficiary's MVI will be reviewed each year taking into account his/her income information of the previous year. As a result, 67% of the beneficiaries saw the amount revised last year and 16% had their benefits withdrawn after the revision, for which they were asked to return an average of EUR 2,500.[67]

There is scepticism regarding the potential of the MVI to overcome the poverty threshold, as the amounts of this benefit are recognised as insufficient to cover basic needs and household supplies.[68] Ironically, it has been pointed out that this is a benefit that is minimal rather than vital.[69]

b) Revaluation

Since the amount of the MVI is calculated on the basis of the amount of the non-contributory pension, it is revalued annually in the same amount as the non-contributory pensions. And pursuant to Article 62 of the General Social Security Law, non-contributory social security pensions will be updated in the corresponding General State Budget Law by at least the same percentage as that established by said law as the general increase in contributory social security pensions. The annual revaluation of contributory pensions is made in accordance with the evolution of the Consumer Price Increase.

Non-contributory pensions, once revalued in accordance with the quoted Article 62, will be increased each year by multiplying by 0.75 the poverty threshold of a single-person household. The poverty threshold for these purposes is calculated in accordance with the latest available data from the Living Conditions Survey of the National Statistics Institute, updated up to the corresponding year in accordance with the average year-on-year growth of that income over the last eight years (Additional Provision 53 of the General Social Security Law).

67 Autoridad Independiente de Responsabilidad Fiscal, 'Opinión 2/2023 Ingreso mínimo vital' (June 2023), p. 46.

68 J. Mª Prieto Lobato and P. de la Rosa Gimeno, 'Convivencia entre IMV y rentas mínimasbalance y propuestas desde los profesionales de la intervención social' Cuadernos de Trabajo Social 36 (2023)2, pp. 293-304, p. 302.

69 M. Básica, 'IMV: más Mínimo que Vital' Rescoldos 41 (2020), p. 10.

The concretisation of the amounts referred to in the previous paragraphs will be made by the respective general State Budget Laws for each year: in 2024 non-contributory pensions and the minimum vital income have increased by up to 6.9%.

3. Activation Mechanism

Initially, it had been a prerequisite to be registered with the Public Employment Services in order to receive the MVI, but this requirement was later abolished. Currently, the National Social Security Institute sends the identification of beneficiaries over 18 and under 65 years of age to the Public Employment Services of the Autonomous Community in which these persons are domiciled, in order to proceed to register them as job seekers.[70] However, the receipt of the MVI is not conditional on a commitment to accept a placement offer.

Since 2021[71], the state government has promoted pilot projects implemented by Autonomous Communities, local entities and the third sector to create itineraries of socio-labour inclusion linked to the MVI and financed by Next Generation EU funds (EUR 212 million). These projects have dealt with work and entrepreneurship, social accompaniment and non-take up, education, comprehensive care, digital training and housing, and fuel poverty. According to the report published in 2024 by the government[72], 76,000 beneficiaries have participated in 32 projects, mainly in Andalucía, Cataluña, Galicia and Madrid, and 80% were not working at the time of setting up the itinerary. 57% of participants were women and 30% of participants were foreigners.

On September 2022, Royal Decree 789/2022 improved the opportunities for social and labour inclusion of the MVI's beneficiaries guaranteeing that their disposable income will be higher than what they would have had if they had not taken up work. Royal Decree 789/2022 entered into force in January 2023 with the objective of serving as a stepping stone to facilitate the transition from a state of exclusion and poverty to a situation of social and occupational inclusion that allows people to integrate themselves

70 Eleventh Additional Provision of the Royal Decree-Law 19/21.

71 Royal Decree 938/2021 and Royal Decree 378/2022.

72 Ministerio de Inclusión, 'Palancas para la Inclusión' (30 May 2024), <https://www.inclusion.gob.es/documents/d/inclusion/20240530-laboratorio-de-politicas-de-inclusion-1 > accessed 19.11.2024.

better in the society in which they live. The amount of exempt income is calculated by applying certain percentages to the increase in income from employment or self-employed economic activity obtained in the two tax years prior to the review of entitlement. The incentive is greater in households with children than in households without children, or in households with only one adult (single-parent families) as opposed to those with two or more adults.[73]

As long as the statistics published by the government do not include the number of people who receive the MVI and work at the same time, it is not possible to assess the impact of the reform introduced by Royal Decree 789/2022. The fact that 62% of MVI beneficiaries in 2022 have maintained their benefit since 2020 does not suggest that collecting the MVI is a guarantee for getting out of poverty.[74] Moreover, it has been pointed out that MVI does not seem to overcome the distinction between unemployed people, people in need and households at risk of exclusion.[75]

4. Infringements and Penalties

Chapter VIII of Law 19/2021 regulates infringements and penalties for MVI beneficiaries. Infringements are classified in terms of minor, serious and very serious. Minor infractions shall be sanctioned with a warning to the offender.[76] Serious infractions shall be sanctioned with the loss of the benefit for a period of up to three months.[77] When the infractions give rise to

73 Trade union USO, 'Ingreso Mínimal Vital, compatible con un empleo a partir del 1 de enero' (11 October 2022) <https://www.uso.es/ingreso-minimo-vital-compatible-con-un-empleo-a-partir-del-1-de-enero/> accessed 13.10.2024.

74 Autoridad Independiente de Responsabilidad Fiscal, 'Opinión 2/2023 Ingreso mínimo vital' (June 2023), p. 75.

75 J. Mª Prieto Lobato and P. de la Rosa Gimeno (n 68), p. 300.

76 Failure to provide the documentation and information necessary to accredit the requirements and the preservation of the benefit, as well as to guarantee the receipt of notifications and communications, when this has not resulted in the undue receipt or preservation of the benefit, are minor infringements.

77 Among which are: failure to provide the necessary documentation and information or to communicate changes that would give rise to the modification, suspension or termination of the benefit, when these would have resulted in an undue receipt less than or equal to 50% of the due amount; the committing of a minor offence for the third time; failure to comply with the obligation to participate in the inclusion strategies promoted by the Ministry of Inclusion, Social Security and Migration, under the terms established; as well as failure to comply with the conditions associated with

the extinction of the right, the sanction will consist in the obligation to pay back three monthly payments of the benefit. Very serious infractions[78] shall be sanctioned with the loss of the benefit for a period of up to six months.[79] In particular, failure to comply with the obligation to participate in the inclusion strategies promoted by the Ministry of Inclusion, Social Security and Migration is also considered an infraction. When the infractions give rise to the extinction of the right, the sanction will consist in the obligation to pay back six monthly payments of the benefit.

In addition to the corresponding sanction and obligation to reimburse the amounts unduly received, and without prejudice to the criminal, civil and civil liability responsibility, the National Institute of Social Security may decree the extinction of the right, as well as the impossibility for the offending party to become a beneficiary for a period of two years.

5. Practical Aspects

a) Non-Take-Up

According to the Independent Authority for Fiscal Responsibility Opinion 2/2023[80], 58% percent of households that could potentially benefit from the MVI have not applied for the benefit (57% in 2021). These are concentrated in the Autonomous Communities with the largest number of potential beneficiaries (Andalucía, Cataluña, Valencia and Madrid). Only one in four applications for the MVI are approved by the Administration. Seventy-six

the compatibility of the minimum living income benefit with income from work or economic activity.

78 As, for instance, failure to notify any change or situation that could lead to the modification, suspension or termination of the benefit, when this would have resulted in an undue receipt of more than 50% of the amount entitled; travel abroad for more than ninety days a year, without having previously notified or justified such departure from Spain to the National Institute of Social Security; repeated failure to comply with the obligation to participate in the inclusion strategies promoted by the Ministry of Inclusion, Social Security and Migration.

79 On 27 March 2024, the media report the news of an Algerian who was receiving Spanish minimum incomes when he had been living in the south of France since 2014. He is accused of having unduly collected EUR 140,281, see J. Izarra, 'La Policía Nacional detiene a dos argelinos por cobrar 140.281 euros de ayudas vascas desde Francia' (27 March 2024) <https://www.elmundo.es/pais-vasco/2024/03/27/66047240e9cf4a9a638b458d.html> accessed 17.04.2024.

80 Autoridad Independiente de Responsabilidad Fiscal, 'Opinión 2/2023 Ingreso mínimo vital' (June 2023), pp. 12-74.

percent of households that could receive Child Supplement have not yet applied.

There is no single cause that explains this situation; among those that have been alleged are: lack of information for potential beneficiaries, difficulty in bureaucratic procedures, and fear of having to pay back money to social security if resources are obtained while collecting the benefit. In the meantime, more people without resources are sleeping on Spanish streets than before the pandemic.

b) Overlapping of Different Schemes

When the MVI was created in 2020, Royal Decree-Law 20/2020 required beneficiaries to have previously applied for all the pensions and benefits to which they may be entitled. This requirement no longer exists in the current Law 19/2021 that regulates the MVI. Therefore, nowadays the MVI is not really a last safety net after all benefits have been exhausted, because it can be applied for as a first option without having to have applied before for any other non-contributory benefit from the social security or social assistance system.

The most relevant difference between the MVI and other non-contributory means-tested social security benefits is that the MVI does not offer protection against a specific social risk, a feature it shares with the social assistance benefits regulated by the Autonomous Communities. So, a certain overlap will be inevitable as long as there has not been a reorganisation of non-contributory social security pensions and non-contributory social assistance benefits[81], something that does not seem likely since the Autonomous Communities are protective of the competences attributed to them by the Constitution, as is the case with social assistance.

There is no shortage of voices calling for the unified management of the MVI and regional minimum incomes, suggesting that the processing of the regional minimum income should always be a step prior to the application

81 M. Ramírez Bendala, 'IMV y Rentas Autonómicas. Un Nuevo Marco para una Recomendable Armonización aún Pendiente', in: I. Villar Cañada (ed.), *Renta Mínima y Democracia Sustantiva. De los Derechos de Pobreza a los de Ciudadanía Social* (Universidad de Jaén, 2021), pp. 137-151.

for the MVI, which would simplify the application process and speed up the resolution procedure.[82]

Moreover, since each non-contributory social security and social assistance benefit is subject to different rules for determining the poverty line and its amounts, it can be complicated for beneficiaries to know which would be more profitable for them. For example: it is true that compared with unemployment allowances, MVI has the advantage that it recognises an indefinite entitlement as long as the circumstances that led to it being granted persist. But the latter also applies to non-contributory pensions. On the other hand, MVI differs from the Active Inclusion Income and unemployment allowances which guarantee a fixed amount identical for all beneficiaries, regardless of whether they are single persons or members of a cohabitation unit.

c) Gender Dimension

It is mainly women who need to resort to minimum income schemes in Spain: two-thirds of MVI beneficiaries are women and they are, on average, 45 years old.[83] As Spain leads the unemployment ranking in Europe, it is not surprising that the largest segment of the population receiving the regional minimum incomes and/or the MVI is of working age.[84] In addition, persons in this group have a low employability profile due to their low level of education and training.

IV. Concluding Remarks

The Spanish social security system has been built on the basis of legal reforms and counter-reforms that have obeyed more the political or electoral

82 J. Mª Prieto Lobato and P. de la Rosa Gimeno (n 68), p. 299.

83 Secretaría de Estado de la Seguridad Social y Pensiones, 'El Ministerio de Inclusión publica una nueva estadística del Ingreso Mínimo Vital, que llega a cerca de 1,7 millones de personas en febrero' (29 February 2024) <https://revista.seg-social.es/-/nueva-estad%C3%ADstica-del-ingreso-m%C3%ADnimo-vital-febrero-2024> accessed 02.04.2024.

84 54% of beneficiaries had not received salaries in any of the three years prior to receiving the MVI in 2020: Autoridad Independiente de Responsabilidad Fiscal, 'Opinión 2/2023 Ingreso mínimo vital' (June 2023), p. 5.

interests of the moment than focused on long-term programming. This consideration applies to minimum income schemes as well.

The constitutional basis for the right to adequate benefits in case of need is not Article 10.1 (human dignity) but Article 41 of the 1978 Constitution, which establishes that the public authorities shall maintain a public social security system for all citizens which will guarantee adequate social assistance and benefits in situations of hardship. However, this right has no direct effect insofar as it could only be invoked before the ordinary courts in accordance with the legal provisions implementing them.

Without a doubt, the interrelationship between all the social protection measures analysed in this chapter is a bit chaotic: although the MVI was intended to homogenise the diversity of minimum income systems that existed throughout the territory, the fact is that all pre-existing minimum incomes (with the exception of the non-contributory family allowance for non-disabled children) remain in place. The MVI is a very important step forward for the non-contributory branch of social security. However, the multiplicity of existing non-contributory benefits and allowances implies that the social security system needs to be coordinated and regulated in order to clarify the relationship between all the social protection measures analysed.

The complexity of the Spanish minimum income system derives, on the one hand, from the large number of benefits, and on the other, from the variety of administrations involved in its design, management and financing, in accordance with the competences attributed to each one by the Spanish Constitution, which implies diversity in benefit amounts, access requirements, duration of benefits, etc. The Minimum Vital Income is, for the time being, the last non-contributory and means-tested cash benefit to be added to the list of non-contributory social security level payments. Its originality is that it is not directly linked to any typical social security risk and that it is the first one to incorporate the term "minimum income" in its name, but it would be a mistake to consider the MVI to be the only social security benefit to guarantee a minimum income.

A characteristic feature of the Spanish social protection system is that it does not recognise a universal basic income, insofar as all minimum incomes schemes are linked to a poverty line (which is different for each specific benefit).

It is worth noting that three quarters of the beneficiaries of minimum income, both state and regional, are women and most of them are of working age. Admittedly, the best way to combat poverty would be to incorporate them into the labour market, something extremely complex in a country that has one of the highest unemployment rates in the European Union. Therefore, the improvement of the minimum income schemes currently in place is, ultimately, the best way to adapt social protection to a system where full employment is currently not possible.

Regressive and Precarious? – (Legal) Protection of a Subsistence Minimum in the United Kingdom

Nikola Wilman

I. Introduction

The United Kingdom (UK),[1] like many other advanced industrialized nations, has experienced significant social and economic change in the past 60 years.

1 Social security is mostly a reserved matter in Great Britain (England, Scotland and Wales). However, the responsibility for certain benefits have been devolved to the Scottish Parliament. Any and all benefits not explicitly devolved by the Scotland Act 2016 continue to be reserved, which include means-tested benefits such as Universal Credit and the benefits and tax credits it is replacing. In Northern Ireland social

The UK's modern welfare[2] state was established gradually in the first half of the 20th century, based primarily on the contributory principle. Prior to the 20th Century, social security provision took the form of means-tested *Poor Law* provision, administered in local parishes and often delivered in workhouses. The provision of relief, as much a church and charitable duty as a state one, was geographically dispersed and, for the able-bodied poor, it was more concerned with discouraging uptake than facilitating access.[3]

This dynamic was transformed by a series of reforms between 1906 and 1948, when the state focus shifted to citizen welfare. According to *Marshall*, these 20th-century reforms established a social right of citizenship, which included a "right to welfare" ensuring that every member of society has the opportunity to live "the life of a civilized being in accordance with the standards prevailing" or at the very least, "a modicum of economic welfare and security".[4]

The National Insurance System, first introduced in 1912, was extended significantly as part of the post-Second World War welfare state, based on the model proposed by William Beveridge. In contrast to other European models of social security, Beveridge had advocated that social insurance should provide "flat-rate", rather than earnings-related, benefits, in exchange for the payment of "flat-rate" contributions. In Beveridge's opinion, this was the best approach to guarantee that the state provided a "basis minimum" while encouraging citizens to make further provisions for themselves through private insurance or savings.[5]

The *National Assistance Act 1948* imposed an explicit duty on the state "to assist persons in Great Britain who are without resources to meet their requirements, or whose resources [...] must be supplemented in order to meet their requirements".[6] The *Ministry of Social Security Act 1966* conferred a "right to benefit" upon "every person... whose resources are

---

security is almost entirely devolved (or "transferred") and is the responsibility of the Department for Communities (aside from the HRMC benefits and tax credits). By long-standing convention, however, Northern Ireland maintains "parity" with social security, child maintenance and pension systems in Great Britain.

2 In this paper, the term "welfare" refers to the individual's ability to attain a minimum standard of living. Means-tested benefits for the relief of poverty, often described as 'welfare' are referred to by name or collectively as 'social assistance'.

3 S. Hardy, *Social Security Law in the United Kingdom* (3rd ed. Wolters Kluwer 2019), pp. 25 ff.

4 T. H. Marshall and T. Bottamore, *Citizenship and Social Class* (Pluto Press 1992), p. 8.

5 S. Hardy (n 3), p. 26.

6 *National Assistance Act 1948*, c29 s4.

insufficient to meet his requirements" and gave the *Supplementary Benefits Commission (SBC)* authority to provide "benefit [...] by way of a single payment to meet an exceptional need".[7] The Act, for the first time, "framed the citizen's claim for means-tested benefits as a legal entitlement" rather than something which was within the discretion of government.[8] Case law reinforced the fundamental principle that the state had a responsibility to ensure, by some means, that those lawfully residing in the United Kingdom could meet their needs by bridging any gap between the household's available resources and its needs, although it was not necessarily required to do so by providing cash.[9]

However, this statutory duty to provide a subsistence minimum has been weakened by the political ideology of individual responsibility for welfare provision held by successive governments, and later exacerbated by austerity and post-pandemic provisions that restrict the financial and public resources available to those without independent means of support.[10] This ideology was driven by concerns about rising public spending and that benefits were leading to a "dependency culture".[11] The statutory obligation, established in 1948 (see above) to provide a subsistence minimum began to be eroded with the exclusion of those on strike due to a labour dispute.[12] 1980 regulations primarily precluded strikers and their families from receiving supplementary benefits.[13] In *Donnison's* analysis this was the point where the government broke with "a centuries old tradition that those who administer the poor laws must in last resort prevent people from starving, no matter what the cause of their plight."[14] In subsequent years, the protection afforded by a subsistence minimum would be further

7 *Ministry of Social Security Act 1966*, c20 s4, 7; *Supplementary Benefits Act 1976*, c71 s1, 3.

8 T. Buck, *The Social Fund: Law and Practice* (3rd ed. Sweet & Maxwell 2009), para.1.25.

9 *Supplementary Benefits Commission* v *Jull; Y* v *Supplementary Benefits Commission* [1981] AC 1025 at 1031 (Viscount Dilhorne); 1037 (Lord Salmon).

10 M. Simpson, G. McKeever, C. Fitzpatrick, 'Legal Protection Against Destitution in the UK: the Case for a Right to a Subsistence Minimum' Modern Law Review 86 (2022) 2, pp. 465-497, 495.

11 A. Le Sueur, 'Constitutional Protection of Rights to Social Security in the United Kingdom' Queen Mary School of Law Legal Studies Research Paper 108 (2012), p. 9.

12 *Ministry of Social Security Act 1966*, c20 s10.

13 *Supplementary Benefit (Trade Disputes and Recovery from Earnings) Regulations 1980*, S.I. 1980 No. 1641.

14 D. Donnison, 'The Politics of Poverty' (Blackwell Publishers 1982), p. 73.

eroded. A growing number of non-UK nationals were ineligible to receive income support, the successor to supplementary benefit, along with restrictions on access to paid employment and certain other benefits.[15] The *Social Fund*, which was introduced in 1986 and provided a discretionary system of loans and payments for one-off expenses, was abolished in 2012, with powers devolved to local authorities in England and regional legislatures in Scotland, Wales, and Northern Ireland – albeit without a legal obligation to replace the abolished national scheme or a ring-fenced budget.[16]

Since the mid-1990s, there has been a striking cross-party continuity of approach between governments (first Conservative, then, in succession, Labour, Coalition, and again Conservative), all of whom appear to have adopted the dominant ideology of conditionality, linking entitlement to social security benefits to an individual's behaviour.[17] Job seeking requirements having been progressively tightened and extended to ever more groups of out-of-work benefit claimants in successive reforms since the late 1990s.[18] However, "in-work-benefits" for low-income households were also promoted through the development of a large and complex system of tax credits administered by the UK Treasury, which combined the goals of encouraging people to move into low-paid employment and combating poverty, particularly among families with children.[19] By the time of the introduction of the tax credit policy in 1997, wage levels of the lowest percentile of the workforce had fallen to historically low levels; this was the result of deregulatory measures such as abolition of Wages Councils and the

15 *Income Support (General) Regulations 1987*, S.I. 1987 No. 1967, reg 21; sch 7 para 17; *Asylum and Immigration Act 1996*, c49 ss 8-11: Migrants in the UK on visas, illegally or seeking asylum are usually ineligible for most social welfare benefits and public housing, referred to as having 'no recourse to public funds' (NRPF). A few categories of people, including those granted permission to remain in the UK for human rights reasons, can apply for a 'change of conditions' granting them recourse to public funds. A successful application requires evidence of destitution, child welfare concerns or exceptional financial circumstances.

16 See G. McKeever, C. Fitzpatrick, et al., *Independent Review of Discretionary Support* (Department for Communities 2022).

17 M. Adler, *Cruel, Inhuman or Degrading Treatment? Benefit Sanctions in the UK* (Palgrave Pivot 2018), p. 23.

18 D. Clegg, 'Convergence from below? The reform of minimum income protection in France and the UK' Journal of International and Comparative Social Policy 30 (2014) 2, pp. 147-164, 154 ff.

19 Ibid., p. 149.

legislative neutralisation of trade unions during the years of Conservative government.[20]

The *Welfare Reform Act 2007* and its successor, the *Welfare Reform Act 2012*, reflect this prevailing ideology which has shaped a significant portion of welfare reform legislation in the last forty years. These acts have aimed to diminish the significance of national insurance benefits and simultaneously make them more challenging to access, by introducing stricter conditions for eligibility.

II. Overview

1. Normative Background

The question, whether there is a right to a subsistence minimum or at least a recognized principle or concept of a subsistence minimum in UK law is not a straightforward question to answer.

a) Constitutional Norms Providing Protection of a Subsistence Minimum

The UK does not have a codified[21] constitution. Instead, the UK's constitutional system is one of Parliamentary Sovereignty, i.e. there is no higher order of constitutional law above ordinary legislation to limit Parliament or protect individual rights. Thus, in relation to social security the UK has an essentially "political" constitution[22] in which rights to social welfare benefits are exclusively creatures of statute and as such the product of legislative discretion. In this way they are always precarious and subject to policy change. Such changes can be rapid and extreme, given the fact that the UK's legislature is dominated by the political party that makes up the executive.[23]

20 P. Larkin, 'Relationship between Employment Status and Scope of Social Security Protection: The United Kingdom Example', in: U. Becker and O. Chesalina (eds.), *Social Law 4.0* (Nomos 2021), pp. 117-146, 124.

21 i.e. enacted by a legislative body.

22 A. Le Sueur (n 11), p. 2.

23 Ibid.

This is subject to two caveats arising originally from the processes of European integration: EU law (at least as far as it has been retained[24] as domestic law at the end of the Brexit transition period) and the European Convention on Human Rights (ECHR). Both of these sources provide a framework of constraints on policy and law that can be regarded as "constitutional" in effect, even though they emanate from supranational bodies and they have had impacts on policy and law-making on social security.[25]

There is therefore no clearly expressed constitutional obligation of the state to ensure a subsistence minimum. The law and a potential state obligation is defined through legislation, common law[26] and/or international legal instruments. These can each play a role in identifying a minimum standard of living, but with variable degrees of precision and enforceability – and always subject to the ability of the legislature to set its own social floor.[27]

Various pieces of domestic legislation exist that in some fashion define a subsistence minimum. What they usually refer to in this context is "protection from destitution": A legal definition of "destitution" can be found in immigration as well as social security legislation: For example under the *Immigration and Asylum Act 1999* the Home Secretary is subject to a duty to protect asylum seekers from destitution. "Destitution" is thereby defined as lacking "adequate accommodation or any means of obtaining it" or inability to "meet ... other essential living needs". [28] Also, social security law provides a concept of "hardship", which broadly equates to the definition of "destitution" in immigration and asylum legislation in that it refers to the inability to "meet [one's] immediate and most basic and essential needs" These essential needs are listed as : accommodation, heating, food and hygiene.[29] The law therefore recognizes destitution as a phenomenon, however, it only establishes a right to protection from destitution in the

24 Retained EU Law is a category of domestic law created at the end of the Brexit transition period, consisting of EU-derived domestic legislation and retained directly applicable EU legislation (such as EU regulations) as well as directly effective rights in EU treaties that was preserved by the European Union (Withdrawal) Act 2018.

25 A. Le Sueur (n 11), pp. 10 ff.

26 i.e. the interpretation of law by judges in individual cases.

27 M. Simpson, G. McKeever, C. Fitzpatrick (n 10), p. 465.

28 *Immigration and Asylum Act 1999*, c33, s95; *Asylum Support Regulations 2000*, SI 2000/704.

29 *Universal Credit Regulations 2013* no 376 reg 116; *Jobseeker´s Allowance Regulations 1996* no 207 part ix.

very specific circumstances the legislation refers to.[30] These definitions have, however, not been recognized by the courts as a universal destitution threshold. For example, the Court of Appeal did not recognise the standard set by the immigration and asylum legislation as a destitution threshold for the purposes of assessing the adequacy of social security benefits.[31]

There are some indications in the case law that the common law principle of "the law of humanity"[32] provides protection against destitution where there is a threat to family life or a risk of degrading treatment. If such a right exists however, it can be, due to the principle of Parliamentary Sovereignty, overridden by statute.[33]

The UK is signatory to social right treaties such as the European Social Charter (ESC) and the International Covenant on Economic, Social and Cultural Rights (ICESR). However, they have not been incorporated into UK law, and so they act as persuasive rather than binding interpretation of the law.[34] Thus, violation of social rights – including the right to social security – are neither subject to ex-ante constraints nor to ex-post challenges in the UK.

The key test for the UK courts therefore remains, whether European Convention on Human Rights (ECHR) rights are affected. The ECHR clearly has domestic force. Most of its component rights have been incorporated into UK law through the *Human Rights Act 1998 (HRA 1998)*. This requires courts to interpret national legislation "so far as possible" to be in accordance with Convention rights.[35] As a last resort, the courts may make a "declaration of incompatibility"[36] about a provision in an Act of Parliament, which does, however, not affect the continuing validity of the

30 For more details, see M. Simpson, G. McKeever, C. Fitzpatrick (n 10), p. 470 ff.

31 *R (on the application of SG) v Secretary of State for Work and Pensions* [2014] EWCA Civ 156; [2014] HRLR 10 at [101-105])).

32 The principle of the "law of humanity" was defined in *R v Inhabitants of Eastbourne* (1803) 4 East 103,107, where Lord Ellenborough famously proposed that 'the law of humanity, which is anterior to all positive laws, obliges us to afford [people] relief, to save them from starving.

33 M. Simpson, G. McKeever, C. Fitzpatrick (n 10), pp. 474 ff.

34 M. Simpson, 'Assessing the Compliance of the UK Social Security System with the State's Obligations Under the European Social Charter' Human Rights Law Review 18 (2018)4, pp. 745-769, 749.

35 *Human Rights Act 1998*, s 3.

36 *Human Rights Act 1998*, s 4.

provision but is a clear signal to government that amending legislation ought to be introduced in Parliament to remedy the situation.[37]

However, unlike the social rights treaties mentioned above, the ECHR contains no provision that can be interpreted as providing an explicit right to a subsistence minimum. Also, the European Court of Human Rights (ECtHR) has traditionally been reluctant to read specific social entitlements into the Convention rights.[38]

Nevertheless, it has been suggested that some doctrinal progress has been made towards using the ECHR as a vehicle for some degree of social rights protection, driven largely by the UK courts[39]. However, looking at the UK case law, the ECHR has not been interpreted as requiring the protection of a subsistence minimum in all circumstances. Rather, the consequences of the most extreme manifestations of destitution may in some circumstances include the violation of certain rights within the ECHR. Correspondingly, these rights can then carry an implicit obligation on the state to provide a subsistence minimum in some circumstances.[40]

The ECHR rights primarily relied on in case law in this context are: inhuman and degrading treatment (Art. 3 ECHR) and respect for family life (Art. 8 ECHR). The judgment in *W* suggests both the courts and the Government now treat it as uncontroversial that inhuman and/or degrading treatment, which is prohibited by article 3 ECHR, can result from "lack of resources."[41] In *Limbuela*[42], the House of Lords held that that the Secretary of State's discretion to support failed or late asylum seekers has to be exercised in respect of an individual's ECHR rights. Also, the UK judiciary may be slightly more receptive than the Strasbourg courts to the

37 A. Le Sueur (n 11), p. 11.

38 A. Williams, 'The European Convention on Human Rights, the EU and the UK: Confronting a Heresy' European Journal of International Law 24 (2013) 4, p.1157, 1187; D. Kagiaros, 'Vulnerability as a Path to a "Social Minimum"? An analysis of ECtHR jurisprudence', in: T. Kotkas, I. Leijten and F. Pennings (eds.), *Specifying and Securing a Social Minimum in the Battle Against Poverty* (Hart Publishing 2019), p. 246.

39 C. O'Cinneide, 'A Modest Proposal: Destitution, State Responsibility and the European Convention on Human Rights' European Human Rights Law Review (2008) 5, pp. 583-605, 584.

40 M. Simpson, G. McKeever, C. Fitzpatrick (n 10), p. 479.

41 *R (on the application of W) v Secretary of State for the Home Department)* [2020] EWHC 1299 (admin); [2020] 1 WLR 4420 at [60] (Bean LJ and Chamberlain J).

42 *R (Adam and Limbuela) v Secretary of State for the Home Department* [2015] UKHL 66.

possibility of a positive right to a minimum – or minimal – income under article 8 ECHR, at least where the welfare of children is at stake.[43] However, the threshold interpretations for violation of these rights has been set very high so that they offer protection against destitution only to a very limited extent.[44]

Also, with the case law in this area clearly dominated by immigration and asylum cases there is no evidence of the courts requiring a similar state obligation where social security benefits are concerned. Whether, for example, benefit sanctions could constitute a violation of Art. 3 ECHR has not been tested in the courts. Claimants whose income is reduced for non-compliance with benefit conditions can seek a hardship payment, but these are contingent on compliance with set conditions and inability to access familial support.[45]

In sum, the UK currently recognises no absolute legal obligation to provide a subsistence minimum. In particular, there is no right to a home or to financial assistance to achieve a given standard of living.

b) Institutional Arrangements for the Constitutional Protection of a Subsistence Minimum

aa) Parliamentary Scrutiny

With the UK constitutional system being essentially "political", Parliament plays an important role in protecting constitutional norms against the misuse of ministerial power or the enactment of legislation that contravenes constitutional norms. This happens mainly through the work of committees, such as the *House of Common's Select Committee* on the *Department of Work and Pensions* or the *Joint Committee on Human Rights (JCHR).*[46]

The latter examines proposed government legislation to assess risks of potential violations of human rights norms: "[...] individuals enjoy a minimum right to social security which supports an adequate standard of

43 *Anufrijeva* v *Southwark LBC* [2003] EWCA Civ 1406; [2004] 2 WLR 603 at [43] (Lord Woolf CJ); *R (on the application of JS)* v *Secretary of State for Work and Pensions* [2013] EWHC 3350 (QB); [2014] PTSR 23 at [66] (Elias LJ).

44 M. Simpson, G. McKeever, C. Fitzpatrick (n 10), p. 480.

45 *Universal Credit Regulations 2013* no 376 reg 116; *Jobseeker´s Allowance Regulations* no 207 reg 140.

46 A. Le Sueur (n 11), pp. 17 ff.

living.[...] In the light of the Government's view that it is principally for Parliamentarians to secure compliance with the right to social security and the right to an adequate standard of living, we consider that it is important that Parliamentarians subject the Government's analysis of these provisions to close scrutiny for compliance with these minimum standards."[47] In 2011 for example, the *JCHR* made a series of criticisms of the *Welfare Reform Bill.* It stated, inter alia, that "there is a risk that the conditionality and sanction provisions in the Bill might in some circumstances lead to destitution, such as would amount to inhuman or degrading treatment contrary to Article 3 ECHR if the individual concerned was genuinely incapable of work".[48]

However, the Government is not required to follow the committees' recommendations. Also, Committee impact is complex, and may often be indirect, making it difficult to assess.[49]

bb) Judicial Control

There is a continuing debate about whether British courts should have greater powers to enforce human rights norms on social security and other social rights. One view is that Britain's "unwritten" constitution currently provides insufficient judicial control over fundamental rights and freedoms. The contrary view is that for courts to have any greater powers to adjudicate on broadly defined positive social rights would undermine Parliamentary Sovereignty and that the executive and legislative branches of government are better placed to deal with complex matters like economic and social rights that involve competing priorities and the allocation of scarce resources.[50] Former Supreme Court Judge Lord Sumption has argued against excessive judicial activism in the name of social justice, stating that Parliament was really the only place where these issues could be

47 UK Parliament (2009), Welfare Reform Bill. Conclusions and Recommendations, para.1.13, < https://publications.parliament.uk/pa/jt200809/jtselect/jtrights/78/7807.htm>, accessed 21.3.2025.

48 *JCHR*, 21st Report of 2010-2012, HL 233/HC 1704, para.1.45, < https://publications.parliament.uk/pa/jt201012/jtselect/jtrights/233/233.pdf> accessed 21.3.2025.

49 M. Russel and M. Benton, *Selective Influence: The Policy Impact of House of Commons Select Committees* (The Constitution Unit 2011).

50 M. Adler (n 17), p. 112.

decided on collectively.[51] This was echoed by the JCHR: [...] we recognise that the democratic branches (Government and Parliament) must retain the responsibility for economic and social policy, in which the courts lack expertise and have limited institutional competence or authority. It would not be constitutionally appropriate, in our view, for example, for the courts to decide whether a particular standard of living was "adequate" [...]. Such questions are quite literally non-justiciable: there are no legal standards which make them capable of resolution by a court."[52] Thus, capacity of the courts to block or inhibit welfare reforms has been very limited.

2. Social Benefits

a) General Structure of the Social Benefit System

Structurally, the UK's social benefit system provides an income safety net for all its citizens, i.e. ensuring that citizens will receive an income enabling them to survive, at least at a subsistence level.[53] The system provides contributory and means-tested benefits as well as benefits which are neither means-tested nor contributory (sometimes referred to as "categorical" benefits).

The so-called "categorical" benefits, which do not depend upon contribution records or the resources of the recipient, are generally paid to certain categories of people deemed to require or deserve additional financial support. Examples include: *Child Benefit*[54] (paid to households with children); *Attendance Allowance* (for people above State Pension age); *Disability Living Allowance* (to help with the extra costs of care and mobility for disabled children under the age of 16); *Personal Independence Payment* (intended to help people of working age with extra costs of disabilities and health

51 Lord Sumption, *The Limits of Law, The 27th Sultan Azlan Shah Lecture*, Kuala Lumpur, 20 November 2013.

52 *JCHR*, 29th Report of 2007-08, A Bill of Rights for the UK?, HL 165-I/ HC 150-I, chapter 5, p. 52, < https://publications.parliament.uk/pa/jt200708/jtselect/jtrights/165/165i.pdf> accessed 21.3.2025.

53 D. Hirsch, 'After a Decade of Austerity, does the UK have an Income Safety Net worth its Name?' Social Policy Review 32 (2020), p. 211.

54 Since 2013, the *High Income Child Benefit Charge* (*HICBC*) provides for *Child Benefit* to be clawed back through the tax system from families where the highest earner has an income above GBP 50,000. The *HICBC* is collected through self-assessment. Individuals who are liable to pay it are required to file an annual tax return if they do not already do so. See *Finance Act 2012*, s 8 and sch1.

conditions) and *Carer's Allowance* (paid to full-time carers of people with disabilities or health conditions receiving certain extra costs benefits).

Means-tested (also referred to as "income-related" or "social assistance" benefits) are only paid to people who have limited income and capital. *Pension Credit*, which was introduced in October 2003, is the main means-tested benefit for pensioners, replacing pensioner Income Support. For people who reached state pension age before 6 April 2016 it has two elements: the *Guarantee Credit* and the *Savings Credit*.[55] Savings Credit was removed for people reaching *State Pension* age from 6 April 2016, when the *new State Pension (nSP)* was introduced. The rationale was, inter alia, to "simplify means-tested support and help to ensure Pension Credit is re-focused on providing a safety net targeted at the poorest and most vulnerable."[56] Since 2013, *Universal Credit (UC)* is the only means-tested benefit for new claimants of working age, gradually replacing six existing means-tested benefits and in-work tax credits (including Working Tax Credit) for working-age households.[57]

Contributory benefits (sometimes referred to as "social insurance") are funded centrally through the National Insurance Fund by contributions from workers and employers, and in some years with a supplement from the Treasury. The most significant contributory benefit in the UK – accounting for expenditure of almost GBP 100 billion a year – is the *State*

---

55 *State Pension Credit Act 2002*, s 2-3; *State Pension Credit Regulations 2002* (SI 2002/1792). Guarantee Credit provides financial help for people aged over the "qualifying age" for Pension Credit (linked to the State Pension age) whose income is below a set amount. Savings Credit is an extra amount for people aged 65 or over, who have made some provision for their retirement (such as savings, or a second pension).

56 Department for Work and Pensions, The Single Tier Pension – A Simple Foundation for Saving, Cm 8528, January 2013, chapter 2, para 40 < https://assets.publishing.service.gov.uk/government/uploads/system/uploads/attachment_data/file/181229/single-tier-pension.pdf> accessed 21.3.2025.

57 UC replaces six former means-tested 'legacy' benefits and tax credits: *Income-based Job Seeker´s Allowance* (an unemployment benefit available to people looking or preparing for work), *Income Support* (a benefit for certain groups of people not expected to look for work, including carers and lone parents with younger children), *Income-related Employment and Support Allowance* (an income-replacement benefit for people whose capability for work is affected by disability or ill health), *Housing Benefit* (a benefit to help people on low incomes and in rented accommodation pay their housing costs), *Working Tax Credit* (a benefit paid by HMR to low income households who are in work,) and *Child Tax Credit* (a benefit paid to lower income families with children). The abolition is contained in the *Welfare Reform Act 2012*, s 33. Since the caseload rollout of UC is not yet complete, individuals and families continue to receive these benefits, although their numbers are declining.

Pension. The main contributory benefits for people of working age are[58]: *"New Style" Employment and Support Allowance (ESA), "New Style" Jobseeker´s Allowance (JSA)*[59] and the *Bereavement Support Payment.*[60]

Despite being the founding basis of the modern social security system in the UK, contributory benefits for people of working age have gradually become less important. Beveridge's vision of a mainly insurance-based welfare system was never fully realised, for various reasons. Benefit rates were never set at full subsistence levels and so could not provide enough income protection. And some of Beveridge's assumptions have been eroded over time, including reliance on a largely male workforce acting as breadwinners. Also, from the 1970s, other forms of social security, including in-work benefits, tax credits, and non-contributory, non-means-tested disability and carer benefits (see above), have also crowded out contributory benefits for people of working age.[61]

The same, however, has not happened in pension-age provision, where the contributory *State Pension* accounts for over four fifths of social security support. This has happened because, in contrast to working-age

58 For further information see F. Hobson, S. Kennedy and A. Mackley 'An Introduction to Social Security in the UK' Briefing Paper no CBP 9535 (1 June 2022), p. 15 < https://researchbriefings.files.parliament.uk/documents/CBP-9535/CBP-9535.pdf> accessed 21.3.2025.

59 *Income-based Job Seeker's Allowance* and *income-related Employment and Support Allowance (ESA)* have been replaced by *UC*. However, it is still possible to submit a new claim for *contribution-based JSA* and *contributory ESA* for those claimants who have made sufficient national insurance contributions in the last two years before the claim When these are paid under the UC system, the DWP refers to them as *new-style JSA* and *new style ESA*. The rules are the same that apply in the *UC* system (e.g. rules on overpayments, claimant responsibilities and sanctions). However, unlike *UC, new style JSA* may be claimed even if the claimant or their household have more than GBP 16.000 in savings. See *Welfare Reform Act 2012* (Commencement No. 11 and Transitional and Transitory Provisions and Commencement No. 9 and Transitional and Transitory Provisions (Amendment)) Order 2013, SI 2013/1511. For further information see P. Larkin (n 20), p. 126.

60 Since their introduction in 2017, *Bereavement Support Payments* have comprised an initial lump sum payment of GBP 3,500 for those with dependent children, followed by 18 monthly payments of GBP 350; and a lump-sum payment of GBP 2500 plus 18 monthly payments of GBP 100 for those without children.

61 Spending on contributory benefits currently accounts for around 9% of social security expenditure on working-age adults and children (£8 billion in 2019/20). For further information, see A. Mackley and R. McInnes, 'Contributory benefits and social insurance in the UK' (House of Commons Library Insight 2020) < https://commonslibrary.parliament.uk/contributory-benefits-and-social-insurance-in-the-uk/> accessed 21.3.2025.

contributory benefits, the real value of the State Pension has significantly increased since the 1970s. More favourable treatment of the basic *State Pension* compared to the *Unemployment Benefit* (and its successor, the *Jobseeker´s Allowance*) over the past 50 years has meant that the former is paid at more than twice the rate (GBP 221.20 a week in 2024/25) of the latter (GBP 90.50 a week), despite having been at the same level until 1973.[62] Policies such as the voluntary *National Insurance Contributions* also allow the vast majority of people of pension age to qualify for contributory benefits – nearly all pensioners (97%) are in receipt of the *State Pension*.[63] *Pension Credit* – the means-tested benefit designed to top-up pensioner incomes (see above) – plays a much less significant role, and has declined as a proportion of social security support for people of pension age.[64]

Be that as it may, for people of working age, the post-war insurance system has been gradually superseded (although not completely replaced) by means-tested benefits, culminating in the introduction of *Universal Credit* from 2013.

b) Universal Credit (UC)

aa) General Introduction

UC has been available in every part of the UK since December 2018 and is now the only option for any working-age individual or family wishing to apply for a means-tested benefit.

In March 2020, 3 million people were on UC. Numbers rose substantially during the coronavirus crisis, reaching 5.8 million people by the end of 2020 and staying fairly steady up to August 2021. As of 12 August 2021, there were 5.9 million people on Universal Credit in Great Britain.[65]

While the Coalition Government argued that *UC* would be the most significant welfare reform since the Beveridge Report and the post-Second World War Labour Government's reforms, it does not in fact begin from

---

62 F. Hobson, S. Kennedy and A. Mackley (n 58), pp. 6 and 16.

63 Ibid., p. 17.

64 Ibid.

65 A. Mackley, R. McInnes et al., 'Opposition Day Debate: Universal Credit and Working Tax Credit' Debate Pack no 2021/0138, House of Commons Library (15 September 2021), p. 3 < https://researchbriefings.files.parliament.uk/documents/CDP-2021-0138/CDP-2021-0138.pdf> accessed 21.3.2025.

a completely blank sheet.[66] Several features were adopted or adapted from former systems, and many of the policy's aims were familiar from previous rounds of reform: *UC* continues the provision of in-work benefits to supplement the income of low-wage families which had been expanding since the 1970s through the introduction of tax credits under the last Labour Governments.[67] For the most part, *UC* does not expand support to or withdraw support from, any large group of people[68] nor does it completely transform the amount of support most of its claimants receive.[69]

Instead of fundamentally changing the aims of social security, the introduction of a single benefit is designed to help the Government meet some long-held policy goals. The main aim of *UC* is to end the historical problem of the 'poverty trap' in the United Kingdom by ensuring that it is more financially rewarding for low-paid households to engage with the labour market than to receive benefits.[70] In conjunction with the introduction of the *National Living Wage* in 2016[71] (which replaced the *National Minimum Wage* for citizens over the age of 25) the Government anticipated that *UC*, with its considerably lower claw back rates when recipients' number of working hours and wages rise, would lead to both an alleviation of poverty among low-paid families and individuals and an increase in the number of UK citizens accepting lower-paid positions in the labour market.[72]

Like the legacy benefits and tax credits that it is replacing[73], *UC* is available to those who are in work but on low incomes, as well as those who

---

66 F. Hobson, 'Universal Credit: Ten Years of Changes to Benefit Claims and Payments' Briefing Paper no 9109, House of Commons Library (16 July 2021), pp. 5 and 7 < https://researchbriefings.files.parliament.uk/documents/CBP-9109/CBP-9109.pdf> accessed 21.3.2025.

67 P. Larkin (n 20), p. 124.

68 There are some exceptions. The design of the *UC* single taper rate means that some relatively higher earners are eligible who would not have received support under legacy benefits, and current tax credit claimants with savings above GBP 16.000 will not be eligible for *UC*.

69 The calculation of awards is different – some elements in legacy benefits are different or not replicated in *UC*, capital rules apply whereas tax credits are unaffected by savings and a new single taper rate means that benefits interact with earnings differently.

70 P. Larkin, 'Universal Credit, `Positive Citizenship` and the Working Poor: Squaring the Eternal Circle?' The Modern Law Review 81 (2018)1, pp. 114-131, 116.

71 The National Living Wage entitles workers aged over 23 to pay of GBP 10.42 per hour < https://www.gov.uk/government/publications/the-national-minimum-wage-in-2023/the-national-minimum-wage-in-2023> accessed 21.3.2025.

72 P. Larkin (n 70), p. 116.

73 See above at n 57.

are unemployed or whose health conditions or disabilities as well as caring responsibilities affect their capability to work.[74] As such, *UC* harmonizes systems of social support and social assistance. The six legacy benefits being phased out and replaced by *UC* since 2013 serve different groups of low-income households with different needs. Where a household was eligible for more than one legacy benefit, each was claimed and paid separately.[75] Legacy benefits were therefore criticized by the incoming Coalition Government for their complexity and for creating poor work incentives for some groups.[76]

bb) Basic Structure

UC is designed to reduce this complexity by requiring claimants apply for just one benefit, providing all the information required to decide what support they are entitled to.[77] Unlike the legacy benefits it is replacing, *UC* is claimed online by default.[78] Stakeholders welcomed the opening up of a digital channel to claim benefits where paper-based forms had previously been the norm. However, concerns were expressed about vulnerable claimants' access to the system, particularly disabled citizens and those with poor literacy skills.[79]

UC can be awarded to single persons and couples jointly, both in and out of work.[80] UC is paid at standardized basic individual and couple rates (standard allowance), differentiated for the over- and under-25s, with addi-

74 P. Larkin (n 70), p. 116.

75 For a brief outline of how each of the legacy benefits or tax credits was claimed and paid, see F. Hobson (n 66), Section 2.

76 Department for Work and Pensions, '21st Century Welfare' (July 2020), pp. 13-16 < https://assets.publishing.service.gov.uk/government/uploads/system/uploads/attachment_data/file/181139/21st-century-welfare_1_.pdf> accessed 21.3.2025.

77 F. Hobson (n 66), p. 13.

78 *The Universal Credit, Personal Independence Payment, Jobseeker's Allowance and Employment and Support Allowance (Claims and Payments) Regulations 2013*, SI 2013/380, as amended, reg 8.

79 See: Work and Pension Committee, 'Universal Credit implementation: meeting the needs of vulnerable claimants' (12 November 2012) < https://publications.parliament.uk/pa/cm201213/cmselect/cmworpen/576/57603.htm> accessed 21.3.2025.

80 *Welfare Reform Act 2012*, ss 1(2)(a) and (b).

tional payments for those with dependent children, disabilities, childcare costs and caring responsibilities.[81]

It is paid monthly in arrears, following a monthly assessment of income.[82] This is supposed to reflect the labour market reality where some 75% of the population now receive their earnings monthly and in arrears.[83] This is, however, problematic for *UC* claimants who are paid on non-month cycles such as non-standard contract workers as their earning in each calendar month may vary which will lead to fluctuating *UC* payments and subsequent household budgeting challenges.[84]

There is also a processing period of up to seven days before people can claim. With the benefit paid monthly in arrears, this results in an in-built wait of five weeks[85] before claimants can first be paid – three times as long as under the old system.[86] From the early stages of *UC* rollout, the wait for the first payment has been controversial, with MPs and campaigners arguing that it causes financial difficulties for claimants: "The rollout of full service Universal Credit [...] has been associated with increases in rent arrears, problem debt and foodbank use."[87] As a result, changes were made,

---

81 *Welfare Reform Act 2012*, ss 1 (3) (a) – (d). The detailed rules on claims for UC are contained in the *Universal Credit, Personal Independence Payment, Jobseeker´s Allowance and Employment and Support Allowance (Claims and Payments) Regulations 2013, SI 2013/380* and *Welfare Reform Act* 2012, ss 3 and 4.

82 *Department for Work and Pensions*, 'Universal Credit: different earning patterns and your payments (payment cycles)' (13 March 2019) < https://www.gov.uk/guidance/universal-credit-and-earnings> accessed 21.3.2025.

83 DWP, 'Universal Credit: welfare that works' (11 November 2010), p. 34 < https://www.gov.uk/government/publications/universal-credit-welfare-that-works> accessed 21.3.2025.

84 J. Tucker and D. Norris, *Rough Justice: Problems with monthly assessment of pay and circumstances in universal credit, and what can be done about them* (Child Poverty Action Group 2018), p. 3. See also the court decisions in Secretary of State for Work and Pensions v Johnson & Others [2020] EWCA Civ 778; R (Pantellerisco and Others) v SSWP [2020] EWHC 1944 (Admin.).

85 Before February 2018, there were an additional seven 'waiting days' after the claim was made and before the first assessment period began. This is what was meant when people refer to the then 'six-week wait'.

86 See M. Adler (n 17), p. 35. Legacy benefits are paid to different frequencies – weekly, fortnightly, four-weekly, or monthly – meaning that separate payments might be made at different times, often sooner than five weeks from the registration of the claim.

87 *Work and Pensions Committee*, 'Universal Credit: The Six Week Wait. First Report of Session 2017-19' (25 October 2017), para. 6 < https://publications.parliament.uk/pa/cm201719/cmselect/cmworpen/336/336.pdf> accessed 21.3.2025.

such as making advances more accessible with larger amounts available and longer repayment periods as well as introducing so-called benefit 'run-ons' allowing people moving from legacy benefits to UC to continue to receive these benefits for a period at the beginning of their UC claim.[88]

The claimant must be at least 18 years old, be below pension age, be in Great Britain, not receiving full-time education[89] and has accepted a relevant claimant commitment with the Department for Work and Pension (DWP).[90]

Like tax credits, *UC* can also be claimed by the self-employed: this is subject to them being deemed "gainfully self-employed"[91]; a process which involves potential claimants undertaking a "Gateway Interview" carried out by Jobcentre Plus Work Coaches who often lack specialist knowledge in assessing small business plans and activity for viability.[92]

cc) Calculation and Deductions

The amount of an award of *UC* consists of the "maximum amount" less "the amounts to be deducted".[93]

The current standard monthly allowance for a single person of 25 years and over is GBP 393.45 (GBP 617.70 for couples of 25 and over). The maximum amount is the total of the *standard allowance*[94] plus additional components for specific household circumstances such as disability, childcare or caring responsibilities. Allowances are also added for housing costs for both tenants and owner-occupiers.[95] There is, for example, a child element, by which an amount is allowed for each child or qualifying young person for whom a person is "responsible", normally for the first and second child

---

88 F. Hobson (n 66), p. 26.

89 Claimants cannot usually get Universal Credit if they are studying full-time, although some exceptions are provided, for instance for claimants who are studying and are responsible for a child, see Department for Work and Pensions, 'Guidance Universal Credit and Students' < https://www.gov.uk/guidance/universal-credit-and-students#studying-full-time> accessed 21.3.2025.

90 *Welfare Reform Act 2012*, s 4.

91 Defined in Regulation 64 of the *Universal Credit Regulations 2013*, SI 2013/376.

92 P. Larkin (n 20), p. 137.

93 *Welfare Reform Act 2012*, s 8(1).

94 See Government UK, 'Universal Credit: What you'll get' < https://www.gov.uk/universal-credit/what-youll-get> accessed 21.3.2025.

95 *Universal Credit Regulations 2013*, reg 36.

only.[96] *UC* also includes a childcare costs element covering up to 85% of childcare costs, with the maximum amount payable being GBP 1014.63 a month for one child, or GBP 1739.37.15 a month for two or more children.[97] To be eligible for the childcare costs element, claimants must meet the work condition and the childcare costs condition, i.e. the costs must be incurred to allow the claimant to take up or continue paid work. There is no minimum working hours requirement. In addition, there is a housing costs element to *UC* (which mainly replaces housing benefit), designed to meet the cost of household rent or mortgage interest payments.[98] Housing benefit claimants and *UC* claimants who receive the housing cost element in the private rented sector have their rent support capped by *Local Housing Allowance (LHA)* rates, which depend on the location of the property in the UK. On 1st April 2020, *LHA* rates were increased to match the 30th percentile of market rents. Previously, *LHA* rates had been frozen since April 2016.[99]

Once the maximum amount is ascertained, the amounts to be deducted have to be calculated. This includes all the claimant's (or claimants combined) unearned income, and 55 % of the earned income, or, if the claimant is responsible for a child, or is deemed to have incapacity for work, all of their income above the *work allowance* (so-called *taper cut*).[100] It allows for much higher earnings disregards than under other means-tested benefits such as *IS* or *ESA* and thus is believed to enhance the financial incentives for families and certain individuals to engage with the labour market.

Also, the DWP has the power to make direct deductions from benefit payments to pay certain debts and costs owed by claimants, for example due to a benefit overpayment or loan. Welfare rights groups have argued that these deductions are creating hardship. In response, the Government

---

96 *Universal Credit Regulations 2013*, reg 35. The current extra amount for a first child is GBP 333.33 (born before 6 April 2017) or GBP 269.58 (born on or after 6 April 2017) and GBP 287.97 for a second child and any other eligible children. See Government UK, 'Universal Credit: What you'll get' < https://www.gov.uk/universal-credit/what-youll-get> accessed 21.3.2025.

97 See Government UK, 'Universal Credit: What you'll get' < https://www.gov.uk/universal-credit/what-youll-get> accessed 21.3.2025.

98 *Welfare Reform Act 2012*, s 11 and *Universal Credit Regulations 2013* regs 25 and 26, and sch 1 to 5.

99 W. Wilson and F. Hobson, 'Housing Costs in Universal Credit' Briefing Paper no 6547, House of Commons Library (18 August 2021) < https://researchbriefings.files.parliament.uk/documents/SN06547/SN06547.pdf> accessed 21.3.2025.

100 *Welfare Reform Act 2012*, s 8(3) and *Universal Credit Regulations 2013*, reg 22.

has introduced reforms including reducing the cap on the total amount that can be deducted each month, and increased the period of time claimants have to repay advance payments. Currently, the maximum amount deducted cannot usually exceed 25% of the standard allowance, which was reduced from 40% in October 2019.[101] They argue, however, that deductions help claimants to manage their finances, and that a balance has to be found between helping people out of debt and affordability. Various think tanks and other stakeholders have reported findings about the proportion of *UC* (and other benefits) claimants subject to deductions: The *Trussel Trust* found, for example, in a report published in November 2019 that 40% of people who had been referred to their food banks said that their benefit income was subject to deductions.[102] A *Joseph Rowntree Foundation* report on destitution published in December 2020 found that half of people surveyed experiencing destitution were claiming or had applied for *UC*, and that debt deductions were a key driver of destitution.[103]

Self-employed claimants are subject to the *"Minimum Income Floor" (MIF)* which assumes they are making a certain minimum of monthly income.[104] For the majority of claimants the *MIF* is the equivalent of a full-time worker's (which equals 35 hours weekly) wage on the national living wage. For the first year of business new self-employed persons are exempt from the *MIF* ("Start-up Period"). The rationale for the *MIF* given by the DWP was to "encourage individuals to increase their earnings through developing their self-employment" and to address " [...] flaws in legacy benefits which allowed self-employed claimants to receive state support while declaring low or zero earnings".[105]

101 Department for Work and Pensions, 'Advice for Decision Making Chapter D2: Third Party deductions UC, JSA&ESA' (18 June 2021) < https://assets.publishing.service.gov.uk/media/64a6b13cc531eb000c64ffa6/admd2.pdf> accessed 21.3.2025.

102 The Trussel Trust, 'State of Hunger: A study of poverty and food insecurity in the UK' (November 2019), p. 70 < https://www.stateofhunger.org/wp-content/uploads/2019/11/State-of-Hunger-Report-November2019-Digital.pdf> accessed 21.3.2025.

103 Joseph Rowntree Foundation, 'Destitution in the UK 2020' (December 2020) < https://www.jrf.org.uk/deep-poverty-and-destitution/destitution-in-the-uk-2020> accessed 21.3.2025.

104 *Universal Credit Regulations 2013*, SI 2013/376, reg 62.

105 P. Larkin (n 20), p. 138.

c) Localism

Another prominent characteristic of the social security reforms was the emergence of *localism*, whereby responsibility for the administration of some of the new measures was devolved to local governmental authorities (*Local Authorities*).The prominent characteristic of this phenomenon was to tie austerity measures to the grant of discretionary authority to Local Authorities in the distribution of "last resort benefits" to those impacted by restrictive measures, yet still deserving of heightened protection.[106]

One example are *Discretionary Housing Payment (DHPs),* payments made at the discretion of the local authority to help people with rent. To be eligible, the person must be in receipt of some *Housing Benefit* or housing cost element in their *UC.* Intention is to give short-term assistance whilst a person seeks a longer-term solution. It is generally paid to those affected by the benefit cap or those who receive reduced *Housing Benefit* due to the size of their current house. Local authorities each set their own criteria for eligibility and awards.[107]

Local authorities are also responsible for administering *Housing Benefit* and, since April 2013, their own *Council Tax reductions schemes.* Following the abolition of the discretionary *Social Fund* in 2013, local authorities in England are also responsible for local welfare assistance schemes in place of Crisis Loans and Community Care Grants (national schemes exist in Scotland and Wales).[108]

Localism has proven controversial. Far from compensating the effects of austerity measures, the policy move has been viewed by many as merely an astute move on the part of the central government whereby they pass the burden of their harshest consequences onto *Local Authorities.*[109] One might argue, indeed, that it is reminiscent of the localism of the old *Poor Laws* which saw uneven and inadequate responses to what had become a national

---

106 J. Meers, 'The Localism- and Austerity-Hybrid: The Case of Discretionary Housing Payments' (21 October 2015) < https://ukconstitutionallaw.org/2015/10/21/jed-meers-the-localism-and-austerity-hybrid-the-case-of-discretionary-housing-payments/> accessed 21.3.2025.

107 Z. Hays, F. Hobson, 'Discretionary Housing Payments' Briefing Paper no CBP 06899, House of Commons Library (20 August 2020), p. 3 < https://researchbriefings.files.parliament.uk/documents/SN06899/SN06899.pdf> accessed 21.3.2025.

108 F. Hobson, S. Kennedy and A. Mackley (n 58), p. 9.

109 Ibid.

and unified welfare problem.[110] In any event, many of the legal challenges regarding the UK's new welfare rules have revolved around the meaning, scope, and use of such local discretion.[111]

b) Devolution

Recent devolution of some social security powers to Scotland[112] has altered the structure of welfare provision in the UK. The *Scotland Act 2016* gives the *Scottish Parliament* and *Government* powers over benefits falling within certain categories, including extra-cost disability, industrial injuries and carer benefits, as well as the power to top-up reserved benefits and create other new social security benefits.[113]

The *Scottish Parliament* is introducing a suite of new devolved benefits: mostly direct replacements for *Department for Work and Pensions* benefits, including extra-costs disability benefits such as the *Personal Independence Payment* (replaced by the *Adult Disability Payment* from 2022); but also benefits which do not have a direct equivalent in the UK, such as the *Scottish Child Payment* – a weekly payment for low-income families with children.[114]

Any and all benefits not explicitly devolved by the *Scotland Act 2016* continue to be reserved, which include: means-tested benefits such as *Universal Credit* and the benefits and tax credits it is replacing; contributory benefits for people of working age, such as the *New Style Jobseeker´s Allowance*; retirement age benefits such as the *State Pension*; HMRC benefits such as the *Child Benefit* and *Guardian´s Allowance.* This amounts to over 80% of social security expenditure in Scotland.[115] *UC* therefore remains a reserved benefit, but under *Universal Credit Scottish Choices,* the *Scottish Government* has used powers conferred by the *Scotland Act 2016* to change payment arrangements *Scotland for UC* (*UC* being paid twice a month rather than monthly) and to vary the housing cost element for rented

110 Ibid.
111 Ibid.
112 See n 1.
113 F. Hobson, S. Kennedy and A. Mackley (n 58), p. 7.
114 Ibid.
115 Ibid., p. 26.

accommodation (having the UC housing element paid directly to their landlords).[116]

III. Analysis

1. Benefit Rates and their Adaptation

a) Benefit Rates

Today's benefit levels in the UK are not the result of any regular, systematic assessment of minimum needs, instead they have emerged from successive rounds of welfare reform since the Second World War and, above all, political choices made at periodic benefit upratings, compounding over time.[117]

William Beveridge intended his proposed benefit rates to be "sufficient without further resources to provide the minimum income needed for subsistence in all normal cases".[118] The proposed rates were informed by a pre-war *Ministry of Labour* survey based on the expenditure of working-class households by poverty researcher *Seebohm Rowntree*, but the minimum budgets only included amounts necessary for the maintenance of mere physical subsistence. *Rowntree* himself had, by the late 1930s, proposed a more generous "human needs" scale based on social as well as physical needs.[119] Slightly adapted in the *National Assistance Act 1948,* Beveridge's recommendations formed the benchmark for the means-tested safety net that later transformed into *Supplementary Benefit* and then *IS*.[120]

In the 1960s civil servants undertook two internal reviews of the adequacy of means-tested *National Assistance* benefit rates in recognition of the lack of an evidence base for policymaking. The reviews concluded that rates for adults in particular could not provide for a satisfactory standard of

116 Ibid., p. 27.

117 F. Hobson, S. Kennedy and A. Mackley, 'How Benefit Levels are Set' Briefing Paper no CBP 9498, House of Commons Library (14 April 2022), p. 5 < https://researchbriefings.files.parliament.uk/documents/CBP-9498/CBP-9498.pdf> accessed 21.3.2025.

118 W. Beveridge, 'Social Insurance and Allied Services' (1942), para 307 < https://pmc.ncbi.nlm.nih.gov/articles/PMC2560775/pdf/10916922.pdf> accessed 21.3.2025.

119 B. Rowntree, *The Human Needs of Labour* (Thomas Nelson and Sons 1937).

120 D. Hirsch (n 53), p. 213.

living. The reviews were not published and resulted in minimal change. All administrations since then have rejected the idea of setting benefits based on an objective assessment of needs.[121] The 1997-2010 Labour Government significantly increased the amount of benefit many households received, particularly those with children, through the introduction of tax credits and the *Minimum Income Guarantee* (later subsumed within Pension Credit).[122] However, they also rejected proposals to link benefit levels to estimates of minimum needs, arguing there was no objective way to determine what constituted a minimum acceptable income.[123]

Despite successive governments rejecting such an approach[124], independent researchers have attempted to determine *Minimum Income Standards.* The most recent example of this is the project undertaken by the *Centre for Research in Social Policy (CRSP)* at Loughborough University, founded by the *Joseph Rowntree Foundation*, which has published *"Minimum Income Standards for the UK"* reports since 2008. The process combines expert knowledge with in-depth consultation with members of the public, to determine the level of income needed for a minimum acceptable standard of living in the UK in different households.[125] The analysis suggests there is a significant – and growing- shortfall between minimum safety net benefits for non-working households and the amount deemed necessary for a minimum acceptable standard of living.

b) Adaptation of Benefit Rates

To prevent inflation from reducing their purchasing power, most benefits are usually increased – *uprated* – each year, following a review carried out in the preceding Autumn to determine whether they have retained their value relative to either prices or earnings.

121 J. Veit-Wilson, 'The National Assistance Board and the 'Rediscovery' of Poverty', in: H. Fawcett and R. Lowe (eds.), *Welfare Policy in Britain. The Road from 1945* (Palgrace Macmillan 1999), pp. 116-157.

122 J. Hills, 'Labour`s Record on Cash Transfers, Poverty, Inequality and the Lifecycle 1997-2010' CASE paper 175 (2013).

123 See for example HC Deb 23 February 1998 c119w.

124 Ministers in the current Government argue that MIS budgets include items that many people would not consider to be necessities.

125 The most recent report: A. Davis, J. Stone, et al., 'A Minimum Income Standard for the United Kingdom in 2022' (September 2022) < https://www.jrf.org.uk/a-minimum-income-standard-for-the-united-kingdom-in-2022> accessed 21.3.2025.

The practice of increasing benefits regularly in line with prices or earnings was first put on a statutory basis in the 1970s[126] and has evolved since then. Before this, benefits had generally been increased at irregular intervals by a series of Acts.[127] Working-age benefits have generally been increased in line with prices, while *State Pensions* have received more favourable treatment with additional uprating guarantees – most recently with the "triple lock", which ensures an increase in line with inflation, earnings or 2.5% annually.[128] Different measures of prices have also been used.

Current practice is to uprate benefits by reference to year-to-September inflation figures (since 2011, the *Consumer Price Index*), and annual earnings growth measured between May and July, in uprating orders coming into force the following April. The explanation successive governments have given for this that it takes several months to apply uprating through the various systems through which benefits operate.[129]

Although the effect of the upratings in most individual years is undramatic, uprating decisions and rules compound, and have over time had a dramatic impact on the level and shape of benefit provision afforded by the social security system.

Also, not all benefits are uprated each year. Over the past decade, a series of below inflation increases and freezes were applied to working-age benefits. In 2012 the link between inflation and working-age benefit uprating was broken and replaced by three years of fixed-rate 1 per cent increases and then by a four-year freeze. Thus, between April 2012 and April 2019 benefits rose 3 per cent in total, while the *Consumer Price Index (CPI)* rose by a cumulative 13 per cent. If *IS/JSA* were assumed to exactly provide subsistence in 2012, they therefore fell 10 per cent short of doing so by 2019.[130]

In addition, some benefits are not uprated annually, and have therefore fallen (sometimes substantially) over time. These include *Winter Fuel Pay-*

---

126 *Social Security Act 1973*, s 39 (as enacted).

127 For example the *National Insurance Act 1974*.

128 In the *Social Security (Up-rating of Benefits) Act 2021*, the earnings element of the "triple lock" was suspended for the 2022/23 tax year. As a result, the State Pension increased by 3.1% in April 2022.

129 F. Hobson, S. Kennedy and A. Mackley (n 117), p. 6.

130 D. Hirsch (n 53), p. 213.

ments[131] and the *Christmas Bonus*[132] available to certain claimants, which has remained at GBP 10 since 1972.[133]

The adequacy of UK benefits rates over the last few years has been subject to more intensified debate. In particular, the economic consequences of the coronavirus pandemic and the rise in the cost of living in 2021 and 2022, following a period of real-terms cuts to the level of many working-age benefits, have prompted debate about whether current benefit rates provide adequate support.

The economic impact of the coronavirus pandemic prompted the Government to increase the standard living allowance of *UC* and the basic element of *Working Tax Credit* temporarily by GBP 1,000 in the 2020/21 financial year.[134] This was interpreted by some think tanks as a tacit admission that benefit levels are too low. The *Joseph Roundtree Foundation* noted, for example, that before the uplift was introduced, the main rate of out-of-work social security support had been at its lowest level in real terms since 1990, and its lowest ever as a proportion of average wages.[135] Nevertheless, the Government said its focus was on "supporting people back into work and supporting those already employed to progress in their careers."[136] The

131 The Winter Fuel Payment is a tax-free annual payment to help older people pay their winter heating bills. Most payments are made automatically between November and December to individuals who get the State Pension or certain other benefits. It is not uprated annually with inflation. The 'standard rates for winter 2021/22' were GBP 2000 per eligible household where the oldest person is under 80, and GBP 300 for households with someone aged 80 or over.

132 The Christmas Bonus is a one-off, tax-free GBP 10 payment made before Christmas, paid automatically to people who get certain working-age and pensioner benefits, normally in the first full week of December.

133 F. Hobson, S. Kennedy and A. Mackley (n 117), p. 6.

134 HM Treasury, 'The Chancellor Rishi Sunak Provides an Updated Statement on Coronavirus' (20 March 2020) < https://www.gov.uk/government/speeches/the-chancellor-rishi-sunak-provides-an-updated-statement-on-coronavirus> accessed 21.3.2025.

135 L. Bannister, '#KeepTheLifeline: Urging the Government Not to Cut Universal Credit' (23 July 2021) < https://www.jrf.org.uk/social-security/keepthelifeline-urging-the-government-not-to-cut-universal-credit> accessed 21.3.2025.

136 Social Justice and Social Security Committee, 'Letter from the Secretary of Work and Pensions to Stephen Timms' (5 August 2021) < https://www.parliament.scot/chamber-and-committees/committees/current-and-previous-committees/session-6-social-justice-and-social-security-committee/correspondence/2021/letter-about-the-universal-credit-uplift-from-the-secretary-of-state-for-work-and-pensions> accessed 21.3.2025.

uplift was subsequently withdrawn from the beginning of October 2021[137], although the generosity of *UC* for in-work claimants was improved from 24 November 2022 with the reduction of the UC taper rate to 55% and the increase in work allowances by GBP 500 a year.[138] The *Resolution Foundation* calculated the combination of this and the withdrawal of the uplift would result in 73% of families on *UC* in 2022/23 being worse off, with 27% better off.[139]

Campaigners have also questioned uprating practices in light of the current cost of living squeeze – basing the benefit uprating for 2022/23 on a year-to-September 2021 inflation measure does not account for subsequent price rises. In early 2022, inflation reached its highest recorded level since 1992. In March 2022, consumer prices as measured by the *Consumer Price Index (CPI)* were 7% higher than the year before, and are forecast to rise still further, whereas in April 2022 inflation-linked benefits and tax credits rose by 3.1%.[140] The Universal Credit standard allowances have increased by 6.7% from April 2024, in line with the Consumer Prices Index (CPI) rate of inflation in September 2023.[141] The Government has not increased benefits beyond regular inflation linked uprating, but has introduced other temporary measures such as additional funding for the *Household Support Fund* which enables local authorities in England to make discretionary payments to people most in need to help towards the rising cost of food and utilities.[142] It has been allocated funding in tranches since October 2021. The latest allocation of GBP 1 billion (including allocations for devolved

137 For further information, see A. Mackley, R. McInnes, et al, 'Universal Credit and Working Tax Credits' Debate Pack no 2021/0138, House of Commons Library (15 September 2021) < https://researchbriefings.files.parliament.uk/documents/CDP-2021-0138/CDP-2021-0138.pdf> accessed 21.3.2025.

138 E. Kirk-Wade, 'Reducing the Universal Credit Taper Rate and the Effect on Incomes' (1 February 2022) < https://commonslibrary.parliament.uk/reducing-the-universal-credit-taper-rate-and-the-effect-on-incomes/> accessed 21.3.2025.

139 M. Brewer, K. Handscomb and L. Try, 'Taper Cut. Analysis of the Autumn Budget Changes to Universal Credit' (6 November 2021) < https://www.resolutionfoundation.org/app/uploads/2021/11/Taper-cut.pdf> accessed 21.3.2025.

140 F. Hobson, S. Kennedy and A. Mackley (n 58), p. 7.

141 E. Kirk-Wade, R. Harker, 'Benefits uprating 2024/25' Briefing Paper no 9680, House of Commons Library (30 November 2023) < https://researchbriefings.files.parliament.uk/documents/CBP-9872/CBP-9872.pdf> accessed 21.3.2025.

142 Department for Work and Pensions, 'Household Support Fund: Final guidance for County Councils and Unitary Authorities in England' (11 November 2021) < https://www.gov.uk/government/publications/household-support-fund-guidance-for-local-councils> accessed 21.3.2025.

governments to use as they see fit) for the 2023/24 financial year was announced alongside the 2023/24 *Cost of Living Payments.* One-off *Cost of Living Payments* for recipients of certain benefits were first announced in May 2022 and were paid in the second half of that year. In the November 2022 *Autumn Statement,* a further package of *Cost of Living Payments* was announced, to be paid over the course of the 2023/24 financial year.[143]

c) The Benefit Cap

All welfare benefit recipients and their family are, since 2013, subject to a legislative *benefit cap* which limits the maximum amount in benefits a household can receive per year, with certain exceptions. Originally set at GBP 26,000 per household, the benefit cap was reduced in autumn 2016 to GBP 20,000 for families (or GBP 23,000 in London due to higher living costs).[144] In April 2023, it was increased for the first time since its introduction—by 10.1%, matching the inflation-linked rise in social security benefits.[145] The *Coalition Government* argued that the benefit cap would increase incentives to work: "Our reforms are creating an alternative to life on benefits and already we are seeing an increasing number of people changing their circumstances so they are no longer subject to the cap."[146] There is no statutory duty to uprate the benefits cap. However, Section 96A of the *Welfare Reform Act 2012* requires that the Government "must at least once in each Parliament review the [levels of the cap] to determine whether it is appropriate to increase or decrease any one or more of those sums." The *benefit cap* has been subject to legal challenge on the grounds that it infringed provisions of international human rights law, but in two major

143 F. Hobson, S. Kennedy and A. Mackley (n 58), p. 7.

144 *Welfare Reform Act 2012*, ss 95-96 and *Benefit Cap (Housing Benefit) Regulations 2012*, SI 2012/2994 and the *Benefit Cap (Housing Benefit and Universal Credit) (Amendment) Regulations 2016*, SI 2016/909.

145 S. Kennedy, 'Benefit Cap' (14. June 2023) < https://commonslibrary.parliament.uk/benefit-cap/> accessed 21-3-2025.

146 Lord Freud, Minister of Welfare Reform, cited in BBC News, ''Thousands' Hit by Government Benefit Cap Now in Work' (6 February 2014) < https://www.bbc.com/news/business-26065080> accessed 21.3.2025.

decisions the Supreme Court ruled that the relevant human rights law had not been breached.[147]

d) Capital Rules

For most working-age means-tested benefits, capital (savings, investments, property, land, and other assets) above a lower limit of GBP 6000 results in inferred *tariff income*, where GBP 1 of income per week is assumed for every additional GBP 250 of capital, reducing the level of benefit paid. Where a household has more than an upper limit of GBP 16.000 in capital, they will not be eligible for means-tested support.[148] The capital limits for means-tested benefits are not uprated annually or at any other interval laid out in statute. Instead, they have been increased on an ad hoc basis since they were first introduced in the 1930s. The last time they were updated was in 2006 when the lower capital limit was increased from GBP 3000 to GBP 6000, and the upper capital limit from GBP 8000 to GBP 16.000.[149]

e) The Two-Child Limit

UC awards can include additional amounts for each child or "qualifying young person" in education up to the age of 19 in a claimant's household.[150]

As part of a series of measures announced in the Budget after the *2015 General Election* to make savings in the welfare system, a *two-child limit* was imposed on these additional amounts.[151] The policy was designed both to reduce the cost of the benefit system and to ensure households on

147 R (SG and Others) v Secretary of State for Work and Pensions [2015] UKSC 16 and R (DA & Ors) v Secretary of State for Work and Pensions [2019] UKSC 21.

148 S. Kennedy, 'How Savings Can Affect Benefits' (23 June 2020) < https://commonslibrary.parliament.uk/how-savings-can-affect-benefits/> accessed 21.3.2025.

149 F. Hobson, S. Kennedy and A. Mackley (n 58), p. 31.

150 See above n 96.

151 For more on this see F. Hobson, 'The Aims of Ten Years of Welfare Reform (2010-2020)' Briefing Paper no 9090, House of Commons Library (18 December 2020), section 3 < https://researchbriefings.files.parliament.uk/documents/CBP-9090/CBP-9090.pdf> accessed 21.3.2025.

means-tested benefits would "face the same financial choices about having children as those supporting themselves solely through work."[152]

With some exceptions, households with a third or subsequent child born from 6 April 2017 claiming *Universal Credit* or *Child Tax Credit* no longer receive additional amounts for these children. Exceptions are made for some claimants who did not choose to have a third or subsequent child, for example due to multiple births or non-consensual conception, and to encourage adoption where children might otherwise be looked after by a local authority.[153]

The policy only applies to children born from 6 April 2017, so not all families with a third or subsequent child claiming Universal Credit will be affected until the mid-2030s. In April 2021, 317,500 (38%) of the 836,020 families with three or more children claiming Universal Credit or Child Tax Credit were affected.[154]

Relative poverty among larger families with three or more children, which has been rising since 2013, has continued to increase since April 2017.[155] The *Resolution Foundation* estimates that nearly half of families with three or more children were in relative poverty in 2021/22, up from a third in 2012/13.[156]

A challenge to the lawfulness of the two-child policy was brought by two single mothers and their children, arguing that it unlawfully discriminates against certain groups, in breach of the European Convention on Human Rights (ECHR). Following an earlier unsuccessful appeal of the policy to the Court of Appeal[157], the case was unanimously dismissed by the Supreme

152 HM Treasury, 'Summer Budget 2015' (8 July 2015), para 1.245 < https://assets.publishing.service.gov.uk/government/uploads/system/uploads/attachment_data/file/443232/50325_Summer_Budget_15_Web_Accessible.pdf> accessed 21.3.2025.

153 *Welfare Reform Act 2012*, s. 10 as amended by s. 14 of the *Welfare Reform and Work Act 2016*. Regulation 24 and Schedule 12 of the *Universal Credit Regulations 2013*, SI 2013/376 (as amended) contain the detailed provisions.

154 HMRC, 'Child and Working Tax Credits Statistics: Provisional Awards- April 2021' (23 June 2021) < https://www.gov.uk/government/statistics/child-and-working-tax-credits-statistics-provisional-awards-april-2021> accessed 21.3.2025.

155 K. Stewart, A. Reeves and R. Patrick, 'A Time of Need: Exploring the Changing Poverty Risk Facing Larger Families in the UK' CASE 224 (July 2021), pp. 29-30 < https://sticerd.lse.ac.uk/dps/case/cp/casepaper224.pdf> accessed 21.3.2025.

156 A. Corlett and L. Try, 'The Living Standards Outlook 2022' (8 March 2022), figure 21 < https://www.resolutionfoundation.org/publications/the-living-standards-outlook-2022/> accessed 21.3.2025.

157 R (SC & Ors) v Secretary of State for Work and Pensions & Ors [2019] EWCA Civ 615 (16 April 2019).

Court in July 2021.[158] The Court held that the question of whether Parliament had made the right choice could not be answered by any process of legal reasoning. There was no basis, consistent with the separation of powers, on which the Court could overturn Parliament's judgment that the two-child limit was an appropriate means of achieving its aims.

f) Bedroom Tax

The *2010 Coalition Government* used powers contained in the *Welfare Reform Act 2012* to provide that, since 1 April 2013, working age social tenants in receipt of *Housing Benefit* or the housing element of *UC* experience a reduction in their benefit entitlement if they live in housing that is deemed too large for their needs, usually defined in terms of excess bedrooms.[159] Affected tenants face a reduction in their eligible rent for Housing Benefit purposes of 14% for one additional (spare) bedroom and 25% where there are two or more additional (spare) bedrooms. Restrictions on entitlement to Housing Benefit based on the size of accommodation occupied have applied to claimants living in privately rented housing since 1989.[160]

The policy is highly controversial. Legal challenges have concerned whether disabled children and adult couples should be required to share a bedroom[161] and the question of whether very small rooms[162] and "panic" rooms[163] should be treated as bedrooms.

---

158 R (SC, CB and 8 children) v Secretary of State for Work and Pensions and others [2021] UKSC 26.

159 *Housing Benefit (Amendment) Regulations 2012* (SI 2012/3040); *Housing Benefit and Universal Credit (Size Criteria) (Miscellaneous Amendments) Regulations 2013* (SI 2013/2828).

160 *Rent Officers (Additional Function) Order 1989*, sch 3.

161 See for example MA & Ors, R (on the application of) v Secretary for Work & Pensions [2016] UKSC 58.

162 See for example M v Secretary of State for Work & Pensions (2017) UKUT 443 (AAC).

163 Case of J.D. and A. v United Kingdom (Applications No. 32949/17 and 34614/17), (24 October 2019).

2. Conditionality and Sanctions

Although in the UK, welfare-to-work schemes and their underlying principles are not a new phenomenon, the *Welfare Reform Act 2012* adopted a particularly punitive regime.[164] The Act extended work-related requirements to certain groups, including single parents with younger children.[165] The biggest change is the application of conditionality up to a specified earnings threshold, i.e. for the first time conditionality applies to those who are already employed but are on a low income. This *in-work conditionality* is likely to create strong incentives for people to enter low hours work, further blurring the line between independence and state support. The Act also increased the length of sanctions for certain groups and introduced the concept of escalating sanctions, with longer sanction periods for second and third sanctionable failures within a 12-month-period. [166] The conditionality and sanction regimes for *JA, ESA and UC* claimants are now broadly aligned.[167]

Claimants are placed in one of four conditionality groups ranging from full to no conditionality, depending on their individual capabilities and circumstances: (1) No Work-Related Requirements; (2) Work Focused interview only; (3) Work Preparation; (4) All Work-Related Requirements. For example, the primary caregiver of a child under the age of one has no work-related requirements. As the child grows, these requirements gradually increase, transitioning to work-focused interviews and work preparation activities until the child reaches the age of three.[168] The group having all work-related requirements comprises job seekers, namely individuals able and willing immediately to take up paid work,[169] and those doing some work (but not earning enough to take them above their individual

---

164 V. Mantouvalou, 'Welfare-to-Work, Structural Injustice and Human Rights' Modern Law Review 929 (2020)83, pp. 929-954, 933.

165 S. Kennedy, F. Hobson, et al, 'Department of Work and Pensions Policy on Benefit Pensions' Debate Pack No CDP 0230, House of Commons Library (12 December 2022), p. 5 < https://researchbriefings.files.parliament.uk/documents/CDP-2022-0230/CDP-2022-0230.pdf> accessed 21.3.2025.

166 Ibid.

167 Ibid., p. 3.

168 UK Government, 'Universal Credit and your claimant commitment' (12 February 2025) < https://www.gov.uk/government/publications/universal-credit-and-your-claimant-commitment-quick-guide/universal-credit-and-your-claimant-commitment> accessed 21.3.2025.

169 *Welfare Reform Act 2012*, s. 18.

or household *Conditionality Earnings Threshold, CET*[170]) and who do not fall into one of the categories of person covered by other conditionality groups.[171] Claimants placed in this group will have to "do all [they] can to find a job or earn more. This includes looking for jobs, applying for jobs and going to interviews".[172] A person's work-related requirements are set out in their *Claimants Commitment* [173] – a "record of the responsibilities that [they] have accepted in return for receiving Universal Credit, and the consequences of not meeting them"[174].

For some claimants their *conditionality threshold* may be lowered in accordance with their personal circumstances on a case-by-case basis. E.g., while lone parents as well as couples with young children will be subject to conditionality arrangements, they will be permitted a certain level of flexibility in their engagement with the labour market, e.g. seeking employment compatible with their caring requirements.[175]

Non-compliance with UC requirements incurs the second harshest sanctions in the world[176], with 100% reductions in benefits for each day the sanction is in place for those failing to comply with any work preparation requirement until the time of compliance, and a minimum full suspension of benefits of three months (or longer for "repeat offences") for some so-called serious failures, including to accept a job offer or even to apply for a job.[177] Depending on their duration, sanctions are classified as low, medium or high level. The lowest level applies to claimants who miss a meeting with their job coach, who will be sanctioned until they attend

---

170 The CET is calculated on an individual basis by multiplying the National Minimum Wage (NMW) or National Living Wage (NLW) by the hours a claimant would normally be expected to undertake work related activity up to a maximum of 35.

171 S. Kennedy, F. Hobson, et al (n 165), p. 7.

172 UK Government, 'Universal Credit: detailed information for claimants' (12 February 2025) < https://www.gov.uk/government/publications/universal-credit-and-you/draft-uc-and-you> accessed 21.3.2025.

173 *Welfare Reform Act 2012*, s 4 (1)(e).

174 *Welfare Reform Act 2012*, s 14.

175 *Welfare Reform Act 2012*, ss 19-25 and *Universal Credit Regulations 2013*, regs 89-91.

176 The US has the harshest sanctions in the world. See H. Immervoll and C. Knotz, 'How demanding are activation requirements for jobseekers', OECD Social, Employment and Migration Working Papers 215 (July 2018), p. 47, < https://www.oecd.org/en/publications/how-demanding-are-activation-requirements-for-jobseekers_2bdfecca-en.html> accessed 21.3.2025.

177 *Welfare Reform Act 2012*, ss 26(2) (a) (b) and (c). The sanctions are substantiated by the *Universal Credit Regulations 2013*.

the next meeting.[178] When a sanction is imposed, only the standard basic amounts for adults are affected, not amounts payable for other reasons (e.g. children, housing costs). In *UC*, this is usually the full amount of the standard allowance for a single person, or half the standard allowance if it is a couple claim.[179]

Sanctioned claimants may be able to receive so-called *hardship payments*, paid at 60% of normal entitlement, if they are in a financially "vulnerable group". They must demonstrate that they have "no cash in hand" and payments will only be made to those who cannot meet their most basic and essential needs (e.g. accommodation, heating, food or hygiene).[180] Although vulnerable claimants can apply immediately, most claimants are not allowed to apply for the first two weeks after the sanction is imposed and the Department for Work and Pensions has itself acknowledged that the two weeks wait will often damage the claimant's health.[181] Under *UC*, hardship payments are not paid automatically, and claimants may need to justify their need for them on an ongoing basis. Hardship payments take the form of a loan, as *UC* claimants will also usually[182] have to repay any payments they receive by deductions from their ongoing *UC* award.[183]

All work-related requirements for benefit claimants were suspended in response to the coronavirus pandemic at the end of March 2020. From 1 July 2020, the Department for Work and Pensions began to reintroduce conditionality and sanctioning on a phased basis. Statistics show the number of sanctions imposed has increased rapidly since then.[184] At August

178 K. Harrison, 'The Sanctions Spiral: The Unequal Impact and Hardship Caused By Sanctions in Universal Credit' Citizens' Advice (July 2023), p. 4 < https://assets.ctfassets.net/mfz4nbgura3g/3BHkqTaFYS4XMj7sBsJWsj/d5df7a015adc3b59781dfb97dd4e07ba/Sanctions_20report.pdf> accessed 21.3.2025.

179 S. Kennedy, F. Hobson, et al (n 165), p. 3.

180 M. Adler, 'Do Benefit Sanctions Have a Future?' Journal of Social Security Law 1 (2024), pp 15-31, 26.

181 M. Adler (n 17), p. 46.

182 The DWP has a discretion to waive recoverable hardship payments, see M. Adler (n 180).

183 P. Larkin, 'Universal Credit: Route To "Virtuous" Citizenship or Engine of Dependency' Journal of Social Security Law 2 (2024), p. 151; Department for Work and Pensions, 'Recoverable Hardship Payments – Guidance' < https://www.parliament.uk/globalassets/documents/commons-committees/work-and-pensions/benefit-sanctions/annex-5-recoverable-hardship-guidance.pdf> accessed 21.3.2025.

184 M. Adler (n 180), pp. 24-25.

2022, 6.4% of UC claimants subject to conditionality had a benefit sanction – more than twice the pre-pandemic rate.[185]

In the last decade, a large amount of research has been conducted or commissioned, and various reports published, about different aspects of the benefit sanctions regime. In a report in 2018, the *Work and Pensions Committee* said that the evidence on the role of sanctions in achieving the goal of motivating people to take steps to move closer to work was "patchy" and required further research. The Committee also noted that sanctions, when applied inappropriately, can have a profoundly negative effect on people's financial and personal wellbeing. It found that some claimant groups – such as single parents and people with health conditions or disabilities – are disproportionately affected by sanctions.[186] Further research shows that sanctions create a "cycle of financial difficulty"[187] and have a counterproductive effect on the search for work.[188] Transportation costs are a major barrier, with no financial support available. Many struggle to afford travel to their Jobcentre, leading to sanctions that further reduce income and make future appointments even harder to attend.[189]

IV. Conclusions

In the UK, with an essentially "political" constitution, the executive has considerable freedom to develop policy and law on welfare benefits. Concerning the protection of a (right to) a subsistence minimum, supranational obligations deriving from EU law and the ECHR do not provide sufficient constraints on policy and law. The creation of stronger judicial controls as part of a redesign of the British constitution, called for by some academics and politicians, seems unlikely to be realized in the foreseeable future.[190]

The *Beveridge Report*, which laid the foundations of the British welfare state, regarded the main aim of social security as being the prevention of poverty which was referred to as "the abolition of want". The development

185 S. Kennedy, F. Hobson, et al (n 165), p. 4.

186 House of Commons Work and Pensions Committee, 'Benefit Sanctions – Nineteenth Report of Session 2017-19' (31 October 2018) < https://publications.parliament.uk/pa/cm201719/cmselect/cmworpen/955/955.pdf> accessed 21.3.2025.

187 K. Harrison (n 178), p. 17.

188 P. Larkin (n 183), p. 151.

189 K. Harrison (n 178), pp. 24-25.

190 A. Le Sueur (n 11), p. 2.

of eligibility and entitlement conditions and benefit sanctions in the UK reflect a shift away from this approach, towards an approach in which the main function of social security is to "activate" unemployed people and get them back into work. The shift has involved the integration of social security policies and employment policies which were formerly relatively autonomous policy areas.[191]

Since the late 1990s there has been a relative consensus in British politics over the goals and principles, if not all the details, of welfare reform for people of working age. British minimum income policies for working-age people have long been focused on promoting work through make work pay and labour market activation measures. Means-tested benefits have thus played a crucial role in social protection for British people of working age for many decades now. The old Poor Law principle of "less eligibility", i.e. ensuring that the differential between benefit levels and wages is sufficient to provide adequate incentives to work, has never been far from the centre of public debate.[192] Also, what counts as a "safety net" has no systematic relationship with actual living costs or need, whether at subsistence or other level. Also, since the 1990s some more "deserving" groups have seen their entitlements rise faster than others, so that a child, a working adult and a pensioner have entitlements today whose respective levels vary dramatically relative to their needs.[193] Moreover, throughout the 2010s, a growing range of claimants have not been able to access the level of disposable income implied by standard entitlement rates through the capping of benefits according to a household's circumstances e.g. the number of children or level of housing costs.[194]

In addition, particular households or groups are excluded from a basic level of support relating to "holes" in the safety net which are growing in size and number. Household that fail conditionality rules or where the administration of the system fails to provide income in a timely way: e.g with *UC* new claimants spend time waiting for payment. Emergency hardship payments have been cut back and are not always available and conditionality has been imposed in a more draconian way.[195] There are indications

191 P. Larkin, 'Incapacity, the Labour Market and Social Security: Coercion into "Positive Citizenship"' Modern Law Review 74 (2011)3, pp. 385-409.

192 D. Clegg (n 18), p. 149.

193 D. Hirsch (n 53), p. 212.

194 Ibid.

195 Ibid.

that UC has not significantly changed claimant attitudes toward workforce participation, and concerns remain about the UK's tight labour market. Research also suggests that the approach taken by DWP work coaches hinders claimants' ability to enter work, highlighting the need for greater investment in education, skills training, and labour market reforms.[196]

Concluding, one could say that there are definite signs that the establishment of a comprehensive welfare state and a certain guarantee of a minimum subsistence level which had advanced throughout the greater part of the 20th century, has been eroded by a series of social security reforms, with local, discretionary and charitable welfare again playing a significant role for the support of the "undeserving" and unemployed poor. Dramatic growth in food bank use is the best publicised example of this tendency[197], but also the increased reliance on discretionary support systems such as the *Discretionary Housing Payments.*[198]

196 P. Larkin (n 183), pp. 140-145 and 155-157.

197 See for example A. Jitendra, E. Thorogood and M. Hadfield-Spoor, *Early Warnings: Universal Credit and Foodbanks* (Trussell Trust 2017); R. Loopstra and D. Lalor, Financial Insecurity, *Food Insecurity, and Disability: The Profile of People Receiving Emergency Food Assistance from the Trussell Trust Foodbank Network in Britain* (Trussell Trust 2017).

198 C. Fitzpatrick, G. McKeever and M. Simpson, 'Conditionality, discretion and TH Marshall's 'right to welfare'' Journal of Social Welfare and Family Law 41 (2019)4, pp. 445-462.

Part III:
Latin American Perspective

Putting People First: How Brazil's Minimum Income Program Promotes Human Rights

Flavia Piovesan, Julia Cunha Cruz and Daniel Wainstock

I. Introduction

Brazil experienced a period of economic and social progress between 2003 and 2014, when over 29 million people were lifted out of poverty and inequality significantly declined.[1] During this time, the income level of the poorest 40% of the country increased by an average of 7.1%, compared to a 4.4% increase in the income of the population as a whole.[2] Cash transfer

1 T.F.L. do Nascimento and B.J.B. Silva, 'A Dívida Pública Brasileira (2003–2014)' Revista Economia e Políticas Públicas 8 (2020)1, p. 73.

2 The World Bank, 'Brazil Poverty and Equity Assessment' (2022) <https://documents1.worldbank.org/curated/en/099230007062256153/pdf/P1746910e33a8407d0b0850b8f0f5bcf18c.pdf> accessed 14.10.2024.

policies and other social programs lifted tens of millions out of poverty. Since 2015, however, the pace of poverty and inequality reduction has stagnated because of a severe recession lasting from 2014 to 2016.[3] While recovering from the economic recession, the country continued to face a serious economic crisis with around 8 million of its citizens unemployed in 2023.[4] Poverty and income inequality remain high; the Northeast, North, and Center-West, along with women, and black, mixed race, and indigenous populations, are all disproportionately affected.[5]

The COVID-19 pandemic significantly worsened the conditions of the most vulnerable people in Brazil, increasing power asymmetries and social inequalities[6]. For instance, due to the pandemic, Brazil had in 2020 and 2021 the worst unemployment rates in its history, with 13.4 million people unemployed in 2020 and a staggering 15.2 million in the first trimester of 2021.[7] There were some attempts by government and civil society to minimize the worst socioeconomic effects of the pandemic. The most relevant of such policy measures was the expansion of Brazil's flagship conditional cash transfer program, the *Bolsa Família* (Family Grant),[8] which grew both in terms of coverage (eligibility criteria were expanded) and in the amount paid to families.

There is consensus that such measures have been crucial and partly effective in avoiding the worst effects of the pandemic, even reducing poverty levels for some periods.[9] There is also some consensus, however, that a significant part of the most vulnerable population was either not reached by

3 Ibid.

4 J.R. de Souza Gentil, T.F. do Nascimento Melo, et al., 'Modelos com erros das variáveis: estudo de simulação e aplicação à dados de taxa de desemprego no Brasil' Peer Review 5 (2023)11, p. 260.

5 A. Salata, 'Race, Class and Income Inequality in Brazil: A Social Trajectory Analysis' (2020) <https://doi.org/10.1590/dados.2020.63.3.213> accessed 14.10.2024.

6 M.G. Corrêa, S. Rego, et al. 'Os impactos sociais da Covid-19 no Brasil: populações vulnerabilizadas e respostas à pandemia', in: Fiocruz, *Série Informação para ação na Covid-19* (Rio de Janeiro 2021).

7 Agência Senado, 'Segue para a Câmara seguro-desemprego extra durante epidemias' (22 November 2022) <https://www12.senado.leg.br/noticias/materias/2022/11/22/segue-para-a-camara-seguro-desemprego-extra-durante-epidemias> accessed 08.11.2024.

8 The name of the program was changed by the 2019-2022 government to Brazil Aid and renamed back to *Bolsa Família* by the current government (2023-2026).

9 L.H. Paiva, P.H.G. Ferreira de Souza, et al. 'Evitando a pandemia da pobreza: possibilidades para o programa Bolsa Família e para o Cadastro Único em resposta à COVID-19' Revista de Administração Pública 54 (2020)4, pp. 1097-1110.

these measures or not sufficiently protected by them.[10] After the pandemic, federal cash transfer programs continue to play a key role in providing income to the poorest segments of society and reducing poverty rates.[11]

II. Overview

1. Normative Background

a) National Provisions

Following a 21-year-long authoritarian dictatorship with a track record of severe human rights violations, Brazilians placed human dignity at the centre of the country's re-democratization process. Adopted in 1988, the current Brazilian Constitution is anchored on the principle of the prevalence of human dignity. The Constitution determines that human dignity is one of the five foundations of the Republic, along with sovereignty, citizenship, "the social values of labour and free enterprise", and political pluralism (Article 1). This means that the right to live a dignified life shall guide all actions of the Brazilian state, constituting both a beacon and a limit for decision-making, policy, and practice.

The Brazilian Constitution directly protects a comprehensive set of human rights, dedicating a chapter to individual and collective rights (including the prohibition of torture, freedom of thought, religious freedom, the right to privacy, the right to access information, freedom of association, the right to property, and due process of law). Social rights have been part of Brazil's Constitution since its promulgation in 1988, covering education, healthcare, social security, and labour rights (Article 6) as fundamental rights. In 2021, the social rights chapter has been amended to include a specific provision on the *right to a basic family income*, which shall be guar-

10 R.P. de Barros and L. Muller Machado, 'A pandemia e o início do fim da invisibilidade', in: L. Muller Machado, *Legado de uma Pandemia: 26 Vozes Conversam Sobre os Aprendizados Para Política Pública* (Autografia 2021).

11 C.B. Silva, L. Hasenclever, R.P.S. Marcia. 'O programa Bolsa Família e seus efeitos na pobreza e na desigualdade socioeconômica no Brasil' Editora Científica Digital 9 (2022), p. 1072.

anteed by a *permanent cash transfer program* encompassing every Brazilian in a condition of social vulnerability (Article 6, § 1º).[12]

Significantly, the Constitution expressly clarifies that the list of rights provided in the constitutional text is non-exhaustive, and that there may be other constitutional rights which – even if not textually included in the Constitution – derive from its principles or from the international treaties to which Brazil is a party (Article 5, § 2º). Therefore, one of the defining features of the Brazilian constitutional order is its openness to human rights norms, including those formulated in international treaties.

There is therefore a human rights nucleus within the Constitution, encompassing the human dignity principle, the rights expressly listed in the constitutional text, and those rights indirectly protected by the Constitution, including the rights established by international treaties. These human rights norms are the axiological centre of the Brazilian legal system, guiding the interpretation and application of all its norms.

b) International Provisions

In Brazil, human rights treaties that have been ratified by the country hold the status of constitutional norms. This means that these treaties are incorporated into the Brazilian legal system with the same legal weight as the Federal Constitution. Therefore, Brazilian courts, including the Supreme Federal Court (STF), must abide by and apply these treaties as if they were an integral part of the Constitution, ensuring that the human rights established in them are fully protected and respected on a national level. In other words, internationally proclaimed fundamental rights have normative force and are immediately enforceable in Brazil.

As mentioned above, Brazil has joined the international community in repeatedly proclaiming and reaffirming the human dignity principle. In the very first article of the Universal Declaration of Human Rights, the foundational basis of the modern international human rights regime, the international community declared that "[a]ll human beings are born free

12 Constitution of The Federative Republic of Brazil, Article 6, § 1º: "Every Brazilian in a situation of social vulnerability is entitled to a basic family income, guaranteed by the government in a permanent income transfer program, whose rules and access requirements will be determined by law, in compliance with fiscal and budgetary legislation", < https://legis.senado.leg.br/norma/579494/publicacao/33296461 > accessed 23.04.2025.

and equal in dignity and rights". With the further development of international norms, states unpacked the meaning of *dignity*, making a clear stance that it included both civil and political rights and economic, social, cultural, and environmental rights. The latter category includes provisions assuring that every individual shall have access to adequate standards of living (see, e.g., the International Covenant on Economic, Social and Cultural Rights, Article 11).

The right to an adequate standard of living is also protected by the Additional Protocol to the American Convention on Human Rights in the Area of Economic, Social and Cultural Rights, which Brazil signed and ratified. The protocol is known as Protocol of San Salvador and it recognizes in particular the right to minimum income as a key aspect of the right to an adequate standard of living (Article 9).[13] The right to minimum income is defined as the right of every person to receive an income that provides for their basic needs and those of their family, without discrimination. This includes not only financial resources, but also access to social security systems and other forms of assistance. The Protocol recognizes that the right to minimum income is closely linked to other economic, social, and cultural rights, such as the right to work, the right to health, and the right to housing.

To fulfil its obligations under the Protocol of San Salvador, states are required to adopt measures to ensure that everyone has access to a minimum income that provides for their basic needs. This includes measures to eliminate discrimination and other forms of exclusion that may limit the access to minimum income. States are also required to ensure that their social security systems and other forms of assistance are available to everyone who needs them.[14]

The Inter-American Court of Human Rights has issued several important decisions regarding the right to minimum income as recognized in the Protocol of San Salvador. These decisions have established strong precedents on the interpretation and application of this right in the Americas.[15]

---

13 Protocol of San Salvador (1988), Art. 9, OAS Treaty Series No. 69, <https://www.oas.org/juridico/english/treaties/b-32.html> accessed 25.09.2024.

14 Ibid.

15 Inter-American Court of Human Rights, *Yakye Axa Indigenous Community v. Paraguay*, 17 June 2005, Series C No. 125, para. 141; *Case of the Girls Yean and Bosico v. Dominican Republic*, 8 September 2005, Series C No. 130, para. 144; *Case of the Kaliña and Lokono Peoples v. Suriname*, 25 January 2010, Series C No. 214, para. 140.

For example, in the case of the *Street Children vs. Guatemala*, the Inter-American Court found that the state has an obligation to provide adequate protection for children, including those living in poverty, and to take measures to guarantee their right to minimum income. The Court held that the state must take steps to ensure that these children have access to adequate food, housing, health care, and education, and that the state has a positive obligation to provide these necessities where necessary to ensure that the right to minimum income is fulfilled.[16]

The Inter-American Court's jurisprudence on the right to minimum income serves as an important reference for states, civil society organizations, and individuals seeking to protect and promote this right in the Americas.

c) The Brazilian Supreme Court and the Right to Minimum Income

In 2021, the Brazilian Supreme Court issued a decision ordering the federal government to take all appropriate measures to effectively implement the right to minimum income, including by updating the value of *Bolsa Família* payments (*Supremo Tribunal Federal, Mandado de Injunção 7300 ED / DF, 2021*). The decision resulted from a legal suit filed by the Public Defender's Office (DPU) on behalf of a citizen who lacked the resources needed to maintain a dignified existence. According to the DPU, the government was failing to implement the claimant's constitutional rights. In his opinion, Justice Gilmar Mendes wrote that, given the poor implementation of the law on universal basic income, in practice this law had nothing but "symbolic effects". Considering that 9 million Brazilians live in extreme poverty, he concluded that "[n]o great argumentative effort is needed to demonstrate the indispensability of welfare programs in a booming but extremely unequal economy such as Brazil's". The Court agreed, mandating the federal government to take measures to improve minimum income policies.

2. Social Benefits

a) Schemes Relevant for Minimum Income Protection

Brazil has implemented several programs aimed at protecting vulnerable populations and ensuring that they are able to live in dignity. These pro-

16 Inter-American Court of Human Rights, *Case of the "Street Children" (Villagrán Morales et al.) v. Guatemala*, 19 November 1999, Series C No. 63.

grams not only provide financial assistance to families in need, but also aim to break the cycle of poverty by promoting education, health, and employment.

aa) Bolsa Família

Bolsa Família is a Brazilian social welfare program that provides financial assistance to low-income families, focusing on poverty alleviation and promoting education and healthcare through conditional cash transfers. As of June 2024, the program covers approximately 20.8 million families.[17] Conditions include requirements for children to attend school and for families to participate in preventive healthcare programs. The impact on minimum income is significant, helping to reduce extreme poverty and promoting social and economic inclusion.[18] As explained below, this program will be the main focus of this analysis, as it represents the largest and most comprehensive minimum income scheme in Brazil.

bb) Minha Casa, Minha Vida

Minha Casa, Minha Vida is a housing program in Brazil that offers affordable housing options to low-income families, addressing housing instability and promoting economic stability. Since its inception, the program has financed over 4 million housing units, benefiting about 10 million people. Conditions include income verification and prioritization of families in vulnerable situations. While the program does not directly guarantee a minimum income, it indirectly supports economic stability by reducing housing costs and improving living conditions. [19]

---

17 Secretaria de Comunicação Social, 'Bolsa Família de julho chega a 20,8 milhões de famílias a partir desta quinta' (18 July 2024) <https://www.gov.br/secom/pt-br/assuntos/noticias/2024/07/bolsa-familia-de-julho-chega-a-20-8-milhoes-de-familias-a-partir-desta-quinta-18> accessed 25.09.2024.

18 F.V. Soares, 'Brazil's Bolsa Família: A Review' Economic and Political Weekly 46 (2011)21, pp. 50-60.

19 C. Krause, R. Balbim, V. Correia Lima Neto, 'Minha Casa Minha Vida, nosso crescimento: Onde fica política habitacional?', in: Instituto de Pesquisa Econômica Aplicada (IPEA), *Texto para Discussão No. 1853* (Rio de Janeiro 2013).

cc) Programa de Aquisição de Alimentos (PAA)

This program supports family farming and food security by purchasing produce from local farmers to distribute to vulnerable populations, ensuring access to nutritious food. In 2023, the PAA benefited around 300,000 farmers and provided food for approximately 10 million people. This program helps to stabilize the income of family farmers and enhance food security among the poorest segments of the population. The impact on minimum income is more indirect, through supporting farmers' livelihoods and providing food to those in need.[20]

dd) Programa Saúde da Família

It provides primary healthcare services to poor populations, enhancing healthcare access and improving overall health outcomes. The program serves more than 70% of the Brazilian population, focusing on preventive care and health education. While the program does not directly influence minimum income, it reduces healthcare costs and improves quality of life, which can have a positive impact on the economic stability of families.[21]

ee) Programa de Proteção e Atendimento Integral à Família (PAIF)

This program focuses on protecting and assisting families, especially those facing social vulnerabilities, by providing a range of support services, including healthcare, education, and social assistance. The PAIF aims to strengthen family ties and improve the social and economic conditions of the most vulnerable families. Although it does not directly guarantee a minimum income, it provides critical support that helps families achieve greater stability and resilience, indirectly supporting economic security.[22]

---

20 R.A. de Medeiros Hespanhol, 'Programa de Aquisição de Alimentos: limites e potencialidades de políticas de segurança alimentar para a agricultura familiar' Sociedade & Natureza 25 (2013)3, pp. 469-483.

21 M.C.M. Senna, 'Eqüidade e política de saúde: algumas reflexões sobre o Programa Saúde da Família' Cadernos de Saúde Pública 18 (2002), pp. 203-211.

22 V.R.S. Ferreira, 'Fatores influenciadores do comportamento de decisão e ação dos implementadores do serviço de Proteção e Atendimento Integral à Família (PAIF)' (Universidade de Brasília, 2016).

b) Bolsa Família in Particular

The legal basis for the *Bolsa Família* program has been established by Law No. 10.836, enacted on 9 January 2004. This law consolidated various social programs into a single framework to provide financial assistance to low-income families, aiming to reduce poverty and promote social inclusion. Additionally, Decree No. 5.209 of 17 September 2004 regulates *Bolsa Família*, outlining the program's objectives, eligibility criteria, and operational guidelines. The policy design of Bolsa *Família* is based on targeting the poor, cutting complexities, and requiring heath checks and school attendance for children. This scheme shares with the above-mentioned programs the common goal of reducing poverty and improving the well-being of low-income families through various means, such as financial assistance, healthcare access, housing stability, and support services.

However, the chapter will focus only on *Bolsa Família.* This program stands out as the largest and most comprehensive one, both in terms of value and the number of people it serves. In term of number of beneficiaries, *Bolsa Família* reaches a significant portion of Brazil's low-income population. The program was recently expanded and, in 2024, covers 20.8 million families in Brazil, compared to the 13.9 million covered in 2020.[23] As for its benefits, *Bolsa Família* provides financial assistance to families facing various economic challenges. While the other above-mentioned social programs in Brazil are also extremely important, their impact is not as broad as *Bolsa Família*'s. This is because the other programs cover only specific needs, target smaller segments of the population and do not have the same scale or financial resources as *Bolsa Família. Bolsa Família* is therefore considered the focal point in discussions of social assistance in Brazil. Moreover, the program aims not only to address immediate needs like food but also imposes conditionalities, which require families to meet certain conditions related to education and healthcare, which are supposed to allow a transition out of poverty.[24]

23 Secretaria de Comunicação Social, 'Bolsa Família de julho chega a 20,8 milhões de famílias a partir desta quinta' (18 July 2024) <https://www.gov.br/secom/pt-br/assuntos/noticias/2024/07/bolsa-familia-de-julho-chega-a-20-8-milhoes-de-familias-a-partir-desta-quinta-18> accessed 25.09.2024.

24 M. Morgandi, K. Fietz, L. Superti, 'Beneficiary Dynamics in the Bolsa Família Conditional Cash Transfer-Capabilities, Constraints and the Local Labor Market' (Washington D.C. 2023).

III. Analysis

As illustrated above, Brazil has codified its cash transfer policy as a permanent program, protected by the Constitution (as mentioned above), as well as by legislation (see Law 10.836/2004, establishing the right to minimum income, and Provisional Measure 1164/23, which recreates the *Bolsa Família* program). However, with the right to minimum income guaranteed in the books, it is important to analyse how the Brazilian state implements such a right.

1. Eligibility and Conditionalities

In order to receive *Bolsa Família*, the beneficiary families must meet at least one of the following socio-economic criteria:

(i) live below the poverty line, if family members include pregnant women and children or adolescents between the ages of 0 and 17; or
(ii) live below the extreme poverty line.

The poverty line is calculated based on household income per capita. The government establishes thresholds that categorize households into different poverty levels. These thresholds are typically updated periodically to reflect changes in the cost of living and economic conditions. The poverty lines are defined as follows: the extreme poverty line is defined as a monthly per capita income that is insufficient to meet basic food needs. The threshold for extreme poverty is R$ 200 (reais, around 33 euros) or less, per month per person. The poverty line is a higher threshold than the extreme poverty line and includes those who can meet basic food needs but may struggle with other essential expenses such as housing, education, and healthcare. The poverty line is set at R$ 637.00 (reais, around 105 euros), per month per person.

The calculation method for determining the poverty status involves several steps. First, household income data is collected through surveys and administrative records, encompassing all sources of income such as wages, pensions, social benefits, and any other earnings. Next, the total household income is divided by the number of household members to calculate the per capita income. Finally, this per capita income is compared with the established poverty and extreme poverty thresholds to determine the household's poverty status.

For the eligible recipients, cash transfers are conditioned on school attendance for children and adolescents between 6 and 17 years old, health checks and timely vaccination on all children aged 0-5, and prenatal and postnatal health checks for pregnant women.[25]

The program is designed to provide long-term support; thus, its duration is not fixed, but is contingent on the family's compliance with the eligibility criteria and conditionalities. If families fail to meet the program's requirements, their benefit is suspended or terminated. However, the program provides warnings and opportunities for families to rectify issues before benefits are cut off.

The conditions of *Bolsa Família* implicitly reflect a definition of a dignified life by ensuring that families have the financial support to meet their basic needs while promoting long-term improvements in education and health. Utilizing conditionalities related to school attendance and healthcare encourages families to prioritize their children's education and ensure they receive essential medical care. This generates long-term benefits by breaking the cycle of poverty through improved access to education and enhanced health outcomes. Additionally, by establishing conditionalities, the program ensures that financial assistance is used for its intended purpose, reducing the risk of misuse or dependency. This promotes responsible resource utilization and contributes to a more sustainable path towards self-sufficiency. Therefore, the program empowers families, promotes social inclusion, and aligns with the principles of dignity and self-reliance.

2. Benefit Amounts and Adaptation

The minimum benefit, or basic bonus, is non-variable and is R$ 600 for each family, but additional payments of R$ 50 are given to families with children and young people aged between 7 and 18 years and pregnant or breastfeeding women. Families with children aged up to 6 years receive an extra R$ 150 per child.

Bolsa Família also includes an adaptation mechanism to address changing economic conditions and evolving beneficiary needs. This mechanism is not automatic, but it encompasses regular updates to the benefit amount to keep pace with inflation and the cost of living.

The program also recognized the importance of directing cash transfers to women, since the money goes directly to the families, preferably to the

25 Ibid.

mothers, or other women in charge of the household, through so-called Citizen Cards. By prioritizing payments to the female members of the household, the government aimed to foster the autonomy of women and reduce gender inequalities.

3. Ministerial Oversight

The Ministry of Development and Social Assistance (*Ministério do Desenvolvimento e Assistência Social*) is responsible for overseeing *Bolsa Família*. Its evaluation process is comprehensive and involves several steps to ensure accuracy and effectiveness. First, families must update their information in the Unified Registry (*Cadastro Único*) regularly, typically every two years. This registry includes details about income, household composition, and other relevant factors.

The information provided by families is then cross-checked with various government databases, such as social security, tax records, and employment databases, to prevent fraud. Additionally, social workers or authorized personnel may conduct home visits to verify the living conditions of beneficiary families and ensure the accuracy of the information provided.

Schools report attendance data to the Ministry of Education, while health units report compliance with vaccination schedules and health check-ups to the Ministry of Health. This approach ensures the accuracy of information and the effectiveness of the *Bolsa Família* in reaching and supporting eligible families.

4. Assessment

a) Positive Impacts

Bolsa Família has significantly reduced poverty and income inequality in the country. Already in the decade following the launch of the program, the poverty rate in Brazil had declined by nearly 20 percentage points, from 42.7% in 2003 to 23.8% in 2014.[26] During the same period, the income of

26 The World Bank, 'Strengthening Conditional Cash Transfers and the Single Registry in Brazil: A Second-Generation Platform for Service Delivery for the Poor' (22 April 2020) <https://www.worldbank.org/en/results/2020/04/22/strengthening-conditional-cash-transfers-and-the-single-registry-in-brazil> accessed 28.10.2024.

the poorest 40% of households in Brazil increased by 56%.[27] According to a study published by the Institute for Applied Economic Research (IPEA) in 2019, *Bolsa Família* contributed to raising 3.4 million people out from under the extreme poverty line, and 3.2 million out from under the poverty line.[28]

Moreover, *Bolsa Família* has also been documented to yield positive impacts on food availability: in a study based on a representative sample of the Brazilian population, it was observed that the Program contributed for higher per capita expenditure on food, higher per capita availability of total calories and higher availability of *in natura* or minimally processed foods and processed culinary ingredients among low-income households.[29] The increase in food availability is positive both because the energy availability among low-income families in Brazil is below the national average (1,611 kcal) and because the increased availability of food items such as meat, roots, tubers, and vegetables can diversify and improve the nutritional quality of the diet.[30]

Several studies have also demonstrated a trend of increasing gains in education associated with the *Bolsa Família* program. A 2014 study shows that *Bolsa Família* contributed to improvements in school performance in test scores and pass grades, as well as reductions in dropout rates for 4th grade children.[31] Another analysis suggests that, among girls, the *Bolsa Família* program significantly increased school attendance (by 8 percentage points) and grade progression (by 10 percentage points), with large, significant

---

27 P.H.G. de Souza, R.G. Osório, et al. 'Os efeitos do Programa Bolsa Família sobre a pobreza e a desigualdade: um balanço dos primeiros quinze anos', in: Instituto de Pesquisa Econômica Aplicada (IPEA), *Texto para Discussão No. 2499* (Rio de Janeiro 2019).

28 Ibid.

29 A.P.B. Martins and C.A. Monteiro, 'Impact of the Bolsa Família Program on Food Availability of Low-Income Brazilian Families: A Quasi Experimental Study' BMC Public Health 16 (2016)827, pp 1-11.

30 Ministério da Saúde, 'Guia alimentar para a população brasileira' (2nd ed. Brasília 2014), pp. 26-30.

31 A.A. Simões and R. Sabates, 'The Contribution of Bolsa Família to the Educational Achievement of Economically Disadvantaged Children in Brazil' International Journal of Educational Development 39(2014), pp. 151-166.

effects across both younger and older girls in rural areas.[32] In urban areas, a positive impact was documented among girls aged 15-17 years.[33]

Bolsa Família also significantly increased women's decision-making power in spheres related to children's school attendance and health expenses, household durable goods purchases, and contraception use.[34] In this regard, *Bolsa Família* increased the share of women who report exclusive control over contraception decisions by 10 percentage points.[35]

The program has also had a positive impact on health-related indexes. By conditioning cash transfers to health checks, *Bolsa Família* increased children's visits to preventive health services.[36] In children under age 7, it was also associated with increases in the number of growth monitoring visits, check-ups, and vaccination.[37] It also had an impact on dental hygiene: children who received *Bolsa Família* for a period up to two years had substantially lower odds of having dental caries than those who had never received *Bolsa Família*.[38]

b) Bolsa Família as an International Benchmark

Brazil's cash transfer policy has been instrumental in poverty reduction, becoming a model for other countries.

According to the World Bank, *Bolsa Família* is a form of investment in human capital. It notices how "[c]onditional cash transfers provide money directly to the poor, via a 'social contract' with the beneficiaries – for example, keeping children in school, or taking them regularly to health

32 A. de Brauw, D.O. Gilligan, et al., 'The Impact of Bolsa Família on Schooling' World Development 70 (2015), pp. 303-316.

33 Ibid.

34 A. de Brauw, D.O. Gilligan, et al., 'The Impact of Bolsa Família on Women's Decision-Making Power' World Development 59 (2014), pp. 487-504.

35 Ibid.

36 A. Shei, F. Costa, et al., 'The Impact of Brazil's Bolsa Família Conditional Cash Transfer Program on Children's Health Care Utilization and Health Outcomes' BMC International Health and Human Rights 14 (2014)10, pp. 1-9.

37 Ibid.

38 P. Calvasina, P. O'Campo, et al., 'The Association of the Bolsa Familia Program with Children's Oral Health in Brazil' BMC Public Health 18 (2018)1186, pp. 1-10.

centers. For the extremely poor this money provides emergency relief, while conditionals promote long-term investment in human capital."[39]

The United Nations has recognised the potential of the program to address poverty and inequality on a global scale better than other interventions.[40] Additionally, the Inter-American Development Bank has expressed strong support for the program, further validating its effectiveness and importance. The positive outcomes associated with *Bolsa Família* have transformed it into an international reference point, frequently cited as an exemplary model of good practice. Countries facing poverty challenges similar to those in Brazil are encouraged to look to *Bolsa Família* for inspiration and guidance in developing their own social assistance programs.[41]

c) Addressing Inefficiencies and Non-Take-Up

Although *Bolsa Família* has admittedly been instrumental in addressing the poverty issue in Brazil, the delivery system of this scheme as well as of other social benefits in Brazil faces several challenges that hinder the effective implementation of the right to minimum income. These challenges include bureaucratic inefficiencies, lack of coordination among different levels of government, and difficulties in targeting and reaching the most vulnerable populations.

First, bureaucratic inefficiencies can result in delays in benefit distribution and create obstacles for those in need to access the programs. Streamlining administrative processes and reducing unnecessary paperwork can help mitigate these issues, ensuring that benefits reach recipients more promptly and efficiently.

The lack of coordination among federal, state, and municipal governments is also an issue, as it can lead to gaps in service delivery and overlapping program implementations. Improving communication and collaboration between these levels of government is crucial. Establishing clear roles and responsibilities, as well as integrating databases and information

39 A. Fiszbein, N. Schady, et al., 'Conditional Cash Transfers: Reducing Present and Future Poverty', in: The World Bank, *World Bank Publications* (Washington D.C. 2009).

40 UNICEF, 'The Role of Child Benefits in Enabling Family-Friendly Policies to Achieve the Triple Bottom Line' (2019), pp. 2-3 and 7-8, <https://www.unicef.org/sites/default/files/2019-07/UNICEF-Child-Benefits-Family-Friendly-Policies-2019.pdf> accessed 08.11.2024.

41 Ibid.

systems, can enhance the efficiency and effectiveness of social benefit programs.

Second, there are difficulties in reaching all potential recipients. Accurately identifying and including the most vulnerable populations, such as those in remote areas or those without proper documentation, is a significant challenge. Enhancing data collection methods and employing technologies like geographic information systems (GIS) can improve targeting accuracy. Additionally, outreach initiatives and partnerships with local organizations can help identify and reach those who are often excluded.

Moreover, the complexity of the eligibility criteria and the requirement for extensive documentation can be barriers for the poorest families. Simplifying the application process and offering assistance to applicants can help overcome these barriers. Providing clear information and support through community centres or mobile units can also ensure that more families can navigate the system successfully.

To enhance the delivery and management of social programs, a multifaceted approach is necessary. First, developing user-friendly digital platforms for the application and management of benefits is crucial. This reduces paperwork and processing times, making the process more efficient and accessible for beneficiaries. Additionally, providing comprehensive training programs for local officials is essential for improving their capacity to manage and deliver social programs efficiently. Well-trained staff can significantly enhance the effectiveness of these programs.

Launching public awareness campaigns to inform eligible populations about their rights and how to access benefits is also vital. Utilizing various media channels and community networks will help reach a broad audience and ensure that information is widely disseminated. Furthermore, establishing decentralized assistance points in remote and underserved areas is necessary to ensure that all eligible individuals have access to the support they need.

Conducting regular monitoring and evaluation of the programs is also important. This process helps identify bottlenecks and areas for improvement, ensuring continuous optimization of the delivery system and better outcomes for beneficiaries. Implementing these strategies can help the social programs to become more efficient, effective, and accessible to those who need them most.

IV. Conclusions

The right to minimum income in Brazil is recognized as a fundamental right under the Brazilian Constitution (Article 6), and the country has implemented several programs and initiatives aimed at reducing poverty and ensuring that vulnerable populations live with dignity. These programs include the *Bolsa Família* program, which provides financial support to low-income families, as well as other initiatives aimed at creating job opportunities and improving access to education and health services.

However, despite these efforts, significant challenges remain in effectively implementing the right to minimum income in Brazil. One of the main challenges is ensuring continued adequate funding for these policies. The cost of implementing a minimum income policy can be substantial, and finding the resources necessary to provide adequate support to vulnerable populations can be difficult. Additionally, the delivery of the policy must be efficient, transparent, and equitable. If the delivery system is bureaucratic, cumbersome, or prone to corruption, it can undermine the effectiveness of the policy and discourage people from participating. [42]

In some circumstances, political opposition to the policy may also be a challenge. Some groups may view a minimum income policy as an undeserved handout or a threat to their own financial stability, and addressing these concerns and building support for the policy is essential to its success. It is important to note that Brazil has been able to create a political consensus to overcome this challenge. Despite initial resistance from some groups who perceive a minimum income policy as an unjustified giveaway, the country has been successful in addressing these concerns and building support for the policy. This has been an important factor in the *Bolsa Família* program success and continued implementation.[43]

Economic constraints, especially in times of economic uncertainty or recession, can also make the implementation of a minimum income policy challenging, as resources are scarce and governments are under pressure to balance their budgets. [44]

Having accurate data and information systems in place is critical to effectively implementing a minimum income policy. These systems are

42 M. Morgandi, K. Fietz, L. Superti (n 24).

43 T.L.S Pinto, B.M. Tabak, D.O. Cajueiro, 'How Politics can Influence the Allocation of Social Program Benefits: A Case Study of the Brazilian Poverty Reduction Program Bolsa Família' Economic Analysis and Policy 80 (2023), pp. 77-89.

44 M. Morgandi, K. Fietz, L. Superti (n 24).

necessary to target support to those who need it most and ensure that resources are being used effectively.

To address these challenges, a strong political commitment is essential, along with the establishment of an efficient delivery system, the building of support among key stakeholders, economic stability, and accurate data and information systems. It requires consistency in the public budget allocation for these programs. Additionally, the government must ensure that financial support and social services are adequate to meet the basic needs of families and that these programs are accessible to all those in need.

Looking to the future, there is still much work to be done in terms of effectively implementing the right to minimum income in Brazil. Some potential areas of improvement include increasing the amount of financial support provided to families, expanding eligibility criteria to reach more individuals in need, and strengthening the monitoring and evaluation of the program to ensure that it is achieving its goals. Additionally, there are opportunities to collaborate with other social programs to provide more comprehensive support to families, such as access to healthcare, education, and job training.

Investing in programs and initiatives that address poverty and support vulnerable populations allows the country to progress towards ensuring that all individuals have access to a dignified life. The right to minimum income is a crucial component of a society that values equality, justice, and human dignity.

Social Protection in Chile: Building a Life in Dignity?

Viviana Ponce de León Solís

I. Introduction

Chile has been one of the fastest-growing economies in Latin America in recent decades and is considered a model for development in the region. This growth has allowed the country to significantly reduce poverty, with the proportion of the population living below the national poverty line having fallen from 36% to 10.8% between 2000 and 2020.[1] According to World Bank estimates, by 2020, 0.7% of the national population was

1 World Bank, 'Poverty headcount ratio at national poverty lines (% of population) – Chile' < https://data.worldbank.org/indicator/SI.POV.NAHC?locations=CL> accessed 27.10.2023.

living on less than US$ 2.15 per day[2] and 1% on less than US$ 3.65 per day.[3] While these figures are relatively positive in comparative terms, they distract attention from the fact that more than 30% of the population is economically vulnerable and income inequality remains high, with the richest 1% of Chileans earning 49.6% of the country's total income.[4] The high level of economic inequality has negatively impacted many areas of society, including education, health, social protection, and employment.

To a large extent, these results can be attributed to historical factors that have decisively influenced the architecture of social protection in Chile, with a particular emphasis on the objective of enabling 'marginal groups in society as rights-bearing subjects to access the means to meet their own needs'.[5] In this view, poverty and social exclusion were seen as a direct result of an individual's 'lack of skills or opportunities' to master 'their own destiny', which had to be remedied through social assistance policies that promoted empowerment.[6] Hence, despite recent efforts to increase social spending and significantly extend social protection, considerable gaps remain in the development opportunities of different population segments, irrespective of whether they live above the poverty line or not.

Against this backdrop, this chapter discusses the extent to which existing social protection policies and benefits in Chile are intended and designed to secure a life in dignity. In order to reach its objective, we will examine the current normative framework in order to answer the following questions: Is there a real system of social protection in Chile or just a loose set of anti-poverty policies? Does the state have an obligation to guarantee a dignified life? How is such an obligation legally constructed? Do individuals have a corresponding subjective right to demand a minimum subsistence level? What does a dignified life entail?

---

2 World Bank, 'Poverty headcount ratio at $ 2.15 a day (2017 PPP) (% of population) – Chile' < https://data.worldbank.org/indicator/SI.POV.DDAY?locations=CL> accessed 27.10.2023.

3 World Bank, 'Poverty headcount ratio at $ 3.65 a day (2017 PPP) (% of population) – Chile' < https://data.worldbank.org/indicator/SI.POV.LMIC?locations=CL> accessed 27.10.2023.

4 L. Chance, T. Piketty et al., *World Inequality Report 2022* (World Inequality Lab 2022), p. 189.

5 V. Schild, 'Engendering the New Social Citizenship in Chile: NGOs and Social Provisioning under Neo-Liberalism', in: M. Molyneux and S. Razavi (eds.), *Gender Justice, Development, and Rights* (OUP 2002), p. 172.

6 V. Schild, 'Neo-Liberalism's New Gendered Market Citizens: The "Civilizing" Dimension of Social Programmes in Chile' Citizenship Studies 4 (2000), pp. 275-305, 286.

To address these questions, the remainder of this chapter is divided into three sections. Section II provides the background for understanding the evolution of the system, its normative basis, and its major structural components. This section is further divided into two parts. The first part presents some relevant milestones in the historical development of social protection in Chile and describes the applicable constitutional and international normative framework. The second part describes in broad terms how the system is organised into different sub-systems and how they relate to each other. Section III develops a detailed analysis of the system's distinctive design features. This section is divided into four parts. The first part reviews the landscape of existing minimum social protection schemes and benefits. The second part describes the technical mechanism for assessing the needs of social protection beneficiaries in Chile: the Social Register of Households. The third part examines the set of non-economic or behavioural conditions to which social assistance is subject and discusses their implications in terms of guaranteeing a decent life. The fourth part examines the activation policies aimed at preventing welfare dependency and promoting the economic self-sufficiency of their beneficiaries. Part IV closes the chapter with concluding remarks.

II. Overview

1. Normative Background

a) Historical Context

Chile has been ranked amongst the pioneering Latin American countries in the development of welfare policies, together with Argentina, Brazil and Uruguay.[7] Until the 1970s, the country had several social policy regimes, with varying conditions and levels of protection for different classes of workers, covering the vast majority of the population through the social security system, basic health services and extensive levels of access to primary and secondary education.[8] These developments peaked during the administration of former socialist president Salvador Allende (1970-1973),

7 C. Mesa-Lago, *Social Security in Latin America* (Inter-American Development Bank, Economic and Social Progress in Latin America 1991).

8 F. Filgueira, *Welfare and Democracy in Latin America: The Development, Crises and Aftermath of Universal, Dual and Exclusionary Social States* (UNRISD 2005), p. 13.

when social spending increased by up to 30% and redistributive policies were intensified.

This trend towards the expansion of the welfare state came to an abrupt halt with the military coup led by Augusto Pinochet, which resulted in a dictatorship that lasted more than fifteen years (1973-1989). Pinochet's dictatorship activated several mechanisms of welfare state retrenchment, which included anti-inflationary policies, as well as a so-called long-term development strategy implemented by the military regime that was dependent on the private sector and the reduction of the state to its minimum expression.[9] In turn, these mechanisms led to a drastic reduction of public social expenditure, decreasing from 24.8% to 14.3% of GDP between 1971 and 1981.[10]

To prevent future reforms and secure his political legacy, Pinochet also enacted a new constitution in 1980 that encouraged the market provision of social rights and promoted a 'residual welfare regime' based on targeted public policies for low-income groups and the neoliberal ideal of individual responsibility for welfare.[11] This regime led to 'a privatised and highly criticised pension system, segmented education, and healthcare, with lower-quality public services for the majority and expensive private [services] for the well-off'.[12] Ultimately, social policy in Chile took the form of a last safety net, targeted at those living in extreme poverty, offering below-minimum and patchy support. While the dictatorship is credited with positive economic results, its impact on the social agenda was dramatic: by 1989, 44% of the national population was living in poverty.[13]

With the return to democracy in 1990, welfare institutions and the offer of social protection programmes were substantially scaled up. A new strategy of 'growth with equity' (*crecimiento con equidad*) was devised, premised on the continuity of neoliberal policies, but supplemented with

9 J. Arellano, 'Social Policies in Chile: An Historical Review' Journal of Latin American Studies 17 (1985), pp. 397-418, 415.

10 J.P. Arellano, *Políticas Sociales y Desarrollo* (CIEPLAN 1988), pp. 45-46.

11 O. Larrañaga, *Las nuevas políticas de protección social en perspectiva histórica. Documento de Trabajo, 4* (PNUD 2010), p. 11.

12 N. Somma, M. Bargsted et al., 'No Water in the Oasis: The Chilean Spring of 2019–2020' Social Movements Studies 20 (2020)4, pp. 495-502.

13 P. Vergara, 'In Pursuit of "Growth with Equity": The Limits of Chile's Free-Market Social Reforms' International Journal of Health Services 27 (1997)2, pp. 207-215.

social policies aimed at promoting greater equality.[14] Although there was a substantial reduction in poverty in Chile between 1990 and 2000, the strategy of 'growth with equity' eventually proved to be limited. After 1996, the reduction of extreme poverty remained stagnant[15] and at the beginning of the 2000s, the existence of a 'hard core of poor households, marginalised from the benefits of economic growth and social policy networks' was already apparent.[16] Moreover, inequality in income distribution rose, evidencing the scant redistributive impact of this period's social policy.

During the 2000s, a number of international development agencies began to acknowledge social protection as a policy tool for poverty eradication and development promotion.[17] The crucial milestones in consolidating this new paradigm were the launch of the United Nations' Social Protection Floors, in 2009, and the adoption of the ILO's Social Protection Floors Recommendation N° 202, in 2012. These initiatives were backed by 'ever-increasing calls for a rights-based development agenda',[18] followed by a 'rapid expansion of social protection', amounting to 'a quiet revolution' in the region.[19]

Chile promptly joined this trend, expanding and integrating its social protection offer, with a view to ensuring 'universal access to benefits' in education, health, childcare, unemployment, and pensions, from a 'rights-based perspective'.[20] Against the backdrop of this universalist momentum, the country saw the emergence of some of the social protection programmes that are still in place to this day. Whereas initially these programmes focused exclusively on eradicating extreme poverty, they progressively began to expand their coverage to other vulnerable sectors of the population.

---

14 United Nations, *Promoting Inclusion through Social Protection. Report on the World Social Situation 2018* (Department of Economic and Social Affairs 2018), p. 7.

15 MIDEPLAN, *Conceptos Fundamentales Sistema de Protección Social Chile Solidario* (Ministerio de Planificación y Cooperación 2004).

16 O. Larrañaga, D. Contreras, G. Cabezas, *Políticas Contra la Pobreza: de Chile Solidario al Ingreso Ético Familiar* (PNUD 2014), p. 1.

17 United Nations, *Promoting Inclusion through Social Protection. Report on the World Social Situation 2018* (Department of Economic and Social Affairs 2018), p. 7.

18 M. Sepúlveda, *The Rights-Based Approach to Social Protection in Latin America: From Rhetoric to Practice* (Nations 2014), p. 7.

19 Ibid.

20 MIDES, *Análisis de la distribución del gasto en subsidios monetarios y de su incidencia en el ingreso de los hogares 2013 y 2015. Panorama CASEN 2015* (Ministerio de Desarrollo Social 2015), p. 20.

b) Constitutional Law and Constitutional Case Law

The Chilean Constitution does not deal explicitly with the protection of a minimum subsistence. However, a few constitutional provisions could be relevant for the construction of a state obligation to offer the necessary conditions for a life in dignity. For instance, Article 1 paragraph 1 of the Constitution stipulates that 'individuals are born free and equal in dignity and rights'. Article 1 paragraph 4 also establishes that 'the state is at the service of human beings and its purpose is to promote the common good, for which it must contribute to create the social conditions that allow each and every one of the members of the national community their greatest possible spiritual and material fulfilment, with full respect for the rights and guarantees established in this Constitution'. Furthermore, Article 1 paragraph 5 imposes on the state the duty 'to protect the population and the family, to strengthen it, to promote the harmonious integration of all sectors of the nation and to ensure the right of individuals to participate with equal opportunity in national life'.

In addition, the Constitution guarantees several fundamental rights that relate to the protection of a minimum subsistence and the promotion of a life in dignity. Article 19 N° 2 enshrines the right to equality before the law, establishes that in Chile there are no privileged individuals or groups, and specifies that neither the law nor any authority whatsoever may establish arbitrary differences. Article 19 N° 9, in turn, enshrines the right to health protection and places a duty on the state to protect free and equal access to actions for the promotion, protection and recovery of health and rehabilitation of individuals. Finally, and perhaps more significantly for the purposes of this chapter, Article 19 N° 18 guarantees all individuals the right to social security. This article also specifies that 'state action will be directed to ensure the access of all inhabitants to uniform basic benefits, whether they are granted through public or private institutions'; that 'the state shall supervise the proper exercise of the right to social security'; 'the laws governing the exercise of this right shall be of qualified quorum'; and that 'the law may establish compulsory contributions'.

The vague statements devised in the Constitution depict a weak constitutional commitment to social security in general, unlike other constitutional provisions in Latin America including detailed policy instructions for the provision of this right.[21] The Constitution does not list any guidance for social security policy on risk or contingency coverage, level of benefits, and social security system governance or financing. Moreover, the Constitution does not explicitly impose a duty on the state for fulfilling the right to social security. Instead, it limits the state's role to simply supervising its proper exercise and enables the private provision of social security without mentioning any standards for such provision, in alignment with neoliberal policies, such as privatisation and deregulation.[22]

In interpreting this provision, the Constitutional Court has defined social security as 'the set of principles that recognises the right of every human being to the essential goods to prevent social contingencies and to cover their effects, and that regulates the institutions necessary for this purpose'.[23] Likewise, the Court has identified four guiding principles of social security that constitute the basis or foundation on which it must be institutionalised, namely: universality (subjective and objective); integrity or sufficiency; solidarity and unity.[24]

Regarding the connection between this right and other constitutional principles, the Court has also pointed out that the duty of the state to protect individuals against various contingencies constitutes a direct and close projection of human dignity, referred to in Art. 1 paragraph 1 of the Constitution.[25] In this sense, social security meets states of need, is aimed at the maintenance of the beneficiaries, and has a social interest component that involves it in the search to protect the weakest.[26] Nonetheless, the Court has cautioned that the Constitution does not recognise a right to unrestricted access to a universe of unlimited benefits, but rather a right to the provision of benefits that must be matched by their corresponding legal, equitable and proportionate sources of financing. Accordingly, social rights and, in particular, the right to social security, only seek to guarantee

21 A. Ben-Bassat and M. Dahan, 'Constitutional Commitment to Social Security and Welfare Policy' Review of Law & Economics 12 (2016)1, pp. 165-201, 172-173.

22 D. Harvey, *A Brief History of Neoliberalism* (OUP 2005), pp. 64-86.

23 STC 790 c. 33, STC 1287 cc. 25 and 30, STC 2025 c. 41, STC 2275 c. 4, STC 3227 c. 33.

24 Ibid.

25 STC 790 c. 31, STC 3058 c. 12, STC 7442 c. 7, STC 7548 c. 6.

26 STC 576 cc. 29 and 31, STC 3249 c. 36, STC 3058 c. 36, STC 3539 c. 9, STC 3540 c. 9, STC 3541 c. 9, STC 5822 c. 13, STC 6166 c. 14, STC 6167 c. 14, STC 6469 c. 13, STC 5679 c. 7, STC 6879 c. 12, STC 7140 c. 10, STC 7275 c. 10, STC 7400 c. 11, STC 7535 c. 11, STC 7694 c. 8, STC 8134 c. 8.

minimum benefits, which are directly linked to the level of economic development of a country and to political decisions expressed in legal norms.[27]

To date, the Constitutional Court has never been directly confronted with the issue of whether Article 19 N° 18 also encompasses the right to social assistance or non-contributory social protection, or whether such right could be implied from other constitutional rights or principles at all.

c) International Law and International Case Law

Pursuant to Article 5 paragraph 2 of the Constitution, 'the exercise of sovereignty recognises as a limitation the respect for the essential rights that derive from human nature. It is the duty of the state bodies to respect and promote such rights, which are guaranteed by this Constitution, as well as by the international treaties ratified by Chile and which are in force'. This provision leads to the conclusion that international human rights treaties ratified and in force are binding on the state and must be considered as applicable legislation by the courts.

To date, Chile is a signatory to two treaties in which legal scholars consider the right to social assistance to be enshrined: the UDHR (Article 25) and the ICESCR (Articles 9 and 11).[28] Nevertheless, these provisions have never been invoked before the courts as a source of a human right to social assistance, nor is there any national case law suggesting such an interpretation.

As far as the Inter-American Human Rights System is concerned, the American Convention on Human Rights (ACHR) – ratified by Chile in 1990 – does not contain explicit references to a life with dignity, minimum subsistence, social protection, social security, or social assistance. However, the Inter-American Court of Human Rights has developed an interpretation of the right to life, understood as the right to a life worth living, which could be of interest for our analysis. According to this interpretation, the

27 STC 2337, STC 3, STC 7585, STC 12, STC 14.

28 L. Leisering and T. Böger, 'Case Study: Social Pensions in the Global South', in: L. Leisering (ed.), *The Global Rise of Social Cash Transfers: How States and International Organizations Constructed a New Instrument for Combating Poverty* (OUP 2019), p. 219; G. Vonk and M. Olivier, 'The Fundamental Right of Social Assistance: A Global, a Regional (Europe and Africa) and a National Perspective (Germany, the Netherlands and South Africa)' European Journal of Social Security 21 (2019)3, pp. 219-240, 223.

right to life also includes the integral realisation of individuals, both in the material and spiritual sphere, considering their vocation, aptitudes, circumstances, potentialities and aspirations, which allow them to reasonably set certain expectations and to have access to them.[29] Consequently, the state has the duty to generate the minimum living conditions compatible with the dignity of human beings and not to generate conditions that hinder or impede it. Yet, to date, there are no cases in which the Inter-American Court's right to a life worth living has been specifically projected to social protection, and its case law does not provide further indications as to the precise content of the aforementioned minimum living conditions compatible with the dignity of human beings.

We do, however, find explicit references to a life in dignity in the Additional Protocol to the ACHR in the Area of Economic, Social and Cultural Rights, ratified by Chile in 2022. For example, Article 6.1. of the Protocol states that the right to work 'includes the opportunity to secure the means for living a dignified and decent existence', while Article 7.a. adds that remuneration must guarantee all workers 'minimum [...] dignified and decent living conditions for them and their families'. On the other hand, Article 9.1. establishes that the right to social security must secure individuals 'the means for a dignified and decent existence'. In a similar vein, Article 13.2. declares that the right to education 'ought to enable everyone to [...] achieve a decent existence'. Moreover, the Protocol also enshrines the rights to the formation and the protection of families,[30] the rights of children,[31] the right to special protection in old age,[32] and the protection of persons with disabilities.[33]

The Protocol establishes a monitoring mechanism that requires States Parties to submit periodic reports to the Secretary General of the Organisation of American States on the progressive measures they have taken to ensure due respect for the rights set forth in the Protocol.[34] The Secretary

29 *Case of Loayza Tamayo v. Peru, Reparations and Costs,* IACHR Series C No. 42, 27 November 1999, para. 147. Although this judgment was passed in a case to which Chile was not a party, pursuant to the so-called conventionality control, the interpretation contained therein could have a general scope.
30 Additional Protocol to the ACHR in the Area of Economic, Social and Cultural Rights, Art. 15.
31 Ibid., Art. 16.
32 Ibid., Art. 17.
33 Ibid., Art. 18.
34 Ibid., Art. 19.1.

General then forwards these reports to the specialised bodies of the Inter-American Human Rights System, who examine them and formulate the general recommendations they deem appropriate.[35] In addition, the Inter-American Commission on Human Rights may formulate observations and recommendations on the status of the economic, social and cultural rights set forth in the Protocol in all or some of the States Parties, which may be included in its annual report to the General Assembly or in a special report, as the Commission deems appropriate.[36] Chile has yet to submit its initial report.[37]

2. Social Benefits

a) Minimum Income Protection in Old Age

In 1980, the dictatorship imposed a mandatory individual capitalisation system, which required each worker to pay a contribution equivalent to 10% of their salary or monthly income into a personal account held by a pension fund administrator (AFP), which invests the pension savings for a return. This system profoundly transformed the Chilean social security landscape, replacing a public defined-benefit system with an individually funded system run by private administrators and regulated by the state. The system also implied a radical change in the understanding of the state's role in social protection, whereby authorities would be concerned only subsidiarily with poverty in old age, through the granting of targeted assistance pensions and guaranteed minimum pensions. Thus, the then-new system rewarded savings and personal effort, as those who contributed the most would get the highest pensions, while leaving the rest of the population behind.

The system's original design envisaged that the pensions of workers who were able to contribute systematically throughout their working lives would be similar to their active income, indexed to inflation. In addition, since

35 Ibid., Art. 19.7.

36 Ibid.

37 According to the General Norms for the preparation of the periodic reports under the Protocol of San Salvador, approved by Resolution AG/RES. 2074 (XXXV-O/05), as updated by Resolution AG/Res. 2713 (XLII-O/12), the first report was due within one year of ratification or accession to the Protocol, i.e. 25 October 2023. As of the closing date of this chapter (August 2024), the first report is in preparation but has not yet been submitted.

there would be a substantially lower contribution compared to the old system, this would increase the worker's liquid income and reduce the cost of labour for employers, which, added to the greater control over accumulated savings, would encourage employment, formality, and contributions on the part of self-employed workers. Meanwhile, by financing pensions with the savings of the workers themselves, the state would be freed from its financial commitments so that it could concentrate its efforts on lower-income pensioners.

However, for these conditions to be met, the system had to behave according to certain assumptions. In particular, dependent and self-employed workers would have an additional incentive to contribute by being able to control and own their capitalisation funds; workers would contribute all their wages throughout their working lives, up to a maximum of UF$ 60,[38] with interruptions only for unemployment; low-income workers would contribute for at least 240 months during their working lives, thus gaining access to the state guarantee of a minimum pension; and women, who used to be mainly housewives, would contribute to the family income during their old age, as they did in previous years. Furthermore, available data showed that without significant changes, more than half of AFP pensioners would not reach a minimum pension and require some public funding.[39]

These shortcomings were partially addressed by a legal reform in 2008, which created the Solidarity Pillar (i.e. the non-contributory, publicly funded tier of Chilean social security), a state-funded basic invalidity and old-age pension scheme designed to complement the contributory pension system.[40] The Solidarity Pillar was targeted at the most vulnerable sections of the population who did not contribute sufficiently or at all to any social security scheme, with the aim of preventing poverty in old age, ensuring a

38 The Unidad de Fomento (UF) is an inflation-indexed unit of account, calculated and published by the Central Bank of Chile (BCCh). It is authorised for pricing credit operations in national currency by banks and credit and savings cooperatives. The BCCh calculates the value of the UF for each calendar day between the tenth day of the current month to the ninth day of the subsequent month. These values are derived from the CPI month-on-month percentage change, as published by the National Institute of Statistics (INE), or the institution who replaces it, of the month preceding the month in which the UF is calculated and published.

39 Observatorio de Igualdad de Género de América Latina y el Caribe, 'La Reforma Previsional de Chile. Un avance en la garantía de la autonomía económica de las mujeres' (2012) <https://oig.cepal.org/sites/default/files/analisis_reforma_previsonal_de_chile2.pdf> accessed 23.3.2023.

40 O. Larrañaga (n 11).

reasonable level of social protection and economic autonomy, and guaranteeing a decent standard of living. The rationale behind its creation was to support those left behind, as ageing and withdrawal from the labour market should not be equated with poverty or an abrupt drop in living standards.[41]

While the Solidarity Pillar effectively increased the coverage of population groups excluded from the individual capitalisation system, the quality of benefits was still lacking and the number of pensioners receiving pensions below the minimum wage increased.[42] In fact, by 2020, around 80% of pensions were below the minimum wage and only 12.5% were above the minimum wage.[43] In response to these challenges, a reform introduced the Universal Guaranteed Pension in 2022, a publicly funded 'universal' benefit for all adults aged 65 and over who are not in the richest 10% of the population aged 65 and over, with the aim of improving the pensions of current and future pensioners. This new benefit has already proved effective in increasing both the level of old-age pensions and their net replacement rate.[44]

b) Social Protection

Social protection in Chile takes the form of a complex scheme of non-contributory means-tested benefits, integrated through the *Sistema Intersectorial de Protección Social* (Cross-Sectoral System of Social Protection). The System represents an attempt to transition from a targeted approach to a rights-based approach to social protection.[45] To that effect, it comprises several actions and social benefits, executed and coordinated by different administrative entities, destined for the socioeconomically most vulnerable[46] national population, to secure them access to better living conditions.

---

41 Bill N° 558-354.

42 C. Andrade, '¿Cuánto más soporta el Pilar Solidario? La experiencia de la vejez en el Chile actual', in: K. Araujo (ed.), *Hilos tensados: para leer el octubre chileno* (Editorial USACH 2019), p. 232.

43 R. Gálvez and M. Kremmerman, *Pensiones bajo el Mínimo: Los montos de las pensiones que paga el sistema de capitalización individual en Chile (Datos 2020)* (Fundación SOL 2021), p. 5.

44 K. Fernández, N. Rojas, A. Weber, *Impacto de la PGU en las pensiones actuales y desafíos para el debate previsional* (Universidad San Sebastián 2023).

45 Bill N° 1162-356.

46 On the notion of socio-economic vulnerability, see Section III.2, below.

Its key features are laid down in Act no. 20.379, which establishes the System's basic institutional and substantive structure. This Act incorporates the recommendations and methodological guidelines provided by international development agencies, such as the Inter-American Development Bank and the World Bank, thus adopting a multidimensional and dynamic approach to poverty and vulnerability.[47]

A central entity is in charge of administering, coordinating, supervising and implementing the System: the Ministry of Social Development and Family. However, for the operation of the System, the Ministry may enter into agreements with municipalities, with other bodies of the State Administration, or with private non-profit entities.

Three subsystems coexist within the System:

- The *Chile Solidario* (Solidarity Chile) subsystem, aimed at promoting the incorporation of families and individuals living in extreme poverty into social networks and providing them access to better living conditions. *Chile Solidario* was established in 2004, as a first attempt at developing an integrated approach to existing social protection programmes, thus addressing the barriers faced by poor households struggling to access a piecemeal, fragmented and sectoral offer for poverty reduction.[48]
- The *Protección Integral de la Infancia – Chile Crece Contigo* (Integral Child Protection – Chile Grows with You) subsystem, intended to support the development process of children who are treated in the public healthcare system, who study in a public educational system establishment, or whose adult caregivers are deprived of liberty, from their first gestational checkup until they reach 18 years of age. This subsystem was created along with the System itself in 2009, to widen the coverage and to further strengthen the integration of social protection programmes.
- The *Seguridades y Oportunidades* (Safeties and Opportunities) subsystem, devised for vulnerable individuals and families, whose monthly per capita income is less than what is necessary for an individual to meet their food needs. The incorporation of this subsystem in 2012 resulted in two major innovations to the country's anti-poverty strategy: the introduction of socio-labour support programmes and the increase in conditional and non-conditional cash transfers.

---

47 MIDES, *Informe de Desarrollo Social 2017* (Ministerio de Desarrollo Social 2017).

48 A. Barrientos, 'Protecting Capability, Eradicating Extreme Poverty: Chile Solidario and the Future of Social Protection' Journal of Human Development and Capabilities 11 (2010)4, pp. 579-597, 586.

Each of these subsystems involves a set of actions and social benefits – including cash and in-kind benefits – cross-sectorally executed and coordinated by state entities, focalised on a specific group of socioeconomically vulnerable people and/or families. Participation of individuals and households in each subsystem is compatible with participation in other subsystems within the System.[49] In fact, in some cases, participation in a subsystem entails preferential or guaranteed access – that is, without application – to other subsystems or to one or more of its specific benefits. Conversely, ceasing to participate in one of the subsystems does not necessarily preclude access to or continued participation in other subsystems.[50]

Since each subsystem was created independently, at different times and under different administrations, each reflects a specific set of normative and political underpinnings, whose realisation requires a variety of techniques and approaches. Hence, some subsystems place a strong emphasis on service provision while others focus on cash transfers or impose greater and more stringent conditionalities.

In addition to the benefits of the *Sistema Intersectorial*, Chilean legislation provides for more than a hundred additional scattered benefits in the form of vouchers and subsidies, support for caregivers and persons with disabilities, training and help for entrepreneurship, student support, and care and counselling programmes for victims of sexual violence or crime.

III. Analysis

1. Benefits and Adaptation

a) Chile Solidario

Due to its narrow targeting and modest results in terms of increasing beneficiaries' incomes, *Chile Solidario* was ultimately destined to be phased out and many of its benefits were absorbed by the Seguridades y Oportunidades subsystem.[51] However, the *Chile Solidario* subsystem is still for-

49 Act no. 20.595 Art. 3 para. 4.

50 Ibid.

51 N. Brandt, 'Reducing Poverty in Chile: Cash Transfers and Better Jobs' OECD Economics Department Working Papers, No. 951 (2012)13 < www.oecd-ilibrary.org/reducing-poverty-inchile_5k9bdt4pld6h.pdf?itemId=%2Fcontent%2Fpaper%2F5k9bdt4pld6h-en&mimeType=pdf > accessed 12.3.2023.

mally in place, and some of its benefits remain to this day: psychosocial support, preferential access to the family allowance, access to the Universal Guaranteed Pension or Basic Solidarity Disability Pension, access to a drinking water consumption and sewage service subsidy, and access to a school retention subsidy.[52]

Preferential access to the family allowance is intended for low-income persons belonging to the 60% of the most socio-economically vulnerable national population, according to the Social Register of Households.[53] The monthly amount of the family allowance is CLP$ 20,328 per each dependent, but it is doubled for persons with disabilities.[54] Family allowance recipients are also entitled to free preventive and curative medical and dental care. Pregnant women can apply for maternity benefit from the fifth month of pregnancy, after which they must stop receiving the family allowance. The family allowance is granted for three years and is readjusted in the same proportion as the minimum income, according to the variation of the Consumer Price Index (CPI) within a given period, defined by law.[55]

b) Chile Crece Contigo

All the benefits provided by the *Chile Crece Contigo* subsystem are services rather than cash transfers, as illustrated by the Biopsychosocial Development Support Programme, which provides personalised guidance and monitoring of the development of its beneficiaries under the age of seven.[56] This programme aims to promote, protect and provide multi-sectoral support for exclusive breastfeeding, ideally up to six months for breastfed infants, and its continuation at least up to two years of age, complemented

52 Except for the preferential access to the family allowance, all other benefits of *Chile Solidario* are also included in *Seguridades y Oportunidades* and therefore, in order to avoid redundancies, they will be treated under the latter subsystem.

53 Act no. 19.949 Art. 7 para. 1. For the functioning of this instrument see below, Section III.2.

54 All figures are updated to their value as of October 2023. For reference, the average exchange rate of one Chilean peso (CLP$ 1) was USD$ 0.001205 and EUR 0.0010964 in that period.

55 In Chile, there is no regulation that determines the periodicity with which the minimum income must be readjusted, but in practice it is usually readjusted annually (except in 1998 and 2005). Nor is there a rule that determines the criteria according to which the minimum income must be readjusted, although in practice factors such as the Consumer Price Index and GDP growth are usually taken into account.

56 Act no. 20.379 Art. 11 para. 1.

by other foods. Protection also extends to the methods of obtaining human milk other than direct breastfeeding, in particular with regard to hygiene, safety and security in the collection, handling, storage and distribution of human milk to infants.

In addition, this subsystem provides children in vulnerable situations with access to technical aids if they have a disability; free access to crèche or equivalent services; free access to full-day kindergarten or equivalent services; free access to half-day kindergarten or equivalent services if the child's caregiver works from home; and guarantees families of unborn children living in extreme poverty access to the *Chile Solidario* subsystem.[57] This subsystem also provides beneficiary families with preferential access to public services, according to the developmental needs of their children, in programmes such as educational equalisation, insertion in dependent or independent work, improvement of housing and living conditions, mental health care, family dynamics, legal assistance, prevention of and care in case of domestic violence and child abuse.[58]

c) Seguridades y Oportunidades

The *Seguridades y Oportunidades* subsystem includes a variety of cash transfers that can be divided into three categories. The first corresponds to dignity transfers, which are unconditional cash transfers aimed at providing immediate relief to families in extreme poverty in order to ensure a life compatible with human dignity. The second corresponds to transfers for obligations, which are conditional cash transfers linked to the fulfilment of obligations that contribute to the development of children as human capital. The third corresponds to transfers for achievements, which are also conditional cash transfers and whose aim is to reward the achievement of goals that are crucial for overcoming poverty, such as those related to education and work. Each of these in turn comprises a number of benefits, as explained below.

---

57 Ibid., Art. 12.

58 Ibid., Art. 13 para. 1.

aa) Dignity Transfers

Dignity transfers include several unconditional cash transfers that are meant for general subsistence, such as the base transfer and the protection transfer; they can be spent in any way the beneficiary deems appropriate. These benefits are widely labelled in the literature on the topic as unconditional, in contrast to duty transfers (see Section III.1.c.bb, below), the granting of which is subject to the attainment of certain achievements or performances. However, dignity transfers are still subject to certain conditions, in a broad sense, including the signing of a letter of commitment by the beneficiary (see Section III.3.i, below), declaring his or her intention to enter and remain in the subsystem and its programmes.

The base transfer is a benefit for users of the subsystem living in extreme poverty who participate in the Socio-Labour Support Programme or in the Psychosocial Support Programme that are part of the subsystem. Its amount is variable, as its purpose is to reduce the magnitude of the gap between the income of beneficiary households and the extreme poverty line (CLP$ 152,338 per individual), covering only 85% of the difference. In order to calculate beneficiary households' income, their autonomous per capita income, the estimated amount of their rent and the subsidies received by their members are taken into account. This transfer is provided for 24 months and its amount decreases by one-sixth per month from the 17th month of the contribution, as long as the requirements continue to be met, which is verified on a monthly basis. These values are readjusted on 1 February of each year, at 100% of the variation of the Consumer Price Index (CPI) of the previous year. As per the most recent official figures available, during the year 2021, a monthly average of 68,126 households received the base transfer, at a total of CLP$ 36,110 million.

The protection transfer, also known as *bono dueña de casa* (housewife's transfer)[59], in turn, is a benefit for users of the subsystem who participate in its Psychosocial Support Programme, provided that they comply with a commitment letter and an intervention plan set out at the beginning of

59 Although Act no. 19.949, which regulates the protection transfer, does not restrict its scope of beneficiaries exclusively to women, the administrative regulation for the application of the Act establishes that only in the cases of families where no adult is female over 18 years of age, the social protection transfer may be assigned to an adult male member of the family'. Hence the name 'housewife transfer'. See Decree 235 Art. 41.

the program. This transfer is granted for 24 months, and its amount varies according to the following time brackets: the first 6 months, the transfer totals CLP$ 21,823; from month 7 to month 12, it totals CLP$ 16,608; from month 13 to month 18, it totals CLP$ 11,419; and from month 19 to month 24, it totals CLP$ 20,328. These values are readjusted on 1 February of each year, at 100% of the variation of the Consumer Price Index (CPI) of the previous year. In the year 2021, a monthly average of 111,578 households received protection transfers, at a total of CLP$ 19,260 million.[60]

Dignity transfers also include tied cash transfers which can only be spent in the context of a specific need.[61] A first illustration of this kind of transfer is the subsidy for the payment of drinking water consumption and sewage services, which favours residential users of scarce resources.[62] The subsidy is applied to the fixed and variable charges related to the beneficiaries' consumption, which cannot be less than 25% or exceed 85% of these charges and must be the same for beneficiaries in the same region who are subject to the same maximum tariffs and have a similar socio-economic level.[63] A second illustration is the educational grant for the retention of students, which is paid to educational institutions that certify that they have enrolled and ensured the permanence in classes or the regular graduation of students between the 7th grade of elementary school and 4th grade of high school who belong to families classified as indigent, according to the Social Register of Households.[64] This grant is awarded each year in April to the sponsors of subsidised educational establishments that have retained students from 7th to 8th grade of elementary education, amounting to CLP$ 50,000; from 1st to 2nd grade of high school, to CLP$ 80,000; from 3rd to 4th grade of high school, to CLP$ 100,000; and from 4th grade of high school for students that have successfully graduated, to CLP$ 120,000.[65] These values are readjusted in January of each year by the same

---

60 MIDES, *Balance de Gestión Integral* (Ministerio de Desarrollo Social y Familia 2021), p. 57.

61 L. Leisering, 'Basic Social Security: From Poor Relief to Social Assistance, to Social Cash Transfers', in: L. Leisering (ed.), *The Global Rise of Social Cash Transfers: How States and International Organizations Constructed a New Instrument for Combating Poverty* (OUP 2019), p. 81.

62 Act no. 18.778 Art. 1, Act no. 19.949 Art. 2, Act no. 20.595 Art. 15 para. 1.

63 Act no. 18.778 Art. 2.

64 Act no.19.837 Art. 43, Act no. 19.949 Art. 2.

65 Subsidised educational establishments are those that are financed by state contributions and monthly co-payments from parents.

percentage by which the Educational Subsidy Unit was readjusted in the immediately preceding year.[66] Users of the *Chile Solidario* subsystem also have access to these benefits.

As for the sufficiency of the amounts of these transfers to meet the objective of enabling the general subsistence of households living in extreme poverty and ensuring living conditions compatible with human dignity, a word is in order. Considering that the base transfer only covers 85% of the difference between the monthly per capita income of the beneficiary household and the value of the extreme poverty line (CLP$ 151.485), this benefit does not even guarantee that the latter threshold will be reached. There is no justification in Act no. 20.595 or in its draft for the base transfer only covering 85% of the gap that families must bridge to overcome the extreme poverty line. A qualitative study carried out in 2018 on the perceptions of the subsystem's beneficiaries suggests that this 85% cut-off represents an individual rather than collective understanding of the causes of poverty, which assumes that families and individuals are primarily responsible themselves for their situation of poverty and vulnerability, as well as for overcoming it.[67]

For its part, the highest value of the protection transfer (CLP$ 21,823 for the first 6 months of the total of 24 in which it is granted) only reaches about 15% of the value of the extreme poverty line. As for the tied cash transfers, these only cover up to 85% of the fixed and variable charges related to the beneficiaries' drinking water consumption or are directly given to individuals other than the beneficiaries, as is the case with the educational grant for the retention of students. These observations suggest that the system is not generous enough and may be unable to fulfil its purposes.

66 The Educational Subsidy Unit is a measure that expresses the amount to be subsidised per pupil, which is readjusted in December of each year or when public sector salaries are readjusted by the same percentage.

67 Subsecretaría de Evaluación Social, 'Evaluación de Impacto del Subsistema de Protección y Promoción Social Seguridades y Oportunidades (Ley N°20.595) – Usuarios Egresados' (2018) < http://www.chileseguridadesyoportunidades.gob.cl/docs/Evaluacion_impacto_SSOO_CSP_Informe_final.pdf > accessed 9.8.2024.

bb) Duty Transfers

The *Seguridades y Oportunidades* subsystem comprises two conditional cash transfers for users who meet certain conditions in the areas of health and education: the healthy child control transfer and the transfer for school attendance, respectively. The healthy child control transfer is a benefit intended for households covered by the subsystem who are entitled to the base cash transfer and have children under 6 years of age as members of the family group, with an up-to-date health check-up. In 2021, 31,695 families obtained this benefit, at a total of CLP$ 3,309,143,000 per year.[68] The transfer for school attendance is a monthly benefit aimed at families who are users of the *Seguridades y Oportunidades* subsystem who are entitled to the base monetary transfer and whose children from 6 to 18 years of age regularly attend educational establishments recognised by the state, whether they are in elementary or secondary education. To qualify for the benefit, the child's monthly school attendance must be equal to or greater than 85% of the total number of days established in the school calendar. Throughout 2021, these transfers benefited a monthly average of 51,213 families, at a total of CLP$ 7,983,436,000 annually.[69]

The amount of each of these transfers is CLP$ 11,000 per month for each child who meets the relevant requirements and the transfer is compatible with the receipt of any other subsidy or transfer provided by the state. This value is readjusted on 1 February each year by 100% of the variation experienced by the Consumer Price Index (CPI) of the previous year.

cc) Achievement Transfers

The *Seguridades y Oportunidades* subsystem includes four kinds of achievement transfers that reward specific accomplishments. The first is the formalisation transfer, a one-time benefit paid to users of the subsystem who have effectively participated in its social and labour support programme and register at least four continuous contributions for health and pensions, or for the Unemployment Insurance established in Act no. 19.728, as appropriate, provided that they are declared and paid within the period of

68 MIDES, *Balance de Gestión Integral* (Ministerio de Desarrollo Social y Familia 2021), p. 57.

69 Ibid., p. 58.

effective participation. Its maximum amount is CLP$ 200,000, in a single instalment, which is adjusted on 1 February of each year, considering 100 percent of the variation of the Consumer Price Index. In 2021, this bonus reached 3091 beneficiaries, at a total of CLP$ 648,950 million.[70]

The second is the high school graduation transfer, also a one-time benefit for users of the *Seguridades y Oportunidades* subsystem who are over 24 years of age and who, within the period of their effective participation in the subsystem, obtain a high school diploma or equivalent recognised by the Ministry of Education. Its amount equals CLP$ 50,000, which is also readjusted on 1 February of each year, considering 100 percent of the variation experienced by the Consumer Price Index. During the year 2021, this transfer reached a coverage of 1306 beneficiaries, at a total of CLP$ 74,103,000.[71]

The third is the effort transfer, which benefits users of the subsystem who belong to the socioeconomically most vulnerable 30% of the population, who show outstanding performance or improvement in the areas of education, health, employment, savings, and monthly adherence to intensive or residential drug rehabilitation programmes. It amounts to CLP$ 50,000, which is readjusted on 1 February of each year, considering 100 percent of the variation experienced by the Consumer Price Index, and may be received by each beneficiary only once in each calendar year. In case the effort transfer can be granted for two or more achievements, the beneficiary will receive the transfer for only one of them. For 2021, 227,310 effort transfers were issued, totalling CLP$ 11,735,836,000.[72]

The fourth and last benefit comprised in this category is the women's employment transfer. This benefit is granted to salaried and self-employed female workers who are between 25 and 60 years of age and belong to the socioeconomically most vulnerable 40% of the population, as well as their respective employers. The monthly payments of this transfer vary according to the minimum and maximum brackets of the gross income of the beneficiary workers, up to a maximum of CLP$ 570,825 per year and are recalculated year by year. During 2021, 390,763 female workers received this benefit, at a total amount of CLP$ 54,509,159,000.[73]

70 Ibid.
71 Ibid.
72 Ibid.
73 Ibid., p. 59.

d) Solidarity Pension System

The Solidarity Pension System is the non-contributory tier of the Chilean pension system, aimed at preventing poverty in old age and invalidity, as well as at increasing the adequacy and equity of pensions. It currently comprises three benefits: the Universal Guaranteed Pension, the Basic Solidarity Invalidity Pension, and the Solidarity Invalidity Pension Contribution. A common denominator of these benefits is that they all target people whose self-financed pension amounts are low or non-existent. By April 2023, the total number of recipients of all the benefits provided by the Solidarity Pension System reached 2,331,467, who collectively received a total of CLP$ 473,354 million.[74] Among them, 59% were men and 41% were women.

The Universal Guaranteed Pension is a publicly funded monthly cash transfer that replaces the old-age benefits of the Solidarity Pillar. It is aimed at all persons 65 years of age or older, who do not belong to the richest 10% of the population and have a base pension of less than CLP$ 1,114,446. The base pension results from adding the beneficiary's self-financed pension and any additional survivor's pensions they may be receiving at retirement age, regardless of whether the beneficiary retires or not.[75] For those with a base pension lower or equal to CLP$ 702,101 per month, the benefit will amount to CLP$ 206,173; while for those with a base pension higher than CLP$ 702,101 but lower than CLP$ 1,114,446, its amount will be variable, depending on the beneficiary's vulnerability level.[76] By April 2023, 1,878,035 individuals received the Universal Guaranteed Pension, a figure representing 80.55% of the beneficiaries of the Solidarity Pension System. The total amount spent on this concept reached CLP$ 381,693 million.[77]

The second benefit included in the Solidarity Pension System is the Basic Solidarity Invalidity Pension, a monthly monetary contribution for people between 18 and 65 years of age who have a certified invalidity, who are

74 Unidad de Políticas Previsionales de la Dirección de Estudios, 'Beneficiarios del Pilar Solidario – Información del mes' (July 2024) < www.previsionsocial.gob.cl/sps/visualizacion-sistema-de-pensiones/ > accessed 30.4.2023.

75 This benefit is available to all eligible individuals, regardless of whether they continue to work or receive a pension from any pension system, except for CAPREDENA and DIPRECA.

76 See Section 2, below.

77 Unidad de Políticas Previsionales de la Dirección de Estudios, 'Beneficiarios del Pilar Solidario – Información del mes' (July 2024) < www.previsionsocial.gob.cl/sps/visualizacion-sistema-de-pensiones/ > accessed 30.5.2023.

not entitled to a pension under any social security system – whether as a pensioner or as a beneficiary of a survivor's pension – and who are part of a household belonging to the poorest 80% of the population. Its amount is the same as that of the Universal Guaranteed Pension. Official figures updated to April 2023 show that 187,578 individuals, equivalent to 8.05% of the users of the Solidarity Pension System, have received this benefit. The total amount paid reached CLP$ 38,652 million.[78]

Finally, the Solidarity Invalidity Pension Contribution is a benefit that supplements an Invalidity Pension[79] until it reaches a final amount equivalent to the Universal Guaranteed Pension. Therefore, its beneficiaries must meet the same requirements to qualify as for the Basic Solidarity Invalidity Pension, except that they must have contributed to a pension scheme and, in addition, receive a base pension lower than the amount of the Universal Guaranteed Pension. Up to April 2023, 94,790 people have accessed this benefit, which represents 4.07% of the beneficiaries of the Solidarity Pension System. Overall, they have received CLP$ 16.4 million.[80]

All benefits of the Solidarity Pension System are readjusted every year on 1 February, according to the variation of the Consumer Price Index.

2. Situation of Need

Access to the *Sistema Intersectorial de Protección Social* and the Universal Guaranteed Pension, among other benefits,[81] is determined by 'socio-economic vulnerability,' which is the legal term used to describe the respective target population.[82] Although the law does not expressly define it, the literature on the topic understands the term as referring to the loss of well-being caused by income variability and the risk it poses to households.[83]

78 Ibid.

79 Invalidity pensions are paid to those who have contributed to any pension scheme, have not reached retirement age, and suffer a permanent impairment in their ability to work due to a common (non-work-related) illness or accident. Its amount depends on the degree of invalidity and is calculated on the basis of the pensioner's average taxable income, excluding allowances, of the last 6 months preceding the accident or diagnosis of illness.

80 Ibid.

81 Over 160 social benefits are assigned using information from the Social Register of Households.

82 Act no. 20.379 Art. 1.

83 P. Henoch, 'Vulnerabilidad social. Más allá de la pobreza' Serie Informe Social 128 (2010), p. 11.

Socio-economic vulnerability is in turn determined by the System of Support for the Selection of Beneficiaries of Social Benefits.[84] The purpose of the System is to provide information that enables a process to classify the target population of the various benefits, programmes and social services created by law, in order to determine whether they meet the conditions for eligibility. This process, legally referred to as 'characterisation',[85] is carried out using information from the Social Register of Households, a functional database for the storage and processing of self-reported information, as well as information from administrative databases. In order to ensure its accuracy and validity, the self-reported information contained in the register may be subject to verification – mainly by comparison with public databases such as those of the Internal Revenue Service, the Ministry of Education and the Land Registry Offices, among others – and updating, rectification, completion or cancellation.

The characterisation itself involves a socio-economic qualification process, which consists of placing each individual or household in one of seven brackets: 40%, 50%, 60%, 70%, 80%, 90% and 100%. The four lowest brackets – between 40% and 70% – represent the lowest income and most vulnerable individuals and households, while the three highest brackets – between 80% and 100% – represent the highest income and least vulnerable individuals and households. Each individual or household included in the Register is assigned to one of these brackets according to a three-stage procedure and a methodology based on several variables, as laid down in an administrative regulation.[86]

The first stage is to determine the total income of the individual or household, also known as equivalent income. Equivalent income is the average monthly income from dependent or independent work, contributory and non-contributory pensions, and physical and financial capital of each household member aged 18 or over in the previous 12 months. In order to determine equivalent income, information from administrative databases is preferred to self-reported data in the Social Register of Households in order to promote efficiency and reduce the risk of fraud.[87]

The second stage is to determine the needs of each individual or household according to the number of members and their characteristics, such

84 Decree 22.

85 Act no. 20.379 Art. 5 para. 1.

86 Resolución 47 exenta.

87 Ibid., B.

as age, level or degree of disability (mild, moderate or severe), level or degree of dependency (mild, moderate or severe) or special educational needs. A coefficient is applied to these attributes and their interactions in order to accurately reflect the real cost to each individual or household of maintaining their standard of living.[88] The application of this coefficient also allows for a more precise grouping of individuals or households, taking into account not only their per capita income but also their composition and characteristics.

The third stage involves an assessment of means, which aims to verify the consistency between the income of the individual or household, their socio-economic level and their access to services and goods. This test takes into account the value of one or more of the following: health insurance, enrolment in an educational institution, vehicles, property and the income of parents who are not part of the household of children under 21 years of age or between 21 and 24 years of age if they are students. For these purposes, a distinction is made between 'high value' and 'very high value' resources, according to tranches defined in an administrative regulation.[89] If two or more of these resources under consideration in the assessment of means are classified as high or very high value, the individual or household will be placed in one of the top four socio-economic brackets, making them ineligible for minimum income support and some social protection benefits.[90]

It should be noted that the vulnerability brackets assigned on the basis of the information entered in the Social Register of Households are relatively independent from the definition of poverty. Thus, some of the target groups for certain benefits or programmes are determined according to socio-economic vulnerability (e.g. the Universal Guaranteed Pension and achievement transfers), while others are determined according to poverty (such as *Seguridades y Oportunidades* benefits) or extreme poverty (such as *Chile Solidario*). The focus of the Register on assessing socio-economic vulnerability allows targeting social assistance benefits not only as a means to respond to poverty but also to prevent it.

Regarding poverty measurement, the value of the poverty line and the extreme poverty line are measured on the basis of the Basic Food Basket, made up of a set of food goods, whose value is the same throughout the

88 Ibid., I.
89 Ibid., III.
90 Ibid.

country and considers a requirement threshold of 2,000 average daily calories per person. The value of the Basket is updated monthly according to the variation of the prices of the products that compose it in the Consumer Price Index (CPI), discounting the food consumed outside the home. Thus, a household in the income poverty bracket is one whose monthly income is below the poverty line per person, or the minimum income established to satisfy basic food and non-food needs in that same period, according to the number of household members. In turn, a household in a situation of extreme income poverty is one whose monthly income is below the extreme poverty line, or with a minimum income established according to the number of household members which corresponds to 2/3 of the value of the poverty line. Although households in poverty or extreme poverty tend to be concentrated in the 10-20% vulnerability brackets, there is no strict correspondence between them.

While the implementation of the system is a step forward, there are still some challenges to overcome. The process of cross-checking self-reported information with information available in administrative databases increased the workload of the bodies responsible for the provision of social assistance and minimum income benefits, which initially hampered their timely delivery.[91] More recently, measures have been taken to reduce delays. However, given that the Register is updated once a month, even if information is reported and cross-checked in a timely manner, it can take up to five weeks to be recorded.[92]

On the other hand, there is self-reported information that is not verifiable through cross-checking with other public databases and that is decisive for the process of socio-economic qualification and eligibility for certain social benefits, such as the number of household members. As a result of these difficulties, the practice of falsifying information is widespread among beneficiaries.[93] The absence of official data to cross-check this information is not only a problem in that it may distort the targeting of the social

---

91 Boreal, *Estudio Evaluación de la Implementación del Sistema de Apoyo a la Selección de Usuarios de Prestaciones Sociales* (2017) < https://biblioteca.digital.gob.cl/server/api/core/bitstreams/de9308c4-a0c7-407c-89ac-1cdf024611a5/content > accessed 15.4.2023.

92 MDSF, *Informe Final: Panel de Expertos para mejoras al instrumento de focalización* (2022) < https://registrosocial.gob.cl/docs/220117_Informe_de_Comisión_CSE_VF.pdf > accessed 15.8.2024.

93 J. Contreras and K. Figueroa, 'Desde la ficha de protección social al registro social de hogares, el nuevo instrumento de focalización en Chile. Una perspectiva desde los

assistance system, but also because it potentially makes benefit recipients liable to sanctions and loss of benefits, including fines[94] and exclusion from some of the subsystems of the *Sistema Intersectorial de Protección Social.*[95]

3. Non-Economic Conditions

As with most social protection systems, access to income support and social assistance in Chile is conditional on the fulfilment of specific status conditions, which define the universe of potential recipients of a given benefit.[96] As a result, it is not enough to establish that a person is socioeconomically vulnerable, poor, extremely poor or, more generally, in need, in order for him or her to have access to social protection benefits. In this regard, membership in a defined support category determines that in practice there are no fully universal social benefits.

a) Age is one of the most common status indicators, as exemplified by the Universal Guaranteed Pension, restricted to those aged 65 and over, and the Basic Invalidity Pension, restricted to those aged between 18 and 65. In the latter case, the status condition of age is accompanied by the status condition of invalidity, i.e. the permanent impairment of a person's working capacity as a result of illness or weakening of the person's physical or intellectual strength. The same is true for the *Chile Crece Contigo* subsystem, which targets children from their first health check-up until they reach 18 years of age. Here too, age is accompanied by other factors, such as being a user of the public health system, being enrolled in public educational establishments, or that the respective significant adult is deprived of liberty. Similarly, some of the potential groups of users of the *Seguridades y Oportunidades* subsystem are defined on the basis of age status together with the lack of support networks – people aged 65 or over, living alone or with a single person – or together with homelessness – people over 18 years of age living on the street. Furthermore, a number of cash transfers provided by the *Seguridades y Oportunidades* subsystem are reserved for individuals belonging to certain age groups, as illustrated by the high school graduation bonus, aimed at beneficiaries over 24 years of age who have graduated from

actores locales' Documentos y Aportes en Administración Pública y Gestion Estatal 30 (2018)18, pp. 129-163, 137-145.

94 Act no. 20.379 Art. 5 para. 2.

95 Act no. 19.949 Art. 10, Act no. 20.595 Art. 25 para. 2.

96 B. Watts and S. Fitzpatrick, *Welfare Conditionality* (Routledge 2018), p. 18.

high school, or the women's employment transfer, aimed at women aged between 25 and 60.

b) While residency is often used as a status indicator for social protection purposes in other countries, in Chile it is not very common for it to be expressly incorporated in the eligibility requirements. An exception to this rule is found in the eligibility requirements for the Universal Guaranteed Pension, which include proof of residence in Chile for a period of at least twenty continuous or discontinuous years since the applicant reached the age of 20, or for a period of at least four years in the last five years immediately preceding the date of application.[97] Similar requirements apply to the Basic Solidarity Invalidity Pension and the Solidarity Invalidity Pension Contribution, the beneficiaries of which must prove that they have resided in Chile for at least five years out of the last six years immediately prior to the date of application.[98]

Nonetheless, in order to apply for inclusion in the Social Household Register, proof of residence in the country must be provided. This proof may consist of the deed or certificate of ownership in force, tax appraisal certificate or lease contract of the property in which the applicant resides, or the bill of basic services (electricity, water, gas), or statement of account issued by the company providing fixed or mobile telephone, Internet, or television services, among others. Given that inclusion in the Registry is a necessary condition for accessing all the benefits of the *Sistema Intersectorial de Protección Social*, in practice, residence implicitly becomes an eligibility requirement for all available social protection offered.

4. Activation

Contemporary social protection systems are designed with an underlying concern about the risk of welfare dependency. As a consequence, they often include activation policies in which the notions of autonomy, desert and self-responsibility take on special prominence. Based on the systematisation proposed by Besharov and Call, the Chilean social protection system incor-

97 Act no. 21.419 Art. 10 c).
98 Act no. 20.255 Art. 16 c).

porates a number of activation policies[99] that can be seen as either punitive, undermining citizenship, or as supportive, enhancing citizenship.[100]

a) Requirements for Job Search, Job Preparation and Job Training

In order to obtain free access to nursery or equivalent services and free access to extended day nursery or equivalent services within *Chile Crece Contigo*, the parents or carers of the children who require them must be working, studying or looking for work.[101] On the other hand, users of *Seguridades y Oportunidades* must undergo a social-work accompaniment programme aimed at improving their ability to generate an independent income, their employability and their participation in the labour market.[102]

b) Reinforced Case Monitoring

Chile Solidario offers its beneficiaries the Psychosocial Support Programme, which consists of personalised coaching by a qualified professional or technician to promote the development of the personal and family skills necessary to meet the minimum conditions of a decent quality of life, and an intervention strategy aimed at strengthening the beneficiaries' effective links with social networks and access to available services.[103] Failure to comply with the Psychosocial Support Programme is grounds for termination of participation in the subsystem.[104] Similarly, *Seguridades y Oportunidades* includes an axis programme aimed at all its users, with the aim of coaching them and evaluating their performance and achievements during their participation in the subsystem. The programme includes a diagnosis, an intervention plan, a follow-up of the participation and an

99 D. Besharov and D. Call, 'Introduction: European and US Experiences with Labor Activation', in: D. Besharov and D. Call (eds.), *Work and the Social Safety Net: Labor Activation in Europe and the United States* (OUP 2023), p. 7.

100 L. Leisering (n 61), p. 95.

101 Act no. 20.379 Art. 12 para. 2.

102 Act no. 20.595 Art. 8 para. 1.

103 Act no. 19.949 Art. 4.

104 Act no. 19.949 Art. 11 para. 3.

evaluation.[105] Acceptance of the intervention plan is mandatory for participation in the subsystem.[106]

c) Incentives

Users of *Seguridades y Oportunidades* who take part in the socio-labour accompaniment programme are entitled to a one-off formalisation bonus, provided that, during their participation in the programme, they register continuous contributions, declared and paid, for a minimum of three months and a maximum of twelve months. Those who meet these requirements will be entitled to the formalisation transfer until the nineteenth month of participation in the programme.[107] In addition, users of the same subsystem who are over 24 years old are entitled to a one-off bonus for obtaining their high school diploma or equivalent, as long as they or members of their household remain users of the subsystem.[108] Finally, *Seguridades y Oportunidades* also includes a publicly financed employment subsidy for female employees and workers aged between 25 and 60 who belong to the most socio-economically vulnerable 40% of the population, as well as for their employers.[109]

d) Time Limits on Benefit Receipt

The family allowance included in *Chile Solidario* is assigned for three years.[110] Equally, the base cash transfer and the protection transfer included in the *Seguridades y Oportunidades* subsystem are granted for a period of 12 or 24 months, depending on the duration of the user's participation in the Psychosocial Support Programme and the Social Work Accompaniment Programme.[111] Both programmes have a maximum duration of 24 months.[112] However, users who successfully complete the socio-labour

105 Act no. 20.595 Art. 6 para. 1.
106 Act no. 20.595 Art. 6 para. 2.
107 Act no. 20.595 Art. 19 para. 1.
108 Act no. 20.595 Art. 19 para. 2.
109 Act no. 20.595 Art. 21 para. 1.
110 Act no. 19.949 Art. 7 para. 2.
111 Act no. 20.595 Art. 14 para. 2 and Art. 15 para. 2, respectively.
112 Act no. 20.595 Art. 11 para. 2.

accompaniment programme early are rewarded and retain access to the basic cash transfer, conditional cash transfers and other social benefits of the subsystem for up to 24 months.[113] Participation in the *Seguridades y Oportunidades* subsystem ends entirely within 12 months of the end of the axis programme.[114] The female employment transfer, on the other hand, is paid to the worker herself for four consecutive years and triggers a subsidy for her employer for up to 24 months.[115]

e) Benefit Step-Downs

Some of the benefits included in the *Seguridades y Oportunidades* subsystem decrease over time. For instance, the amount of the subsystem's base cash transfer decreases linearly at a rate of one-sixth per month, from the 17th month after its commencement.[116] Likewise, the subsystem's accomplishment bonuses decrease linearly at a rate of one-fifth per month, from the 10th month after their first grant.[117]

f) Other Behavioral Conditions

Some benefits are also linked to the fulfilment of behavioural conditions on the part of their recipients, as illustrated by the large number of conditional cash transfers included in the *Seguridades y Oportunidades* subsystem. The behavioural dimension of this type of conditionality is determined by the fact that it aims at modifying or influencing the behaviour of its recipients, as it is supported by monitoring and sanctioning mechanisms,[118] which may amount to social control devices.[119] Furthermore, the literature on the subject suggests that behavioural conditions and sanctions can have a significant impact on other rights and can be counterproductive to the social reintegration of their beneficiaries in terms of opportunities to access

113 Act no. 20.595 Art. 9 para. 2.
114 Act no. 20.595 Art. 18 a).
115 Act no. 20.595 Art. 21 para. 1.
116 Act no. 20.595 Art. 14 para. 2.
117 Act no. 20.595 Art. 19 para. 1.
118 B. Watts and S. Fitzpatrick (n 96), pp. 18-20.
119 Ibid., p. 11.

formal employment, potentially leading to homelessness, drug dealing and crime.[120]

Another source of conditionality is reflected in the fact that to enter and participate in both the *Chile Solidario* and the *Seguridades y Oportunidades* subsystems, eligible individuals and households must expressly declare their willingness to do so and to comply with the conditions of the system by signing a commitment letter.[121] The commitment letter is a technical instrument that sets out the conditions of participation in the program, the family's rights and responsibilities, general information about the services and social programmes to which they may have access and the grounds for suspension and termination of their participation. Failure to comply with this letter may result in termination of participation in the subsystem or programme, loss of benefits and, potentially, lack of access to all forms of social protection.[122] Consequently, some commentators have argued that it is not entry into the scheme itself that ensures access to social protection benefits, but rather compliance with the conditions set out in the commitment letter.[123]

This is one of the most glaring weaknesses of the system, as it could lead to the total deprivation of the minimum basic level of social assistance benefits for the target population, in open contradiction to international human rights standards and to the system's own fundamental objective of providing better living conditions to the most socio-economically vulnerable national population.[124] To illustrate the scope of this issue, it should be borne in mind that Chilean social assistance includes benefits related to the provision of drinking water, education, health, housing and access to justice.[125] Against this background, it is essential to define minimum levels of social protection and to raise awareness of the specific contribution

---

120 J. Griggs and M. Evans, *Sanctions within Conditional Benefit Systems: A Review of Evidence* (Joseph Rowntree Foundation 2010); M. Adler, *Cruel, Inhuman or Degrading Treatment? Benefit Sanctions in the UK* (Palgrave 2018); WelCond, *Final Findings Report, Welfare Conditionality: Sanctions, Support and Behaviour Change* (ESRC 2018).

121 Act no. 19.949 Art. 5.

122 Act no. 19.949 Art. 11 N° 2, Act no. 20.595 Art. 18 c).

123 D. Giambruno, *Anti-Poverty Social Policies in Chile and Concerns for Social Justice in Neo-Liberal Times: A View from Below* (University College London 2020), pp. 148-149.

124 Act no. 20.379 Art. 1.

125 Act no. 20.379 Art. 13.

that such minimum levels make to the realisation of all other fundamental rights.

The fact that conditionality is a regulatory technique applied only to the most vulnerable population may be questionable from the perspective of the right to equality and non-discrimination. Through this technique, the state provides resources to beneficiary households in order for them 'to do something they did not do before, from taking children to health check-ups to enrolling them in school, thus breaking the cycle of poverty and giving children more opportunities to overcome their vulnerability in the future'.[126] While this may be a legitimate objective, there is a risk of succumbing to the irresistible temptation to 'improve' the recipients of the systems by 'imposing virtuous behaviour' on them, rather than simply offering them social assistance.[127] In the Chilean case, this risk could be illustrated by the regulation of the effort transfer, which is granted to those belonging to the 30% of the most socio-economically disadvantaged segments of the population who achieve outstanding achievements or improvements in the areas of education, health, employment, savings and monthly compliance with intensive or residential drug rehabilitation programmes.[128]

It is also worth noting that some forms of conditionality may end up reinforcing traditional gender roles, for example by targeting social assistance benefits at women, mainly in their role as mothers.[129] Take, for instance, some of the duties and benefits transfers of the *Seguridades y Oportunidades* subsystem: the healthy child monitoring transfer, the school attendance transfer and the female employment transfer. Given that the majority of social assistance recipients in Chile are single mothers, and that the system does not provide mechanisms for reconciling wage or salaried work with caring responsibilities, the simultaneous fulfilment of these conditions could prove too burdensome, if not impossible. As a result, the potential beneficiaries of these transfers access them at the cost of a double workload or do not access them at all, thus defeating the very purpose of the former.

126 C. Huneeus and A. Repetto, 'Los desafíos pendientes del Ingreso Ético Familiar', in: M. Fantuzzi (ed.), *Ingreso ético familiar: Innovando en la lucha contra la pobreza* (Ediciones LyD 2013), p. 219.

127 C.A. Reich 'Individual Rights and Social Welfare: The Emerging Legal Issues' The Yale Law Journal 74 (1965)7, pp. 1245-1257, 1246.

128 Act no. 20.595 Art. 20 para. 1.

129 N. Jones and R. Holmes, 'Why is Social Protection Gender-Blind? The Politics of Gender and Social Protection' IDS Bulletin 42 (2011)6, pp. 45-52, 46.

IV. Concluding Remarks

Although the declared purpose of the various components of the social policy system is to adopt a rights-based approach, neither the Constitution nor the case law of the Constitutional Court provides any further parameters for determining exactly what requirements such an approach entails. Nor does the constitutional text in any way indicate that the state has a constitutional duty to ensure a certain level of subsistence and that there is a corresponding individual subjective right to demand it. This gap could be partially filled by international human rights law standards, and in particular the Inter-American system's standards, which could provide some grounds for building the state's obligation to ensure a dignified life.

In practice, the definition of a dignified life encompasses a wide range of transfers and services aimed at enhancing social citizenship of vulnerable segments of the population. Access to education, work, housing, health services and a minimum subsistence level, among others, are at the core of this aim. Nevertheless, structural causes of inequality, such as lack of affordable quality education or healthcare, lack of housing and social mobility, poorly paid jobs, among others, receive scant attention. Thus, while the system has been effective in targeting scarce resources and improving economic growth rates, the high levels of poverty and inequality in the country remain an unresolved challenge.

By and large, the system continues to reinforce an ideal of deservingness that tends to undercut the recognition of the poor as genuine right holders. Traces of this ideal can be found not only in conditional cash transfers, but also in unconditional transfers, as illustrated by the fact that the dignity transfers in the *Seguridades y Oportunidades* system only covers 85% of the gap between household income and the value of the extreme poverty line. Underlying the design of both transfers is an understanding of poverty that emphasises individual responsibility and effort.

On the other hand, it is not entirely clear what level of recognition of individual autonomy a dignified life requires. For example, while in most cases the system allows recipients of cash transfers to freely determine the purposes for which their funds are spent, in other cases access to a life in dignity and to minimum subsistence depends on a series of activation policies and behavioural conditionality. These policies can either have a punitive character and undermine citizenship, insofar as they rely on sanctions and surveillance techniques, or have a supportive character and enhance citizenship, insofar as they aim to educate and help achieve self-sufficiency.

Highlighting this difference is crucial, as over-reliance on the use of punitive policies could render the system unable to provide a floor below which no one should fall. Therefore, sanctions such as permanent expulsion from a subsystem or the loss of and duty to repay received benefits must be carefully assessed.

In conclusion, while Chile's social protection has managed to expand its coverage and benefits over the years, there is still considerable room for improvement. The constant reforms and adjustments to the system, without prior thorough evaluation of what already exists, have led to its inorganic and disjointed growth, complexity and, ultimately, to greater difficulty regarding access to it. On the other hand, although efforts have been made to refine the instruments for assessing socio-economic vulnerability, other factors that should be relevant for access to social protection, such as territorial and cultural context, do not receive any attention. Despite these areas for improvement, the results of the Chilean social protection system in terms of decreasing poverty rates over the years have helped to shield this issue to some extent from public scrutiny.[130] Consequently, the political and academic debate centres predominantly on increasing old-age pensions, either by raising individual contributions[131] or, at most, by increasing the Universal Guaranteed Pension.[132] By contrast, a profound reflection on the minimum conditions necessary to allow the most vulnerable to build a life in dignity in Chile is still pending.

---

130 This phenomenon may be due to the fact that non-contributory social protection in Chile is often seen only as an 'initial nudge' to overcome poverty, which must then be replaced by social security contributions and tax payments. Giambruno (n 123), pp. 186 and 262; N. Martínez, 'Pobreza en Chile: conceptualización, discurso y política' (DPhil thesis, Universidad de Salamanca 2016), p. 377.

131 S. Hormazábal, *9 propuestas para un nuevo sistema previsional* (Horizontal 2022), pp. 15-18; G. Ugarte and R. Vergara, *PGU y tasas de reemplazo* (CEP 2022), p. 19.

132 This is the position officially taken by the government and the National Congress.

A Life in Dignity for Vulnerable Populations in Mexico

Gabriela Mendizábal Bermúdez

I. Introduction

The scope of the state obligation to guarantee minimum subsistence protection is currently discussed in Mexico with regard to the action of each of the three branches of government (legislative, executive, and judicial), as it is clearly reflected in case law. First, minimum income benefits are established and provided for by the legislative branch, which guarantees them through legal reforms to the Political Constitution of the United Mexican States (CPEUM), labour laws, social security laws and tax laws. Second, the federal executive establishes a large number of social assistance programmes through executive orders, which are then emulated by state governments to provide income to different vulnerable social groups of the Mexican population and are sometimes elevated to the rank of law. Finally, the judiciary expands the scope of existing provisions through its interpretation of them, providing a comprehensive approach in granting social security benefits and social programmes aimed at guaranteeing the right to the minimum conditions for life and thereby ensuring a life in dignity.

The country's social policy objectives regarding minimum income are reflected in the slogan "The Poor First"[1], which has imbued government actions aimed at implementing legislative changes, assistance programmes and political campaigns, while permeating judicial rulings. The allocated budget for all social programmes in the category "wellbeing" (welfare) in 2024 was MXN$ 543.93 billion[2] (US$ 32,113,746,258.346),[3] a 25.2% increase from the previous tax year, in which it was MXN$ 414.63 billion (US$ 24,479,846,732.4).[4] A large part of these resources will be earmarked for the programmes analysed in Section II.2. of this chapter. However, all these measures are primarily targeted at people living in conditions of poverty and belonging to a vulnerable group, and are not designed for the general population.

In this context, data on the socioeconomic context of poverty in the country becomes critically important. The National Institute of Statistics and Geography (INEGI) and the latest measurement report from the National Council for the Evaluation of Social Development Policy (CONEVAL) from 2023 show that 46.83 million out of 129 million Mexicans[5] were living in income poverty (36.3% of the total population), and 9.16 million of these were living in extreme poverty. [6]

---

1 This slogan has been incorporated into the National Development Plan 2019-2024 of the current administration.

2 Cámara de Diputados, 'Ramo 20 Bienestar' (2024) < https://www.cefp.gob.mx/publicaciones/nota/2024/notacefp0232024.pdf> accessed 2 June 2024.

3 The exchange rate used for this chapter is MXN$ 16.9377 (Mexican pesos) = US$ 1 (American dollar), data from the Bank of Mexico from 1 June 2024, < https://www.banxico.org.mx/tipcamb/tipCamIHAction.do?idioma=sp&fechaInicial=dd/mm/aaaa&fechaFinal=dd/mm/aaaa&salida=HTML > accessed 20.6.2024.

4 Cámara de Diputados, 'Ramo 20 Bienestar' (n 2).

5 INEGI, 'Estadísticas a propósito del día mundial de la población. Datos Nacionales' (2023) <https://www.inegi.org.mx/contenidos/saladeprensa/aproposito/2023/EAP_DMPO23.pdf.> accessed 20.6.2024.

6 CONEVAL is a decentralized public entity of the Federal Public Administration, with autonomy and technical expertise to generate objective information about the state of social policy and poverty measurement in Mexico; CONEVAL, '¿Quiénes somos?'

To examine the state's obligation to guarantee a life in dignity and the connections between minimum income schemes and other social protection systems in Mexico, this chapter is divided into 4 sections. After this short introduction, it will delineate the constitutional framework on dignity, poverty and its relationship with minimum income, social security, social assistance, in particular the scope of the state's obligation to guarantee a minimum of subsistence to poor people, whether it be workers or people in vulnerable conditions. The third section analyses the state's obligation in social protection schemes for vulnerable individuals and covers the following three aspects: enforceability and accessibility of the benefits, levels of protection, and conflicting arguments between protection for vulnerable groups and the universalism of benefits to ensure a life in dignity as well as the outcome of the social programmes on poverty. Finally, some conclusions are drawn on the consequences of the lack of a universal programme regarding the guarantee of a life in dignity for the Mexican population.

II. Overview

1. Normative Background

a) Dignity in the CPEUM

The Mexican Constitution (CPEUM) embraces the idea that dignity is an essential quality of human beings, a universal attribute common to all. Because it is intrinsic to human beings, dignity is not something that can be granted by a legal system, i.e., it exists and is enforceable for all individuals, regardless of whether it appears in a rule.[7] In this sense, "dignity" appears in several articles of the CPEUM, including Article 1, which prohibits discrimination of any kind that threatens human dignity; Article 3, which states that education must be provided with full respect for the dignity of persons; Article 4, which stipulates that all families have the right to decent housing; and Article 25, which establishes that dignity should be a guiding principle of national development.

(2022) <https://www.coneval.org.mx/quienessomos/Paginas/Quienes-Somos.aspx > accessed 20.6.2024.

7 G. Mendizábal-Bermúdez and M.J. López, 'Análisis de la dignidad del trabajador en el contexto de la globalización. El ejemplo de México' Revista Chilena de Derecho del Trabajo y de la Seguridad Social 3 (2012) 6, pp. 165-194.

In line with constitutional provisions, the Supreme Court of Justice of the Nation (SCJN) has established case law that analyses and recognises dignity from various perspectives. First, dignity must be considered as a legal principle and right. Dignity should not be confused with a moral precept because it is considered a guiding principle that shall permeate all national laws. It is also a fundamental right and as such has the rank of a legal principle that imposes a constitutional mandate on all entities in the country – authorities, institutions and individuals – obliging them to respect and protect all individuals as persons, and thereby prohibiting that they be humiliated, degraded, debased or objectified in any context.[8] In this sense, dignity is also to be considered as a limit to rights. Dignity restricts the exercise and enjoyment of rights so as not to infringe on the dignity of another person, recalling the Kantian maxim that human beings must always be treated as an end, never merely as a means. The Court also considered dignity as an objective guarantee, and establishes the link between basic needs and dignity since a person can only live in dignity when their basic needs are met. Only then can they develop their potential as human beings.[9]

b) Relevant Constitutional Provisions

The Mexican Constitution does not explicitly mention a universal minimum income, nor does it provide for the obligation to guarantee income protection mechanisms. While it does call on the state to ensure human rights for all people and provide dignified living conditions and specific rights to vulnerable groups, the lack of a constitutional inclusion of a universal minimum income as a subjective right means that these rights are often unattainable for many, as seen in the high rates of poverty and social deprivations mentioned above.

However, Article 1 of the CPEUM establishes that "all authorities, within the scope of their competencies, have the obligation to promote, respect, protect, and guarantee human rights in accordance with the principles of universality, interdependence, indivisibility, and progressivity". A life in dignity is inextricably linked to human rights. Moreover, in 2020, the CPEUM established the state's responsibility to provide a minimum in-

8 Tesis, Jurisprudencia, 1a./J. 37/2016 (10a.).
9 Tesis aislada 1a. XCVII/2007 (9a.).

come through: a non-contributory pension for older adults; scholarships for students at all levels coming from poor families; and financial support for persons with disabilities. After this reform, the following social human rights are now explicitly recognised in the Mexican Constitution: Article 4 acknowledges the right to the minimum conditions for life by declaring the state's responsibility to ensure access to nourishing, sufficient, and quality food; comprehensive and free health services; sufficient and safe water and sanitation services; dignified housing; the means to access, spread, and develop culture; as well as the guarantee of a minimum income for vulnerable groups (financial support to persons with permanent disabilities, with priority given to indigenous peoples, Afro-Mexicans, people living in poverty; non-contributory pensions for individuals over the age of 68; scholarships for students at all levels of the public education system). It should be noted that Article 4, while not defining a national minimum income, has been established as the grounds for the judicial rulings on the right to the minimum conditions for life on the one hand, and as the basis for the minimum income of certain social groups, on the other.

Article 3 provides for the right to education, Article 5 enshrines the right to work, and Article 123 covers labour rights, including minimum wages and the right to social security for workers.

Likewise, Article 2, Section B, clause VII, of the CPEUM focuses on the state's obligation to protect the income of indigenous peoples and communities by establishing the necessary institutions and policies to guarantee their rights, support their productive activities to achieve economic self-sufficiency, create new jobs, and increase their productive capacity, among other things.

Following the constitutional precepts, the legislature has regulated these rights in different pieces of legislation, such as the General Health Law, General Education Law, Federal Labor Law, Social Security Law, and General Social Development Law.

c) Concurrent Competences of the States

Article 124 of the CPEUM establishes the residual powers of the states by providing that all matters not expressly reserved to the federal government may be the subject of legislation by the federated entities and concurrent policies may also exist. There is a General Law on Social Development, applicable to both the federal and federated entities, which sets out in more detail how these concurrent competencies are distributed and coordinated across the three levels of government. Article 9 of the General Law of Social Development specifies that the municipalities, the governments of the federated entities and the federal executive branch, in their respective spheres, will formulate and apply assistance policies for the benefit of individuals, families, social groups and, where appropriate, indigenous and Afro-Mexican peoples and communities in vulnerable situations, allocating the necessary budgetary resources and establishing quantifiable goals.

An example of particularly forward-thinking policy is the recently drafted Political Constitution of Mexico City. It establishes a general system of social well-being, which includes mechanisms to ensure the right to a minimum subsistence income for a life in dignity, prioritising persons living in poverty. Within the competence of the state, the legislation on the issue shall define the criteria and procedures for public social programmes and cash transfers, while guaranteeing their efficient and transparent use.[10]

However, in designing their welfare policies, federated entities must conform to the national policy of the General Law on Social Development. Moreover, the scope and scale of the states' schemes are not comparable with those of the federal programmes, because the economic resources are allocated and exercised on the part of the federation. Therefore, this contribution focuses on federally provided schemes of assistance.

d) Case Law and Consequences of the Limited Existence of Subjective Rights

The judicial branch is made up of various jurisdictional bodies, with the SCJN as the highest court in Mexico. Given that there is no explicit concept of minimum income in the CPEUM, the extent of the state obligation to guarantee basic living conditions is unclear, thus opening up the possibility for the judicial branch to interpret the existing constitutional legal provisions. As mentioned above, only few social benefits in Mexico are enshrined in constitutional subjective rights and have established regulatory provisions. These include, on the one hand, the workers' right to a minimum wage and to social insurance and, on the other hand, a guaranteed minimum income for vulnerable groups, such as people with permanent

10 Constitución Política de la Ciudad de México, Section 3A (Regarding Social Policy), Article 17 (Social Welfare and Distributive Economy).

disabilities, indigenous peoples, Afro-Mexicans, people living in poverty, people over 68 years of age with non-contributory pensions, as well as scholarships for students in the public education system.

The actual implementation of these subjective rights exhibits important shortcomings, and this is even more pronounced for people who cannot be identified as belonging to a vulnerable group and often require judicial intervention to safeguard their rights.

In this framework, some SCJN judgments have set certain precedents framing minimum income as an individual right. In particular, the Court has elaborated the concept of a "vital minimum" (mínimo vital). First, it has established that the minimum conditions for life consist of the skills, basic conditions, and social benefits a person needs to be able to live unfettered by fear and the burdens of poverty, in such a way that the scope of the right to the minimum conditions for life extends to all the positive or negative measures needed to prevent a person from being unconstitutionally reduced in terms of their intrinsic value as a human being for not having the material conditions that allow them to lead a dignified existence.[11] In other words, certain minimum conditions for life are considered necessary for human dignity.

Second, the right to the minimum conditions for life has been derived from a systematic interpretation of the fundamental rights enshrined in the General Constitution, among which are Articles 1 (dignity), 3 (education), 4 (social human rights), 27 (private property) and 123 (right to decent work and minimum wage).[12] In other court precedents, the SCJN has mentioned that the right to the vital minimum entails the state's obligation to ensure access to minimum living conditions, including food, housing, health, education and a healthy environment.[13] Third, in cases related to the vital minimum the judiciary has reminded the legislature of their obligation for Mexican constitutional law to be consistent with the Universal Declaration of Human Rights and the International Covenant on Economic, Social, and Cultural Rights to ensure the right to a dignified standard of life.[14]

11 Tesis I.9o.A.1 CS (10a.) (2016) and Tesis 1a. XCVII/2007 (9a.).
12 Tesis 1a. XCVII/2007 (9a.).
13 Tesis 2a./J. 27/2017 (10a.) and Tesis III.2o.T.62 L (11a.) (2024).
14 Tesis I.9o.A.1 CS (10a) (2016).

However, the implications and consequences of the doctrine of a vital minimum have not been properly elucidated.[15] Moreover, it should be mentioned that these SCJN judgments are binding, but they only benefit the citizen who files an *amparo* and not the entire population.

It is important to observe that case-law criteria continue to evolve. For example, in 2018, it was debated whether increases to pensions should be proportional to increases to the minimum wage, on the grounds that both are intrinsically linked to the right to a vital minimum. Although the SCJN initially dismissed this appeal,[16] in April 2024, the relationship between increases to the minimum wage and to pensions was subsequently upheld, marking progress towards the direct enforceability of these rights.[17]

These developments underscore the continued importance of case law and court interpretation in strengthening the effective protection of constitutional rights related to well-being and a dignified life for people in Mexico.

e) Importance of the Minimum Wage

The one aspect of the vital minimum that is clearly regulated by the legislature and elaborated by the case law is related to the minimum wage. This, according to Mexican law, is the lowest amount a worker may receive in cash for services rendered in a workday.[18]

The minimum wage is of paramount importance in Mexico. It helps bridge the gaps of inequality that emerge in societies by creating conditions to prevent or eradicate poverty across various aspects of life in a society. The right to a minimum wage is enshrined in Article 123 of the Mexican Constitution. According to this provision, the general minimum wage must be sufficient to guarantee the material, social and cultural needs of a family and to cover the compulsory education of the children.

15 E. Ferrer Mac-Gregor and R.S. Gil, 'Foreign Precedents in Mexican Constitutional Adjudication' Mexican Law Review 4 (2012) 2, pp. 293-307.

16 SCJN, amparo directo en revisión 2373/2018, available at: <https://www.scjn.gob.mx/sites/default/files/listas/documento_dos/2022-09/42.pdf.> accessed 20.6.2024.

17 Tesis, la I.2o.T.15 L (11a.) 8 (2024).

18 Article 90 Federal Labor Law.

2. Social Benefits

The protection of a life in dignity in Mexico is still linked to poverty and vulnerability, or to the status of a worker. In other words, some measures protect persons living in poverty and belonging to a vulnerable group (indigenous, Afro-Mexican, older adults or youth); other benefits protect low-income workers in a way that prevents them from receiving less than the minimum wage in addition to ensuring their access to social insurance coverage.

It is clear that the benefits directed at ensuring a life in dignity are not really interconnected. Some benefits only apply to workers in the formal sector while others like social programmes and tax exemptions are aimed at the poorest or the most vulnerable. The only exceptions are contributory and non-contributory old-age pensions, which are cumulative, in the sense that will be explained below.[19]

The structure for organising and delivering social benefits in Mexico consists of public social insurance and government agencies providing social assistance at both federal and state levels. The following description will concentrate on the federal level. The different benefits available, how they work and their relevance for protecting workers, as well as programmes and measures to alleviate poverty for the most vulnerable and the few existing tax measures are described below.

a) Protection for Workers

aa) Minimum Wage and Social Security

The concept of a life in dignity in terms of a minimum subsistence for workers is based on the legal construct of the state's obligation as established in Article 123, which provides both the right to a minimum wage and the guarantee of social security for workers.

The minimum wage, as mentioned before, is of paramount importance in the constitutional construction of the minimum conditions of life and is supposed to guarantee a life in dignity to Mexican families.

As of the second quarter of 2023, more than 20 million workers among the economically active population in Mexico (approximately 34.80%) were

19 See below, Section II.2.b) ee).

paid the equivalent of only one minimum wage for their work.[20] The CONASAMI, the National Minimum Wage Commission, sets the minimum amount to be received per workday (8 hours of work), categorised into professional minimum wages assigned to the different occupations, such as bricklayer, carpenter or nurse. There are 61 categories, and the corresponding wages range from MXN$ 250.00 (US$ 12.28) per day to MXN$ 557.00 (US$ 27.4) per day in 2024.

General minimum wages are also sorted into geographical areas. The Northern Border Free Zone, which corresponds to the states of Baja California, Sonora, Chihuahua, Coahuila, Nuevo León, and Tamaulipas, offers a minimum wage of MXN$ 374.89 per day (US$ 22.13) which means a monthly income of MXN$ 11.246.7 (US$ 664) in 2024. Meanwhile, in the rest of the country, the minimum wage for the same year is MXN$ 248.93 per day (US$ 14.7), which means a monthly income of MXN$ 7,468.00 (US$ 440.9).[21]

The relevance of the minimum wage appears, however, limited if one compares the monthly minimum wage with the monthly cost of the basic food basket per person of MXN$ 2,304.27 (US$ 136) in urban areas and MXN$ 1,767.03 (US$ 104.32) in rural areas[22]. If we take into account that the average Mexican family is made up of 3.6 members, with 2.1 and 3.2 children in urban and rural areas, respectively, it follows that the minimum wage is not enough to cover even the minimal basic food needs of three people in urban areas, and that it much less covers other needs such as culture, education, and so on.

As for the national and state social security institutions, these are organised into 3 national social insurance programmes that provide comprehensive coverage (occupational hazard insurance; sickness and maternity insurance; severance at old age, old age, retirement, disability, and life insurances; childcare, and social benefits), one national insurance programme that awards housing benefits, and 26 state social insurance programmes, some offering comprehensive coverage and others only covering old age.

---

20 INEGI, 'Ocupación 2022' (2022) available at: <https://www.inegi.org.mx/app/tabulados/default.html?nc=602 > accessed 20.6.2024.

21 CONASAMI, 'Incremento a los Salarios Mínimos para 2024' (2024), available at: <https://www.gob.mx/conasami/articulos/incremento-a-los-salarios-minimos-para-2024?idiom=es> accessed 20.6.2024.

22 Cf. CONEVAL, 'Valor de la canasta alimentaria' (2022), available at: <http://blog coneval.gob.mx/wordpress/index.php/category/canasta-alimentaria/> accessed 20.6.2024.

Unfortunately, they are not linked to each other in such a way for them to work together as a comprehensive system. Social insurance programmes are still employment-based (depending on the type of work relationship and the labour regulations for workers) with the exception of social groups that receive medical care without being workers, such as students or people enrolled in the IMSS voluntary family health insurance.

In 2022, 64.7 million people (50.2% of the population) did not have access to social security.[23] This is largely due to the high rates of informal economy jobs in the country. In August 2023, the number of people working in the informal economy stood at 32.7 million.[24]

bb) Old-Age Contributory Pension

Within the social insurance programmes, special mention must be made of cash transfers for the elderly. These benefits are especially relevant to the guarantee of a life in dignity for the Mexican population, as the poverty rate for this age group is very high (31.1%) and Mexico is an aging country: in 1990, the population aged 60 and older represented 6.4% of the total population, a percentage that rose to 9.9% in 2010 and will reach 21.5% in 2050.[25]

For the contributory pension, the 2021 reform to the Social Security Law reduced the required number of contribution weeks from 1,250 to 750 (with 25-week increments each year to reach 1,000 weeks of contributions by 2031) and increased employer contributions from 5.15% to a maximum of 13.87% of the worker's salary. This has enabled 38,000 workers[26] who would otherwise not have been able to meet the requirements to obtain an old-age or severance at old age pension in 2021 and 2022. This same reform

23 Secretaría de Bienestar, '5 Informe de labores' (2023) p. 93, available at: <https://www.gob.mx/cms/uploads/attachment/file/853167/BIENESTAR-5to-Informe-de-Labores.pdf> accessed 20.6.2024.

24 INEGI, 'Comunicado de prensa número 568/23' (2023) p. 9, available at: <https://www.inegi.org.mx/contenidos/saladeprensa/boletines/2023/enoen/enoen2023_09.pdf> accessed 20.6.2024.

25 K.D. González, 'Envejecimiento demográfico en México: análisis comparativo entre las entidades federativas' (2015) p. 115, available at: <http://www.conapo.gob.mx/work/models/CONAPO/Resource/2702/06_envejecimiento.pdf> accessed 20.6.2024.

26 IMSS, 'Reforma a la Ley del Seguro Social de 2020 ha recuperado la esencia del sistema pensionario' (2022), available at: <https://www.imss.gob.mx/prensa/archivo/202207/367> accessed 20.6.2024.

also modified the requirements needed to obtain a guaranteed pension, as well as the amounts to be granted.

It should first be noted that the law defines a guaranteed pension as one granted by the state to persons who meet the age requirement (above 60) and a minimum of at least 825 weeks of contributions,[27] but whose individual account funds are insufficient to secure a pension paid by an insurance company (so-called lifelong annuity) or a Retirement Funds Administrator (so-called programmed withdrawal)[28].

This guaranteed pension provides a minimum amount variable by law[29] to be paid based on the individual's age, weeks of contribution, and salary range. If a worker meets the requirements, the amount of the guaranteed pension ranges from a minimum of MXN$ 2,622.00 per month (US$ 154.8) to a maximum of MXN$ 8,241.00 per month (US$ 486.58). In other words, a distinction is made based on the number of contributions, age, and salary.

This reform is designed to allow workers with insufficient resources to secure their severance at old age or an old-age pension so they can enjoy a decent income through a guaranteed pension, seeing that in the past, this pension was only equal to the general minimum wage.

Lastly, it should be noted that Mexican social security provides family allowances to pensioners based on their family ties and the amount of the pension: an additional 15% of the amount of their pension for a spouse, 10% for each child under 16 years of age, 10% for children between 16 and 25 years of age who are students without an insurance of their own, 10% for children unable to work, and 10% for each ascendent, if there is no descendant or spouse. In the absence of these beneficiaries, an additional 15% is granted as welfare assistance. These economic allowances are part of the social security benefits to financially help pensioners and their families as per their needs and circumstances.[30]

27 Article 170 of the Social Security Law.

28 Gobierno de México, 'Pensión por Régimen 97' (2021), available at: <https://www.gob.mx/consar/articulos/por-regimen-de-97#:~:text=La%20Pensi%C3%B3n%20Garantizada%20es%20aquella,Vitalicia%20o%20un%20Retiro%20Programado> accessed 20.6.2024.

29 Article 170 of the Social Security Law.

30 Cf. Article 138 of the Social Security Law.

b) Programmes and Measures to Alleviate Poverty

Social policy in Mexico has been implemented through actions to create better living conditions for the country's most vulnerable groups. Although the design of social assistance schemes for vulnerable populations changes with each change of government, their objective remains that of eradicating conditions of socioeconomic inequality and reducing poverty levels to create conditions to access a life in dignity at various stages of a person's life.

The current National Development Plan (NDP) 2019-2024 establishes the general focus on "well-being"; which aims to "guarantee the effective exercise of economic, social, cultural, and environmental rights", with a special focus on bridging gaps of inequality and conditions of vulnerability.[31]

Several social transfers have been established at the federal level in order to fulfil the aim presented in the NDP as well as the constitutional obligations enshrined in 2020 in Article 4. The available programmes can be classified by the age group of the targeted beneficiaries and families, which are always associated with poverty as a contributing factor to vulnerability: children, youth, the elderly, and persons with disabilities.

aa) Benito Juárez Scholarship Programme for Basic Education

This scholarship is part of a much more extensive programme called the Family Well-Being Programme, which replaced the internationally acclaimed "*Prospera*" programme. It is currently a conditional educational cash transfer programme for children and adolescents under 14 years of age,[32] administrated by the Ministry of Welfare. Its main objective is to guarantee the children's right to education by providing families with children or adolescents in their basic education (approximately between 6 to 15 years old) with a scholarship of MXN$ 920.00 (US$ 54.31) a month per family in 2024. Although it is not stipulated whether it is only for families

---

31 Gobierno de México, 'Anexo XVIII-Bis del Plan Nacional de Desarrollo 2019-2024' (2019) p. 83, available at: <https://gaceta.diputados.gob.mx/PDF/64/2019/abr/20190430-XVIII-1.pdf > accessed 20.6.2024.

32 SEP, 'Reglas de Operación del Programa de Becas de Educación Básica para el Bienestar Benito Juárez para el ejercicio fiscal 2023' (2022), available at: <https://www.dof.gob.mx/nota_detalle.php?codigo=5676024&fecha=29/12/2022#gsc.tab=0 > accessed 20.6.2024.

living in poverty, the decree establishing the scholarship does mention its objective to strengthen inclusive and equitable education, aimed at people living in poverty or vulnerable conditions.[33] Moreover, the requirements to obtain the scholarship do establish two conditions of vulnerability. First, schools are prioritised based on their location in indigenous communities, in areas of high marginalisation, or with fewer than 50 inhabitants with no degree of marginalisation. Second, it accords priority also to children who are not enrolled in schools considered priorities but who are nonetheless considered 'victims' in the sense of the decree.[34]

It should be noted that the funds allocated to this programme are distributed in this order, based on the marginalisation index calculated by the National Population Council (CONAPO),[35] and are subject to the availability of resources.

Another noteworthy feature is that it does not formally establish a residency requirement. However, it does require submitting a birth certificate or equivalent document; certificates and/or report cards that attest to studies completed abroad, a document that accredits their school record, and the corresponding registration payments,[36] which makes this benefit also accessible to foreigners, as long as they are legally residing in the country.

As of August 2023, this programme has only extended to 3,336,323[37] beneficiaries out of the 33,145,240 students in basic education nationwide in the 2022-2023[38] school year. This means that approximately 10% of students

---

33 DOF: 31/05/2019, DECRETO por el que se crea la Coordinación Nacional de Becas para el Bienestar Benito Juárez.

34 A person who has directly or indirectly suffered harm or the impairment of their rights as a result of a human rights violation or the commission of a crime. In addition, a victim or person with the status of victim shall be understood to be a migrant, refugee and/or displaced person.

35 Cf. CONAPO, 'Índices de marginación 2020' (2021) available at: <https://www.gob.mx/conapo/documentos/indices-de-marginacion-2020-284372> accessed 20.6.2024.

36 Cf. Gobierno del México, 'Revalidación de estudios de Primaria y/o Secundaria' available at: <https://www2.aefcm.gob.mx/mstr/revalidacion/mas_informacion.jsp> accessed 20.6.2024.

37 Gobierno de México, 'Programas para el Desarrollo. Becas para el Bienestar Benito Juárez Educación Básica' (2023), available at: <https://pub.bienestar.gob.mx/pub/programasIntegrales> accessed 20.6.2024.

38 INEGI, 'Matrícula escolar por entidad federativa según nivel educativo, ciclos escolares seleccionados de 2000/2001 a 2022/2023' (2023), available at: <https://www.inegi.org.mx/app/tabulados/interactivos/?pxq=ac13059d-e874-4962-93bb-74f2c58a3cb9> accessed 20.6.2024.

in basic education receive this scholarship and that it can therefore not be classified as a universal programme.

bb) Assistance Programme for the Well-Being of Children of Working Mothers

This programme aims to contribute to improving access to care and education to enable children, adolescents, and young people up to the age of 23 living in vulnerable situations due to the absence of one or both parents, to fully exercise their social rights by providing them with financial support, which can be used for their care and to further their education.[39] As a precondition, the parent or guardian must be working, studying or looking for a job.

This programme is subject to the availability of resources, and priority is given to people living in indigenous municipalities or in populations with more than 40% Afro-Mexicans, areas of high deprivation, or marginalised zones.

The financial amounts provided vary depending on the conditions for which the support is granted. Minors without any type of disability receive the amount of MXN$ 1,600 (US$ 94.46) per child every two months with a maximum of three simultaneous allowances per family unless it involves multiple births.

In the case of minors with qualifying disabilities in this programme, MXN$ 3,600 (US$ 212.54) are provided every two months until the day before the child turns 6 years old. Finally, support for orphaned minors is granted according to the beneficiary's age range, going from MXN$ 800 (US$ 47.23) to MXN$ 1,200 (US$ 70.84) every two months.

As of August 2023, this programme had 200,947 beneficiaries under the category of children of working mothers and 41,428[40] under the category of maternal orphans. The programme is expected to continue throughout 2024.[41]

---

39 Gobierno de México, 'Programa para el Bienestar de las Niñas y Niños, Hijos de Madres Trabajadoras' (2022), available at: <https://www.gob.mx/bienestar/acciones-y-programas/programa-para-el-bienestar-de-las-ninas-y-ninos-hijos-de-madres-trabajadoras> accessed 20.6.2024.

40 Ibid.

41 Cf. López-Castro Fernanda, INFOBAE, 'AMLO afirma que presupuesto del 2024 incluirá aumento en apoyos del Bienestar; analiza ampliar becas para estudiantes'

cc) Youth Building the Future

Implemented in 2019 under the Ministry of Labor and Social Welfare, this programme aims to give young people between 18 and 29 years of age, who are not studying or employed at the time of applying for or while enrolled in the programme, the opportunity to acquire job training. The young beneficiaries receive professional training, financial assistance in the form of a monthly scholarship, which in 2024 was MXN$ 7,572 (US$ 447.05), and access to medical services provided by the IMSS by means of benefits granted for illness, maternity, and work-related accidents,[42] for a maximum of 12 months. [43]

Data from August 2023 shows that 246,808[44] young people have benefited from this programme. The only official data, presented in President Andrés Manuel López Obrador's fourth government report (2022),[45] indicates that 46% of apprentices have either been employed or take part in productive activities. However, this information has not been updated in the most recent report.

dd) Youth Writing the Future

This Ministry of Public Education programme provides scholarships to students from priority public higher education institutions. Targeted at students under the age of 29 from low-income families, it aims to help them stay in school and graduate. For 2024, this scholarship awards MXN$

(2023), available at: <https://www.infobae.com/mexico/2023/09/05/amlo-afirma-que-presupuesto-del-2024-incluira-aumento-en-apoyos-del-bienestar-analiza-ampliar-becas-para-estudiantes/> accessed 20.6.2024.

42 IMSS, 'Acuerdo acdo.as2.hct.270219/93.p.dir, DOF: 29/03/2019' (2019), available at: <https://dof.gob.mx/nota_detalle.php?codigo=5555926&fecha=29/03/2019&print=true> accessed 20.6.2024.

43 STPS, 'Reglas de Operación del Programa Jóvenes Construyendo el Futuro' (2024), available at: <https://www.gob.mx/cms/uploads/attachment/file/878411/Reglas_de_Operacio_n_del_Programa_Jo_venes_Escribiendo_el_Futuro_para_el_ejercicio_fiscal_2024.pdf> accessed 20.6.2024.

44 Gobierno de México, 'Programas para el Desarrollo' Jóvenes Construyendo el Futuro, (2023), available at: <https://pub.bienestar.gob.mx/pub/programasIntegrales> accessed 20.6.2024.

45 A.M. López Obrador, Cuarto informe de gobierno' (2022) available at: <https://www.gob.mx/cuartoinforme> accessed 20.6.2024.

2,800.00 per month (US$ 165.31), payable for 10 months of the fiscal year, which means that students can receive up to 45 monthly payments throughout the duration of their university studies.[46] As of August 2023, a total of MXN$ 403,145[47] have been granted.

ee) Well-Being Pension Programme for Older Adults

In 2020, the Mexican Constitution established a new non-contributory pension for older adults.[48] This pension is granted through the Well-Being Pension Programme for Older Adults intended for persons aged 68 (or aged 65 for indigenous peoples and Afro-Mexicans) and older of Mexican nationality and residing in Mexican territory.[49] This programme is aimed at guaranteeing the "well-being" of the recipients, whereby "well-being" is defined as having the minimum conditions for a dignified life.[50] In 2024, beneficiaries receive MXN$ 3,000.00 (US$ 177.11) per month, paid every two months.[51] This benefit is not means-tested, which implies that the contributory and non-contributory old-age pensions are cumulative: it can happen that former workers are entitled to the maximum amount for contributory pensions and still receive a non-contributory pension. In the event of the beneficiary's death, a one-time payment of the same amount is made to the beneficiary's caregiver.

46 SEGOB, 'Acuerdo número 25/12/23, 'Reglas de Operación 2024' (2023), available at: <https://dof.gob.mx/nota_detalle.php?codigo=5676229&fecha=30/12/2022#gsc.tab=> accessed 20.6.2024.

47 Gobierno de México, 'Programas para el Desarrollo' Jóvenes Escribiendo el Futuro, available at: <https://pub.bienestar.gob.mx/pub/programasIntegrales> accessed 20.6.2024.

48 CPEUM, Article 4.

49 ACUERDO por el que se emiten las Reglas de Operación del Programa Pensión para el Bienestar de las Personas Adultas Mayores, para el ejercicio fiscal 2024, DOF: 29/12/2023.

50 Ibid.

51 Secretaría del Bienestar, '2024 inicia con aumentos a Pensiones de Bienestar, anuncia Ariadna Montiel', (2024), available at: <https://www.gob.mx/bienestar/prensa/2024-inicia-con-aumentos-a-pensiones-de-bienestar-anuncia-ariadna-montiel?idiom=es> accessed 20.6.2024.

Up until August 2023, a total of 10,981,247[52] older adults have benefited from this programme, receiving a steady lifelong income every two months and with annual increments. This serves as an important supplement to a Mexican family's income since 14% of the total population is 60 years old or older,[53] and 31.1% of this sector live in poverty.[54]

ff) Pension Programme for the Well-Being of Persons with Permanent Disabilities

This social programme is aimed at contributing to the income of Mexican families caring for a child, youth, or adult with a permanent disability.[55] The programme is reserved for people of Mexican nationality and residing in Mexico. Beneficiaries, in order of prioritisation, are young people from zero to twenty-nine years of age; people from 30 to 65 years of age who live in indigenous or Afro-Mexican municipalities and localities or in municipalities or localities with a high or very high degree of marginalisation, and persons between 30 and 65 who reside in a state whose government has signed the Agreement for the Universalisation of the Pension for Persons with Permanent Disability.[56] It is not means-tested.

In the 2024 fiscal year, the programme provides MXN$ 3,100.00 (US$ 183.02) in financial support every two months. In the event of the beneficiary's death, the officially registered caregiver receives a one-time payment of MXN$ 1,550.00 (US$ 91.51) to help with funeral expenses. Additionally, the programme offers "well-being vouchers" for rehabilitation services in National Health System-accredited public or private healthcare centres. Each voucher corresponds to an individually tailored rehabilitation session

52 Gobierno de México, 'Programas para el Desarrollo' Pensión para el Bienestar de las Personas Adultas Mayores' (2023), available at: <https://pub.bienestar.gob.mx/pub/programasIntegrales> accessed 20.6.2024.

53 INEGI, 'Estadísticas a propósito del día internacional de las personas adultas mayores' (2022), available at: <https://www.inegi.org.mx/contenidos/saladeprensa/aproposito/2022/EAP_ADULMAY2022.pdf> accessed 20.6.2024.

54 CONEVAL, 'Medición de la pobreza' (2022), available at: <https://www.coneval.org.mx/Medicion/MP/Paginas/AE_pobreza_2022.aspx> accessed 20.6.2024.

55 Cf. SEGOB, 'Acuerdo por el que se emiten las Reglas de Operación del Programa Pensión para el Bienestar de las Personas con Discapacidad Permanente, para el ejercicio fiscal 2024', (2024), available at: <https://www.dof.gob.mx/nota_detalle.php?codigo=5713347&fecha=29/12/2023#gsc.tab=0> accessed 20.6.2024.

56 Ibid.

and can be redeemed for medical appointments, inclusive of educational therapy and rehabilitation for persons with disabilities up to 17 years of age. [57]

Since the launch of the programme in January 2019 to June 2023, assistance has been provided to 1,431,498 beneficiaries.[58] Between 2019 and 2024, the pension amount went from MXN$ 1,275 (US$ 75.27) to MXN$ 1,550 (US$ 91.51), an 21% increase.

gg) IMSS-BIENESTAR Programme

IMSS-BIENESTAR is a social welfare programme in Mexico that provides health services to those without social security. Created in 1973 with non-contributory benefits, it has evolved under different administrations, reforming and shaping federal, state and municipal guidelines. Formerly known as IMSS-COPLAMAR (1979), IMSS-Solidaridad (1989), IMSS-Oportunidades (2002), and IMSS-PROSPERA (2014), it acquired its current name in 2018. This programme adapts to political and social changes, while preserving its objective of improving access to health for those who lack social security in Mexico.

The April 2024 report stated that IMSS-BIENESTAR operates in 23 states with a network of 635 hospitals, 11,913 clinics and 131,000 workers attending to 53.2 million Mexicans, that is, 84.8% of those without social security,[59] with an operating budget of MXN$ 128,623,931,279 (US$ 7593943172.86) for this purpose.[60]

---

57 Ibid.

58 A.M. López Obrador, 'Quinto informe de gobierno, Presidencia de la República' (2023) p. 216, available at: <https://framework-gb.cdn.gob.mx/informe/760e7dab2836853c63805033e514668301fa9c47.pdf> accessed 20.6.2024.

59 IMSS, 'IMSS-Bienestar opera en 23 entidades para atender a 53.2 millones de mexicanos que no tienen seguridad social' (2024), available at: <https://www.imss.gob.mx/prensa/archivo/202404/170#:~:text=IMSS%2DBienestar%20es%20una%20instituci%C3%B3n,por%20ciento%20de%20quienes%20no> accessed 20.6.2024.

60 Proyecto de presupuesto de egresos de la federación 2024 septiembre de 2023, available at: <https://www.ppef.hacienda.gob.mx/work/models/7I83r4rR/PPEF2024/oiqewbt4/docs/47/r47_ayo_afpefe.pdf > accessed 20.6.2024.

c) Tax Exemptions

It must be pointed out that there are very few tax exemptions for lower income taxpayers. To that effect, Article 151 of the Income Tax Law[61] establishes the items that can be deducted in annual tax returns, including medical and dental fees, education expenses, housing expenses, and pensions. The exemption is only available for persons who do not, during the calendar year, receive income in an amount equal to or greater than that resulting from calculating the general minimum wage of the taxpayer's geographical area. Thus, this benefit is targeted at taxpayers in the lowest income levels, and is considered to profit only individuals in a condition of poverty.

III. Analysis

1. Enforceability and Accessibility of the Benefits

From the perspective of the enforceability of rights, it is hard to hold the state truly responsible for providing social benefits. Although the above-mentioned social protection programmes are based on the human rights enshrined in the Constitution, such as the right to education or to food, beneficiaries in practice do not have an accessible legal mechanism to enforce their rights in the event of non-compliance in granting cash transfers.

Admittedly, if an authority or public institution does anything that violates human rights, such as denying access to a social programme even if the person applying meets the legal requirements, [62] interested parties can file an *amparo* trial,[63] the constitutional legal remedy to safeguard rights by means of federal protection. Unfortunately, however, this remedy is

61 SHCP, 'Decreto por el que se reforman, añaden y derogan diversas disposiciones de la Ley del Impuesto sobre la Renta, de la Ley del Impuesto al Valor Agregado, del Código Fiscal de la Federación y de la Ley Federal del Impuesto sobre Automóviles Nuevos' (2016), available at: <https://www.diputados.gob.mx/LeyesBiblio/ref/lisr/LISR_ref02_30nov16.pdf> accessed 20.6.2024.

62 One example is the judgment under review 42/2022, by the Second Chamber of the SCJN regarding a human rights violation under the Pension Programme for the Well-Being of Persons with Permanent Disabilities, available at: <https://www2.scjn.gob.mx/juridica/engroses/2/2022/2/2_292884_6001.docx> accessed 20.6.2024.

63 *Amparo* trial: Articles 103 and 107 of the Constitution define it as a procedural means in the Mexican legal system specifically used to protect the human rights established in the Constitution and in the international treaties to which Mexico is a party against

practically beyond the reach of the part of the population made vulnerable by poverty. Given the complexity of the procedure, it is indispensable to hire a lawyer specialised in the field, making a lawsuit unaffordable for people living in conditions of poverty, although free legal assistance can be obtained through national or state human rights commissions or legal clinics. Therefore, while an *amparo* is legally available to everyone, its scope and effectiveness may largely depend on having access to legal representation.

In addition to this, the rulings of the Supreme Court of Justice do not automatically apply to the entire population because the judicial system is based on the idea that judicial decisions should arise from specific cases and abide by the principle of appeal[64] and judicial independence.[65] While judgments can establish case-law currents[66] and inform future judicial decisions, their outreach depends on how lower courts interpret and apply them in similar cases.

Lastly, the number of requirements for each social programme beneficiary often imposes a considerable administrative burden on them, making it difficult to access benefits. For example, the programme for persons with permanent disabilities calls for a birth certificate, a valid identification card, the unique population registry code, proof of address, a completed registration form (downloaded from a website), and a disability verification form validated by a federal, state, or municipal health institution.

---

any act of any national authority, when said authorities violate said fundamental rights and their guarantees. This resource is based on Article 103 of the Mexican Constitution and the corresponding regulatory law (Amparo Law, which regulates Articles 103 and 107 of the Political Constitution of the United Mexican States).

64 This means that people can go to court to challenge government decisions or actions that they believe violate their rights (Article 107 of the CPEUM, fraction I).

65 The Mexican judicial system is based on judicial independence and the principle of separation of powers. This means that courts, including the SCJN, make decisions based on the law and the Constitution, and do not have the authority to issue general resolutions (Article 107 of the CPEUM, fraction II).

66 Case law is made up of criteria arising from SCJN and Collegiate Court rulings (Article 215 of the Ley de Amparo) that courts can follow in similar cases. However, even in these cases, the rulings do not apply automatically to the entire population. The lower courts may choose whether or not to follow the case law established by the SCJN (Article 215 of the Ley de Amparo). The case law established by the Supreme Court of Justice of the Nation shall be binding for all judicial authorities of the Federation and the federal entities, with the exception of the Supreme Court itself (Article 217 of the Ley de Amparo).

2. Level of Protection

The cash transfers distributed by social programmes are complementary. There is no regulation establishing that each family should receive a minimum income to be able to live in dignity, based on the number of family members. In 2023, the federal budget explicitly stated that social programmes are exclusively targeted at those parts of the population living in conditions of poverty, vulnerability, old age, underdevelopment, and marginalisation. Thus, a link can clearly be established between the financial benefits given to the poor through social programmes and the specific precarious situations that the beneficiaries are facing. In fact, these programmes are not directly designed to lift people out of poverty, but rather aim to improve at least one aspect of their vulnerability (a social deprivation established by the CONEVAL), such as access to education, health care or subsistence.

Accordingly, the amounts of financial transfers of the social programmes discussed above (with the exception of the "Youth Building the Future" programme) are not directly related to the cost of the basic food basket or to the general minimum wage established for the country. Nor are there any legal provisions or a clear policy in place for progressive increments to the amount of the financial benefits, so they are increased every year at the discretion of the executive branch.

When comparing figures from recent years, it is evident that increases to financial support are effected arbitrarily. For instance, while, scholarships provided by the "Youth Building the Future" programme have increased each year, those of other programmes like the "Assistance Programme for the Well-Being of Children of Working Mothers" have not increased since 2019. Meanwhile, the "Young People Writing the Future" programme has only seen minor changes, as seen in the following table:

Table 1: Monthly amount of cash transfers of social programmes aimed to reduce poverty in Mexico 2019-2024 (in MXN$)

Programme	2019	2020	2021	2022	2023	2024
Benito Juárez Scholarship Programme for Basic Education	NA	$800.00	$800.00	$840.00	$875.00	$920.00
Assistance Programme for the Well-Being of Children of Working Mothers	$1,600.00	$1,600.00	$1,600.00	$1,600.00	$1,600.00	$1,600.00
Youth Building the Future	$3,600.00	$3,748.00	$3,748.00	$5,258.13	$6,310.00	$7,572.00
Youth Writing the Future	NA	$2,400.00	$2,400.00	$2,450.00	$2,575.00	$2,800.00
Well-Being Pension Programme for Older Adults	$1,275.00	$1,310.00	$1,550.00	$1,925.00	$2,400.00	$3,000.00
Pension Programme for the Well-Being of Persons with Permanent Disabilities	NA	$1,310.00	$1,350.00	$1,400.00	$1,475.00	$1,550.00

Source: Based on the Rules of Operation of each social programme sorted by year.

The cash transfers provided for by the Well-Being Pension Programme for Older Adults have increased, but are still not enough to cover the basic food basket for a large family. This can lead to situations where elderly persons find themselves in extreme poverty even when they receive both pensions. Meanwhile, others can receive the maximum amount for contributory pensions (currently proportional to a payment of 25 minimum daily wages for 30 days,[67] which amounts to a total of MXN$ 186,697.50 [US$ 11,022.60]) and still receive a non-contributory pension. On average, however, contributory and non-contributory pensions in tandem do ensure a minimum level of subsistence for older adults, at least by means of measurable income, since issues related to access to healthcare have yet to be resolved.

An attempt to restructure the contributory and non-contributory pension system has been made in the form of a series of reforms introduced by the outgoing president through executive orders (and not established through legislative reforms) with a sharp tinge of electioneering – which paid off in the recent presidential election.

The first reform, implemented in 2024, seeks to allow workers to retire with 100% of their pre-retirement wages, as long as it is equal to or less than the average national monthly wage – calculated by the IMSS – currently standing at MXN$ 16,777 (US$ 990.5).[68] The second one, created on 30 April (2024), established the Pension Fund for Well-Being entrusted with collecting, administrating and distributing the resources. This fund will be used to, first, finance the increase for future pensioners who find themselves in the above category of contributory pensions[69] and, second, contribute to the financing of non-contributory pensions. This fund will be made up of the seizures made by the Institute to Return to the People what was Stolen, resources from the liquidation process of the National Agricultural, Rural, Forestry and Fishing Development Financial Institution, and profits from state-owned entities like the Felipe Angeles International Airport (AIFA) and the Mayan Train. It also obliges *Afores* (Retirement Funds Administrators authorised to manage Mexican individual retirement accounts) to transfer the resources of workers over 70 years of age who have not requested their retirement, severance at advanced age, and housing subaccount balances to the Pension Fund for Well-Being. It is calculated that a total of MXN$ 40 billion (US$ 2,361,595.7) will be collected this

67 IMSS, 'H. Consejo Técnico del IMSS ratifica criterio de 25 salarios mínimos como límite para el pago de pensiones' (2020), available at: <https://www.imss.gob.mx/prensa/archivo/202002/064> accessed 20.6.2024.

68 DOF, 'DECRETO del Fondo de Pensiones para el Bienestar' (2024), available at: <https://www.dof.gob.mx/nota_detalle.php?codigo=5725285&fecha=01/05/2024#gsc.tab=0> accessed 20.6.2024.

69 Ibid.

way.[70] This is a clear violation of workers' acquired rights since these are individual savings accounts. Although the Executive Order has already come into force, the controversy it triggered is still being discussed in bar associations, *amparo* proceedings are underway, and other legal measures are expected to be taken.

3. Group Vulnerability vs. Universalism

Government agencies provide financial assistance benefits as stipulated by the public policies laid down by the current government. For the current administration, poverty is the issue guiding public policies, as well as government programmes and benefits. However, as illustrated above, constitutional provisions only mandate the state's obligation to provide minimum income through financial support for persons belonging to a vulnerable group, as well as a minimum wage for workers. As a result, there is no universal system aimed at improving conditions for a life in dignity. Instead, there are individual systems such as targeted social insurance and assistance programmes that are not linked to each other, which makes it difficult to describe a specific legal construct as a system protecting people's right to a life in dignity.

Among the social programmes to alleviate poverty, two individual systems have a certain degree of universality: non-contributory pensions for older adults and financial support for persons with disabilities. These are based on the Constitution and they fulfil the state obligation explicitly included in Article 4 of the CPEUM in 2020. They are not means-tested and the related cash transfers are thus not conditioned to poverty. However, they still address recipients that belong to specific vulnerable groups: the original argument that led to the incorporation of this constitutional right took into account the high levels of marginalisation that both categories of beneficiaries face.

As for the other social programmes, access to them depends on whether the beneficiaries, families or individuals classified by age, such as children

70 DOF, 'DECRETO por el que se reforman, adicionan y derogan diversas disposiciones de la Ley del Seguro Social, etc.' (2024), available at: <https://www.dof.gob.mx/nota_detalle.php?codigo=5725265&fecha=30/04/2024#gsc.tab=0> accessed 20.6.2024.

or youth, meet the requirement of being within the marginalisation index established by the National Population Council (CONAPO).[71]

Except for the non-contributory and disability pension, it should be noted that in general, none of the social programmes impose a nationality requirement. However, they do require proof of current address without specifying a length of stay in the country, a birth certificate and the Unique Population Registry Code (CURP), which restricts access to foreigners in irregular migratory conditions.

4. Outcomes: Measuring Poverty in Mexico

In Mexico, poverty is measured by the CONEVAL. Poverty is not seen as simply a lack of economic income, but as a multidimensional phenomenon which comprises aspects related to living conditions that threaten the dignity of people, limit their rights and freedoms, prevent the fulfilment of their basic needs and hamper their full social integration.[72] Hence, through the CONEVAL, the government identifies poverty based on the following measurable dimensions: educational lag, lack of access to health services, lack of access to social security, inadequate quality housing or space, unavailability of basic housing services and the lack of access to food.[73] The General Law for Social Development states that "poverty, in its broadest sense, is associated with living conditions that undermine people's dignity, limit their fundamental rights and freedoms, prevent them from satisfying their basic needs and make it impossible for them to be fully integrated into society."[74]

Unfortunately, upon analysing the data presented in Table 1 below, it is clear that the percentages of poverty, and thus the threat to a life in dignity for the Mexican population, remain high.

71 This index measures the deprivations a population experiences as a result of a lack of access to education, health, residence in inadequate housing and the lack of goods and services related to Information and Communication Technologies (ICT), essential for the development of their capabilities, CONAPO, 'Índices de marginación 2020' (n 35).

72 CONEVAL, 'Medición de la pobreza. Anexo estadístico de la pobreza en México 2022' (n 54).

73 Ibid., p. 4.

74 CONEVAL, 'Anexo único de los "lineamientos y criterios generales para la definición, identificación y medición de la pobreza"' (2018), available at: <https://www.coneval.org.mx/Normateca/Documents/ANEXO-Lineamientos-DOF-2018.pdf > accessed 20.6.2024.

Table 2: Multidimensional poverty measurement in Mexico from 2018 to 2022

	Percentage			People (in millions)		
Poverty Indicator	2018	2020	2022	2018	2020	2022
Population living in poverty	41.9	43.9	36.3	51.9	55.7	46.8
Population living in moderate poverty	34.9	35.4	29.3	43.2	44.9	37.7
Population living in extreme poverty	7.0	8.5	7.1	8.7	10.8	9.1
Indicators of social deprivation						
Educational lag	19.0	19.2	19.4	23.5	24.4	25.1
Lack of access to health services	16.2	28.2	39.1	20.1	35.7	50.4
Lack of access to social security	53.5	52.0	50.2	66.2	66.0	64.7
Lack of access to basic housing services	19.6	17.9	17.8	24.3	22.7	22.9
Lack of housing quality and space	11.0	9.3	9.1	13.6	11.8	11.7
Lack of access to nutritious and quality food	22.2	22.5	18.2	27.5	28.6	23.4

Based on CONEVAL Poverty Measurement Report 2022, statistical appendixes.[75]

People living in moderate poverty are those with one or two social deprivation indicators (e.g., education lag or a lack of access to health services, social security, basic housing services or nutritious and quality food) and who, moreover, do not have a minimum income to cover the basic food basket.[76] Meanwhile, extreme poverty refers to those with three or more social deprivations, and who, additionally, have insufficient income and resources to acquire the basic food basket.[77]

75 Ibid.

76 Since it is used as an indicator, the cost of the basic food basket is updated for both rural and urban areas every month. In May 2024, the basic food basket per person was said to cost MXN$ 2,304.27 in urban settings while in a rural setting this figure went down to MXN$ 1,767.03 per person. Cf. CONEVAL, 'Valor de la canasta alimentaria' (n 22).

77 CONEVAL, 'Anexo único' (n 74), under this criterion – as reported by the CONEVAL – poverty in Mexico has gone down by 7.6% in just 2 years. However, it should be kept in mind that the period between 2020 to 2022 was affected by the COVID-19 pandemic and by the ensuing post-pandemic economic reactivation.

Analysing the data on the social deprivation parameters in the light of the provided minimum income schemes enables us to gauge how these programmes impact the vulnerability and the dignity of millions of Mexicans.

First of all, it should be noted that the educational gap does not necessarily indicate illiteracy but refers to the number of children and adolescents between the ages of 3 and 15 who are not enrolled in basic education institutions. In this sense, the percentage of Mexicans lacking basic academic education, far from dropping, has seen a 0.2% growth every two years, going from 19% in 2018 to 19.4% in 2022, despite the provision of Benito Juarez Scholarships for Basic Education.

The lack of access to health services reveals an interesting fact, especially considering that the social programmes aimed at granting access to health have been in place uninterruptedly for more than 45 years in Mexico, only changing names, but preserving the operational bases or extending their scope. Surprisingly, when the IMSS PROSPERA programme changed its name in 2018 to IMSS[78] BIENESTAR (to date), the number of people without access to basic health services increased by 150%, going from 20 million to 50 million people with this specific social deprivation.

Access to social security has improved with a 3.3% decrease in the number of people without coverage. This means that more workers have contributed for their old age through the Retirement Savings System and have an individual account at a Retirement Fund Administrator, thereby also obtaining medical services for themselves and their families through social insurance. However, this raises a contradiction in terms: an increase in the number of people with social security would imply a reduction in the figures for those lacking health services, but it has yet to be factored in that the Youth Building the Future social programme gives recipients access to social insurance for only one year without providing it for their families. So, although social insurance has increased, it has not been possible to narrow the gap in the area of health care.

Deprivations in housing quality and space, as well as in access to basic housing services, have decreased by almost 2% each, improving conditions like solid floors, slab roofs, and access to public services like water, sewage and electricity during the period of the last administration.

The indicator of deprivation due to lack of access to nutritious and quality food has gone down by 4%. This indicator is based on the Mexican

78 Acronym of the Mexican Social Security Institute [Instituto Mexicano del Seguro Social].

Food Security Scale, which assesses whether people have skipped a meal (breakfast, lunch or dinner), have gone a whole day without eating, have been hungry but did not eat, or have had to ration their food in the three months prior to the survey.

IV. Concluding Remarks

Constitutional provisions do not expressly provide for a minimum subsistence income for all Mexicans, but they do lay down specific social rights such as housing, food, employment, education, and access to healthcare for those within Mexican territory. The implementation of such rights, in line with international human rights instruments, help individuals lead a life in dignity.

Even though the CPEUM protects all persons within Mexican territory, some guarantees are targeted at people who are part of vulnerable groups only, such as the right to minimum income introduced in 2020. As a result, social programmes put in place by the executive branch are designed to address some of the specific vulnerabilities affecting the population, which may include age-related considerations, such as being part of the population group of older adults, youth, or children, as well as belonging to vulnerable social groups, such as young people who are not studying or are unemployed, indigenous communities, Afro-Mexicans, persons with disabilities, or those residing in geographic areas of extreme poverty. The poverty gap is thus addressed by means of a variety of social programmes that provide cash transfers that are supposed to contribute to leading a life in dignity. As observed in the analysis of social programmes, each particular benefit (scholarships, pensions, etc.) does alleviate a social deprivation of poverty, but when measured against the cost of the basic food basket, it does not guarantee a life in dignity for people living in poverty.

Moreover, there is no universal programme to ensure that people can lead a life in dignity. Generally speaking, each programme focuses on protecting vulnerable groups. However, often administrations have used social assistance as a political instrument to tout their activities, as well as an electoral quid pro quo. Therefore, the target population for such programmes is not always the poor. For example, the universalisation of certain social programmes such as the non-contributory pension for older adults marks a departure from the purpose of poverty alleviation, since anyone can receive these benefits without experiencing financial insecurity. Thus, persons with disabilities and older adults receive cash transfers without having to belong to a community marginalised by poverty.

Despite the fact that various international instruments like the ICESCR and the Protocol of San Salvador stress the need to progressively guarantee social rights, we can see how the social programmes analysed herein that regularly confer financial benefits do indeed contribute to leading a life in dignity, but only provide relief while being delivered. Hence, they also lead to dependency and transgress their very nature by creating a form of clientelism. The minimum conditions for these programmes to exist (regulatory framework, financing, and implementation) need to be sustainable to avoid falling into assistentialism, a consideration that is not foreseen in most of the social programmes analysed here.

An important point to consider is the protection of subordinate employees, which is based on the emblematic Article 123 of the Mexican Constitution. While this article does not expressly discuss the protection of a minimum existence, it introduces two contributing figures: the minimum wage and the right to social security for workers and their families. The regulation of both is found in various secondary laws.

Lastly, it should be noted that the issue of a minimum income has been controversial, considering that its effective materialisation in the right to minimum conditions for life was only possible through a judicial interpretation of the law and the CPEUM. The right to minimum conditions of life, or the vital minimum, is only recognised in single rulings issued by the Supreme Court of Justice of the Nation (spanning the last decade) on the grounds of human dignity as a condition for people to fully enjoy their rights. These rulings draw attention to the fact that individuals need a minimum level of financial security and the ability to satisfy their basic needs.

Part IV:
Asian Perspective

Life in Dignity in Japan – How Can the Constitutional "Right to Life" Be Adequately Guaranteed?

Eri Kasagi

I. Introduction

At the end of World War II, Japan faced extreme poverty as well as food and housing shortages. Measures to fight poverty became a pressing issue. In December 1945, four months after the end of the war, the government adopted a cabinet decision on the "outline of emergency livelihood assistance for the needy", a temporary emergency measure for individuals in need, which was implemented in April of the following year. Furthermore, the first public assistance law (hereinafter referred to as the 'old public assistance law') was enacted in September 1946 to fundamentally amend several existing laws and regulations.[1] Although the subsequent period of strong economic growth and the subsequent expansion of the social security system helped alleviate extreme and absolute poverty, it continues to remain an important issue in Japan today: the country's relative poverty rate was 15.7 per cent in 2017,[2] one of the highest among OECD countries. Against this backdrop, ensuring a life in dignity has remained a priority in Japanese society for over 70 years since the end of World War II; however, the nature of this issue has gradually evolved and the level of political attention it has received has fluctuated considerably over time. Due to the low unemployment rates achieved during Japan's period of strong economic growth, stable employment and substantial corporate welfare for regular workers, the issue of poverty in Japan seems, until very recently, to have been understood as being limited to single-parent families, persons with disabilities, the elderly, etc., *i.e.* persons who comprise a large part of public assistance recipients.[3] Regular workers benefitted from seniority wages and various corporate benefits, while their spouses were also supported through such corporate welfare. In other words, the Japanese welfare state has been underpinned by this unique corporate model and family structure.[4] In this context, the issue of poverty has, in some respects, faded from political discourse. It was only in the 2000s, triggered by the increase in the number of informal workers and the global economic crisis, that the issue of poverty

1 S. Naito, 'Seikatsu-hogo no genjō to kadai/The Current Status and Challenges of Public Assistance' Rippō to chōsa (2012)331, pp. 78-79.

2 According to data provided by the Ministry of Health, Labour and Welfare. The poverty rate of children in the same year was 13.9 per cent.

3 In fact, many of today's public assistance recipients in Japan belong to these categories.

4 This entire structure is often called 'Japanese-style welfare society'. M. Ōsawa, *Kigyō chûshin syakai wo koete*/Beyond a Corporate-Centered Society (Iwanami Gendai Bunko Jijitsushin-sha 2020).

received renewed political attention. In 2009, for the first time in its history, the Japanese government published data on the relative poverty rate, revealing significant gaps and inefficiencies in the country's social security system, which had previously been considered well-developed.[5]

Today, Japan's minimum income schemes are characterised by their relatively simple framework. As a reflection of the constitutional right to life, the Public Assistance Act (enacted in 1950 to replace the previous legislation) guarantees a minimum standard of living for all citizens. Due to the principle of subsidiarity, this law provides different forms of minimum income guarantees for each eligible individual. The mechanism for determining such personalised benefits is complex, despite the simple framework described above. In addition to minimum income guarantees, there are various social insurance schemes form another key pillar of Japan's social security system. One of the schemes' primary objectives is the prevention of poverty. This chapter begins with an overview of Japanese law (Section II). It focuses first on the constitutional right to life (Art. 25 of the Constitution), its scope and its impact on the development of Japanese social security law (Section II.1). An overview of existing social benefits, including the Public Assistance Act, which is inseparably linked to the constitutional right to life is provided in Section II.2. In the next section (Section III), the Public Assistance Act, which plays a central role in Japanese legislation in ensuring a minimum standard of living, is explored.

II. Overview

1. Normative Background: The Constitutional Right to Life and its Impact on the Evolution of Japan's Social Security System

After World War II, Japan's legal system underwent significant transformations. While these transformations covered a wide range of important changes, such as the shift from imperial sovereignty to popular sovereignty (Preamble, Art. 41, Art. 44), the redefinition of the Emperor as the symbolic head of State (Art. 1), the adoption of pacifism (Art. 9) and fundamental human rights,[6] this chapter focuses on social benefits and social protection.

5 See Section II. 2. b) cc) below.

6 See S. Wagatsuma, 'Guarantee of fundamental human rights under the Japanese Constitution' Washington Law Review 26 (1951), p. 145.

The new Constitution of 3 May 1947 established the foundation for Japan's post-war social welfare system, introducing the right to life（生存権 – *seizonken*, Art. 25 of the Japanese Constitution).[7] Although the Constitution was drafted under the strong influence of the American authorities, Article 25 was primarily introduced on the Japanese deputies' initiative, who were inspired by Weimar-era social law.[8] Article 25 states that "all people shall have the right to maintain the minimum standards of wholesome and cultured living" (para. 1). It also provides that, in all spheres of life, the State shall promote and expand social welfare, security and public health (para. 2). Sakae Wagatsuma, one of Japan's most influential jurists of the time, argued that this provision marked a shift in line with a global trend towards 20th century fundamental rights. This shift reflected a greater emphasis by the State on the individual's well-being compared to 19th century fundamental rights, which prioritised guaranteeing individual freedom.[9] However, there has not always been a fruitful debate about what type of standard of living this right specifically guarantees. Although the phrase "wholesome and cultured living" clearly signifies that the right to life is not limited to mere physical survival, judicial precedents have established that defining the specific scope of a 'wholesome and cultured life' falls within the broad discretion of the legislature. According to the Supreme Court, "the minimum standards of wholesome and cultured living" is a highly abstract and relative concept, with its scope determined in relation to the country's level of cultural development, economic and social conditions, and the general standard of living during each period. It has therefore been interpreted that both the legislature and the executive branch (through delegated powers under the Welfare Act as discussed below)[10] are granted considerable discretion in defining and implementing this human right.

7 In the field of labour law, it provides for the right and duty to work, the requirement for minimum working conditions to be fixed by law, the prohibition of child labour (Article 27), the right to organise collective bargaining and collective action (Article 28).

8 A strong influence of Anton Mengar's works is noted as well. T. Yamamori and Y. Vanderborght, 'Introduction: Income Security and the "Right to Subsistence" in Japan', in: T. Yamamori and Y. Vanderborght (eds.), *Basic Income in Japan: Prospects for a Radical Idea in a Transforming Welfare State* (Palgrave Macmillan 2014), pp. 2-3.

9 S. Wagatsuma, Kenpō Fukyukai (ed.), *Shin-kenpō to kihon-teki-jinken/* The New Constitution and Fundamental Human Rights (Kokuritsu Shoin 1948), pp. 110. See also S. Wagatsuma (n 6), pp. 159 ff.

10 See Sec. III. 1. b) cc).

Nonetheless, Article 25 has, since its introduction, remained one of the major political and legal driving forces behind the development of social welfare in Japan, despite its slightly ambiguous judicial effect.[11] Hence, the establishment and ongoing development of the social security system are regarded as the State's efforts to realise or give concrete expression to this constitutional right, which is guaranteed to all Japanese citizens.[12] This perception of social security as the embodiment of a human right that is enjoyed equally by all citizens seems to have significantly influenced the character of Japan's social security system.

It also seems that the legislative, political and administrative leaders of the time acknowledged certain links between this new constitutional right and the social security model proposed by William Henry Beveridge in the United Kingdom in November 1942, and which garnered considerable attention among Japanese leaders shortly after the publication of the Beveridge report, even before the end of war. Several documents indicate that as early as 1943—at the height of the war—the Beveridge report was translated and studied by the Ministry of Health and Welfare, which had already begun drafting a social policy framework for the post-war period.[13] In 1947, a committee set up within the Ministry at the central government's request published Japan's first concise social security plan,[14] serving as the foundation of the country's post-war social security system. This plan was strongly influenced[15] by the Beveridgian idea, even reflecting a quasi-direct adoption of its principles.

Thus, the committee concluded that social health insurance and old-age pensions should ideally be guaranteed for the entire population, acknowledging that, at the time, it was unavoidable and acceptable to keep these systems separate for workers and the rest of the population, with the level of benefits for workers' insurance substantially higher than for the rest of pop-

---

11 See Sec. III. 1. b) cc) on judicial control on legislation.

12 S. Wagatsuma (n 6), p. 163.

13 E. Kasagi, 'Comprendre le développement de la sécurité sociale japonaise: l'incarnation des idées occidentales dans le contexte japonais de différentes époques', in: I. Daugareilh and M. Badel (eds.), *La sécurité sociale – Universalité et modernité: Approche de droit comparé* (Pedone 2019).

14 Syakaihosyōseido chōsa kai/ Social Security System Research Council, *Syakaihosyō seido yōkō/* Outline of the Social Security System (Investigation Committee on Social Security Systems, October 1947).

15 Y. Matsuzaki, 'On "The Beveridge Report" and Social Security Policy in Japan: How "The Report" was the Origin' Shukutoku University bulletin 27 (1993), pp. 14 ff (in Japanese).

ulation. While the plan ultimately proposed a segmented social insurance system for workers and the rest of the population, universal coverage for both health insurance and pension insurance (including for the elderly, persons with disabilities and survivors) became a cornerstone of Japanese social policy from that point onwards. By 1966, both the health insurance and the basic (old-age, invalidity and survivors) pension schemes had achieved universal coverage, *i.e.* ensuring the entire population is covered, despite maintaining the segmented structure between employed workers and the rest of population. Unemployment insurance and occupational accident insurance were also proposed for workers in the post-war legislation.

The starting point of Japan's modern social security system highlights that its entire structure is underpinned by a universal, state-driven approach, influenced by the Beveridgian model and the constitutional right to life. At the same time, it incorporates elements of the Bismarckian social insurance concept (with contributions from both employees and employers based on wage level, and the amount of benefits is determined accordingly). This Bismarckian influence, which shaped Japanese social security legislation even before the war,[16] continued to leave its mark on the evolution of Japan's social security system throughout the post-war period and into the present day.

As regards the minimum income benefit (currently referred to as "state assistance"), the abovementioned plan outlined its purpose as ensuring a minimum standard of living for all individuals facing poverty, with the State assuming responsibility. The plan specified that while this system shall cover all citizens who are facing poverty, assistance is only provided if a minimum standard of living cannot be maintained through other means. These basic principles of the public assistance system—universality, subsidiarity and State responsibility—were enshrined in the Public Assistance Act of 1950[17] and have remained unchanged to this day. The following sections[18] explore the Public Assistance Act in more detail, a legal act that embodies this fundamental human right, and explicitly refers to Article 25 of the Constitution.

16 See E. Kasagi (n 13).

17 Public Assistance Act (Act No. 144 of 1950), English translation available at: < https://www.japaneselawtranslation.go.jp/en/laws/view/24/en> accessed 10.12.2024.

18 See Sec. II. 2. b) bb) and Sec. III.

2. Different Social Benefits and their Interconnections

Before exploring the public assistance system in more detail (Section III), which is the primary, direct mechanism for guaranteeing minimum income in Japan, we first provide a general overview of the country's social security system, and explore how each scheme within the system contributes indirectly and preventatively to ensure a minimum standard of living for all citizens. Three points should be highlighted here. First, the public assistance system serves as a last resort and only takes effect after all other preventive measures have been exhausted. Second, Japan's social security system aims to prevent poverty through universal social insurance schemes. Third, there are several limitations and gaps in the country's poverty prevention policy, and the connection to the public assistance system is not always seamless.

a) Contributory Schemes – Social Insurance

A number of social benefits have been introduced and developed to guarantee the constitutional right to life since its adoption. Today, these benefits fall into two main categories: 1) five different social insurance schemes based on type of risk each covers, namely i) health insurance, ii) pension insurance (old-age, survivors and disability pensions), iii) unemployment insurance, iv) workers' accident insurance, and v) sickness compensation, and 2) long-term care insurance. Only four of these social insurance schemes are considered here.

aa) Health Insurance

All persons who legally reside in Japan (except for short-term and temporary residents, *i.e.* tourists and those on short-term visas) are covered by social health insurance. Coverage is provided through different insurance schemes depending on age and professional status (employed or not).[19] Japan's health insurance system is divided into three schemes: 1) the health

19 Foreigners illegally residing in the country are not eligible for any medical insurance scheme (see bb) for details on their exclusion from public assistance benefits).

insurance scheme for employed workers (Kenkō-hoken)[20], 2) the health insurance scheme for the elderly aged 75 and older (Kōki-kōreisya-iryō-seido), and 3) the national health insurance scheme for all individuals who are not covered by the other two schemes (Kokumin-kenkō-hoken).

These social health insurance schemes provide both medical services in kind and various financial benefits, including—albeit only for employed persons—income support during periods of absence from work due to sickness and maternity. Income compensation in case of sickness and maternity benefits are not provided to self-employed persons.[21] However, in terms of benefits in kind, the scope and level of insurance benefits are largely the same across all schemes. Only for the elderly and children, the out-of-pocket charge of 30 % is reduced to 10 % or 20 % (depending on the level of income for the elderly. For children, the rate of 20% is universally applied). There is a monthly cap on out-of-pocket charges, which depends on the beneficiary's age and income level.

Insurance premiums vary according to insurance scheme. Both workers and employers contribute equally to the scheme for employees based on the worker's wage level.

Among these different health insurance schemes, the National Health Insurance scheme is the most important one, ensuring access to medical insurance for low-income and unemployed persons. However, when insurance premiums are in arrears, benefits are partially restricted (requiring the insured person to initially cover any medical costs out of pocket and receiving reimbursement later). Those who are unable to pay their premiums or who do not have the necessary resources to pay out-of-pocket costs receive livelihood assistance (health assistance).

bb) National Pensions

The National Pension scheme, which is administered by the government, covers all residents of Japan, aiming to provide basic income security for

20 This health insurance scheme for employed workers has the same limited coverage as the pension insurance scheme for employed workers (see below, sec. cc)). See also n 26 for details on the recent reforms concerning the application of social insurance for employed workers).

21 Insurers (municipalities, prefectures or associations established by self-employed persons within the same industry) can provide these benefits voluntarily.

the elderly, persons with disabilities and survivors (basic old-age pension, basic disability pension, basic survivors' pension).[22] This system offers a flat-rate, rather small pension (the full amount is around EUR 440 per month), and covers a share of the beneficiary's basic income. Covering all citizens through contributions, including those without a job or income (although there are many exceptions, as discussed below), pension insurance is a key feature of Japan's pension system, and highlights the significance of social security as a poverty prevention policy.

Although this pension system is intended to be universal, it does not, in practice, provide coverage for every resident of Japan. Nor does the old-age pension guarantee the same benefit amount for all, despite the fact that the full benefit amount is standardised, as discussed above. In fact, in the case of basic pensions, each insured person—aside from workers whose basic pension premiums are included in the premiums for workers' pensions (see next section)—is required to pay a fixed premium to the insurance provider (JPY 16,520, around EUR 105 in 2023). As a result, some individuals are unable to pay contributions. In such cases, the pension is reduced (only for the basic old-age pension) or not paid at all, depending on the duration of the period of non-payment. However, legal provisions allow for a reduction or full exemption of insurance premiums under certain conditions, such as low income, but this consequently also reduces the benefit amount up to a certain limit (this also only applies to the basic old-age pension). For instance, individuals who are categorically unable to contribute—typically public assistance recipients—are automatically and fully exempt from contributions to insurance premiums (Art. 89 I, para. 2 of the National Pension Act).[23] Those who do not automatically qualify for full exemption can apply for a graduated exemption ranging from one-quarter, one-half, three-quarters and full exemption, depending on their income level. In such cases, the pension amount is reduced in proportion to the duration of the exemption. For example, for periods of full premium exemption, the benefit amount

22 Similar to medical insurance, short-term and temporary residents, *i.e.* tourists and those on short-term visas, as well as foreigners illegally residing in the country, are excluded from coverage.

23 In other words, recipients of public assistance retain their status of insured person and continue to accumulate pension contributions. In addition, under the exemption scheme for students, the benefit is reduced by an amount in direct proportion to the amount of exempt contributions. However, deferred contributions can be made for up to 10 years after the original payment due date.

is calculated as if only half the premiums had been paid.[24] In a universal pension system that covers individuals with little or no income, there will always be insured persons who are unable to contribute. These exemptions (and a mechanism that calculates premiums as having been partially paid during exemption periods) play an important role in ensuring coverage for all residents, particularly those with a low income, and in guaranteeing a certain benefit amount for all residents. However, the pension amounts provided may be lower than the full benefit amount, especially in cases where the exemption period extended for a significant duration.

For disability and survivors' pensions, the non-payment of contributions may also result in loss of pension payments, but when entitlement requirements are met, the full benefit is provided, irrespective of the individual's contribution history. This is why income security is not always universally achieved by pension schemes for the elderly, persons with disabilities and survivors, despite the system's goal of universal coverage.

The basic pension includes a special and often controversial provision for financially dependent spouses of employees. Spouses who are financially dependent (and subject to certain income requirements) on the individual insured under the employees' pension insurance[25] are exempt from the obligation to pay contributions. If they maintain this status for 40 years, the dependent spouse may be eligible to receive a full pension without having made any contributions. This provision was introduced in 1986, primarily to resolve the problem of poverty among women (even though male spouses may also be eligible for this scheme), who often struggle to sufficiently contribute to a pension scheme. Nevertheless, this provision has long faced strong criticism for potentially discouraging women from working full time and reinforcing part-time work among women. Spouses earning a salary over JPY 1.3 million (about EUR 8,000) are required to pay their own pension contributions. Some spouses deliberately change jobs to limit their income and ensure that it does not exceed the established threshold. This provision has also been strongly criticised from a fairness perspective, as only spouses of employed workers can benefit from this scheme. Those who are not married to an employed worker are required to pay contributions; even though they can opt for the exemption scheme

24 For periods of half premium exemption, the benefit amount is calculated as if 75 per cent of the premium had been paid. For further details, see Art. 28 of the National Pension Law (*kokumin-nenkin-hō,* Act No. 141-1959).

25 See Sec. II. 2. b) cc).

in some cases, their final pension amount as noted earlier will in that case not be the full amount. Despite these valid concerns, the system has played a role in providing full old-age basic pensions for certain insured persons who were unable to pay contributions (or who lost the ability to pay contributions at specific period(s) during their lives).

It is also important to note that 50 per cent of the financial resources for the pension system come from tax revenue.

cc) Employees' Pension Insurance (*Kōsei-nenkin*)

In addition to the National Pension scheme, employees are mandatorily enrolled in the Employees' Pension Insurance scheme (Kōsei-nenkin-hoken). Under this scheme, workers pay contributions in accordance with their earnings and receive a pension amount that corresponds to their contribution level and duration of their contributions. Contributions are equally shared between the worker and the employer. This scheme also provides three types of pensions – i) old-age pension, ii) disability pension, and iii) survivors' pension. The pension amount is determined, within a set range, in proportion to the worker's wage level during their years of employment and the length of their period of affiliation (contributions).

Workers covered by this pension insurance scheme do not directly contribute to the National Pension scheme, but contribute indirectly through the Employees' Pension Insurance scheme which transfers funds to the National Pension scheme, theoretically covering the national pension benefits for employees and their spouses. This means that half of the contributions to the pensions of workers and their dependent spouses are theoretically shouldered by the employer, even the share of the basic pension.

One notable characteristic of Japan's Employees' Pension Insurance scheme is the exclusion of certain part-time workers from its scope of application. In the past, all workers who worked less than two-thirds of the hours and days of full-time workers were excluded from coverage. While coverage has gradually expanded since the 2000s, workers who work less than 20 hours per week or earn less than JPY 88,000 per month continue to remain excluded from this insurance. The abovementioned two-thirds criterion continues to apply for smaller entities.[26] Part-time student work-

26 Under the 2025 legislative amendments, the exemptions applicable to small-scale entities will be phased out by 2035 for both pension and health insurance (see n 20).

ers are also excluded from this pension insurance scheme. As a result, a significant number of long-term part-time workers do not receive an income-proportional pension upon retirement, having to rely solely on the basic pension.

dd) Pensions as Poverty Prevention

Social insurance schemes are often referred to as "poverty prevention" measures and differ from and contrast with "poverty relief" schemes, which do not depend on contributions and apply *a posteriori* and residually, are based on a means test, and are provided if the individual falls into poverty. Among the two abovementioned pillars of the pension system, the National Pension scheme plays a distinct and vital role in "poverty prevention" by ensuring a contributory pension for all residents, including those who are unemployed or have not worked at all. However, failure to pay contributions may ultimately result in a significantly reduced pension or no pension at all.

Within the framework of this contributory pension scheme, the provision allowing the employee's spouse to receive a full pension on a non-contributory basis has, to some extent, addressed the problem of female poverty.

ee) Unemployment Insurance

Unemployment insurance (referred to as "employment insurance" – *koyō hoken*),[27] is a social insurance scheme administered by the government, in which workers and employers pay 50 per cent of premiums. The law entitles all insured workers to unemployment insurance, with some legally defined exceptions (see below on short-time workers). It classifies insured persons into four categories, with distinct regulations for each, including the scope of benefits and how they should be financed: i) ordinary insured persons (all insured workers who do not fall into the following three special categories), ii) elderly insured persons (workers aged 65 and over who do not belong to the following two categories), iii) insured persons with

The condition regarding the salary level (JPY 88,000) will be totally removed before 2028, also for both pension and health insurance.

27 Employment Insurance Act, Act No. 116 of 28 December 1974.

seasonal employment, and iv) insured persons with daily jobs. Here, we will focus on ordinary insured persons and the 'basic benefit' (Art. 13 of the Employment Insurance Act). To be eligible for this benefit, an individual who is "unemployed" 1) has left his/her job, 2) has the intention to work, 3) has the capacity to work, and 4) is unable to find employment. The individual must have been affiliated with an employment insurance and paid contributions for at least 12 months within the two years preceding the date of his/her job loss (in case of job loss due to insolvency of the employer, dismissal, harassment, etc., the required contribution period is reduced to six months). The benefit amount is calculated as a percentage of the insured person's wage level (between 45 per cent to 80 per cent, depending on age and wage level), which is determined based on the wages earned in the six months preceding loss of employment (Art. 16 and 17 of the Employment Insurance Act).

Two key characteristics of this insurance scheme should be highlighted. First, workers who work less than 20 hours per week are not covered by employment insurance.[28] This exclusion is based on the notion that part-time workers with short working hours have a relatively lower need for income security in case of unemployment. However, due to the rise in non-regular employment and the growing number of workers who hold multiple jobs, the need for reform to extend employment insurance coverage to include such workers has been repeatedly discussed in recent years.[29]

The second key characteristic is that the duration of Japanese unemployment insurance benefits is relatively short compared to European countries. This duration is based on age, the reason for leaving employment, and the period of contributions, with the maximum standard duration being 330 days (for workers aged between 45 and 65 who have at least 20 years of insurance contributions and who have left employment due to dismissal or company insolvency, for example). One notable exception applies to workers with disabilities, who are eligible for unemployment benefits for up to 360 days, provided they have been insured for at least one year.

These characteristics of Japan's employment insurance system—the relatively short duration of unemployment benefits and the limited scope of insurance coverage—increase the likelihood that part-time workers, who

28 Due to the 2025 legislative amendments, the eligibility for employment insurance will be extended to part-time workers under 10 hours per week in 2028.

29 See the report of the expert committee established within the Ministry of Health, Labour and Welfare (27 December 2018) < https://www.mhlw.go.jp/content/11601000/000469766.pdf > accessed 10.12.2024.

are not covered by employment insurance, long-term unemployed, or those who receive benefits for a very short time only due to insufficient contribution periods, may fall into poverty in case of unemployment, and may subsequently require public assistance.

b) Non-Contributory Schemes

aa) Child Allowance and Allowance for Single-Parent Families

All other social benefits are non-contributory, *i.e.* they are financed through taxes, and include various social services for persons with disabilities (personal care, caregiver services, daycare, residential care facilities, transportation services, etc.) as well as services for children (nursery care, children's homes), which will not be described in detail here.

On the other hand, there are also financial allowances, such as child allowance (*jidō-teate*)[30] and single-parent family allowance (*jidō-fuyō-teate*),[31] which are provided based on income criteria. While we will not delve into the technical details of the eligibility conditions of these two allowances here, it is important to note that the two allowances serve quite distinct purposes, which is clearly reflected in their differing eligibility criteria.

The single-parent family allowance focuses primarily on addressing poverty, based on the assumption that single-parent families are at a higher risk of falling into poverty. This allowance is therefore provided to a parent raising a child (or children) on their own, and is subject to stringent income conditions (an income of around EUR 11,000 annually to be eligible for the full benefit amount, for a single parent raising one child. The amount can vary depending on the number of children). Additionally, the absence of one parent from the child's household is a central criterion for eligibility for this allowance, with "parent" being interpreted in a relatively broad sense. Consequently, if the parent who lives with the child marries someone other than the child's other parent, the parent that is living with the child will no longer be eligible for the single-parent family allowance, even though the new spouse has no legal obligation to support the child.

30 Act on Child Allowance, Act No. 73 of 1971.
31 Child-rearing Allowance Act, Act No. 238 of 1962.

In contrast to the single-parent family allowance, the purpose of the child allowance is not as clear-cut and has, at times, been subject of controversy. When child allowance was introduced in 1971, its primary aim was to prevent poverty in families with a large number of children. Thus, the allowance was initially only granted to families with three or more children depending on household income. In 1978, a supplementary allowance was introduced for families with low incomes. However, the legislator at the time explained that this allowance was not exclusively reserved for low-income families;[32] the income condition had been introduced due to budgetary constraints rather than as a fundamental principle of the scheme (the allowance is financed by both the State and employers). The ambiguity surrounding the aim of this allowance has since persisted and even increased, particularly since the 1990s, when attention and expectations shifted towards its role as a measure to address the declining fertility rate. The allowance was thus expanded in terms of three aspects: i) the number of children (since 1992, child allowance is provided from the first child), ii) the amount of benefit provided, and iii) the income threshold (the income condition was abolished in 2010, but reintroduced one year later). Parents raising a child under the age of 15 are entitled to a benefit amount of JPY 15,000 (for children aged 0-3) or JPY 10,000 (for children aged 3-15), subject to an income condition that is relatively less stringent compared to the single-parent family allowance (the gross income threshold for eligibility ranges from around JPY 6,000,000 to 8,000,000 (between EUR 38,000 to EUR 51,000) annually, depending on the number of family members living in the beneficiary's household). The government is currently discussing an increase of this benefit in an effort to boost the stagnant birth rate. Today, the significance of child allowance as a poverty alleviation measure has largely been relativised and diluted. In other words, the justification at the time the scheme was first introduced that the allowance was not exclusively intended for low-income families has been confirmed in the meantime by the significant expansion of the benefit's scope.

32 M. Sato, 'Jidō-teate-seido no hensen ni kansuru ichi-kōsatsu/Study on the Changes in the Child Allowance System' Nenpō Kō-kyō-seisaku-gaku (2022)16, pp. 79-99.

bb) Minimum Income – Public Assistance

Since its enactment in 1950, the Public Assistance Act (*Seikatsu hogo ho*) has played a key role in guaranteeing the constitutional right to life. This has been repeatedly, explicitly or implicitly, referenced within the act itself (Art. 1, Art. 3, Art. 8, para. 2), and consistently recognised in extensive case law since the 1960s.[33] The Public Assistance Act is a direct embodiment of the constitutional guarantee of the right to life as stipulated in Art. 25, para. 1 of the Constitution.

The Public Assistance Act holds a unique legal status as an embodiment of the constitutional right to life, requiring careful interpretation. For example, courts tend to apply relatively strict interpretations when assessing administrative discretion, particularly in decisions concerning the withdrawal of public assistance benefits from those in need.[34]

The purpose of public assistance is to ensure that a minimum standard of living is guaranteed by the State to all citizens in need (Art. 1). The same law applies to the elderly, persons with disabilities, single-parent families, etc. The universal character of this law needs to, however, be nuanced in two key aspects. First, according to both the Ministry of Health, Labour and Welfare (MHLW) and the Supreme Court, the law does not extend to foreign nationals, including long-term visa holders and asylum seekers.[35] However, since 1954, the MHLW has applied the law to certain foreign nationals mutatis mutandis, and this treatment, based on administrative circulars, continues to apply to this day. This mutatis mutandis application of public assistance is restricted to foreign nationals with permanent residence or a similar status. Asylum seekers are excluded from such treatment and are only granted minimal assistance payments (amounting to less than

---

33 See the Asahi case, Supreme Court (24 May 1967) 21-5 *Minshû,* 1043. The Supreme Court has repeatedly held that the standard of living guaranteed by the right to life (Art. 25) is abstract and relative in nature and does not grant courts the authority to require legislators to enact specific legislation, and that under current law, it is the Public Assistance Act that embodies this constitutional right.

34 See, for instance, Supreme Court (23 October 2014) 2245-10 *Hanreijihō 10.* In this judgment, the Supreme Court ruled on the guidance provided by the welfare office, which is discussed below (III. 2. b)): unless the instructions a recipient is required to follow are explicitly set out in writing, an unfavourable measure, such as the suspension or termination of assistance, cannot be imposed on them, as though they had violated these instructions. See Section III.1.c) cc) for a discussion on the limited judicial oversight over executive and parliamentary legislative discretion.

35 Supreme Court (18 July 2014) 386 *Hanrei-Chihō-Jichi* 78.

welfare benefits) and access to residential accommodation in case of hardship. Access to such support is not a legal right of asylum seekers; they can claim such support in court. In a 2001 ruling, the Supreme Court stated that based on the provisions and objectives of the law, public assistance does not extend to illegal aliens, asserting that this exclusion does not violate Art. 25 of the Constitution.[36]

Second, access to benefits is strictly limited by the subsidiarity principle, meaning that some individuals and households may not be eligible for protection, even if they are facing poverty. As explored in more detail in the analysis, public assistance is only available as a last resort, *i.e.* after the individual in need has already exhausted all of his/her assets, income, work capacity, and all other social benefits (Art. 4 of the Public Assistance Act). For instance, an individual in need may be denied welfare benefits if, regardless of the reason, he or she does not relinquish all assets (that exceed the minimum standard of living). In addition, young people, especially those without health problems or disabilities, may be deemed as not having fully exploited their earning capacity and may be denied public assistance, even if they are at risk of poverty. Therefore, in case of continued unemployment—once the relatively short period of unemployment insurance benefits mentioned above[37] has ended—public assistance is not always readily and immediately available for unemployed persons. In reality, there is a large gap between the two systems, which means there is a certain number of unemployed persons who do not receive any social benefits at all.[38] It is also important to note that more than half of current public assistance recipients are aged 65 or older.[39] In other words, despite being designed as a universal system, the strict application of the subsidiarity principle sometimes makes the welfare system inaccessible, especially for younger people. Moreover, as a consequence of the principle of subsidiarity, other social benefits outlined in this section take priority over public assistance. For example, if the basic pension described above is insufficient to meet the

36 Supreme Court (25 September 2001) 1768-47 *Hanrei-Jihō* 47.

37 See Sec. II. 2.

38 Additionally, it is often pointed out that the take-up rate of public assistance in Japan is relatively low (with estimates varying widely among experts. Experts' estimates range from 10 per cent to 30 per cent, and in some cases even lower). See, for example, the detailed observation of H. Ogawa, 'Hinkon Setai no genjo /The Current Situation of The Households in Poverty' *Keizai Kenkyu* 51 (2000)3, p. 220.

39 See data of the Ministry of Health, Labour and Welfare, <https://www.mhlw.go.jp/content/12201000/000908527.pdf> accessed 10.12.2024.

minimum standard of living, public assistance is provided as a supplement to the basic pension to make up the shortfall.

While the Public Assistance Act's primary objective is to guarantee a minimum standard of living, its second key objective is to promote the autonomy of those living in poverty. Despite the various academic debates about the significance of 'autonomy' in this context, we will focus here on its central and foundational significance only. In other words, autonomy refers to the ability of a person in need to regain independence and to no longer have to rely on welfare. Public assistance, at least as envisioned by the law, is not intended to be a permanent solution, and courts have repeatedly emphasised this point in their interpretations of the Public Assistance Act. These interpretations have been highlighted not only in cases where social welfare offices encourage public assistance recipients to work, but also in various other cases, such as educational opportunities for young recipients,[40] as well as cases in which the judges allow public assistance recipients to put aside savings for their children's education.[41]

While public assistance is the responsibility of the State, its actual implementation is left to local authorities and the social welfare offices (*Fukushi-jimusho*) established by them.

cc) Support System for Autonomy of Individuals in Need (Seikatsu-Konkyusha-Shien-Seido)

In the 2000s, the issue of the 'working poor' gained significant attention in Japan as a result of the rise in the number of non-regular workers, combined with the impact of the Lehman shock. In this context, there was growing awareness about the limitations of public assistance, particularly for the younger generations. Partially related to this situation, a debate arose about the advantages of providing public support to individuals before they fall into extreme poverty. It was argued that public assistance could help prevent individuals from falling into poverty or make it easier for them to get out of poverty. Concerns about providing assistance to vulnerable population groups even before their standard of living falls below the threshold to qualify for public assistance were expressed in particular during the reform of 2013, which introduced a "system of support for the

40 Kumamoto District Court (4 October 2022) 1819 *Chingin-to-Shakaihoshō* 42.
41 Supreme Court (16 March 2004) 58-3 *Minshū* 647.

autonomy of individuals in need".[42] The lack of sufficient employment support within the public assistance framework was also raised as problematic. The new law introduced a series of services (counselling, short-term housing allowance, support for (re)entering the labour market, etc.), giving these benefits a provisional and anticipatory character, providing access to support for vulnerable population groups that are not yet eligible for public assistance.

The law also introduced a housing allowance for this population group, which is quite novel in the context of Japan's social security system, even though the scope of coverage and duration of benefits are admittedly quite modest. This allowance (*jy ū-taku kakuho kyūfu kin,* Housing Security Benefit) covers beneficiaries' actual rent amount up to the housing assistance's threshold for, in principle, a period of three months (renewable for up to nine months). This benefit is granted in cases of job separation, business closure or a decrease in income that is comparable to the aforementioned events, provided the household meets the income requirements and the recipient is actively seeking employment (or working to restore their business). The eligibility is extended to not only employed workers but also to self-employed workers. This is a new approach within Japanese law, which now recognises income reduction as a risk that is comparable to job separation.

Finally, the law places strong emphasis on assisting recipients in securing employment. Combined with the large number of elderly recipients, as previously mentioned, concerns have been raised that the public assistance system lacks adequate employment support for recipients. The new law aims to enhance early employment support for those in need who have not yet received any public assistance, enabling them to quickly (re)enter the labour market.

dd) Exceptional Allowance Related to the COVID Pandemic

Finally, an exceptional benefit introduced during the pandemic is worth mentioning. On 20 April 2020, the government decided to grant a one-time allowance of JPY 100,000 to all residents of Japan (*Tokubetsu-kyūfukin*, special lump-sum allowance) to "support households quickly and efficiently

42 Act No. 105 of 2015. For more information on this law and the context of legislation, see also E. Kasagi, 'L'aide sociale au Japon à la recherche d'un niveau de vie minimum' Droit Social (2020)10, p. 842.

through a simple system", according to the Ministry of Internal Affairs and Communications. Initially, the government considered making the payment conditional on a significant reduction in the beneficiary's income due to the COVID-19 pandemic, but this idea was later abandoned. Given strong public opposition and the need to speed up the payment process, the government ultimately adopted a uniform allowance for all residents. Although this benefit was created within the scope of a simple administrative "programme" that was of a discretionary nature, and was paid only once (*i.e.* it is not a periodic allowance), it has the potential to re-launch and reignite the debate in Japan on a universal, flat-rate income referred to as "basic income", borrowing the Anglo-Saxon term. Such a basic income would differ significantly from Japan's existing public assistance system, which while universal, remains highly targeted and individualised.

ee) (Quasi) Absence of Housing Allowance

One notable characteristic of the Japanese social security system, particularly compared to European countries, is the near-total absence of a housing allowance. There is no social benefit to offset the costs of housing, with two exceptions, namely i) housing assistance, which is available to public assistance recipients, and ii) the housing grant, which is provided for a limited period (in principle, three months with a possible extension up to nine months) within the scope of the support system to promote the autonomy of people in need, as mentioned above, sec. II. 2. b) cc). This housing grant is provided if the main breadwinner i) has left his/her employment or closed his/her business within the past two years or ii) when his/her ability to earn a wage or other income has been reduced to the same extent as if he/she had left his/her job or closed his/her business, provided that this reduction is not due to personal responsibility or personal circumstances. As a result, the benefit is quite restrictive in terms of both eligibility and the duration of the benefit.

In other words, Japan's social security system has historically paid little attention to the financial burden of housing, except for those who are living in poverty or at risk of poverty.[43]

43 At the same time, the recently introduced housing grant has gained significance in recent years as the eligibility criteria for the benefit have been relaxed.

One reason for this situation is the traditional employment practice in Japan, whereby companies, especially large corporations, have covered housing costs for permanent employees through corporate housing allowance. However, with the transformation of these employment practices and the rise in the number of non-regular employees, the lack of universal housing security is becoming an increasingly important policy issue, though this topic will not be discussed here in detail.

III. Analysis

In this section, we provide a detailed analysis of Japan's public assistance system (Public Assistance Act), which ensures a minimum standard of living.

1. Social Assistance Benefits

a) Various In-kind and Cash Benefits

The Public Assistance Act provides various in-kind and cash benefits, aiming to offer a comprehensive guarantee of a minimum standard of living. More specifically, the act provides for eight types of benefits: i) livelihood assistance, ii) education assistance, iii) housing assistance, iv) health assistance, v) long-term care assistance, vi) maternity assistance, vii) occupational assistance, and viii) funeral assistance (Art. 11 of Public Assistance Act). Among these, livelihood assistance—primarily provided in cash—plays a central role, as it is designed to cover the costs of basic daily needs such as food, clothing, transportation and other essentials to maintain a basic standard of living (Art. 12). Education assistance covers the costs of school materials and school meals during the years of compulsory education. Housing assistance covers the costs of rent and, for homeowners, the costs related to maintenance. As a component of public assistance, housing assistance subsidises a limited amount of rent and remains the primary social benefit for housing costs within Japan's broader social security system.[44] Health assistance, which is provided in kind, is intended to cover

44 Except for the very limited allowance described above in Section II. 2. b) ee).

the cost of healthcare with no out-of-pocket expenses for the recipient[45] (Art. 15). Long-term care assistance provides in-kind services similar to those provided by long-term care insurance.[46] Maternity assistance is a cash benefit that covers childbirth expenses.

The payment of these eight types of assistance is limited. In other words, the costs or services that do not fall within these categories are not covered by social assistance. The existing categories are interpreted relatively flexibly. For instance, the high school education fee (which is not covered by education assistance as it is not part of compulsory education) can be covered under the occupational assistance scheme if deemed helpful for the recipient to increase his/her chances of finding employment.

b) Standards for Public Assistance

The law grants the Minister of Health, Labour and Social Affairs the authority to determine the scope of welfare benefits (Standards for Public Assistance, Art. 8 (1) of the Public Assistance Act). The welfare standards must meet but not exceed individuals' minimum basic needs according to age, sex, household size, area of residence and other relevant circumstances according to type of assistance (Art. 8, para. 2).[47] This administrative norm plays a central role in the public assistance system, as these standards define

45 As mentioned above, social health insurance requires the insured person to pay 30% of the medical fee.

46 Long-term Care Insurance Act, Act No. 123-1997. All individuals aged 65 and older, including those receiving social assistance, are also covered by long-term care insurance. Individuals aged 40-65 years who remain covered by social health insurance (as explained below, recipients of social assistance can maintain their affiliation with their health insurance if they are employed) are also covered by long-term care insurance. Long-term care assistance is primarily intended for those under 65 who are not covered by social health insurance for workers.

47 Public Assistance Act No. 144 of 1950: "Article 8, para. 1: Public assistance shall be provided, based on the level of the demand of a person requiring public assistance, which has been measured according to the standard specified by the Minister of Health, Labour and Welfare, to the extent that makes up the shortfall thereof that cannot be satisfied by the money or goods possessed by said person.(2)The standard set forth in the preceding paragraph shall be one that sufficiently satisfies but shall not exceed the demand pertaining to a minimum standard of living, taking into consideration the age, sex, household composition and location of the person requiring public assistance and any other necessary circumstances according to the type of public assistance", English translation from: < https://www.japaneselawtranslation.go.jp/en/laws/view/24/en> accessed 10.12.2024.

the scope of welfare benefits and the eligibility criteria for receiving public assistance, particularly the amount of livelihood assistance, ensuring that individuals whose income falls below a given threshold qualify for public assistance. Article 8, para. 1 of the Public Assistance Act stipulates that public assistance should be provided based on the need for support, assessed according to the criteria specified by the Minister, to the extent that it compensates for the shortfall that the person's financial capacity cannot cover. From this legal provision, it can be inferred that the criteria for determining both eligibility for public assistance and the level of assistance granted are generally aligned. In practice, however, subtle differences exist between the two; for instance, the assessment of eligibility for public assistance does not initially account for special expenditures, such as housing assistance. These specific benefits are added after determining the total amount of public assistance the individual is eligible to receive.

Despite the critical importance of this administrative norm, the law outlines only very few regulations on how the level of assistance should be determined, leaving significant discretion to the Minister of Health, Labour and Welfare. The law only states that assistance must be set at a level 'capable of maintaining the minimum standards of wholesome and cultured living' (Art. 1), and that the standards for public assistance must consider elements such as age, sex, type of household and place of residence (Art. 8, para. 2). This requirement means that the criteria for determining the minimum standard of living are numerous and varied, while the Public Assistance Act aims to guarantee a universal minimum standard of living for all. The "minimum standard" the law intends to provide is not uniformly defined for everyone.

As mentioned above, the law requires public assistance standards to take several elements such as age, sex, type of household and place of residence into account. Different supplements are provided for certain categories of recipients, including persons with disabilities, single-parent households, or for certain life events, such as pregnancy, childbirth, etc., to address very specific needs. Consequently, the scope of benefits provided is highly personalised.

Table 1 – Example 1
Household consisting of three persons (a couple with one child) [33, 29 and 4 years old] (monthly amount: yen)

District	1st grade-1	1st grade-2	2nd grade-1	2nd grade-2	3rd grade-1	3rd grade-2
Livelihood assistance	158,760	153,890	149,130	149,130	142,760	139,630
Housing assistance (max.)	69,800	44,000	56,000	46,000	42,000	42,000
Total amount	228,560	197,890	205,130	195,130	184,760	181,630

Table 2 – Example 2
Household consisting of three persons (a single parent with two children) [30, 4 and 2 years old] (monthly amount: yen)

District	1st grade -1	1st grade -2	2nd grade-1	2nd grade-2	3rd grade-1	3rd grade-2
Livelihood assistance (including additional allowance for single-parent households)	190,550	185,750	179,270	179,270	171,430	168,360
Housing assistance (max.)	69,800	44,000	56,000	46,000	42,000	42,000
Total amount	260,350	229,750	235,270	225,270	213,430	210,360

Table 3 – Example 3
Single-person household [68 years old] (monthly amount: yen)

District	1st grade-1	1st grade-2	2nd grade-1	2nd grade-2	3rd grade-1	3rd grade-2
Livelihood assistance (including additional allowance for elderly persons)	77,980	74,690	70,630	70,630	67,740	66,300
Housing assistance (max.)	53,700	34,000	43,000	35,000	32,000	32,000
Total amount	131,680	108,690	113,630	105,630	99,740	98,300

Source: Ministry of Health, Labour and Welfare.

The districts are established within municipalities, based on the level of consumption expenditure of the residents in each municipality.

c) How Are Minimum Standards Determined and Adjusted?

aa) Maintaining a Certain Distinction Between these Standards and those of the Average Household

Although there are no legal requirements on the frequency of revisions, the minimum standards are typically reviewed every five years.[48] As mentioned earlier, this ministerial decision only includes a few legal provisions, leaving the Minister with significant room for discretion. Within this broad discretion, the Minister has revised these standards by sometimes explicitly and sometimes implicitly combining various considerations. Until 1961, the minimum living standard was determined in absolute terms (known as the "market basket" method), but this approach has since 1965 gradually shifted towards a method that aligns the welfare standard more closely with the standard of living of ordinary households. A significant shift occurred in Japan's understanding of poverty, moving from the concept of absolute poverty to relative poverty. There has not been a complete break, however, as the minimum standards continue to be determined based on the previous standards set by the market basket method, while adjusting the overall amounts.[49] Since 1984, the living standards of households receiving public assistance have been considered to have reached a certain baseline. As a result, according to the Ministry's official explanation, welfare standards have been adjusted to maintain the then-existing level of disparity with the living standards of ordinary households. Specifically, the revision of the minimum standards has generally been based on the growth rate of private final consumption expenditure, incorporating a wide range of available statistical data.[50] In recent revisions, the adjustments made have ensured that the amount of assistance provided aligns with the consumption levels of the bottom 10 per cent of households. Not surprisingly, there has been considerable criticism of the lack of democratic control in the determina-

48 Nevertheless, this does not mean that the amount of all types of assistance is revised and modified every five years.

49 During the revision process, the discussions on relative and absolute poverty are often blurred. For more details, see R. Iwanaga, *Seikatsu-hogo ha saitei-seikatsu wo dō kō-sō shitaka*/ How Has Public Assistance Conceived Minimum Living Standards? (Mineruva Shobō 2011), pp. 157 ff.

50 "The National Household Income and Expenditure Survey" conducted by the Ministry of Internal Affairs and Communications is the main source used, but other materials and data have not been excluded.

tion of these minimum standards as well as the intransparency of the decision-making process.[51]

As mentioned earlier, these minimum standards serve as both criteria for determining the level of public assistance and for determining the conditions for eligibility, meaning that public assistance is granted if the applicant's income and assets fall below this threshold.

bb) Welfare Level and Minimum Wage

In Japan, the Minimum Wage Act[52] provides for the setting of minimum wages in each region (prefecture). According to Article 9 (para. 2), workers' cost of living is one of the factors considered when setting the minimum wage, in addition to the wages and financial capacity of enterprises in the region. The Act further stipulates that the consideration of workers' cost of living must align with measures related to public assistance to ensure that workers can maintain the minimum standard for a wholesome and cultured life (para. 3). Prior to the 2000 amendment, which introduced this provision, the minimum wage level was so low that even full-time workers who earned minimum wage made less than the amount provided by public assistance. The minimum wage level has gradually but steadily increased since this amendment and has largely resolved this so-called "reverse phenomenon" for full-time workers.

cc) Constitutional Review of the Standards for Public Assistance

The level of welfare benefits and any reductions can be challenged in court. As the level of public assistance is determined by ministerial decree based on the criteria described above,[53] the issue is whether the administrative legislation falls within the scope of the discretion conferred on the Minister by the Public Assistance Act, and whether the right to subsistence, as required by the Constitution, is adequately reflected in the welfare benefits being provided.

---

51 See R. Iwanaga (n 49), pp. 302, 303.
52 Minimum Wage Act (Act No. 137 of 1959).
53 See Section III.1.b).

Japanese courts, including (and especially) the Supreme Court, have generally been reluctant to review the constitutionality of legislation,[54] a tendency that is even more obvious in cases concerning social security legislation related to Article 25 of the Constitution.[55] As noted above, the Supreme Court has repeatedly held that "the minimum standards of wholesome and cultured living" is an extremely abstract and relative concept, the specific scope of which must be determined in relation to the level of cultural development, economic and social conditions, and the general standard of living. According to the Supreme Court, when translating such provisions into actual legislation, the State's financial situation cannot be ignored and thus requires complex, multifaceted and highly technical considerations, along with policy judgments based on these considerations. Therefore, the decision on specific legislative measures to fulfil the purpose of Article 25 of the Constitution is left to the broad discretion of the legislature and is generally not subject to judicial review, except in cases where it is deemed extremely unreasonable and must be considered a clear excess or abuse of discretion.[56] The Supreme Court has also recognised that these principles apply not only to parliamentary legislation but also to administrative legislation.[57]

In a Supreme Court decision of 2012, where the reduction of welfare payments for the elderly was challenged as contradicting Article 25 of the Constitution as well as Article 3 and 8, para. 2 of the Public Assistance Act,[58] the Court reviewed the criteria for judicial oversight of the Ministry's broad discretion on public assistance standards. According to this decision,

---

54 The Supreme Court has so far declared only 11 laws to be unconstitutional. See also K. Tonami, 'Judicial review in Japan and its problems' Waseda Bulletin of Comparative Law 33(2015), pp. 1-11, available at < https://www.waseda.jp/folaw/icl/assets/uploads/2015/09/1-11-Judicial-Review-in-Japan-and-its-Problems.pdf.> accessed 10.12.2024.

55 T. Yamamori and Y. Vanderborght (n 8), p. 3. See also H. Sasanuma, 'La justiciabilité des droits sociaux au Japon, la revue des droits de l'homme' (2012), pp. 195 ff. < https://revdh.files.wordpress.com/2012/04/la-justiciabilitc3a9-des-droits-sociaux-au-japon.pdf> accessed 10.12.2024.

56 The Horiki case, Supreme Court (7 July 1982) 36-7 *Minshū* 1235.

57 The Asahi case (n 33), Supreme Court (28 Feb. 2012) 66-3 *Minshū* 1240.

58 Decision of Third Petty Bench, 28 February 2012, *Minshū*, vol. 6, n° 3, p. 1240. As mentioned above, sec. II. 2. b) bb), these two articles directly refer to the constitutional right to life guaranteed by Art. 25 of the Constitution. Therefore, the Supreme Court has, in litigation concerning the minimum standard of living, assessed consistency not directly with Art. 25 of the Constitution but with these two provisions of the Public Assistance Act.

determining whether there has been an excess or abuse of administrative discretion requires consideration of the following two factors: 1) errors or omissions in the Ministry's decision-making procedure and process, and 2) whether the decision to adopt measures such as a gradual reduction of benefits based on recipients' expectations and the impact on their life. In other words, while the judiciary remains reluctant to determine the minimum standard of living guaranteed by the Constitution, it is willing to exercise a certain, albeit limited, degree of oversight over the ministerial decision-making process.

Today, litigation is underway over the reduction in public assistance levels between 2013 and 2015 on the grounds of falling prices due to deflation. The decision-making framework set out by the Supreme Court in 2012 has been used by the lower courts, with several of their judgments finding that the reductions violated the Public Assistance Act due to errors and omissions in the decision-making process.[59] In June 2025, the Supreme Court ruled that the drastic cuts in public livelihood assistance benefits infringed upon the Public Assistance Act (Art. 3 and Art. 8, para 2),[60] marking the first recognition that the government's livelihood assistance standards could be unlawful. According to the decision, the indicators used to adjust welfare benefit levels to account for deflation were not in line with experts' opinions. The Court has therefore recognised "errors and omissions in the decision-making procedure and process",[61] following the framework proposed by the Supreme Court decision in 2012.

dd) Adjusting Public Assistance Benefits to the Circumstances of Individuals and Households

The scope of benefits is determined once the social welfare office has reviewed the individual's application and approved his/her request for assistance. To define the precise scope and type of support needed, the social welfare office applies the benefits standards outlined in Article 8

59 See, for example, Nara District Court (11 April 2023), available on the Courts' website < https://www.courts.go.jp/app/files/hanrei_jp/040/092040_hanrei.pdf> accessed 10.12.2024. One of the key issues at stake is which data to use to determine the average household's level of consumption.

60 See n 58.

61 Decision of Third Petty Bench, 27 June 2025.

of the Public Assistance Act. This ensures that the assistance provided to the individual meets his/her needs: in line with the Public Assistance Act, which requires that the assistance provided is 'effective and adequate' (Art. 9), the social welfare office reviews the needs of the individual and the household in terms of age, sex, health conditions, etc.[62] The Public Assistance Act places strong emphasis on addressing the specific needs of each individual and household, which underpins both the criteria for defining the minimum standard of living and the individual decision to grant the applicant public assistance. The law thus ensures that the assistance provided to each beneficiary (individual or household) must correspond, as closely as possible to his/her individual and specific needs.

For example, an applicant with a child in school, who owns an own home, and suffers from health problems, may receive a combination of livelihood assistance, education assistance and healthcare assistance. An applicant without children and no health problems, but who has difficulty paying rent, may be eligible for housing assistance in addition to livelihood assistance. The provision of only health assistance is also possible if the out-of-pocket costs for medical care impose a heavy financial burden on the applicant, who is otherwise capable of supporting him-/herself.

2. Conditions for Receiving Benefits

One important feature of public assistance is its subsidiary nature (principle of subsidiarity, Art. 4 of the Public Assistance Act). Welfare payments are subject to a strict means test and are only provided when the household's income and assets fall below a minimum standard of living. A situation of need is thus a primary condition for eligibility for public assistance benefits. In addition, as a general rule, individuals are required to utilise any available assets and explore all feasible employment opportunities (b), and apply for any other available social benefits (c). Furthermore, within the scope of the maintenance obligations under the Civil Code, support from family members is, in principle, given priority (d).

---

62 Public Assistance Act (Act No. 144 of 1950), Article 9: "Public assistance shall be provided effectively and appropriately by taking into consideration the differences between the actual needs of individuals or households, such as the age, sex and health conditions of the person requiring assistance".

a) Situation of Need (Means Test)

aa) Standards for Public Assistance as an Income Threshold

Since the Public Assistance Act protects all individuals in need, the only condition an applicant must fulfil to receive welfare benefits is to be in a situation of need (for example, there is no condition related to age).

When the standard of living of the applicant's household falls below the threshold established by these criteria, the social welfare office provides support to bridge the gap between the household's standard of living and the minimum standard of living. The livelihood assistance criteria play a decisive role in practice. As mentioned above, the amount of public assistance, including livelihood assistance, is determined based on various factors related to the applicant's household (household size, the age of household members, location of the household, etc.). The social welfare office primarily assesses whether the household's income falls below the established threshold for the minimum standard of living, while ensuring that all of the applicant's assets exceeding the minimum necessity have been fully exploited. Regarding assets, by way of example, the applicant may keep his/her residence, unless its disposal value is significantly higher than its use value. The determination of whether household necessities, such as household appliances, meet the minimum necessity standard is based on whether they are widely owned by the average household in the area where the applicant lives.

In some cases, the social welfare office may advise applicants to relinquish certain assets to qualify for public assistance. For example, the possession of a car is not permitted unless a special need for one is recognised.

bb) Households

Whether an individual qualifies for public assistance and, if so, what type/level of assistance he/she is entitled to, is determined on a 'household-by-household' basis (Art. 10 of the Public Assistance Act). This approach is justified by the notion that the need for and scope of assistance should align with the individual's actual living conditions. However, the application of this rule, in many cases, has a similar de facto effect of requiring members of the same household to support each other financially, which raises theoretical concerns about its relationship with both the legal obligation to support family members and the principle of subsidiarity (supra.).

In certain situations, the law also allows for the exceptional division of a household into separate units. One example of this is when a child from a household that receives public assistance wishes to attend university and earns his/her own tuition fee or has received a scholarship. In such cases, the child can be formally excluded from the household for public assistance purposes. This allows the child to attend university on his/her part-time salary or scholarship, while continuing to live with his/her family. The child's income is not included in the calculation of the household's income. The social welfare office has a certain degree of discretion in deciding whether to separate a household into different units.

b) Exhausting One's Earning Capacity

The requirement to exhaust one's earning capacity is not easy to apply, given each applicant's distinct and complex situation. Depending on the applicant/recipient's circumstances, three factors are considered in practice: i) his/her ability to work, ii) his/her willingness to work, and iii) the availability of job opportunities. For the sake of simplicity, let us assume that the individual is currently unemployed (although, in reality, public assistance may be provided even while an individual is employed, if his/her wage income is insufficient to maintain a minimum standard of living). When the applicant is 65 years or older, the social welfare office generally treats the individual as lacking capacity for work. In other words, the requirement to exhaust one's earning capacity does not, in practice, apply to elderly persons in need. This is also the case for those with a significant disability and are therefore considered to lack capacity for work. For individuals who are theoretically able to work, both their willingness to work and the availability of job opportunities are examined. If the individual is willing to work but no job opportunity is available, he/she is deemed to have exhausted his/her earning capacity. Some scholars argue that an individual's willingness to work is an irrelevant factor, erroneously emphasising moral judgment. However, it seems that this factor might, in some cases, be useful when considered in relation to available job opportunities; if a person is actively seeking employment (*i.e.* is willing to work) but cannot find a job, it can logically be inferred that no suitable job opportunities are available for him/her.

The principle of subsidiarity applies not only when making the decision to grant public assistance but also throughout the period during which the recipient receives assistance. In this context, the social welfare office can give instructions to recipients to undertake efforts to find employment (or to increase their income if they are already working; Art. 27 of the Public Assistance Act).[63] If the recipient fails to comply with these instructions and does not undertake the necessary efforts to find a job, public assistance can be reduced, temporally suspended or terminated (Art. 62, paras. 1 and 3). The instructions must be clear and documented to justify any unfavourable decisions regarding the recipient's eligibility for assistance.[64] The social welfare offices have broad discretion over these instructions, including their content (such as specifying the use of savings, if any, for certain purposes or reminding recipients of their legal obligation to accurately declare their income, etc.) and the timing of the issuance of instructions (if and when such instructions are given), as well as the content and timing of any measures taken in response to non-compliance.[65]

c) Exploitation of All Other Social Benefits

The Public Assistance Act also requires all other social benefits to have been fully exploited before the person is granted public assistance benefits (Art. 4, para. 2 of the Public Assistance Act). Individuals in need should

---

63 Article 27 of the Public Assistance Act states that "a public assistance implementing agency may give a recipient guidance or instructions necessary for maintaining or improving his or her livelihood or otherwise achieving the objectives of public assistance." This means that the guidance and instructions are not limited to those related to the principle of subsidiarity. However, the guidance and instructions related to this principle are a typical and significant example of instructions given on the basis of this article.

64 Apart from these instructions, which may be linked to unfavourable measures, social welfare offices can also offer advice to individuals in need (including those not yet receiving public assistance), but only upon their request (Art. 27-2), without any negative consequences if the individual does not follow the office's advice. Thus, communications of a varied legal nature coexist in the casework routinely carried out by social welfare offices.

65 This, however, does not exclude the possibility that certain instructions and unfavourable measures may be annulled if they exceed the scope of discretion granted by the Public Assistance Act. Courts often deem the termination of assistance illegal when such a measure is taken without first considering more moderate alternatives, such as a reduction in the level of assistance. See, for example, Yamaguchi District Court judgment, 19 October 2022.

first apply for and make use of the different social benefits indicated above (Section II.2.) and can only access public assistance if they are still unable to maintain a minimum standard of living. The accumulation of public assistance with other social benefits is only possible to the extent that they are insufficient for maintaining the minimum standard of living.

d) Support Obligation of Family Members

The Public Assistance Act stipulates that assistance from family members who have a legal obligation to support the person in need as defined in the Civil Code (*Miinpo*) should take precedence over the provision of public assistance (Art. 4, para. 2 of the Public Assistance Act). This component of the principle of subsidiarity differs slightly in nature from this principle's other elements mentioned earlier; it is not a requirement for the public assistance applicant to request or ensure that his/her support obligations are fulfilled by family members. However, the social welfare office can contact the applicant's family members if they have the financial means to support him/her and encourage them to support the person in need – without, however, being able to enforce this obligation. They may also inquire with public authorities or private entities, such as banks or the family members employers, to determine whether they have the capacity to support the applicant (Art. 28, para. 2, Art. 29 of the Public Assistance Act). If the family member(s) agree(s) to support the applicant but this support it is still insufficient to meet the minimum standard of living, the applicant can receive public assistance benefits to cover the difference.

The Civil Code establishes support obligations for two groups of relatives; the first group includes immediate family members, including brothers and sisters (Art. 877, para. 1 of the Civil Code). The second group consists of third-degree relatives, who may be required to provide support if ordered to do so by a family court ruling (Art. 877, para 2). Current administrative practice encourages the fulfilment of support obligations without differentiating between these two groups, which is considered problematic in legal doctrine because it contradicts the abovementioned family law framework established by the Civil Code (family members in the second group are only required to provide support if ordered by a family court).

IV. Concluding Remarks

Japan's social security system is designed to uphold the universal and constitutional right to life guaranteed by Article 25 of the Constitution based on two primary pillars: 1) social insurance as a mechanism for preventing poverty and 2) public assistance as a means of alleviating poverty. As mentioned in the introduction, the system's structure appears relatively straightforward on paper, with Article 25 serving as its foundation. From a social insurance perspective on poverty prevention, one key feature is the universal applicability of the two main social insurance schemes – healthcare and pensions. However, as discussed in this contribution, significant gaps exist in this so-called "universal" social insurance system, particularly concerning part-time workers. On the other hand, public assistance is regulated by the strict principle of subsidiarity, making access to the system challenging, especially for the working poor. Moreover, the level of public assistance does not, in practice, guarantee a uniform minimum standard of living for all citizens; instead, it varies according to each individual's circumstances. Thus, Japan's social security system, which on paper appears to have a simple structure, must be understood and discussed in a more nuanced way.

From a legal perspective, Japan's system of minimum income guarantee is implemented by the Public Assistance Act, which directly embodies and realises Article 25 of the Constitution. On the other hand, its role in judicial review remains relatively limited. In other words, the minimum standard of living guaranteed by Article 25 of the Constitution is in most cases determined by the Public Assistance Act and by the Minister of Health, Labour and Welfare (who sets the standards for public assistance). As pointed out several times already, the Public Assistance Act, which plays a crucial role, is characterised by very broad administrative discretion in two aspects: first, ministerial discretion determines the scope of the minimum standard of living, meaning that the scope of constitutional human rights is left almost entirely in the hands of the executive; as noted in the analysis, this process for exercising such discretion lacks transparency, and despite longstanding criticism in the past, there have so far been no indications of reform. Second, the social welfare offices have broad discretion in applying the minimum standards set by the executive to individual recipients, in conducting the casework and following up with the recipient households to ensure that public assistance is provided appropriately. Although this mechanism aligns with the law's purpose—ensuring that minimum living standards are tailored as closely as possible to the needs of individuals and households—the broad discretion places a burden on caseworkers, and unfortunately, there have also been numerous court rulings deeming the exercise of this discretion is unlawful.[66] Despite the compelling constitutional declaration of the right to life, there is still much room for improvement towards fully realising a life in dignity in Japan.

66 See n 65.

The Guarantee of a Minimum Standard of Living in the Republic of Korea: A Constitutional and Social Security Law Perspective

Kwang Seok Cheon

I. Introduction

The Republic of Korea is still falling behind in its mission to guarantee a minimum standard of living for its citizens. According to a 2021 survey, the national poverty rate stood at 23.2 per cent, yet only 4.8% per cent of the population were recipients of social benefits.[1] The poverty rate among the elderly is particularly severe at around 38 per cent, the highest among OECD member states.[2] However, only about 10 per cent in this group receive welfare support.[3]

Several questions arise in relation to the right to a minimum standard of living. The first concerns whether the right to a minimum has binding force within the legal system, and how it can be effectively implemented. This is fundamentally a question of constitutional interpretation, specifically whether the normative and practical limitations that typically apply to the implementation of basic social rights also apply to the enforceable right to a minimum standard of living, or whether the unique characteristics of this right lead to a different conclusion in a constitutional review. Second, the relationship between the legal and policy spheres must be explored, specifically how each sphere contributes to the broader goal of guaranteeing a minimum standard of living. Within this comprehensive understanding, the guarantee of the right to a minimum standard of living could be integrated into the constitutional framework, transforming abstract principles and guidelines into concrete criteria for policymaking, legislation and constitutional review. Given that the constitutional clauses on human dignity (Art. 10) and the basic social right to a decent life (Art. 34), later illustrated, permeate nearly all legal and institutional domains, it is important to include them in this analysis. This will further deepen our understanding of the guarantee of a minimum standard of living, which is an essential step towards effectively understanding, evaluating and advancing the core principles of the welfare state. It should be also noted that the provision of personal social services for the elderly, children and persons with disabilities plays a leading role in functionally complementing social insurance

1 T. Kim and S. Han, *Basic research on social security reform to eliminate welfare no-care zone* (Korea Institute for Health and Welfare 2023), p. 72, 171.

2 Ministry of Health and Welfare, *The Health and Welfare White Book* (2023), p. 408. This estimation was, however, to some degree inflated because it was based on income without taking assets into account.

3 Ministry of Health and Welfare (n 2), p. 105.

and public assistance schemes. The same holds true for the functional cooperation between national health insurance and public health policy.

This chapter, however, focuses exclusively on public assistance and social insurance, which are the primary instruments to realise individuals' subjective right to a decent life and serve to fulfil the State's corresponding responsibilities. Public assistance belongs to the last-resort safety net within the social protection system and aims directly to guarantee a minimum standard of living. In the face of social and economic changes, public assistance today evolves to target specific groups of individuals (e.g. the elderly poor) and those in need of support (e.g. the working poor). But social insurance to some extent also contributes in its own way towards ensuring a minimum standard of living.

II. Overview

The constitutional aspects of a minimum standard of living protection must be examined from two perspectives. First, the relevant principles and basic social rights of the constitution need to be deductively translated into social security legislation, with universal protection against poverty and adequacy of benefits and of their amount as elements. These aspects are expected to guide legislative discretion, which is generally afforded wide recognition, on the one hand, and to provide criteria for effective judicial review, on the other. Second, constitutional law is developed inductively, with stable and meaningful content formed by concrete social security legislation and institutions that refine the interaction between the two. The legislative and institutional consensus around specific goals, such as maintaining minimum living standard for a healthy and cultural life (Art. 4 of the National Basic Livelihood Security Act), serves to innovate the constitutional ideas and principles. Constitutional law is thereby enriched by socially favourable elements that are necessary to ensure the continued vitality of the constitution. This reduces the discrepancy between higher and lower norms, as well as between legal norms and fact.

1. Constitutional Law

a) Basic Social Rights Related to the Guarantee of a Minimum Standard of Living

The Republic of Korea's constitutional law enshrines the protection of human dignity as a core constitutional principle (Art. 10), which is closely tied to the basic social right to a decent life through social security (Art. 34). Every citizen is entitled to this right (Art. 34, para. 1), and the State has the obligation to promote social security and welfare (Art. 34, para. 2). The Constitution specifically mandates the protection of citizens who are unable to earn a livelihood due to physical disability, illness, old age or other causes under the conditions prescribed by the act (Art. 34, para. 5). Additionally, the State has the obligation to establish a social and economic order that extends beyond the political one. This obligation is articulated through the guarantee of various basic social rights (Arts. 31-36) and through a separate chapter in the Constitution that covers the economic order (Chapter 9, Arts. 119-127). Taken together, these provisions affirm that every citizen has the right to a minimum standard of living, with the State bearing responsibility to ensure its protection.

In addition to the right to a minimum standard of living in Art. 34, other basic social rights, such as the right to education (Art. 31), the right to work (Art. 32), and the right of workers to organise, bargain collectively and take collective action (Art. 33) are importantly linked to the State's obligation to guarantee a minimum standard of living. The right to education is related with the task of the guaranteeing a minimum standard of living in two ways. Above all, it provides individuals with the chance of an equal starting point, equipping them with the general and professional knowledge and skills necessary to be able to lead a decent life. Passively speaking, it prevents them from falling into poverty. This right should be reflected in social policies aimed at ensuring a minimum standard of living, for example, by being treated as a distinct component among the benefits provided to guarantee a minimum standard of living.

The right to work (Art. 32) entails more than just access to employment; it also guarantees the working conditions necessary for individuals to be able to lead a decent life. In the Republic of Korea, the main instruments of social security are the social insurances. They are predominantly financed through contributions based on workers' incomes. Consequently, individuals without employment cannot afford to maintain their current standard of living due to lost income, let alone prepare for their future living expenses with the help of social insurance benefits. This increases their risk of falling into poverty. Workers' rights (Art. 33) are functionally related to the right to work. In the bargaining process on working conditions, workers generally do not have equal bargaining power compared to their employers. Workers' rights to association, collective bargaining and action empower them to counterbalance this disparity. Based on this they will be able to reach improved working conditions at either their individual workplaces or across the entire industry. If such improvements are expanded over time, they can, in turn, contribute to strengthening the relevant legislation, such as the Labour Standards Act, in favour of workers. The foundations of social security would thereby be further solidified. In order to maintain the effects of such reforms, it is essential that the solidarity and scope of labour union activities are sustainable. If part-time workers are separated from regular workers in the process of bargaining over working conditions, the labour force becomes fragmented. As a result, improving their working conditions and expanding their access to social security would remain a distant goal.

b) Economic Order

Article 119 of the Constitution declares the principle of a free market economy order (para. 1) while also empowering the State to regulate and coordinate economic activities to maintain balanced growth and stability of the national economy, ensure proper distribution of income, prevent market domination and abuse of economic power, and finally the democratization of the economy through harmony among the economic actors (para. 2). Preventing market dominance and the abuse of economic power are essential for the market to function properly. From a social order perspective, such measures also contribute to guaranteeing the social protection of labour which is inherently shaped by market dynamics. In addition, a proper distribution of income aligns with the goals of the social order, ensuring that workers' incomes cover substantially both their present and future livelihood needs. The Constitution generally conceives the relationship between capital and labour as one of confrontation and cooperation. From this constitutional conception, it could be inferred that the capital supports and protects workers' social problems. This is particularly discussed in terms of the possibility of social insurance protection for labour providers who are not employed by a particular employer but economically dependent on him, and the need to protect them against the risk of falling into poverty.[4]

c) Constitutional Review

aa) Overview

The Constitution of 1987 introduced the possibility of lodging constitutional complaints. Several such complaints have challenged whether delayed legislative and administrative measures in public assistance violate related basic social rights. None of the constitutional complaints in these cases were successful,[5] but the possibility of a constitutional review on this theme as such sparked much of the constitutional discourse about the conformity of State action with basic individual rights.

Until the late 1990s, legislation guaranteeing minimum standard of living lacked the appropriate norm structure to provide recipients with the necessary benefits. As a result, constitutional complaints were often filed against the low benefits levels that fell below the minimum cost of living. However, the Constitutional Court hesitated to acknowledge the right to a minimum standard of living as one that is directly enforceable. Since then, this position has essentially remained unchanged.[6]

The reasons were multiple. First, the constitutional nature of the right to a minimum standard of living standard has been negated, inferring that the general logic inherent to basic social rights is applicable to the right to a minimum standard of living as well. This means that the State's obligation to guarantee a minimum standard of living only turns into an individually enforceable right once concretely enacted by the legislature taking various factual circumstances such as public financial capacity, into account. Second, the concept of a decent life is an abstract and relative

4 For a detailed analysis of reforms addressing these challenges in industrial accident compensation insurance and employment insurance, see II.2.a) dd) and II.2.a) ee).

5 On an analysis and critical review of constitutional decisions on the National Basic Livelihood Security Act, see K. Cheon, *Social Security Law and Constitutional Review* (Gyphyenjae 2021), pp. 291 ff.; S. Hong, 'Study on the Conditional Livelihood Benefits in the National Basic Living Security Act – With Comment on the Decision of Korean Constitutional Court on the Article 15 of National Basic Living Security Act' Journal of Legislation Studies 16 (2019)2, pp. 54 ff.

6 On the first case, see Decision of 1997.5.29., 94 Hun-Ma 33, 9-1, pp. 543 ff.

one, and its realization largely depends on cultural development, historical background and socio-economic circumstances. As a result, both the scope and level of the minimum measures required to secure a minimum standard of living are open and variable. Third, the minimum measures required to ensure a decent life vary significantly, depending on elements such as national awareness, socio-economic circumstances and their ongoing changes. Accordingly, when determining the level of benefits required to ensure a minimum standard of living, complex and various elements such as national income, national living standard, public financial capacity and policy, and conflicting interests should be comprehensively taken into account as a whole. In this context, the legislature and executive enjoy a broad scope of discretion.

Against this background, the Constitutional Court reviewed constitutional complaints using moderate criteria and less intensively. It has repeatedly stated that the provisions concerned violate the state obligation only if their content is deemed so obviously unreasonable as to clearly deviate from the broadly approved discretion. The constitutional scrutiny typically proceeded as follows. First, the constitutional conformity cannot be judged by the low level of livelihood benefits under the National Basic Livelihood Security Act alone. Instead, the assessment must consider the aggregate level of support, including benefits, allowances, subsidies or exemptions from payments provided under other regulations and institutional policies as well. Secondly, it then examines whether this aggregated amount corresponds to a minimum standard of living calculated in a reasonable way, and whether it deviates from the legislative and administrative discretion. In contrast, the significance of the state obligation to guarantee a minimum living standard, from the ideal, normative and factual perspective described below, was not speculated on.

bb) Critical Remarks

Ideally, the minimum standard of living should be absolutely guaranteed, as it is the most fundamental precondition for human dignity and the free development of the individual. From the perspective of equality, all individuals should be equal at least in terms of the minimum standard of living. It is also worth considering that citizens should be able to participate in social life and integrated into social communication. In this sense, the guarantee of a minimum standard of living represents an essential foundation for further social integration.

The normative obstacles to realising basic social rights as enforceable legal entitlements do not generally apply in the same way and degree of intensity to the right to a minimum standard of living. The concept of basic social rights expressed in the constitutional provisions is admittedly understood as being open-ended and adaptable, largely leaving their substantive concretisation to legislative discretion. In contrast, the scope and level of benefits necessary to guarantee a minimum living can, to some extent, be directly derived from constitutional provisions and their interpretation.

Basic needs for physical subsistence, a healthy and cultural living, and opportunities for socio-economic participation are indispensable for ensuring human dignity. In this respect, the principle and normative guidelines of the basic social right to a minimum standard of living are clearly articulated in the Constitution. However, this aspect has often been neglected in the constitutional review process, which tends to emphasise the ambiguity of the concept and the varying factual circumstances that contribute to the difficulties in its realisation.[7]

Determining the level of benefits necessary to ensure a minimum standard of living is undoubtedly primarily left to legislative and administrative discretion. However, the possibility to review scope, content and level of benefits based on constitutional law remains. This is justified by the fact that the content of the minimum standard of living can, at least in principle, be derived from the relevant constitutional clause and its interpretation as has been shown above. On this normative ground, the Constitutional Court should be authorised and in fact obligated, even taking the policy discretion into account, to apply the constitutional guidelines, and at the very least to establish a baseline that is applicable in constitutional reviews. The intensity of constitutional review may vary depending on the issue under review and whether it concerns basic needs for physical subsistence or the opportunity to participate in socio-economic and cultural life.[8]

Normative challenges surrounding the realisation of basic social rights through state action arise due to potential conflicts between third parties' competing interests and the general interest. The right to work serves as a

7 To date, the Constitutional Court has hesitated to enforce this perspective, see Decision of 2004.10.28, 2002 Hun-Ma 328, 16-2(2), p. 204.

8 In the decision concerning the subjective right to benefits for veterans, the Constitutional Court implied this position, which, however, has not been further developed, see Decision of 1995.7.21., 93 Hun-Ga 14, 7-2, p. 31.

notable example, insofar as it has to be balanced against the employer's occupational freedom (Art. 15). The right to work cannot be enforced by imposing unreasonable obligations or financial burdens on employers. However, this is not the case for the right to a minimum standard of living, because its realisation is grounded in a more straightforward, bilateral relationship of right and obligation between the individual and the State.

Lastly, it is important to acknowledge that public financial capacity generally plays a significant role in the implementation of basic social rights; however, in the case of the right to a minimum standard of living its role is not as decisive as it may be for other basic social rights. Accordingly, the logic of public finance should not be treated as absolute. Instead, it should be reserved to decision making determining financial priorities across different policy fields. Given the fundamental significance of the right to a minimum livelihood from both an ideal and normative perspective, policy priorities should rather centre around it.

2. Social Benefits

a) Overview of Social Insurance Schemes

Since the mid-1970s, the Republic of Korea has actively advanced legislation across various branches of social insurance. The National Health Insurance Act, the National Pension Service Act, and the Employment Insurance Act were enacted in 1976, 1986 and 1993, respectively. In response to the growing need for long-term care, the Long-term Care Insurance Act for the Elderly was introduced in 2007.

aa) National Health Insurance Act

The National Health Insurance (NHI) aims to support the prevention and treatment of diseases, thereby promoting the population's overall health. However, it does not cover loss of income resulting from illness. Currently, around 97 per cent of the population is covered by the NHI, while the remaining citizens are supported under the Medical Care Assistance Act. The NHI does not fully cover the costs of medical treatment. Insured individuals must cover a share of the costs on their own (co-payment). The co-payment rate ranges from 30 per cent to 50 per cent, depending on type of healthcare facility. Medical treatment is provided in accordance with the criteria and procedures specified by the Act. However, due to the co-payment system and the extensive range of uninsured costs, the share of medical costs covered by the NHI remains low at around 63 per cent. The NHI is funded through both employer and employee contributions. In 2024, the contribution rate was 7.07 per cent for insured employers. This rate may be reduced for insured individuals with limited financial ability.

bb) Long-Term Care

Long-term care is provided to insured individuals aged 65 and older, who are no longer able to live their ordinary life independently. Individuals are classified into one of five ratings depending on their level of need. Initially, 4.2 per cent of individuals aged 65 or older were beneficiaries, but this number has rapidly increased in recent years, reaching 10.87 per cent of all persons aged 65 and older in 2022.[9] All individuals insured under the NHI are also insured under the Long-term Care Insurance for the Elderly. Those who are eligible for medical care assistance can also apply for benefits under this scheme.

cc) National Pension Service

Employees, as well as all residents between the ages of 18 and 60, are insured under the National Pension Service (NPS). While the NPS's income security scheme seemingly covers the entire economically active population, many low-income earners do not enrol in the scheme, and legislation does not yet take non-standard forms of employment into account. As a result, the coverage gap within the NPS is significantly wider compared to the NHI. Moreover, the rate of the factually insured individuals among those eligible for the NPS shows a conspicuously large gap between regular work and irregular work. In 2023, 92.7 per cent of regular workers were covered compared to only 40-50 per cent of irregular workers. Accordingly, only 51.2 per cent of eligible individuals are recipients.[10] The scheme is financed through contributions from both the insured workers and their employers. The NPS Act sets the contribution rate at 9.0 per cent. In recent

9 Ministry of Health and Welfare (n 2), p. 397.
10 Ibid., p. 406.

years, discussions have increasingly focused on the possibility of raising this rate to between 13 per cent and 15 per cent over the long term.[11]

The NPS provides pensions to insured persons and their dependents. Dependent pensions are paid as flat-rate payments. Children are eligible under the strict condition; they must be under the age of 19 or severely disabled. The annual benefit amount remains low, namely KRW 293,580 for the beneficiary's spouse, and KRW 195,660 for the beneficiary's children in 2024.[12] Following legislative reforms in 1998 and 2007, the income replacement rate was reduced from approximately 70 per cent to around 60 per cent and finally to 40 per cent. As a result, the pension provided under NPS no longer guarantees recipients belonging to the lower category of income to live a minimum livelihood. This shortfall resulted in the introduction of a basic pension for the elderly, which is discussed below.[13]

When recipients of an old-age pension engage in economic activities that generate income exceeding a prescribed threshold, their pension benefits are reduced by up to 50 per cent. However, this reduction contradicts both the policy objective of occupational promotion for the elderly and the constitutional right to occupation (Art. 15). The discussion about whether it should be abolished is ongoing.

dd) Industrial Accident Compensation Insurance

The Industrial Accident Compensation Insurance (IACI) is a social insurance designed to compensate workers who have suffered an accident at work, including accidents that occurred during their commute to and from work.[14] At the same time, the IACI covers the employer's liability for compensation in case of work accidents, thus exempting the employer from liability to the extent that IACI provides benefits to the worker. The IACI applies in all workplaces that employ workers, with limited exceptions

11 On the reform discussion, see H. Sung, 'Measures and effects of Introducing Automatic Adjustment Mechanism for Financial Stabilization of the National Pension System' Korean Social Security Studies 40 (2024)3, pp. 30 ff.

12 EUR 1 is approximately KRW 1,470 in 2024.

13 See Sec. II.2.b) cc).

14 The IACI was revised to cover this risk, as the Constitutional Court had declared the clause unconstitutional, which does not explicitly enumerate the accidents that occur during the commute to and from work. See Decision of 2016.9.29, 2014 Hun-Ba 254, 28-2(1), pp. 316 ff.

based on factors such as risk level, employer's size, or location of the workplace.

The benefit amount provided by the IACI are based on the average wage. When a worker sustains an illness or injury from a work-related accident, the IACI provides temporary layoff benefits amounting to 70 per cent of the worker's average wage. In case of permanent disability, the worker may receive either a disability pension or a lump-sum compensation, with the pension level ranging from the equivalent of 138 to 329 days of the worker's average wage, depending on the degree of the disability. If the worker dies as a result of a work accident, survivors are entitled to 47 per cent of the deceased's average annual wage.

The IACI is financed through contributions solely paid by employers. The contribution rate varies by industry. In 2022, the average contribution rate across all industries was 1.43 per cent.[15] In order to incentivise employers to invest in the prevention of work accidents, the rate is raised or reduced depending on the individual workplace. If an employer's benefit claims exceed 85 per cent of its contributions or fall below 75 per cent, the contribution rate may be adjusted upward or downward by up to 50 per cent.

ee) Employment Insurance

Employment insurance (EI) was already introduced in 1995. The EI covers the workers and contributions are shared between both employees and employers. During the foreign exchange crisis of 1997 and the global financial crisis of 2008, the Republic of Korea experienced unprecedented levels of unemployment.[16]. Facing this problem, it became urgent to rapidly extend coverage to workers, irrespective of their workplace, as well as to self-employed persons, who can now be insured upon approval by the EI administration.[17]

15 Ministry of Employment and Labour, *Yearbook of Industrial Accident Compensation Insurance* (2022), p. 104.

16 On this emerging problem of unemployment and its social effects, see H. Youn, 'The Current State of the Working Poor and Policy Assessment' Health and Welfare Policy Forum 197 (2013) 3, pp. 33 ff.

17 Employment Insurance Act, No. 19591, 08 Aug, 2023, Art. 2 < https://www.law.go.kr/LSW/eng/engLsSc.do?menuId=2&section=lawNm&query=Employment+Insurance+Act> accessed 22.03.2025.

The EI provides employment security and vocational skills development programmes as active labour market policies. To compensate for loss of income, insured persons are entitled to unemployment benefits and maternal protection benefits. Employment security and vocational skills development programmes are designed to prevent unemployment caused by business fluctuations and industrial restructurings. These programmes are implemented through individual or facility-based support. Unemployment benefits are granted to insured persons who have lost their jobs and are unable to find employment despite being willing and having the capacity for work. Unemployment benefits include job-seeking benefits and employment promotion incentives. Employment promotion allowances include an early reemployment allowance, vocational skills development allowance, wide-area job-search allowance, and relocation allowance. The basis for calculation of the unemployment benefit is the basic daily wage. The maximum of the basic daily wage is in 2024 of KRW 110,000 per day. Job seekers receive 60 per cent of the basic daily wage. The duration of the job-seeking benefits differs according to the recipient's insurance periods. For example, a worker aged 50 or older who has an insurance contribution period of at least 10 years receives job-seeking benefits for a total of 270 days, while those with less than one year of insurance contributions receive such benefits for only 120 days.

b) Overview of Public Assistance Instruments

aa) National Minimum Standard of Living: Historical Overview

The first legislation guaranteeing the minimum standard of living was enacted in 1961. However, its effectiveness was undermined by significant normative shortcomings and financial constraints. At the time, the to a minimum standard of living standard lacked political recognition. Consequently, judicial review was not activated due to insufficient understanding of the specific features of this basic social right.

In light of these challenges and strong criticism, a fundamental reform became necessary. Civil movements advocating for the guarantee of a national minimum standard of living gained traction in the 1980s and contributed to bringing the issue onto the political agenda. The Act of 1961 was repealed in 1999 and replaced by the National Basic Livelihood

Security Act.[18] Under this Act, individuals with a 'recognised income' below the established minimum cost of living become eligible for benefits, regardless of their capacity for work. 'Recognised income' comprises both the individual's assessed income and the value of assets converted into income. This approach has clarified eligibility criteria for benefits, thereby enhancing institutional and legal stability as well as improving practical effectiveness. Benefits are calculated based primarily on the price of a comprehensive basket of goods deemed necessary to maintain a minimum livelihood. The value of this basket is determined annually through a notice issued by the Ministry of Health and Welfare. Consequently, some degree of administrative discretion is inevitable.

The provision of a minimum income has been designed to enable recipients with a capacity for work to continue maintaining their livelihood. This emphasis on self-support aims to empower individuals to overcome their situation of need through their own efforts. Accordingly, individuals who have a capacity for work only receive benefits if they participate in self-support programmes provided by the Act. Through this mechanism, the guarantee of a minimum standard of living was closely connected with employment services. This conditional eligibility did not apply to those who lack the capacity for work.

Despite these reforms, a significant number of individuals remained ineligible for coverage,[19] prompting demands for further reform. This resulted in the amendment of 2014, which is illustrated below. The primary factors that contributed to the gap in coverage were unreasonable subsidiarity clauses concerning family support obligations, on the one hand, and an unrealistic income conversion rate from asset value on the other.[20] Individuals with little or no income were excluded from benefit eligibility if the income converted from their assets' value—primarily housing—exceeded the recognised income threshold, leading them to be practically forced to dispose of their assets. In addition, the assistance for self-support was not

---

18 National Basic Livelihood Security Act, Act No. 6024, Sep. 7, 1999. This was improved by the 2014 reform, as described below in Section III.1.

19 On the achievements and challenges of the 1999 legislation, see K. Cheon (n 5), pp. 310 ff. From the comparative perspectives, this development is reminiscent of the 1954 decision of the Federal Administrative Court of Germany concerning the legal character of social assistance benefits, see BVerwGE p. 1, 159 ff.

20 On the impact of these factors on the Act's disfunction, see M. Kim, 'The Coverage of the National Basic Livelihood Security and Its Policy Implications' Health and Welfare Policy Forum 292 (2021)2, pp. 10 ff.

as effective as intended or anticipated by the legislature at that time. There were concerns that the work incentive would decrease because of livelihood benefits provided to individuals who are capable of work. Consequently, livelihood benefits were disapproved of, when recipients of self-support would earn more than the minimum cost of living, namely the poverty line as defined by the National Basic Livelihood Security Act. Recipients were often found to intentionally avoid economic activities which would raise their income above that minimum threshold, or to not report their full income. These consequences ran counter to the conceptions underlying the National Basic Livelihood Security Act. In addition, the infrastructure and program for employment services were insufficient both in quality and quantity. Resources were largely concentrated on ensuring a minimum standard of living mainly with recipients participating in public works, so that the goal to lift them out of poverty by integrating into the labour market could not be achieved.

These problems prompted the 2014 reform.[21] Until then, eligibility for various types of benefits had been decided according to an integrated requirement, meaning that those who did not meet this requirement were excluded from all kinds of benefits including self-support and medical care assistance. This so-called integrated benefit system discouraged recipients from engaging in economic activities to remain eligible for essential benefits, especially medical care assistance. The reform abolished the integrated requirement, provided mechanisms to expand coverage and revised the method for the calculation of benefits.[22]

bb) Emergency Welfare Assistance

Benefits aimed at guaranteeing a minimum standard of living must be provided in a timely manner to those in need of help or support. The Emergency Welfare Assistance (EWA) Act was enacted in 2005 for those in need who do not meet the eligibility requirements for benefits or where the provision of such benefits is delayed.[23]

---

21 Act No. 12933, Dec. 30, 2014.

22 See Section III.1 below.

23 Emergency Aid and Support Act No. 7739, Dec. 23, 2005.

cc) Basic Pension

Since the 1990s, poverty among the elderly has been widespread in the Republic of Korea and has worsened over time.[24] The ageing society proceeded rapidly. The share of elderly persons in the population increased from 7.2 per cent in 2000 to 11 per cent in 2010, and 14.3 per cent in 2018. By 2023, that share had grown to 18.4 per cent, and projections indicate it will rise further to 20.8 per cent by 2026.[25] The national pension service has been limited in its function to protect the elderly from poverty for both institutional and practical reasons. In the national pension service, the elderly are only entitled to a short period of insurance. Accordingly, the level of pension acquired was low, namely only KRW 594,000 on average. Furthermore, the national minimum standard of living still left the many individuals uncovered mainly due to unreasonable and unrealistic requirements, which were in place until 2014. The basic pension was introduced in 2007 in an attempt to face the problems of ensuring the risk of old age.

dd) Occupational Promotion and Social Assistance Act

Although the working poor emerged as a social issue, the self-support programme under the National Basic Livelihood Security Act of 1999 was not effectively implemented due to the various reasons previously discussed. Employment insurance also failed to address this problem, because its coverage was limited by nature, as social insurance benefits are provided for a relatively short period. In 2019, 45.2 per cent of the employed population remained uncovered, with an even higher rate among irregular workers. The limited function of employment insurance was exemplified by the low rate of recipients: only 1.8 per cent of the working poor aged 20 to 39, and 3.9 per cent of those aged 40 to 64 received the benefit.[26] These gaps in coverage as well as the short duration of the benefits prompted discussions about the need for a new public assistance scheme for unemployed persons. This ultimately resulted in the enactment of the Occupational Promotion and Social Assistance Act in 2020. The Act is targeted at covering individ-

24 See Section I.

25 See Statistics Korea (2025) < http://kostat.go.kr> accessed 22.3.2025.

26 On these statistics, see S. Kang, *A Study on the Establishment of Income Security System Database: Extension and Systematization* (Korea Institute for Health and Welfare 2022); T. Kim and S. Han (n 1), p. 151.

uals who are capable of work and is designed to provide comprehensive job-seeking support services. The content of this legislation and its interaction with the National Basic Livelihood Security Act is discussed below.

III. Analysis

1. Protection of a Minimum Standard of Living

a) Guarantee of the National Minimum Standard of Living

aa) Conditions

Since the 2014 reform, eligibility criteria have been linked to the country's median income rather than to the minimum cost of living. This means that poverty is now taken as relative concept instead of absolute one. This shift assumes the commitment to achieving welfare equality as a dominant idea. The use of median income enhanced institutional stability by reducing the administrative discretion previously granted in determining the minimum cost of living. In 2023, the median income of a single-person household was KRW 2,077,892, and KRW 5,400,964 for a four-person household.[27] The conditions concerning recognised income, family responsibility, and the minimum benefit amount are now applied separately for each type of benefit. To qualify for the minimum livelihood benefit, medical care assistance, education benefit, and housing benefit, recognised income may not exceed 32 per cent, 40 per cent, 50 per cent and 48 per cent of the median income, respectively. The application of the clause of the family responsibility was intended to be discontinued. This requirement was abolished for eligibility to education benefits in 2015 and for housing benefits in 2018. The family responsibility provision continues to apply to the livelihood benefit, if the annual income of the applicant's parental or child household exceeds KRW 100,000,000 or if the value of assets exceeds KRW 900,000,000. This revision has to some extent increased the coverage rate.[28] The next step should be a realistic adjustment of the criteria to the value of assets.

To be eligible for the livelihood benefit, the applicant's recognised income may not exceed KRW 623,368 for a single-person household, and

27 Ministry of Health and Welfare (n 2), p. 32.
28 M. Kim (n 20), pp. 10 f.

KRW 1,036,846 for a two-person household in 2023.[29] However, these thresholds are still unrealistic as the actual minimum living costs amount to KRW 1,166,888 for a single-person household, and KRW 1,956,051 for a two-person household. This benefit applies to foreigners only under very specific circumstances.[30]

bb) Benefits

Various types of benefits are available, including the livelihood benefit, medical care assistance, housing benefit, education benefit, childbirth benefit, funeral benefit and self-support benefit, to ensure recipients can maintain a minimum standard of living.

Benefits provided under the National Basic Livelihood Security Act are intended to guarantee recipients a minimum level of a healthy and cultural life (Art. 4, para. 1). This legislative framework provides a foundation for interpreting the constitutional right to a minimum standard of living as one that protects individuals not only by ensuring mere physical subsistence, but by also enabling meaningful participation in socio-economic and cultural life.[31]

The livelihood benefit aims to secure essential daily needs such as clothing, food, heating, and other forms of cash or in-kind support necessary for basic subsistence. However, this focus on physical subsistence highlights the National Basic Livelihood Security Act's limitation, which tends to neglect the broader aspect of participation in social and cultural life derived from constitutional law. The benefit level is calculated on the statistic base of the median income. This was a peculiar feature of the 2014 reform. Before that the calculation of the benefit amount was based on the minimum cost of living, allowing for a degree of administrative discretion. The minimum livelihood benefit provides the difference between the eligibility threshold and the recipient's recognised income. Nevertheless, questions persist about whether the level of the benefits calculated according to the median income adequately meets the needs for the minimum standard of living. The housing benefit consists of support for rent, maintenance and repair costs necessary to ensure housing stability. The education benefit is provided to individuals who are entering and attending educational

29 Ministry of Health and Welfare (n 2), p. 32.
30 Specified in Act No. 12933, Dec. 30, 2014, Articles 5-2.
31 On the relevant suggestions of the Constitutional Court Decision, see n 8.

institutions such as elementary, middle, and high school, as well as for lifelong learning establishments, etc. It covers school admission and tuition fees, school supplies and other related expenses in cash or in kind. The childbirth benefit provides maternity services and other forms of support before and after childbirth. In the event of a recipient's death, the funeral benefit covers costs for post-mortem examination, transport of the body and cremation or burial. These benefits are paid to the person actually responsible for the funeral arrangements.

Medical care assistance is regulated in the separate Medical Assistance Act (MCA). Under this Act, recipients receive the same medical care as those covered by the National Health Insurance. The costs are fully subsidised by the Medical Care Fund for Type 1, and partially for Type 2 recipients. That means that Type 2 recipients are subject to a co-payment. Recipients of the minimum livelihood benefit are basically classified as Type 1 recipients, while those who are recognised by the Ministry of Health and Welfare as requiring medical care assistance are classified as Type 2 recipients. When the co-payment amount for medical services to be covered by a Type 2 recipient exceeds a specified threshold, the Medical Care Fund of the respective local government covers 50 per cent of the costs. In case recipients are unable to pay even this reduced amount, the Medical Care Fund may cover the costs through subrogation, with recipients expected to repay the amount later without interest.

cc) Self-Sufficiency Support Programmes

Self-support is also recognized among the benefits provided under the National Basic Livelihood Security Act. However, support in the search of employment is provided through a dual system. In 2020, the Act for Occupational Promotion and Social Assistance was introduced for recipients capable of work, functioning as a type of employment policy instrument, as discussed below.[32] This Act replaced relevant provisions of the National Basic Livelihood Security Act to more effectively implement employment services, on the one hand, and to complement the lack of employment insurance benefits for uninsured persons, on the other. However, the National Basic Livelihood Security Act still takes responsibility for recipients

32 See below, Sec. III.2.

of the livelihood benefits.[33] In practice, some overlap between recipients under the Occupational Promotion and Social Assistance Act and those receiving self-support benefits under the National Basic Livelihood Security Act is unavoidable. In practice, the self-support provisions under the National Basic Livelihood Security Act primarily aim to ensure a minimum livelihood on the condition of recipients' participation in the working project provided. The goal to support recipients' integration in the labour market and to thereby lift them out of poverty has not been effectively implemented by the National Basic Livelihood Security Act, which merely provides payments or loans, support for improvement of vocational ability and acquisition of skills, information about job placement, employment opportunities, the leasing of facilities and equipment, support for business start-ups, and benefits for asset-building necessary for self-support.

b) Emergency Welfare Assistance

Under the emergency welfare assistance (EWA) scheme, individuals are eligible for benefits if they are unable to maintain a minimum livelihood for any of the reasons enumerated in the Act, such as the death of the breadwinner, a fire or natural disaster or the breadwinner's loss of employment.[34] Its difference from the national minimum standard is that EWA provides benefits to persons in need of help preliminarily, and then conducts a need and means test afterwards. Benefits are provided not only through applications by individuals themselves or by a third party aware of the person in need's situation, but also ex officio. The EWA also covers foreigners and refugees residing in the country, unlike the minimum livelihood benefit, which primarily applies to Korean citizens. The benefits under the EWA are similar to those available under the National Basic Livelihood Security Act. The livelihood benefit is provided for three months, while other types of benefits are paid for only one month. Coverage can be extended up to twice by one month.

33 On the objective of occupational promotion and social assistance, on the one hand, the self-support of the National Basic Livelihood Security, on the other, see. T. Kim and S. Han (n 1), pp. 129 ff.

34 On the limited function of emergency welfare assistance resulting from this list, see. T. Kim and S. Han (n 1), pp. 84 ff.

2. The Working Poor and the Occupational Promotion and Social Assistance Act

Services aimed at encouraging job-seeking are provided under the Occupational Promotion and Social Assistance Act. To be eligible for these services, individuals must have the ability and willingness to work; their household income may not exceed 120 per cent (for a person aged 18 to 34 years) or 100 per cent (for persons aged 34+) of the average median income. Unlike the more stringent eligibility criteria of the National Basic Livelihood Security Act, the value of assets is not considered. These more moderate eligibility criteria for employment services compared to those for the minimum livelihood benefit is expected to strengthen the work incentives. Moreover, social assistance in the form of a basic livelihood benefit is provided to recipients participating in employment services. However, the income threshold for eligibility to this benefit is stipulated in a stricter way than for access to employment services, as the value of assets is included in the calculation. In addition, applicants must demonstrate a prior work history of at least 100 days or 800 hours. This is considered an indication of their willingness to work.

Occupational promotion services are implemented based on the individualised work activity plan developed in consultation with the recipient. These services include programmes designed to strengthen recipients' willingness to work, enhance their job adaptability and help them acquire the necessary skills for job-seeking. Examples include career motivation counselling, vocational training, start-up support, skills development programmes, etc. The services are provided for one year, with a possible extension of six months. Employment incentives may be granted if a recipient secures employment within a specified period.

The basic livelihood benefit is provided to eligible individuals who participate in the development of their own individual work activity plan and carry out any part thereof. The benefit is paid monthly for a period of six months and amounted to KRW 500,000 in 2023. Admittedly, this modest amount is largely symbolic and insufficient to provide meaningful support, particularly as it falls below the level of the minimum livelihood benefit offered under the National Basic Livelihood Security Act. The benefit can be extended for up to one year upon application. If a recipient earns an income exceeding the monthly benefit amount, payment is suspended. After three or more suspensions, eligibility for the benefit is withdrawn. Employment services benefits are also discontinued if the recipient finds employment or starts a business. Eligibility is also terminated if an individual begins receiving minimum livelihood benefits under the National Basic Livelihood Security Act. However, eligibility for employment services remains unaffected, and individuals may reapply for the basic living benefit after a period of three years.

3. Poverty in Old Age and Basic Pension

a) Conditions and Benefits

The Basic Pension Act, enacted in 2007, provides a basic pension to persons aged at least 65 years whose recognised income falls below a threshold set by the Ministry of Health and Welfare. Notably, the Act itself determines the scope of recipients to be covered: the income threshold for eligibility must ensure that 70 per cent of the total number of persons aged at least 65 years would receive the basic pension. In 2024, the income threshold was KRW 2,130,000 for a single-person household, and KRW 3,408,000 for a two-person household. The basic pension is not provided to recipients of a retirement pension under the Public Officials' Pension Scheme or the Military Pension Scheme.

The amount of the basic pension is calculated differently depending on whether the recipient also receives a national pension. Those who are not eligible for the national pension benefit receive the standard basic pension amount. For those who receive the national pension, the standard pension amount is reduced to prevent overcompensation from overlapping redistributive benefits. However, if a recipient's national pension amount is less than 150 per cent of the standard basic pension, they continue to receive the full amount of the basic pension.

The amount of the basic pension is set at KRW 300,000 in the Basic Pension Act. This amount is however regularly adjusted to changes in the national consumer price index. In 2024, the maximum basic pension was KRW 334,810 for a single-person household, and KRW 535,680 for a two-person household. If both individuals of a couple are eligible for the basic pension, 20 per cent is deducted from their respective basic pension amounts. When the sum of both the recognised income and the basic pension exceed the income threshold, the basic pension is reduced by the amount exceeding that threshold.

b) Balancing Income Security and Poverty Relief

In 2007, the Basic Pension Act was introduced in response to the challenges of a reduction in the level of the national pension and rising poverty among the elderly. At the time, its enactment was a prerequisite for the National Assembly's decision to lower the national pension level. While the basic pension has, to some extent, served to alleviate poverty among the elderly,[35] it has also sparked debate about its role within the country's social security framework. There is ongoing debate on policy choices, in particular whether the basic pension should be treated as one layer in a multi-layered income security system meant to compensate for the reduced national pension level, or as a targeted scheme for the elderly living in poverty in functional cooperation with the general scheme of the National Basic Livelihood Security scheme. In fact, the legislative purpose outlined in the Basic Pension Act was not clearly defined, nor was the guiding principle on which that Act evolves.[36] If the basic pension were intended primarily to serve as one component of a multi-layered income security system, it would function as a selective form of social allowance that abstractly compensate for the reduced income replacement rate set in the National Pension Service. In this interpretation, for instance, the basis pension would be granted regardless of whether recipients also receive national pension, the livelihood benefit, etc. The predetermined threshold, targeting coverage of 70 per cent of the elderly (based on their income level) would systematically align with this concept. Alternatively, if the basic pension were designed specifically to ensure a minimum livelihood for low-income seniors, it would be exclusively provided on account of their low level of recognised income, irrespective of any family responsibility. In that case, the basic pension would be deducted from the minimum livelihood benefit, meaning that if the beneficiary receives a basic pension, the minimum livelihood benefit is reduced proportionally. In the Basic Pension Act, both elements co-exist without any clear coordination.

---

35 To this effect, see W. Lee, *The Elderly Poverty and the Basic Pension: Towards the Reform to Alleviate the Elderly Poverty* (Korea Institute for Health and Welfare 2022), pp. 113 ff.

36 On the related policy choice, see S. Kim, 'A Study on Restructuring of Basic Pension, National Pension and Basic Livelihood Security Program' Korean Social Security Studies 37 (2012)4, pp. 50 ff.; K. Oh, 'A Study on Restructuring of Pension Systems in Korea: Focusing on a 'Multi-Pillar Pensions System by Class' Korean Social Policy Review 28 (2021)4, pp. 139 ff.

It is not the appropriate policy choice to form the basic pension in order to compensate for the reduced income replacement rate of the National Pension Service. For the elderly with a low national pension and for those unable to maintain a minimum standard of living for various reasons, the income replacement rate is not particularly relevant from a social policy perspective. The basic pension should instead be positioned within the system of poverty relief for the elderly, operating in conjunction with the National Pension Service, on the one hand, and with the National Basic Livelihood Security Act, on the other. Within this scenario, the basic pension and the national minimum standard of living standard would stand in a special and general relationship. That is, the elderly should first be eligible for the basic pension with the moderated condition regards the family responsibility as well as the assets assessment, and then subsidiarily for the benefits under the National Basic Livelihood Security scheme as a last-resort social safety net to mitigate poverty among the elderly. In addition, the scope of coverage should be narrowed while increasing the benefit level, thereby ensuring that the basic pension effectively fulfils its purpose of protecting the elderly from falling into poverty.

The concept of a social allowance scheme, or something provisional towards this direction, is completely different and would entail corresponding contents, as mentioned above. The debate surrounding a 'basic income' falls into this category, but represents a departure from the Republic of Korea's current social security framework, which is built on a complex institutional arrangement. Whether adopting such an approach would be appropriate remains a fundamental question.[37]

4. Minimum Wage

The Constitution explicitly mandates the enforcement of a minimum wage scheme (Art. 32, para. 1). An Act on minimum wage was already enacted in 1986 and it applied to all kinds of workplaces. In this respect it differs from the Labour Standards Act, which only covers workplaces with five or more employees. The minimum wage is determined by the Minister of Em-

37 On the discussion about basic income, see H. Noh, 'A Legal Review on Basic Income' Korean Social Security Law 9 (2020)1, pp. 143 ff.; S. Back and S. Lee, 'Debating Universal Basic Income in South Korea' Korean Social Policy Review 25 (2018)3, pp. 37 ff.; J. Lee, *Constitutional Review on Basic Income* (Constitutional Research Institute 2018).

ployment and Labour, subject to deliberation by the Minimum Wage Commission. In determining the minimum wage, factors such as the employee's cost of living, the wage of comparable employees, labour productivity, income distribution, etc. must be considered. The Commission consists of representatives of employees, employers and the public interest. The minimum wage was unrealistically low for quite some time, but has been raised significantly in recent years. In 2018, it was 16.4 per cent while by 2024, it amounted to KRW 9,860 per hour, or KRW 2,060,740 per month.

The minimum wage is intended to serve as both an economic benchmark for workers' livelihoods and a financial resource of contributions to social insurance. Through this, a functional cycle of adequate income distribution in the labour market and corresponding welfare provision evolves.

5. Social Insurance and the Guarantee of a Minimum Standard of Living

a) Elements for Guaranteeing a Minimum Standard of Living in Social Insurance

As mentioned above, social insurance does not directly aim to guarantee a minimum standard of living for the entire population or even for all insured persons. It is inherent to social insurance to maintain, at least to some extent, the standard of living the individual achieved during his or her working years, even when faced with various social risks. In other words, income disparities among individuals in the labour market tend to be reflected in the welfare production. However, due to the social character of this insurance scheme, some of its elements are designed to meet the minimum standard of living of insured persons. First, for those with a low income, the financial burden of contributions is partially subsidised by public institutions to help them obtain and maintain membership in social insurance. Second, efforts have been made to extend social insurance coverage to irregular and part-time workers. In addition, some initiatives are launched to include jobs located between employment and self-employment, namely non-standard work such as platform work. These developments illustrate how social insurance, traditionally designed for standard employment relationships, is adapting in response to different forms of work and ongoing changes in the labour market. Third, a minimum level of benefits or redistributive elements in the calculation of benefits have been introduced.

b) National Health Insurance and Long-Term Care Insurance for the Elderly

Disease and injuries result in medical treatment costs and loss or reduction of income. This is particularly challenging for individuals who earn a low income. In this context, the National Health Insurance (NHI) scheme is insofar an important instrument to guarantee a minimum livelihood as it partly alleviates financial burdens related to medical costs. Today, nearly the entire Korean population is covered under the NHI scheme. To ensure that persons assumed as economically vulnerable individuals can obtain and maintain eligibility, the contribution amounts can be partially reduced. Reductions apply for residents of agricultural and fishery districts, persons aged at least 65 years, individuals with a registered disability, etc. For instance, contributions may be reduced by 10–30 per cent for those aged 65 or older, depending on their income. However, daily wage earners and non-standard workers are excluded from the category of 'insured employee', and must instead pay the full contribution as district-based insured persons.[38] It is largely observed that this financial burden often discourages them from making contributions, resulting in their exclusion from NHI benefits.

Another shortcoming lies in the fact that medical care benefits are provided only in accordance with the relevant regulations. This means that certain types of medical treatments are classified as non-benefit and are excluded from coverage and must be paid by the patient in full. In addition, patients are required to partially cover the costs of medical care benefits (co-payment). The rate of co-payment varies by type of medical facility, namely clinics (30 per cent), hospitals (40 per cent), general hospitals (50 per cent) and tertiary hospitals (60 per cent). This may prevent patients from receiving adequate medical care benefit, potentially leading to the deterioration of their illnesses. To address this deficit, the NHI partially covers patient expenses that exceed a certain threshold. Due to these restrictions related to non-benefit services and co-payments, the NHI's overall cost coverage remains approximately 63 per cent, which disproportionately impacts low-income earners.

Insured persons under the Long-term Care Insurance for the Elderly (LCI) scheme are also required to make a co-payment. Beneficiaries who

---

38 On the constitutionality of this differentiated approach to levying contributions between employed and district-based insured persons in the National Health Insurance scheme, see. Decision of 2003.10.30, 2000 Hun-Ma 801, 15-2(2), pp. 134 ff.

receive home care pay 15 per cent, while those in care facilities bear 20 per cent of the costs. This co-payment requirement does not apply to recipients of medical care assistance, who are also exempt from paying contributions. The co-payment amount is reduced for individuals whose income and asset value fall below a given threshold. From the beginning, the LCI has prioritised financial stability; unlike the NHI, long-term care benefits are subject to a monthly cap. In 2024, it was set at KRW 1,672,700 for individuals with a long-term care rating I, and at KRW 597,600 for individuals with a long-term care cognitive assistance rating V. Expenses exceeding the monthly cap must be borne by the insured persons. If recipients are unable to cover these additional costs, they must rely on benefits provided under the Act on Welfare for the Elderly. The limited of the LCI inevitably places especially low-income earners in a difficult position. Recognising the gaps in protection against the long-term care needs of the elderly, the debate on reforms is ongoing to supplement the LCI and introduce a so-called integrated care system for the elderly. However, this initiative is still in its infancy.

c) National Pension Service

Under the National Pension Service (NPS), the guarantee of a minimum standard of living for insured individuals following retirement is reflected in partial subsidies for contributions of low-income earners. Contributions from employees and employers are partially subsidised, ranging from 40 per cent to 80 per cent, depending on the employer's size and the employee's income level. In addition, the NPS subsidizes three-fourths of the contributions for recipients of the job-seekers' benefit under the Employment Insurance Act for one year, helping them maintain their insurance coverage. The NPS incorporates redistributive elements in its pension calculation by factoring in both the insured individual's average monthly income and the overall average income of all insured members. This approach results in a more favourable pension calculation for low-income earners. For instance, the income replacement rate of pensions amounted to 92 per cent for the lowest income group compared to just 15 per cent for the highest income group. However, following the reforms of 1998 and 2007, the pension level for low-income earners has significantly declined. For instance, the average monthly pension of recipients with over 20 years of insurance contributions amounts to KRW 1,036,854 per month. For those with only 10 to 20 years of insurance contributions, it amounts to KRW 419,461 monthly.[39] It is important to note that the livelihood benefit under the National Basic Livelihood Security amounts to KRW 623,368 for a single-person household.[40] This means that the national pension, particularly for low-income earners with shorter contribution periods, does not guarantee even the minimum means necessary to maintain a minimum standard of living.

Given that the national pension does not ensure a minimum livelihood, especially for low-income insured persons, there have been ongoing discussions in recent years about raising both the income replacement rate and the contribution rate. However, in light of the declining birthrate and ageing population in the Republic of Korea, the possibility of increasing the income replacement rate appears unlikely. Ultimately, it should be admitted that the NPS's capacity to guarantee a minimum standard of living for insured members is clearly limited, and this shortfall needs to be supplemented by adjusting the basic pension and the national minimum standard of living. This has been partly discussed above.[41]

d) Industrial Accident Compensation Insurance

Under the Industrial Accident Compensation Insurance (IACI) scheme, the guarantee of a minimum livelihood is provided through the provision of a minimum level of compensation. If an employee's average wage, which is used as the basis for calculating the benefit amount, is less than 50 per cent of the national average wage across all employees, they qualify for the minimum compensation benefit (a maximum limit of compensation benefits exists as well). As of 2024, the daily minimum amount was set at KRW 78,880, while the maximum daily amount was KRW 253,354. This mechanism introduces a degree of redistribution among beneficiaries, favouring low-income earners.

In recent years, efforts have been made to include new forms of employment, including platform work. The scope of this protection was expanded by the amendments of 2007 and 2022. In 2007, the concept of 'employee'

39 Ministry of Health and Welfare (n 2), p. 380.

40 See above n 29.

41 See Section III. 3. b).

under the IACI was decoupled from that in the Labour Standards Act, allowing IACI coverage to apply independently of labour law regulations. The IACI now covers specific forms of non-standard employment, regardless of the type of contract. This, however, falls short of providing comprehensive coverage for all individuals concerned, given that potential beneficiaries are enumerated in the legislation. They included, for instance, insurance solicitors, learning-aid tutors, golf caddies, door-to-door couriers, solicitors of credit card holders, drivers engaging in a designated service, etc. In 2022, a general coverage clause was introduced to extend protection to all forms of work, making it possible to include platform workers as well. Despite this legislative development, a significant number of individuals remain uncovered. This is largely due to the reluctance of both employers and employees to report employment relationships to the competent agency or their choice to apply for exemptions from the insurance.[42]

e) Employment Insurance

Employment insurance has followed a similar trajectory as the IACI by expanding its coverage to include atypical forms of employment, such as platform-based work. Efforts are also underway to transition to income-based insurance,[43] with the aim of covering all income earners, regardless of the type of work they perform. However, the problem of implementation in the IACI, as mentioned above, holds true in the employment insurance system as well. Employment insurance includes a minimum benefit clause. If the recipient's daily wage based on which the benefits are calculated, is lower than the statutory minimum daily wage set by the Minimum Wage Act, the benefit is calculated on the basis of that minimum. The contribution rate of insured persons is partially subsidised for low-income earners.

42 On this issue, see. J. Cho, 'Application of Industrial Accident Compensation Insurance System for Platform Workers' Social Security Law Review 10 (2021)2, pp. 156 ff.; S. Cho, 'Legal Protection for Platform Workers – Focusing on the Industrial Accident Compensation Insurance Act and the Employment Insurance Act' Labor Law 79 (2021), pp. 111 ff.

43 On this policy direction, see J. Do, 'Issues and Tasks of Employment Insurance System' Korean Social Security Law 12 (2023)2, pp. 47 ff.

IV. Conclusions

The primary social security instruments in the Republic of Korea include a range of social insurance schemes, including the National Health Insurance, Long-term Care Insurance for the Elderly, the National Pension Service, the Industrial Accident Compensation Insurance, and Employment Insurance. These are supplemented by a scheme aimed at guaranteeing a minimum standard of living. This approach offers a distinct advantage: social insurance provides both normative and institutional stability, because it is financed primarily through contributions from the insured persons themselves. These benefits are protected under the constitutional right to property (Art. 21), and any changes to them receive political attention. However, it is evident that social insurance schemes do not explicitly aim to ensure a minimum livelihood for all citizens, nor is this objective a political goal. Within this limited function and based on their social character, social insurance schemes in the Republic of Korea contribute to ensuring a minimum standard of living by incorporating elements designed for this specific purpose. Moreover, social insurance schemes are currently focused on expanding coverage to include a broader range of insured individuals affected by evolving social and employment conditions. The reform measures have been outlined above. It remains to be seen whether they will ultimately fulfil their intended objectives in the future.

The emergence of poverty among new population groups, especially the working poor and the elderly poor, highlighted the urgent need to develop new social policy instruments. This was driven by the functional limitations of the traditional scheme for the guarantee of a minimum standard of living standard calling for innovative ideas and new measures. In response, the Basic Pension Act was enacted in 2007, followed by the Act for Occupational Promotion and Social Assistance in 2020. However, the Basic Pension Act still needs to clarify its policy choice between providing income security and offering relief for the poor. Meanwhile, the Act for Occupational Promotion and Social Assistance should establish its own system to complement both employment insurance, on the one hand, and the general scheme for guaranteeing of a minimum standard of living on the other.

Part V:
Conclusions

Life in Dignity Through Minimum Income Protection: Conclusions from a Comparative Perspective

Irene Domenici

I. Relevance and Challenges of Minimum Income Protection

The chapters in this volume show that minimum income protection has, in various forms, become a consolidated component of modern welfare states. Minimum income measures now play a central role not only in 'mature' welfare regimes, but also in countries with less-developed social protection systems. In most of the countries examined, minimum income schemes serve as essential pillars of last-resort support, particularly during times of socioeconomic crisis. They have, in many cases, demonstrably contributed to reducing poverty,[1] or at the very least, mitigated certain dimensions of deprivation among the most vulnerable population groups.

Yet, despite their presence and recent expansion, minimum income schemes continue to exhibit significant shortcomings across the countries analysed. Their ability to lift individuals and households out of poverty remains severely constrained. These findings reinforce the results of previous

1 See Ireland, where social transfers play a significant role in reducing poverty (chapter on Ireland, p. 195) and Brazil, where figures show that *Bolsa Família* contributed to lifting 3.4 million people out of extreme poverty, and 3.2 million out of poverty (Brazil, p. 427), or Chile, where the share of the population living below the national poverty line fell from 36 per cent to 10.8 per cent between 2000 and 2020 (Chile, p. 433).

research which has found that minimum income protection – particularly for the non-working, working-age population – often falls short of providing adequate protection against poverty.[2] In many of the countries analysed, the share of those living below the poverty threshold is particularly high or exceeds regional averages.[3] A comparative legal analysis supports this factual conclusion from both a normative and institutional perspective: in several countries, minimum income schemes are, often by deliberate design, characterised by insufficient benefit levels, strict and invasive means testing rules, structural exclusions from eligibility and stringent (labour-related) conditionalities and sanctions. Particularly noteworthy is the recent reform in Italy, where, in contrast to general trends elsewhere, the approach to inclusiveness and universality of minimum income protection has been reversed. Consequently, income inequality remains persistently high in several of the countries analysed, and minimum income protection remains far from meeting its promise of securing a life in dignity for all.

The authors in this volume attribute these shortcomings to various structural and design-related factors, such as the schemes' limited coverage due to strict means testing or eligibility reasons,[4] persistent structural determinants of inequality,[5] and the inadequacy of the benefits provided.[6] Importantly, each country faces its own specific set of challenges. For example, countries with comparatively effective minimum income schemes may struggle to ensure stable and adequate funding (as in Brazil), or to regularly adjust benefit levels (as in Ireland). In several countries, including Brazil and Mexico, overly bureaucratic and complex delivery mechanisms undermine accessibility to benefits. Political polarisation and narratives of welfare dependency continue to shape debates in countries including Bulgaria and Italy, while in others, such as Brazil and Chile, measurable success in poverty reduction has cultivated broad political consensus. The poverty rate in some countries is characterised by profound territorial (e.g. Brazil and Italy) or racial (e.g. Brazil and Mexico) disparities, while in others, there is a recognised need to improve the situation of particularly

2 See, *inter alia*, S. Marchal and I. Marx, *Zero Poverty Society: Ensuring a Decent Income for All* (Oxford University Press 2024), pp. 1-14.

3 Especially high or above the regional average poverty levels have been highlighted in particular in the chapters on Bulgaria, Poland, Mexico, Spain, Italy and Greece.

4 This is the case, for instance, in Mexico, Greece, Italy, Poland, Bulgaria, the Republic of Korea and Japan.

5 As noted in particular in South American countries.

6 *Inter alia* in Greece, the United Kingdom, Poland, Mexico and Italy.

vulnerable groups, such as the elderly (in Poland or Chile) or children (for instance in Germany). While these examples are illustrative rather than exhaustive, they highlight the diversity of policy contexts and institutional challenges in which minimum income protection schemes operate today.

Bearing in mind each country's diverse factual and normative contexts, the comparative insights do not aim to assess the minimum income schemes' "effectiveness" or generosity.[7] Instead, they seek to examine these schemes through a normative lens grounded in the idea of safeguarding the recipients' dignity. This reflects the principle of a rights-based approach to social assistance which was developed in the years following the Second World War.[8] From a dignity perspective, individuals should have access to the means necessary to lead a minimally decent life by virtue of the dignity they possess as human beings, and not as a reward for compliance, a tool to achieve behavioural improvement, a means to boost the country's economic growth or to improve overall societal well-being. From this perspective, it becomes increasingly clear that, depending on their design and implementation, social protection measures intended to guarantee a "life in dignity at all stages of life"[9] may, paradoxically, threaten the very right they seek to uphold.[10] The safety net of minimum income protection can become a trapping net, if the individual recipient's dignity is disregarded.

Drawing from the country-specific studies, we can critically reflect on how dignity is either operationalised or neglected in the design and implementation of minimum income schemes. When looking at minimum income through a dignity-based lens, a pressing need to rethink the multiple layers of minimum income protection measures becomes clear: from benefit levels to eligibility criteria and the narrative of deservingness that

7 This is a task more suitably undertaken by social policy research. See, for example, the substantial work conducted by the OECD in assessing the reliability and adequacy of minimum income protection schemes in several developed countries, with results available here: OECD, 'How reliable are social safety nets in situations of acute economic need?' (20 December 2024) < https://www.oecd.org/en/publications/how-reliable-are-social-safety-nets-in-situations-of-acute-economic-need_568bb35b-en.html > and here: OECD, 'Income support, redistribution and work incentives' < https://www.oecd.org/en/topics/income-support-redistribution-and-work-incentives.html> both accessed 14.6.2024.

8 See Introduction, pp. 17-18.

9 Council Recommendation of 30 January 2023 on adequate minimum income ensuring active inclusion (2023/C 41/01), recital 1).

10 G. Vonk and E. Bambrough, 'The human rights approach to social assistance: Normative principles and system characteristics' European Journal of Social Security 22 (2022)4, pp. 376-389, 377.

underpin conditionalities. Applying this lens requires an analysis not simply of whether given population groups receive certain benefits, but also whether they possess an enforceable or subjective right to claim these, or whether the benefits are provided as discretionary charity. It also requires examining whether the aim is to ensure recipients a life in dignity or to limit the opportunity to rise above the poverty threshold to "deserving" individuals only. If we are to take the normative claim that all individuals are entitled to a life in dignity seriously – regardless of whether they have "earned" this entitlement – then the architecture of minimum income protection must be restructured accordingly.

II. Insights from the Normative Frameworks

1. Minimum Income Protection as a State Obligation

Not all jurisdictions investigated have an explicit constitutional background that grounds minimum income protection as a declination of human dignity. While constitutional protections of human dignity exist in Spain, Ireland and France, for instance, these do not serve as a basis for granting social rights and minimum income protection is not considered a realisation of a right to dignity.[11] Countries where (constitutional) legislation, case law or literature have explicitly identified a normative basis for minimum income protection in the guarantee of human dignity include Germany,[12] Norway,[13] Poland,[14] Slovenia,[15] Greece,[16] the Republic of Korea,[17] Chile[18]

11 Ireland, p. 178, Spain, p. 345, France, pp. 80 ff.
12 Where "the fundamental right to the guarantee of a subsistence minimum is derived from the principle of human dignity in Article 1.1 of the Basic Law in conjunction with the principle of the welfare state in Article 20.1 of the Basic Law", Germany, p. 116.
13 Norway, pp. 256 ff.
14 "The principle of social justice is normatively and axiologically linked to the principle of human dignity that is formulated explicitly in Article 30 of the Constitution. Both principles are invoked in the jurisprudence of the Constitutional Court, in order to specify the scope of the legislator's freedom in defining social rights", Poland, pp. 275-276.
15 Slovenia, p. 315.
16 Greece, pp. 150 ff.
17 The Republic of Korea, p. 540.
18 Chile, p. 439.

and Mexico,[19] although the precise scope and expression of this dignity-based approach, as well as its implications for the right to a minimum income, vary considerably. In some countries, dignity is only invoked in relation to specific social benefits.[20]

What is of relevance for this analysis is not so much whether the concept of dignity in a given country is explicitly linked to minimum income, but rather whether the guarantee of a minimum income is treated as a subjective right of the individual, or is at least a constitutional obligation of the State to protect the rights of the individual. This distinction allows us to assess whether minimum income is guaranteed as a discretionary hand-out or as the fulfilment of a rights-based obligation by the State.

A right to social assistance, which is either directly enshrined in the Constitution or derived from constitutional case law, exists in Brazil, Bulgaria, Greece, Norway, Japan and Germany. In many cases, this recognition is the result of relatively recent reforms or shifts in case law. In Brazil and Greece, for example, recent amendments explicitly frame the right to social assistance as a right to minimum income. Brazil's 2012 constitutional provision not only recognises a right to a basic family income, but also stipulates that it must be guaranteed through a permanent and universal cash transfer programme.[21] In Greece, the 2019 constitutional reform introduced an obligation for the State to ensure decent living conditions through a guaranteed minimum income system established by law.[22] Thus, in these countries, the abolition of the minimum income scheme would be considered unconstitutional. Similarly, a fundamental right to a minimum level of subsistence that safeguards human dignity has also been recognised by the German Federal Constitutional Court following its landmark judgment of February 2010.[23] This constitutional right is subjective and enforceable. In Norway, a 2014 constitutional reform introduced, for the first time, provisions on the enforceable right to a minimum level of subsistence for children and

---

19 "[T]he right to the minimum conditions for life has been derived from a systematic interpretation of the fundamental rights enshrined in the General Constitution, among which are Articles 1 (dignity), 3 (education), 4 (social human rights), 27 (private property) and 123 (right to decent work and minimum wage)", Mexico, p. 475.

20 See Italy, where dignity has been interpreted as a constitutional standard relevant to the granting of a right to housing, p. 203.

21 Brazil, pp. 417-418.

22 Greece, p. 157.

23 Germany, p. 116.

for those unable to support themselves.[24] In Japan, the constitutional right to life includes the right to maintain a minimum standard of living and explicitly forms the normative basis of the social assistance system.[25] In Bulgaria, the Constitution provides for a right to social security and social assistance, framed as an objective obligation of the State.[26]

Other constitutional frameworks do not explicitly guarantee the right to minimum income or social assistance but express a broader commitment to social protection by declaring a right to social security. In some cases, this has been interpreted broadly by constitutional case law to include social assistance. For instance, Chile's Constitution refers to the right to social security, but provides a very weak constitutional basis for non-contributory assistance.[27] The Constitutional Court has not yet ruled on whether the right to social security encompasses non-contributory social protection. In Slovenia, on the other hand, although the right to social assistance is not explicitly mentioned, the Constitutional Court has interpreted the State's duty under the principle of the social state to include an obligation to support those in need as a matter of human dignity.[28] Similarly, the Spanish Constitutional Court has affirmed that the "social security system's" scope is not limited to insurance-based social protection, but also encompasses social assistance benefits.[29] In Italy, while Article 38 of the Constitution does not establish an explicit right to minimum income, the Constitutional Court has acknowledged the State's responsibility to provide benefits that are essential for alleviating situations of extreme deprivation.[30] The Republic of Korea offers a more robust constitutional commitment: Article 34 explicitly guarantees the right to a decent life through social security, interpreted as imposing a constitutional duty on the State to ensure a minimum standard of living for all citizens.[31] In Mexico, the Constitution guarantees the right to social security for workers, without establishing a universally enforceable right to social protection that applies to all citizens. Instead, the constitutional right to a vital minimum is limited to particularly vulnerable groups – such as persons with permanent disabilities, indigenous peoples, Afro-

24 Norway, p. 249.
25 Japan, pp. 503 ff.
26 Bulgaria, pp. 42 ff.
27 Chile, pp. 439-440.
28 Slovenia, pp. 317-318.
29 Spain, p. 346.
30 Italy, pp. 202 ff.
31 The Republic of Korea, p. 540.

Mexicans, the elderly and students.[32] This "categorical" approach, which singles out specific vulnerable population groups and guarantees them a higher standard of social protection, is a recurring pattern across many of the countries analysed. In Bulgaria, constitutional protection is provided for children and mothers.[33] Similarly, marriage, family and motherhood are explicitly protected in Poland.[34] In Norway, children are covered by a specific constitutional provision regarding minimum income.[35] In Greece, "special care" and "special measures" are provided to several vulnerable population groups, as well as to large families and persons with disabilities.[36] In general, provisions for persons with disabilities and the elderly are common across the constitutional frameworks analysed.[37] In Ireland, the Constitution also makes explicit reference to widows and orphans.[38]

As noted by several authors, these particular groups often find themselves in a situation of need through no fault of their own.[39] This points to a distinction between "deserving" and "undeserving" poor. Typically, protection is extended to citizens who are deemed disadvantaged due to circumstances that are beyond their control, such as age, disability or caregiving responsibilities. While these groups are undoubtedly in need of support, the underlying rationale reinforces a logic of conditional deservingness, implying that assistance is primarily warranted for those not responsible for their socio-economic situation. From a normative perspective grounded in dignity, such fragmentation undermines the idea that all individuals are entitled to a minimum level of subsistence and a decent life simply by virtue of their human dignity.

Among the countries analysed, only the United Kingdom lacks specific recognition of an enforceable right to social security or social assistance. However, Articles 3 and 8 of the European Convention on Human Rights which has been incorporated into the country's national legislation, impose an obligation on the State to provide a minimum subsistence in certain situations, albeit granting the legislature an exceptionally broad margin

32 Mexico, p. 473.
33 Bulgaria, p. 42.
34 Poland, p. 277.
35 Norway, pp. 257-258.
36 Greece, p. 155.
37 See, *inter alia*, the chapters on Poland, the Republic of Korea, France and Ireland.
38 Ireland, p. 180.
39 Bulgaria, p. 45.

of discretion.[40] Yet, even in countries where enforceable rights are constitutionally recognised, they often protect only the minimum core of the right to a life in dignity. Legislatures retain broad discretion in defining key elements such as the amount of cash benefits and what constitutes a minimum level of subsistence,[41] influenced by budgetary constraints[42] and Constitutional Courts' deference to legislative authority.[43] Consequently, the scope, strength and practical enforceability of these rights vary significantly across countries, with accessible or adequate minimum income protection largely left to legislative discretion.

2. Normative Conceptions of a Life in Dignity

Regardless of whether a constitutional obligation to guarantee a minimum level of subsistence exists – as we have seen, its scope and purpose vary considerably – the normative conceptions of what constitutes a dignified and decent life differs markedly in the countries analysed. One way to understand the definition of a "life in dignity" is by examining the underlying assumptions embedded in the design of the different countries' minimum income benefits. In other words, the answer to the question "What does a life in dignity entail?" is rooted in the choices about what minimum income benefits are intended to cover: whether they are aimed at covering to basic nutritional needs only, or also at enabling participation in social and cultural life, including access to transport, the internet or leisure activities. Depending on the legal system, the normative guidelines for defining a minimum standard of living are either shaped directly by the country's constitutional framework or largely left to the legislature's discretion.

40 The United Kingdom, pp. 381-382.

41 See, for instance, Bulgaria, where the realisation of the right to social assistance is subject to the legislature's wide margin of discretion, p. 43; Ireland, where the judiciary habitually avoids interfering in the legislature's prerogatives, p. 178; Poland, where constitutional social rights are subject to the limits set by law, p. 277; Spain, where constitutional social rights can only be enforced before ordinary courts with respect to the legal provisions that implement them, p. 347; Japan, where it is at the legislature's discretion to define the specific scope of a "wholesome and cultured life", p. 504; the Republic of Korea, where the Constitutional Court does not recognise the right to a minimum standard of living as directly enforceable, see p. 542; and Germany, where the determination of the minimum level of subsistence falls under the legislature's responsibility, p. 117.

42 See Italy, p. 204 and Slovenia, p. 318.

43 See France, p. 79, Ireland, p. 181 and the Republic of Korea, p. 542.

Nearly all countries analysed acknowledge, at least nominally, the need to cover basic subsistence requirements, typically defined as food, clothing and housing;[44] in some cases, these extend to health and hygiene. The case law in Mexico, for instance, includes health and a healthy environment within the right to a vital minimum.[45] Similarly, health is a cornerstone of the assistance schemes in Chile and Brazil.[46] In the United Kingdom, minimum subsistence usually refers to immediate and most basic and essential needs, such as accommodation, heating, food and hygiene.[47]

While situations of poverty that threaten the full enjoyment of the individual's fundamental right to life and health certainly undermine human dignity, it follows from the assumption that human beings are social creatures that their dignity is only fully guaranteed when they are also able to actively participate in society. Accordingly, not only poverty but also social exclusion constitutes a violation of human dignity. From this perspective, a dignified life entails not only the right to physical existence but also the right to be included in socio-political life and to be recognised as a "full" member of society.[48]

Several national constitutions link dignity with societal participation. For example, Italy's Constitution affirms that all citizens possess equal "social" dignity and the State has a duty to remove economic and social obstacles to individuals' effective participation in the country's political, economic and social life. The German Federal Constitutional Court also states that

44 See Bulgaria (where the basic needs are understood as "sufficient food, clothing and housing, according to the socio-economic development of the country"), p. 57 and Poland (where the social intervention threshold aims at avoiding a biological threat to human life and psychophysical development), pp. 284-285.

45 Mexico, p. 475.

46 Chile, p. 452 and Brazil, p. 425.

47 The United Kingdom, p. 380.

48 See, *inter alia*, C. Fabre, 'Social Rights in European Constitutions', in: G. de Búrca, B. de Witte and L. Ogertschnig (eds.), *Social rights in Europe* (Oxford University Press 2005), p. 17; U. Becker, 'Sozialmodell und Menschenbild in der „Hartz-IV"-Gesetzgebung', in: O. Behrends and E. Schumann (eds.), *Gesetzgebung, Menschenbild und Sozialmodell im Familien- und Sozialrecht* (De Gruyter 2008), p. 62; F. Ferraro, 'The Social Dimension of Fundamental Rights in Times of Crisis', in: S. Civitarese Matteucci and S. Halliday, *Social Rights in an Age of Austerity: European Perspectives* (Routledge 2017), pp. 197, 205, S. Huster, 'The Universality of Human Dignity and the Relativity of Social Rights', in: D. Grimm, A. Kemmerer and C. Möllers (eds.), *Human Dignity in Context* (Nomos 2018), p. 417; T. Bahle, 'Mindestsicherung im europäischen Vergleich', in: F. Blank, C. Schäfer and D. Spannagel (eds.), *Grundsicherung weiterdenken* (transcript Verlag 2021), p. 246.

the right to dignity implies the "possibility of maintaining inter-human relations and a minimum of participation in social, cultural and political life".[49] Hence, minimum income benefits must cover costs that are essential for ensuring such participation and the maintenance of social contacts.[50] In the Republic of Korea, the Constitutional Court suggests that the right to a minimum standard of living includes not only physical subsistence, but also opportunities to participate in socio-economic and cultural life.[51] In countries lacking explicit constitutional guidance in this regard, the legislative framework may provide guidance on the need to include societal participation within minimum income protection. For instance, in France, education, training and access to culture are included in the aims of the poverty alleviation measures. Telephone and internet connections are explicitly mentioned as essential components of decent housing.[52] In Japan, cash assistance must be sufficient to not only purchase food and clothing, but for transportation costs as well,[53] which is often crucial for full societal participation. In the South American countries analysed, the normative definition of minimum subsistence typically includes participation in education and culture. Education is explicitly part of the minimum income schemes of Chile, Brazil and Mexico.[54] More generally, in both Chile and Brazil, assistance measures are differentiated by their purpose: alleviation of extreme poverty or of poverty, respectively, understood as an inability of the individual to meet basic food needs or as a lack of access to a broader range of goods and services, such as education, culture or technologies.[55]

Whether these normative ideas are reflected in the concrete design and adequacy of the benefits provided by the different minimum income measures, however, is another matter, as will be illustrated below.[56] In many cases, a gap emerges between the normative ideal and the benefits actually provided. This discrepancy may not only be due to shortcomings in legislative implementation, but also to the balancing between competing

49 German Federal Constitutional Court, Judgment of 9 February 2010 (BVerfGE 127, 175), available in English at < https://www.bundesverfassungsgericht.de/SharedDocs/Entscheidungen/EN/2010/02/ls20100209_1bvl000109en.html>, accessed 14.6.2025.

50 Germany, p. 117.

51 The Republic of Korea, pp. 543 ff.

52 France, p. 84.

53 Japan, p. 521.

54 Chile, p. 452, Mexico, pp. 481 ff., Brazil, p. 425.

55 Brazil, pp. 424 ff., Chile, p. 457.

56 See Sec. III.2.a) of these Conclusions.

interests at the constitutional level. In Italy, for instance, despite the above-mentioned connection between dignity and social inclusion, the Constitutional Court acknowledged that the "irreducible core" of social assistance is limited to enabling beneficiaries to meet their basic dietary needs.[57] The Constitutional Court in Slovenia has also embraced both dimensions of minimum subsistence: while meeting beneficiaries' cultural and other personal needs is recognised as representing a constitutional right to dignity, the legislature's intent to limit coverage to the most immediate basic needs only is also upheld.[58] Norway provides a contrasting example in that the minimum level enshrined in the constitution is interpreted as providing only food, water, clothing, housing and healthcare, whereas ministerial regulations for social assistance explicitly include communication, hygiene, leisure and social needs. As a result, the level of benefits in Norway tends to exceed the constitutionally required subsistence minimum.[59]

III. Dignity in the Implementation of Minimum Income Protection

1. A Collaborative Task: Between Social Insurance, Targeted Schemes and Safety Nets

Reflections on the differing normative conceptions of a life in dignity reveal a wide spectrum of basic needs to be met by minimum income protection. These range from food and housing to clothing, hygiene, recreational activities and education. As a result, guaranteeing a life in dignity through social protection is only comprehensively achievable when all of these different dimensions and circumstances are adequately addressed. At present, there is a certain degree of fragmentation within minimum income protection systems. One of the starkest results of this comparative study is that minimum income protection systems are multifaceted. They may take the form of a universal scheme, categorical benefits aimed at specific vulnerable population groups, or targeted assistance designed to address individuals' specific needs.[60] In some cases, minimum income functions

57 Italy, pp. 203-204.
58 Slovenia, p. 318.
59 Norway, p. 265.
60 As correctly pointed out in the chapter on Slovenia: "the challenge of offering means for a dignified life to all members of society seems much broader than the challenge

are embedded within broader social insurance instruments.[61] Furthermore, certain social benefits, such as child allowances, initially introduced to achieve another objective, such as increasing fertility rates, have become functional to ensuring a minimum standard of living for families. This is evident in Bulgaria, Poland and Japan.[62]

The country reports also show that the fragmentation of social benefits is not necessarily negative, and might even be inevitable, given that a one-size-fits-all approach often fails to comprehensively address diverse needs and various life situations.[63] Admittedly, the most reliable method for ensuring a minimum level of subsistence for all individuals who fall below a certain poverty threshold remains the implementation of a universal minimum income scheme. This approach effectively establishes a uniform baseline of assistance, thereby eliminating any gaps in the social safety net. It should be noted that such schemes have now been adopted in nearly all of the countries analysed.[64] However, even countries that have adopted universal minimum income schemes supplement them with targeted programmes to address specific needs. Brazil, for instance, has implemented *Bolsa Família* as a safety net with universal coverage, but also provides distinct housing and food programmes.[65] This is considered an opportunity to provide more comprehensive assistance.[66] In Poland, purpose-specific allowances can be provided to cover certain expenses,

of offering minimum income protection alone", Slovenia, p. 313. See, also, the considerations by H. M. Adzakpa *Realising the Human Right to a Social Minimum? A Comparative Socio-Legal Study of EU Member States* (Nomos 2024), p. 276.

61 In the Republic of Korea, for instance, social insurance schemes include a minimum income function by establishing a minimum level of benefits, see p. 561. Similarly, Bulgaria provides minimum unemployment benefits and minimum contributory pensions, although these are set below the at-risk-of-poverty threshold, see p. 60. In contrast, Germany, does not define a minimum standard of benefits within its social insurance instruments, as noted on p. 121.

62 Bulgaria, p. 41, Poland, p. 303 and Japan, pp. 514-515.

63 See also H. M. Adzakpa (n 60), pp. 276-278.

64 See, *inter alia*, *Bolsa Familia* in Brazil, the universal minimum guaranteed income scheme in Greece, Universal Credit in the United Kingdom, the Supplementary Welfare Allowance in Ireland, the Spanish MVI, the active solidarity income in France, the subsidiary social assistance scheme in Slovenia, periodic allowances in Poland, the *Chile Solidario* system in Chile and the *Bürgergeld* in Germany. Among the countries analysed, only Italy and Mexico do not have a universal social assistance instrument.

65 Brazil, pp. 421-422.

66 Brazil, p. 423.

including food, medicine, house repairs, funeral costs and similar items.[67] In Bulgaria, heating and rent allowances target individuals' housing and energy-related needs.[68] In several countries, inclusion in the minimum income scheme facilitates or entitles individuals to additional benefits, thereby institutionalising a systematic connection between the different schemes and programmes. This is exemplified by Chile's system of social protection.[69] In Greece, individuals who are eligible for minimum income benefits also have access to social tariffs for electricity and water.[70] In many cases, specific needs are already covered through the calculation of the cash benefit amount provided under the minimum income scheme. This ensures comprehensive protection for diverse living situations within the same social protection instrument. The United Kingdom is a good example, where the Universal Credit includes not only a standard allowance, but also provides supplementary components tailored to specific circumstances, such as disability, caregiving responsibilities, childcare and housing needs.[71] In Germany, recipients of the *Bürgergeld* are eligible for additional support to cover the costs of accommodation and heating beyond the standard levels of need.[72] Similarly, in Norway, children's needs are accorded particular consideration in the calculation of benefits. For instance, costs for activities for children and youth may be included in the calculation, even if the same would not be covered for adults.[73]

The relationship between minimum income measures and other social protection instruments plays a crucial role. The different systems must be effectively coordinated to cover all possible life circumstances and income fluctuations over an individual's lifetime. For instance, various social benefits designed primarily for purposes other than providing a minimum standard of living should be compatible with social assistance. This is usually the case with social insurance benefits,[74] particularly when they are provided at amounts insufficient to guarantee minimum subsistence. In several countries, allowances meant to address specific needs

67 Poland, p. 298.
68 Bulgaria, p. 57.
69 Chile, pp. 444 ff.
70 Greece, p. 170.
71 The United Kingdom, pp. 392 ff.
72 Germany, p. 134.
73 Norway, p. 268.
74 See Spain, p. 360, Slovenia, p. 330, Poland, p. 290, Greece, p. 160 and Germany, pp. 121 ff.

are excluded from the means test for eligibility for social assistance.[75] For instance, non-contributory disability benefits are excluded when they serve to compensate for specific needs arising from a disability.[76] In all of the countries examined, the elderly are recognised as a group requiring special protection,[77] which in some cases results in higher benefit amounts.[78] These two groups usually receive enhanced support in both types of countries, i.e. those with and those without a universal minimum income scheme. In Mexico, for instance, the only two poverty alleviation instruments with a universal character are non-contributory pensions for the elderly and financial support for persons with disabilities.[79]

However, depending on the design and interaction of the different schemes, substantial disadvantages may arise. A tangled network of measures may, first, obstruct the effective pursuit of coherent social policy goals, and second, accessibility to and effective coverage of the system.[80] The complex institutional landscape arising from overlapping schemes may undermine beneficiaries' ability to navigate the system and access the support they are entitled to. In instances where different social benefits are not cumulative, individuals often struggle to determine which benefit best suits their individual situation. Choosing one scheme might disqualify them from access to another.[81] This complexity is particularly pronounced

75 In Greece "certain allowances, such as non-contributory disability benefits, education, vocational training and job-search allowances for unemployed persons, emergency financial assistance for natural disaster victims and support for labour market integration of homeless persons and domestic violence victims, are excluded from the calculation of household income", p. 160. In France, housing benefits are partially excluded from means test, p. 88. In Ireland, income from other social assistance or benefits payments are not included in the means test, p. 189. Similarly, in Italy, the Inclusion allowance "can be combined with unemployment insurance benefits and various social assistance benefits that are not counted as income. It is, moreover, fully compatible with the universal child benefit", p. 212. This differs in several countries, for instance, in Slovenia, where all social security and other benefits are taken into account when determining the amount of applicants' personal income, p. 327.

76 See for instance Bulgaria, p. 41, Greece, p. 160, France, p. 93.

77 See for instance Bulgaria, pp. 65 ff. and Chile, p. 442.

78 See France, where the benefits provided to elderly persons are higher than the Active Solidarity Income, p. 96 and Italy, where means testing is more lenient for old-age benefits, and social protection is more generous for beneficiaries that have reached the age of 70, p. 235.

79 Mexico, p. 493.

80 As already mentioned in the Introduction, p. 30.

81 In some cases, the interplay between different benefits is not only difficult for individuals to navigate, but also lacks clarity in the legislation, as in the case of the Republic

in countries where national minimum income schemes coexist with regional or local assistance measures.[82] The intricacies of these schemes might influence take-up rates and, more worryingly, create real gaps in the safety net.[83] Bulgaria is a clear example of this, as the minimum income function is provided through both social security, in the form of a guaranteed minimum amount, and through social assistance instruments. However, these schemes are mutually exclusive, and their combined eligibility requirements may exclude certain segments of the population from receiving any support.[84]

From the perspective of human dignity, the crucial concern goes beyond mere effective implementation issues and includes the normative assumptions underlying the fragmented protection schemes. Compartmentalised protection can undermine the principles of equality and reinforce narratives of "deservingness". When benefits are fragmented, needs and entitlements could be assessed inconsistently, resulting in some individuals being deemed more deserving of support than others based on their life situation or on the specific social protection scheme they fall under.

2. Design of Minimum Income Schemes

a) Benefit Amounts and their Adequacy

The definition of what constitutes a "minimum" within a minimum income protection system reflects the normative conception of a life in dignity endorsed by the State, as described above.[85] This conception should logically guide not only the system's underlying principles but also the concrete determination of benefit amounts and types. The country reports demonstrate that in most cases, this normative understanding is not effectively translated into practice. The benefits provided under such systems

---

of Korea, where the relationship between benefits to ensure a minimum standard of living with, for instance, the basic pension, remains unclear, see p. 559.

82 The most obvious examples are Italy (see p. 223) and Spain (see p. 350).

83 This is clearly the case in Mexico, where the various targeted social insurance and assistance programmes are not interconnected and fail to ensure coverage for the entire population, and in Italy, where the abolition of the *Reddito di Cittadinanza* has left gaps in protection despite the existence of several other social assistance benefits.

84 Bulgaria, p. 70. A similar problem is evident in Japan, where "there is a large gap between the two systems, which means there is a certain number of unemployed persons who do not receive any social benefits at all", p. 517.

85 See above, Sec. II.1. of these Conclusions.

frequently fall short of enabling recipients to attain the standard of living that the State's own normative framework appears to support.

Disentangling this gap calls for a closer examination of the specific methods and criteria used to determine benefit levels. Three distinct approaches to calculating cash benefits have been identified and found to be connected to the concept of minimum subsistence adopted by the legislature.

Firstly, in countries where the legislative definition of minimum subsistence is limited to basic subsistence needs, benefits are typically calculated using poverty or income thresholds. For instance, the Bulgarian legislature defines basic necessities to be food, clothing and accommodation, and calculates minimum income benefits based on a social assistance baseline as a percentage of the at-risk-of-poverty threshold. This amount is then adjusted according to the individual's health condition and family situation.[86] Similarly, in Chile, the base transfer for meeting basic food needs is calculated as a percentage of the extreme poverty threshold.[87] In Slovenia, where the legislative intent is to provide means to cover immediate basic needs,[88] the baseline amount corresponds to the at-risk-of-poverty threshold.[89] In the Republic of Korea, the levels guaranteed by the National Basic Livelihood Security Act are primarily focused on ensuring physical subsistence – although social and cultural participation should also be covered according to constitutional law – and are calculated as percentages of the median income.[90]

Secondly, countries that incorporate elements of social participation into their concept of minimum subsistence often use the basket of goods or reference budget method. In Germany, the standard needs for the Citizen's Income, which encompass participation in social and cultural life, are determined using the basket of goods method based on income and consumption surveys.[91] In Norway, although the final decision rests with municipalities, ministerial guidelines provide detailed suggested rates which are based on the costs of food, beverages, household products, media and communication, leisure activities, etc.[92] In Japan, minimum standards are set using the basket of goods method and are adjusted according to

86 Bulgaria, p. 56.
87 Chile, p. 449.
88 Slovenia, p. 324.
89 Ibid.
90 The Republic of Korea, p. 554.
91 Germany, p. 137.
92 Norway, pp. 265 ff.

consumption levels of comparable households, although the actual benefit amount provided to recipients is highly individualised based on relevant circumstances.[93] Additionally, support for funerals is also provided as part of ensuring a minimum and dignified standard of living.[94]

Thirdly, in a surprisingly large number of jurisdictions, the calculation of benefit amounts is "arbitrary" or lacks a concrete basis that is not influenced by political discretion or budgetary constraints. This is particularly pronounced in Greece, where there is a significant gap between the intended purpose of minimum income protection and its practical implementation. Although the guaranteed minimum income amounts vary according to the number and age of household members, these amounts lack "clear legislative justification" and are determined by "fiscal constraints rather than a calculation based on poverty thresholds or actual living costs".[95] As a result, although the guaranteed minimum income scheme in Greece was designed to fight poverty in a broad sense, encompassing both economic deprivation and lack of access to cultural goods, education and new technologies, its adequacy in achieving these goals remains questionable.[96] A similar pattern is observed in Italy, where the benefit level appears to be derived from the distribution of a predetermined amount of tax revenue among potential beneficiaries.[97] In Ireland, the rate of the supplementary welfare allowance is set annually through the national budget based on the government's perception of need.[98] The United Kingdom also establishes the standard monthly allowance explicitly rejecting the idea of setting benefits it based on an objective assessment of needs.[99] In France, the amount of the RSA lacks a precise calculation and is left to political discretion, originally fulfilling an electoral promise. However, the minimum wage is intended to serve as a benchmark to encourage recipients to seek employment.[100] In Brazil, the basic benefit under *Bolsa Família* is a fixed amount for each household, with additional top-ups for families with children.[101] Another indication of arbitrary determination is evident in

---

93 Japan, pp. 528-529.
94 Japan, p. 521.
95 Greece, p. 167.
96 Greece, p. 173.
97 Italy, p. 227.
98 Ireland, pp. 182 and 188.
99 The United Kingdom, pp. 397-398.
100 France, p. 98.
101 Brazil, p. 425.

the benefit caps observed, particularly in Italy and the United Kingdom. In Italy, the coefficient used to calculate benefits is capped, preventing larger families from receiving amounts proportional to their size and needs.[102] In the United Kingdom, households are subject to a legislative cap that limits the maximum annual amount of benefits that can be received.[103] These mechanisms effectively decouple the benefits provided from recipients' actual needs.[104]

In terms of adequacy of benefits over time, the amount provided cannot be considered sufficient if it is not subject to regular indexation. Automatic annual adjustments are ideal, as they allow benefit levels to keep pace with inflation without being subject to political discretion. Without regular and automatic indexation, benefit levels become disconnected from actual living costs, leaving recipients' dignity contingent on political priorities and budgetary constraints. The lack of regular and frequent indexation is particularly problematic in Ireland,[105] Italy[106] and Poland.[107] While benefits are usually increased in most countries to reflect inflation, this occurs arbitrarily in some countries without an automatic mechanism in place. Although no automatic mechanism exists in Brazil, the Supreme Court has ordered the government to regularly update benefit levels to effectively uphold the right to a minimum income.[108] In Norway, the United Kingdom, Slovenia, Spain, France and Chile, adjustments are made annually based on changes in consumer prices or inflation.[109] In Bulgaria, the at-risk-of-poverty threshold used to calculate social assistance benefits is established every year by governmental decree.[110] In Germany, standard needs are adjusted annually, based on the development in both prices and wages.[111] In Mexico,

---

102 Italy, p. 228.

103 The United Kingdom, p. 402.

104 J. King, 'The Future of Social Rights. Social Rights as Capstone', in: K. Young (ed.), *The Future of Economic and Social Rights. Globalization and Human Rights* (Cambridge University Press 2019), p. 306.

105 Ireland, p. 188.

106 Italy, p. 237.

107 Where indexation takes place regularly, but only every three years, see Poland, p. 285.

108 Brazil, p. 420.

109 Norway, p. 265, Chile, p. 450, the United Kingdom, pp. 398 ff., France, p. 97, Spain, p. 367, Slovenia, p. 324.

110 Bulgaria, p. 56.

111 Germany, p. 139.

while benefits are increased yearly, these adjustments are made at the complete discretion of the executive and are based on arbitrary criteria.[112]

Another important factor for assessing adequacy is the duration of benefit payments. While benefits are provided in most countries for as long as the need persists, some impose time limits or waiting periods, which can undermine the right to a life in dignity by implying that individuals are no longer deserving of support after having received a given amount of benefits for a given period of time. In Chile, for example, most benefits are granted for a maximum of 24 months, after which the amount gradually decreases each month by a certain percentage.[113] In Italy, the duration of benefits is limited to 18 months, with the possibility of renewal for an additional 12 months following a one-month break.[114] There is a three-month waiting period in Bulgaria for working-age applicants after registering with the employment office before they can apply for assistance.[115] In other countries, while the duration of benefits is fixed, participation in the scheme can be renewed for as long as a situation of need persists.[116]

Irrespective of the calculation method or the existence of an adjustment mechanism, concerns about the adequacy of benefits to cover basic needs or to lift beneficiaries out of poverty, let alone enabling a full and meaningful participation in social life, are prevalent in most countries analysed.[117] Even in European countries renowned for strong protection of social rights, our findings show that the existing safety nets often fail to ensure a life in dignity.[118] The comparative analysis gives rise to two main reflections in this regard.

First, regardless of the method used to determine benefit levels, amounts that remain merely symbolic undermine the very purpose of minimum

112 Mexico, p. 490.
113 Chile, p. 462.
114 Italy, p. 212.
115 Bulgaria, p. 58.
116 In Greece, for instance, beneficiaries must reapply after six months, see p. 169.
117 See, for instance, the chapters on Bulgaria (p. 60), Chile (p. 451), Greece (p. 173), Mexico (p. 490), Ireland (p. 186) Slovenia (p. 324), Spain (p. 367), the Republic of Korea (p. 554) and Italy (p. 227).
118 In this regard, the results of our comparative analysis directly challenge the "complacency exist[ing] as to the adequacy of the European social model", as cautioned by C. O' Cinneide, 'The Present Limits and Future Potential of European Social Constitutionalism', in: K. Young (ed.), *The Future of Economic and Social Rights. Globalization and Human Rights* (Cambridge University Press 2019), pp. 324-352, 349.

income schemes as instruments to guarantee a life in dignity. If the final amount received by the beneficiaries is insufficient to cover their minimum subsistence needs, it fails to uphold their dignity. This failure is even more troubling when symbolic amounts are instrumentalised to advance political narratives of generosity, treating beneficiaries as mere policy tools.

Second, to give material effect to their normative conceptions of a dignified life as reflected in constitutional or legal frameworks, states must assume responsibility for defining, in concrete terms, what this entails. Otherwise, the process of setting benefit levels risks rendering the normative content of minimum income protection practically meaningless. While the definition of this standard can be country-specific, it should not remain implicit or be determined arbitrarily. In this respect, reference budget methods hold significant potential. By systematically identifying the goods and services necessary for a dignified life, they promote transparency and foster an open public debate about the essential elements of a life in dignity. Moreover, they support the justiciability of minimum income schemes by providing a standard against which the adequacy of benefits can be assessed in light of states' obligations.[119]

b) Eligibility

aa) Means Testing

Means testing, by definition, is an essential feature of minimum income schemes, and is crucial for directing available resources towards individuals in situations of need. However, due to the extensive personal information required by authorities to conduct means testing, the very burden of proving deservingness threatens applicants' dignity, subjecting them to intrusive scrutiny of their private lives and personal circumstances. Against this background, designing a means testing system that ensures effective targeting while fully respecting beneficiaries' dignity remains a fundamental challenge.

First, means tests for eligibility within the scope of universal minimum income schemes is conducted at the household level in all countries. Just to mention a few examples: in Brazil, the poverty threshold that is used

119 Ibid, pp. 348-349.

to determine eligibility is calculated by dividing total household income by the number of household members.[120] In Greece, poverty is assessed on the basis of household income over the six months preceding the application for support.[121] Italy applies a dual means testing approach, relying on the family Equivalent Economic Situation Indicator (ISEE) as well as ADI-specific income limits, both of which are based on total household income.[122] While this makes sense for identifying situations of need within constellations where resources are typically shared, conducting means testing at the household level also means setting individual autonomy and personal agency aside. This approach risks denying protection to individual applicants who lack personal income and have no control over the household's resources. In Italy, for instance, childless adults who live on their own and have no income are automatically included in their parents' household for calculating both the ISEE and the ADI-specific income threshold.[123] Some countries address this issue by allowing discretion in treating individuals separately from their household for means testing purposes, as is the case, for instance, in Japan.[124] Moreover, determining eligibility based on the entire household results in sanctions for individual behaviour affecting the entire household. In several schemes, the combination of eligibility rules and sanctions for non-compliance creates situations where the entire family is held accountable for the misconduct of a single member.[125]

The issue of family responsibility is especially pronounced in countries where access to minimum income support is conditional on exhausting all possibilities of support from family members. In some cases, there are very far-reaching maintenance obligations, including members of the extended family. This is the case in Italy, as seen in the example of childless adults with no income of their own, and in Bulgaria, where the obligation to seek family support first is particularly strict. There, eligibility for social benefits is excluded if the applicant has any relatives legally obliged to support them.[126] In Slovenia, individuals are generally also required to first seek family support, including from former spouses.[127] Similarly, in Greece,

---

120 Brazil, pp. 424-425.
121 Greece, pp. 164 ff.
122 Italy, p. 211.
123 Italy, p. 230.
124 Japan, pp. 530-531.
125 Bulgaria, p. 65, Greece, p. 172 and Italy, p. 232.
126 Bulgaria, p. 55.
127 Slovenia, p. 327.

access to guaranteed minimum income is denied if the recipient can obtain assistance from family members.[128] While support from family members must be prioritised in Japan as well, discretion is granted to caseworkers in contacting the applicant's family members and assessing their resources.[129] In the Republic of Korea, livelihood assistance is subsidiary to family support only when relatives' income exceeds certain thresholds, whereas other benefits, such as housing and education allowances, do not require applicants to first seek family support.[130]

Secondly, if means testing is overly strict, it may create significant coverage gaps by targeting only those who face severe physical subsistence risks, while neglecting individuals who are at risk of poverty or social exclusion. In this sense, means testing is considered particularly strict, *inter alia*, in Bulgaria[131] and the Republic of Korea.[132] Chile addresses this challenge by implementing a system of "vulnerability brackets": an instrument allowing to expand access to certain social programmes beyond individuals who are at risk of poverty and to also include households characterised by other socio-economic vulnerabilities.[133] Mexico stands out in this regard, as eligibility for certain programmes is determined by residence in designated areas where vulnerability and marginalisation are higher than in other parts of the country.[134]

Third, means testing typically includes an assessment of assets and capital based on different approaches. If the criteria for capital and assets are too stringent, applicants may end up having to dispose of personal assets, including those that will be essential for meeting their basic living needs after ceasing to receive minimum income support. In Chile, households that possess two or more "high value" assets, including vehicles, private health insurance and properties, may be deemed ineligible for social benefits.[135] In Greece, eligibility is limited by thresholds on the total taxable value of the household's assets and vehicles.[136] The "bedroom tax" sparked controversy in the United Kingdom by reducing benefits for households

128 Greece, p. 164.
129 Japan, p. 533.
130 The Republic of Korea, p. 553.
131 Bulgaria, pp. 55 ff.
132 The Republic of Korea, pp. 553-554.
133 Chile, p. 456.
134 Mexico, pp. 482-483.
135 Chile, p. 457.
136 Greece, p. 166.

with more living space than deemed necessary.[137] In Italy, no household member may have full availability of certain high-value movable goods.[138] In Japan, the possession of a vehicle is generally prohibited, except in special cases of recognised need.[139] Many tools can be used to mitigate the effect of requiring applicants to dispose of essential assets, while still ensuring that assistance is targeted to cover those who are genuinely in situations of need. Certain types of income and assets can be partly or fully excluded from the means test, such as the primary residence in some countries.[140] In Slovenia, both transport vehicles and the place of residence are excluded up to a certain threshold.[141] In Germany, household effects, vehicles and the place of residence are exempt from the means test if they are deemed adequate.[142] Other mechanisms to avoid an overly stringent means test for assets include granting more discretion to caseworkers or applying different timelines for evaluating different asset types. In Norway, for instance, the means test for assets is very strict, but caseworkers have some discretion, and the requirement to liquidate assets depends on the expected duration of receipt of benefits.[143] In Germany, a one-year period from the initial receipt of benefits applies, during which only significant assets are taken into account.[144]

bb) Residence and Age

Among the additional eligibility requirements, a link to the state providing the scheme in the form of residency is commonly required for access to minimum income protection. Even where this is not explicitly required by law, applicants are generally presumed to be legal residents of the country, or it is a factual requirement to file the application. In some countries, simple proof of current residence in the country is necessary to apply for

137 The United Kingdom, p. 405.
138 Italy, p. 211.
139 Japan, p. 530.
140 Ireland, p. 190.
141 Slovenia, p. 326.
142 Germany, p. 131.
143 Norway, p. 264.
144 Germany, p. 131.

benefits, such as in Brazil[145] and Chile[146]. Legal residence status is required in other countries such as Norway, Mexico and the United Kingdom. In most countries, however, eligibility requires a qualified period or legal title of residency, or the prospect of long-term residence in the country. In Ireland, applicants must demonstrate habitual residence with a proven link to the country, implying that the applicant must have resided in the country for a longer period of time and must prove an intention to stay.[147] In Slovenia, in addition to permanent legal residence, there must be a demonstrated link between the applicant and the community of tax payers.[148] Similarly, in Poland, foreigners can only receive assistance if they possess a qualified residence permit.[149] In Spain, beneficiaries must have legally resided in the country for at least one uninterrupted year prior to applying.[150] In Greece, households that are legally and permanently established in the country are eligible for minimum income protection, but no previous period of residence is required and the homeless are explicitly recognised as a category of beneficiaries.[151] In Bulgaria, eligibility is limited to those who hold a long-term or permanent residence permit.[152]

In some cases, concerns about potential abuse or the intention to restrict access for non-nationals have led to stricter residence requirements. In France, the continuous and effective residency condition requires foreign applicants to have held a residence permit with work authorisation for at least five years.[153] Moreover, periods of absence from the country exceeding three months may result in a proportional reduction of the minimum income benefit, based on actual time spent in the country.[154] In Italy, applicants must have resided in the country for at least five years, with the last two years without interruption.[155] In Japan, although assistance was traditionally only conceived for nationals, it is now interpreted to include foreign nationals with permanent residence status.[156]

145 Brazil, p. 426.
146 Chile, p. 460.
147 Ireland, pp. 191 ff.
148 Slovenia, p. 328.
149 Poland, p. 296.
150 Spain, p. 362.
151 Greece, p. 163.
152 Bulgaria, p. 55.
153 France, p. 86.
154 France, p. 87.
155 Italy, p. 210.
156 Japan, p. 516.

Eligibility for minimum income benefits is usually also linked to age, often requiring recipients to be of adult and working age. While most countries require the beneficiary to be over 18, some jurisdictions exclude young adults from eligibility to minimum income benefits, based on the assumption that they remain under their families' responsibility. The minimum age for eligibility is 23 in Spain[157] and 25 in France,[158] though both countries allow for certain exceptions. In Italy, young adults living alone are generally excluded from receiving minimum income support independently, as they are considered to be part of their parents' household for means testing purposes.[159] In some jurisdictions, such as the United Kingdom, Germany and France,[160] pursuing university studies or other forms of education leads young adults to be excluded from general minimum income schemes. In Chile, this is achieved through a means testing mechanism comparable to that in Italy, whereby the income of students up to the age of 24 is assessed on the basis of their parents' income, even if they do not live in the same household.[161] In only a few cases is the exclusion of students from minimum income protection offset by their inclusion in other schemes specifically designed for them.[162] All of the countries analysed provide targeted schemes for recipients who are no longer of working age (the elderly).[163] In some cases, measures targeting the elderly have proven to offer more generous benefits and more lenient means testing criteria.[164]

157 Spain, p. 363.

158 France, p. 87.

159 As mentioned above, sec. III.2.b)aa) of these Conclusions.

160 See the United Kingdom, where those in full-time education are usually not eligible for Universal Credit, see p. 392; Germany, where students are excluded from receiving the Citizen's Income, see p. 137 and France, where students and trainees are excluded from the RSA despite recent expansions of eligibility for active young adults, see p. 87.

161 See Chile, p. 457.

162 In Germany, for instance, educational support benefits are provided to university students under the *BAföG*, see p. 124. Mexico, despite not having a universal minimum income scheme, provides a programme targeted at students below the age of 29, p. 484.

163 For a legal comparison of minimum income protection measures specifically for the elderly, see S. Devetzi (ed.), *Minimum Income in Old Age: A legal comparison of selected European countries* (Sakkoulas Publications 2023).

164 See *supra*, n 78.

c) Activation Measures

The tension between the principles of dignity and deservingness is most evident in the design of activation conditionalities attached to minimum income schemes, in particular those involving labour market participation, behavioural requirements and sanctions for non-compliance. The aim of lifting individuals out of poverty is a double-edged sword. On the one hand, the principles of dignity and autonomy support State efforts to empower individuals to secure their own means of sustenance, achieve independence from public assistance, and participate fully in the labour market and social life. On the other hand, the right to a minimum income grounded in human dignity[165] limits the State's ability to withhold basic means of subsistence from individuals who fail to meet certain behavioural requirements.[166]

Against this backdrop, this comparative analysis identifies three main patterns of beneficiary activation, each reflecting a distinct role assumed by the State in relation to recipients. Conditionalities in minimum income schemes can function as instruments of paternalism, coercion and sanction, or support. While the role of conditionalities varies depending on a country's stage of economic development,[167] no State exclusively follows any one of these models. In all countries analysed, minimum income measures combine elements of all three approaches, incorporating various mechanisms of conditionality and sanctions into their design. The aim is thus not to rigidly categorise countries' measures, but rather to highlight the convergences and divergences in how each model embodies the underlying tension between the logic of deservingness and the principle of human dignity.[168]

---

165 See above, sec. I of these Conclusions.

166 Several other compelling arguments have been made for renouncing conditionality, see, *inter alia*, S. White, 'Should a Minimum Income be Unconditional?', in: S. Civitarese Matteucci and S. Halliday (eds.), *Social Rights in an Age of Austerity: European Perspectives* (Routledge 2017), pp. 181–196; M. Adler, *Cruel, Inhuman and Degrading Treatment? Benefit Sanctions in the UK* (Palgrave Macmillan 2018); S. Marchal and I. Marx (n 2), pp. 245 ff.

167 See H. Immervoll, F. Antía, et al., 'Welfare Conditionality in the OECD and in Latin America: A Comparative Perspective' IZA DP No. 17869 (April 2025), p. 3.

168 The combined analysis of sanctions and conditionalities has already inspired more nuanced models of minimum income schemes systematisations in the social sciences. *Inter alia*, Natili's model offers a particularly compelling framework, distinguishing between passive, workfare, paternalistic, enabling, inadequate, sanctiona-

Paternalistic conditionalities are contained in provisions that tie the receipt of cash benefits to recipients' compliance with prescribed "virtuous" behaviours, or that restrict the use of cash benefits only to purchase certain approved categories of goods. This model of conditionalities is widespread in South American states, reflecting the distinct role that minimum income protection plays in these jurisdictions, where conditionalities are considered an integral component of the support provided by the State to beneficiaries.[169] In Brazil, cash transfers are conditional on school attendance, health and dental check-ups and vaccinations.[170] Similarly, in Chile, conditional cash transfers are provided to individuals who meet specified health and education obligations.[171] Evidently aimed at nudging individuals towards adopting certain virtuous behaviours are the "effort transfers", offered to beneficiaries who "show outstanding performance or improvement in the areas of education, health, employment, savings, and monthly adherence to intensive or residential drug rehabilitation programmes".[172] In both Brazil and Chile, health and education conditionalities are seen as essential to help lift individuals out of poverty.[173] However, imposing behavioural requirements also serve a paternalistic function aiming to "improve" the beneficiary while ensuring that the resources provided are used for virtuous purposes and to not be misused.[174] Similar paternalistic conditionalities linked to health and education are found in some Eastern and Southern European schemes as well. In Bulgaria, social assistance schemes for families include health and education conditionalities, designed to encourage parents towards a "responsible upbringing and education of the child".[175] In Greece, the household is also held accountable for ensuring that minors attend compulsory education.[176] Similarly, in Italy, benefits have recently been made conditional on children's regular school attendance.[177] State control over how cash benefits are used reflects an element of paternalism

tory and protective models, see M. Natili, 'Worlds of last-resort safety nets? A proposed typology of minimum income schemes in Europe' Journal of International and Comparative Social Policy 36 (2020)1, pp. 57–75.

169 H. Immervoll, F. Antía (n 167), p. 5.
170 Brazil, pp. 425 and 428.
171 Chile, p. 452.
172 Chile, p. 453.
173 Brazil, p. 425 and 428.
174 Brazil, p. 425 and Chile, p. 465.
175 Bulgaria, p. 63.
176 Greece, p. 171.
177 Italy, p. 210.

in Southern European countries. In Greece, half of the monthly benefit must be used for purchasing consumer goods and cannot be saved.[178] In Italy, the use of cash benefits is restricted to in-person purchases of food, pharmaceutical and para-pharmaceutical products, as well as rent and utility payments, with monthly caps on cash withdrawals.[179]

The coercive and sanction-based model includes measures primarily aimed at preventing individuals from relying on State support for extended periods and at swiftly pushing them out of the safety net. This is typically enforced through strict labour obligations, underpinned by the threat of significant sanctions. In some countries, coercion also takes the form of compulsory participation in community or voluntary work, implying that individuals must give back to society to deserve assistance. This is the case, for instance, in Bulgaria and Norway.[180] These countries also impose additional labour activation requirements backed by sanctions. In particular, in Bulgaria, access to social assistance is conditional on strict job search or training requirements and non-compliance with these obligations is sanctioned with suspension or termination of benefits.[181] Labour activation requirements of varying scope and intensity are a common feature across all European countries analysed. In Slovenia, beneficiaries may lose or even be required to repay benefits if they refuse suitable employment.[182] In Greece, beneficiaries who have capacity for work must accept suitable job offers from the employment office or participate in any offered activities such as counselling or vocational training. Failure to comply with these requirements results in the loss of benefit entitlement.[183] The United Kingdom also imposes stringent labour activation requirements on beneficiaries in the higher conditionality group, with non-compliance harshly sanctioned, potentially resulting in full suspension of benefits.[184] In Ireland, beneficiaries must demonstrate willingness to accept any reasonable job offer and actively pursue employment opportunities, with possible sanctions including reductions in benefit payments.[185] Similarly, in France, recipients are required to actively seek employment, with potential sanctions ranging from benefit

178 Greece, p. 168.
179 Italy, p. 212.
180 Bulgaria, p. 65 and Norway, p. 267.
181 Bulgaria, p. 65.
182 Slovenia, p. 326.
183 Greece, p. 171.
184 The United Kingdom, pp. 406 ff.
185 Ireland, pp. 193 ff.

reductions to suspension of benefits,[186] and a recent reform has further expanded beneficiaries' obligations and the applicable sanctions.[187] In Italy, work-related conditionalities have also been recently tightened through a stricter sanction regime, which allows for the suspension or termination of benefits in a number of cases, for instance, if recipients refuse low-paid job offers anywhere in the country.[188] Sanctions also play an important role in Germany, although their scope has been curtailed following the sanctions ruling of the Federal Constitutional Court, which held that cuts to benefits must not exceed 30 per cent in line with the fundamental right to a dignified minimum subsistence.[189] In contrast, South American countries generally do not apply strict, sanction-based labour activation requirements. However, failure to comply with the above-mentioned health and education conditions may lead to the suspension or withdrawal of conditional benefits. Moreover, in Chile, the terms of participation in the system are formalised through a commitment letter, and violations may result in exclusion and loss of benefits.[190] In Japan, recipients' failure to comply with job activation measures may lead to a reduction or temporary suspension of benefits; however, welfare offices retain significant discretion in determining both the timing and content of such instructions and any associated sanctions.[191]

Finally, a model of supportive conditionality is designed to empower individuals to regain full participation in the community's labour and integrate into social life by providing the targeted support they need, while also ensuring their livelihood throughout the reintegration process. The focus is not only on short-term activation measures but on achieving long-term and sustainable social inclusion. To this end, the model offers personalised assistance and access to services such as training and coaching, aiming to address the structural obstacles that caused the situation of poverty or social exclusion in the first place. To facilitate smooth reintegration into the labour market, positive incentives are preferred over sanctions, such

---

186 France, p. 91.

187 France, p. 102.

188 Italy, pp. 232-233.

189 Although "this regulation was corrected again by the new provision reducing the benefits to zero (Section 31a, para. 7 SGB II) for so-called 'total objectors' who deliberately refuse to accept an actual and direct offer of employment", see Germany, p. 145.

190 Chile, p. 464.

191 Japan, pp. 531-532.

as means testing mechanisms that exclude income earned from work and additional monetary incentives that support transition into employment.[192] Several instruments inspired by this approach exist in the jurisdictions analysed. Chile's social protection system offers coaching, labour and social support programmes, while also rewarding beneficiaries for active participation and employment uptake.[193] In many countries, a shift away from strict workfare models to more supportive approaches has occurred in recent years, driven by evidence that coercion alone is ineffective. Germany has recently moved away from a policy prioritising job placement in favour of offering a range of integration and education programmes, along with holistic support for individuals.[194] Moreover, employed beneficiaries receive supplementary allowances designed to positively incentivise work take-up.[195] Similarly, the Republic of Korea has recently shifted towards a more supportive model by providing individualised activation plans and offering counselling, vocational training, start-up assistance and other services.[196] In Greece, the means test for the recently introduced minimum income scheme excludes a percentage of the applicant's income from any work-related activities, also to address the problem of the working poor.[197] Employment counsellors are expected to provide support in a personalised and individualised manner.[198] In Bulgaria, a recent provision allows individuals who enter employment to continue receiving social assistance for a transitional period of three months.[199] Similarly, in France, income earned during the first three months after re-entering employment is excluded from the means test,[200] and a progressive formula is applied to gradually phase out benefits as the individual's earnings increase.[201] Spain has also introduced a new calculation mechanism that ensures beneficiaries' disposable income increases when they take up work.[202] Significant earning disre-

192 A supportive model of conditionality can also involve elements of paternalism, as it may be justified by the notion that such conditions serve the best interests of the recipient, see S. White (n 166), p. 183.
193 Chile, p. 462.
194 Germany, pp. 140 ff.
195 Germany, p. 130.
196 The Republic of Korea, p. 557.
197 Greece, p. 166.
198 Greece, p. 171.
199 Bulgaria, p. 59.
200 France, p. 88.
201 France, p. 90.
202 Spain, pp. 368-369.

gards are offered in the United Kingdom,[203] while beneficiaries in Slovenia, who work a certain number of hours, are entitled to higher monthly benefits as an incentive to remain in the labour market.[204]

IV. Concluding Remarks

The results of this comparative study confirm that in all countries analysed, the design of minimum income protection poses several potential threats to the dignity of individuals in need of social assistance. Implementing a minimum income scheme that guarantees a life in dignity in all individual life situations is a complex task, especially given the unstable political landscape and financial constraints modern welfare states face today. Beyond the key issues explicitly discussed in this conclusion, the country reports highlight additional dimensions that warrant further investigation. Notably, they underscore the realisation that respect for individuals' right to dignity depends not only on the substantive design of the scheme but also on the procedural aspects governing access to it. In situations of extreme need and high vulnerability, beneficiaries often face complex and discouraging procedural challenges. Bureaucratic inefficiencies delay access to benefits,[205] while complex and burdensome applications procedures[206] or full digitalisation without adequate safeguards[207] create significant obstacles for vulnerable population groups. Effective coordination among the State, regional and local entities remains essential but difficult to achieve in a seamless way.[208] In countries where local authorities play a key role, the broad discretion granted to caseworkers allows for more personalised assessments, but also introduces an element of uncertainty that may undermine the principle of minimum subsistence as an enforceable right.[209] Moreover, the imperative to prevent fraud and verify self-reported information may lead to invasive procedures that scrutinise beneficiaries' living conditions,

203 The United Kingdom, p. 393.
204 Slovenia, p. 325.
205 Brazil, p. 430.
206 Slovenia, pp. 322-323.
207 The United Kingdom, p. 390.
208 Spain, pp. 352 ff., Italy, pp. 223 and 233 and Brazil, p. 429.
209 Norway, pp. 267-268, Japan, pp. 528-529, Bulgaria, p. 48 and the United Kingdom, p. 395.

posing risks to personal autonomy and dignity.[210] Non-take-up of benefits, driven by stigma, fear of scrutiny or repercussions, or procedural barriers, remains a major concern. Several country reports also highlight the gendered dimensions of minimum income schemes,[211] noting their potential to reinforce stereotypes or to increase the mental load carried by mothers.[212]

Despite these limitations, minimum income schemes, in the form of universal and means-tested safety nets, remain a crucial instrument for upholding the fundamental right to a dignified minimum subsistence for all. Their institutional design, however, must consistently prioritise respect for individuals' dignity over the mere tightening of the safety net at every stage of the process.

---

210 See Greece, p. 172, Brazil, p. 426 and Bulgaria, p. 48.
211 See Spain, p. 372.
212 See Chile, p. 465 and Brazil, pp. 425-426.

List of Authors

Ulrich Becker, Dr., LL.M. (EUI), Director at the Max Planck Institute for Social Law and Social Policy and Professor at the Law Faculty of the LMU, Munich

Julia Cunha Cruz, Master of Laws (Harvard Law School), University of São Paulo

Elaine Dewhurst, Dr., Professor of Equality Law and Social Justice, University of Manchester

Irene Domenici, Dr., Senior Research Fellow at the Max Planck Institute for Social Law and Social Policy, Munich

Agnieszka Górnicz-Mulcahy, Dr., Professor at the Faculty of Law, Administration and Economics at the University of Wrocław

Yaroslava Guenova, Dr., Associate Professor at the Law Faculty, University of Plovdiv "Paissii Hilendarski"

Linxin He, Dr., Professor at the Law Faculty, University of Strasbourg

Eva Maria Hohnerlein, Dr., Senior Research Fellow at the Max Planck Institute for Social Law and Social Policy, Munich

Eri Kasagi, Professor of Law at the University of Tokyo and Research Fellow at CNRS

Ute Kötter, Dr., Professor at the University of Applied Sciences, Munich

Monika Lewandowicz-Machnikowska, PhD, Associate Professor, Legal Sciences, Faculty of Law and Communication in Wrocław, SWPS University

Gabriela Mendizábal Bermúdez, Dr., Professor of Law at the Universidad Autónoma del Estado de Morelos

Luka Mišič, Dr., Assistant Professor at the Faculty of Law, University of Ljubljana

Teodora Petrova, Dr., Regulatory Affairs Specialist and former Research Fellow at the Max Planck Institute for Social Law and Social Policy

Flavia Piovesan, Dr., Professor of Human Rights and Constitutional Law at the Pontifical Catholic University of São Paulo

Viviana Ponce de León Solís, Dr., Professor of Law at the Universidad Diego Portales of Santiago de Chile.

Anastasia Poulou, Dr., Judge at the Administrative Court of First Instance of Athens and former Senior Research Fellow at the Max Planck Institute for Social Law and Social Policy, Munich

Ariel Przybyłowicz, Dr., Assistant Professor at the Faculty of Law, Administration and Economics at the University of Wrocław

María Dolores Ramírez Bendala, Assistant Professor of Labour Law and Social Security at the University of Sevilla

Cristina Sánchez-Rodas Navarro, Dr., Professor of Labour Law and Social Security at the University of Sevilla

Anika Seemann, Dr., Associate Professor of Modern European History at the University of Bergen

Kwang Seok Cheon, Dr., Professor at Yonsei University Law School

Henriette Sinding Aasen, Dr., Professor of Law at the University of Bergen

Grega Strban, Dr., Professor of Law at the University of Ljubljana, Senior Research Associate at the University of Johannesburg, Member of the European Committee of Social Rights

Daniel Wainstock, Bachelor of Laws (LLB), Pontifical Catholic University of Rio de Janeiro

Nikola Wilman, LL.M., MJur (University of Durham, UK), Taskforce Infektiologie, Bayerisches Landesamt für Gesundheit und Lebensmittelsicherheit and former Senior Researcher at the Max Planck Institute for Social Law and Social Policy